# ESSAYS ON
# CHINESE CIVILIZATION

# ESSAYS ON
# CHINESE CIVILIZATION

## Derk Bodde

EDITED AND INTRODUCED BY
Charles Le Blanc and Dorothy Borei

PRINCETON UNIVERSITY PRESS
PRINCETON, NEW JERSEY

Library of Congress Cataloging in Publication Data will be
found on the last printed page of this book

Clothbound editions of Princeton University Press books
are printed on acid-free paper, and binding materials are
chosen for strength and durability

Printed in the United States of America by Princeton
University Press, Princeton, New Jersey

ISBN 0-691-03129-0
ISBN 0-691-00024-7 (pbk.)

# CONTENTS

# PREFACE

Journals and those books that embody the scholarship of more than one author are obviously of great immediate value to contributors and readers alike. In the longer run, however, I have noticed that the articles they contain often tend to fall into gradual neglect and sometimes even virtual oblivion amid the outpourings of new scholarship. My growing awareness of this phenomenon caused me, during the early 1970s, to begin to think of bringing together a representative collection of my own essays on China for possible publication as a book-length anthology.

On approaching the University of Chicago Press with this idea, the Press appeared interested, the more so because of the favorable opinion of a reader who, to my keen regret, still remains unknown to me. The view expressed by this reader was that although the essays might well be published as they stood, their value would be considerably enhanced if their author would preface each with some new introductory remarks, in which he would explain how the essay came to be written, assess its value from his candid present viewpoint, and bring its scholarship up to date. This suggestion, of inestimable value to me, has been carried out to the best of my ability in the present book.

Beginning in 1974, however, the whole project had to be shelved for three years while I worked at Cambridge University upon a particular portion of Joseph Needham's *Science and Civilisation in China*. Only after returning to the United States in mid-1977 did I again consider the idea. Then, to my surprise, I discovered that a similar idea was in the minds of two of my one-time students, Dorothy V. Borei and Charles Le Blanc, both now professors in the Chinese field. The twenty-one essays in the present book are, in selection and arrangement, the joint result of the thinking of these two friends and of my earlier planning. This time we approached Princeton University Press, in part because the Press was then planning the series of scholarly anthologies to which the present book belongs, and in part because it had already published several of my books.

In order to reduce the price of the present book, some features in it have been materially altered from our original planning. One such change is deletion of an introductory section, "Why Be a China Specialist?" in which I had described what such specialization meant in the United States of fifty years ago, when I began my Chinese studies. Another is elimination of the paginations of individual articles as found in their original publications, which I would have liked to accompany the single continuous pagination now covering all of the articles. The most conspicuous change, however, is the grouping together within a single general Introduction of those new introductory remarks for each article which I had originally intended would in each instance be located immediately before the particular article to which they pertain. Because of this change, I would now urge readers not to read the general Introduction from beginning to end as a single whole, but instead to read only that particular part of it at any given time dealing with the particular article in which the reader then happens to be interested.

To Dorothy Borei and Charles Le Blanc I am happy to express my hearty thanks for their friendship, cooperation, and especially the writing of a very perceptive, although unduly laudatory, Foreword. This I shall always prize. To Cecilia Lee, Instructor in Chinese formerly at the University of Pennsylvania and now at Swarthmore College, I am grateful for taking the trouble to make copies of certain texts in the present book when these were badly needed and when she was particularly busy.

Thanks are also expressed here to the following publishers, publications, and scholarly organizations for permission to reprint the essays in this book:

American Council of Learned Societies for essay 2, reprinted from *Far Eastern Leaflets, Numbers 1-6*;
American Oriental Society for essays 5-7, 9, and 17-18, reprinted from *Journal of the American Oriental Society*;
American Philosophical Society for essay 8, reprinted from *Proceedings of the American Philosophical Society*;
*Asia Major* for essay 20;
Association for Asian Studies for essays 10 and 19, reprinted from the *Far Eastern Quarterly*;
Chinese University Press, Chinese University of Hong Kong, for essay 21, reprinted from David T. Roy and Tsuen-hsuin Tsien, eds., *Ancient China: Studies in Early Civilization*;
Columbia University Press for essay 13, reprinted from the *Review of Religion*;
Doubleday and Company, Inc., for essay 3, reprinted from Samuel Noah Kramer, ed., *Mythologies of the Ancient World*;
Gemini Smith, Inc., for essay 1, reprinted from Bradley Smith and Wan-go Weng, *China: a History in Art*;
*Harvard Journal of Asiatic Studies* for essays 12 and 14;
Princeton University Press for essay 4, reprinted from Rushton Coulborn, ed., *Feudalism in History*;
*Studia Serica Bernhard Karlgren Dedicata* for essay 15;
University of Chicago Press for essay 11, reprinted from Arthur F. Wright, ed., *Studies in Chinese Thought*, copyright 1953 by Robert Redfield; also for essay 16, reprinted from the *History of Religions*.

The foregoing essays cover a considerable variety of topics and nearly half a century of scholarly activity (1933-1979). Inevitably, inconsistencies will be found between some of them not only in such matters as bibliographical citations, but also in their approaches to topics, points of emphasis, and degrees of scholarly maturity. Taken as a whole, however, my colleagues and myself hope that the essays will provide interest, stimulation, and sinological relevance for those who read them.

*February 1, 1981*                                  Derk Bodde
*Washington, D.C.*               *Professor Emeritus of Chinese Studies*
*University of Pennsylvania*
and first
*Dr. Sun Yat sen Distinguished Visiting*
*Professor of China Studies*
*Georgetown University*

# CHRONOLOGY OF CHINESE DYNASTIES

PRE-DYNASTIC
  Archaeology: a series of cultures ranging from early Palaeolithic (Peking Man and other hominids, half a million or more years ago) down to late Neolithic (19th or 18th c. B.C.)
  Literary sources: a series of legendary sage-rulers and culture heroes, including Huang Ti, the "Yellow Sovereign" (trad. 27th c. B.C.)

HSIA dynasty (trad. 2205-1766 B.C.): unconfirmed by archaeology

SHANG dynasty (trad. 1765-1123 B.C.): confirmed by archaeology; earliest script and bronze

CHOU dynasty (trad. 1122-256 B.C.; actual founding date is probably around a century later): China's age of "feudalism"; many principalities nominally under Chou suzerainty
  Western Chou (trad. 1122-771 B.C.)
  841 B.C. onward: a single standard chronology
  Eastern Chou (770-256 B.C.)
    "Spring and Autumn" (Ch'un-ch'iu) period (722-481 B.C.)
    Warring States (Chan-kuo) period (403-222 B.C.): increasing interstate warfare, rise of iron technology, classical age of philosophy

CH'IN dynasty (221-207 B.C.): creation of China's first universal empire; a centralized bureaucratic form of government and a unified script; building of the Great Wall

HAN dynasty (206 B.C.-A.D. 220): age of classical empire; elaboration of Ch'in system of government, geographical expansion, rise of Confucianism to orthodoxy
  Former or Western Han (206 B.C.-A.D. 5)
  Wang Mang as Regent and Acting Emperor (A.D. 6-8); then as Emperor of "Hsin" dynasty (A.D. 9-23)
  Later or Eastern Han (A.D. 25-220)

PERIOD OF DISUNITY (190/220-589): "mediaeval" China; spread of Buddhism and creation of non-Chinese "barbarian" states in North China
  Three Kingdoms (190/220-280)
  Chin dynasty (265-316)
  Northern and Southern Dynasties (317-589)

Sᴜɪ dynasty (590-617): China reunited

Tʼᴀɴɢ dynasty (618-906): political grandeur, cultural brilliance, cosmopolitanism, apogee of Buddhism, beginning of printing

Fɪᴠᴇ Dʏɴᴀsᴛɪᴇs (907-959)

Sᴜɴɢ dynasty (960-1279): political weakness coupled with economic development, urbanization, spread of printing, rise of Neo-Confucianism, decline of Buddhism
  Northern Sung (960-1125)
  Southern Sung (1126-1279)

Yüᴀɴ (Mongol) dynasty (1280-1367): China's first total rule by outsiders

Mɪɴɢ dynasty (1368-1643): restoration of Chinese rule, with growing autocracy and crystallization of culture

Cʜʼɪɴɢ (Manchu) dynasty (1644-1911): China's second total rule by outsiders, this time ones who became strongly Chinese in culture; heavy impact of West from early 19th c. onward

Rᴇᴘᴜʙʟɪᴄ (1912-    )
  Republic of China (1912-1949): Sun Yat-sen, the warlords, and Chiang Kai-shek
  People's Republic of China (1949-    ): Mao Tse-tung and the Chinese Communists

# FOREWORD

A productive scholar and inspiring teacher creates his own intellectual biography through the ideas and methodology contained in his formal writings and, less tangibly but equally as importantly, through the manner in which he has communicated his knowledge to colleagues and students. As both scholar and teacher, Derk Bodde (1909-    ), Professor Emeritus of Chinese Studies at the University of Pennsylvania, has left an indelible mark on the field of Sinology. The present volume, a selection of articles from journals and collected works, delineates the main intellectual features of almost half a century of Derk Bodde's contributions to Sinology.

By experience and academic training Derk Bodde belongs to a dying breed of Western Sinologists. As a young boy he accompanied his parents to China, where his father taught in a college on the edge of Shanghai from 1919 to 1922. Later, following four years of undergraduate study of English literature at Harvard and then one year of Chinese studies there in the Graduate School, Bodde returned to China. There he spent the next six years (1931-1937) immersing himself, with very little formal supervision, in ancient Chinese history and literature. After receiving his Ph.D. from the University of Leiden in 1938, he began his lengthy teaching career at the University of Pennsylvania, retiring in 1975 to devote himself to full-time research.

While contemporary graduate students receive professional training in a specific academic discipline, Bodde's education, like those of his generation of prewar China scholars, was scattered and general. His lack of specialized methodological training, however, has been more than compensated for both by his lengthy residence in China and by his rigorous mind. A Sinologist par excellence, he is a humanist in the broadest sense, with a comprehensive knowledge of China's classical language and culture.

Sinology implies an integrated, interdisciplinary approach to the study of China as a coherent whole. This approach is largely necessitated by the close interrelatedness of the many aspects of China's culture—language, social structure, political and economic institutions, the arts, religious and philosophical beliefs, and so on. A Sinologist is one who has grasped the fundamental "organic" character of Chinese civilization and whose study of any particular element of that culture is integrated into a larger vision of the society. Derk Bodde's scholarship is a prime example of Sinology at its best, for it provides detailed knowledge of various facets of the Chinese experience at the same time that it expresses an acute awareness of their interconnectedness.

The Sinologist relies extensively upon the critical and painstaking examination of texts in order to draw conclusions about China's past.

Language skill is thus the Sinologist's indispensable tool. The textual aspect of research, so central to Bodde's scholarship, has, as a methodology, come under attack in recent decades as trivial, even obsolete. Whereas social scientists with their quantitative methodologies appear to reign supreme in contemporary academic circles, China scholars of the prewar generation were essentially humanists who, due in part to the underdeveloped nature of the field, felt obliged to translate and annotate a vast number of Chinese texts in order to become sufficiently familiar with the culture to draw verifiable conclusions. For Bodde, as for many of the older generation of Sinologists, translation is predominantly an art. Although an imprecise and often frustrating exercise, translation, and language proficiency in general, is crucial in their minds to a clear understanding of an alien culture. What Bodde's training may have lacked in discipline specialization is more than counterbalanced by his exceptional grasp of the Chinese language and by his ability to comprehend and interpret Chinese culture on the basis of textual analysis.

Yet at no point does the textual nature of Bodde's research become an end unto itself. The translations, while they may be intellectually challenging in themselves, always serve as a basis from which to draw broader conclusions about China's cultural experience. In other words, Bodde never loses sight of the forest for the trees—his meticulous marshaling of textual evidence allows him to draw what are for him the most valid conclusions on a given subject. Many of the selections in this volume are excellent illustrations of Bodde's philosophy of translation and of his use of textual criticism as the bedrock of his interpretations.

A cursory glance at the bibliography in this volume reveals the fecundity of Derk Bodde's scholarly career. Upon closer examination the diversity of his research, in terms of both subject matter and chronology, is evident. In the course of the last half century many fields of Chinese studies have come under his scrutiny, among them philosophy, intellectual and cultural history, law, science and religion. He has written as both the detached scholar, as in his writings on Chinese philosophy, and as historical participant, as in his *Peking Diary*. He has enumerated for us some of the unique aspects of China's civilization, yet has been sufficiently grounded in Western history and thought to make pertinent intercultural comparisons and has been intrigued with tracing the impact of Chinese intellectual and material culture on the West. Chronologically, his inquiry has extended from the ancient and early imperial periods, his central emphasis, to the last imperial dynasty and modern China. In almost every instance, Bodde's research delves into the intellectual world of the elite, but certain of his contributions, notably those on legal institutions and popular festivals, relate directly to the nonelite substratum of Chinese society.

Bodde's most significant contributions to Sinology have been in the fields of early Chinese history and law. The work for which he will be most gratefully remembered by generations of students and teachers of Chinese culture is his translation of Fung Yu-lan's *History of Chinese Philosophy*. This collaborative project required a thorough knowledge of both classical and modern Chinese, as a very large part of Fung's text consists of long passages quoted from the works of two-and-a-half millennia of Chinese thinkers. In addition, this translation necessitated a mind capable of penetrating the conceptual nuances and complexities of very diverse philosophical schools, as well as a firm grounding in Western philosophical traditions.

The present volume reveals some of the major changes in Derk Bodde's thinking and research in the past fifty years. Perhaps the most perceptible change is his growing sense of social and political concern and commitment. Initially apolitical, he paid little attention to the revolutionary forces about to engulf China and instead riveted his attention on the old society. This political aloofness is clearly evident in the content of his earliest professional contributions to Sinology, which deal exclusively with the abstract world of ideas. They are the product of the detached philosopher, the lover of antiquity.

In 1937, however, Bodde left China for Europe and passed en route through Southeast Asia, then under white colonial rule. His antipathy toward economic, racial, and social exploitation emerged during this trip, and was heightened in 1948 when he returned to China where he witnessed the collapse of the Nationalist government the following year. It is particularly revealing that his published research in the years 1949 and 1950 deal almost exclusively with the catalytic events then sweeping China. These first-hand experiences shifted the focus of Bodde's research away from more abstract subjects (philosophy) toward more concrete fields of thought (intellectual and institutional history). In doing so, he buried himself less often in the classical philosophers of antiquity and investigated more often recent historical phenomena.

Related to these changes is his growing interest in drawing sharp comparisons and contrasts between premodern and contemporary China, thus helping us to understand better the significance of the revolutionary changes since 1949. Further, as Bodde himself notes in his introduction to one article, his vision of premodern Chinese history, highly idealized at the outset of his career, has matured over the years and he is now able to recognize the weaknesses that existed in China's traditional institutions.

Finally, Derk Bodde's deep sense of social and political commitment has not been confined to scholarly research, for he has emphatically voiced his opinions on some of the most critical issues facing American society during the last thirty years. His defense of Owen Lattimore, his published attacks on United States actions in Vietnam, his opposition to McCarthyism and its sequels, all attest to his great social and political concern.[1] These and other such writings and activities have played a major role both in Bodde's personal life and his career as a scholar.

Any attempt to evaluate Derk Bodde's contribution to Sinology must take into account the brevity and lucidity of his style. The fact that his writing is more readable than a great deal of recently published Sinological literature is no doubt due in part to the nature of his academic training. Bodde's writing is not overburdened with jargon understandable only to those initiated in the discipline. By intentionally striving to be as clear and straightforward as possible, Bodde has succeeded in making his ideas accessible to both the specialist and the nonspecialist. This volume includes technical articles of primary interest to the academic world as well as several selections of an introductory nature which the lay audience will readily understand.

Selections included in this volume represent but a few of the considerable Sinological output of Derk Bodde, of which a complete listing is provided in the bibliography. Published in a host of periodicals and books over an almost fifty-year period (1933-1979), they will be far more accessible to a greater number of readers in the present collection. The articles have been chosen on the basis of their intrinsic worth, their relevance to contemporary Chinese studies, and their integration into a systematic outline of Chinese culture. Like a tapestry, the essays reveal manifold intricate designs within an overall pattern. Each section focuses on a major facet of the culture: the "Formation of Chinese Culture" delineates some of the forces—such as kinship and humanism—that were deeply rooted in preimperial Chinese society; "Man in Society" depicts some of the institutional, particularly legal, aspects of imperial China; "Man in the Cosmos," which deals largely, but not exclusively, with some of the philosophical and religious beliefs of the elite, reinforces the concepts discussed in the first two sections; and "Text Studies" vividly illustrates the analytical skills and imagination needed to translate classical Chinese, and exemplifies how the Sinologist uses a text as historical evidence to support his interpretations.

The value of the present collection is greatly enhanced by the addition of editorial comments to each article by Bodde himself. In these he recalls the circumstances under which the article was written, briefly discusses its main points, sometimes revising his earlier interpretations on the basis of new evidence, and updates the bibliography

[1] Representative are letters by him in the *New York Times* of 16 September 1963, 27 May 1964, 18 March 1965, 26 January 1966, 25 December 1967, 9 February 1969, 26 January 1971, and 25 December of the same year.

on each topic, pointing out the relevance of recent publications. So, although the articles cover a time-span of more than forty years, the reader may rest assured that he has in hand not only the best, but the latest of Derk Bodde's Sinological writings.

Dorothy V. Borei
*Assistant Professor of*
*Far Eastern History*
*Guilford College*

Charles Le Blanc
*Director, Centre*
*d'Etudes de*
*l'Asie de l'Est*
*Université de*
*Montréal*

# ESSAYS ON
# CHINESE CIVILIZATION

# INTRODUCTION:
# THE ESSAYS REASSESSED

## THE FORMATION OF CHINESE CULTURE

### 1. Introduction to the History of China

BIBLIOGRAPHY, A-85; from Bradley Smith and Wan-go Weng, *China: a History in Art* (New York: Harper & Row, 1973), pp. 10-13.

It is appropriate that this essay, originally written to introduce a handsome volume of historically arranged reproductions of Chinese art, should now become the first study in the present book. Like other compressed introductions, it has the merit of presenting basic facts and ideas in brief and lucid form. Also like such introductions, it is open to possible criticism on grounds of over-generalization, over-simplification, and inadequate attention to detail.

Quite aside from this possibility, the essay errs in its very first paragraph by equating our word "civilization" with the Chinese term *wen hua*, regarded as an ancient equivalent. The attempt founders on the fact that this usage of *wen hua* is not ancient in China at all. On the contrary, it was borrowed by China from Japan, probably in the late nineteenth century, where it had no doubt been originally formulated in response to new ideas and words entering Japan from the West.[1]

Curiously, however, the invalidation of the first paragraph of this essay by no means invalidates the generalization drawn from it in the second. For it remains an incontrovertible fact, as there stated, that China throughout its history was an overwhelmingly scribal rather than verbal civilization—one where culture was regarded as coterminous with the written word. Thus this episode illustrates the occasional truth that a generalization may remain valid even when its supporting illustration has been proven to be invalid.

Some readers, remembering how the eunuch Ts'ai Lun is recorded in Chinese history as having reported on paper-making to the Chinese emperor in A.D. 105, may wonder why the invention of this product is attributed in the present essay (p. 39) to the preceding century. However, this and even considerably earlier dating is now confirmed by archaeology.[2] On the other hand, archaeology also now confirms

---

[1] This fact was first suggested to me by Janusz Chmielewski, of the University of Warsaw. Professor Chmielewski's supposition is confirmed by Li Yu-ning, *The Introduction of Socialism into China* (New York: Columbia University Press, 1971), p. 84.

[2] Fragments of paper of Former Han date, ranging in time from probably the late second century B.C. to the late first century B.C., have been found in 1934 at Lopnor

the fact that some of China's neolithic cultures are probably earlier than the date of "early third millennium B.C." suggested midway in the essay.

The status of China's merchant class is a subject of controversy. Such status undoubtedly differed considerably at different periods, though with an admitted trend toward improvement during the later dynasties. Nevertheless, the essay's central assertion remains true that at no time were merchants in China ever seriously able to challenge the status and values of the dominant gentry elite. An excellent summary of changing merchant status during roughly the first half of the Chinese empire is given in Denis Twitchett, "Merchant, Trade and Government in Late T'ang," *Asia Major*, n.s. 14 (1968), 63-95. Another important survey is Yang Lien-sheng, "Government Control of Urban Merchants in Traditional China," *Tsing Hua Journal of Chinese Studies*, n.s. 8 (August 1970), 186-206.

The four major patterns or movements of Chinese history described in the latter part of the essay are all matters of controversy, especially the last. A good brief anthology of scholarly writings on the general nature of Chinese history has been compiled by John Meskill, *The Pattern of Chinese History: Cycles, Development, or Stagnation?* Problems in Asian Civilization series (Boston: D.C. Heath & Co., 1965).

As to the first of the four historical patterns enumerated in the essay, that of the creation of the first Chinese empire in 221 B.C., further detailed information will be found in my *China's First Unifier* (Bibliography, A-12); see also, for broader and more up-to-date treatment, my chapter, "The Ch'in State and Empire," in the forthcoming first volume of the *Cambridge History of China*. The second pattern, that of the dynastic cycle, has been taken for granted by many writers, past and present, but is now seriously questioned by Hans Bielenstein, "Is There a Chinese Dynastic Cycle?" *Bulletin of the Museum of Far Eastern Antiquities*, 50 (1978), 1-23. See also Arthur F. Wright's discussion of Chinese traditional views of history, supplemented by comments by myself (Bibliography, A-73). For the third pattern, that of the age-old struggles between the agrarian Chinese within the Great Wall and the pastoral peoples outside, the classic work remains Owen Lattimore's *Inner Asian Frontiers of China* (New York: American Geographical Society, 1940; 2nd ed., 1951). Finally, the fourth pattern, that of the growing urbanization and commercialization of Chinese life from around the ninth century onward, is the most controversial

(in eastern Sinkiang); in 1957 at Pa-ch'iao (some 25 kms. east northeast of Sian, Shensi); in 1973-1974 at Chü-yen (in present northern Kansu); and in 1978 in Fu-feng (175 kms. west of Sian). See Thomas Francis Carter, *The Invention of Printing in China and Its Spread Westward*, 2nd ed. rev. by L. Carrington Goodrich (New York: Ronald Press, 1955), pp. xvii, 5-6, 132-133; Tsuen-hsuin Tsien, "Raw Materials for Old Papermaking in China," *Journal of the American Oriental Society*, 93 (1973), p. 511; *Wen Wu* (Cultural Relics), 1978, no. 1, p. 6; and *Wen Wu*, 1979, no. 9, pp. 19-20.

of all. Besides several writings in the above-cited Meskill anthology, mention may be made of two articles: Edward A. Kracke, Jr., "Sung Society: Change within Tradition," *Far Eastern Quarterly*, 14 (1954-55), 479-488; and Miyakawa Hisayuki, "An Outline of the Naito Hypothesis and Its Effects on Japanese Studies of China," *ibid.*, pp. 533-552. A book-length discussion, ingenious and stimulating but also, in important respects, unconvincing or inadequate, is Mark Elvin, *The Pattern of the Chinese Past* (Stanford: Stanford University Press, 1973). On a significant aspect of Sung society, see Peter J. Golas, "Rural China in the Song," *Journal of Asian Studies*, 39 (February 1980), 291-325.

The present essay, I venture to hope, remains essentially sound in its main contentions despite its brevity, broadness of scope, and the initial error about *wen hua*.

## 2. The Chinese Language as a Factor in Chinese Cultural Continuity

BIBLIOGRAPHY, A-21; from *Far Eastern Leaflets, Numbers 1-6* (Washington, D.C.: American Council of Learned Societies, 1942), pp. 28-29.

This tiny essay is one of a dozen written by seven American scholars in the early 1940s on various phases of East Asian history and culture. Their particular aim was to induce social scientists to bring that part of the world within their frame of reference. Apparently the essays were well received because in 1942, during the depths of World War II, they were reprinted as a single pamphlet under the editorship of John K. Fairbank of Harvard and his wife Wilma, aided by Mortimer Graves, then director of the American Council of Learned Societies.

What is said in this essay about the Chinese language has often been said before and suffers from over-simplification. Its two main contentions, however, are important for any adequate understanding of the development of Chinese civilization. Worth reading on the language, in addition to the three items listed at the end of the essay, are Bernhard Karlgren, *The Chinese Language, an Essay on Its Nature and History* (New York: Ronald Press, 1949), which describes in particular Karlgren's own very important researches on ancient Chinese; Robert A. D. Forest, *The Chinese Language* (London: Faber & Faber, 1948), which deals primarily with modern Chinese as a spoken language; and the pamphlet by Herrlee Glessner Creel, *Chinese Writing*, Asiatic Studies in American Education no. 2 (Washington, D.C.: American Council on Education, 1943), which focuses on the characteristics of the Chinese script, especially in its early development.

## 3. Myths of Ancient China

BIBLIOGRAPHY, A-72; from Samuel Noah Kramer, ed., *Mythologies of the Ancient World* (Chicago: Quadrangle Books, 1961), pp. 367-408;

paperback edition: Garden City, N.Y.: Doubleday Anchor Books, 1961.

Late in December 1959, at the joint annual meetings of the American Anthropological Association and the American Folklore Society (held that year in Mexico City), one Mexican scholar and nine from the United States—seven of them from the University of Pennsylvania—participated in a single all-day session. Their papers covered the major mythologies of the ancient world, ranging from Egypt and Greece to China and Japan, and jumping across the Pacific to ancient Mexico. From this session resulted the book cited above and the present article.

The book was well received in scholarly circles and has continued to sell in hardback and paperback editions. Yet of the American reviews, none can compare in length, insight, and sympathetic interest with that written in Russian by E. M. Meletinsky for the Moscow scholarly journal, *Narody Azii i Afriki* (Peoples of Asia and Africa), 1962, no. 5, pp. 194-198. As translated into English by my wife, this review amounts to eight single-spaced typescript pages.

Perhaps a major reason for the Russian scholar's approval is that the book, though non-Marxist, tries to be factually precise, stresses the historical development of its mythologies, and avoids one-sided theorizing. On this last point, in particular, Mr. Meletinsky compares it very favorably with another American symposium on mythology published in 1955, whose contributors he describes as "followers of the outdated meteorological theory, and of the now fashionable concepts of the ritualists, semanticists, structuralists, and psycho-analysts." In 1977, *Mythologies of the Ancient World* was published in Moscow in Russian translation under the title, *Mifologii Drevnego Mira*. Its edition of 30,000 copies contains a new lengthy introduction on the origin of myths by I. M. Diakonov, a well-known Russian scholar.

As to the present article, it, like the book as a whole, strives to be factual and stresses the historical development of its subject. In particular, it discusses at some length the major problems involved in trying to reconstruct ancient Chinese myths from the fragmentary materials scattered in early Chinese literature. This emphasis on problems and methodology renders the article useful, I hope, as a general introduction to its subject before going on to other more particularized studies.

A very few examples of such studies, in addition to those listed in the article's bibliography, may be cited here. They include N. J. Girardot, "The Problem of Creation Mythology in the Study of Chinese Religion," *History of Religions*, 15 (1976), 289-318; Girardot, " 'Returning to the Beginning' and the Arts of Mr. Hun-tun in the *Chuang Tzu*," *Journal of Chinese Philosophy*, 5 (1978), 21-69; and John S. Major, "Myth, Cosmology, and the Origins of Chinese Science," *ibid.*, pp. 1-

20. Among articles in Chinese, see Chang Kwang-chih, "The Chinese Creation Myths: a Study in Method," *Bulletin of the Institute of Ethnology, Academia Sinica*, no. 8 (Autumn 1959), 47-76 (English summary, pp. 77-79); Chang, "A Classification of Shang and Chou Myths," *ibid.*, no. 14 (Autumn 1962), 47-74 (English summary, pp. 75-94); Chang, "Changing Relationships of Man and Animal in Shang and Chou Myths and Art," *ibid.*, no. 16 (Autumn 1963), 115-132 (English summary, pp. 133-146); and Lin Heng-li, "The Analyses of the Myth of Shooting Suns," *ibid.*, no. 13 (Spring 1962), 99-114 (English summary, pp. 116-122). The second and third Chang articles are republished in English versions in Chang's *Early Chinese Civilization: Anthropological Perspectives* (Cambridge, Mass.: Harvard University Press, 1976), pp. 149-173 and 174-196, respectively.

Since the publication of this article in 1961, numerous texts have been recovered from tombs by Chinese archaeology. Thus the discovery of significant mythological texts is now an ever-present possibility which, when and if it takes place, will effectively invalidate the final point made in the Conclusion.

## 4. Feudalism in China

BIBLIOGRAPHY, A-60; from Rushton Coulborn, ed., *Feudalism in History* (Princeton, N.J.: Princeton University Press, 1956), pp. 49-92, 404-407.

In 1950 a group of twenty-three scholars, including Alfred L. Kroeber as chairman and Arnold Toynbee, met at Princeton for a two-day conference on feudalism. Its purpose was to gain, by comparing possible instances of feudalism in various civilizations, a better understanding of uniformities in history. The book that resulted, *Feudalism in History*, opens with a brief introductory essay, "The Idea of Feudalism," by Joseph R. Strayer and the book's editor, Rushton Coulborn; continues with essays by eight scholars on feudalism or quasi-feudalism in Western Europe, Japan, China, Ancient Mesopotamia, and elsewhere; and concludes with a lengthy study based on these essays, "A Comparative Study of Feudalism," again by Coulborn.

A conspicuous omission is any chapter on Islam—the result of unavoidable circumstances. Nevertheless, the book aroused considerable interest among historians and generated some lengthy book reviews, among them several of particular interest to China specialists. These include reviews by James T. C. Liu in *Pacific Affairs*, 29 (June 1956), 181-186; Joseph R. Levenson in *Far Eastern Quarterly*, 15 (August 1956), 569-572; Etienne Balazs in the same, 16 (1957), 329-332 (reprinted in Balazs, *Chinese Civilization and Bureaucracy* [New Haven: Yale University Press, 1964], pp. 28-33); and Owen Lattimore in *Past & Present*, no. 12 (November 1957), pp. 45-57. All four reviews are still worth reading today. The one by Balazs is largely a commentary on Levenson, while Lattimore refers more briefly both to Levenson and Balazs.

The conference and the book both demonstrated, if demonstration was needed, that feudalism remains a highly controversial subject. The word was first coined in the eighteenth century to designate a set of social, economic, and especially political circumstances said to have characterized Western European government and society many centuries earlier. However, after the appearance of Marxism, the same word began to be used by Marxists in a primarily economic (not political) sense to designate one of the several fixed stages of production through which, it was alleged, all advanced societies had passed. How greatly this interpretation of feudalism differs from the usual non-Marxist interpretations is indicated by the standard chronology of Chinese history which, when I visited China in 1978, I found posted in the Museum of Chinese History in Peking as well as other museums throughout the country:

| | |
|---|---|
| Primitive Society | ca. 1,000,000-4,000 years ago |
| Slave Society | ca. 21st century-476 B.C. |
| Feudal Society | 475 B.C.-A.D. 1840 |
| Semi-colonial and Semi-feudal Society | A.D. 1840-1919 |

James Liu, in his review of *Feudalism in History*, criticizes the book for making no reference to the Marxist concept. The criticism is justified except, perhaps, for the last two pages of my own contribution, wherein I briefly touch on the concept, without, however, specifically identifying it as Marxist. Aside from this reference, my study, like the others in the book, adheres to the book's introductory assertion that feudalism is "primarily a method of government, not an economic or social system." Keeping this definition in mind, I looked for evidence of Chinese feudalism in 1. the early centuries of the Chou dynasty (trad. 1122-256 B.C.), often referred to as China's "classical" age of feudalism, and 2. the Period of Disunity (A.D. 221-589). My conclusions, to which I still adhere, are that the term "feudalism," in a non-Marxist sense, may properly be applied to the early centuries of the Chou but not to its later centuries, when only remnants of feudalism remained; and that the Period of Disunity, though characterized by phenomena reminiscent of feudal ages elsewhere, was nevertheless not actually an age of feudalism according to the criteria enunciated in the book's introductory essay.

Not all scholars, of course, accept the labeling of the first half of the Chou as "feudal." Sceptics include, for example, Jacques Gernet and Perry Anderson.[1] A larger number of scholars, however, do seem

[1] Gernet, with respect to Chou China of the ninth to seventh centuries B.C., writes on p. 55 of his *Le Monde chinois* (Paris, 1972) that "the term feudal has been so much

to accept the equation, among them all four of the reviewers mentioned earlier (Levenson somewhat grudgingly), as well as such specialists as A.F.P. Hulsewé, Cho-yun Hsu, and Timoteus Pokora.[2] A good illustration of the persistence of conflicting views is a 1973 book edited by John T. Meskill, in which the editor concludes that the differences between the political systems of Chou China and medieval Europe "seem too great for them to be considered of the same type," whereas two of the book's contributors express a contrary opinion.[3] Among Japanese scholars there is a similar bifurcation, with the added complication that quite a number accept the Marxist view of feudalism as applied to China. A German scholar solves the dilemma neatly by regarding both the early Chou and imperial China as "feudal."[4] A Chinese scholar repeatedly uses the same word while surveying Chinese premodern intellectual attitudes toward "feudal" as against centralized Chinese political institutions.[5] Conversely, an American scholar, with regard to Chou China, urges caution and further study before using the word "feudal" at all.[6]

The longest and most detailed account of early Chou feudalism to appear in English since my article is the chapter "Feudalism," in H. G. Creel's *Origins of Statecraft in China* (Chicago: University of Chicago Press, 1970), I, 317-387. This study provides greater detail on the Western Chou period (the period before 770 B.C.) than was possible in my article, and on certain points what it says indicates the need for correction in the article. For example, it offers convincing evidence (pp. 371-373) for the existence of subinfeudation in Chou feudalism, as against the article's citation (pp. 93-94) of the contrary opinion of Henri Maspero. Generally speaking, however, I believe

---

abused that it has lost all meaning"; thereafter he never uses the term, although he does speak of fiefs. Anderson, in his *Lineages of the Absolutist State* (London, 1974), discusses Chinese historical and economic development with regard to the "Asiatic mode of production" (pp. 520-549), but says nothing about feudalism.

[2] See Hulsewé, "China im Altertum," in Golo Mann and Alfred Heuss, eds., *Propyläen-Weltgeschichte*, II (Berlin: Propyläen-Verlag, 1962), 503, section entitled "Chou-Gesellschaft und Feudalismus"; Hsu, *Ancient China in Transition* (Stanford University Press, 1965), pp. 2ff.; Pokora, "China," in H.J.M. Claessen and P. Skaln'ik, eds., *The Early State* (Paris and The Hague: Mouton, 1978), pp. 201, 203, 206 (where Pokora speaks of early Chou "fiefs," "feudatories," and "feudal rulers," though he does not actually describe the Chou itself as "feudal").

[3] Meskill, ed., *An Introduction to Chinese Civilization* (Lexington, Mass.: D.C. Heath, 1973), p. 13 of his own historical essay and, for the two contributors (Nairuenn Chen and Charles O. Hucker), pp. 464-465 and 553-554, respectively.

[4] Ernst Schwartz, "Zum Feudalismus in China," *Ethnographisch-Archäologische Zeitschrift*, 16 (1975), 655-657.

[5] Lien-sheng Yang, in the first half of his article, "Ming Local Administration," in Charles O. Hucker, ed., *Chinese Government in Ming Times* (New York: Columbia University Press, 1969), pp. 1-10.

[6] Barry B. Blakeley, "On the 'Feudal' Interpretation of Chou China," *Early China*, 2 (1976), 35-37.

that the article's main points are sustained by Professor Creel's data. This seems true, for example, concerning a transition (posited on p. 90 of the article but touched on only briefly) from a "proto-feudalism" in very early Chou times to a subsequent "fully feudal stage."

Both Liu and Lattimore, in their reviews of *Feudalism in History*, comment on the editor's readiness, from time to time, to ignore or contradict in his interpretative essay what has been said in some of the regional essays. I believe this readiness is particularly apparent in his discussion of China, probably because some of the features of Chou feudalism as described by me do not readily accord with the editor's general criteria for feudalism. To cite but two examples: on p. 364 Professor Coulborn writes that "feudalism has been found here to be a mode of revival of a society whose . . . disintegrating polity was in every known case a great empire." This contradicts my own statement (p. 109; see also p. 119) that "in the case of Chou feudalism, it is highly doubtful whether any . . . antecedent 'highly organized political system' did in fact exist." Again, Professor Coulborn writes on pp. 365-366 that "feudalism is invariably a phenomenon occurring in an age of faith." This too contradicts my statement (p. 96; see also p. 120), according to which "one striking difference between Chou China and medieval Europe was that the former possessed neither a universal church nor a professional priesthood."[7]

Other statements surely occur in the article, however, that call for correction. Examples are the references on p. 68 to the eighteen degrees of honor instituted in the state of Ch'in, whereas the correct number is probably only seventeen; or the statement on the same page that the *hsien* (county) was first instituted in Ch'in in 688 and 687 B.C., whereas it now seems possible that the earliest instance may have been in Ch'u in 598. For the most part, however, I believe that despite the passage of time, the article still provides a reasonably good introduction to its subject—from which, however, interested readers should proceed to other later studies such as that of Creel.

## 5. Dominant Ideas in the Formation of Chinese Culture

BIBLIOGRAPHY, A-30; from *Journal of the American Oriental Society*, 62 (December 1942), 293-299.

"Dominant Ideas in the Formation of Asiatic Cultures" was the name of a symposium held in Boston on April 8, 1942, as part of the centennial celebration of the founding of the American Oriental Society. Besides this paper on China, the symposium included others on dominant ideas in India, in Judaeo-Christian culture, and in Islam.

---

[7] The two references made in this paragraph to the Coulborn article are to this article as paginated in the original Coulborn book, whereas the six page references made in the same paragraph and that before it to my own article are made in accordance with the new pagination for the article provided in the present book.

Symposia such as this provide welcome occasions for bringing together several succinct and clear presentations all neatly focused on the same general topic. The present China paper, in my opinion, has its share of these desirable qualities. On the other hand, it also, it seems to me, displays three major weaknesses which, as I now read it again after thirty-seven years, are readily apparent.

The first weakness—one admittedly hard to avoid in any very brief presentation—is that of making sweeping generalizations that ignore any exceptions, inconsistencies, or minority views. In discussing "The World of Nature," for example, the paper treats the views of the Taoists and the cosmologists as the norm, while ignoring Confucian and Buddhist views. In "The World of Man," on the other hand, the situation is reversed: Confucianism moves to the center of the stage while the other schools are disregarded. The fact that the Chinese responsible for the ideas labeled "dominant" under one rubric were not always the same Chinese who formulated the "dominant" ideas under another rubric is not clearly brought out. Or again, brevity almost always leads to omission. A good example from "The World of Nature" is the failure to mention an idea—or absence of an idea—of major and continuing importance in Chinese philosophical thinking. This, of course, is the customary absence of any theory of initial cosmic creation; most Chinese thinkers have viewed the universe as self-created and thus always existent, even though ever undergoing cycles of change. In view of this prevalent concept, it is wrong to describe the *Tao* or Way as "an impersonal first cause or prime mover" (Section 2); *Tao* is simply the name for the cosmic process in its total variety, ever changing but uncreated, and never coming to an end.

The second weakness is the paper's failure to live up to its initial pledge: that of presenting as "dominant" only those ideas common to large numbers of Chinese, illiterate as well as literate. On the contrary, the paper gives too much weight to the thinking of sophisticated intellectuals and not enough to that of the unlettered man or woman. This is particularly apparent in its treatment of "The World of the Supernatural," where, despite some qualifications, it unduly emphasizes the attitudes of intellectuals toward death and the supernatural, as against more popular attitudes. Religion *did* play an important role in Chinese life, despite the validity (but only within certain limits) of the statements made within the paper's first two pages. A major distinction between religion in China and, say, the monotheistic religions familiar to us, is that the former was more amorphous and eclectic, the latter more tightly organized and demanding more commitment from their adherents. Here it may be added that the eleventh article in this book ("Harmony and Conflict in Chinese Philosophy") is superior to the present article in that it explicitly confines itself to "philosophy," thus making no pretense, like the present paper, of covering *all* Chinese "dominant" ideas, low as well as high.

The third and most important weakness is the article's over-idealization of Chinese thinking and ways of life. This appears, for example, in its favorable remarks about Chinese historiography, unbalanced by any mention of such unfavorable features as the use of clichés, omission of important topics, or failure to provide individualized portrayal of historical figures. Or yet again, the bias appears in the favorable account of the Chinese governmental system within the main text, while all weaknesses of the system are relegated to two lengthy footnotes (notes 15 and 16). I remember, after presenting the paper in Boston, that somebody in the audience got up and remarked that the paper's picture of China was not too far removed from that conveyed by eighteenth-century Jesuit writers on China. Of course the commentator was entirely correct. In 1942, when I wrote this paper, I was still quite close to my student days in Peking, when anything Chinese seemed to me almost automatically to be better than anything Western. In the years that followed, I gradually matured and changed my thinking. This change is very apparent, for example, if one compares this 1942 production with the ninth article below ("Prison Life in Eighteenth Century Peking"), written in 1969.

Once one keeps these limitations in mind, however, I believe this paper still provides a useful survey of some ideas very important in the old Chinese ways of thinking.


## MAN IN SOCIETY

### 6. Types of Chinese Categorical Thinking

BIBLIOGRAPHY, A-15; from *Journal of the American Oriental Society*, 59.2 (1939), 200-219.

The thinking discussed in this article was long prevalent in China, and was especially important during the Han dynasty (206 B.C.-A.D. 220). Its central feature was the grouping of things, qualities, and ideas into classes, many of them numerically determined. Such classifications were applied just as much to the natural as to the human world, so that this article could well have been grouped with articles 15 and 16 under "Man in the Cosmos." Because, however, its particular examples belong mostly to the human world, it was chosen instead to head the present section.

The reader, before beginning his labors, should be warned of two matters. The first is that the word "categorical" in the title has nothing to do either with logic or a moral imperative. It refers solely to the above-mentioned practice of linking together seemingly unrelated things and ideas into groupings or categories. The second warning is that only the first third of the article discusses its topic in general terms. The remainder concentrates on a notable example occurring in the *History of the Former Han Dynasty*; some readers may regard the analysis as overly long and detailed. For another briefer but more technical article about thinking of a similar sort, see J. L. Kroll, "The Term *Yi-piao* and 'Associative' Thinking," *Journal of the American Oriental Society*, 93 (1973), 356-359.

Were I writing this article today, I would avoid citing earlier writings to support matters already well known. Particularly objectionable is note 10, with its reference to an immature and superficial article that should never have been published. On the other hand, a good deal of the article's first few pages about Chinese fondness for numerical categories and order and balance has recently been treated by me, in greater detail and I hope more maturely, in the course of preparing a lengthy section for the future final volume of Joseph Needham's *Science and Civilisation in China*. This section has to do with the sociological and intellectual factors that may either have encouraged or inhibited scientific ways of thinking in China before roughly 1600.

The present article's fourth note, remarking on the acute sense of direction possessed by the Chinese, reminds me irresistibly of the November afternoon in 1978 when, in company with thousands of others, I filed through the mausoleum of Mao Tse-tung in Peking. This structure is located due south of the major entrance to the imperial palace, the T'ien An Men or Gate of Heavenly Peace, and is itself on the major north-south axis of the old Peking. In former times all buildings of any importance in Peking, including private houses, faced southward in the direction of the life-giving sun, as did the emperor on his throne. Persons entering these buildings, and especially those being received by the emperor, always faced northward and moved from south to north. Remembering this from my earlier years in Peking, I was considerably struck by the fact that the long lines of people filing into Mao's mausoleum entered it from the north side and exited on the south. Whether or not this arrangement was deliberately made, it impressed me as one of the sharpest psychological breaks with the old China. Even during the pre-1949 years of the Republic, such an idea would have been inconceivable. Sun Yat-sen's mausoleum, for example, faces southward on the Purple Mountain outside Nanking.

Returning to the article, a slight typographical error should be noted in note 13, where the ninth item, *cheng lien*, should be corrected to *cheng chien*.

## 7. Authority and Law in Ancient China

BIBLIOGRAPHY, A-57; from *Authority and Law in the Ancient Orient*, Supplement No. 17 (July-September 1954), 46-55, of *Journal of the American Oriental Society*.

The symposium that prompted this paper belonged to one of the annual meetings of the American Oriental Society, and was held at Columbia University on April 14, 1954 as part of the bicentennial celebration of that institution. The symposium's other papers dealt with Egypt, Mesopotamia, the Hittite Kingdom, Canaan-Israel, and India. In their totality, the papers still constitute an excellent brief introduction to concepts of authority and law in the ancient orient.

I venture to hope that my own paper meets the criteria implied by this judgment, with the important single exception of its remarks on law in its last four paragraphs. In preparing for the symposium, I was handicapped by the fact that in 1954 my knowledge of Chinese law was still not really adequate for the task. The result, I fear, is that the actual role of law in imperial China was a good deal weightier than these last paragraphs might suggest, written as they were more on the basis of widespread opinion than of specialized knowledge. This fact, I hope, will become apparent through comparison of the present article with the much longer one that immediately follows in this book. By the time that second article was published nine years later, I had devoted a good deal of attention to Chinese law.

Other than this, I believe the only minor error calling for correction in the present article is the date of 1955 indicated in note 2 for the then forthcoming publication of the study of feudalism; the actual date was 1956.

## 8. Basic Concepts of Chinese Law: The Genesis and Evolution of Legal Thought in Traditional China

BIBLIOGRAPHY, A-74; from *Proceedings of the American Philosophical Society*, 107 (15 October 1963), 375-398.

The Western study of Chinese law, especially pre-modern Chinese law, still remains relatively undeveloped despite the considerable progress made since this article was published in 1963. Even today, so far as I know, the article remains the most comprehensive and detailed survey of its kind in English. It originated from a course on Chinese legal thought taught from 1961 onward in the University of Pennsylvania Law School—probably the first such course ever given in an American law school. In 1963 I presented the article in abbreviated form at the annual spring meeting of the American Philosophical Society, to which I had been elected a member. Later the same year it was published in the Society's *Proceedings* and then, in 1967, reprinted as the first chapter of *Law in Imperial China* (see Bibliography, A-79). Clarence Morris, my collaborator on the book, describes in its Preface how, beginning in 1959, he and I, together with my colleague W. A. Rickett, became interested in Chinese law and joined in its teaching and study.

There are only a few differences between the article and its reincarnation in the book. The most important comes at the end of sub-section 9.1, where the reincarnation, at p. 32 of the book, adds two paragraphs concerning the use of analogy in Ch'ing legal procedure and the development of sub-statutes in the Ming and Ch'ing codes. At subsection 9.4, near the beginning, the book version adds a new note 66 in which it enumerates the names and funeral garbs of the five degrees of mourning. In section 2, the book version adds two new sentences (pp. 44 and 47).

At different points in the article it seems desirable to call attention to a few new publications and developments.

At the end of section 1, concerning the loss of legal texts predating the T'ang code of 653: this statement requires revision as the result of the discovery in 1975 of extensive legal texts in the grave of a Ch'in dynasty official excavated at Yün-meng, Hupei province. The texts include numerous laws, many of them probably belonging to the otherwise long lost code of Ch'in as it existed shortly before the Ch'in creation of the first unified Chinese empire in 221 B.C. These materials are of highest importance for studying legal and administrative procedures and social conditions in Ch'in at that time. For a preliminary survey, see A.F.P. Hulsewé, "The Ch'in Documents Discovered in Hupei in 1975," T'oung Pao, 64 (1978), 175-217 and 338.

Note 8: of the *Hsing-an hui-lan* cases here mentioned, 190 have since been translated in *Law in Imperial China*.

Note 11: the T'ang code is now being translated by Wallace S. Johnson, Jr.; see his *The T'ang Code*, Vol. I: *General Principles* (Princeton: Princeton University Press, 1979).

Note 12: to Hulsewé's book on Han law add the article by J. L. Kroll, "Notes on Han Law," *T'oung Pao*, 51 (1964), 125-139.

Section 2, at note 16: Kauṭilya's *Arthaśāstra*, according to recent scholarship, is probably a composite text of varying date and author-ship, brought together into its present form somewhere around A.D. 250. See Thomas R. Trautmann, *Kautilya and the Arthaśāstra* (Leiden: E. J. Brill, 1971), pp. 174ff. (especially pp. 176 and 183).

Section 9, "The Imperial Codes": on codes and legal procedures, especially for the Ch'ing dynasty, see also William C. Jones, "Studying the Ch'ing Code—the Ta Ch'ing Lü Li," *American Journal of Comparative Law*, 22 (Spring 1974), 330-364; Brian E. McKnight, "A Sung Device for Encouraging Speedy Trial," *Journal of the American Oriental Society*, 95.3 (1975), 483-484; and Shūzō Shiga, "Criminal Procedure in the Ch'ing Dynasty—with Emphasis on Its Administrative Character and Some Allusion to Its Historical Antecedents," *Memoirs of the Research Department of the Toyo Bunko*, no. 33 (1975), pp. 115-138.

Section 8, Legalist influences on Han law: see also J. L. Kroll, "Chang T'ang's Statutes on Going beyond the Official Functions," *Archiv Orientalni*, 38 (1970), 313-331.

Note 83: to the Bünger article now add one by myself, "Age, Youth, and Infirmity in the Law of Ch'ing China" (Bibliography, A-84 and 92).

Note 86: to the Kennedy study now add M. H. van der Valk, "Voluntary Surrender in Chinese Law," *Law in Eastern Europe*, 14 (1967), 359-394; also W. Allyn Rickett, "Voluntary Surrender and Confession in Chinese Law: the Problem of Continuity," *Journal of Asian Studies*, 30 (August 1971), 797-814.

Section 11, "Law and Cosmic Harmony": A strong criticism of what is said here (and has been said by other scholars) comes from the late Hsu Dau-lin in his "Crime and Cosmic Order," *Harvard Journal of Asiatic Studies*, 30 (1970), 111-125. The article provides lively reading but suffers, in my opinion, from carelessness in citations, irrelevance of a good part of what it says, and failure to address itself to the main point of my exposition, namely, the correlation in early China of legal procedures with the rise and fall of animal and plant life through the seasons of the year. Above all, Dr. Hsu's article suffers from a reluctance to admit that ancient Chinese law (like much ancient law elsewhere) may in some measure have embraced elements of magic as well as reason. How, one wonders, would he explain the continued presence in the Chinese codes down to the present century of harsh penalties for manufacturing magic poisons or practicing other forms of black magic unless there was belief in such magic?

Section 11, paragraph after note 89: on Han ceremonies connected with the solstices, see now my *Festivals in Classical China* (Bibliography, A-87), chapters 6 and 13.

Note 95: to the references here listed now add Edouard J. M. Kroker, translator and commentator, *Die amtliche Sammlung chinesischer Rechtsgewohnheiten (Min shang shih hsi kuan tiao ch'a pao kao lu)*, *Untersuchungsbericht über Gewohnheiten in Zivil- und Handelssachen*, 3 vols. (Bergen-Enkheim bei Frankfurt/M., 1965). This is a compendium of civil and commercial customary law as reported from many areas by late Ch'ing and early Republican officials.

At note 78 of the article, the sentence pointing out the apparent parallel with American practice should say that wives are not compelled to testify against their husbands. I am grateful to Professor Morton Fried for this suggestion.

The article, unlike its reincarnation in book form, lacks Chinese characters. The following are those for a few of its technical terms:

> *chün tzu* 君子 (superior man)
> *chung* 忠 (loyalty)
> *fa* 法 (law)
> *hsiao* 孝 (filial piety)
> *hsing* 刑 (punishment)
> *li* 禮 (ceremony, politeness, etc.)

*liang jen* 良人 (commoner)
*lü* 律 (statute or pitchpipe)
*pa yi* 八議 (eight considerations)

## 9. Prison Life in Eighteenth Century Peking

BIBLIOGRAPHY, A-82; from *Journal of the American Oriental Society*, 89 (April-June 1969), 311-333.

In shortened form, this article served as my presidential address at the 1969 annual meeting of the American Oriental Society. It remains one of my favorites because it translates and evaluates a very rare kind of Chinese personal narration concerning an important aspect of Chinese government about which little is known. The somber picture of human brutality and resulting suffering depicted by it contrasts sharply with the idealization that all too often characterizes the expositions—my own included—of Chinese thinking on its higher "inspirational" levels.

Besides the very few written glimpses of Chinese prison life mentioned in the article's first footnote, mention might be made of the following (chronologically arranged):

C. R. Boxer, ed., *South China in the Sixteenth Century* (London: Hakluyt Society, 1953), pp. 17-25 and 175-185. These pages contain remarkably favorable accounts of Chinese prisons and judicial procedure written by a Portuguese trader and a Portuguese friar—the former an inmate of a Chinese prison during a good part of his sojourn in south coastal China, 1549-1552.

Niida Noboru, *Chūgoku hōsei-shi kenkyū* (Studies in the History of Chinese Legal Institutions), 3 unnumbered vols. (Tokyo: University of Tokyo Press, 1959-1964). Chapter 14, pp. 615-675 of the first volume (called in English *Criminal Law*) presents a wealth of material from Chinese plays, stories, and legal texts concerning the instruments of torture used in prison for interrogating prisoners, instruments of confinement, male and female prisons, and the carrying out of punishments ranging from beating to death by slicing. On Niida Noboru's very important researches on Chinese law, see Denis Twitchett, "Niida Noboru and Chinese Legal History," *Asia Major*, n.s. 13 (1967), 218-228.

Judy Feldman Harrison, "Wrongful Treatment of Prisoners: a Case Study of Ch'ing Legal Practice," *Journal of Asian Studies*, 23 (1964), 227-244. This is a study of thirty cases involving harsh treatment of prisoners by judicial authorities, taken from the *Hsing-an hui-lan* (Conspectus of Penal Cases), a compilation mostly of the nineteenth century. The article deals primarily with the legal principles involved in the judgment of cases, and therefore does not provide a vivid picture of Chinese prison life itself.

Bodde & Morris, *Law in Imperial China* (1967; Bibliography, A-79).

Three cases from the same compendium, in which harsh treatment of prisoners leads to their suicide, are translated on pp. 450-453; on pp. 455-460 are given two of the cases that are discussed (not translated) by Harrison.

L. Carrington Goodrich, "Prisons in Peking, *circa* 1500," *Tsing Hua Journal of Chinese Studies*, n.s. 10 (June 1973), 45-53: A translation of a French translation of an account by a Muslim merchant, Aly Ekber, describing his visit to China around 1500. What he says of prisons is vivid and horrifying, but at the same time filled with so many palpable errors as to make Professor Goodrich himself admit (in note 5) that "some of it strikes me as hardly credible."

Other less relevant writings include Fu-mei Chang Chen, "Local Control of Convicted Thieves in Eighteenth-century China," in Frederic Wakeman, Jr. & Carolyn Grant, eds., *Conflict and Control in Late Imperial China* (Berkeley and Los Angeles: University of California Press, 1975), pp. 111-142; and Chauncey S. Goodrich, "The Ancient Chinese Prisoners' Van," *T'oung Pao*, 61.4-5 (1975), 215-231.

Returning now to the article, the following are a few corrections and added comments:

Section II, at Fig. 1, the location of the Board of Punishments in Peking was not far west of the present mausoleum of Mao Tse-tung.

Note 55: the article here mentioned was published in 1973 (see Bibliography, A-84).

Subsection IV.4, second paragraph, lines 6-8: a translation error means that these lines should be reworded to read:

> he encountered an imperial amnesty. On the day he was about to be released, he had a party with his [prison] companions, at which they drank and

This change invalidates my statement following note 75. Other lesser errors are:

> Section I, sixth paragraph, line 5: *for* May 12 *read* May 5
> Note 56: for *Che jung* read *Che shu*
> Last paragraph, line 9: *for* of the West *read* by the West.

## 10. Henry A. Wallace and the Ever-Normal Granary

BIBLIOGRAPHY, A-34; from *Far Eastern Quarterly*, 5 (August 1946), 411-426.

I am glad to have this article included in the book, because it is the sole representative of one of my major research interests: the influence of Chinese ideas and things on the Western world. Three other items in the Bibliography (A-31, 41, and 49) also reflect this interest. The second of them, *Chinese Ideas in the West* (a pamphlet prepared for high-school use), stimulated the research that led to the present article.

This article appeals to me in the second place because the Chinese institution it describes was exactly two thousand years old in 1946 when the article was published; also because the article links the institution with the "New Deal" period of American history via the work and ideas of Henry A. Wallace (1888-1965) when he was Secretary of Agriculture (1933-1940). Many instances can be found from earlier times in which the influence of Chinese inventions and ideas on the West seems very probable but cannot be definitely proven; Joseph Needham's *Science and Civilisation in China* contains numerous examples. In the present instance, however, the chain of influence is very clear and was acknowledged by the late Mr. Wallace himself. Thus the Chinese ever-normal granary was initially mentioned by him in 1918 as an idea that might be worth trying in the United States, whereas, as pointed out in note 27 of the article, it was not until 1934 that he publicly mentioned Joseph in Egypt and the Mormons in Utah as parallels to the Chinese idea. No doubt institutions similar to the Chinese ever-normal granary can be found in other times and cultures; the marketplace operating in Mexico City in the seventeenth century, as alluded to in note 32, is a good example. Apparently nowhere else but in China, however, was the institution so well worked out and so long-lasting.

The last several pages of the article describe how Wallace in 1941, when he was vice president, conceived of an international "ever-normal granary" that would function as a world institution. Soon after the end of the Second World War, as the article goes on to describe, the idea was momentarily revived in 1946 in conjunction with the United Nations. Sadly, however, by that year the Cold War was already well under way, and since then the growth of divisive nationalisms has effectively prevented that "brotherhood of nations" that Chen Huan-chang, author of the book from which Wallace learned about the Chinese ever-normal granary, predicted in 1911 would some day come (see the article at note 6). Thus in recent decades not only the name but also the idea of the ever-normal granary have been largely forgotten. The latest reference I have seen is an Associated Press dispatch from Washington in the *New York Times* of November 2, 1961. This reports how Wallace, in a lecture the preceding day at a graduate training center in the Department of Agriculture, advocated that an "ever-normal granary" program "be put to use on an international scale to help the needy and make use of farm surpluses." Today, almost two decades later, the need for such a program is, if anything, greater than when Wallace spoke.

Turning now to a few small points in the article: the above-mentioned Chen Huan-chang died at fifty in 1931 in Peking, probably quite unaware of Wallace's interest in the institution he had described. Wallace himself died in 1965, by then ignored and largely forgotten after his 1948 unsuccessful campaign for the presidency. In note 9, the passage cited from the *Han shu* is now available in the translation of Nancy Lee Swann, *Food and Money in Ancient China* (Princeton: Princeton University Press, 1950), pp. 143-144; the same work, pp. 139-140, also describes the effort by Li K'o which is referred to earlier on the same page of the article. And the correct name of the famous statesman mentioned above note 9a is of course Sang Hung-yang, not San Hung-yang.

# MAN IN THE COSMOS

## 11. Harmony and Conflict in Chinese Philosophy

BIBLIOGRAPHY, A-56; from Arthur F. Wright, ed., *Studies in Chinese Thought* (Chicago: University of Chicago Press, 1953), pp. 19-80.

The book to which this article belongs is a symposium of nine papers originally presented at a conference in Aspen, Colorado in 1952. The article itself makes considerable use of quotations from Chinese philosophical texts contained in my translation of Fung Yu-lan's two-volume *History of Chinese Philosophy* (Bibliography, A-52 and 55). Of course, however, the article is far shorter and less comprehensive. It approaches Chinese philosophy in terms of a few basic themes labeled "The Cosmic Pattern," "The Pattern of History," "Good and Evil," and so on.

Both the book and the article have generally been well received. The late Kenneth Scott Latourette, writing in the Sunday Book Review of the *New York Times* of March 28, 1954, generously termed the book "the best volume on Chinese thought thus far written in the United States," and the article "as good an introductory brief account of Chinese thought as we now have." I myself recognize the dangers of making sweeping generalizations in such a broad field as Chinese philosophy, and no doubt some readers may question some of those in the article. Other very different approaches to harmony and conflict in Chinese philosophy are of course quite possible. Several are exemplified by the issue of the *Journal of Chinese Philosophy* (vol. 4.3, October 1977) containing four chronologically and topically diverse expositions of the subject. Their authors are Chung-ying Cheng, Maurice Meisner, James C. Hsiung, and Jan Yün-hua, with comments by H. G. Creel.

To touch on lesser matters: at the beginning of Section 1, the sketchy discussion of "Laws of Nature" is of course quite superseded by the detailed next article in the present book. In the tables of elements and their correlatives, I now believe that the color of the element wood should more properly be termed blue or azure rather than green. Concerning Chinese cyclical patterns of history (see Section 2), Joseph

Needham expresses a somewhat different opinion in his *Time and Eastern Man* (London: Royal Anthropological Institute of Great Britain and Ireland, 1965). At note 23, with respect to K'ang Yu-wei's utopian treatise, there is now the partial translation and partial paraphrase of this work by Laurence G. Thompson, *Ta T'ung Shu, the One-World Philosophy of K'ang Yu-wei* (London: Allen & Unwin, 1958); see also the articles in Lo Jung-pang, ed., *K'ang Yu-wei: a Biography and a Symposium* (Tucson: University of Arizona Press, 1967). As to Chinese social mobility and the civil service, a good anthology of relevant statements will be found in Johanna M. Menzel, ed., *The Chinese Civil Service: Career Open to Talent?*, Problems in Asian Civilizations (Boston: D.C. Heath & Co., 1963). At note 36, concerning Tung Chung-shu's correlations, see also Yao Shan-yu, "The Cosmological and Anthropological Philosophy of Tung Chung-shu," *Journal of the North China Branch of the Royal Asiatic Society*, 73 (1948), 40-68. Finally, in Section 6-E, the otherwise excellent quotation from Bruce is marred by his rendition of *li* as "Law"—very misleading, because of its erroneous suggestion of "Laws of Nature" in a Chinese environment. A better rendition is "principle."

The article contains a few minor typographical errors:

Section 3-A, second paragraph: *Mencius*, VI*a*, 3 should be *Mencius*, VI*a*, 2

Note 9, fifth line: *for* Chun-shu *read* Chung-shu.

Incidentally, the full title of the work by Hsi Wen-fu referred to in note 34 will be found in note 22.

## 12. Chinese "Laws of Nature": A Reconsideration

BIBLIOGRAPHY, A-91; from *Harvard Journal of Asiatic Studies*, 39 (1979), 139-155.

Basic to Joseph Needham's history of Chinese science known as *Science and Civilisation in China* is his lengthy analysis, at the end of Vol. II (1956), of the concept of "laws of nature" as it developed (or failed to develop) in China and the West. Inspired by what he wrote, I published an article in 1957 on the Chinese aspect of the subject (Bibliography, A-62). More recently, while spending three years (1974-1977) at Cambridge University preparing most of one section for the future final volume of *Science and Civilisation*, I had occasion to examine once more the question of whether the conception or near-conception of "laws of nature" can be found in early Chinese philosophical writings. This examination is the basis for the present article. It, rather than its 1957 predecessor, has been chosen for republication here because it not only sums up the earlier article but adds considerable new material. The topic, "laws of nature," is of some importance for evaluating Chinese and Western thinking alike and therefore should be of interest to historians of science in the West as well as in China.

Since the publication of this article, two further references to *t'ien fa*, "laws of Heaven," have come to my attention besides the two discussed in the section on Passage 8 in the article.

1. The Han statesman K'uang Heng 匡衡, in a memorial submitted to Emperor Ch'eng in 32 B.C., quotes a sentence (now no longer extant) from the *T'ai shih* 太誓 (Grand Declaration) section of the *Shu ching* (Documents Classic). See *Ch'ien Han shu* (History of the Former Han Dynasty), 25B.11a-b (Po-na ed.). The sentence reads: "Correctly observe antiquity, establish achievements, and establish affairs; thereby may Heaven's great statute (*lü* 律 ) be received for untold years." The commentator Yen Shih-ku (581-645) glosses *lü*, "statute," as *fa*, "law," and therefore explains the latter part of the sentence as meaning: "Thereby may Heaven's great law *(fa)* be received." The fact that men (and not the creatures and things of the nonhuman universe) are to receive this "statute" or "law" is enough to indicate that it has nothing to do with "laws of nature." The same passage and gloss are cited in the T'ang legal Code of A.D. 653. See translation of Wallace Johnson, *The T'ang Code*, Vol. I: *General Principles* (Princeton: Princeton University Press, 1979), p. 51, where by typographical error the words *lü* and *fa* are interchanged.

2. The *T'ai-p'ing ching* 太平經 (Classic of Grand Peace), a text of religious Taoism possibly dating from the second century A.D., though many scholars regard it as considerably later, contains the following passage in its thirty-sixth chapter: "They [the sages] did not dare to deviate however slightly from the laws of Heaven (*t'ien fa*)." See Max Kaltenmark, "The Ideology of the T'ai-p'ing ching," in Holmes Welch and Anna Seidel, eds., *Facets of Taoism: Essays in Chinese Religion* (New Haven: Yale University Press, 1979), p. 22 (where, however, *t'ien fa* is rendered as "celestial norm," not "laws of Heaven"). Here, as in the preceding instance, the fact that it is human beings (the sages) who are said to conform makes it once more evident that *t'ien fa* does not, in this sentence, signify "laws of nature."

In addition to these two negative instances, David Hawkes employs the term "heaven's laws" when translating the first two lines of a poetic riddle in the twenty-second chapter of the famed eighteenth-century novel, *Hung lou meng* (Dream of the Red Chamber). See David Hawkes, tr., *The Story of the Stone, a Chinese Novel by Cao Xueqin* (Harmondsworth: Penguin Books, 1976), I, 448. The lines read in his translation:

Man's works and heaven's laws I execute.
Without heaven's laws, my workings bear no fruit.

However, the Chinese term misleadingly rendered "heaven's laws" is actually *t'ien yün* 天運 , "cycle of Heaven" (meaning heavenly fate).

Thus this passage too has nothing to do with "laws of nature" in the Western sense.

### 13. The Chinese View of Immortality: Its Expression by Chu Hsi and Its Relationship to Buddhist Thought

BIBLIOGRAPHY, A-27; from *Review of Religion*, 6 (May 1942), 369-383.

Chu Hsi (1130-1200) is of course the great Neo-Confucian philosopher, and this article is a by-product of my translation of the Chu Hsi chapter in the second volume of Fung Yu-lan's *History of Chinese Philosophy*. The chapter was separately published in 1942 in advance of the volume (Bibliography, A-26).

The article's subject matter is divided into three roughly equal parts: one on non-Buddhist Chinese views of immortality, one on Chinese Buddhist views, and one on Chu Hsi's view and his attitude toward Buddhism. Several fairly extended discussions of various aspects of these topics have been published since 1942. On non-Buddhist attitudes, for example, see Hu Shih, "The Concept of Immortality in Chinese Thought," *Harvard Divinity School Bulletin*, 1946, pp. 26-43 (a very sketchy and somewhat superficial survey from the beginnings to the eleventh century A.D.); Yü Ying-shih, "Life and Immortality in the Mind of Han China," *Harvard Journal of Asiatic Studies*, 25 (1964-1965), 80-122; and Joseph Needham, *Science and Civilisation in China*, Vol. V/2 (Cambridge University Press, 1974), 71-127 (on immortality-theory in China and the West).

On Chinese Buddhist views, see Walter Liebenthal, "The Immortality of the Soul in Chinese Thought," *Monumenta Nipponica*, 8 (1952), 327-396 (despite its title, a discussion limited to the opinions of Buddhists and their opponents, with valuable translations of thirteen different texts, some quite lengthy); Kenneth Ch'en, "Anti-Buddhist Propaganda during the Nan-ch'ao," *Harvard Journal of Asiatic Studies*, 15 (1952), 166-192, and his *Buddhism in China* (Princeton: Princeton University Press, 1964), pp. 46-47, 111-112, and 138-139; Fung Yu-lan, *A History of Chinese Philosophy*, II, 284-292 (especially on a major critic of Buddhism, Fan Chen); and Etienne Balazs, "The First Chinese Materialist," in his *Chinese Civilization and Bureaucracy* (New Haven: Yale University Press, 1964), pp. 255-276 (a detailed discussion and translation of Fan Chen).

On Chu Hsi's attitude toward Buddhism, see Fung Yu-lan's *History*, II, 566-571, and especially Galen Eugene Sargent, *Tchou Hi contre le Bouddhisme* (Paris: Imprimerie Nationale, 1955); the latter makes it evident that Chu Hsi's understanding of Buddhism did not go very far.

Returning to my own article, a serious error is its repeated rendition of the Neo-Confucian word *li* or "principle" as "Law," thus wrongly evoking a suggestion of "Laws of Nature" in Chinese thinking. In my translation of Fung's *History* (but not the separate translation of the Chu Hsi chapter, published earlier), this rendition was corrected to "Principle."

There are two minor typographical errors: on the first page, last line, *change* Chi Hsi *to* Chu Hsi; at note 2, *change* letters *to* letter.

## 14. Some Chinese Tales of the Supernatural: Kan Pao and His *Sou-shen chi*

BIBLIOGRAPHY, A-22; from *Harvard Journal of Asiatic Studies*, 6 (February 1942), 338-357.

The Chinese thinking so far discussed in this book has been mostly of a refined, "philosophical" sort. In the present article, however, the intellectual environment sharply changes. Although the fourth-century writer Kan Pao is an official of aristocratic background, the stories he records in his *Sou-shen chi* (Researches into the Supernatural) combine spirits, ghosts, and magic with a great deal of earthiness and zest for everyday living. Thus it is evident that they reflect the popular beliefs of their day quite as much as the mentality of a Confucian scholar. Kan Pao, indeed, appears to have recorded his stories very seriously because he really believed in them. Unlike somewhat similar compilations of a much later time, they were by no means written simply to entertain.

The present article follows its discussion of Kan Pao and his compilation with translations of eight representative stories. Later the same year (1942) I published another more technical and less interesting article (Bibliography, A-29), further discussing Kan Pao's name and the date of his compilation, in refutation of views advanced by Lionel Giles in the *New China Review*, 3 (1921), 378-385 and 460-468.

The present article, as indicated in its note 31, is the by-product of a translation I had been preparing of a sixth-century text on annual festivals. A first draft of the translation had been completed when the 1941 Japanese attack on Pearl Harbor pulled me and countless other American academics into various kinds of war activity. Following World War II, I never had time to return to this translation, but perhaps I will eventually try to bring it into final shape.

Kan Pao's *Sou-shen chi* is of considerable interest from the point of view of religion and folklore as well as literature. A popular rendition of twenty-five of its stories (including four contained in the present article) appears in the anthology of translations by Yang Hsien-yi and Gladys Yang, *The Man Who Sold a Ghost; Chinese Tales of the 3rd-6th Centuries* (Peking: Foreign Languages Press, 1958), pp. 1-2, 6, and 11-54.

The *Sou-shen chi* deserves further attention from scholars, and the translation of more of its stories. So far as I know, the only person who has made much use of it for scholarly purposes is E.T.C. Werner in his *Myths and Legends of China* (London, 1922). Of the relationship of this work to the *Sou-shen chi* it has been written: "The Chinese work was the source for the materials in Werner's book. There are frequent unidentified quotations and summaries throughout."[1] This sounds as if Werner had used the *Sou-shen chi* without making any acknowledgment. However, he explicitly names the text in the first paragraph of his Preface, together with three other Chinese works on supernatural beings, and then states: "In writing the following pages I have translated or paraphrased largely from these works." His account of the goddess of silkworms *(Myths and Legends,* pp. 168-169) is similar to, but more elaborate than, the version of the same story translated in my article, story 3.

## 15. The Chinese Cosmic Magic Known as Watching for the Ethers

BIBLIOGRAPHY, A-69; from Søren Egerod and Else Glahn, eds., *Studia Serica Bernhard Karlgren Dedicata, Sinological Studies Dedicated to Bernhard Karlgren on His Seventieth Birthday October Fifth, 1959* (Copenhagen: Ejnar Munksgaard, 1959), pp. 14-35.

I feel privileged to have had this opportunity to contribute to the Festschrift in honor of one of the greatest of all Western sinologists. It was likewise my privilege to meet Karlgren for the first and last time in December 1975 at his office in the Museum of Far Eastern Antiquities, Stockholm. On that occasion, though feeble, he spoke well and was in good spirits. Among his statements I particularly remember the remark that China's two greatest literary productions are the *Tso chuan* history (on which he himself had conducted such important research) and the *Chuang-tzu.* Less than three years later, in October 1978 when I myself was in China, he died, blind, in a Swedish nursing home.

I believe that Karlgren appreciated the present article because, following its appearance and until a year or two before his death, he annually sent me a copy of the invaluable *Bulletin of the Museum of Far Eastern Antiquities* (the locus of so many of his own writings). I too have a liking for the article inasmuch as it deals with a very basic Chinese concept: that of the "sympathetic attraction" or "mutual action and response" operating between the interrelated components of an all-embracing "organismic" universe. Further, it studies this subject by tracing the history of a very curious magical practice from the first century B.C. until its final rejection by rationalists in the seventeenth and eighteenth centuries A.D.

[1] Martha Davidson, *A List of Published Translations from Chinese into English, French, and German*, Pt. 1: *Literature, Exclusive of Poetry* (Ann Arbor, Mich.: J. W. Edwards, 1952), p. 87.

A shorter and less detailed treatment of the same subject appears in Joseph Needham, *Science and Civilisation in China*, IV/1 (Cambridge University Press, 1962), 186-189. Exchanges between Dr. Needham and myself prior to publication of our respective studies enabled each to benefit to some extent from the work of the other.

On the second and third pages of my article, mention is made of the thesis of Edouard Chavannes that the Chinese untempered chromatic scale, identical with that of Pythagoras, might have been brought from Greece to Asia and eventually to China through the conquests of Alexander the Great. This thesis is strongly rejected by Needham in the work just mentioned, pp. 176-183. At several places in my article, the name of the mathematician Hsin-tu Fang (with a two-character surname) wrongly appears as Hsin Tu-fang; it is correctly given in Needham's opus.

## 16. Sexual Sympathetic Magic in Han China

BIBLIOGRAPHY, A-76; from *History of Religions*, 3 (Winter 1964), 292-299.

Like the preceding article, this one discusses the manner in which Han thinkers viewed the relationship of man to nature. In this case, however, the relationship is more tenuous and, to us moderns, less rational, because it rests on puns made between allegedly related words. Such puns, as we shall see, often appear in the thinking of Han cosmologists. Of particular interest is the sexual frankness of the sentence of text which is the core of the article, because such frankness runs counter to usual Confucian prudery on the subject.

Note 12 of the article cites several instances in which Han scholars interpret the chronological terms *keng* and *tzu* as puns. The following are two further instances: (1) *Shih chi*, chap. 25 (E. Chavannes, tr., *Les Mémoires historiques de Se-ma Ts'ien*, III [Paris, 1898], p. 305, note 2: *Tzu* [the chronological term] is said to be equivalent to *tzu*, "to engender"); (2) the Han apocryphal text, *Shih-wei t'ui-tu-tsai* 詩緯推度災 , as quoted by P'ei Sung-chih 裴松之 (372-451), commentary on the *San-kuo chih* (History of the Three Kingdoms), 2/3b, states: "*Keng* [the chronological term] is *keng* [again]; *tzu* [the chronological term] is *tzu* [to engender]."

One typographical error occurs at note 10, where "making use hairpins" should read "making hairpins."

# TEXT STUDIES

## 17. A Perplexing Passage in the Confucian Analects

BIBLIOGRAPHY, A-7; from *Journal of the American Oriental Society*, 53.4 (1933), 347-351.

This, my earliest scholarly publication on China, was by no means the product of a spontaneous burst of energy on my part. My second year in Peking as a Harvard-Yenching Institute Fellow was also the year (1932-1933) when a grim warning reached me from Harvard: get something into print if you want your fellowship renewed. This threat stimulated the writing of two articles: the one printed here and another (which I thought more interesting) on the uncertain paternity of Confucius. I sent both to the *Journal of the American Oriental Society*, whose Far Eastern editor, John K. Shryock, was then teaching Chinese at the same institution (the University of Pennsylvania) where I was later to do the same.

I am deeply grateful for the sound advice this scholar sent back to me. The paternity article, he thought, *might* perhaps be published in the *Journal*, but it was so vague in subject matter and uncertain in conclusions that he believed I would ultimately regret it. The *Analects* article, on the other hand, was clearer, more specific and more concrete. Retrospectively, I can now say further that it demonstrated an ability to use untranslated Chinese sources, which made it an ideal first effort for the neophyte. I accordingly wrote back asking to have it published, forgot all about Confucius' paternity, and enjoyed the happy reward of a renewal of my fellowship for another two years by Harvard.

This article may have won me a renewal of my fellowship, but it made remarkably little impact on the sinological world. Several post-1933 translators of the *Analects* simply ignored it entirely, among them Arthur Waley (1938), Lin Yutang (1938), and Daniel Leslie (1962). The one translator who apparently tacitly accepted its interpretation was James R. Ware, judging from his *Sayings of Confucius* (New York & Toronto: Mentor, 1955), in which the key sentence reads: "The Master rarely spoke of profit; his attachment was to fate and to Manhood-at-its-best."

Nevertheless, the article *did* attract the attention of two scholars who were not primarily translators. The first was Berthold Laufer (whom I had never met), whose brief note, "*Lun Yü* IX, 1," appeared in the very next issue of the *Journal of the American Oriental Society*, 54 (1934), 83. The note is still cherished by me, the more so because it was one of the final writings by this great scholar prior to his tragic death the same year.

After agreeing that the traditional understanding of IX, 1 is wrong, Laufer objected to equating the key word *yü* with *hsü* (see note 18 of the article). "There is no other example known," he wrote, "where *hsü* would represent *yü*." This statement, however, is wrong. For example, there are three other places in the *Analects* (V, 8, iii; VII, 28; XI, 25, vii) in which *yü* occurs and is glossed by Chu Hsi in his commentary as equivalent to *hsü*; Legge accepts the equation in all three instances.

Laufer's own interpretation of *yü* in IX, 1 was that it means "in comparison with, proportionately with." Hence, he believed, the passage should be rendered: "The Master rarely discussed material gain compared with the will of Heaven and compared with humaneness." To support this interpretation, he cited Friedrich Hirth, *Notes on the Chinese Documentary Style* (2nd ed., Shanghai, 1909), Sect. 158. Unfortunately for Laufer's argument, however, the *yü* discussed by Hirth in this section is not that of IX, 1 at all but another quite different *yü* 於.

The other critic is my friend Wing-tsit Chan, who refers briefly to my article on pp. 296-297 of his "The Evolution of the Confucian Concept Jen," *Philosophy East and West*, 4 (1954-1955), 295-319. The major cause of Professor Chan's criticism is my statement (fourth page) that *yü*, used as a conjunction, is uncommon. Of course he is right with respect to the functioning of *yü* as a mere *single conjunction* (A *yü* B, that is, A and B). But he is *not* right with respect to what I really intended to say and was remiss in not saying clearly. This is, that the alleged use of *yü* in IX, 1 as a *double conjunction* is in fact most unusual (A *yü* B *yü* C, that is, A and B and C). Professor Chan's negative viewpoint leads him to the lame conclusion that "unless better evidence is discovered, we had better leave the contradiction unsolved." I see little reason for accepting such a defeatist attitude when there is another interpretation that not only resolves the contradiction, but does so simply and in a grammatically acceptable manner.

Still another reading appears in Göran Malmqvist's new interpretation of *Analects*, IX, 1. It appears on p. 154, note 7 of his "What *Did* the Master Say?" in David T. Roy and Tsuen-hsuin Tsien, eds., *Ancient China: Studies in Early Civilization* (Hong Kong: The Chinese University Press, 1978). In the *Analects'* relevant sentence, *Tzu han yen li yü ming yü jen*, Professor Malmqvist believes that only the first *yü* functions as a conjunction ("and"), whereas the second is to be understood as a preposition ("compared with; than"). In this way he arrives at the rendition: "The Master spoke more rarely of profit and *(yü)* human destiny than *(yü)* of humanity." Such an interpretation, though ingenious, I nevertheless find unconvincing. In the first place, it seems quite unlikely that two *yü* words, being so closely spaced, would still function quite differently. Second, even if they did, I believe that such a construction would then probably require a shift in word order. The resulting sentence—still quite awkward, in my opinion—might then read: *Tzu, yü jen, han yen li yü ming* ("As to the Master, compared with *(yü)* humanity, he rarely spoke of profit and *(yü)* human destiny").

Regardless of how readers may react to all this, they can at least find in the article and these added comments a good illustration of how the meaning of a short sentence in classical Chinese can be completely changed by a single key word, depending on how one decides to interpret it. The article suffers from quite a number of minor errors and misprints, probably in part because I was too far away in Peking to read it in proof, including:

note 8: for *Kung-tse* read *Kungfutse Gespräche*
note 14: change the third character to 化,
note 15: change the second character to 了.
note 19: *for* XVIII, 4 *read* XVIII, 6
last page, ninth line from bottom: *for* Yüan Yüan *read* Juan Yüan.

## 18. Two New Translations of Lao Tzu

BIBLIOGRAPHY, A-58; from *Journal of the American Oriental Society*, 74 (1954), 211-217.

The little text called the *Lao Tzu* after its putative author, and later canonized as the *Tao Te Ching* or *Canon of the Way and the Power*, has been translated more times into Western languages than any other Chinese work. In English alone there must by now be well over fifty versions, a few of them good, many more mediocre or worse. Yet translations will continue to be made simply because the text is so short, so mysterious, so profound, so beautiful, and so deliberately ambiguous. For the same reasons it will never be possible to produce a really "definitive" translation.

Within this plethora of renditions, the two here selected for extended review are unusual because they both come from a distinguished scholar translating into two languages (French and English), neither of which happens to be his own. Let it be added that this scholar is the late J.J.L. Duyvendak, Professor of Chinese at the University of Leiden when I took my Ph.D. there in 1938, that he made these translations (as well as an earlier one in Dutch) during the years of Nazi occupation of his native Holland, and that they were his last works of substantial scholarship, published close to his sudden death in 1954. It should be clear from all this why these two translations are very close to me.

Duyvendak, like all earlier scholars, was of course confined in his work on the *Lao Tzu* to a very few transmitted literary versions. In 1973-1974, however, three royal tombs of early Han date were excavated at Ma-wang-tui, on the outskirts of Ch'ang-sha, capital of Hunan province. The third tomb, containing a written date corresponding to 168 B.C., yielded a large number of texts written both on wood and silk; among them were two similar but far from identical copies of the *Lao Tzu*. These, then, provide the first opportunity of comparing the literary versions of the *Lao Tzu* with true archaeological texts belonging to the early decades of the second century B.C.

The most revolutionary feature of Duyvendak's translations is his willingness either to shift phrases and clauses of the text from one chapter to another according to what he thinks was their probable original sequence, or when a phrase or clause is repeated in two different chapters, to delete it from one of them. Emendations of this sort, as carried out by Duyvendak, affect twenty-seven of the *Lao Tzu*'s eighty-one chapters. I have compared eight of the emendations with the corresponding readings in the two Ma-wang-tui texts.[1] The results are not favorable to Duyvendak. Thus the Ma-wang-tui texts confirm his judgment in two emendations (those involving chapters 52/56 and 23/17), but contradict it in all six of the others. Indeed, in two of the latter (chapters 27/62 and 56/81), the Ma-wang-tui texts call for transfers of material in the *reverse direction* from that proposed by Duyvendak (i.e., from 27 to 62 instead of 62 to 27, and from 56 to 81 instead of 81 to 56). This sampling thus obliges me to modify my favorable opinion of Duyvendak's rearrangements expressed in the article. It also seems to indicate that duplications of phrases or clauses were actually not uncommon in early versions of the *Lao Tzu*, so that their presence does not necessarily justify the making of deletions.

Besides matters of rearrangement or deletion, the Ma-wang-tui texts are important because their readings of individual characters or phrases often differ from those in the received literary versions. Not infrequently, in fact, they also differ between themselves. For example, the phrase *hsi ming* 襲明 , "twofold understanding" (see my article, second page left column), appears in the first of the Ma-wang-tui texts as *shen ming* 忡明 and in the second as *yi ming* 曳明 . Although neither reading makes sense as it stands, it seems probable that the *shen* of the first is a graphic distortion of *shen* 神 , "divine," thus yielding a new phrase, *shen ming*, "divine spirituality" (or possibly "divine understanding"). It is likewise possible that *yi* in the second version is a graphic distortion of the right-hand side of *shen*, "divine," and is intended to stand for that word. This would then mean that the phrases in both versions have the same meaning and that this meaning is quite different from the *hsi ming* of the received literary versions.

Although the Ma-wang-tui readings often seem superior to those in the traditional literary versions, this is by no means always so and

---

[1] The eight emendations involve chaps. 52/56 and 42 (discussed on the third page of my article, left column), as well as chaps. 2/43, 4/56, 10/51, 23/17, 27/62, and 56/81. The *Lao Tzu* texts from Ma-wang-tui are transcribed into modern Chinese in *Wen Wu* (Cultural Relics), 1974, no. 11, pp. 8ff.; also in *Ma-wang-tui Han-mu po-shu* (Silk Texts from the Han Tomb at Ma-wang-tui) (Peking: Wen-wu, 1974), vols. (*ts'e*) 2, pp. 2a-26a, and 6, pp. 2a-25b.

sometimes the Ma-wang-tui texts contradict one another. Generally speaking, the first of them seems to have been written more carelessly than the second, which approaches more closely the traditional literary versions. Despite these or other limitations, however, it is evident that any future studies or translations of the *Lao Tzu*, if they are to advance beyond previous scholarship, will have to pay very serious attention to these two archaeological texts.[2]

## 19. On Translating Chinese Philosophic Terms

BIBLIOGRAPHY, A-59; from *Far Eastern Quarterly*, 14 (February 1955), 231-244.

This article was initially written to defend the renditions of certain terms used in my translation of Fung Yu-lan's *History of Chinese Philosophy*, Vol. II (Bibliography, A-55), which had been criticized by the late Peter A. Boodberg in a review of that work. However, the article goes on to discuss general principles of translation as formulated not only by Boodberg but by Edward H. Schafer, and ends by formulating several principles of its own.

Translation, being an art rather than a science, can never enjoy any full measure of agreement, especially when it attempts to bridge such linguistic dissimilarities as Chinese and the Indo-European languages. In addition to the articles on Chinese translation listed in the first note of the article, there has since accumulated a growing literature of varying value. The following examples (arranged chronologically and some of them more concerned with language per se than with actual translation) are representative:

Arthur Waley, "Notes on Translation," *Atlantic Monthly*, 202 (November 1958), 107-112.

A. C. Graham, " 'Being' in Western Philosophy Compared with *Shih/ Fei* and *Yu/Wu* in Chinese Philosophy," *Asia Major*, n.s. 7.1-2 (1959), 79-112. This is technical but of high quality. Graham's conclusion (not shared by me) is that neither English nor classical Chinese is better than the other as an instrument of thought. Elsewhere, however, he sees a probable connection between the structure of the Chinese language and the traditional indifference of Chinese thinkers to logical problems. See p. 55 of his "The Place of Reason in the Chinese Philosophical Tradition," in Raymond Dawson, ed., *The Legacy of China* (Oxford: Clarendon Press, 1964), pp. 28-56.

---

[2] The growing scholarly literature on the Ma-wang-tui texts, including the two *Lao Tzu* texts, comprises, to cite only a few items in English: Jan Yün-hua, "The Silk Manuscripts on Taoism," *T'oung Pao*, 63 (1978), 65-84 and esp. pp. 66-69; Robert G. Henricks, "A Note on the Question of Chapter Divisions in the Ma-wang-tui Manuscripts of the *Lao-tzu*," *Early China*, 4 (1978-1979), 49-51; and Tu Wei-ming, "The 'Thought of Huang-Lao': a Reflection on the Lao Tzu and Huang Ti Texts in the Silk Manuscripts of Ma-wang-tui," *Journal of Asian Studies*, 39 (November 1979), 95-110 and esp. pp. 99-102.

Tsu-lin Mei, "Chinese Grammar and the Linguistic Movement in Philosophy," *Review of Metaphysics*, 14 (March 1961), 463-492.

A. C. Graham, *Poems of the Late T'ang* (Harmondsworth: Penguin Books, 1965), pp. 13-37, "The Translation of Chinese Poetry."

Chung-ying Cheng, "A Generative Unity: Chinese Language and Chinese Philosophy," *Tsing Hua Journal of Chinese Studies*, n.s. 10 (June 1973), 90-104.

Wing-tsit Chan, *A Source Book of Chinese Philosophy* (Princeton University Press, 1963), pp. 783-791, "On Translating Certain Chinese Philosophical Terms": This concentrates on justifying the English renditions of specific terms but says little about general principles.

Manfred Porkert, *Theoretical Foundations of Chinese Medicine* (Cambridge, Mass. & London: MIT Press, 1974): Porkert's radical translation procedure consists of latinizing most Chinese medical or other technical terms and sometimes even replacing them by phonemes of his own invention. Thus the "ten celestial stems" (*chia, yi, ping*, etc.) become *ust, bust, cust*, etc., and their counterpart "twelve terrestrial branches" (*tzu, ch'ou, yin*, etc.) become *ast, bast, cast*, etc. The result, as one reads this book, is that one can readily forget it is dealing with a Chinese subject. Worth reading in conjunction with it is the lengthy review article by Joseph Needham and Lu Gwei-Djen, "Problems of Translation and Modernization of Ancient Chinese Technical Terms," *Annals of Science*, 32 (September 1975), 491-501, followed by Porkert's rebuttal, pp. 501-502.

Returning to my own article, the fourth page contains a serious error in the supposition that the term *t'i-yung* (substance and functioning) is probably of Chinese Buddhist origin. Of course the term actually originates with the Neo-Taoist Wang Pi (226-249), who uses it in his commentary on the thirty-eighth chapter of the *Lao-tzu*. Thereafter, as pointed out by Chan (*Source Book of Chinese Philosophy*, pp. 322-323), the term becomes an important one both in Chinese Buddhism and Neo-Confucianism.

Owing to printing difficulties in the *Far Eastern Quarterly* at the time, my article suffers from several typographical errors. Most serious is the omission of note 26a which should read:

26a. Cf. *Chou Yü* C/2: "To love (*ai*) others is to be capable of *jen*."

Other errors include:
Section 4, paragraph 4, second line: *delete* mi
note 38: *for* Gabenlentz *read* Gabelentz

## 20. Lieh-Tzu and the Doves: A Problem of Dating

BIBLIOGRAPHY, A-70; from *Asia Major*, n.s. 7.1-2 (1959), 25-31.

The volume of *Asia Major* in which this article first appeared was published in honor of the seventieth birthday of the late Arthur Waley, and the article discusses an episode about which Dr. Waley had commented. By putting together several seemingly unrelated phenomena, the article attempts to prove that a particular anecdote recorded in the Taoist work *Lieh-tzu* could hardly have been written prior to the first or second century A.D. (the Later Han dynasty), and could conceivably have been composed a century or so later. This conclusion runs counter to that of Waley who, like most Western scholars as late as 1959 (original date of the article), believed the *Lieh-tzu* to be a pre-Han text. Sharply different is the opinion of most modern Chinese scholars, who regarded (and still regard) the work as a compilation of the third or fourth century A.D., in which, however, some earlier materials are embodied.

The years immediately following 1959 saw the appearance of A. C. Graham's English translation of the entire text, *The Book of Lieh-tzu* (London: John Murray, 1960), followed by his careful and detailed study, "The Date and Composition of Liehtzyy," *Asia Major*, n.s. 8.2 (1961), 139-198. The latter convincingly demonstrates that the *Lieh-tzu* was in all probability deliberately forged at the very end of the third century A.D. or early fourth century; its style is homogeneous, aside from about one-quarter of the total, which the forger copied or adapted from earlier known sources. It is to be hoped that Professor Graham's study has changed the opinions of some believers in the early dating. It has certainly made me more open to the idea than I was when I wrote the article that the episode there discussed may have been composed as late as around A.D. 300 rather than a century or two earlier, as I then thought more probable.

It should be further noted that the article's section on "Presentation of Dove-staffs to the Aged" is now treated in considerably greater detail in chapter 16, pp. 341-348, of my 1975 book, *Festivals in Classical China* (Bibliography, A-87).

A curious parallel to the episode in which doves save the life of the founder of the Han dynasty occurs in the traditions about Fanca 范察, a sixteenth-century ancestor of the Ch'ing (Manchu) ruling house who, it is said, was once protected from his enemies by a "divine magpie" (*shen ch'iao* 神鵲). Having been pursued by these enemies, Fanca fled to the wilds, where a divine magpie settled on his head. The pursuers, seeing the roosting bird from afar, mistook the human form beneath it for a dead tree and so abandoned their pursuit. See the *Ta Ch'ing T'ai-tsu kao huang-ti shih-lu* 大清太祖高皇帝實錄 (Veritable Records of the Great Ch'ing Grand Ancestor and Lofty Emperor; preface dated 1686), 1/3b (1964 Taipei reprint, p. 2). The tale is also recounted in J. Macgowan, *The Imperial History of China* (2nd ed., Shanghai, 1906), note on p. 501. (For these references I am indebted to Professor Franz Michael, letters of March 16 and April 21, 1959.) As also told in the same *Shih-lu* (1/

2a-b or 1964 reprint, p. 1), another divine magpie at an earlier date had once deposited a red fruit on the clothing of one of three girls while the three were bathing. The girl ate the fruit, became pregnant, and thus gave birth to Aisin Gioro, first ancestor of the later imperial Manchu clan.

## 21. Marshes in *Mencius* and Elsewhere: A Lexicographical Note

BIBLIOGRAPHY, A-90; from David T. Roy and Tsuen-hsuin Tsien, eds., *Ancient China: Studies in Early Civilization* (Hong Kong: Chinese University Press, 1978), pp. 157-166.

The book to which this article belongs is a Festschrift for my friend Herrlee G. Creel. The article itself resulted from my puzzlement when reading with students a passage in the *Mencius* contained in a textbook prepared by Professor Creel and his colleagues. In themselves, the findings of the article are not highly important. Nevertheless, the process of reaching them illustrates rather neatly, I think, how, by being willing to explore many texts, one can learn something completely new about a seemingly everyday word. In this case it is a word which, though used with a peculiar touch in the *Mencius*, was left unexplained there by some two thousand years of commentators. No doubt this was because the *Mencius* is an ethical text and this ordinary word possesses no ethical significance. The moral, perhaps, is that new insights and information are still to be gained from the classics, provided only that we moderns are willing to approach them with questions different from those that were central in traditional scholarship.

An anthropologist and cultural ecologist at the University of California at Riverside, Professor E. N. Anderson, Jr., has kindly commented on this article in a letter to me of December 13, 1979: "A unitary, sensible translation of *tse* that fills all the bills might be 'river-bottom.' Early Chinese agriculture was probably often carried out in wooded river-bottoms because of the rich soil. A river-bottom would have marshes, pools, and dry forested ground, as well as thickets and patches of grass; it would contrast, very appropriately, with mountains."

As thus described, "river-bottom" seems indeed to meet many of the criteria postulated for *tse* in various contexts. I am therefore happy to add it to the list of possible English equivalents proposed for *tse* near the end of the article. On the other hand, I question whether "river-bottom" was ever the only, or even necessarily the most common, meaning intended by *tse* in the early texts. Such a supposition would carry with it the further implication that such *tse* were usually or always associated with rivers, and hence usually or always long and relatively narrow in shape. To me it seems more probable that already in rather early times, as suggested in the article, some *tse* were true marshes but others were pools or lakes; some were meadows or plateaus, probably in many cases largely devoid of water; and some were probably of irregular shape, extending perhaps several miles in various directions and not necessarily river-centered at all, even though one or several waterways may sometimes have run through them.

In short, I am ready with much appreciation to accept the suggestion that "river-bottom" was quite possibly one of the more important early significations of *tse*. However, it does not follow from this, in my opinion, that such a single term can serve as a "unitary" (if this means all-inclusive) translation.

# THE FORMATION OF
# CHINESE CULTURE

# Introduction to the History of China

Our word "civilization" goes back to a Latin root having to do with "citizen" and "city." The Chinese counterpart, actually a binom, *wen hua*, literally means "the transforming [i.e., civilizing] influence of writing." In other words, for us the essence of civilization is urbanization; for the Chinese it is the art of writing.

The ramifications of this capsulized distinction have been many and significant. Throughout their literate history, the Chinese have been much more interested in the written than the spoken word. Famous Chinese orators have been rare, famous calligraphers legion. Whereas in India it was the oral recitation of a sacred composition that made it efficacious, in China it was above all its reproduction in written or printed form. Papers bearing writing could not be indiscriminately discarded in the streets of the old China. This was not so much because they polluted the streets as that such an act showed disrespect to the written word. As late as the 1930's it was still possible, in Peking, to see public trash receptacles inscribed with the traditional exhortation: *"Ching hsi tzu chih,"* "Respect and spare written paper."

No doubt this attitude stems from the nature of Chinese writing: a nonalphabetic and basically ideographic script whose thousands of separate symbols or characters each signifies a distinct object or concept and therefore, like the Arabic numerals (1, 2, 3, 4, etc.), are immediately understandable to the eye irrespective of the pronunciations the reader may attach to them. This fact explains why the Chinese script could become the written medium of peoples adjoining the Chinese: not only those, like the Vietnamese, closely related to the Chinese linguistically, but also peoples, like the Koreans and Japanese, whose spoken languages belong to totally different linguistic families.

Because each Chinese ideograph carries from its cultural past its own distinct connotations, the acceptance of Chinese writing by others meant, to a considerable extent, their acceptance of Chinese cultural and moral values as well. Conversely, the Chinese script proved a major barrier to the free *entry* of foreign ideas and values into Chinese culture, because it meant that these values and ideas could reach the Chinese consciousness only through the filter of the ideographs. Resulting frequent failures and distortions of communication were as well known to Buddhist missionaries fifteen hundred years ago as they were to those from the Christian West of the seventeenth century onward.

The prime place of calligraphy among the Chinese arts and its intimate relationship with Chinese painting are both well known. But the significance of their concern with writing has a far wider cultural range. There seems to be a consistent pattern, for example, in the fact that the Chinese were the inventors of paper (first century A.D.), of block printing (ninth century or earlier), and of movable type (eleventh century). Or that, prior to around 1750, they are said to have produced more printed books than the rest of the world put together.

Of particular interest to us here, however, are the social and political consequences. The high prestige of the written language, combined with the tremendous difficulties attached to its mastery, gave to the scholar in China a status unequaled in any other society. During the past two thousand years, speaking very broadly, the Chinese ruling elite consisted neither of nobles, priests, generals, nor industrial or commercial magnates, but rather of scholar-officials. These were men educated from childhood in the Confucian classics who, ideally, became members of officialdom through success in the government's civil service examinations. These examinations, which were written, humanistic in content, and exceedingly rigorous, were conducted periodically throughout the empire at county, provincial, and national levels. In name they were open to all but a very few members of the total male population. In actuality, of course, it was only a tiny fraction of that total who were educationally qualified to take them.

If any single word can describe the imperial state system, it is *bureaucracy*. The government maintained a complex network of official positions which were specialized, ranked according to a fixed scale in the civil service, salaried accordingly, and staffed on the basis of demonstrated intellectual qualifications rather than birth. Career officials moved upward, or sometimes downward, on the bureaucratic ladder according to the merits or demerits regularly entered on their dossiers by their superiors; of course the usual principle of seniority operated as well.

It would be wrong, however, to suppose that these officials were commonly unimaginative, rigid, or lacking in initiative simply because some people today associate these characteristics with the word "bureaucracy." It should be remembered that governmental service was the most highly regarded of all professions for the Chinese educated man and that he came to it trained as a humanist rather than as a technician. As a rule, he had a good appreciation of the accepted literary and artistic accomplishments—notably poetry, calligraphy, and painting— and not infrequently he was a competent practitioner of them. Thousands of Chinese bureaucrats have been passable poets, and most great poets have at some time been bureaucrats.

Like every bureaucracy, that of China generated enormous amounts of paper work, often in multiple copies. These documents, preserved in the official archives, provided much of the raw material that was periodically incorporated into the official or dynastic histories. These histories, normally compiled under imperial auspices from dynasty to dynasty (hence their name), constituted a historical record more continuous, detailed, and precise than those available for any of the other long-lived ancient civilizations.

Although the Chinese bureaucratic system formally began with the creation of the first centralized empire in the third century B.C. (about which more below), tendencies toward bureaucratism may be already detected in the feudal period centuries earlier. If, in fact, the Chinese were not the world's first bureaucrats, they can at least be credited with the creation of governmental forms more complex, more sophisticated, and longer-lived than anywhere else prior to the Industrial Revolution. Indeed, recent research increasingly indicates that certain features hitherto deemed unique in modern bureaucracies were anticipated, and in some cases perhaps even inspired, by Chinese example. There is little doubt that the Chinese form of government has been a major factor in the remarkable continuity of Chinese civilization, both culturally and politically. Another, less formal institution of sterling importance for the lengthy maintenance of Chinese social stability, of course, has been the famed Chinese family system.

We began these pages with the proposition that the Westerner sees civilization as a process of urban development, the Chinese as that of spreading the written word. The role of the city-based bourgeoisie in the rise of modern Western society is known to all. In traditional China, on the contrary, society was strongly rooted in the countryside, cities served often more as administrative than as commercial centers, and the scholar-officials, though necessarily spending much of their lives in an urban environment, usually continued to regard the small rural village of their ancestors as their real "home." Many of them invested their surplus capital in farmland, which they rented to tenant peasants. Perhaps they might retire to their rural communities as landlords or, if continuing an official career, might allow their estate to be managed by a rural branch of the family. Thus our earlier definition of China's dominant elite as consisting of scholars and officials needs to be broadened to include rural landlords as well. Because of the extraordinary cohesiveness and dominance of this interlocking scholar-official-landlord class, Chinese traditional society has sometimes been referred to as Chinese gentry society.

The orthodox ideology of the gentry was Confucianism, but its social and political norms widely permeated all social classes. At the same time, however, the Chinese, perhaps because of their closeness to the soil, were unusually aware of the intimate relationship between man and nature, and the consequent need to harmonize man's movements with the cosmos. Taoism (pronounced "dow-ism") was the major philosophy for achieving this goal. Its spirit imbues much of Chinese imaginative literature, especially poetry, and Chinese art, especially painting.

Despite gentry dominance, a great many merchants and entrepreneurs individually succeeded in acquiring great wealth. Never, however, did they achieve sufficient class cohesiveness to seriously challenge the status and values of the dominant elite. On the contrary, in the very course of reaching success, they tended to adopt these values for themselves and thus eventually to convert themselves into members of the elite. Traditionally, Confucianism favored agriculture as the prime basis of national wealth, while showing suspicion toward large-scale private commercial activity. The history of imperial China is filled with examples of the imposition of bureaucratic limitations upon such activity. The resulting contrast with Japan is instructive. Probably it is no accident that modern Japan, with very little bureaucratic tradition, moved successfully from feudalism to massive industrial capitalism, whereas modern China largely jumped the capitalist stage by moving directly from preindustrial agrarian bureaucratism to what might be called socialized bureaucratism. (Of course there is very much more to the present government than this rather forbidding term by itself would suggest.)

How old is Chinese civilization? Roughly, perhaps, the same age as that of India but considerably younger than the major civilizations of the ancient Near East. Neolithic cultures have been uncovered in China, some of them probably going back to the early third millennium B.C., or possibly earlier. They have produced some artifacts of amazing beauty (notably the burial urns of the "painted pottery" culture), but none of the cultures can as yet be identified with any stages of early Chinese history as recorded in later traditional historiography. The earliest confirmation of history by archaeology comes only in the second half of the second millennium B.C., with the discovery of the divination bone inscriptions pertaining to the bronze civilization of the Shang dynasty.

Many major hallmarks of ancient Eurasian civilizations—among them the use of bronze and later iron, the invention of the wheel, the idea of writing, and the cultivation of wheat—all appear many centuries earlier in the ancient Near East than they do in China. This fact has led to a continuing and inconclusive debate between the diffusionists (most of them, unsurprisingly, Westerners), who believe that these techniques and ideas were invented only once in the Near East and then transmitted across the continent to East Asia, and those other scholars (most of them, unsurprisingly, Chinese) who believe in independent invention.

What are the major patterns or movements of Chinese history? Space permits a summary description of only four. By far the most important is the passage from feudalism to empire during the first millennium B.C. During most of this millennium, the then "China" consisted of a coterie of small principalities mostly clustered in the north around the Yellow River valley and westward, plus one or two others in the Yangtze valley farther south. These principalities were ruled by hereditary noble houses. The social and political relationships operating within and between them, as well as with their nominal overlords above, the Chou dynasty kings, were in some ways remarkably similar to those characterizing feudal Europe during the Middle Ages. Endemic warfare, coupled with other factors, gradually produced increasingly acute social, political, and economic changes. The later centuries of the Chou (fifth to third centuries B.C., appropriately named the Warring States period) were the age of China's greatest intellectual diversity, when many competing schools of thought, including Confucianism and Taoism, arose in response to the needs of the time.

The most important single date in Chinese history before the abolition of the monarchy in 1912 is 221 B.C. In that year the state of Ch'in brought Chinese feudalism to an end by conquering the last opposing principality and creating for the first time a truly universal Chinese empire. (The name "China," from Ch'in, commemorates the Ch'in achievement, but has never been used by the Chinese themselves, who have always termed their land *Chung kuo*, "the Central Country.") This event begins the age of imperial China and with it the bureaucratic state—the roots of which, however, as indicated above, actually go back centuries earlier.

Since the founding of empire, the historical pattern most emphasized by Chinese historians themselves has been that of the dynastic cycle: a sequence of major dynasties, each having a usual duration of somewhat under three hundred years, in the course of which it would come into being, flourish and expand, then decline, and finally disintegrate. Each such cycle would usually be closed by a much briefer period of political disorder and warlordism, out of which, eventually, a new dynasty would arise. Overemphasis on this recurrent pattern has created the traditional belief that nothing much has ever changed in China. That this notion needs correction should, in art at least, be apparent to anyone who turns these pages.

A third pattern has been that of the recurring tension between the agrarian Chinese and the pastoral peoples of the steppes and deserts north and northwest of China proper. The Great Wall was first built under the Ch'in empire as an arbitrary and only partially effective attempt to demarcate the two ways of life. In the long run, neither the Chinese nor the nomads could impose their life patterns on each other, but in the short run (which in China might mean a century or more), China proper repeatedly expanded to embrace greater China during the peaks of major dynasties, but contracted again under "barbarian" pressure during the intervening troughs. Twice in late imperial times, all of China fell under barbarian rule: first under the Mongols (the Yuan dynasty, 1279-1368) and again, more effectively, under the Manchus (the Ch'ing dynasty, 1644-1912).

A fourth and very significant but little understood development is that of the growing urbanization and commercialization of Chinese life beginning during the late T'ang dynasty (ninth century) and perhaps reaching its peak under the Sung (960–1279). During these centuries, commercial and industrial activity, especially in Central and South China, enormously increased. The circulation of metal coins reached a level never equaled before or since, and was supplemented in the eleventh century by extensive issues of the world's first paper currency. A new bourgeois class swelled the population of the great cities, which became major centers of trade as well as administration. The spread of printing brought literacy to a widening sector of the population and fostered the growth of new popular forms of literature. In short, what was to begin in Renaissance Europe several centuries later seemed already to be beginning in China, with all the potential changes this implied. But then something happened or rather failed to happen: the forces that were to lead to capitalism and industrialism in Western Europe failed to achieve ongoing momentum in China. The West was to change into a modern society, China did not. Why this should have been—whether it resulted from the Mongol invasions or the resiliency of the Confucian bureaucratic state or other factors—is one of the major unanswerables in Chinese history.

In the nineteenth century, beginning with the Anglo-Chinese Opium War of 1839–42, the industrializing West came to China in force and irrevocably broke or changed the traditional historical patterns. The monolithic imperial polity disintegrated after more than two thousand years, followed first by Sun Yat-sen's Republic in 1912, and then eventually by the People's Republic of China in 1949. To what extent China today continues to be influenced by more than three thousand years of recorded history is a matter of controversy. At first sight, certainly, the changes seem total. Yet as implied above, when comparing China with Japan, the strength of the past may still be more weighty than appears on the surface. But that is another story.

# THE CHINESE LANGUAGE
# AS A FACTOR IN
# CHINESE CULTURAL CONTINUITY

In the present age of rapid change and uncertainty, it is not amiss to investigate what may be some of the factors that have given Chinese civilization that remarkable continuity and vitality which make of it the oldest of the world's living civilizations. These factors are, of course, many, but one of the most fundamental is probably the peculiar nature of the Chinese language, and especially of its script, which sets it so sharply apart from our own types of language.

Chinese writing consists of isolated characters or "ideographs," each of which represents a single unchanging word. A similar phenomenon is to be found in our Arabic numerals 1, 2, 3, etc., which are written the same in many countries, although they may be pronounced one, two, three, in English, un, deux, trois, in French, and so on.

ADVANTAGES OF THE CHINESE SCRIPT

There are certain features inherent in the Chinese language which bring their own definite compensations. The first and most important of these is that each word remains eternally the same regardless of how it is used, the tense of a verb or number of a noun usually being indicated by the context of the sentence. For such a language as this, an ideographic type of script is ideally suited, since it need not represent inflectional changes. For inflected languages like our own, on the contrary, phonetic symbols of some sort are a necessity.

As a result of this and other factors, Chinese has really developed into two forms of language widely differing from each other: (1) a colloquial "spoken" language, which has undergone constant phonetic and other changes through the centuries; and (2) a "classical" written language, which was under no necessity to follow the changes in the colloquial language, and which therefore crystallized early into a relatively stable form of expression, having a grammar and even vocabulary widely different from the colloquial. This unique phenomenon has resulted in two effects of incalculable importance upon the development of Chinese cvilization:

(1) It has given to China an unexampled literary and hence cultural *continuity in time,* inasmuch as an educated Chinese could, once he possessed a knowledge of the written language, read ancient classics, written thousands of years ago, with little less facility than contemporary documents. This meant that the early classics came to be revered as the highest models of style and thought, and exerted a profound and uninterrupted ideological influence upon countless generations of Chinese scholars.

(2) It also gave to China an equally striking literary and cultural *unity in space.* For though many of the dialects spoken in China differ from each other as widely as do English and French, yet the domination of the literary classical language prevented the emergence of regional types of literature, and so assured a means of communication that was equally accessible to every literate Chinese.

In Europe during the Middle Ages, the use of Latin acted similarly as a unifying agent. But the alphabet in which Latin words were written was equally suitable for recording the languages of separate regions. Hence with the beginnings of nationalism in Europe, national literatures arose in each country which gradually supplanted the use of Latin.

In China, during the past few decades, there has also been a movement to discard the classical language in favor of a more flexible form of literary expression modelled closely on the grammar and vocabulary of the spoken language. The resulting style will probably be neither wholly "classical" nor "colloquial" in form, but will aim to combine certain good elements in both, and thus form an adequate link between China's literary past and the living colloquial language.

*References:* Excellent brief summaries on the Chinese language are to be found in Bernhard Karlgren's *Sound and Symbol in Chinese* (London, 1923) and his *Philology and Ancient China* (Oslo, 1926). H. G. Creel's Introduction to *Literary Chinese by the Inductive Method, vol. 1, the Hsiao Ching* (University of Chicago Press, 1938), is good for its study of the earliest forms of Chinese script.

# MYTHS OF
# ANCIENT CHINA

## I. INTRODUCTION

The student of Chinese religion quickly learns that there is a world of difference between the gods of classical China (ending with the fall of the Han dynasty in A.D. 220) and those of post-classical times. The latter are large in number, diverse in origin (Buddhist, Taoist, or numerous local cults), have clearly defined anthropomorphic traits, and belong to a spiritual hierarchy which, in its gradations, closely parallels the terrestrial hierarchy of bureaucratic imperial China. These gods are portrayed for us in art, described in religious literature, and even satirized in works of fiction such as the great sixteenth-century novel *Hsi yu chi* (translated by Arthur Waley as *Monkey*). It is notable that relatively few of them are known as early as the classical period. This means that though several compendia have been published under such generalized titles as "Chinese mythology," they are of little relevance for the study of *ancient* Chinese myth since, despite their titles, they limit themselves very largely to these later gods.\*

The gods of ancient China, by comparison, are fewer in

---

\* For these compendia, see the Selected Bibliography under Ferguson, Maspero, and Werner. In this bibliography will be found all modern studies mentioned in this essay, as well as others not mentioned. Primary Chinese sources, however, are not listed, since for the specialist this is unnecessary, whereas for the general reader it has little purpose.

number, appear very rarely or not at all in art, and are commonly described so vaguely or briefly in the texts that their personality, and sometimes even their sex, remains uncertain. Side by side with them, on the other hand, appear a good many figures who, at first sight, seem to be human beings, yet on closer examination are found to display more than ordinary human qualities. They are gods or demigods who, through a process to be discussed presently, have been largely stripped of their divine attributes and transformed into men.

It would be tempting but erroneous to conclude from this that there are no myths in ancient China. More accurate would be the statement that individual *myths* certainly do occur, but not a systematic *mythology*, meaning by this an integrated body of mythological materials. On the contrary, these materials are usually so fragmentary and episodic that even the reconstruction from them of individual myths—let alone an integrated *system* of myths—is exceedingly difficult. Before discussing the myths themselves, we shall in the following section elaborate on some of the factors which may throw light on this peculiar situation. First of all, however, some definitions and explanations are in order.

In this essay we shall confine our attention to the field covered by what Stith Thompson calls a "minimum definition" of myth. "Myth," he has written (in an article appearing in *Myth: A Symposium,* 1955), "has to do with the gods and their actions, with creation, and with the general nature of the universe and of the earth. This is a minimum definition." Even within this minimum definition, moreover, reasons of space will compel us to limit ourselves still further to myths of a cosmogonic nature. This means that, aside from their mention in connection with cosmogonic phenomena, we shall be obliged to disregard the much larger category of ancient Chinese *hero* myths: those of the culture hero who enjoys supernatural birth, is sometimes aided by protective animals, becomes a sage ruler or otherwise performs great deeds for mankind, and so on.

Chronologically, our attention will be focused for the most

part on myths believed to have existed during the pre-imperial epoch of Chinese "feudalism," in other words, during the Chou dynasty (ca. 1027–221 B.C.). (For the preceding Shang dynasty, trad. 1766–ca. 1027, the extant inscriptional material is unfortunately too limited to be serviceable for our subject.) This means that whenever possible we shall base ourselves on texts belonging to the Chou dynasty itself. Because, however, these are often inadequate, we shall in case after case supplement them with the more abundant sources dating from the Han dynasty (206 B.C.–A.D. 220)— an age of empire which, though still forming a part of China's "classical" period, differs in many respects from the pre-imperial Chou dynasty. The question of textual chronology is an exceedingly complicated one, on which we shall have more to say in a later section (II, 3).

Finally, a word about the seemingly precise dates given for many of the personages to appear in these pages. These dates, when marked as "trad." (traditional), should not, of course, be accepted literally, nor even as necessarily signifying that the personages in question ever historically existed. They derive from the traditional chronology formulated by Chinese historians of a later time, and as such are indicative of that same euhemerization about which we shall speak in a moment. We give them here, therefore, simply to show how the Chinese historians have tried to fit their ancient traditions into a chronological framework.

## II. THE PROBLEMS

Though ancient Chinese myths have been studied by some of the best known scholars of East and West alike, the nature of the available data has prevented anything like a generally accepted consensus from emerging. What we have, instead, are diverse theories which, though often ingenious, are rarely conclusive and sometimes exceedingly fanciful. In writing a brief essay such as this, therefore, we are at once confronted by an almost impossible task: that of synthesizing and simplifying where no really reliable basis exists for so doing; of compressing into a few pages what would ideally require a good-sized volume of analysis and exposition. The manifold factors responsible for this situation can perhaps be summarized under three main headings: those of euhemerization, of fragmentation and language, and of chronology.

## 1. The Problem of Euhemerization

The theory to which Euhemerus has given his name maintains that the origin of myth is to be found in actual history, and that the gods and demigods of mythology were, to start with, actual human beings. As commonly used by writers on Chinese mythology, however, "euhemerization" denotes precisely the opposite process: the transformation of what were once myths and gods into seemingly authentic history and human beings. Unquestionably, a fair amount of what purports to be early Chinese history has been subjected to this kind of euhemerization, the literal acceptance of which by most people until recent years has led to gross misunderstandings concerning the beginnings of Chinese civilization. Not infrequently, to be sure, the literalists might encounter certain mythological elements not wholly concealed beneath their euhemerist dress, but when this happened, these could always be explained as mere later accretions to what in essence was genuine history. Henri Maspero, in the opening paragraph of his notable study, "Légendes mythologiques dans le *Chou king*" (1924), has vividly described the situation as follows:

> Chinese scholars have never known more than one way of interpreting legendary accounts, that of euhemerization. Under the plea of recovering from such accounts their historical kernel, they eliminate those elements of the marvellous which seem to them improbable, and preserve only a colorless residue, in

which gods and heroes are transformed into sage emperors and sage ministers, and monsters into rebellious princes or evil ministers. Such are the lucubrations which, placed end to end according to a sequence imposed upon chronology by various metaphysical theories, especially that of the five elements, constitute what is called the history of Chinese origins. In this there is nothing but the name of history; actually there are only legends, sometimes mythological in origin, sometimes coming from the ancestral temples of the great families, sometimes emanating from local religious centers, sometimes the accounts—more or less learned—which have been elaborated to explain a rite, sometimes simple stories borrowed from folklore, etc. All these phantoms ought to disappear from the history of China, whose origins they encumber; rather than persist in the search for a non-existent historical basis beneath the legendary form, we should seek to recover the mythological basis or the popular story beneath the pseudo-historical account.

It should be added that since 1924, when this was written, the Chinese scholars themselves have done wonders along these lines. In many cases, indeed, they have been more iconoclastic toward their own early history than have the Western scholars—sometimes, one might add, overly iconoclastic.

That euhemerization was already a recognized process in Chou dynasty China, and that it was then viewed with skepticism by some, is clearly indicated by several amusing anecdotes preserved in literature ranging from the fourth to around the first century B.C. In all of them, significantly, Confucius (551–479 B.C.) is made the exponent of euhemerism. The first story (contained in *Ta Tai li-chi*, ch. 62; compiled i cent. B.C. from earlier materials) concerns the legendary sage ruler Huang Ti, the "Yellow Lord" or "Yellow Emperor" (trad. xxvi cent. B.C.). "Was the Yellow Lord a man or was he not a man?" asks a disciple of Confucius.

"How is it that he reached (an age of) three hundred years?" To which Confucius is made to reply that this is a misunderstanding: what is actually meant is that during the Yellow Lord's own life of one hundred years, the people enjoyed his benefits; during the first hundred years after his death, they revered his spirit; and during the next hundred years after that, they continued to follow his teachings. "And this is why there is mention of three hundred years."

The next anecdote, also about the Yellow Lord, is based on a double meaning of the word *mien*, primarily signifying "face," but also meaning a "side, direction, quarter." In a passage from the fourth century B.C. *Shih-tzu* (now missing from the text, but quoted in a later encyclopedia), another disciple asks Confucius: "Is it true that the ancient Yellow Lord had four faces [*ssu mien*]?" To which Confucius replies that this is not at all true. What is meant is that the Yellow Lord used four officials to govern the four quarters (*ssu mien*) of his empire, so that he was "four faced" in the sense that the four "faces" or "sides" of his empire were controlled by these officials on his behalf.

The third anecdote again rests on a double meaning, this time of the word *tsu*, ordinarily meaning "foot" but in some contexts meaning "enough." This anecdote (recorded in *Han Fei-tzu*, ch. 33, and *Lü-shih ch'un-ch'iu*, XXII, 6; both iii cent. B.C.) has to do with a curious being called K'uei. In the euhemerized histories he is the human Music Master of the sage ruler Shun (trad. xxiii cent. B.C.), but from other scattered references we can see that he was actually a mythological creature having only one foot. In the story, the ruler of Confucius' native state of Lu is made to ask Confucius: "I have heard that K'uei was one-footed [*yi tsu*]. Is this really so?" To which Confucius replies: "K'uei was a man, so why should he have one foot?" Then he goes on to explain that because K'uei's royal master Shun was greatly pleased with K'uei's musical ability, he once exclaimed of him: "As to K'uei, one (like him) is enough [*yi erh tsu*]." By later people, however, this saying came to be misconstrued as meaning that K'uei had but one foot (*yi tsu*).

These anecdotes are surely apocryphal, yet the fact that they all center around Confucius is no accident. For it is precisely the Confucianists who, more than any other school of thought, were historically minded and assumed prime responsibility for conserving and editing the ancient texts which eventually became the Chinese classics. In so doing they were, on the one hand, always intensely interested in the search for historical precedents which would confirm their own social and political doctrines; on the other hand, their strong humanism tended to make them either indifferent toward supernatural matters, or to seek to explain them in purely rationalistic terms. The results have been disastrous for the preservation of early Chinese myth, for they mean that it is precisely in those classical texts which might otherwise be expected to be prime repositories of myth, that such myth has either vanished entirely or (more probably) suffered grievous distortion.

Obviously, therefore, our search for myth must go beyond the Confucian-dominated classics to include the writings of the several non-Confucian schools. Among such writings, those of the Taoists, because of their iconoclasm toward Confucian tradition, their greater interest in popular beliefs, and their richly imaginative mode of expression, are by far the most promising. Here again, however, there is a limitation imposed by the philosophical assumptions of Taoism: its denial of teleology and anthropocentrism, and insistence upon a natural rather than a supernatural explanation for the universe. This in practice means that though mythological allusions abound in Taoist writings, they are introduced as a rule only for philosophical or literary effect, and not because the Taoist authors actually believe in them themselves. Rarely, therefore, do these authors bother to narrate at length the myths to which they allude. Rather, they take from them those elements which can be used for allegories of their own invention, thereby to express the philosophical ideas in which they themselves are interested.

A good example is the conversation in the seventeenth chapter of the *Chuang-tzu* (iii cent. B.C.) between a centipede

and that same K'uei whom we have just encountered in
Confucian dress. There is no doubt that Chuang Tzu's K'uei
is a mythological creature, for he is made to complain to the
centipede about his own difficulties in hopping around on
one foot, and to ask the latter how he succeeds in controlling
those many feet of his. The allegory's purpose, however, is
not at all mythological but philosophical. From it we learn
the Taoist moral that every creature should be satisfied with
his own native endowment, but nothing whatsoever concerning the K'uei himself, other than the basic fact that he is
one-footed.

## 2. The Problems of Fragmentation and of Language

Not only does pre-Han literature lack any separate genre
which might be called myth, but within any single literary
work it is not easy to find a myth recorded in consecutive
entirety. All that we have are casual references and tantaliz-
ing fragments, widely scattered among texts of diverse date
and ideological orientation. No wonder then that scholars can
rarely agree as to how to fit these pieces into some kind
of unity.

This fragmentation is characteristic even of what is probably the richest single storehouse of Chou mythological lore:
the anthology of imaginative and sensuous poems known as the
Ch'u tz'u or Songs of Ch'u (wherein, however, are to be found
Han as well as Chou poems). A striking example, to which
we shall refer many times, is the T'ien wen or "Heavenly
Questions" (prob. iv cent. B.C.), whose 185 lines are packed
with mythological allusions, all, however, presented in the
form of enigmatic riddles. Typical are the following lines
(as translated by David Hawkes, Ch'u Tz'u, the Songs of the
South, Oxford, 1959, pp. 49, 56):

> Where is the stone forest? What beast can talk?
> Where are the hornless dragons which carry bears
>     on their backs for sport? (ll. 47–48)
> P'eng Chien made a drink-offering of pheasant's
>     broth. How did the Lord eat of it?

*He received the gift of long-lasting life. Why*
*then was he still sad?* (ll. 171–72)

Other than that P'eng Chien may be identified with fair
certainty as the Chinese Methuselah, P'eng Tsu, practically
nothing is known of what is here alluded to (aside from the
very uncertain guesses of much later commentators).

The difficulties produced by such fragments are enhanced
by linguistic difficulties inherent in the Chinese classical
language. In the first place, its many homophones and characters easily confused for one another make very tempting the
search for new readings and identifications, usually based on
such arguments as: character X of text A appears as character
Y of text B; character Y appears in turn as character Z in
text C; hence character X of text A and character Z of text C
are equivalents. This kind of work, brilliantly performed by
a long line of Chinese scholars, has done wonders in eluci-
dating the ancient texts. On the other hand, conducted too
exuberantly it can lead to quite startling results.

In the second place, the telegraphic brevity of classical
Chinese, coupled with its inflectional inability (without the
use of added words) to indicate gender, number, or tense,
makes it often possible to translate a small fragment in several
ways, with no assurance as to which is correct unless a larger
clarifying context can be found. A good example is the fifty-
sixth line of the *T'ien wen* poem, wherein most scholars see
an allusion to the myth of the shooting of the ten suns by
Archer Yi (see III, 4 below), and therefore translate: "Why
did Yi shoot down the suns? Why did the ravens shed their
wings?" Bernhard Karlgren, however (in his encyclopedic
"Legends and Cults in Ancient China," 1946, p. 268), believes
that the motif of *ten* suns came to be associated with Archer
Yi only in Han times. Therefore he translates in the singular:
"Why did Yi shoot at [and not "down"] the sun? Why did
the raven shed its feathers?" Either translation is grammatically possible; which one we accept, however, determines our
entire decision as to whether or not the two themes originally
formed a single myth.

## 3. The Problem of Chronology

The year 221 B.C., because it saw the final unification of "feudal" China into a truly centralized empire, is the great watershed of early Chinese history. Before that year, the country was divided into mutually warring, independent states, each ruled by a hereditary house and divided in turn into lesser domains also held by noble families. Politically, most of this pre-imperial age was covered by the Chou dynasty (ca. 1027–221 B.C.). Following 221, on the other hand, the next several centuries saw the consolidation of a new form of centralized empire, in which an official bureaucracy which was non-hereditary and centrally appointed took the place of the landed aristocracy of Chou times. The patterns of empire then laid down remained the norm until the present century, but the classical phase of Chinese history came to an end with the disintegration of the Han dynasty (206 B.C.–A.D. 220).

Culturally speaking, the Chou dynasty was the creative age of China's great classical and philosophical literature, whereas the Han dynasty, though also notably creative, was at the same time the first age when the writings of the past were systematically collected, edited, and commented upon. It was likewise the epoch which saw the appearance (ca. 100 B.C.) of China's first "universal" history. To what extent the Han scholars changed the texts they edited, sometimes introducing (perhaps quite unconsciously) ideas reflecting their own environment, and to what extent they may even have forged works which they then attributed to Chou or earlier times, still remains a subject of great controversy. Fortunately, much has been done by Chinese and Western scholars alike in recent decades to clarify the situation. Nonetheless, many points of uncertainty still remain.

In the field of mythology, the differences between the two dynasties are equally striking. Thus what, in the Chou literature, is fragmented and frequently euhemerized, often becomes, in Han times, so greatly elaborated that though the personages in the myths remain in large part the same, what is said of them may be totally new. It would seem, in many cases, that the Han writers were tapping new sources of living popular tradition, hitherto neglected by the more aristocratically oriented writers of the Chou. Likewise, for the first time, a very few of the mythological figures are portrayed in sculptured reliefs. A notable example of the new imaginative trend is the *Shan-hai ching* or *Classic of Mountains and Seas* (trad. ascribed in part to the Chou, but probably all of Han date), wherein not only the lands of China proper, but those extending to the far reaches of the earth, are populated by hundreds of strange new gods and monsters. So fantastic and prolific, indeed, are the beings of this book, that one may fairly ask whether many of them are not simply the fanciful creations of their author (or authors), rather than based upon actual popular belief.

On the other hand, we can also often see the Han scholars manfully grappling with a body of older tradition which apparently has lost its living reality. They strive to reconcile seeming differences, to fill in lacunae, to put into order (according to their own ideological preconceptions) matters that they no longer truly understand. These efforts are particularly conspicuous in the disagreements often found among the Han commentators on the Chou classics.

All these developments, it should be kept in mind, are entirely distinct from the phenomenon noted at the very beginning of this essay: the gradual fading, in post-Han times, of most of the ancient gods from popular consciousness, and their replacement by a new and more clearly defined pantheon (no doubt stimulated in part by the advent of Buddhism).

What, then, is the scholar of early Chinese myth to do when confronted by these two very different bodies of literature? Two general approaches are possible, one of which we may term the "historical," the other the "sociological." As respective examples of these approaches, let us briefly contrast the theories of Bernhard Karlgren (expressed in his large "Legends and Cults in Ancient China," 1946), and of Wolfram Eberhard (expressed in several works, notably his two-volume *Lokalkulturen im alten China,* 1942, which, however, covers much else besides myth proper).

According to Karlgren, the main reason for the recording of ancient Chinese traditions in Chou literature is the fact that the personages in these traditions were regarded by the many grandee houses of Chou times as their ancestors. As a consequence, their memory was kept alive in the ancestral cults maintained by these houses. This, Karlgren believes, explains why they are portrayed neither as outright gods nor yet quite as ordinary mortals, but rather as "supermen," that is to say, as cultural heroes who are definite historical figures, but who at the same time possess something more than purely human characteristics. With the destruction of the old social order at the end of the third century B.C., however, the ancestral cults of these grandee houses lost their social significance, with the result that the memory of the ancient legends and heroes became divorced from living tradition. Thus was the way paved for the fanciful elaborations or antiquarian speculations of the Han writers.

In discussing these legends and heroes, therefore, Karlgren distinguishes sharply between what he calls the "free" texts of Chou times (texts in which the legends and heroes appear casually, without any tendentious purpose), and the fanciful or "systematizing" texts of Han times (in which materials are arranged according to set systems and theories, notably that of the five elements; among these "systematizing" texts Karlgren would also include a few late Chou works). For the study of genuinely early myth and legend, therefore, Karlgren believes that only the pre-Han "free" texts have any real validity.

Eberhard, on the other hand, sees the rise of Chinese civilization as resulting from the interaction and intermixture of various cultural components which, he believes, were in early times ethnically and regionally distinct from one another. Therefore, though by no means indifferent to the problem of historical development, his main interest lies in trying to isolate (regionally rather than chronologically) what he believes to be these basic cultural components. For his purposes, therefore, what is recorded in a Chou text, and what may be said by a writer many centuries or even a millennium later, may both be valid provided they both point toward a common cultural cluster. Basing himself on this standpoint, Eberhard, in a lengthy review (1946), has severely criticized Karlgren's methodology on several counts, two of which in particular may be mentioned:

(1) The mere fact that version A of a given myth happens to appear in an older text than version B, does not necessarily mean that *developmentally* speaking version A is the earlier or more primitive. On the contrary, as Eberhard points out, the Han writers could and did utilize long-existent popular oral tradition to a greater extent than did the more aristocratically oriented writers of the feudal age. (2) Karlgren's belief that most of the beings in the myths were originally human heroes, who only later, in some cases, acquired the attributes of gods or even animals, is at variance with modern ethnological and sociological theory. "If this opinion were correct, Chinese mythology would be the greatest exception hitherto known in the whole field of ethnology: the Chinese would first have created heroes and later only have made them into gods or even animals!"

Karlgren's strictly historical approach does indeed seem overly mechanical when, for example, he accepts or rejects a text simply according to whether it happens to have been written before or after the dividing line of 221 B.C., instead of evaluating, in each case, the particular ideology and other individual circumstances of the text itself. Furthermore, his rigid approach would seem to overlook the possibility of persistence or recurrence of a given motif (perhaps in varying forms) over a very long period of time.

On the other hand, Eberhard's use of chronologically widely separated data for reconstructing an ancient myth (in contrast to his main endeavor, that of isolating a cluster of long-term cultural components) has its obvious dangers. No doubt Eberhard is correct in asserting that "a myth reported only in a later text, may very well represent a form reflecting quite an early stage of development." However, as he himself then goes on to say, "Of course, we have to prove this in every single case." Unfortunately, the proofs presented by followers of this methodology are by no means always convincing, nor are they sometimes even seriously attempted. In many cases, indeed, they can never be really convincing, simply because the data themselves make this impossible.

In what follows, therefore, we shall try to steer a middle course: that of limiting ourselves (save for the first myth, which is a special case) to those myths for which at least *some* factual basis can be found in the Chou literature. However, we shall not hesitate to add to this what the Han writers have to say, in every instance being careful to warn the reader accordingly.

## III. THE MYTHS

The following are five examples of cosmogonic myth; as explained earlier, space does not permit us to discuss, more than incidentally, those having to do with cultural heroes, unless (as in the fifth myth) they also have cosmogonic significance.

### 1. The P'an-ku Creation Myth

In the *San-wu li-chi* (Record of Cycles in Threes and Fives), an obscure work of the third century A.D. now known only through quotations in later encyclopedias, there appears the following story (here paraphrased):

Heaven and Earth were once inextricably commingled (*hun-tun*) like a chicken's egg, within which was engendered P'an-ku (a name perhaps meaning "Coiled-up Antiquity"). After 18,000 years, this inchoate mass split apart, what was bright and light forming Heaven, and what was dark and heavy forming Earth. Thereafter, during another 18,000 years, Heaven daily increased ten feet in height, Earth daily increased ten feet in thickness, and P'an-ku, between the two, daily increased ten feet in size. This is how Heaven and Earth came to be separated by their present distance of 90,000 *li* (roughly 30,000 English miles).

Other texts, probably somewhat later in date, add the further information that after P'an-ku died, his breath became the wind and clouds, his voice the thunder, his left and right eyes the sun and moon respectively, his four limbs and five "bodies" (fingers?) the four quarters of the earth and five great mountains, his blood the rivers, his muscles and veins the strata of the earth, his flesh the soil, his hair and beard the constellations, his skin and body-hair the plants and trees, his teeth and bones the metals and stones, his marrow gold and precious stones, and his sweat the rain. The parasites on his body, impregnated by the wind, became human beings. In graphic portrayals of much later date, he is often shown as a horned demiurge who, with hammer and adze, chisels out the universe.

Here, in these works of the third century A.D. and later, we find China's *only* clearly recognizable creation myth. Most Chinese scholars believe it to be of non-Chinese origin and link it to the ancestral myth of the Miao and Yao tribal peoples of South China (also first recorded in the third century), in which these tribes trace their origin to a dog named P'an-hu. This dog, a pet of the Chinese legendary ruler Ti K'u (trad. ca. 2400 B.C.), succeeded in bringing to his imperial master the head of a certain troublesome barbarian general, and in accordance with a previously promised reward was given the emperor's own daughter as wife. The dog then carried her off to the mountain fastnesses of South China, where the progeny of the two became the ancestors of the present Miao and Yao tribes. Aside from the phonetic similarity between the names P'an-ku and P'an-hu, however, and the fact that both cults seem to have been centered in South China, where they were sometimes confused with one another, there is little apparent similarity between the myths.

Similarities to the P'an-ku story do appear, however, if we

look farther afield, for example at India and ancient Sumer.
Thus the *Rig Veda* tells us that the cosmic waters were
originally restrained within a shell, but that the fashioner god,
Tvaṣṭṛ, created Heaven and Earth, who in turn engendered
Indra. By drinking the soma, Indra became strong and
forced Heaven and Earth apart, himself filling up the space
between them and also slitting open the cover within which
lay the cosmic waters, so that they could issue forth. Another
later story in the *Rig Veda* also tells us that when Puruṣa
was sacrificed by the gods, the parts of his cut-up body became the sun, sky, atmosphere, earth, four quarters, four
social classes of mankind, and so forth.

In Sumer, similarly, it was believed that there first existed
the primeval sea, which engendered the cosmic mountain,
consisting of Heaven and Earth in undivided form. They in
turn produced the air-god Enlil, who separated Heaven from
Earth, carried off Earth for himself, and through union with
his mother Earth set the stage for the organization of the
universe.

Though in China itself the P'an-ku myth does not appear
before the third century, Eberhard (in his *Lokalkulturen*, II,
467 ff.) would relate it conceptually to what he believes to
be a much earlier Chinese idea: that of a primeval egg or
sac, the splitting of which permits its undifferentiated. con-
tents to assume form as an organized universe. In its sophisticated version, this conception may well underlie the astronomical theory, current in Han times, according to which
Heaven and Earth are shaped like an egg, Earth being enclosed by the sphere of Heaven just as the yolk of an egg is
enclosed by its shell.

The first of our texts, it will be remembered, says that
Heaven and Earth were once inextricably commingled (*hun-
tun*) like a chicken's egg. In late Chou and Han philosophical
texts, the same onomatopoeic term *hun-tun* is used to designate the state of undifferentiated chaos before an organized
universe came into being. Curiously enough, the term appears again in modern Chinese parlance as the name for a
small *sac*-like dumpling (a thin shell of dough enclosing

chopped-up meat), used as the basic ingredient of the popular *hun-tun* soup served in Chinese restaurants.

In the *Shan-hai ching* or *Classic of Mountains and Seas* (bk. 2), of Han date, Hun-tun is personified as a being living southwest of the Mountain of Heaven (T'ien Shan), who has six feet and four wings, is the color of fire, lacks a face or eyes, and is *shaped like a sac.* Among Chou dynasty texts, the *Tso chuan* history (iv cent. B.C., with later additions), under the year 618 B.C., euhemerizes Hun-tun as the evil son of an early sage ruler. Describing his undesirable characteristics, it says, among other things, that he "screens [i.e., covers over or bottles up] righteousness." The best-known Chou reference to Hun-tun, however, is the charming allegory in the seventh chapter of the Taoist work *Chuang-tzu* (iii cent. B.C.). There we are told that Hun-tun or Chaos was the Ruler of the Center, and that he lacked the usual seven openings of other men (eyes, ears, nostrils, and mouth). Therefore his friends, Shu and Hu, having been well treated by him, decided to bore such openings in him. Each day they bored one hole, but on the seventh day Hun-tun died.

Such are the scattered data from which we must decide whether or not the cosmogonic *conception* underlying the P'an-ku myth (and not, of course, the myth as such) possibly goes back to early times. Marcel Granet, for his part (in his *Danses et légendes de la Chine ancienne*, 1926, p. 540 ff.), would link the *hun-tun* idea to another mythical theme in which, though the term *hun-tun* itself does not appear, a leather sack plays a central role. It concerns King Wu-yi (trad. reigned 1198–95 B.C.), one of the last evil rulers of the Shang dynasty, who made a human figure which he called the Spirit of Heaven (T'ien Shen), and played a game of counters with it, which he won. To show his contempt, he then hung up a leather sack filled with blood and shot at it with arrows, saying that he was shooting at Heaven. Soon afterward, while hunting, he was killed by lightning. The same theme recurs almost a millennium later in connection with the last king of Sung, a state which in Chou times was ruled by descendants of the Shang royal house. This king too hung up a leather blood-filled sack and shot at it, saying that he was shooting at Heaven. Shortly afterward, in 282 B.C., he was attacked by a coalition of other states, killed, and his state annihilated.

Possibly Granet is correct in believing that this theme is related to the *hun-tun* conception. On the other hand, a parallel has also been suggested between it and the theme of Archer Yi's shooting at the sun (see III, 4 below).

### 2. *The Fashioning Deity Nü-kua*

Nü-kua, the "Woman Kua," though fairly prominent in Han times, appears only twice in earlier literature. Despite her name, it is only in the first century A.D. that her sex is positively stated. At about the same time she also becomes identified as either the sister or consort of the much better known Fu-hsi (Subduer of Animals), a sage (trad. ca. 2800 B.C.) said to have taught men how to hunt and cook, to make nets, and so on. On the stone reliefs of the Wu Liang offering shrines (ca. A.D. 150), Fu-hsi and Nü-kua appear together; their upper bodies are human, but merge below into serpent tails that are intertwined with one another. Fu-hsi holds a carpenter's square in his hand and Nü-kua a compass, apparently as symbols of their constructive activities. The constructive work of Fu-hsi, however (other than as inventor and ruler), has not come down to us, and we may wonder whether the purported association between him and the fashioning deity Nü-kua really goes back before Han times.

The best account of the latter's activities occurs in the sixth chapter of the Han Taoist work, *Huai-nan-tzu* (ii cent. B.C., a work rich in mythological materials):

> In very ancient times, the four pillars [at the compass points] were broken down, the nine provinces [of the habitable world] were split apart, Heaven did not wholly cover [Earth], and Earth did not completely support [Heaven]. Fires flamed without being extin-

guished, waters inundated without being stopped, fierce
beasts ate the people, and birds of prey seized the old
and weak in their claws. Thereupon Nü-kua fused
together stones of the five colors with which she
patched together azure Heaven. She cut off the feet of
a turtle with which she set up the four pillars. She
slaughtered the Black Dragon in order to save the
province of Chi [the present Hopei and Shansi provinces in North China]. She collected the ashes of reeds
with which to check the wild waters.

The text goes on to say that thereafter there was universal
harmony: the seasons followed their due course, beasts
sheathed their claws and teeth and serpents hid their poison,
the people lived lives of undreaming sleep and uncalculating
wakefulness.

The "four pillars" mentioned in this myth belong, of course,
to the cosmological belief, found in many cultures, that
Heaven is supported on pillars or some other kind of foundation. In China (where the pillars were thought of as mountains), the earliest mention is that in the *T'ien wen* poem
(iv cent. B.C.), which, however, speaks not of four but of
eight pillars. The same poem, as well as the Kung-kung story
below (and other texts as well), further makes mention of
the *wei* or "cords" of Earth. As a technical term, *wei* desig-
nates the cords which, on a chariot, secure its canopy to the
frame or body. By analogy, therefore, the *wei* of Earth
(sometimes stated to be four in number) must likewise serve
to attach the canopy of Heaven to Earth below. (The comparison of Heaven to a chariot's canopy and Earth to its
body is a common one in the texts.) Just how the *wei* function in relation to the (four or eight) pillars of Heaven is,
however, unstated.

The story of Nü-kua is by several Han writers linked to
the cosmic struggle between Chuan-hsü (legendary ruler,
trad. xxv cent. B.C.) and Kung-kung (euhemerized in Chou
writings as a human "rebel," but in late Han times described
as a horned monster with serpent's body). Wang Ch'ung

(A.D. 27–ca. 100), for example, in his *Lun heng* or *Critical Essays* (chs. 31 and 46), says that anciently, when Kung-kung fought unsuccessfully with Chuan-hsü to become ruler, he blundered in his rage against Mount Pu-chou (in the northwest quarter), thereby causing the pillar of Heaven and the cord of Earth to break off at that point. It was then that Nü-kua patched up Heaven with melted stones and cut off a turtle's feet to hold it up. Nonetheless, Heaven and Earth have since that time sloped toward one another in the northwest, but have tilted away from one another in the opposite direction. This is why the astral bodies of Heaven continue to this day to move in a westerly direction, whereas the rivers (of China) on Earth flow toward the ocean (in the east). In the *T'ien wen* there is already mention of the gap in the southeast between Heaven and Earth, from which we may infer that at the time of this poem the story of Kung-kung was already current.

We may question, however, whether this story and the Nü-kua myth properly belong together. In the *Huai-nan-tzu* (ch. 3), for example, the Kung-kung story appears alone, without any mention of Nü-kua at all, and though the two are joined in the fifth chapter of *Lieh-tzu* (a Taoist work, trad. Chou but prob. Han), their order is there reversed (the story of Nü-kua given first, followed by that of Kung-kung). This, of course, destroys any logical connection between them.

In a passage (now known only through later quotation) from the *Feng-su t'ung-yi* (Comprehensive Meaning of Customs), by Ying Shao (ca. 140–ca. 206), Nü-kua is also portrayed as the creator of mankind:

> It is popularly said that when Heaven and Earth had opened forth, but before there were human beings, Nü-kua created men by patting yellow earth together. But the work tasked her strength and left her no free time, so that she then dragged a string through mud, thus heaping it up so as to make it into men. Therefore the rich and the noble are those men of yellow earth,

whereas the poor and the lowly—all ordinary people—
are those cord-made men.

Another passage from the same work (likewise now known
only in quotation) tells us further that Nü-kua is prayed to
as the goddess of marriage, because it is she who first instituted marriage. (In other words, having created men, she
taught them how to propagate.)

Finally, we are told in the *Shan-hai ching* (bk. 16) that
beyond the northwest sea there are ten spirits, called "Nü-
kua's intestines," because (after she died) they were transformed into spirits (from her intestines).

Whether or not Nü-kua as the creator of mankind represents simply a popular addition to the primary theme of
Nü-kua as the repairer and organizer of the world, it is evident that neither theme constitutes a true creation myth (in
the sense of the P'an-ku myth), since both take place in an
already existing universe. We might assume the entire Nü-
kua cult to be a Han creation, were it not for two bare references to her occurring in Chou literature. The more important of these is one of the riddles in *T'ien wen:* "Nü-kua had
a body. Who formed and fashioned it?" This certainly suggests that Nü-kua's fashioning activities were already known
in Chou times if, as seems reasonable, it should be interpreted as meaning: Nü-kua was a fashioner of other things.
Who then fashioned her?

### 3. *The Separation of Heaven and Earth*

We have already encountered the theme of the separation
of Heaven and Earth in the P'an-ku myth. It crops up again,
though in a very different context, in two texts of Chou
date. The first is one of the major classics, the *Shu ching* or
*Classic of History* (sect. *Lü hsing*, trad. x cent. B.C., but
prob. some cents. later). There we are told that the Miao
(a tribe or confraternity, notorious as troublemakers during
the reigns of Yao and Shun, trad. xxiv–xxiii cent. B.C.) created
oppressive punishments which threw the people into disorder. Shang Ti, the "Lord on High" (name of the most

prominent ancient divinity), surveyed the people and found them lacking in virtue. Out of pity for those who were innocent, the August Lord (surely another name for Shang Ti, though the euhemerizing commentators interpret him as either Yao or Shun) had the Miao exterminated. "Then he charged Ch'ung and Li to cut the communication between Heaven and Earth so that there would be no descending and ascending [of spirits and men between the two]." After this had been done, order was restored and the people returned to virtue.

The second much more detailed account—actually an early exegesis of the foregoing—is that in the *Kuo yü* or *Narratives of the States* (iv cent. B.C. with later additions; sect. *Ch'u yü*, II, 1). In it King Chao of Ch'u (515–489), puzzled by the *Shu ching's* statement about the separating of Heaven from Earth, asks his minister: "If it had not been thus, would the people have been able to ascend to Heaven?" To which the minister, after making denial, supplies his own metaphorical explanation:

Anciently, men and spirits did not intermingle. At that time there were certain persons who were so perspicacious, single-minded, and reverential that their understanding enabled them to make meaningful collation of what lies above and below, and their insight to illumine what is distant and profound. Therefore the spirits would descend into them. The possessors of such powers were, if men, called *hsi* (shamans), and, if women, *wu* (shamannesses). It is they who supervised the positions of the spirits at the ceremonies, sacrificed to them, and otherwise handled religious matters. As a consequence, the spheres of the divine and the profane were kept distinct. The spirits sent down blessings on the people, and accepted from them their offerings. There were no natural calamities.

In the degenerate time of Shao-hao (trad. xxvi cent. B.C.), however, the Nine Li (a troublesome tribe like the Miao) threw virtue into disorder. Men and spirits became intermingled, with each household indiscriminately performing for itself the religious observances which had hitherto been conducted by the shamans. As a consequence, men lost their reverence for the spirits, the spirits violated the rules of men, and natural calamities arose. Hence the successor of Shao-hao, Chuan-hsü, charged Ch'ung, Governor of the South, to handle the affairs of Heaven in order to determine the proper places of the spirits, and Li, Governor of Fire, to handle the affairs of Earth in order to determine the proper places of men. "And such is what is meant by 'cutting the communication between Heaven and Earth.'"

Still later, however, the Miao, like the Nine Li before them, stirred up new disorders, obliging the ruler Yao to order the descendants of Ch'ung and Li to resume the tasks of their forebears. Since that time members of the same two families have continued to maintain the proper distinctions between Heaven and Earth. Under King Hsüan of Chou (827–782), one of them remarked of the two ancestors: "Ch'ung lifted Heaven up and Li pressed Earth down."

A detailed comparison of these two texts is unnecessary, other than to say that the first telescopes events which by the second are placed in two different periods (the troubles caused by the Nine Li during the reigns of Shao-hao and Chuan-hsü, and the similar troubles caused by the Miao during that of Yao); that both accounts are in part euhemerized; but that this is especially evident of the second, with its added "human" details and metaphorical explanation of what, in the first text, might be understood as a literal separating of Heaven from Earth. However, the second text also reveals the real state of affairs in its significant final quotation: "Ch'ung lifted Heaven up and Li pressed Earth down."

The idea that Heaven and Earth were once joined together, thereby permitting free communication between men and the divine powers, but later became separated, is extremely widespread among many cultures. It and related concepts have been brilliantly analyzed by Mircea Eliade in his two books, *The Myth of the Eternal Return* (1954; first published in French in 1949) and *Le chamanisme et les techniques archaïques de l'extase* (1951). In the former (p. 12 ff.) he discusses the concept of an *axis mundi*. This

cosmic symbol, widely found among Asian peoples, may take
the form of a mountain, a sacred temple, palace or city, or
a tree or a vine; its distinguishing characteristic is that it is
believed to occupy the center of the world and to connect
Earth with Heaven. Concerning the ideas underlying this
belief, Eliade writes further (p. 91):

> . . . the myths of many peoples allude to a very
> distant epoch when men knew neither death nor toil
> nor suffering and had a bountiful supply of food merely
> for the taking. *In illo tempore,* the gods descended to
> earth and mingled with men; for their part, men could
> easily mount to heaven. As the result of a ritual fault,
> communications between heaven and earth were inter-
> rupted and the gods withdrew to the highest heavens.
> Since then, men must work for their food and are no
> longer immortal.

In his *Le chamanisme,* Eliade has also discussed at length
what it is that motivates the shaman when he enters his
ecstatic trance. It is his desire to be able thereby to ascend
to Heaven and thus momentarily restore, in his own person,
that contact between Heaven and Earth which had more
generally existed prior to the "fall."

It can hardly be doubted that our two Chinese texts are
reflections of these widespread concepts. For in them, too,
the cutting of communication between Heaven and Earth
follows upon a "ritual fault," and the second text, in particular, describes in some detail the male and female shamans
who enjoy contact with the spirits.

There is, however, also an important shift of emphasis:
the fact that in the Chinese story it is the shamans only, and
not the people as a whole, who originally enjoyed communication with the spirits, and that the usurpation of this prerogative by other persons then constituted the "ritual fault"
leading to the cutting of communication between Heaven
and Earth. Conceivably this shift in emphasis is not, after all,
deeply significant, for it may be merely an attempt on the
part of the author (or of the minister whose speech he is

ostensibly recording) to enhance the prestige of the shamans by emphasizing their dominant role in earliest times. We cannot really know. (In his *Le chamanisme,* pp. 396–97, Eliade has also discussed this second text, basing himself, however, on an inexact translation which has led to certain misunderstandings on his part.)

The Miao, it will be remembered, are mentioned in both texts as one of the two groups responsible for the ritual disorder. Maspero ("Légendes mythologiques," pp. 97–98) has already pointed out that in the *Shan-hai ching* (bk. 17) these Miao are described as winged human beings living in the extreme northwestern corner of the world, while in a still later text they are said to have wings but to be unable to fly. Here, perhaps, is a symbolic expression of the "fall": the fact that the Miao had once been able to communicate with Heaven, but lost this power when, because of their ritual fault, the Lord on High exiled them to their distant region and ordered the (shamans) Ch'ung and Li to sever the communication between Heaven and Earth.

Are there other passages in Chinese literature expressive of a paradisal era followed by a "fall"? The Taoists often write about man's state of innocence before the rise of human institutions, but it is hard to know whether this is simply a Taoist philosophical abstraction, or may be inspired, at least in part, by popular traditions concerning a primordial paradise. The latter hypothesis, however, seems quite reasonable.

Among such passages, one of the most vivid is that in the eighth chapter of *Huai-nan-tzu,* describing the era of Great Purity, when men were genuine and simple, sparing of speech and spontaneous in conduct. "They were joined in body to Heaven and Earth, united in spirit to the *yin* and *yang* [the negative and positive cosmic forces or principles], and in harmonious oneness with the four seasons." At that time wind and rain brought no calamities, sun and moon equably distributed their light, the planets did not deviate from their courses. But then came the era of decline: men began to mine the mountains for minerals, to make fire with the fire drill, to fell trees for houses, to hunt and fish, and to do the many other things which destroyed their original purity.

A later passage in the same chapter is even more suggestive of an ancient Chinese Garden of Eden: In ancient times men entrusted their children to birds' nests and left the grain in the fields. Without fear of injury, they could freely grasp the tails of tigers and panthers and tread upon serpents. Then, however, came the inevitable decline. It is notable that nowhere here or elsewhere do the Taoists provide a mythological explanation for the "fall"; it is simply, for them, the inexorable concomitant of the rise of human civilization.

### 4. Sun Myths

Anciently there existed not one but ten suns, each of which would appear in succession on each day of the Chinese ten-day week. Once, however, at a time usually placed in the reign of Yao, all ten suns, through some confusion, appeared simultaneously, so that it seemed as if the world were about to burn up. At this climactic point the Chou texts (*Chuang-tzu*, ch. 2; *Lü-shih ch'un-ch'iu*, XXII, 5; etc.) leave off; for the denouement we must turn to the *Huai-nan-tzu* (ch. 8). There we are told that when the suns appeared, a certain Yi (or Hou Yi), famous as an archer, shot down all but one, thus rescuing the world and leaving the single sun which moves in the sky today. At Yao's bidding he also killed a number of destructive monsters (described in gory detail in works like *Shan-hai ching*). So overjoyed were the people by this happy ending that (somewhat inconsequentially, as we might think) they thereupon established Yao as their ruler.

There is an ambiguous line in the *T'ien wen* which, as usually translated, reads: "Why did Yi shoot down the suns? Why did the ravens shed their feathers?" Here we have the earliest reference to the belief that in the sun (or in each individual sun) there is a raven. (In *Huai-nan-tzu*, ch. 7, it is said to be three-legged.) From this line one might also conclude that the story of Archer Yi's shooting at the ten suns goes back at least to the fourth century B.C.

Karlgren, however, believes the story to have originated only in Han times, and therefore, as we have seen (II, 2 above), would translate the line in the singular: "Why did Yi shoot at the sun? Why did the raven shed its feathers?" His main reason for so doing is the chronological difficulty that, in other Chou texts, Yi appears as a great but arrogant hunter who lived in the early part of the Hsia dynasty (a century or more after Yao), and who, after usurping the throne, came to a bad end. Yi's shooting at a *single* sun (and not ten of them) is, therefore, as interpreted by Karlgren, simply "a sacrilegious act," expressive of Yi's hybris, but having nothing to do with the threatened burning up of the earth; he compares it with the act of the two kings (see III, 1 above) who shot at a leather sack filled with blood, calling it Heaven.

There are several arguments, however, which—at least to this writer—speak in favor of the more usual interpretation. In the first place, Yi's shooting at the ten suns provides a necessary conclusion to a myth which otherwise—quite literally—would leave the several suns dangling in mid-air. In the second place, is it really fair to look for strict chronological and thematic consistency in what, after all, is not history but myth? Yi seems to have been the focus of several cycles of story. There is no real reason to be surprised, therefore, if he appears as a hero in one cycle, but as a villain in another.

Thirdly, and perhaps most important, the theme of saving the world from multiple suns is by no means peculiarly Chinese. On the contrary, as shown by Eduard Erkes ("Chinesisch-amerikanische Mythenparallelen," 1926), it has many parallels on both sides of the Pacific. Among the Battaks of Sumatra and the Semangs of Malaya, for example, the sun is believed to be the parent of several children suns, but is tricked by the moon into devouring them when they threaten to burn up the world. Among the Shasta Indians of California it is the coyote who slays nine of ten brother-suns (a striking numerical agreement with the Chinese myth). And among the Golds of eastern Siberia there is even a national hero who, in the manner of the Chinese story, shoots down two of three suns when they make the world unbearably hot.

Returning to China, we find considerable lore concerning the daily course taken by the sun (or suns) across the sky. Perhaps the earliest source is the opening chapter of the *Shu ching* (Classic of History), which, as usual for this work, is considerably euhemerized:

> He [the sage Yao] then charged Hsi and Ho, in reverent accordance with august Heaven, to calculate and delineate the sun, moon, stars and constellations, and respectfully to give the people the seasons. He separately charged the younger Hsi to reside among the Yü barbarians, [at the place] called the Valley of Light (Yang-ku), there to receive the rising sun as a guest and regulate its activities in the east. . . . He further charged the youngest Hsi to reside in Southern Chiao, there to regulate its doings in the south. . . . He separately charged the younger Ho to reside in the west, [at the place] called the Valley of Darkness (Mei-ku), there respectfully to see off the setting sun and regulate the completion of its work in the west. . . . He further charged the youngest Ho to reside in the Northern Region (Shuo-fang), [at the place] called the City of Obscurity (Yu-tu), there to supervise its operations in the north.

Other Chou texts make it evident that the two sets of three brothers, here spoken of as supervising the movements of the sun and other heavenly bodies, are in actual fact mere multiplications of a single person, Hsi-ho. (The multiplication was no doubt motivated by the desire to provide enough brothers to take care of all celestial operations in all quarters of the sky.) As pointed out by Karlgren, Hsi-ho appears in the Chou texts simply as an ancient cult-master (sex unspecified) who observes the heavenly bodies, creates the calendar, prognosticates by means of the sun, and controls the sun in its movements.

In the *Shan-hai ching* (bk. 15), on the other hand, Hsi-ho for the first time becomes the mother of the sun or suns (for ten are specifically mentioned). She lives beyond the Southeast Sea, in the midst of the Sweet Waters (Kan-shui), where she bathes the suns one by one in the Sweet Gulf (Kan-yüan). The same work (bks. 9 and 14) tells us further that in the eastern Valley of Light (already mentioned in the *Shu ching*) there grows a tree known as the Fu-sang (Supporting Mulberry; other names for it appear in other texts). Its trunk reaches a height of 300 *li* (about 100 miles), yet its leaves are no bigger than mustard seeds. It is in the branches of this tree that the suns (personified, it will be remembered, as ravens) rest when they are not crossing the sky; as soon as one of them returns from its journey, another starts forth.

The daily itinerary of the sun (or suns) is best described in the third chapter of *Huai-nan-tzu* (though several of its place names also occur in other texts, both of Chou and Han time). At dawn, we are told, the sun first emerges from the Valley of Light and bathes in the Hsien Pool (presumably the same as the Sweet Gulf mentioned in *Shan-hai-ching*, and identified in some texts as a constellation). Maspero points out ("Légendes mythologiques," pp. 26–27) that at the Chou royal court there was a Hsien Pool Dance, the details of which are uncertain, but which is said to have been performed at the summer solstice on a square outdoor altar in the middle of a pond.

The *Huai-nan-tzu* goes on to say that after bathing, the sun ascends the Fu-sang tree and from there crosses the sky, passing en route a dozen or more places of which we know little more than the names. Finally it arrives at Yen-tzu, said to be a mountain in the extreme west of the world. There, at its setting place, grows another mythological tree known as the Jo tree, the flowers of which shine with a reddish glow. It has been suggested by modern scholars that these flowers symbolize either the glow of sunset or the twinkling of stars as they appear after sunset.

The *Ch'u tz'u* anthology contains a poem, probably of the

third century B.C., called *Tung chün* (Lord of the East), which, though it never mentions the sun by name, seems to be a hymn sung in its praise. From it we may infer that the sun uses a chariot when it traverses the sky, for the poem's opening lines read (as translated by David Hawkes, *Ch'u Tz'u, the Songs of the South*, Oxford, 1959, p. 41):

> *With a faint flush I start to come out of the east,*
> *Shining down on my threshold, Fu-sang.*
> *As I urge my horses slowly forward,*
> *The night sky brightens, and day has come.*

The last two lines of this hymn give us the one and only hint in all early Chinese literature as to how, after setting, the sun makes its way (perhaps under the earth?) back to its eastern starting point:

> *Then holding my reins I plunge down to my setting,*
> *On my gloomy night journey back to the east.*

### 5. *Flood Myths*

Of all the mythological themes of ancient China, the earliest and by far the most pervasive is that of flood. It appears in writings belonging to the beginning of the Chou dynasty (*Shih ching* or *Classic of Poetry* and *Shu ching*), and thereafter the references are too numerous to be listed here. Though it crops up in localized form in conjunction with several minor figures (including Kung-kung, whom we have already encountered in connection with Nü-kua in III, 2 above), its really universal version is that in which Yü, together with his father Kun, play the major roles. The former is renowned in history not only as conqueror of the flood, but also as founder of China's first hereditary dynasty, that of Hsia (trad. in 2205 B.C.). Though Yü and his father are portrayed in the orthodox accounts as human beings, the written graphs for their names betray their non-human origin: that for Kun contains the element meaning "fish," and that for Yü is written with an element often found in the names of reptiles, insects, and the like.

The euhemerized version of the Kun-Yü myth, notably as found in the early chapters of the *Shu ching*, may be summarized as follows:

"Everywhere the tremendous flood waters were wreaking destruction. Spreading afar, they embraced the mountains and rose above the hills. In a vast flow they swelled up to Heaven. The people below were groaning." In response to their appeals, a being who in the *Shu ching* is referred to simply as Ti, "Lord," rather reluctantly (because he had reservations about his ability) commanded Kun to deal with the flood. (By the commentators this "Lord" is equated with the sage ruler Yao; in all probability, however, he was none other than the supreme divinity, Shang Ti, the "Lord on High.")

For nine years Kun labored without success to dam up the waters. At the end of that time either Yao or his successor Shun (the texts differ) had Kun executed at the Feather Mountain (Yü-shan), and ordered Kun's son, Yü, to continue the task. The latter, instead of trying to dam up the waters in the manner of his father, adopted the new technique of channeling passages for them to drain off to the sea. In this way he eventually conquered the flood and made the land fit for habitation. As a reward, he was given the throne by Shun and became founder of the Hsia dynasty.

In contrast to this "historical" account, we can, by piecing together the fragments found both in Chou and Han literature, produce another version which is much more "mythological":

On being ordered to deal with the flood, Kun stole from the Lord the "swelling mold" (*hsi jang*)—a magical kind of soil which had the property of ever swelling in size. With this he tried to build dams which, through their swelling, would hold back the waters. When his efforts failed, the Lord, angered by his theft, had him executed at Feather Mountain, a sunless place in the extreme north. There his body remained for three years without decomposing, until somebody (unspecified) cut it open with a sword, whereupon Yü emerged from his father's belly. (One tradition says that

Yü was born from a stone, which would apparently signify that Kun's body had turned to stone.) Following Yü's birth, Kun became transformed into an animal—variously said to be a yellow bear, black fish, three-legged turtle, or yellow dragon—and plunged into the Feather Gulf (Yü-yüan). A cryptic line in the *T'ien wen* poem, however, suggests that he subsequently managed to get to the west, where he was restored to life by a shamanness.

Yü, we are told, "came down from on high" to continue his father's work. He was helped by a winged dragon which, going ahead of him, trailed its tail over the ground and thus marked the places where channels should be dug. For some eight or ten years Yü labored so intensely that, though several times passing the door of his home, he had no time to visit his family within. He wore the nails off his hands, the hair off his shanks, and developed a lameness giving him a peculiar gait which in later times came to be known as the "walk of Yü." Nonetheless, he eventually succeeded in draining the great rivers to the sea, expelling snakes and dragons from the marshlands, and making the terrain fit for cultivation. So great, indeed, were his achievements that the *Tso chuan* history, under the year 541 B.C., reports a noble as exclaiming: "Were it not for Yü, we would indeed be fish!"

There are many other stories about Yü, for example, that he used the same "swelling mold" which had brought disaster to his father to build China's great mountains. Or again, we read that he ordered two of his officials (presumably after he became ruler) to pace off the dimensions of the world from east to west and north to south. In this way they determined it to be a perfect square, measuring exactly 233,500 *li* (roughly 77,833 miles) and 75 paces in each direction. Yü himself also traveled extensively. His itinerary included mythological places like that of the Fu-sang tree (where, as we have seen, the sun comes up), as well as the lands of the Black-teeth People, the Winged People, the Naked People, and many more; among the latter he even stripped himself naked so as to accord with local custom. Furthermore, Yü was a mighty warrior who conquered notorious rebels and gained the allegiance of ten thousand states. On one occasion he held a great assembly on a mountain consisting, in its euhemerized version, of dependent nobles, but elsewhere described as an assembly of spirits.

One curious episode concerns Yü's wife, the Girl of T'u, whom he met and married in the course of his flood labors. Later, while digging a passage through a certain mountain, he was changed (for unexplained reasons) into a bear. His wife, seeing him, ran away and herself became changed to stone. She was pregnant at the time, and so when Yü pursued her and called out, "Give me my son!" the stone split open on its north side and a son, Ch'i, came forth. It should be added that the name of this son (who succeeded Yü as second ruler of the Hsia dynasty) means "to open."

Of the foregoing episodes, most are already attested by the Chou texts. Some, however—notably Kun's theft of the "swelling mold," Yü's use of it to build the great mountains, and the measuring of the world by his two officials—are known only from Han works (primarily *Huai-nan-tzu* and *Shan-hai-ching*). Of still later date, moreover, is the story of Ch'i's birth, which first appears only in a seventh-century A.D. commentary, where it is claimed, quite erroneously, to come from the *Huai-nan-tzu*. At first sight the story appears to be nothing more than the clumsy repetition of two already attested themes, since in it Ch'i (like his father Yü) is born from a stone, and Yü (like his father Kun) is changed into a bear. Yet it would be unwise to dismiss it simply as a late and deliberate literary invention, for already in 111 B.C., according to the sixth chapter of *Han shu* (History of the Han Dynasty), Emperor Wu of that dynasty issued an edict in which he said: "We have seen the mother-stone of the Hsia sovereign Ch'i." This can only mean that at that time the belief that Ch'i was born from a stone was already current.

The story of Kun's transformation into an animal also raises a problem: the fact that in its Chou version (see *Tso chuan* under the year 535 B.C.) the animal in question is a bear, whereas in other much later versions it is variously described as a fish, turtle, or dragon. Kun's close associations with water make any one of these latter interpretations much more plausible. Nevertheless, the earlier bear version cannot be rejected out of hand, since its context is a story in which a noble, having dreamed that he was visited by a bear, is told that this is none other than Kun's spirit.

The fact that the bear is associated both with Kun and Yü (if the story of the latter's change into a bear can be accepted as more than literary invention) has been adduced as evidence for an ancient (and possibly totemistic) bear cult in China. Certainly it accords very poorly with the otherwise overwhelmingly aquatic associations of Kun and Yü alike. This contradiction, together with other thematic disparities, suggests that the Kun-Yü myth (aside from its central theme of flood) is by no means a homogeneous entity, but rather an amalgam of several cultural components which, originally, may have been geographically and perhaps ethnically quite distinct from one another. Just how these diverse cultural components should be interpreted and localized, however, is by no means an easy question. To cite only two of several hypotheses: both Maspero ("Légendes mythologiques," pp. 70–73) and Eberhard (*Lokalkulturen*, I, 365; II, 380–81, etc.) believe that the Kun-Yü myth originally had two major centers of development. Maspero, however, would locate these in North China (along the upper and lower reaches of the Yellow River), whereas by Eberhard they would be placed much farther south (very roughly along a west-east axis extending from eastern Szechuan to coastal China).

In closing, let us repeat (in slightly expanded form) two conclusions already suggested by Maspero: (1) The flood motif is by no means uniquely Chinese, for it is widely found among other peoples of East and Southeast Asia. Hence it could not have been inspired by the localized memory of any particular flood, whether along the Yellow River or elsewhere. (2) Between the Chinese and the Biblical or other Near Eastern flood stories there is this basic difference: in the Chinese version the flood is not inflicted as divine retribution for human sin, but simply epitomizes the condition of the world before there yet existed an organized human society. What is emphasized, therefore, is not the flood as such. Rather it is the task of draining the land and rendering it fit for settled human life. In essence, therefore, the Chinese myth is one about the origins of civilization, in which a divine being, Yü, descends from on high, creates a habitable world for mankind, and founds the first civilized state, the perpetuation of which he ensures by marrying a human mortal.

## IV. CONCLUSIONS

1. The fragmentary and episodic nature of China's ancient myths suggests that they are not homogeneous creations, but rather the amalgams—still incomplete at the time of their recording—of regionally and perhaps ethnically diversified materials.

2. The intense historical-mindedness of the Chinese— displayed already in very early times—together with their tendency to reject supernatural explanations for the universe —caused them to "humanize" or "euhemerize" much of what had originally been myth into what came to be accepted as authentic history. No doubt this trend was encouraged by the eagerness of the noble houses of feudal China to find convincing genealogies for themselves among the shadowy figures of ancient tradition. So early did the process begin, in relationship to the development of written literature, that it largely prevented the myths from being recorded in this literature in their pristine mythological form. This situation is perhaps well-nigh unique among the major civilizations of antiquity.

3. Chinese scholars of the past few decades—notably the historian Ku Chieh-kang—have devoted much energy to the problem of the chronological stratification of early Chinese myth. In so doing they have demonstrated a widespread

phenomenon: the fact that the "historical age" of a myth (the period of history to which it purports to belong) usually stands in inverse ratio to its "literary age" (the period when it is first actually recorded in the literature). In other words, the earlier the purported age of a myth, the later is its actual appearance in the literature.

This phenomenon quite possibly reflects the gradual geographical expansion of Chinese civilization, in the course of which it absorbed the cultural traditions—including myths— of peoples originally lying outside the Chinese orbit. As these myths were thus successively acquired, the historically minded Chinese tried to fit them into a chronological sequence, in which each new acquisition had to be dated earlier than its predecessor, since the lower chronological levels had already been pre-empted. Confirmation of this phenomenon is in general supplied by the five myths we have studied (aside from the fourth, that of the ten suns), as shown by the following table (in which, of course, the dates under the middle column are traditional only):

| Myth | Historical Age | Literary Age |
|---|---|---|
| P'an-ku | Beginning of creation | iii cent. A.D. |
| Nü-kua | Fu-hsi (2852–2738) | Only two pre-Han references (one of iv cent. B.C.) |
| Separation of Heaven and Earth | Chuan-hsü (2513–2436) | First half of Chou |
| Ten suns | Yao (2357–2256) | Second half of Chou |
| Flood | Yü (2205–2198) | Early years of Chou |

Of these five examples, the flood myth of Yü, indubitably the oldest in literary age, also has by far the greatest hold on the Chinese consciousness. That of P'an-ku, on the other hand, is both the youngest and the most obviously alien (unless, which is far from certain, it can be *conceptually* linked with the possibly Chou-time notion of the primordial universe as an egg or a sac).

4. It is rather striking that, aside from this one myth, China—perhaps alone among the major civilizations of antiquity—has no real story of creation. This situation is paralleled by what we find in Chinese philosophy, where, from the very start, there is a keen interest in the relationship of man to man and in the adjustment of man to the physical universe, but relatively little interest in cosmic origins.

5. Violence and drama, boisterous humor or morbid macabreness, a frank concern with sex or the other bodily functions: all these are traits often found in other mythologies, but softened or absent in the myths we have examined. No doubt the selectivity of these myths—the fact that they are cosmogonic rather than intimately "human" in their subject matter—is partly responsible for this situation. Yet there also seems to be a reflection here of a broader phenomenon: the didactic tone and concern for moral sensibility found in much early Chinese literature. It is striking, nonetheless, that when it comes to actual human history, the writers of ancient China could, if need be, record quite unflinchingly the raw facts of life.

6. That the themes of ancient Chinese myth are by no means peculiar to China is demonstrated by the outside parallels noted by us for four out of our five examples (all save that of Nü-kua).

7. Virtually the only texts recovered in original form from pre-Han China are the short and restricted inscriptions on Chou bronze vessels or the even shorter and more restricted inscriptions on Shang divination bones. Almost none of the more extensive literature written on bamboo slips has come down to us physically, owing to the North China climate. This fact, coupled with the rarity of anthropomorphic portrayal in pre-Han art, makes it unlikely—though prophesy is admittedly dangerous—that future archaeology will add very greatly to what we already know about the myths of ancient China from traditional literary sources.

# SELECTED BIBLIOGRAPHY

Only modern studies, and not original sources, are here included.

Eberhard, Wolfram. *Lokalkulturen im alten China*, I (Leiden, 1942); II (Peking, 1942).

———. Review of Karlgren, "Legends and Cults in Ancient China," in *Artibus Asiae*, IX (1946), 355–64.

———. *Typen chinesischer Volksmärchen* (Helsinki: FF Communications No. 120, 1937).

All of Eberhard's writings display stimulating originality, admirable organization, and encyclopedic knowledge. They have sometimes been criticized, however, for an occasional tendency toward overly sweeping conclusions and carelessness as to details.

Eliade, Mircea. *Le chamanisme et les techniques archaïques de l'extase* (Paris, 1951).

———. *The Myth of the Eternal Return*, translated from the 1949 French original by Willard R. Trask (New York: Bollingen Series XLVI, 1954).

Salient ideas from these two stimulating works (discussed in III, 3 of our essay) are conveniently summarized in Eliade, "The Yearning for Paradise in Primitive Tradition," *Daedalus* (Spring 1959), pp. 255–67.

Erkes, Eduard. "Chinesisch-amerikanische Mythenparallelen," *T'oung Pao*, n.s. XXIV (1926), 32–54.

A useful comparative study of the Chinese ten-sun myth and its circum-Pacific parallels.

Ferguson, John C. "Chinese Mythology," in J. A. MacCulloch, ed., *The Mythology of All Races*, VIII (Boston, 1928), 1–203.

This and the compendia by Maspero (on "Modern China") and Werner have little relevance for *ancient* Chinese mythology.

Granet, Marcel. *Danses et légendes de la Chine ancienne* (2 Vols.; Paris, 1926).

A notable pioneer work, the results of which, however, are often questioned today, and which should be used only with extreme caution.

Hentze, Carl. *Mythes et symboles lunaires (Chine ancienne . . .)* [Antwerp, 1932].

Listed primarily as an example of the highly questionable theorizing that should be avoided.

Karlgren, Bernhard. "Legends and Cults in Ancient China," *Bulletin of the Museum of Far Eastern Antiquities,* No. 18 (1946), 199–365.

For the controversy between Karlgren and Eberhard, see II, 3 of our essay. Regardless of the validity of Karlgren's theories (presented with uncompromising finality), this monograph is invaluable for its incredibly complete coverage of a huge mass of data.

Ku Chieh-kang. Numerous articles in *Ku shih pien* (which see) and elsewhere.

Ku is one of the greatest of present Chinese historians. See our "Conclusions" for his theory of the stratification of Chinese myth. Though the writings of him and other Chinese scholars here listed are not explicitly cited in our essay, they have been indispensable in its preparation.

Ku Chieh-kang and Yang Hsiang-kuei. *San-huang k'ao* (The History of the "Three Emperors" in Ancient China) [Peiping: Yenching Journal of Chinese Studies, Monograph Series No. 8, 1936].

A notable product of modern Chinese scholarship.

*Ku shih pien* (Symposium on Ancient Chinese History) [Vols. 1–5, Peiping, 1926–35; Vols. 6–7, Shanghai, 1938–41].
A huge repertory of studies by China's best-known scholars.

Maspero, Henri. "Légendes mythologiques dans le *Chou king*," *Journal Asiatique*, CCIV (1924), 1–100.
Like all of Maspero's writings, a fine piece of work, even though open to criticism on particular points.

————. "Mythology of Modern China," in P. L. Couchoud, ed., *Asiatic Mythology* (London, 1932), pp. 252–384.
See comment under Ferguson.

Thompson, Stith. "Myths and Folktales," in *Myth: A Symposium* (Bibliographical and Special Series of the American Folklore Society, Vol. 5, 1955), pp. 104–10.

Werner, Edward T. C. *Dictionary of Chinese Mythology* (Shanghai, 1932).

————. *Myths and Legends of China* (London, 1922).
See comment under Ferguson.

Yang K'uan. *Chung-kuo shang-ku shih tao-lun* (Introduction to Ancient Chinese History), in *Ku shih pien*, Vol. 7, Pt. 1 (Shanghai, 1938), pp. 65–421.
An attempt to prove that some forty personages of ancient Chinese "history" were actually gods or animal divinities. Though not always convincing, the work presents a wealth of valuable material.

Yüan K'o. *Chung-kuo ku-tai shen-hua* (Ancient Chinese Myths) [Shanghai, 1950].
A popular retelling of the myths, untrustworthy as to theory, but convenient for its careful citation of the original texts.

# FEUDALISM IN CHINA

## I. Introduction

THE *Periods of Chinese Feudalism.* In recent years the terms "feudal" or "feudalistic" have become increasingly popular as designations for premodern Chinese society. The justification for such usage is economic rather than political. In traditional China, the basic medium of wealth was grain, produced on small patches of land by peasants who were either petty proprietors or tenant farmers. These peasants, who constituted seventy or eighty per cent of the total population, were economically dominated by a small interlocking oligarchy of government officials, landed gentry, and rural moneylenders; the capital of this oligarchy was commonly invested in land rather than in commercial or industrial enterprise, which for the most part was small, familial, localized, and marginal to the total economy.

This meant that the bulk of the peasants, though legally free to buy and sell land or change their occupation, were in actual fact effectively bound to the land they cultivated by a variety of economic factors. These included population pressure and concentration of land in the hands of the ruling group, with consequent high land taxes and rents; a shortage of capital with consequent high rates of interest; and the failure of industry and commerce to develop to the point where they could provide real alternatives to farming. Traditionally, indeed, most peasants, should they be forced by economic circumstances to abandon the land, had little alternative but to become either soldiers or bandits. Such a society, though obviously precapitalistic, could not properly be called a slave society, since its number of actual slaves was relatively small. How then, so runs the argument, can it be described other than through use of the word "feudal"?[1]

Such an argument, however, disregards the political aspects of feudalism, which are those stressed in the Introductory Essay of this book, and which, if we examine China, are found to be largely or totally

---

[1] The answer, for many scholars, is that it was neither capitalistic, slave, nor feudal, but constituted yet another distinctive form of society, referred to by K. A. Wittfogel as "oriental" society, but which Wolfram Eberhard prefers to describe as "gentry" society. For the theories of these men and of Owen Lattimore, see Sect. IV below; cf. also the remarks in the concluding paragraphs of this paper.

absent under most of its major dynasties. The common characteristic of those dynasties is that they governed a centralized empire through a salaried civilian bureaucracy which was. appointive, non-aristocratic, theoretically non-hereditary, and in many cases recruited by means of the famous Chinese examination system. Between these periods of empire intervened other shorter periods of political disunity and warlordism, which, however, are too brief and obviously transitional to merit discussion here.

From the strictly political point of view, therefore, there are only two major periods of Chinese history in which feudal or quasi-feudal phenomena are prominent. The first, commonly regarded as China's "classical" age of feudalism, is the Chou Dynasty (1122?-256 B.C.), with which, however, it is convenient for our purposes to group the preceding Shang Dynasty (1765?-1123?).[2] The second is the period of A.D. 221-589, during which China was fragmented among more than two dozen short-lived dynasties and states, to designate which it is convenient to use a modern coined term, Period of Disunity. These two ages were separated from one another by the Ch'in (255-207 B.C.) and Han (206 B.C.-A.D. 220) dynasties, under which, beginning in 221 B.C., remnants of the Chou feudal system were destroyed and replaced by a new form of bureaucratic empire. The collapse of Han rule (officially in 220, though actually in 190, when the empire disintegrated into three parts) ushered in the Period of Disunity, which in turn was brought to an end by the re-establishment of centralized empire under the Sui (590-617) and T'ang (618-906) dynasties.

In the following pages we shall first discuss the rise and fall of Chou feudalism, and, more briefly, the subsequent institutional changes of the Ch'in and Han empires; then present theories which try to explain the factors in ancient Chinese society responsible for these changes; and finally, in less detail, describe the resurgence of certain quasi-feudal phenomena during the Period of Disunity.

## II. Feudalism during the Early Chou Period

*The Chinese Term for Feudalism.* The modern Chinese equivalent for "feudalism" is a compound term, *feng-chien chih-tu*, which literally

---

[2] Variant chronologies exist for events prior to 841 B.C., and many scholars believe that the shift from Shang to Chou actually occurred about a century later than the officially accepted date here given. The period prior to the Shang Dynasty is too sparsely documented to permit any fruitful discussion on our topic.

means "*feng*-establishment system." Though this term became really popular in China only in comparatively recent times, following the influx of sociological and historical concepts from the West, the word *feng*, which is its key component, has a history of almost three millennia and carries with it a rich body of associations stemming from indigenous ancient Chinese civilization. As used in literature of the Chou period, *feng* means, among other things: a mound, to raise a mound, to earth up (a plant), a boundary, to determine the boundaries of a fief, to enfeoff. Its ancient written graph represents a hand beside a plant growing from the soil, and apparently is intended to portray the act of heaping earth around a plant, or, more generally, of raising a mound. As we shall see below, a mound of earth played a central part in the Chou ritual of enfeoffment.

*Shang Antecedents.* The word *feng* apparently does not occur on the divination inscriptions of the Shang Dynasty so far discovered. Hu Hou-hsüan, however, on the basis of an exhaustive examination of these inscriptions made from the point of view of feudalism, has arrived at the following conclusions.[3] Certain Shang kings apparently made a practice of conferring territories upon their wives, sons, and prominent ministers, as well as upon a number of unnamed individuals who are simply referred to in the inscriptions as *hou*, or (less frequently) as *po* or *nan*. These terms, as we shall see, were later to become well-known titles of nobility in the Chou feudal hierarchy. Other territorial holders included neighboring tribal leaders who, originally independent of the state of Shang, had in the course of time apparently been reduced to positions of political dependency. These various landholders, whom Hu interprets as vassals of the Shang kings, were, he believes, in general obligated to perform one or several of the following duties: (1) defense of the Shang frontiers; (2) conducting of punitive expeditions against rebels; (3) tribute payment of tortoise shell and other valuable localized products; (4) tax payment of millet and other grains; (5) supplying of *corvée* labor for cultivation of the king's lands.

Hu's inscriptional material is too fragmentary and ambiguous to be as conclusive as he seems to assume. In its totality, however, it lends

[3] In his "Yin-tai Feng-chien Chih-tu K'ao" [Study of Feudal Institutions of the Yin—i.e., Shang—Period], contained in his *Chia-ku-hsüeh Shang-shih Lun-ts'ung* [Collected Essays on Shang History Based on the Bone Inscriptions], 1st Ser. (Chengtu, 1944), 1, Essay 1.

fair probability to the thesis that already during Shang times dependency relations may have existed, perhaps not greatly unlike those which in Chou times were to develop into a feudal structure. Further than this it would be unwise to venture at the present stage of our knowledge.[4]

*Origin and Stages of Chou Feudalism.* The Shang capital was located in northern Honan, somewhat north of the Yellow River, on the present Peking-Hankow Railroad. Some three hundred miles to the west, near the present city of Sian in the basin of the Wei River, the Chou people rose to political prominence on the fringes of Shang civilization. Though little is known of their early history, it is evident that they were then culturally far less sophisticated than the Shang, whose script and advanced bronze-working technique they probably acquired only at the time of, or shortly prior to, their conquest of the Shang. Other cultural differences, too, seem to have existed between the two groups.

It is still a moot point, however, with the scanty evidence presently available, whether these cultural differences are sufficiently decisive to point to clear-cut ethnic differences as well. Scholars like Creel and Lattimore think that they are not. According to these writers, both the Chou and the Shang stemmed from an essentially uniform human stock common to North China in neolithic times, and the cultures of the two groups were in good part derived from common antecedents. This means that the Chou, at the time of their conquest of the Shang, were not "barbarians" in the sense of being an intruding, definitely alien group, but only in the sense of being the provincial and culturally rather backward cousins of the Shang.[5]

Eberhard, however, strongly disagrees. "Our present knowledge," he maintains, "indicates that the Chou were originally of Turkish

[4] It is not hard to find writers who assert that the Shang possessed a feudal system, but in so doing they are merely following traditional accounts composed long after the Shang period itself, and therefore far from trustworthy. H. G. Creel, writing some eight years earlier than Hu, but basing himself on essentially the same Shang inscriptional material, strongly doubts that feudalism goes back to the Shang. As pointed out by him, the mere occurrence in the Shang texts of titles which later appear in the Chou feudal hierarchy does not prove that in Shang times these titles had the same connotations as they did during the Chou. See his *Birth of China* (New York, 1937), pp. 135-136.

[5] Creel, p. 221, and Owen Lattimore, *Inner Asian Frontiers of China* (2nd edn.; New York, 1951), pp. 307-308.

stock."[6] This thesis, to which we shall revert in Section IV below, is central to Eberhard's whole theory of Chou feudalism.

When the Chou, following their gradual political consolidation in the Wei valley, finally launched their eastern expedition in the twelfth or eleventh century B.C., they not only succeeded in overthrowing the state of Shang, but also in overrunning considerable areas which had probably lain outside the Shang domain proper. Then, because of the difficulties involved in maintaining personal control over these large new territories, the Chou conquerors retired to their homeland in the west, where they thereafter exercised direct rule only over a limited area known as the "royal domain." Of their newly acquired eastern territories, a part was parcelled out to various Chou leaders and the allies who had helped them in the conquest, but much was apparently simply left in the continued possession of those indigenous clan leaders who, during the Chou advance, had either been conquered or had voluntarily tendered their submission. Even the descendants of the house of Shang, in fact, were not exterminated, but were allowed to continue ruling over a state reduced in size.

In this way there came into being a host of small states or principalities—at least one hundred are known to have existed in the eighth century B.C., when we begin to have detailed historical records—each consisting of a walled capital, surrounded by tilled lands from which it derived its sustenance. During the early Chou Dynasty, most of these were separated from one another by mountains, marshes, and other uncultivated "no man's land," peopled only by "barbarians" over whom no one exercised clear-cut jurisdiction.

The relationships of the rulers of these principalities to the Chou monarchy, as well as to their own landholding subordinates, seem in a general way to merit the term "feudal" usually applied to them. From the viewpoint of the present book, however, there is less justification for the common assumption that Chou feudalism began as a full-fledged institution immediately with the Chou conquest, and that it ended as such only with the creation of the Ch'in empire in 221 B.C.

The objection to the first half of this assumption is that feudalism, as defined in this book, means something more than the mere existence of vassalship ties between a single group of territorial nobles on the one hand and a single ruling house on the other. In order to constitute a true feudal system, it should include a network of similar ties linking

[6] Wolfram Eberhard, *History of China*, trans. E. W. Dickes (Berkeley, 1950), p. 25.

these same territorial nobles with a descending hierarchy of lesser and more localized dignitaries beneath them, until, ideally, virtually the entire population is integrated into a complex pyramid of delegated powers and responsibilities.

On the face of it there is little likelihood that such an elaborate structure could have sprung into being full-fledged at the time of the Chou conquest—unless, indeed, the Chou at that time merely perpetuated a pre-existing Shang structure, and this, as we have seen, is improbable. Much more likely would seem the hypothesis that Chou feudalism, as known to us a few centuries after the conquest, had resulted from a gradual evolutionary process, though how and when this evolution occurred is almost impossible to say with the existing evidence. One or even two centuries may have been required before a fairly crystallized and broadly inclusive system emerged. Probably, however, the steps in that direction began very soon after the conquest, since it was already then that the house of Chou began to show signs of political weakness.

That such an evolutionary process did, in fact, take place, is suggested by two bits of evidence contained in the data to be presented in later pages. One is the loose manner in which titles of nobility were used in the early days of the Chou Dynasty, as contrasted with the fixed hierarchical sequence they assumed later.[7] Another, and one much more significant, is Maspero's thesis (see note 12 below) that, in early Chou times, the relationships of state rulers to the Chou monarch were quite different in nature from those of these same state rulers to the lesser landholders within their own states. In later times, however, as Maspero then goes on to say, this difference tended to disappear owing to the fact that these lesser landholders assimilated themselves more and more into the hierarchy of the state nobles. Such a phenomenon, if it did occur—and unfortunately the evidence is not too conclusive—would seem to point to a transition from a proto-feudal to a fully feudal stage such as we have been assuming.

Because of the difficulty of tracing this transition, however, we must be content, in the remainder of this section, to draw an over-all picture of feudal institutions as they appear to us down to about the seventh or sixth century B.C. The changes that thereafter occurred, on the other hand, can be outlined with greater assurance. By that time the weakness of the Chou monarchy had become so pronounced that it is questionable whether the word "feudal" should be used at all to describe the relationships to it of the former vassal principalities. To all intents and

[7] Cf. above p. 18 where Strayer finds the same contrast in feudal Europe.—Ed.

purposes these had become completely independent states, and they remained thus until one of them, the state of Ch'in, successively annexed its rivals and established a new type of empire in 221 B.C.

Within the separate states themselves, however, feudal institutions persisted until the end of the dynasty, though to varying degrees according to time and place. Beginning about the sixth century B.C., the impact of a series of social, political, and economic changes forced a gradual transformation and eventual breakdown of the old feudal order, particularly in Ch'in, where it is quite probable that feudalism had already virtually disappeared prior to the creation of the Ch'in empire.

From the point of view of the foregoing analysis, therefore, the traditional statement that Ch'in "destroyed" feudalism in 221 B.C. is only partially true. What it really did was to destroy the localized remnants of feudal institutions and replace them by a centralized bureaucratic form of empire, the roots of which, however, can be traced back earlier, particularly in Ch'in itself. In Section III we shall examine in more detail the changes that led up to this all-important step, as well as the further consolidation of empire that took place under the following Han Dynasty.

*Political Structure.* The Chou rulers ( like their Shang predecessors) held the title of *wang* or "king."[8] Their vassals were collectively known as the *chu hou*, "all the lords" or "all the princes."[9] Individually, however, each bore one of five specific titles: those of *kung, hou* (same as the *hou* just mentioned), *po, tzu*, and *nan*. In the course of time these titles crystallized into a fixed hierarchy of descending rank, for which reason Western scholars have found it convenient to translate them as duke, marquis, earl, viscount, and baron respectively. Some writers of the end of the Chou go so far as to equate them with fixed territorial holdings of similarly descending importance for which they even indicate precise measurements, but this is obviously a late and idealized schematization. There is abundant evidence that in early Chou times the five titles followed no absolute sequence.[10]

[8] The ancient graph represents a man, standing erect with arms outstretched and feet firmly planted on the ground. He is, so to speak, holding a piece of territory against all comers. Though this title, generally speaking, was a prerogative of the Chou kings, Creel points out (*Birth of China*, pp. 343-344) that even in early times cases are known of its use outside the royal family. This practice, as we shall see, was to become well-nigh universal in the latter centuries of the dynasty.

[9] The same *hou* that had already been used as a title during the Shang Dynasty.

[10] All of them, according to Hu Hou-hsüan (pp. 32ff.), occur on the Shang

The territories with which these nobles were invested were known as *kuo*, a word which today still means a state, country, or principality. Rulership of such *kuo* was hereditary, descent being usually by primogeniture, though favoritism or intrigue produced many violations of this principle. Smaller fiefs also existed, known as *fu-yung* or "attached territories," the rulers of which had no direct access to the Chou kings, but rendered their service to the ruler of that particular neighboring *kuo* to which they happened to be attached.

Concerning the exact nature of the ties between the nobles and their Chou overlord we must draw our information from scattered statements, some of rather late date. The nobles were confirmed in the possession of their territory through a ceremony of investiture which took place in the Chou ancestral temple. There the new vassal, after receiving from the king a solemn admonition to be conscientious in his duties, prostrated himself before him and was given a jade scepter and a written tablet bearing the terms of his enfeoffment. Often these were accompanied by other valuable gifts, such as bronze vessels, clothing, weapons, chariots, and the like. During the early part of the Chou Dynasty, at least, this ceremony was apparently commonly repeated whenever the son of a deceased noble succeeded his father as holder of a fief.[11] We shall defer to a later point in this section an account of one of its most significant aspects, that associated with a divinity known as the Lord of the Soil.

In return for their land holdings, the nobles manifested allegiance by going to the Chou court for individual audiences with the king (probably not as frequently or regularly, however, as traditionally supposed), or sent envoys for this purpose. The late ritualistic texts further speak of periodic mass audiences attended by nobles from all parts of the country, but whether or not these actually occurred on the scale described is uncertain. We do know that the nobles offered tribute on occasion, consisting of valuable but easily transportable products indigenous to their territory. In time of rebellion or "barbarian" attack,

---

inscriptions, though the functions attached to each are far from clear. As interpreted by him, *kung* originally meant "patriarch," i.e., the ancestral head of a family; the graph for *hou* pictured an arrow entering a target, and the word was apparently used as a military title; *po* meant "senior" or "elder"; *tzu* meant "son," i.e., the son or sons of the king; *nan* meant "male."

[11] For further details, drawn from contemporary bronze inscriptions as well as the usual literary sources, see Ch'i Ssu-ho, "Investiture Ceremony of the Chou Period" (article in Chinese), *Yenching Journal of Chinese Studies*, Peiping, No. 32 (June 1947), 197-226.

they were expected to provide troops to help the king. Sometimes they were called upon for special services, such as the supplying of men and materials for repairing the city wall of the royal capital. The king had the right, if not always the power, to act as judge in disputes involving two nobles, or to send troops against those who proved recalcitrant.

Within their own states, however, the nobles were for all practical purposes autonomous. They appointed their own officials, levied their own taxes, maintained their own armies, and exercised their own justice, which was based on tradition and personal opinion rather than on any clearly defined body of law.

Much of their land, nonetheless, was further subdivided in the form of domains, known as *yi*, which they distributed to their relatives, officials, and courtiers. The same was true of land within the Chou royal domain. Such *yi* were measured by the number of peasant families occupying them. The early portion of the *Book of Changes*, for example, speaks of an *yi* as having 300 families. However, the fact that in other contexts this word is also used to designate a city, seems to show that it underwent a semantic evolution similar to the Latin *villa*, from which are derived the French *ville, village*, etc.

It was possible for a single individual to hold more than one *yi*, sometimes scattered in different parts of the state to which he belonged. Often he himself lived in the state capital, leaving his domains in charge of an administrator or steward known as *tsai*. Such stewards were sometimes highly influential men, who constituted the *alter ego* of their master.

Instances are known in which a state noble took back a domain that he had given to a subordinate, or transferred it to another man. In general, however, such domains became the hereditary property of those who received them, and were administered by them without external interference. This parallels the fact that the official positions in the various feudal states tended to be held hereditarily by certain families, some of whom ended by becoming more powerful than the nobles they served.

It is commonly assumed that this intra-state subdivision of land was simply a further extension of the process whereby fiefs were allotted by the house of Chou to the state nobles. Maspero, however, believes that the two systems were originally quite distinct. In his opinion, the investiture ceremony which marked the king's granting of a fief to a noble did not take place when a noble conferred a domain on a subordinate. Therefore, such subordinates, strictly speaking, did not belong to the feudal hierarchy, and their status was that of landed proprietors, not of vassals. He points out, for example, that should an official be dispossessed of his property by his master, he then owed him nothing and was free to seek service under another lord, from whom he could obtain a new domain.[12]

Even if this distinction originally existed, however, it seems evident that in the course of time it became obliterated for all practical purposes. Maspero himself admits that there was a constant tendency for the great officials to convert themselves into actual vassal lords. Moreover, he draws attention to an institution, about which we unfortunately know little, whereby an individual could, by swearing a solemn oath, entrust himself to a patron, whom he thereafter served unto death with unswerving fidelity. This practice he compares with that of commendation. "Each great lord thus had his bands of followers who played an important role in the troubles of this epoch."[13] We have indicated above the importance this theory—unfortunately difficult to prove conclusively—may have for tracing the early evolution of Chou feudalism.

Many scholars further assume that all land, in the last analysis, was regarded as actually belonging to the Chou kings. As one piece of evidence they cite the famous early Chou poem (*Book of Odes*, no. 205) which reads:

> Everywhere under vast Heaven
> There is no land that is not the king's.
> To the borders of those lands
> There are none who are not the king's servants.

Here again, however, Maspero disagrees. What this poem expresses, in his opinion, is merely the concept of political sovereignty, not that of any definite right of property. The ancient Chinese philosophical theory, as summarized by him, was that land was not the inalienable property of any one man, but belonged to "everyone." Everyone, in other words, enjoyed the right, varying in degree according to his position in a strongly hierarchical society, to make use of a portion of it. What the sovereign did, therefore, by determining its specific allotments, was merely to regularize this right which was common to all.[14]

---

[12] Henri Maspero, "Le régime féodal et la propriété foncière dans la Chine antique," *Mélanges posthumes sur les religions et l'histoire de la Chine*, III. *Études historiques* (Paris, 1950), 133, 143-144.

[13] "Le régime féodal," p. 144.

[14] Maspero, "Les termes désignant la propriété foncière en Chine." *Mélanges posthumes*, III, 204-205.

*The Aristocracy.* A common designation in Chou literature for members of the upper class is *chün-tzu* or "rulers' sons." Originally this was a term primarily indicative of good birth, but later, under Confucian influence, it acquired a strongly moral coloration in a manner very similar to our word "gentleman." Lowest among the *chün-tzu* was the class known as *shih*, which Creel defines as meaning, among other things, "a young man" or a "stalwart," and which he compares with the word "brave" as used to denote the warriors of an American Indian tribe. Though not all *shih* were warriors, he suggests that as a class they were perhaps roughly comparable to the knights of medieval Europe.[15]

All these aristocrats, regardless of whether or not they bore titles of nobility, differed from the rest of the population in that they maintained family genealogies, performed no agricultural or artisan labor, did not engage in trade, and lived according to an elaborate but (in early times) unwritten code of ceremonial and etiquette known as *li* (variously rendered as rites, ceremonies, traditional mores, customary morality, etc.). These *li*, which took the place of any fixed code of law, were designed to cover all the major activities of life and required much time to learn. On the military side they remind us in some ways of the code of chivalry of European knighthood. Warfare, if we are to believe the historical records, was waged more for prestige than to gain loot or territory. One should be generous to the enemy, not push one's victory too far, and not resort to unfair stratagems. In 638 B.C., for example, we read in the *Tso Chuan* that the Duke of Sung suffered a serious defeat because he allowed the enemy to cross a river before launching his attack. On being criticized for his act, he said: "The superior man[16] does not inflict a second wound, and does not take prisoner anyone with gray hair. When the ancients had their armies in the field, they would not attack an enemy when he was in a defile."[17]

Warfare was endemic during most of the Chou Dynasty. The aristocrats went into battle wearing leather armor and riding in four-horse chariots, each bearing a driver, a lancer, and an archer equipped with the powerful Chinese reflex bow. A company of foot soldiers, recruited from the common people and traditionally said to number 120, accompanied each chariot; seventy-two such chariots, with their infantry

---

[15] *Birth of China*, pp. 278-279.

[16] *Chün-tzu* or "ruler's son," the term that has just been described.

[17] See also Marcel Granet, *Chinese Civilization* (London and New York, 1930), pp. 266-281, for a vivid account of the military code during the early Chou period.

complement, were regarded as comprising the army of a first class state.

When not engaged in warfare, the Chinese aristocrats, like their medieval European counterparts, amused themselves by feasting, hunting, and engaging in such games as archery contests. To a greater extent than in medieval Europe, however, they seem also to have been seriously interested in the administrative affairs of peace. Many were well-educated men who, at diplomatic assemblies or court gatherings, could buttress their arguments with appropriate quotations from such ancient literature as the *Book of Odes*.

One striking difference between Chou China and medieval Europe was that the former possessed neither a universal church nor a professional priesthood. There were, to be sure, certain men who specialized in religious ritual, divination, and the like, but their role was that of assistants rather than chiefs in the great religious ceremonies, in which the aristocrats acted as their own priests. A primary reason, no doubt, is that these ceremonies were in large part concerned with the cult of the ancestors. Such a cult was necessarily divisive rather than unifying, since the ancestors of each aristocratic clan were of immediate concern only to the members of that clan. Hence it was unable to develop into a universal church with an organized priesthood.

Nevertheless, this ancestral cult was probably the most vital psychological factor from which the aristocratic class derived its power and prestige. Each important clan maintained its own elaborate genealogy, through which it traced descent from ancient heroes who were locally and even nationally famous. These ancestors received regular food offerings from their descendants, by whom they were consulted on all important occasions. They were powerful spirits capable not only of aiding their own family, but also of injuring anyone outside the family who might arouse their ire. This, no doubt, is one reason why the Chou conquerors permitted the descendants of the Shang kings to continue ruling as heads of a lesser feudal state, rather than draw possible retribution on themselves by causing the sacrifices to these Shang ancestors to be interrupted.

In a society as ancestor-conscious as that of ancient China, it is obvious that relationship ties between the leading clans were of paramount importance. Political alignments, in fact, were determined more often by these ties than by abstract obligations of vassal to overlord. Or rather, it would perhaps be more correct to say that the vassal-lord relationships were to a large extent based on those of family. To quote

Ch'i Ssu-ho, "the whole empire was converted into a great family system."[18] So strong, indeed, was the stress on family that in later Confucian thinking the state itself was regarded as simply an enlargement of the family system. Even during early Chou times, in fact, we find the ruler commonly referred to as "the parent of the people."

Aside from the ancestral cult, however, other religious ceremonies were psychologically important for the political system. Symbolic of territorial sovereignty, for king and noble alike, were the sacrifices paid by both to a divinity known as Hou T'u, Lord of the Soil. Actually there were many such lords: lesser ones presiding over local villages, a greater one for each fief, and a supreme one (sacrificed to by the Chou king alone) presiding over the country as a whole. Each had its own altar, consisting of a flat open-air square mound of earth. A tree or trees were in ancient times (not later) grown on this altar, and the cult almost certainly originated as one of fertility.

We, however, are concerned only with its political aspects. When a new fief was created, the invested noble received from the king a lump of earth taken from the altar of the national Lord of the Soil, which then became the nucleus for the localized altar built by the noble in his own fief. We have examined at the beginning of this section the meaning of the word *feng* ("a mound," "to raise a mound," etc.), used to designate this ritual. A fief's Lord of the Soil was, like the noble's own ancestors, among the most powerful divinities to whom he sacrificed, and, as long as he retained his fief, these sacrifices continued. Should the fief be annexed, however, its altar of the soil was then roofed over, thereby destroying the power of its divinity, after which the new ruler built another altar of his own. Maspero, as we have seen, believes that this investment ritual did not apply to the lesser domains distributed by fief holders to their subordinates, even though each peasant community within such domains had its own localized Lord of the Soil.[19]

Finally, the Chou kings themselves were specifically confirmed in their rule of the entire country by a further religious sanction, connected

[18] Ch'i Ssu-ho, "A Comparison between Chinese and European Feudal Institutions," *Yenching Journal of Social Studies*, IV (1948), 11-12.

[19] The classical study of this cult still remains that of E. Chavannes, "Le Dieu du Sol dans la Chine antique," Appendix to his *Le T'ai Chan* (Paris, 1910). The reader should beware, however, of the remarks there made regarding the use of the five colors in conjunction with this cult, since Chinese naturalistic speculations centering around the five colors, five directions, five elements, etc., did not crystallize until the fourth or third century B.C.

with their supreme divinity, T'ien or Heaven. The ancient graph for T'ien clearly represents an anthropomorphic figure. It is, indeed, very similar to the early graph for *wang*, "king," save that it omits the latter's lower horizontal line representing the ground on which the figure stands. Already at the beginning of the Chou Dynasty, however, the word was used not only religiously to designate a supreme divine power, but also non-religiously as the term for "sky." Creel suggests that it may have originated as a collective designation for the ancestors of the Chou kings, taken as a group, and that it thereafter became the name for the realm above in which they lived, thus changing into an impersonal supernatural concept very similar to our word "heaven."[20] This theory would explain very conveniently why no one but the Chou kings bore the title of T'ien Tzu, "Son of Heaven," and why, although Heaven could be appealed to by all, sacrificing to it was a Chou royal prerogative.

Certainly there seems no doubt that T'ien was a Chou and not a Shang divinity, and that the Chou were the creators of the important political theory known as that of T'ien Ming, the "Mandate of Heaven." Creel, indeed, believes that this theory was used as political propaganda by the Chou to justify their overthrow of the Shang Dynasty. Their claim was that they had supplanted the Shang because of the latter's moral unworthiness, and that Heaven had therefore transferred its Ming or Mandate to themselves, thus giving them the divine right to rule. This theory, however, proved to be double-edged, for it involved the idea that the Mandate does not necessarily remain "eternal." That is to say, should its holders at any time prove to be incompetent, it could quite conceivably be transferred by Heaven to yet another ruling house. As later elaborated by the scholar-bureaucrats of imperial China, this idea was to become an important instrument for criticizing the ruler and thus strengthening their own influence. It has been repeatedly invoked to justify the many changes of dynasty in Chinese history, and is still perpetuated in the present Chinese term for revolution, *ko ming*, which literally means "transferring the Mandate."

*The Commoners.* The economic basis for the feudal structure we have been describing was the great bulk of non-aristocratic commoners known as *min*, "the people," or as *shu jen* or *chung jen*, "the masses." Unlike the aristocracy, the *min* had no family names or genealogies, no ancestral cult, and but little knowledge of the complex rules of *li*

[20] *Birth of China*, pp. 342-344.

which governed the lives of the ruling class. Between them and the latter, however, there was a series of gradations rather than an absolute gap, for cases are recorded, though admittedly rare, in which commoners were raised to aristocratic status or aristocrats fell to the ranks of the commoners.

This non-aristocratic population belonged to various categories. Some were artisans or menials who served the ruling class. Both groups apparently included slaves, consisting either of war captives or of persons who had been enslaved for crime; these, however, do not appear to have been numerically or economically significant. There were also merchants, a few of whom seem to have succeeded in acquiring a fair amount of wealth. No fixed system of metal coinage yet existed, however, so that trade largely consisted of barter. All these groups lived in walled towns or were attached to the establishments of the landed proprietors in the countryside. Economically they did not play an important role, and there was, during the early Chou, no development of artisan guilds or of an urban bourgeoisie comparable to that of medieval Europe.

Far more vital to the total economy was the great mass of peasants. They appear to have had no formal rights to the land they cultivated, to which they were bound as serfs, and with which they could be transferred whenever its control passed from one overlord to another. There seems to have been no trace of free landholders, as in Europe. It is uncertain whether the serfdom of the peasantry derived from a formally recognized right of the overlord over the lives of those who cultivated his land, or simply from the fact that any peasant desperate enough to flee from his own overlord would have great trouble in obtaining land from another. Maspero tends toward the second view.[21] In any case, we know that the peasants were obligated in peacetime to surrender a portion of their crops to their overlord (said in late texts to be about a tenth, though probably the actual amount was considerably greater), and were subject to conscription for wall and road building, irrigation and flood-control works, and other public construction. In time of war they supplied the foot soldiers who accompanied the chariots of the nobles.

Much has been speculated but little is definitely known about the precise system of land tenure of the early Chou. The difficulty lies in the fact that what little information we have is mostly late, fragmentary, and ambiguous. Much of the discussion centers around the

[21] "Le régime féodal," p. 126.

*ching-t'ien* or "well-field" system, the first comparatively detailed account of which, however, dates only from Mencius (372?-279?). According to what he says, such a *ching* consisted of nine plots of land: eight "private fields" (*ssu t'ien*), each occupied by one peasant family, surrounding a ninth central plot known as the "public field" or "lord's field" (*kung t'ien*; the word *kung* may be translated either as "public" or "lord"). The produce of this central field, which was communally cultivated by the eight families, went to the overlord, whereas that of the "private fields," cultivated by each family individually, was retained for personal use. Traditionally, the term *ching-t'ien* is explained on the basis of the graphic resemblance of the character *ching*, "well," to the layout of the nine plots of land. Conceivably, however, the nine plots may have actually centered around a well used for irrigation.

That such a checker-board pattern could ever have been laid out over wide areas with the mathematical exactness described by Mencius is very improbable. On the other hand, it is the belief of most scholars at present that his account does reflect some kind of actual economic and administrative unit of early Chou times, the essence of which was that part of the land was communally cultivated by the peasants for their overlord and part privately cultivated for their own use. Ch'i Ssu-ho goes so far as to compare the public or lord's field with the "demesne" of the European manor, and the private fields with its "land in villeinage."[22]

Various Chinese scholars have proposed theories to explain this and other ancient land systems ambiguously referred to in Mencius and elsewhere. Though ingenious, they are generally not too convincing and hardly provable, and it would lead us too far afield to discuss them here.[23] One of the more probable, followed by Maspero,[24] is that in very early times, before a fixed land system had yet evolved, the peasants practiced a system of communal cultivation in which they shifted every few years from one piece of land to another, preparing the new land for agriculture by burning off its cover of bush and grass.

[22] Ch'i Ssu-ho, "The *Ching-t'ien* Theory of Mencius" (article in Chinese), *Yenching Journal of Chinese Studies*, Peiping, No. 35 (December 1948), 101-127, esp. 124-126.

[23] That of Hsü Chung-shu, however, will be touched on briefly in Sect. IV below. For a convenient summary of it and several other recent Chinese theories, see Yang Lien-sheng, "Notes on Dr. Swann's *Food and Money in Ancient China*," *Harvard Journal of Asiatic Studies*, XIII (1950), 531-543.

[24] "Le régime féodal," pp. 124-126.

This theory is supported by passages in certain early texts, as well as by modern parallels in Indo-China and elsewhere. It is weakened, however, by the fact that a word occurring on the Shang divination inscriptions, where it has been commonly interpreted as referring to this method of "fire farming," has now been conclusively shown to refer in actual fact to the burning of the fields as a preparation for hunting rather than for agriculture.[25]

## iii. Disintegration and Disappearance of Chou Feudalism

*Decay of Chou Royal Power.* The picture of Chou feudalism which we have been painting necessarily glosses over, for want of adequate information, the many regional and temporal variations that undoubtedly existed. An era of increasingly sharp change perhaps began as early as 771 B.C., when, according to the traditional account, a sudden attack by "barbarians" forced the house of Chou to abandon its capital in the west and to establish a new one some two hundred miles farther east near the present city of Loyang. There, though perpetuating its rule until 256 B.C., it succeeded in doing so only because the question of its continued existence or non-existence no longer had any practical significance. The history of the last several centuries of the Chou is that of the struggles for power between half a dozen or so of the major states—by that time completely free of any Chou overlordship—in which the Chou kings rarely figure at all.

Indicative of this political change in its early stages is the fact that the *Tso Chuan* (an extremely detailed historical chronicle of the period 722-481 B.C.), though mentioning hundreds of nobles by name, records only nine of them as having undergone the ceremony of feudal investiture. In not one of these nine cases, moreover, did the noble in question actually go himself to the Chou capital. On the contrary, the king in every instance sent his own envoy to the noble's home state to perform the ceremony.[26]

Even better known is the way in which, during this same period, the more powerful of the feudal lords endeavored to arrogate to themselves various royal functions. The first step came in 679, when one of them assumed a new title, that of *pa*, "lord protector" or "tyrant" (in the

[25] See Hu Hou-hsüan, "Yin-tai Fen-t'ien Shuo" [On the Burning of Fields during the Yin—i.e., Shang—Period], *Chia-ku-hsüeh Shang-shih Lun-ts'ung*, I, Essay 4.

[26] See Ch'i Ssu-ho, "Investiture Ceremony of the Chou Period," pp. 224-226.

Greek sense). This title was thereafter successively taken by the rulers of four other states before it finally lapsed in 591. Under the aegis of these *pa*, assemblies of the leading nobles were convoked, at which the latter solemnly, and somewhat cynically, signed treaties pledging themselves to maintain the peace and "assist the royal house [of Chou]." These efforts at peacemaking failed, perhaps in part because no one state was powerful enough to retain the title for more than one generation. Had it been otherwise it is conceivable that an institution might have developed comparable to that of the Shogunate in Japan.

*Changes, ca. Sixth Century Onward.* The latter centuries of the Chou were marked by widespread change and innovation which speeded the dissolution of the feudal order, though remnants persisted within the individual states down to the Ch'in unification of 221 B.C.

(1) *Technological changes*: These include the appearance of iron (first mentioned in 513), and of improved agricultural techniques (better plows and fertilizers, building of irrigation and water-control works, etc.). A growth in population was one important result, as evidenced by the increasing size of cities and armies. An impressive indication of technological advance, and of the ability to mobilize large masses of manpower on public works, was the wall-building in which the leading states engaged during the fourth and third centuries B.C. Walled fortifications, hundreds of miles long, were built not only along the northern frontiers to separate China as a whole from the steppe peoples as a whole, but also elsewhere to separate the individual Chinese states from one another.

(2) *Military changes*: With the advent of the appropriately named Warring States period (403-221), warfare lost its chivalric character and turned into large-scale conflict, waged in deadly earnest by armies of tens of thousands for the primary purpose of territorial annexation. It was backed up by political alliances, diplomatic intrigue, and such techniques as bribery and assassination. The result was that by the third century B.C. all but a handful of the larger states had been crowded from the scene. Complex siege engines and other techniques were devised for the assault on walled cities. What is more important, at the end of the fourth century the northern and western states, notably that of Ch'in (now centered at what had been the Chou capital prior to the shift of 771), learned from the neighboring steppe peoples the use of mounted archers in place of the old cumbrous war chariots.

(3) *Economic and social changes*: From the lower fringes of the aristocracy, many members of which had become impoverished through the constant wars, there now arose a new class of unattached politicians, educators, and thinkers, who often travelled from state to state, seeking a ruler who would put their ideas into practice. The golden age of Chinese philosophy owes its genesis to these men, of whom Confucius (552/551-479) was the earliest example. Other members of the aristocracy specialized as professional military warriors and "bravos" attached to the various state rulers.

Yet another phenomenon of the times was the appearance of a money economy based on metal coinage (and with it no doubt a growing merchant class). This development is commonly said to date from the late fifth century.

Most significant evidence of the disintegration of feudalism, however, was the changing relationship of peasant to land, culminating in the disappearance of serfdom. The imposition of new forms of land taxation and military levy in two states (Lu and Cheng) in the years 594, 590, 543, 538, and 483 is probably indicative of this change. Though we know virtually nothing of their precise details, it has been thought that they were attempts, on the part of the state administration, to extract taxes directly from the peasantry, instead of through their immediate overlords, the local landed proprietors.

In the state of Ch'in the changes were most sweeping. There the famous statesman, Shang Yang (died 338), is credited with abolishing the old system of land tenure in at least parts of that state, and giving to the peasants the right to "sell and buy" land. On such land he seems to have instituted a tax-in-kind paid directly to the state in place of the labor services formerly rendered by peasant serfs to their immediate overlords. Through these measures, Ch'in successfully encouraged settlers to migrate from other states.

(4) *Institutional changes*: With the institution of written law codes, mentioned in two states (Cheng and Chin) in 536, 513, and 501, we find a new concept emerging: that of an impersonal body of law, to which all men, high and low alike, should be subject, in place of the old personalized feudal relationships, based on the traditional mores or *li*. This new concept, fostered by the Legalist school of thought, reached its highest development in Ch'in, where it undoubtedly helped that state in its ultimate triumph.

Another phenomenon equally indicative of the increasing complexity of social organization was the trend toward specialization in administration. Civil and military functions, for example, which in earlier centuries had often been conducted by the same men, came to be differentiated during the Warring States period by being allocated to a civil and a military hierarchy, the former headed by a Prime Minister (*hsiang*) and the latter by a Military Commander (*chiang*). This bifurcation was to be perpetuated in imperial times.

In the more important states there was a steady curtailment of the power of local officials and landed proprietors. In Ch'in, for example, this political centralization is evidenced by the land reform described above. It also appears both there and in other states in the rise of a new administrative system based on the *hsien* (prefecture) and *chün* (commandery). These territorial units seem to have originated in land newly annexed from other states, or in the militarized zones of states bordering the steppe peoples on the north. Gradually, however, especially in Ch'in, they were established in territory lying well within the state frontiers as well. What distinguished them from the domains of the landed proprietors seems to be that they, unlike the latter, were directly controlled by the state government by means of state-appointed governing officials who, at least in principle, were non-hereditary. The *hsien* (which was smaller than the *chün*) is first mentioned as early as 688 and 687 in Ch'in, while the *chün* appears considerably later, first in the neighboring state of Wei around 400 and again in 361. Though the *chün* was to give way to the province in later times, the *hsien* survives as an administrative unit to this day.

Yet another innovation, carried out in Ch'in in the year 350, was the institution of a new aristocratic hierarchy of eighteen degrees, having purely honorary rather than territorial or hereditary significance. These degrees were acquired, not by birth, but by military exploits, or later (the first case is reported in 243) through purchase.

(5) *Concept of a universal empire*: The administrative system of the early Chou, inadequate though it had proved to be in practice, undoubtedly represented an attempt to create a political universality probably greater than any that had previously existed in China. In the last two centuries of the Chou, with the intensification of war and social upset, the dream of almost all thinkers became that of recreating a universal empire that would bring peace to the world. In literature, this dream is manifested in the highly idealized writings of the ritualists and others, purporting to give detailed pictures of early Chou and even pre-Chou institutions and customs.

Politically, the same ideal is symbolized in the history of the words *wang*, "king," and *ti*, "emperor." In 370 B.C. the new ruler of Wei usurped the title of *wang* (hitherto, with few exceptions, a royal designation); his example was speedily followed by other state rulers. This title, however, no longer sufficed to express the aspirations of the leading contenders for power. Hence a new title was looked for and found: that of *ti*, a word rich in religious and historical associations. Ti (or Shang Ti, "Supreme Ti") had been the name of the most powerful divinity of the Shang Dynasty; by the Warring States period it had also come to be attached to the names of certain legendary heroes supposed to have ruled in the predynastic golden age. Finally, during the last decades of the Chou (in the years 288, 286, and 257), several state rulers tried to adopt it as their political title. Though these efforts failed, owing to the jealousy of rival states, the founder of the Ch'in Empire took the word as part of his title in 221 B.C., and it has since remained as the permanent Chinese equivalent for emperor.

*Establishment of Bureaucratic Rule under the Ch'in and Han Empires.* Having conquered the last of the opposing states in 221 B.C., the king of Ch'in adopted for himself the new grandiose title of Shih-huang-ti, "First Sovereign Emperor." At the same time, so we are told by the *Shih Chi* or "Historical Records" (the official history of the period), "he caused the Ch'in [Empire] to be without a foot of land of investiture [*feng*]," and removed "the rich and powerful people of the empire, amounting to 120,000 families," to the Ch'in capital, where they could be kept under the watchful eye of the central government. Their weapons were confiscated and cast into bells and monumental human statues. Though certain noble titles were retained, they were honorary only and had no territorial significance. The empire was divided, in 221 and the years immediately following, into a total of forty-two *chün* or commanderies.[27] Each commandery was governed by a centrally appointed triumvirate of Administrator, Military Governor, and Overseer, and was subdivided into an indeterminate number of *hsien* or prefectures, governed by Prefects.

[27] Thirty-six is the number stated in the *Shih Chi* as having been established in 221, and this figure is repeated in D. Bodde, *China's First Unifier: A Study of the Ch'in Dynasty as Seen in the Life of Li Ssu (280?-208 B.C.)*, Sinica Leidensia, III (Leiden, 1938), pp. 135, 144, 238, which, however, on p. 246 lists four additional commanderies as having been created in 214. From scattered references we can deduce that the actual total number created during the dynasty was probably forty-two.

A major technological achievement of the Ch'in was the Great Wall of China, built by hundreds of thousands of conscript laborers, who in part utilized for this purpose the walls previously erected by several of the major states along their northern frontiers.

When the Ch'in Empire disintegrated only twelve years after its founding, many of the former nobles or their descendants returned to power in the resulting civil wars. Moreover, when the founder of the Han Dynasty (206 B.C.-A.D. 220) mounted the throne, he, though a commoner himself, created a new land-holding aristocracy in 202 B.C. This he did by dividing almost two-thirds of his new empire into "kingdoms" and "marquisates," bestowing these on his brothers, sons, and meritorious assistants, each of whom possessed full authority over the people within his boundaries.

In following decades, however, the power of the new aristocracy proved to be dangerous and so was checked in various ways, especially after the unsuccessful Revolt of the Seven Kings in 154 B.C. Thus a decree of 127 B.C. destroyed primogeniture by compelling all kingdoms to be equally divided among the sons of deceased kings. In 106 the empire, including the kingdoms, was divided into thirteen Circuits, each headed by an imperially appointed Inspector charged with keeping watch over it on behalf of the central government. Many noble families met violent ends as the result of intrigue or attempted rebellion, so that, during the first two centuries of the Han Dynasty, the average noble life-span of such families was only 2.31 generations. In fact, we know that of the marquises created by the Han founder, not a single descendant retained that title by the year 86 B.C.

Furthermore, the *chün* and *hsien* system was continued and gradually extended, so that by the end of the first century B.C. there were 83 *chün* and 1,314 *hsien*, as against only 20 kingdoms and 241 marquisates. (The holdings of the latter ranged in size from 100 to 20,000 families, with 2,600 as the average.) The nobility, to be sure, lived lives of great luxury, but the real administrative power by this time lay in the hands of the centrally appointed bureaucracy, which under Emperor Ai (6-1 B.C.) amounted to 130,285 officials, and which was paid in cash or grain, not in land (though much of its capital was invested in land).

Thus was created the vitally important official-gentry class, which in most later periods has been the effective ruling group in China, and which, though it tended to be self-perpetuating as a class, was non-titled and individually non-hereditary in the government posts it held. The orthodox ideology of this group was Confucianism. The Han also saw the beginnings of the examination system, greatly elaborated in T'ang and later dynasties as the instrument for recruiting the official bureaucracy.

This internal political consolidation was accompanied by a military expansion which pushed the imperial frontiers into modern Indo-China in the south, Manchuria and Korea in the northeast, and the westernmost reaches of Chinese Turkestan in the northwest, thus making of the Han one of the three or four largest empires in Chinese history.

Private ownership and buying and selling of land were now the rule, and resulted in such a concentration in the hands of the wealthy that the government was often urged to impose limitations on the size of landholdings. The climax was reached with the famous decree declaring the nationalization of all farm land, issued by the usurper Wang Mang in A.D. 9, which, however, had to be rescinded three years later owing to the tremendous opposition of the landed gentry.

## IV. The Dynamics of Chou Feudalism

What were the forces that shaped early Chinese society along the lines we have been describing? No answer to such a complex question can, in the present state of our knowledge, be really conclusive. Nevertheless, the theories of Owen Lattimore and (more recently) Wolfram Eberhard, because of the care and detail with which they have been worked out, deserve serious consideration.

We shall begin with Lattimore's theory, as developed in his *Inner Asian Frontiers of China*.[28] Though deriving much from K. A. Wittfogel's concept of what the latter calls "oriental society," it goes considerably further by combining this with Lattimore's own concept of the nature of nomadic society. In this way it seeks to explain what has been a major theme of Chinese history: the interplay of forces between the agrarian society of China proper and the nomadic society of the steppes, mountains, and deserts fronting China's northern periphery.

*The Agrarian Way of Life*. Lattimore's theory begins with the thesis that Chinese civilization evolved in North China out of a relatively uniform antecedent neolithic culture, based on a mixed economy of hunting, fishing, and food-gathering, to which were later added the domestication of the dog and pig and a primitive agriculture. The trend

[28] See especially Chaps. IX-XIII, which are those most pertinent to the period we are discussing.

toward agriculture occurred first in the north rather than in the potentially richer Yangtze Valley, owing to the fact that the loess soil which covers much of the Yellow River basin was comparatively free from vegetation and could be easily worked with stone tools, whereas the Yangtze Valley was still a thick jungle land. Even in North China, however, agriculture did not develop evenly everywhere. At first it tended to be concentrated in certain valleys in the loess highlands, which, being well watered and sheltered, combined favorable conditions for crop growing with continued opportunities for hunting and fishing. Only later, probably, did agricultural communities spring up in the lower reaches of the Yellow River, for there the land, though fertile, was marshy and required drainage.

Somewhere along this line of development, however, a vital factor intruded itself: the comparative sparseness and seasonal irregularity of the rainfall in North China, which meant that agriculture could not progress beyond a certain point without the help of irrigation. We cannot as yet precisely date the beginnings of Chinese irrigation, but when it started, its need for the cooperative labor of communal groups must have powerfully reinforced the already-present tendency of agriculture to develop in a few nuclear areas rather than evenly throughout the country.

The Shang state was one of these nuclei. Another was the Chou, which, starting from the same general neolithic background, matured later than the Shang but eventually outstripped it. Still others were the little principalities—each a self-contained economic cell centered upon the walled city where it could store its precious grain—that came into political existence under the Chou.

From these nuclei the agrarian way of life spread outward wherever the terrain was favorable. The demonstrated ability of grain-production to support a larger population than any other occupation encouraged the use of manpower for increasingly ambitious water-control works. These enabled ever more land to be brought under cultivation, thus in turn making possible a yet greater population. Such works—built not merely for irrigation, but also, especially later, for flood control, drainage, and water transport—enabled the Chinese progressively to overcome environmental obstacles such as in the beginning would have been insuperable.

At the same time, the increasing concern with agriculture caused other economic activities to decline to marginal importance. Hunting, for example, once economically significant, became the sport of the aristocracy. The pig, rather than cattle or sheep, was used as the chief food animal, because, as a scavenger, it did not require extensive land for its pasturage such as could more efficiently be devoted to crop growing. In short, the production of grain—wheat or millet in the north, and, later, rice in the south—became *the* great Chinese way of life.

The amalgamation through military means of smaller states into larger states, characteristic of the Chou period, was a political reflection of the growth of key economic regions. Because, however, this growth was not uniform, but advanced more rapidly in some areas and times than in others, the balance of political power likewise fluctuated between different regions. The culmination was reached with the creation of a single universal empire in 221 B.C.

Having outlined Lattimore's theory, let us now try to formulate some conclusions. In the first place, as pointed out in the Introductory Essay of this book, one of the stimuli for the rise of a feudal system may often be "the decay or weakening of a highly organized political system—an empire or a relatively large kingdom." A few lines later, however, the essay wisely warns us that this is not necessarily true for all feudal societies, and points to China by way of illustration. This warning is well taken because, in the case of Chou feudalism, it is highly doubtful whether any such antecedent "highly organized political system" did in fact exist, irrespective of whether we think of it in terms of the Shang state, or of the hegemony established by the Chou themselves at the time of the conquest (from which, presumably, gradually evolved the later full-fledged feudal system). In the words of Maspero: "Chinese feudalism does not emerge from the decomposition of an antecedent regime more or less strongly centralized."[29]

In the second place, the reason why Chou feudalism was doomed to eventual failure, at first nationally and then locally, was that, initially and nationally, even the moderate political unity demanded by it outstripped the economic integration of the scattered units to which it was applied, whereas, later on and locally, the economic growth of these units outstripped the organizational ability of feudalism to handle them effectively. The resulting tensions brought about the changes and eventual breakdown already described, thus clearing the way, first, for the transformation of the former feudal principalities into states entirely independent of the Chou monarchy, and then, finally, for the amalgamation of these states into a new kind of bureaucratic empire. This,

[29] "Le régime féodal," p. 144. Cf. also Lattimore, p. 370, for a similar view.

however, did not happen without tremendous resistance on the part of the old order. The wall-building activities of different states during the fourth and third centuries B.C., for example, are interpreted by Lattimore as "a general phenomenon of the last phase of . . . feudal separatism in China."[30]

In the third place, the growing economic monoculturism of the Chinese, with its need for the efficient utilization of concentrated manpower, led even in early times to a bureaucratic tendency in Chou feudalism. "It was necessarily interested in public works of a kind that were not characteristic of European feudalism. . . . The labor of the whole community had to be regulated for the maintenance of public works—water rights had to be allotted and grain stored and issued for the labor gangs. Even under feudal conditions, accordingly, there was a more urgent need for clerkly functions than in Europe."[31] In the end, the ruling aristocracy of feudal China successfully transformed itself into the ruling scholar-gentry of imperial China.

Finally, the factors which we have been describing gave to Chou feudalism a homogeneity far greater than that of Europe, with its diverse origins and varied local economies. This fact was to have lasting consequences, for, as pointed out by Lattimore,[32] it is no accident that "Europe changed in a way that led to a money economy and industrialism, while China changed in a way that created a centralized imperial bureaucracy, . . . whose combination of landed interest and administrative interest kept capitalism well in check and prevented industrial development almost entirely."[33]

*The Pastoral Way of Life.* The other side of Lattimore's theory concerns the nomadic steppe peoples of China's northern frontiers. In his view, the pastoral economy of these peoples was in good part an outgrowth of that same general neolithic North China culture from which had arisen the grain economy of the Chinese. This happened because,

[30] p. 404. From our point of view, of course, the term feudal is not entirely accurate at this point, since feudalism had by this time disappeared from the national scene, even though its remnants persisted within the individual states.

[31] Lattimore, pp. 375-376.

[32] p. 393.

[33] This, like most generalizations, requires some qualification. The growing complexity of Han society, for example, inevitably led to an industrial and commercial development which was very considerable, judged by previous standards. Nevertheless it remains true, then and later, that this development was consistently opposed by the state bureaucracy and never reached the position where it dominated the state, as in Europe.

in the beginning, only those groups occupying certain favorable localities had followed the trend toward specialized agriculture which caused
them eventually to become "Chinese." In less favorable intervening
terrain other groups retained their earlier mixed economy, thus becoming the "barbarians" who in early Chou times occupied the uncultivated
no man's land between the feudal states.

It is not surprising that in the Chinese historical accounts of Chinese-
barbarian conflicts during the first half of the dynasty, the latter are
usually pictured as aggressors. Viewed in their larger historical context,
however, what these conflicts really seem to represent is a series of losing
rear-guard actions on the part of the barbarians against the spreading
tide of Chinese agricultural economy. Some "barbarians," engulfed by
this tide, accepted the Chinese way of life and thereby themselves
became "Chinese." Others who resisted, however, were driven progressively farther into the mountains and finally even out into the inhos-
pitable steppe.

It should not be supposed that at this time these "barbarians" were as
yet true nomads. We read in the records, for example, that in their
clashes with the Chinese they fought on foot. But gradually, as they
reached the steppe, their old mixed economy evolved into a new way
of life. They "found themselves in a terrain and environment that
would not tolerate either the old mixed economy as a whole or the
special emphasis on agriculture that had become the mark of 'being a
Chinese.' They were forced, instead, to work out for themselves a new
line of specialization in the control of herded animals in the wide
steppe. This emphasis on a single technique produced in due course
a society even more one-sided than that of China, but sharply different
from it and in the main antagonistic to it."[34]

Thus there developed in the steppe lands fronting northern China a
genuine nomadism which from the time of its appearance powerfully
affected Chinese history. We have already seen, for example, how at
the end of the fourth century B.C. certain of the Chinese states, including Ch'in, learned from their nomad neighbors the use of mounted
archers in place of the former war chariots. The building of the Great
Wall during the Ch'in Dynasty is commonly regarded as an artificial
attempt to demarcate the Chinese from the nomadic way of life.

[34] Lattimore, p. 381. He is careful to point out elsewhere (p. 355), however,
that the pastoral nomadism of Inner Asia derived its origins not only from the
steppe margins of North China, but also from the edges of the Siberian forests
and of the Central Asian oases.

This attempt, however, foundered on the geographical fact that between agrarian China and the pastoral steppe there is no clear-cut physical demarcation, but only an ill-defined transitional zone, to some extent suited for either farming or herding, but ideally suited for neither. In this zone, therefore, a mixed agricultural-pastoral society developed. Politically, its members enjoyed a peculiarly strategic position, because, though conversant with both ways of life, they were definitely committed to neither and therefore were free to join either one in its struggles against the other.

From the Han Dynasty onward, as a result, Chinese and nomads have repeatedly struggled to control this intermediate zone, and from it have gone on to try to establish domination over the other's homeland. In this struggle each has enjoyed temporary but not permanent success, because each, in order to rule the other, has had to accept the other's psychology and way of life, thereby losing its own cultural and political identity. This fact is important for the discussion in Section V of feudalistic phenomena during the Period of Disunity. Before turning to this, however, let us first consider Eberhard's theory of Chinese society and compare it with that of Lattimore.

*Chou Feudalism and Chinese Gentry Society.* Eberhard's theory of Chou feudalism, and of its evolution into what he calls Chinese "gentry" society, is presented in the first chapter of his recently published *Conquerors and Rulers: Social Forces in Medieval China* (Leiden, 1952). There he begins by applying to China A. Rüstow's theory of "superstratification,"[35] i.e., the theory that feudalism results from the stratification produced when there is the conquest of one group by another that is ethnically and culturally different. This, in the case of China, means, for Eberhard, that "Chou society is the result of an *ethnic superstratification.* The Chou rulers came from Western China accompanied by a group of militarily organized tribes of non-Chinese affiliation. . . . They conquered and occupied East China and started an expansionist, colonial activity."[36]

Elsewhere (pp. 24-25), Eberhard emphasizes the wide general applicability of the "superstratification" concept: "We regard feudal conditions as the result of superstratification of a basically agrarian group by an essentially or at least originally pastoral group. . . . Feudalism came into existence when the originally pastoral tribes of the migration period

[35] See A. Rüstow, *Ortbestimmung der Gegenwart*, 1 (Zurich, 1949).
[36] p. 4 (Eberhard's emphasis).

had conquered the Roman Empire; when the originally pastoral Chou and their allies had conquered Shang-China; when nomadic Mongol and Turkish tribes had conquered India, or Persia, or Russia." However, as Eberhard is careful to add, this fact "does not mean that any conquest of nomads inevitably led to feudalism."

In Chou China, Eberhard believes, the conquest resulted in a deep dualism between the rulers and the subject population, manifesting itself in such fields as religion, literature, and law. Above all, however, it is conspicuous in property relations. The Chou conquerors, when they settled on their new fiefs in Central and East China, built city fortresses there which stood like islands in the sea of the indigenous population. Being unable to rely wholly on this population for their food supply, they were obliged to develop alternative sources of food of their own. They therefore "organized their tribesmen in semi-military cadres of eight families each. These groups left the fortress in early spring, cleared a piece of land and cultivated it for one or more seasons until the soil was exhausted, after which a new clearing was made."[37] These clearings, ideally possessing regular size and shape, and quite possibly cultivated collectively by their eight-family occupants, were the *ching-t'ien* or "well-fields" of Mencius and other late Chou writers. Their rigid organization contrasted sharply with the freer organization of the indigenous "natives," who lived in villages of their own more or less independently of the conquest group, to which they merely had to pay sporadic "tribute" as a token of submission.

In the course of time, the fortress cities of the ruling nobles lost their exclusively administrative and military character and became industrial and commercial centers as well, increasingly frequented by the surrounding "natives" who were anxious to acquire the goods produced by the city artisans. This development was accompanied and facilitated by the rise of a merchant class and a money economy. As the result of it and other complex factors, much of the land originally belonging to the "natives" was probably bought or otherwise acquired by the nobles and their city-dwelling followers. In this way new relationships of a landlord-tenant character came into existence. These, though "shaped after the model of feudal institutions," such as had hitherto prevailed, differed from them in the "absence of the moral element (loyalty), [or of] the mutuality of rights and obligations," and in the fact that they were "more or less purely economic" in character.[38]

[37] p. 7.
[38] pp. 10-11.

This development was of crucial importance, for it speeded the cultural assimilation of the ruling group with the subject population, made it possible for the former to regularize the latter's occasional tribute into a fixed tax indistinguishable from the "tithe" received by the nobles from the communally-cultivated "well-fields," and caused these "well-fields" themselves to disappear entirely as separate units. Commissioners—many of them recruited, Eberhard believes, from the merchant class—were now employed by the nobles to travel about the countryside and collect the new taxes. "The lords regarded these collectors as their 'officials' and shaped their relation towards them after the model of their household administration."[39]

These and other changes of the sort we have described in Section III led to the gradual dissolution of the old feudal relationships, and their replacement by a new network of economically-centered landlord-tenant relationships. The process culminated, as we have seen, with the creation of a new type of empire in the third and second centuries B.C., dominated by a new social group to which Eberhard gives the appropriate name of "gentry."

The two major characteristics of this gentry class that distinguish it, in Eberhard's eyes, from the "burgher" society of the West, are that (1) it was economically dependent upon landed property, not industrial capital; (2) its three major professions were those of landowner, scholar, and politician—all normally represented within a single gentry family, and often, indeed, in a single individual. The key to the great stability of this class lay in the fact that a gentry family normally possessed both a city and a country home. The former was occupied by those family members who were engaged in political careers, while in the latter lived other members who administered the family's rented-out landed property. At the same time, this rural seat provided an economic base to which the city members could retire in times of political disfavor or uncertainty. "The extreme stability of Chinese gentry society was the decisive factor which prevented the disintegration of Chinese civilization and militated against the success of foreign rule over China. But it also prevented change. It prevented the development of modern science—the instrument of change."[40]

*The Theories of Eberhard and Lattimore Compared.* Eberhard's description of gentry society differs little in its broad outlines from Lattimore's conception of post-Chou society. Nor does Eberhard object

[39] p. 11.    [40] p. 16.

to Lattimore's theory of the development of pastoral society along China's northern periphery, and its interaction there with Chinese agrarian society; on this point, indeed, he seems to be in essential agreement with Lattimore.[41] It is the agrarian side of the picture, however, that Eberhard in the second chapter of his book heavily attacks. In so doing he by-passes Lattimore himself and concerns himself exclusively with K. A. Wittfogel's formulation of the theory of "oriental" society. This formulation, however, has, as we have noted earlier, been of basic importance in shaping the agrarian side of Lattimore's own theory.

Reasons of space prevent us from considering in detail all of Eberhard's arguments. The more important of them, however, have to do with Wittfogel's central thesis, according to which the preoccupation of the state with water-control works, especially those for irrigation, has been the decisive factor shaping the evolution of Chinese and other examples of "oriental" society. Eberhard, by way of refutation, adduces historical evidence from which he seeks to prove that (1) irrigation was not vital to the wheat and millet culture of North China (where Chinese civilization had its start), but assumed real importance only in connection with the later rice culture of the South; (2) Chinese political interest in water-control works cannot be traced with assurance far back into the feudal period, and became conspicuous only during the imperial epoch, when, moreover, it centered more around canal-building activities (themselves but one aspect of the rising interest of the time in improved communications), than it did around irrigation projects per se; (3) when, as we sometimes read in the literature, purely irrigational projects were undertaken, their initiative usually came from the local populace and not the central government.

Despite questions of detail, Eberhard's total arguments convince this writer that Wittfogel has probably considerably over-estimated the all-embracing role of irrigation in China, at least as far as the North is concerned. Certainly the criticism, made by Eberhard on the final page of his book, seems justified that Wittfogel, by his blanket application of the word "oriental" to a wide range of civilizations—some not even found in Asia at all—has tended to obscure the actual differences among them. The safer course, suggested by Eberhard himself, is to approach each of these civilizations, including China's, as an "individual case."

Eberhard's own socio-political approach, on the other hand, does not—at least to this writer—provide a fully satisfying explanation for

[41] See Eberhard, pp. 8-9, 72.

the evolution of Chinese society from its feudal and pre-feudal stages to its later form. His theory does not, in other words, convincingly explain why, for example, Chinese society from early times displayed tendencies toward an economic monoculturalism and a political bureaucratism, such as eventually transformed it into the gentry-dominated monolithic state of imperial China. For problems such as these, the environmentally-based and economically-based functional approach of Wittfogel and Lattimore seems to provide a more dynamic and consistent rationale.

Even if we accept Eberhard's strictures on Wittfogel, it is perhaps still possible to utilize the Wittfogel-Lattimore theory in a modified form. Thus it seems reasonable to suppose, with Lattimore, that the early development of agriculture in North China tended to be concentrated in those areas that were environmentally favorable to it, and that this concentration encouraged the growth of population in the same areas, thus leading to the rise of local political entities. It seems likewise reasonable to suppose that the thinner population that occupied the less favorable intervening areas tended at first to retain the old general mixed economy, but that it then began to move toward a more exclusively pastoral way of life when it discovered this to be better suited to its environment. In this way the stage was set for that bifurcation, postulated by Lattimore, which led toward a specialized agriculture on the one hand and a specialized pastoralism on the other.

Given the seasonal unevenness and relative sparsity of rainfall in North China, moreover, it would be strange if the occupants of the agricultural areas did not at some stage try to remedy this condition by means of irrigation. This they might very well do even though their irrigation projects were of only marginal importance to the agricultural situation, were neither grandiose nor all-pervasive, and stemmed from private groups rather than from any centralized political authority. The net effect, in any case, would be the stepping up of agricultural productivity, resulting in the further growth and spread of a population now increasingly wedded to an agrarian way of life. These factors would in turn induce the local political structure to develop more and more along bureaucratic lines in its efforts to handle the enlarging population.

In this way a chain reaction would be produced which, once started, could continue under its own momentum until China finally became a centralized empire. All this could plausibly happen even though the state as such waited until the imperial age to play a major role in water-control activities, and even then interested itself more in canal-building than in irrigation-works per se.

We have, moreover, so far said nothing about such forms of hydraulic activity as the drainage of lowlands and flood-control, about which Eberhard himself says relatively little. Yet it is obvious that they must have become of crucial importance to the Chinese when their agrarian way of life expanded from the valleys of the loess uplands out onto the great alluvial plain of the lower Yellow River. The difficulties then encountered must have been so formidable that they could hardly have been overcome by private initiative alone, unaided by centralized political supervision.

If we turn now to Eberhard's own theory of "ethnic superstratification" as the key to Chou feudal institutions, we are confronted by certain difficulties. One is the uncertain support provided by the available data for Eberhard's supposition (see Sect. II above) that the Chou were "originally of Turkish stock," and hence ethnically distinct from the peoples they conquered. Certainly it seems strange, if this be the case, that linguistic traces of the fact have not survived, similar to those found in the case of the many alien invaders of China of later periods.

In the second place, Eberhard's attribution to ethnic superstratification of the "deep dualism" believed by him to characterize Chou society, is to some extent weakened by a factor already noted by us in Section II. This is, that when the Chou people conquered East China, they retained only a part of the new territories as fiefs for themselves and their allies, leaving other portions in the continued possession of indigenous clan leaders. This means that the new ruling aristocracy did not in all areas consist of alien conquerors.

In the third place, Eberhard, it will be remembered, finds the alleged dualism of Chou society most significantly manifested in the *ching-t'ien* or "well-field" system, regarded by him as a semi-military institution created by the Chou conquerors for their own people, in contradistinction to the looser organization of the subject population. At this point Eberhard explicitly acknowledges his indebtedness to Hsü Chung-shu's theories of early Chou land tenure.[42] These theories, however, while extremely ingenious, depend on so many scattered and sometimes dubious bits of evidence that they definitely do not bring

[42] Eberhard, p. 6. Cf. Hsü Chung-shu, "A Study on the Ching T'ien System" (article in Chinese), *Chung-kuo Wen-hua Yen-chiu Hui-k'an* [Bulletin of Chinese Studies], Vol. IV, Pt. I (Chengtu, 1944), 121-156.

conviction to this writer. What is much worse, moreover, is that this complex evidence is used by Hsü to prove, not that the *ching-t'ien* system was inaugurated by the Chou conquerors, but that it was a survival from the Shang dynasty![43] Yet Eberhard reverses this equation for his purposes without a word of explanation.

In summary, we would like to suggest that Eberhard's application of the superstratification theory to Chou China does not really seem to require the ethnic differentiation he himself postulates for it. Such, at least, is the conclusion we might draw from Eberhard's own opinion, quoted earlier, that the source of feudalism lies in the "superstratification of a basically agrarian group by an essentially or at least originally pastoral group." Cultural patterns such as these do not necessarily have to be associated with ethnic differences.

What we ourselves suspect really resulted from the Chou conquest was a superstratification that was primarily political rather than ethnic. Though certain cultural differences no doubt accompanied this process of political superstratification, it would seem wiser to regard most of them as functionally arising out of the very fact that the population was divided into a ruling and a ruled group, rather than as indicative of innate ethnic or cultural differences between the two groups, antedating the conquest.

In this modified sense we are quite ready to accept superstratification as the immediate factor responsible for the rise of feudal institutions in Chou China. At the same time, however, we believe that other longer-continuing forces—probably both environmental and economic—must also be looked for, if we are to explain the processes which finally produced Chinese gentry society. These forces may well have been much more varied and less exclusively "hydraulic" than Wittfogel and Lattimore assume, but that they existed, and in the end proved decisive, seems reasonably certain.

Though we may glimpse the main contours of Chou feudalism, any theory as to its dynamics is necessarily rendered uncertain by the limitations of the available data. With the humbleness of the true scholar, Eberhard admits as much when he concludes his book by saying: "The theory developed here is only an attempt at an interpretation. Our knowledge of Chinese society is still far too limited to make any final explanation possible."

[43] Hsü, pp. 131ff., esp. p. 139. Cf. also Yang Lien-sheng in *Harvard Journal of Asiatic Studies*, XIII (1950), 536, which summarizes Hsü's theory.

## v. Feudalistic Phenomena during the Period of Disunity[44]

*Comparison with the Chou Dynasty and with Medieval Europe.* The Han Dynasty officially ended in A.D. 220 (though the empire had already disintegrated into three parts thirty years earlier). The subsequent Period of Disunity (221-589) falls into three main divisions: (1) the Three Kingdoms (221-280); (2) the Western Chin Dynasty (265-316), during which most of China was momentarily reunited following the year 280; (3) the Northern and Southern Dynasties (317-589), during which South China was ruled by five successive dynasties with capitals at Nanking, while the North was fragmented among almost a score of ephemeral states and dynasties, of which only the Northern Wei (386-535) succeeded in lasting more than a century. Finally the period was brought to an end by the reunification of North and South under the Sui Dynasty (590-617).

The Period of Disunity, as an age of prolonged political division, invites comparison with the Chou Dynasty on the one hand and with medieval Europe on the other. Such comparison shows that whereas it differs from the Chou on several vital points, its similarities with medieval Europe are striking, even though subject to important qualifications.

(1) Like the European Middle Ages but unlike the Chou, the Period of Disunity followed the collapse of a major empire, whose memory and political institutions, however, it preserved to a greater extent than did medieval Europe. The result was twofold: it meant that on the one hand the Period of Disunity differed from the Chou in its political system, but that on the other its break with the past and decline in learning were neither as sharp nor as prolonged as was the case in Europe.

(2) Like the Middle Ages but unlike the Chou (after the conquest itself), the Period of Disunity witnessed a continuing series of major barbarian invasions which destroyed native Chinese rule in North China for almost three centuries, imposing a sequence of alien dynasties ruled by Turks, Mongols, Tibetans, and Tungus. Unlike Europe, however, where barbarian invasion actually helped to overthrow the Roman

[44] The writer is keenly aware of the difficulties involved in the discussion of this period, for which the basic monographic studies are largely lacking, so that the remarks below are necessarily tentative and subject to correction.

Empire, the invasions of China during the Period of Disunity did not begin until the early fourth century, i.e., until a century after the Han Empire itself had already collapsed. Even then, in fact, the term "invasion" is something of a misnomer, for the first alien state, that of the Former Chao (304-329), was not created by the inroads of peoples from the actual steppe, but by a coalition of Hsiung-nu (Hun) tribes who had already been settled in North China for more than a century. There they had acquired military power after having been used as mercenaries by the northernmost of the Three Kingdoms. In other words, they were partially Sinified by the time they founded their state, and were the products of that undefined frontier zone between China proper and the steppe whose importance we have described in the preceding section. Some, though not all, of the subsequent alien states and dynasties of the Period of Disunity were likewise dynasties of "infiltration" rather than dynasties of conquest.[45]

(3) Like the Middle Ages but unlike the Chou, the Period of Disunity was an "age of faith." Buddhism, which had entered China during the Han Dynasty, spread during the Period of Disunity to become *the* great religion of high and low alike. Here again, however, the similarity with Europe must be qualified, for whereas Christianity there became the state religion already under the Roman Empire, Chinese Buddhism did not become really influential until the late third or early fourth century, i.e., again, as in the case of barbarian invasion, until about a century after the collapse of the Han. Even then, in fact, it had to meet the continued challenge of the rival ideologies of Confucianism and Taoism, which, though temporarily weakened, were never permanently submerged. Chinese Buddhism, furthermore, always remained a congeries of different sects and monasteries, rather than a truly universal church united under a supreme spiritual hierarchy. Though spiritually, socially, and even economically, its impact was profound, its political power was much less than that of Christianity in Europe or even Buddhism in feudal Japan.

(4) Unlike the Chou, and also, though to a lesser extent, unlike the Middle Ages, the Period of Disunity had no central pivot of political unity. That is to say, it had no single ruling house to provide political continuity, such as the house of Chou had provided during the earlier period. Dynasty followed dynasty, with little regard for political

[45] The terminology is that of K. A. Wittfogel and Feng Chia-sheng, *History of Chinese Society: Liao* (Philadelphia, 1949), pp. 15-16.

legitimacy, and the schism between the Chinese South and the alien North effectively inhibited any feeling of common allegiance to a single overlord.

*Feudalistic Phenomena.* Aside from these partial similarities with the European Middle Ages, the Period of Disunity displays other phenomena which elsewhere are the frequent, if not invariable, marks of a feudal age. There is, for example, the very fact of political disunion itself. Warfare, coupled with famine and other disasters, exacted an enormous toll, and more than once the historical records contain the grim word "cannibalism." Nevertheless the drop in population from Han times, if it actually occurred, was far less than traditionally supposed.[46]

A by-product of disorder was the southward migration of Chinese—especially those of the upper class—to escape the invasions from the North. It has been estimated that by the end of the fourth century about one million northerners had fled to the south of the Yangtze River. This movement, on a scale heretofore unprecedented in China, gave to the South a growing economic importance which caused it ultimately to outstrip the North.

Another by-product was the widespread dislocation of economic life. Trade, which despite Chinese agricultural monoculturalism had developed to sizable proportions under the Han, was choked off in many places. From the third century onward there was a shrinkage in the use of metal coinage, and between then and the fifth century there were periods when copper coins were reported as being out of circulation. The result was a reversion to barter trade in many places.

With the wane of central authority, governmental functions were often monopolized by powerful local landowning families. Despite decrees to the contrary, it became common practice for wealthy clans to enclose large amounts of public land for their own use. Helpless families and individuals frequently attached themselves as *k'o* or "guests" (retainers) to such a clan, thereby gaining support and security

---

[46] Census figures recorded in the dynastic histories indicate a drop from about 48 million to about 16 million between the years A.D. 140 and 280. The two sets of figures, however, are in actual fact useless for comparative purposes, because only the first seems to be a moderately complete census of the total population, whereas the second is almost surely merely an enumeration of the country's taxpayers. Cf. Hans Bielenstein, "The Census of China during the Period 2-742 A.D.," *Bulletin of the Museum of Far Eastern Antiquities*, Stockholm, No. 19 (1947), 125-163, esp. 128, 139-145, 153-155.

for themselves, as well as exemption from the levies and services imposed by whatever central government existed. Similar reasons caused other people to become Buddhist monks, or to attach themselves or their lands to powerful monasteries. Like the rich families, such monasteries enjoyed special privileges. They commonly owned large amounts of land, and not infrequently acted as trade centers or money lenders.

Individuals who became *k'o* were hereditarily owned and could be transferred as gifts to friends; the chief difference between them and slaves (who also existed) was that unlike the latter they could not be sold. This institution was on several occasions recognized by the ruling dynasty, which tried to regularize it by placing limitations on the number of *k'o* permitted to be held by protectors according to the latters' rank. On the other hand, we also read of cases in which slaves and *k'o* were freed by imperial decree and drafted as soldiers or transport workers in spite of objections from powerful families.[47]

Aside from such general phenomena reminiscent of feudal ages elsewhere, attention should be drawn to a political move on the part of the founder of the Western Chin Dynasty, Emperor Wu (265-289), which, though not "feudal" itself according to the definition of this book, might conceivably, under differing circumstances, have led to the eventual development of an institutionalized feudal system. On his accession, he enfeoffed twenty-seven or more of his relatives as *wang* or kings, giving them *kuo* or principalities converted from former commanderies and ranging in size from 5,000 to 20,000 families. Each had its own private army and staff of administrative officials, modelled on that of the central government. In addition, there was created an indeterminate number of lesser dukedoms and marquisates.

At first the new nobles apparently preferred the pleasures of life in the capital to living on their own fiefs. In 277, however, they were compelled by imperial edict to retire to the countryside. Three years later, following the unification of the empire, the central government

[47] The above data (save those on population, for which see preceding note) are conveniently summarized in Yang Lien-sheng, "Notes on the Economic History of the Chin Dynasty," *Harvard Journal of Asiatic Studies*, IX (1946), 112-117. Cf. also the pertinent data in Wang Yi-t'ung, "Slaves and Other Comparable Social Groups during the Northern Dynasties (386-618)," *ibid.*, XVI (1953), 293-364, and in Etienne Balazs, "Le traité économique du 'Souei-Chou,'" *T'oung Pao*, XLII (1953), 113-329. As clearly indicated by Wang (pp. 344-358), *k'o* or "guests" were in actual fact only one (perhaps the most conspicuous) of several serf-like social groups, whose status was little better than that of slaves.

attempted a general disarmament program, which, however, failed on the one hand to apply to the new aristocracy, and on the other led to the selling of many government arms to the Hsiung-nu or Huns. The combination of these events was disastrous. The Revolt of the Eight Kings, beginning in 291, was not suppressed until 306. This left the dynasty so weakened that it fell an easy prey to the Huns and was completely expelled by them from North China ten years later. Had the Chin rulers proved more competent, it is conceivable that the Period of Disunity might have been shortened by two centuries, and that the domination of the North by the barbarians might have been avoided almost entirely.[48]

*Was the Period of Disunity an Age of Feudalism?* Despite the facts just cited, the answer to this question is definitely no if we accept as valid the central criterion for feudalism advanced in the Introductory Essay of this book. To quote this essay: "Feudalism is primarily a method of government . . . in which the essential relation is not that between ruler and subject, nor state and citizen, but between lord and vassal." Such a relationship did not exist during the Period of Disunity, save in sporadic instances.[49]

During this age the main struggle was no longer really one of bureaucracy against feudalism, or centralism against localism, for this had already been decided in favor of the former several centuries earlier. Rather it was that described by us in Section IV: the struggle between the Chinese agrarian way of life and the nomadic pastoral way of life. In this struggle, the Period of Disunity represented a phase of nomad ascendancy, just as the Han Dynasty before it and the Sui and T'ang dynasties after it represented phases of Chinese ascendancy.

The Chinese migrants who fled southward from the fourth century onward carried with them the typical Chinese social pattern. For those with money and influence it was, despite political uncertainty,

[48] For these events, see Teng Chih-ch'eng, *Chung-hua Erh-ch'ien-nien Shih* [Two Thousand Years of Chinese History] (Shanghai, 1934), ii, 40ff.

[49] It is only fair to point out that this verdict—based as it is on rather specific political criteria—is not universally shared by all scholars. Balazs, *op. cit.*, for example, several times uses the word "féodalité" with reference to the Period of Disunity (without, however, defining what he means by the term). A good example is the sentence on p. 125 of his article which begins: "However, opposed to the feudalism of the Chinese baron emigrés in the South, there is in the North the new feudalism of the Turco-Mongol conquerors. . . ." Concerning possible differing interpretations of the nature of Chinese society during the Period of Disunity, see also the concluding paragraphs of this essay.

a boom period. Great estates were created out of land which, through the efforts of innumerable peasant tenants and "colonizers," was cleared, drained, and put under cultivation. The holders of these estates, the landed gentry, were interlinked or identical with the members of the official bureaucracy. Their common characteristic was that they all belonged to "old families"—families with lengthy pedigrees and cultured backgrounds. Like members of an exclusive club, they were careful to bar all parvenus from their ranks.

An example of how they did this is found in the system known as the "rectification of the nine categories" (*chiu-p'in chung-cheng*), used as a basis for making official appointments. Under this system, government boards in different localities periodically graded the local populace into nine ranks, ostensibly according to their moral and intellectual qualifications, but actually on the basis of family backgrounds. In the words of a Chin Dynasty critic, Liu Yi (died 285): "In the upper categories there are no 'cold gates' [socially insignificant families]; in the lower categories there are no 'hereditary families.'" It is hardly surprising that few people from the "cold gates" ever gained official rank.[50]

Yet though the men who ruled South China thus constituted a privileged oligarchy, for whom family and social connections were of paramount importance, they did not form a titled nobility nor belong to a feudal hierarchy of overlords and vassals. Though their government was weakened by corruption, incompetence, and political strife, its form followed that of the Ch'in and Han bureaucracies. It cannot, therefore, according to the definition used in this book, be said to have been a feudal government.

In the North, the Huns, Tibetans, and other invaders had their own tribal organizations, varying from group to group, but all reflecting to some degree their pastoral background. Beneath them, however, the overwhelming bulk of the population remained Chinese in culture and economy. In dealing with this Chinese population, the aliens had four main alternatives. On the one hand, if they wished to preserve their own way of life, they might drive the Chinese peasants south, convert them into slave herdsmen, exterminate them, or allow them to remain as subjugated peasants, while installing themselves over them as a ruling military caste. On the other hand, they had the

[50] Though statistical data confirming the great stability and exclusiveness of the gentry class during the Chin Dynasty have not yet been made, Eberhard has prepared comparable data covering the Northern Wei Dynasty (386-535). See note 52 below.

possibility of deliberately giving up their own nomadism and assimilating themselves as much as possible to the Chinese way of life.[51]

None of the alien dynasties that attempted any of the three former alternatives succeeded in surviving for more than a few decades. The fourth and peaceful alternative, most notably tried by the comparatively long-lived Northern Wei (386-535), yielded greater success because it enlisted the invaluable cooperation of the Chinese landed gentry. Yet in the end it too led to the same result: through the very fact of making themselves a part of Chinese society, the conquerors lost their political identity and disappeared from history. Thus it is significant that when China was reunited, the dynasty that did this, the Sui, was Chinese and not alien, though it originated in the North. In the long run the tribal organization of the nomad could not withstand its new Chinese environment.[52]

The process of Sinification of the barbarians is reflected in the land policies of North and South. Under the Han, the general policy—formulated but hardly enforced—had been to set limitations on the amount of land owned by wealthy individuals. During the Period of Disunity this policy shifted to that known as the "equalization of land" (*chün t'ien*), under which peasant families received land allotments from the government on the basis of the age, sex, and number of their members, these allotments being periodically equalized through subsequent readjustment.

This policy, which represented an effort to extend centralized control at the expense of local interests, was never, however, more than partially effective. This was not merely because of the technical difficulties involved, but more especially because the policy in general applied only to "government land"—that is, to land not privately owned; in particular, it probably extended only very rarely to the estates of the powerful landed gentry.[53] Significantly, the policy was advocated most

[51] Eberhard, *History of China*, p. 112. In the fourth chapter of his *Conquerors and Rulers*, Eberhard discusses these several alternatives in detail.

[52] In his *Das Toba-Reich Nordchinas: Eine soziologische Untersuchung* (Leiden, 1949), Eberhard has prepared statistical analyses (also touched on in *Conquerors and Rulers*, pp. 116f.), indicating that under the Northern Wei Dynasty, only 28 per cent of the known leading gentry families were of alien stock; that of the remaining indigenous gentry families, no less than 92 per cent had already belonged to the leading political class prior to the establishment of the dynasty; and that as the dynasty wore on, the importance of the alien gentry steadily diminished while that of the Chinese gentry increased.

[53] This point is emphasized by Balazs. Cf. his translation (pp. 278-281) of a Chinese document of c. 577-580, from which we gain a vivid picture of the great gap between theory and application of the land regulations at that time.

actively in the long-settled and heavily populated North, especially during and following the period of Sinification of the Northern Wei Dynasty. In the South, where a sort of "colonial" expansionism was taking place, and where the thinner population made land control less needed, little was done along this line, even on paper. In this respect, then, the alien North was less "feudal" than the Chinese South.

## vi. Conclusion

In the Introductory Essay of this volume, criteria of two sorts have been advanced for the identification of feudalism: those that define it in static terms, i.e., try to tell us what feudalism itself is; and those that define it in dynamic terms, i.e., try to tell us how it operates and what are the attendant conditions under which it is likely to arise.

The static criteria include those of vassal-lord relationships (regarded as particularly important); a personalized government which is most effective on the local level and has little separation of political functions; heredity of functions; a system of landholding consisting of fiefs given in return for service; regularization of the rights of the lord over the peasant; existence of private armies; and a code of honor in which military obligations are stressed.

The dynamic criteria include those of an antecedent empire which has disintegrated; the impact of barbarian invasion; the outstripping of economic unity by political unity, leading to the waning of central authority and rise of local magnates exercising considerable *de facto* authority; monopolization of military techniques by a special group; warfare as a means of building larger political units out of lesser ones; and the existence of a universal religion which makes of the feudal period an "age of faith."

If we apply these criteria to China, a curious fact emerges: the Chou period, on the whole, meets the static criteria better than it does the dynamic criteria, whereas the Period of Disunity, on the whole, meets the dynamic criteria better (though with certain qualifications) than it does the static criteria. In other words, though the Chou Dynasty produced a genuine feudal system, it seems to have done so through forces, some of which, at least, differed considerably from those commonly associated with feudalism elsewhere. The Period of Disunity, on the other hand, though it experienced conditions theoretically favorable to feudalism, did not see the rise of a true feudal system. The superficial conclusion, if we compare this situation with other civilizations, is that differing conditions may give birth to similar institutions, and similar conditions may give birth to differing institutions.

From the point of view of our particular case study, however, the second part of this generalization requires qualification. In Section IV we have already tried to suggest what may have been some of the important forces underlying ancient Chinese society. The important point to remember is that these forces not only operated during the feudal age itself, but also deeply influenced the entire later development of Chinese society. This continuing influence explains why the Period of Disunity developed the way it did, despite the appearance of certain conditions at that time which in a different society might have led to a full-blown feudal system.

In conclusion, the writer would like to draw attention once more to the definition of feudalism made in the Introductory Essay, which has been that followed in the present paper. Feudalism, as thus defined, is "primarily a method of government, not an economic or social system." Because of this political emphasis, the Introductory Essay, while recognizing the importance for feudalism of certain economic phenomena, denies that these phenomena are themselves decisive factors unless occurring in conjunction with a rather specific set of political relationships.

There are many writers, however, who would prefer to broaden the concept of feudalism by applying it to a wider range of landlord-tenant relationships, the common feature of which is that they in effect bind the peasant so closely to the particular land he cultivates as to make him little better than the serf of his landlord proprietor. Such relationships—often based more on economic than on political sanctions—do not necessarily have to occur only within the specific political framework we have been discussing. In recent years wide currency has been given to this broadened interpretation of feudalism by numerous writers who have used it to describe conditions characteristic of many Asian agrarian societies.

In the case of China, such a more generalized concept would almost surely require a modification of some of the conclusions we have been making. It is evident, for example, that the "equalization of land" program of the Northern Wei Dynasty, though no doubt intended, at least in good part, to improve the livelihood of the peasant, at the same time—to the extent that it actually operated—severely curtailed his freedom of economic choice by confining him to whatever plot of land happened to be allotted to him. As such, it could be interpreted as an instrument for the economic control of the peasantry, and hence as a "feudal" institution, even though, since this control operated from the state rather than from a personal overlord, some special term like "state feudalism" or "bureaucratic feudalism" might have to be coined for it.[54]

Such a formulation rests on an interpretation of feudalism which, while often convenient for purposes of ordinary discussion, lacks the precision of the narrower political interpretation, and has the further defect that it tends to obliterate the all-important distinction between China's bureaucratic-gentry form of society and other non-bureaucratic forms found elsewhere. On the other hand, its merit is that it centers attention upon vital economic factors such as the political approach may tend to overlook, and which, despite their importance for China, have hitherto received not nearly the systematic study they deserve.

[54] The latter term has, in fact, already been used. See, for example, Joseph Needham, "The Chinese Contribution to Science and Technology," p. 221 of *Reflections on Our Age* (London, 1948), where Needham remarks that "Chinese society has been called 'bureaucratic feudalism.'" Cf. also the comparable Chinese term, *kuan-liao chu-yi chung-yang chi-ch'üan ti feng-chien chih-tu* or "bureaucratic centralized feudalism," as used in Fan Wen-lan, chief editor, *Chung-kuo T'ung-shih Chien-pien* [A Short General History of China]. Thus in the first (1947) through third (1949) printings of this work, Chap. I of Pt. II bears the title: "Establishment of Bureaucratic Centralized Feudalism—Ch'in." In the 1950 printing, however, this is changed to read: "Establishment of a Bureaucratic Centralized National State." For the relationship of Fan Wen-lan's theory of Chinese society to those of other Chinese scholars, see Eberhard, *Conquerors and Rulers*, p. 50. For a further discussion of the views of various Chinese scholars concerning the nature of Chinese society, see Benjamin Schwartz, "A Marxist Controversy on China," *Far Eastern Quarterly*, xiii (1954), 143-153.

SPACE permits the listing of only major primary sources and, among secondary accounts, only those written in Western languages, thus excluding from the latter the large literature in Chinese and Japanese. References to several Chinese articles and monographs, however, will be found in notes 3, 11, 22, 25, 42, 48, and 54 in the text.

The Shang is the earliest dynasty whose historicity has been confirmed by archaeological remains. These include numerous divination texts inscribed on bone or tortoise shell, which, however, are restricted in content and often obscure, and only a handful of which are available in Western translation. Probably none of the literary sources traditionally said to be of Shang or earlier date actually antedate the beginning of the Chou Dynasty.

For the first half of the Chou (prior to ca. 600 B.C.), the primary archaeological texts are inscriptions on bronze ritual vessels (very few of them available in Western translation). More important, both in size and content, are the following literary works: the original corpus of the *Yi Ching* [Book of Changes], a work of divination; the *Shih Ching* [Book of Odes], a collection of folk and court poetry; portions of the *Shu Ching* [Book of History], a collection of historical documents; and the *Tso Chuan*, a detailed historical chronicle covering the period 722-481 B.C., which, however, did not assume its present form earlier than the fourth or third century B.C. Many gross misconceptions about early Chinese history have been created through indiscriminate use of such idealized accounts as the *Li Chi* [Book of Rites] and *Chou Li* [Rites of Chou], which, though purporting to describe the institutions of the early Chou, were actually compiled only during the last two or three centuries B.C. They and the other major classics listed above have all been translated into Western languages by James Legge, Edouard Biot, Séraphin Couvreur, Arthur Waley, Bernhard Karlgren, and others. Invaluable though they are, they often leave unanswered those questions on which we should most like to be informed.

For the second half of the Chou (ca. 600 B.C. onward), the literature becomes too extensive to be listed here, owing to the rise of many political and philosophical thinkers, among whom Confucius (552/551-479) was the earliest. They contribute much information, not only on their own but on the earlier age. Most of them have been translated into Western languages.

The Han Dynasty saw the appearance of the extremely valuable *Shih Chi* [Historical Records], by Ssu-ma Ch'ien (ca. 145-ca. 86 B.C.), a work traditionally regarded as the first of China's many "dynastic histories," but actually a universal history of China from earliest times to about 100 B.C. Roughly half of it has been translated by Edouard Chavannes as *Les mémoires historiques de Se-ma Ts'ien*, 5 vols. (Paris, 1895-1905). Its successor, the *Ch'ien Han Shu* [History of the Former Han Dynasty], by Pan Ku (A.D. 32-92), contains an important section on Chinese economic history from earliest times until the birth of Christ, which has been translated by Nancy Lee Swann as *Food and Money in Ancient China* (Princeton, 1950).

For the Period of Disunity, the situation is the reverse of that of the Chou: the original sources, while far more bulky, have been far less studied from the point of view of our subject. Of prime importance are the dynastic histories, of which there are no less than eleven for this period—a fact which helps indicate the magnitude of the task involved.

Among secondary materials, there are, first of all, several general historical surveys, of varying value but all covering both the Chou and the Period of Disunity. Among them are Otto Franke, *Geschichte des chinesischen Reiches*, 5 vols. (Berlin, 1930-52); K. S. Latourette, *The Chinese, Their History and Culture*, 3rd rev. edn., 2 vols. in 1 (New York, 1946); Wolfram Eberhard, *A History of China* (Berkeley, 1950), which is particularly detailed on the Period of Disunity; C. P. Fitzgerald, *China: A Short Cultural History*, 2nd rev. edn. (London, 1950); and L. Carrington Goodrich, *A Short History of the Chinese People*, 2nd rev. edn. (New York, 1951).

For the dynamics of Chinese society, important analyses include K. A. Wittfogel, "The Foundations and Stages of Chinese Economic History," *Zeitschrift für Sozialforschung*, IV (Paris, 1935), 26-60 (one of several writings); Owen Lattimore, *Inner Asian Frontiers of China*, 2nd edn. (New York, 1951); and Wolfram Eberhard, *Conquerors and Rulers: Social Forces in Medieval China* (Leiden, 1952). The two latter works have been discussed in detail on pp. 107-118.

General surveys, covering pre-Han China only, include Henri Maspero, *La Chine antique* (Paris, 1927), still excellent in part, though a good deal of it antiquated by reason of later archaeological discoveries; and H. G. Creel, *The Birth of China* (London, 1936, and New York, 1937), which makes full use of archaeology and is by all odds the most reliable account down to ca. 600 B.C.

The numerous works of Marcel Granet, including his *Chinese Civilization* (London and New York, 1930), though widely known, contain some theories of dubious validity and hence should be used with considerable caution. Granet's *La féodalité chinoise* (Oslo, 1952), uncompleted at the time of his death and now published posthumously, unfortunately reached this writer too late to be utilized in the present study. Like all of Granet's writings, its main emphasis is sociological rather than historical. It devotes much space to such matters as the social groupings, the mores, and the mythological, cosmological, and magico-religious conceptions of the early Chou Chinese (especially the aristocracy). On the other hand, it pays but scant attention to the dynamic aspects of Chou feudalism, i.e., those pertaining to its historical growth and decay. Unlike Maspero (in the articles listed below), Granet makes no use of archaeological data (notably the bronze inscriptions), but relies entirely on literary materials, including some that are late and probably considerably idealized, and others that he dates a good deal earlier than most scholars would allow. The result, as far as this writer is concerned, is a book more theoretical, less concretely linked to time and space, and hence less satisfactory, than are the studies of Maspero.

Many of Granet's findings, nonetheless, agree essentially with those presented (necessarily more briefly) in the present study. In particular, Granet rightly insists (pp. 24ff.) on the appropriateness of the word "feudal" to describe the society of the Chou Dynasty, and points to significant institutional parallels between it and medieval Europe. Basic to both societies, in his opinion, is the bifurcation between an elite warrior class on the one hand, living according to an elaborate code of honor and having as its main function the performance of military service on behalf of the suzerains by whom it is invested with landed estates, and, on the other hand, a mass of despised peasants who lack this code of honor, play only a subordinate role in warfare as conscripted footsoldiers, and possess no rights to the land which they cultivate.

Studies particularly pertinent to feudalism, especially for the Chou period, include Otto Franke, "Zur Beurteilung des chinesischen Lehenswesens," *Sitzungsberichte der Preussischen Akademie der Wissenschaften*, XXXI, Pt. I (1927), 359-377, and his summarizing article, "Feudalism, Chinese," in the *Encyclopaedia of the Social Sciences* (New York, 1937), VI, 213-214—both somewhat conventional surveys; Ch'i Ssu-ho, "A Comparison between Chinese and European Feudal Institutions," *Yenching Journal of Social Studies*, IV (Peiping, 1948), 1-13, which is based on earlier articles in Chinese by the same writer; and Yang Lien-sheng, "Notes on Dr. Swann's *Food and Money in Ancient China*," *Harvard Journal of Asiatic Studies*, XIII (1950), 524-557, which contains a useful summary of theories by several contemporary Chinese scholars on Chou systems of land tenure. On the God of the Soil and his connection with the Chou ritual of feudal investiture, see E. Chavannes, *Le T'ai Chan: Essai de monographie d'un culte chinois* (Paris, 1910), Appendix, "Le Dieu du Sol dans la Chine antique." Above all, however, should be cited the three striking articles by Henri Maspero in Volume III of his *Mélanges posthumes sur les religions et l'histoire de la Chine* (Paris, 1950): "Le régime féodal et la propriété foncière dans la Chine antique" (pp. 109-146); "Les régimes fonciers en Chine, des origines aux temps modernes" (pp. 147-192); "Les termes désignant la propriété foncière en Chine" (pp. 193-208).

For the Ch'in Dynasty, the standard work is D. Bodde, *China's First Unifier* (Leiden, 1938). For the Han system of government, see Chapter I of C. Martin Wilbur, *Slavery in China during the Former Han Dynasty* (Chicago, 1943), and Wang Yü-ch'üan, "An Outline of the Central Government of the Han Dynasty," *Harvard Journal of Asiatic Studies*, XII (1949), 134-187, both excellent studies.

For the Period of Disunity, the few available pertinent studies include Yang Lien-sheng, "Notes on the Economic History of the Chin Dynasty," *Harvard Journal of Asiatic Studies,* IX (1946), 107-185 (covering particularly the period 265-419); Wang Yi-t'ung, "Slaves and Other Comparable Social Groups during the Northern Dynasties (386-618)," *ibid.*, XVI (1953), 293-364; Etienne Balazs, "Le traité économique du 'Souei-Chou,'" *T'oung Pao*, XLII (Leiden, 1953), 113-329 (covering primarily the Sui Dynasty, 590-617, but also presenting rich and abundant data on the preceding Period of Disunity); and Wolfram Eberhard, *Das Toba-Reich Nordchinas* (Leiden, 1949) (dealing with the Northern Wei Dynasty, 386-535). See also Eberhard's *History of China* and *Conquerors and Rulers*, both cited above.

## DOMINANT IDEAS IN THE FORMATION OF CHINESE CULTURE *

Innumerable difficulties beset the man daring enough to attempt a subject such as this, quite aside from the obvious ones of facile generalization and limitations of space. Should we, for example, consider as " dominant ideas " those that have been expressed by the relatively small group of articulate Chinese known to us through literature, or should the heterogeneous and often contradictory beliefs held by the anonymous masses also be included? And if the latter, how are we to evaluate their importance as compared with those of the minority? In reply, I can merely say that I shall attempt to present as " dominant " only those concepts that I feel have had genuine importance for a very large number of Chinese, both literate and illiterate; that go far back into the roots of Chinese civilization and are presumably truly Chinese in origin; and that at the same time have continued over long epochs to exert a powerful influence in Chinese thought, in many cases unto the present day. This last criterion means that we shall be forced to disregard certain very early and in themselves interesting concepts (such as some of the magical beliefs current during the Shang dynasty, 1766?-1123? B. C.), simply because, important as they were in their own age, they either disappeared or became greatly changed by the time Chinese civilization assumed a well defined pattern or norm.

As a convenient method of procedure I propose to treat our subject under three heads: (1) the basic concepts of the Chinese as regards the world of the supernatural; (2) as regards the world of nature; and (3) as regards the world of man. In other words, what has been the prevailing Chinese attitude toward religion, toward the physical universe, and toward themselves? Adoption of such a division will give us a convenient framework within which to move, even though we must recognize that some ideas cannot be readily confined to any one of these three categories, while others may conceivably escape the bounds of all of them together.

### 1. The World of the Supernatural

The first observation to be made here is a negative one. It is that the Chinese, generally speaking,

have been less concerned with this world than with the other worlds of nature and of man. They are not a people for whom religious ideas and activities constitute an all important and absorbing part of life; and this despite the fact that there are, nominally, more Buddhists in China to-day than in any other country of the world. The significant point, in this connection, is that Buddhism came to China from the outside, and that before its impact in the first century A. D., China itself produced no thinker, with the doubtful exception of the philosopher, Mo Tzǔ (ca. 479-ca. 381 B. C.), who could be classed as a religious leader. It is ethics (especially Confucian ethics), and not religion (at least, not religion of a formal organized type), that has provided the spiritual basis of Chinese civilization.[1]

The prevailing attitude of sophisticated Chinese toward the supernatural is perhaps best summed up by Confucius himself (551-479 B. C.), who once when asked by a disciple about the meaning of death, replied: " Not yet understanding life, how can you understand death? "[2] Later thinkers have generally tended to adopt a skeptical attitude toward the unknown, and most of them, when they have ventured to express themselves on the subject, have even gone to pains to deny that there can be such a thing as a personal immortality.[3] All of

[1] This does not mean that there have not been periods of intense religious activity in Chinese history; during some five hundred years, from the fourth through the eighth century, many of China's best minds went into Buddhism. Nor does it mean that the Chinese masses have ever been free from a huge accumulation of superstitious belief of all kinds; China is one of the richest storehouses in the world for the folklorist. Nevertheless, I still believe the statement to be true, generally speaking, that religion, as such, has been taken more lightly in China than in most other countries. Also it is certainly significant that Confucianism, despite periods of temporary eclipse, has for the last eight hundred years succeeded in retaining its dominance at the expense of both Buddhism and religious Taoism.

[2] *Analects*, XI, 11.

[3] On this point, which has not been clearly stated before, see my article, " The Chinese View of Immortality: its Expression by Chu Hsi and its Relationship to Buddhist Thought," *Review of Religion* 6. 4 (May, 1942), 369-83. It must be remembered in this connection that this was the view expressed only by a sophisticated minority. The great majority of the masses in China, as elsewhere, held a contrary opinion.

* Paper presented April 8, 1942, at the Centennial meeting of the AOS held in Boston.

which, of course, marks a difference of fundamental importance between China and most other major civilizations, in which a church and a priesthood have played a dominant role.

The preceding remarks do not mean, of course, that before the coming of Buddhism there were no religious manifestations in ancient China. What is important, however, is the fact that, from the very beginnings of Chinese history, the most vital and sincere form of religious feeling has been expressed in the worship of departed ancestors.[4] And this has been of decisive importance, for ancestor worship, through its very nature, was a form of religion that could appeal to and be performed by only the immediate individual family groups concerned. Therefore it could not develop into a national or international organized faith similar to Christianity or other world religions.

Side by side with this ancestral cult, to be sure, various objects and forces of nature were also worshipped, such as sacred mountains, rivers, and the life-giving soil. These, however, were generally conceived of in abstract rather than personified terms, and even the supreme Chinese divinity, *T'ien* 天 or Heaven, very rapidly lost its anthropomorphic qualities and became for most people a purely abstract ethical power. There was, therefore, no elaborate pantheon or mythology in ancient China.[5] Likewise, there was no priesthood, because the worship of these divine forces was performed, not by the common people or by a priestly class, but almost entirely by the ruler himself, who, as the " Son of Heaven," acted as a sort of intermediary between the world of the supernatural and the world of man. Thus a pantheon, a mythology, or a priesthood are all comparatively late phenomena in China, connected either with Buddhism, or with the religious and popularized form of Taoism which developed, in part, as a Chinese imitation of the formal aspects of Buddhism.

It is true that the innumerable divinities of Buddhism and Taoism have in later times found a ready welcome among the Chinese masses, but this testifies more to the highly eclectic nature of the

Chinese mind than to any strongly religious feeling. Because of this eclecticism the Chinese have, like the Hindus, for the most part been remarkably free from religious bigotry. The few persecutions that have occurred have usually been directed, not against religious ideas, but against religion as a social and political institution that might threaten the security of the secular state.

Finally, another fundamental difference between China and the civilizations of the Near East and of India, is the fact that in early China there was no idea of any kind of divine retribution after death. The whole concept of a system of rewards and punishments, meted out in a heaven or hell during a life hereafter, is utterly alien to Chinese thought and appears in China only with Buddhism.[6]

## 2. THE WORLD OF NATURE

If the supernatural world has held a lesser place in China than in most other civilizations, quite the reverse is true of the second of our three categories, the world of nature. For the Chinese, this world of nature, with its mountains, its forests, its storms, its mists, has been no mere picturesque backdrop against which to stage human events. On the contrary, the world of man and the world of nature constitute one great indivisible unity. Man is not the supremely important creature he seems to us in the western world; he is but a part, though a vital part, of the universe as a whole. This feeling conceivably may have originally sprung out of the overwhelmingly agrarian nature of Chinese civilization, and its consequent utter dependence, for survival itself, upon the continued regular succession of the forces of nature. Be that as it may, it is a feeling which has come to permeate a very large part of Chinese philosophy, art and literature.

In Taoism, the philosophy which has best ex-

---

[4] This, of course, contradicts the denial of a personal immortality, discussed above. But see the preceding note.

[5] This, like all sweeping statements, is not absolutely true. Hints of a mythology can be found in early Chinese literature, but it is significant that they have been largely obliterated through the process of euhemerization. Cf. Henri Maspero, " Les légends mythologiques dans le Chou King," *Journal asiatique* 214 (1924), 1-100.

[6] The early Chinese did believe in a celestial realm known as *T'ien*, or Heaven, and a nether world region known as the Yellow Springs (*huang ch'üan* 黃泉), but they apparently conceived of them only in the vaguest terms, and certainly never as abodes of the blest and the damned, respectively. According to various texts, each human being was supposed to have two souls: the *p'o* 魄 or anima, produced at the time of conception, and the *hun* 魂 or animus, which was joined to the *p'o* at the moment of birth. After death the *hun* ascended to Heaven, while the *p'o* remained in the tomb with the corpse for three years, after which it descended to the " Yellow Springs." Cf. Maspero, *La Chine antique* (Paris, 1927), 176-9, 182-3.

pressed this mystic awareness of the oneness of the universe, we find many striking anticipations of the ideas that were propounded in the West by Rousseau some two thousand years later. Like Rousseau, the Chinese Taoists said that human moral standards are artificial and hence invalid; that the appurtenances of civilization are corrupting; and that therefore we must cast off these manmade trammels and return to the state of nature. Yet Taoist naturalism fundamentally differs from occidental romanticism, despite certain remarkable superficial resemblances. In the first place, it avoided the latter's sentimentality, emotional excess, and emphasis upon love between man and woman. In the second place, romanticism has countenanced the breaking of moral restraints in the name of spontaneity and originality. Taoism also did away with human moral standards, but replaced them by a higher standard, that of the *Tao* 道 or Way, the first cosmic principle of the universe which gives the Taoist school its name Man, said the Taoists, must subordinate himself to the *Tao*, that is, to nature. This is not to be done by a facile giving in to one's emotions, but by a process of self discipline (through meditation and other means) that will result in a lessening of the desires and a consequent feeling of calm content amidst the simplicities of the natural life. In the final stage the Taoist devotee aims at entering a state of union with the surrounding universe, in which he is so completely freed from the bonds of human emotions that neither joy nor sorrow, life nor death, longer affect him. In this respect, Taoism remains in accord with the general stream of oriental mysticism.

This Taoist subordination of the self to the universe also differs importantly from another current of modern occidental thought. In the West happiness is to be found by harnessing the forces of nature to the will of man and thus increasing the means for man's material enjoyment. In China, on the contrary, the sage traditionally has been one who accords himself to the universe as he finds it, and thus gains what he considers to be the true happiness of contentment in simplicity. This concept, widely accepted in China, goes far to explain why Chinese, both educated and illiterate, can remain cheerful and even happy under poverty and primitive conditions that to a westerner would be intolerable. It has also been an important reason why the Chinese, though they developed remarkably

scientific techniques in the compilation of their dictionaries, histories, encyclopaedias, and other scholarly works, failed to apply these techniques to the world of nature, and so failed to create a physical science.[7]

Yet this prevailing attitude toward the physical universe—an attitude perhaps best summed up in Wordsworth's phrase as a "wise passiveness"—has not prevented the Chinese from attempting to classify and systematize the natural phenomena which they observed. In simplest terms, the Chinese theory of cosmogony (expressed, of course, with infinite variations by different writers) may be summarized as follows:

Lying behind the physical universe as we see it there exists an impersonal first cause or prime mover, known as the *Tao* or Way, from which all being has been evolved. This *Tao* manifests itself in the form of two all-inclusive principles: the *yang* 陽, which is the principle of activity, heat, light, dryness, hardness, masculinity; and the *yin* 陰, which is the principle of quiescence, cold, darkness, humidity, softness, femininity. Through the eternal interplay and interaction of these two principles, the five primary elements come into existence, these being fire (which is the essence of *yang*), water (which is the essence of *yin*), and earth, wood, and metal (which are combinations in varying degrees of the *yang* and the *yin*). These elements in their turn combine and recombine to produce all things in the universe, including Heaven (the sky, atmosphere, stars, etc.), which is preponderantly *yang*, and the Earth (the soil, plants, animals, etc.), which is preponderantly *yin*. Everything in the universe thus pertains to one or another of the five elements, and the Chinese have compiled long lists of categories in fives, such as the five colors, five smells, five tastes, five tones, five internal organs, etc., with which to correlate the five elements.[8]

This splitting up of the world into sets of fives is a typical manifestation of the rationalistic Chinese mind, which tries to find order and plan in all things, and which has therefore taken a particular delight in inventing numerical categories of all

---

[7] Cf. Bodde, "The Attitude toward Science and Scientific Method in Ancient China," *T'ien Hsia Monthly* 2. 2 (Feb., 1936), 139-60; also Fung Yu-lan, "Why China Has No Science," *International Journal of Ethics* 32. 3 (April, 1922), 237-63.

[8] For a table showing a few of these correspondences, see Alfred Forke, *The World-Conception of the Chinese* (London, 1925), 240-1.

kinds, not only in fives, but in many other numbers.[9] The theory of the *yin* and *yang*, the five elements, and their correlates, has for more than two thousand years been the basis for Chinese medicine, alchemy, astronomy, and naturalistic speculation generally. While it represents a very real attempt at the use of a scientific method, it unfortunately has not led to a true physical science, because, being based upon arbitrary, man-made analogies, it disregarded the all important necessity of using an empirical method of direct observation of nature.

In connection with this theory of cosmogony, it is important that we should distinguish clearly between the Chinese dualistic system based upon the interplay of the *yin* and *yang* principles, and the superficially similar dualisms of light and darkness, good and evil, etc., with which we are familiar in the Near East and in the occidental world. The latter dualisms are all based upon the concept of mutual antagonism between their two conflicting members; of the goodness of the one and the evilness of the other; and of the consequent necessity to conquer the evil so that the good may eventually triumph. They are often closely connected with religion.

The *yin-yang* dualism, on the contrary, is based, not upon mutual opposition, but upon mutual harmony. The feminine *yin* and the masculine *yang* are equally essential if there is to exist a universe. Each is complementary to the other, and neither is necessarily superior or inferior from a moral point of view. In this concept we see a striking manifestation of the Chinese tendency, already alluded to, to find in all things an underlying harmony and unity, rather than struggle and chaos. In it, the Chinese would seem to have come closer to the ideas lying behind much of modern science, than have we in the West with our traditional good-versus-evil type of dualism.

### 3. THE WORLD OF MAN

When we turn to the third of our three categories, that of the world of man, we find ourselves at the heart of the greater part of Chinese philosophical speculation. How to get along equably with one's fellow men: this is the problem that Confucianism set itself to answer, just as Taoism posed for itself the problem of how man can adjust himself to the outer universe. The Chinese, with

sound common sense, have from very early times realized that unless there can be a solution to this central problem of human relationship, material power and progress will but serve to increase the afflictions of mankind. Being a practical, realistic, and pragmatic people, they launched their frontal attack upon this vital question, and in so doing have produced a great mass of ethical and political philosophy.[10] For the same reason they rejected both the abstruse metaphysical speculations of the Hindu, and the explorations into logic that have been one of the major contributions of occidental philosophy. This practical concern with the immediate exigencies of human life helps once more to explain, perhaps, why the Chinese, although they have contributed to the world many inventions of the highest practical value, such as paper, printing, porcelain, and the mariner's compass, have not developed a theoretical natural science.

Coupled with this intense preoccupation with human affairs is the Chinese feeling for *time*; the feeling that human affairs should be fitted somehow into a temporal framework. The result has been the accumulation of a tremendous and unbroken body of historical literature, extending over more than three thousand years, such as is unequalled by any other people. This history has served in China a distinctly moral purpose, for by studying the past one might learn how to conduct oneself in the present and future. Hence the writing of history was commonly not left merely to the whim of a few historically minded individuals. Ever since the founding of the first long lived empire in the second century B. C., one of the first duties of a conquering dynasty has been to compile the history of the dynasty it supplanted, often appointing for that purpose a large board of government-supported scholars, who were set to work upon the historical archives of the preceding dynasty. The resulting

[9] See Bodde, " Types of Chinese Categorical Thinking," *JAOS* 59. 2 (1939), 200-19.

[10] Which, however, did not always attain the pragmatic goal aimed at, because it sometimes fell into the common error of assuming that morality is something that can be realized automatically through the mere preaching of lofty doctrines, without sufficient regard for the practical human difficulties (economic and otherwise) that lie in the way of the realization of these doctrines. Here is perhaps the most serious indictment that can be made of Confucianism, but it is one that is very far from being universally true. This is shown by the fact that a great many Confucian thinkers were not mere philosophers in an ivory tower, but were at the same time men of affairs who were active in government, and who there directly concerned themselves with political programs that would serve to carry their ideals into operation.

dynastic histories were not limited to a bald narration of political events. They included also valuable essays on such subjects as economics, law, water-control works, astronomy, bibliography, geography, and many other topics, as well as the biographies of hundreds of illustrious individuals. This temporal mindedness of the Chinese once more marks them sharply apart from the Hindus.[11]

What was the nature of the society that the Chinese thus took such pains to record? It was not one that believed in what we would call rugged individualism. Rather, Confucianism aimed at teaching each individual how to take his place with the least possible friction in his own social group, and how to perform his allotted duties within that group in such a way as would bring the greatest benefit to the group as a whole. The basic and most important unit of Chinese society was the family or clan, to which the individual owed his first allegiance, and which he served, first by sacrificing to the ancestors who were dead; secondly, by caring for the elder generation who were still living; and thirdly, by rearing descendants of his own who would carry on the family line. In return, the family acted as a protective group of mutual aid, shielding the individual from an often hostile outer world. Through its cohesiveness, it succeeded in maintaining the fabric of Chinese life and culture even in times of almost complete social and political collapse. Because of this stress upon family in China, there has been a correspondingly limited development of nationalistic feeling (save in a vague cultural sense), and little of that fiery patriotism so exalted in the West.

Beyond the family, nevertheless, lay the state, which was regarded simply as an enlargement of the family unit. Thus even to-day the term for "nation" in Chinese, literally translated, means "national family,"[12] while it was common in the past for the emperor to refer to himself as "the parent of the people."[13] In this society each individual occupied a definite position and was held accordingly responsible for the performance of stated duties. Yet paternalistic though it was, the system certainly did not (in theory, at least) operate solely for the benefit of a ruling class. If inferiors were expected to serve their superiors with

loyalty, superiors were equally bound by certain definite obligations toward their inferiors. Confucianism stressed the reciprocal nature of these duties and obligations. It also emphasized that the primary duty of the ruler is to give good government to his people, and that to do this he must himself set a high moral standard and select with care the officials who serve under him. It thus attached great importance to the power of personal example of men in public life, and the need for their moral self cultivation.

Owing to the development of a very intensive agricultural economy, stimulated in part, at least, by a widespread government-fostered system of irrigation works, it was possible in China for a large population to subsist upon a comparatively small amount of land. Having this large population, the Chinese empire spread to huge proportions and developed into an exceedingly complex bureaucracy, employing a vast army of officials. Yet despite its size and all inclusive character, the Chinese state remained sufficiently fluid and flexible to leave a place for considerable social change and individual initiative. It aimed at moral suasion rather than legalistic compulsion, and definitely rejected the somewhat cold and mechanical approach to government, based on law, which has been such a cornerstone of occidental civilization. Law codes, of course, existed, but they were subject to a considerable degree of individual judgment and interpretation, which was based upon the handed-down body of traditional experience and morality known as *li* 禮.

It was quite possible, therefore, in Chinese society, especially in times of political change, for determined individuals to work their way up to high positions, a feat accomplished several times in history by founders of dynasties who rose from quite humble origins. Women, similarly, though before the law they held an inferior position, yet in point of fact quite frequently exercised very considerable power within their family group. Thus China has produced a goodly number, not only of famous beauties, but also of female painters, poets, historians, and empresses. There was, in fact, little in Chinese society suggestive of any hard and fixed stratification into unchanging social groups.

The moral basis for this society was the belief, shared by the majority of Chinese thinkers, that man is by nature fundamentally good; that there is no such thing as original sin; and that therefore any person, even the lowliest, is potentially capable

---

[11] For a good account of this subject, see Charles S. Gardner, *Chinese Traditional Historiography* (Cambridge, Harvard University Press, 1938).

[12] *Kuo chia* 國家.

[13] *Min chih fu mu* 民之父母.

of becoming a sage.[14] Evil, according to the Chinese view, does not exist as a positive force in itself; it is simply the result of a temporary deflection from the essential harmony of the universe. With these concepts go the optimism, the good humor, and the will to live, that are marked characteristics of so many Chinese. The Indian dictum that life is suffering was inconceivable to the Chinese mind, and even with the coming of Buddhism never succeeded in gaining general acceptance.

Because they believed that all men can be taught morality, the Chinese attached an importance hardly paralleled elsewhere upon the value of learning. "Wisdom" was included by them among the five cardinal virtues, meaning by this an understanding of right and wrong and of moral principles generally. Hence the Chinese stress upon their classics, which they regarded as containing deep moral truths; upon history as an instrument whereby man may be taught to avoid the mistakes of his forefathers; and eventually upon all humanistic scholarship.

All this led to the creation of what has been the most distinctive feature of Chinese government, the famed examination system. Other countries have until recent times with few exceptions been ruled by a hereditary aristocracy, a priesthood, a military hierarchy, or a rich merchant class. But in China, ever since the creation of the first long lived empire in the second century B. C., entry into the bureaucracy that governed the country was limited to those who succeeded in passing a series of very strict governmental examinations, based upon a thorough knowledge of the Chinese classics. Service in this official bureaucracy was the highest goal which one could attain, and therefore success in the examinations was the highest aim.

Such, at least, was the theory. In practice, the system naturally operated best in periods of strong political unity, while in times of strife or dynastic change it tended to break down. Likewise, it contained certain manifest defects, such as its undue stress upon memory, and the fact that the wealthy naturally enjoyed superior opportunities to acquire the education that would make success possible.[15]

Nevertheless, when all is said and done, the fact remains that the examinations provided an impartial and purely intellectual test that had to be surmounted by each and every individual through his own efforts alone if he were to enter the coveted ranks of the scholar-officials. Likewise, the examinations were open to all members of society alike, with but trifling exceptions. It is little wonder, therefore, that Voltaire, comparing this system with the political conditions of Europe of his time, acclaimed the organization of the Chinese state as the best the world had ever seen.[16]

---

[14] Not everyone, of course, held this belief. Thus the Confucian, Hsün Tzŭ (ca. 298-ca. 238 B. C.), proclaimed that man's nature is essentially evil. Yet even he maintained that man can be taught goodness. His school, moreover, was eventually rejected in favor of that of Mencius (372?-289? B. C.), who was the chief proponent of the doctrine of the goodness of human nature.

[15] Another weakness of the governmental system was the fact that the officials were often inadequately paid, thus encouraging them to look toward various forms of illegitimate revenue as a means of increasing their income. The same tendency was strengthened by an unfortunate feature of the family system, according to which any successful member of a family was under a moral obligation to give support to his less prosperous relatives. These defects, however, apply more to the bureaucratic system as a whole than to the examinations per se, and they were at least in part compensated for by a very intricate and ingenious system of checks and balances designed to reduce the abuse of office to a minimum. Considering the size and geography of China, its government has operated with a considerable degree of efficiency over a very long period of time, and certainly during many epochs with less corruption than most westerners commonly believe.

[16] Voltaire's exact words are: "One need not be obsessed with the merits of the Chinese to recognize that the organization of their empire is in truth the best that the world has ever seen, and moreover the only one founded on paternal authority." Cf. his Œuvres complètes (Gotha, 1785), XXXVIII, 492; quoted in Adolph Reichwein, China and Europe (translated from the German by J. C. Powell, New York, 1925), p. 89.

Voltaire was not, of course, aware of certain abuses in the Chinese governmental system. One of these, though by no means unique to China, has been of particular consequence owing to the dense concentration of population upon the arable land. This has been the ever present tendency for such land gradually to gravitate into the hands of a comparatively small landowning class; a class largely made up of those same scholar-officials who governed the country, and who owing to their contempt for trade usually preferred to invest their money in land rather than in commercial enterprise. An examination of Chinese history will reveal this process of land accumulation taking place during the course of almost every long lived Chinese dynasty. The result has been the laying of an ever increasing economic burden upon the peasants, leading finally to revolt, overthrow of the dynasty, and a subsequent redistribution of the land. Though many ingenious governmental measures have repeatedly been instituted to check this dynastic cycle, they have never (as might be expected) been permanently successful. Indeed, even to-day one of the most important problems confronting the existing government is this same age old question of the distribution of land.

As a corollary to the Chinese respect for learning has been a corresponding dislike of violence and strife. Reason, arbitration and compromise are (in theory, if sometimes not in practise) the instruments for settling disputes in China, and the man who resorts to force shows by that very fact that he is in the wrong. China has had her share of strife, yet a large anthology could be compiled of the essays and poems that have been written lamenting the suffering and horrors of war. The poor but worthy scholar has been the typical hero of much Chinese literature, while there has been very little of that glorification of the military genius so characteristic of the West. Perhaps the prevailing attitude toward the soldier is best summed up in the popular proverb which says: " Good iron is not beaten into nails; a good man does not become a soldier." [17]

Finally, a few words remain to be said about one of the most fundamental concepts underlying the Chinese theory of government, that of the so-called Right of Revolution. According to this theory, the ruler, being the " Son of Heaven," enjoys a divine sanction for his rule in the shape of a celestial Mandate or Decree which has been conferred on him by Heaven. As long as he rules in the interests of the people he may not be legally overthrown. Bad government, however, is displeasing to Heaven, which then indicates its dissatisfaction through the appearance of inauspicious natural phenomena, such as droughts, floods, or earthquakes. If these warnings go unheeded, heavenly disapproval is further manifested in the form of popular revolts, which may even culminate in the ruler's dethronement and the founding of a new dynasty. Success in such a revolt becomes the criterion of whether or not Heaven has withdrawn its Mandate from the evil ruler and passed it on to the new line.

This theory, which originated in China before the first millenium B. C., was much elaborated by later writers, and is perpetuated at the present time in the term for revolution, *ko ming* 革命, which literally means " changing the Decree." Together with the influence of the non-hereditary scholar class, it has acted as a strong check upon the abuse of power by the sovereign, and thus has given to China a sort of ideological preparation for democratic institutions, which, there is good reason to hope, will enable her in the future to assume her rightful place among the world's great democracies.

## CONCLUSION

We have now reached the end of our lightning journey through the three worlds of the supernatural, of nature and of man, and have gained a fleeting glimpse of their main contours, as they appear to occidental eyes. Before closing, however, I should like to reaffirm the importance of one concept to which I have already more than once alluded, namely, the fundamental oneness and harmony of the Chinese *Weltanschauung*. In the Chinese mind, there is no real distinction between the world of the supernatural, the world of nature, and the world of man. They are all bound up in one all-embracing unity. " All things are complete within me," proclaims the Confucian, Mencius (371?-279? B. C.),[18] thus echoing the sentiment of the Taoist, Chuang Tzŭ (ca. 369-ca. 286 B. C.), who says: " Heaven and Earth came into being with me together, and with me, all things are one." [19]

As applied to social relationships, these concepts manifest themselves in the emphasis of Chinese writers upon restraint, tolerance, equanimity, and pursuit of the golden mean. " Let the states of equilibrium and harmony exist in perfection, and a happy order will prevail throughout Heaven and Earth, while all things will be nourished and prosper." So says the *Doctrine of the Mean,* one of the works that was formerly learned by heart in the traditional system of education.[20] To-day the world is convulsed by a terrifying struggle. But when that struggle is over, may we of the West find it in our heart to exercise these principles in the new world that emerges. It will be a world in which we and the peoples of the East will be working and cooperating together as never before in history. Assuredly it must be one in which all creeds and races of East and West alike live on a basis of justice, equality and brotherhood.

---

[17] *Hao t'ieh pu ta ting;* 好鐵不打丁；
*Hao jen pu tang ping* 好人不當兵.
It is only during the present Sino-Japanese War that this attitude has changed and the Chinese soldier has come to be regarded as something more than a parasite of society and an agent of destruction.

[18] *Mencius,* VIIa, 4.
[19] Transl. of Fung Yu-lan, *Chuang Tzŭ* (Shanghai, 1933), ch. 2, p. 56.
[20] Transl. of Legge, *Sacred Books of the East* (Oxford, 1885), XXVIII, 300-1.

# MAN IN SOCIETY

# TYPES OF CHINESE CATEGORICAL THINKING

ONE OF THE criticisms levelled by westerners against Chinese philosophy is that it has failed to develop a system of logic. Like most sweeping criticisms, this is not absolutely true, for during the fourth and third centuries B. C., the followers of the Mohist school do appear to have experimented with methods of thinking in many ways comparable to our western logic.[1] The statement remains true, however, to the extent that this school did not long survive, and that it failed to leave a lasting impression on Chinese thought.

We may grant, therefore, that the Chinese have made comparatively little use of the logical method, but this by no means implies that they, in their way, are not as orderly and " logical," in the non-technical sense of that word, as we are in ours. There is hardly a people on the face of the earth, in fact, which has tried more consistently to look for balance and harmony in the universe, and hence has striven more zealously to reduce all phenomena under sets of orderly, all-inclusive schemata. This characteristic of Chinese thinking I have elsewhere described as a part of " the Chinese view of the universe, which tends to divide both the human and the physical worlds into a number of fixed categories, and which, in the human world, tries to classify each man under one of these categories." [2] For want of a better term, I should here like to define further this characteristic feature of Chinese thought as " categorical thinking," using the word categorical not in its logical sense of unconditional, absolute, etc., but in the sense of something that is classified or divided.

Nowhere is this feeling of the Chinese for order and balance more apparent than in their classical written language itself, which to a

---

[1] See Fung Yu-lan, *A History of Chinese Philosophy* (Peiping, 1937), English translation by Derk Bodde, vol. 1, ch. 11.

[2] See Derk Bodde, *China's First Unifier, a study of the Ch'in dynasty as seen in the life of Li Ssŭ (280?-208 B. C.)*, Leiden, 1938, p. 99. See also Marcel Granet, *La pensée chinoise* (Paris, 1934), which treats this subject at considerable length.

high degree is characterized by the use of evenly balanced clauses consisting of three, four, five or six words each as the case may be, following each other in a markedly rhythmical progression.[3] It shows itself again in the Chinese dualistic view of the universe, according to which all physical phenomena are the product of the ceaseless interplay of the *Yang* and the *Yin,* which represent respectively the male and the female, the positive and the negative, the light and the dark forces of nature.

There is hardly an aspect of Chinese life, indeed, in which this search for balance is not to some degree evident. It is to be found all the way from the formal arrangement of the furniture in a Chinese room to that rigid layout of city streets along north-to-south and east-to-west axes, which places Chinese cities among the earliest examples of city planning.[4]

The consequence of this very fundamental Chinese feeling for order and harmony is the extraordinary development, both in speech and in literature, of what may be called numerical categories. Under the numeral three, for example, there are such categories as the Three Rituals, Three Sacrificial Animals, Three Auspicious Stars, etc.; under four, the Four Seas, Four Great Rivers, Four Cardinal Points, etc.; under five, the Five Punishments, Five Forms of Taxation, Five Supernatural Creatures, etc.; and so on up to the Ten Thousand Things,[5] which is a generic term signifying all things in the universe.[6]

Among these numerical categories, those in five and nine are the most important. An example of the latter is to be found in the description, given in the *Huai-nan-tzŭ* (second century B. C.), of Heaven as a plate-like body comprising nine parts: a small inner disk, which is surrounded by eight pie-like segments extending

---

[3] For a description of a notable example of this type of prose, that of the Chinese chain-syllogism, see Bodde, *China's First Unifier*, pp. 228-232.

[4] It may be remarked here parenthetically that the Chinese possess an amazingly acute sense of direction. When in China, for example, one wishes to have a table moved to a different part of one's room, one does not tell the servant to shift it to his right or to his left, but to "move it a little east" or west, or whatever the direction may be, even if it is a matter of only two or three inches.

[5] *Wan wu* 萬物.

[6] For an extended list of 319 such categories, see W. F. Mayers, *The Chinese Reader's Manual* (Shanghai reprint of 1924), part 2.

toward the eight compass points.[7] Another example is Tsou Yen's (third century B. C.) conception of the world as being made up of nine large continents, separated from one another by oceans. These nine continents are in their turn each subdivided into nine smaller continents, which are again separated by seas, so that the world as a whole includes a total of eighty-one such small continents, of which China was believed to be one.[8]

As for the categories in five, these are for the most part based on the theory of the Five Agents or Elements (earth, wood, metal, fire, and water), which, through their successive rise and decline in an eternal cycle, are believed to produce all physical and even mental phenomena. With them a long series of other categories in five have been equated, such as the Five Colors, Five Sounds, Five Tastes, Five Smells, Five Tones, Five Directions, Five Planets, etc.[9] This Five Element system, though probably not existing in well developed form much before the third century B. C., has since that time completely dominated all other theories in cosmology, medical science, and Chinese thinking generally.

These attempts to fit the universe into numerical categories, though absurd to us today, represented in their time a very real effort toward the use of a scientific method. Unfortunately, they failed to produce a true physical science, because, being based upon false, man-made analogies, they disregarded the use of the empirical method of direct observation of nature, and thus distorted and forced natural phenomena into an artifical pattern. Indeed, their uncritical acceptance in later times has even tended to discourage the development of a true scientific method.[10] Very much the same situation has existed until recent times in the West, where for many centuries the mere existence of a system of logic by itself failed to produce any very great results in natural science, until it came to be reinforced by the all important empirical method of objective observation and experimentation.

[7] See Alfred Forke, *The World-Conception of the Chinese, their astronomical, cosmological and physico-philosophical speculations* (London, 1925), pp. 134-135.

[8] See Fung Yu-lan, *A History of Chinese Philosophy*, I, 160-161.

[9] For a table showing these correspondences, see Forke, *op. cit.*, pp. 240-241.

[10] See Bodde, "The Attitude toward Science and Scientific Method in Ancient China," in *T'ien Hsia Monthly*, vol. 2, no. 2, Feb., 1936, pp. 151-152.

Chinese categorical thinking, of the sort discussed above, has been for the most part directed to the classification of objective, physical phenomena. Less familiar, but equally interesting, have been the Chinese attempts to classify human beings under various categories, usually according to their mental and moral characteristics, or according to the type of activity which they should pursue in society. Confucius (551-479 B. C.) was probably the originator of classifications of this kind, when he described four types of men as: " Those who are born with knowledge are of the hightest rank. Those who acquire it by study are next. Those who learn despite their natural limitations are next. But those who are of limited ability and yet will not learn—these form the lowest class of men." [11] Some of his other suggestive, though fragmentary, remarks on this subject will be quoted later.

The *Shuo Yüan*, written by Liu Hsiang (79-8 B. C.),[12] is a very well known work in the Confucian tradition, containing a vast number of historical incidents and anecdotes. These anecdotes, though they were not written with the express purpose of classifying human beings according to different categories, do serve in effect to do this, because, being compiled with the definite intention of standing as moral examples to later generations, they are carefully grouped under twenty different chapters, each designed to exemplify one particular type of human character or conduct. The titles of these twenty chapters are as follows: (1) The way of the ruler, (2) The methods of the minister, (3) Consolidating the foundation, (4) Establishing self restraint, (5) Valuing virtue, (6) Returning to kindliness, (7) Principles of government, (8) Honoring the talented, (9) Upright remonstrances, (10) Respectful caution, (11) Virtuous counsels, (12) Deputy emissaries, (13) Wily plots, (14) Extreme public-mindedness, (15) Pointers to the militarists, (16) Collected conversations, (17) Miscellaneous words, (18) Discrimination between things, (19) Cultivation of outword form, (20) Returning to the essential.[13]

---

[11] See the *Lun Yü* (Confucian Analects), XVI, 9.

[12] For these dates, see Charles S. Gardner, *Chinese Traditional Historiography* (Harvard University Press, 1938), p. 33, note 37

[13] The Chinese titles are: (1) *chün tao* 君道, (2) *ch'en shu* 臣術, (3) *chien pen* 建本, (4) *li chieh* 立節, (5) *kuei te* 貴德, (6) *fu en* 復恩, (7) *cheng li* 政理, (8) *tsun hsien* 尊賢, (9) *cheng lien* 正諫, (10) *ching shen* 敬慎, (11) *shan shuo* 善說, (12) *feng shih* 奉使, (13) *ch'üan mou*

It will be noticed that almost all of these titles have to do with governmental and administrative activity, which the Chinese have always placed on the highest plane of human activity, and preparation for which has been the main reason for making moral classifications of this kind. Such, at least, is true in the case of the *Jen Wu Chih*, a very interesting work written sometime between A. D. 240 and 250 by Liu Shao, which has been translated into English by John K. Shryock, under the title of *The Study of Human Abilities*. The chief purpose of this book is to classify statesmen according to their abilities and types of personality, and hence it contains a number of interesting categories. Among these is one that lists the following twelve different types of ability: the man of sublime behavior, the statesman, the strategist, the leader of a state, the man of instrumental ability, the critic, the practical man, the astute man, the literary man, the learned man, the dialectician, and the military hero. Liu Shao goes on to give historical examples for each of these types of men, and then to state what particular office in the government each is best suited for. For example, a person who combines in himself the qualities of the man of sublime behavior, the statesman, and the strategist, should be prime minister; the literary man should be imperial historiographer, and so on.[14]

Classifications of this kind suggest very much the theory of the "humours" which was so prevalent in medieval Europe, and has left its influence on Ben Jonson's two plays, *Every Man in his Humour* and *Every Man out of his Humour*, as well as on much later literature. According to this theory, "Fire was hot and dry, air hot and moist, water cold and moist, earth cold and dry. The effect of these in the human system was that fire produced choler, air produced blood, water phlegm, and earth melancholy. . . . An equable mixture of the four humours produced the perfect, well-balanced temperament. . . . But in average characters, these conflicting elements were blended in varying proportions, and the predominance of any one humour determined the type."[15]

---

權謀, (14) *chih kung* 至公, (15) *chih wu* 指武, (16) *ts'ung t'an* 叢談, (17) *tsa yen* 雜言, (18) *pien wu* 辨物, (19) *hsiu wen* 修文, (20) *fan chih* 反質.

[14] See John K. Shryock, *The Study of Human Abilities, the Jen wu chih of Liu Shao* (American Oriental Series, vol. 11, 1937), pp. 68, 105 f.

[15] See Percy Simpson's introduction to Ben Jonson's *Every Man in his Humour* (Oxford University Press, 1919), pp. xxxvi-xxxvii.

An extremely interesting example of the way classifications based on moral qualities were carried into actual practise in the Chinese government, is described by Robert des Rotours in his book dealing with the development of the civil service examination system during the T'ang dynasty (A. D. 618-906).[16]   According to Rotours's account, it was the custom during this time for the governmental heads of offices in the capital and in the prefectures throughout the empire, to give a public report each year on the moral and intellectual qualities of their subordinates.   The basis of these reports was what were known as the four " Merits," [17] and the twenty-seven " Perfections." [18]   The four Merits were as follows: (1) " His virtue and his righteousness are renowned." [19]   (2) " His integrity and his circumspection are brilliantly displayed." [20]   (3) " His equity and his impartiality are worthy of being praised." [21]   (4) " His diligence and his activity never relax." [22]   These were qualities that were considered universally desirable, and at least one of which should be possessed by every good official.

The twenty-seven Perfections were qualifications of a more specific nature, differing according to the particular position held by the individual official.   They are too numerous to be given in full here, but a few may be quoted as examples.   The first was: " He proposes what is proper, discards what is improper, repairs omissions, and fills up lacunae."   This Perfection would be applied as a standard to the ministers who immediately surrounded the Emperor.   The eighth was: " The soldiers are exercised, and the armies and their clothing are completely ready."   This applied to the troop commanders.   The twenty-seventh was: " In calculating the movement of the stars and the calendar, he has observed the rules with precision and exactness."   This applied to the officials of astronomy in charge of the calendar.

By means of the reports thus made annually all over the empire, subordinate officials were graded into nine classes or categories, according to the number of Merits and Perfections which each

---

[16] See Robert des Rotours, *Le traité des examens, traduit de la Nouvelle histoire des T'ang* (Paris, 1932), pp. 50-55.

[17] *Shan* 善.                              [18] *Tsui* 最.

[19] *Te i yu wen* 德義有聞.

[20] *Ch'ing shen ming chu* 清愼明著.

[21] *Kung p'ing k'o ch'eng* 公平可稱.

[22] *K'o ch'in fei hsieh* 恪勤匪懈.

possessed, as follows: (1) Those possessing at least one Perfection and all four Merits. (2) Those with either one Perfection and three Merits, or with all four Merits. (3) Those with either one Perfection and two Merits, or with three Merits. (4) Those with either one Perfection and one Merit, or with two Merits. (5) Those with either one Perfection or one Merit. (6) Those with neither a single Merit nor a single Perfection, but who had not done badly. (7) Those who had acted unjustly and for their own self interest. (8) Those who had sought only their private interest and had turned away from their duties. (9) Those who had committed a proven fraud.

According to this very curious classification, officials holding a place in the first four ranks received an increase in salary corresponding to one-fourth of their actual salary for every rank above the fifth gained since the preceeding year. The salary of those in the fifth or middle rank was neither increased nor reduced. That of those in ranks six to eight was decreased by one-fourth for every rank below five. Those in the ninth rank were dismissed. Promotions, as well as salary increases, were made according to the same classifications.

For us of the modern world, such a system of classification is so fantastic that it seems almost incredible that it could ever have been seriously applied in actual government. Possibly it was more of an Utopian idea on paper than something that was ever used very widely, and in any case it probably lasted no more than a very short period. Nevertheless, another, though less bizarre, evidence of the Chinese fondness for fixed categories, and one also connected with the examination system, lasted as late as the year 1905, when these examinations were abolished. This concerned the method used for grading the candidates who took the examinations held every three years in Peking and in the provincial capitals. Candidates who were successful were not only marked as having " passed," but were even graded in the exact order in which they had passed, such as first, second, third, fourth, etc. The stupendous task involved in such a grading becomes apparent when we remember that the Peking examinations, for example, might be attended by more than ten thousand candidates on any one occasion.

The remainder of this article will be devoted to another example of Chinese categorical thinking, which, though not as early as that of Liu Hsiang, not as elaborately discussed and developed as that of

Liu Shao, and not carried into actual practise in the government, as was that of the T'ang examination system, is probably the most comprehensive attempt of its kind to be found, not only in Chinese, but in world literature.

This is the curious compilation, known as the " Table of Ancient and Modern Men," [23] which occupies the twentieth chapter in the *Ch'ien Han Shu* (History of the Former Han Dynasty). The greater part of this history was written by the noted historian, Pan Ku (A. D. 32-92), but there is some doubt as to the actual authorship of the " Table " itself. We know that this and the other seven chronological tables contained in the *Ch'ien Han Shu* were left incomplete by Pan Ku at the time of his death, and that his gifted sister Pan Chao (died between A. D. 114 and 120), was then put to work on them. There is also a probability that some of the final touches were added by one of Pan Chao's students, Ma Hsü 馬續, and it is impossible to determine exactly how much of the total should be attributed to Pan Ku, how much to Pan Chao, and how much to Ma Hsü. Perhaps we shall not be far wrong, however, if we assume that the general conception of the " Table of Ancient and Modern Men," and possibly its preface, come from Pan Ku; while Pan Chao, and to a lesser extent Ma Hsü, may have done the actual work of compilation. The exact date is also uncertain, but a year near A. D. 100 may not be far wrong.[24]

In this " Table of Ancient and Modern Men," a total of no less than 1,955 men known to Chinese history have been arranged in chronological order, beginning with the earliest legendary times and coming down to the end of the Ch'in dynasty (255-206 B. C.). These men have each been classified under nine different categories, according to the compiler's opinion of their moral and intellectual worth.

Before going on to discuss this classification in detail, it may be well to allow Pan Ku, its original conceiver, to explain it in his own words. His preface to this chronological table reads as follows:

" Ever since the making of written documents, the people of former times whom we have been able to hear about are those

---

[23] *Ku chin jen piao* 古今人表.
[24] For a discussion of this whole problem, see Nancy Lee Swann, *Pan Chao: Foremost Woman Scholar of China* (American Historical Association, 1932), ch. 5, especially pp. 65-69.

mentioned in the classics and records, (such as) the Emperors and Kings, from T'ang and Yü upward,[25] who bear appellations and posthumous titles. Their ministers have not been so mentioned, but the various philosophers (of later times) have had something to say about these. Although (their lives) have not been studied by Confucius,[26] nevertheless they have been recorded in (other) writings, where they have been classified so as to exemplify virtue, make evil manifest, and serve as encouragement or warning to later men.[27] Therefore I have taken widely (from these writings).

" Confucius has said: ' As to being a Sage or a man of perfect virtue, how can I presume to such a claim? ' [28] Again he has said: ' What has he to do with perfect virtue? Must he not be a Sage? ' [29] ' I do not know why he should be deemed a man of perfect virtue.' [30] ' Those who are born with knowledge are of the highest rank. Those who acquire it by study are next. Those who learn despite their natural limitations are next. But those who are of limited ability and yet will not learn—these form the lowest class of men.' [31]

" Again he has said: ' To men above the middle class one may discourse on higher things.' [32] ' It is only those of the highest wisdom or of the lowest stupidity who cannot be changed.' [33]

" The records say in the cases of Yao, Shun and Yü, that when Chi and Kao acted with them to do good, they carried out (their

---

[25] 唐 and 虞, i.e., the mythical sage-rulers, Yao and Shun.

[26] This is a reference to the brief historical work known as the *Ch'un Ch'iu* (Spring and Autumn Annals), the writing of which has been traditionally, but erroneously, attributed to Confucius.

[27] A reference to the " praise and blame " theory of Chinese history, traditionally believed to be found in historical writings of the type of the *Ch'un Ch'iu* (mentioned in the preceding note), the cryptic sentences of which are supposed by their phraseology to indicate either the historian's praise or censure for the persons and events they describe.

[28] See the *Lun Yü* (Confucian Analects), VII, 33.

[29] This was the answer given by Confucius to the question of a disciple: " Suppose there were one who conferred benefits far and wide upon the people and who was able to succour the multitude, what might one say of him? " See *Lun Yü*, VI, 28.

[30] Another answer by Confucius to a disciple who asked concerning someone whether he were a man of perfect virtue. See *ibid.*, V, 18.

[31] *Lun Yü*, XVI, 9. See also above, p. 144.

[32] *Ibid.*, VI, 19.

[33] *Ibid.*, XVII, 3.

ideas).³⁴ But when Kun and Huan Tou wished to do evil with them, they had them executed.³⁵ Those with whom one may do good, but with whom one cannot do evil, are what are meant by the highest wisdom.

"In the cases of Chieh and Chou, when (Kuan) Lung-feng and Pi Kan wished to do good with them, they had them executed.³⁶ But when Yü Hsin and the Marquis of Ch'ung acted with them to do evil, they carried out (their ideas).³⁷ Those with whom one may do evil, but with whom one cannot do good, are what are meant by the lowest stupidity.

"In the case of Huan, Duke of Ch'i, when Kuan Chung was his minister, he became Lord Protector, but when Shu Tiao assisted him, there was disorder.³⁸ Those with whom one may do (either) good or evil are what are meant by men of the middle class.

"In accordance with these (classifications), I have arranged (the persons listed in my table) into nine grades. I have examined deeply into the classics and records of successive generations, which mutually follow one another, and thus have compiled an all-inclusive outline covering both antiquity and modern times, as follows."

---

³⁴ Yao and Shun are mythical sage-rulers; Yü, also a mythical figure, is supposed to have followed them and to have founded the Hsia dynasty. Chi, whose full name is Hou Chi 后稷, is supposed to have been minister of agriculture under Shun and to have been the first ancestor of the rulers of the Chou dynasty. Kao 高, usually known as Kao Yao 皋陶, was the most famed of Shun's virtuous ministers.

³⁵ Kun 鯀, the unworthy father of Yü, failed in the task assigned to him of draining the great flood which covered China at that time. He was recommended for this task by Huan Tou 讙兜, an evil minister under Yao. Both men were later punished by Shun.

³⁶ Kuan Lung-feng 關龍逢 and Pi Kan 比干 were respectively virtuous ministers under Chieh (1818?-1776?) and Chou (1154?-1123?), the evil last rulers of the Hsia and Shang dynasties, by whom they were put to death for their remonstrances.

³⁷ Yü Hsin 于莘 and the Marquis of Ch'ung 崇候 were evil followers of Chieh and Chou respectively.

³⁸ Kuan Chung 管仲, one of the most famous statesmen of Chinese antiquity, brought his ruler, Duke Huan (685-643), to a position of supremacy (pa 霸) over the other feudal lords. Shu Tiao 豎貂 was a eunuch who waited on the table of Duke Huan, and through whose influence the proper heir to the throne was set aside in favor of another son. This led to a general struggle for the rule of Ch'i, when the Duke died in 643. See the *Tso Chuan* (Couvreur's translation, I, 316).

The numerous quotations from Confucius that appear in the above preface make it evident that Pan Ku has looked to him for inspiration in compiling this table; indeed, it has already been pointed out that Confucius was probably the first who made classifications of humanity in this way. It is to be noted that the types of personality mentioned by Confucius in these quotations are the Sage,[39] the man of perfect virtue,[40] the man of wisdom,[41] and the stupid man.[42]

The distinctions between these types of men are not based on mere material accomplishment, but at the same time take into consideration both moral and intellectual qualities. The man of wisdom, for example, though notable for his learning, must at the same time be a person of high moral standards, if he is to merit the title of "wise." In other words, his knowledge cannot be of the Machiavellian type, used solely for the injury of his fellow creatures. It must be a higher kind of wisdom, giving him an insight into ethical and social problems.

Pure virtue, however, is valued even more greatly by the Confucian than is intellectual knowledge, and therefore the man of *jen* 仁, meaning by that, the man of perfect virtue and goodness, is considered to be higher than the man of wisdom. Nevertheless, the man of *jen* may sometimes conceivably be a person so naïve and guileless that he lacks the understanding of human nature that would make his virtue most effective in the world. Hence the highest rank of all is reserved for the Sage, of whom there have been but a handful in human history, and who combine in their character, wonderfully blended, the perfect virtue of the man of *jen* and the insight and understanding of the man of wisdom.

At the other end of the scale stands the stupid man, whose stupidity is not that of the simple, good-natured idiot, but is a lustful, savage, degenerate kind of stupidity, which blinds him to all goodness in the world and makes him no better than a beast.

These, then, are the main types of personality discussed by Confucius, and all of them appear in the " Table of Ancient and Modern men." This table groups its 1,955 historical figures under three main categories, which are in their turn subdivided into three

---

[39] *Sheng jen* 聖人.
[40] *Jen jen* 仁人.
[41] *Chih jen* 智人.
[42] *Yü jen* 愚人.

minor divisions, thus making a total of nine ranks or classes. These nine ranks are arranged in the text as nine parallel columns, under which the names contained in each are chronologically listed, and are headed by the following titles: (1) upper upper: the Sage; (2) middle upper: the man of perfect virtue; (3) lower upper: the man of wisdom; (4) upper middle; (5) middle middle; (6) lower middle; (7) upper lower; (8) middle lower; (9) lower lower: the stupid man.[43]

The men classified under the above nine categories begin with the mythical sage-emperor, Fu Hsi (traditionally said to have reigned from 2852 to 2738 B.C.), and end with Wu Kuang 吳廣 (died 208 B.C.), one of the revolters who helped to overthrow the Ch'in dynasty. In Pan Chao's original compilation this period of 2,646 years is not subdivided chronologically in any way, but for our own purposes we may break it up as follows:[44] (1) Legendary period (2852-2206 B.C.); (2) Hsia dynasty (2205-1766); (3) Shang or Yin dynasty (1765-1123); (4) Western Chou dynasty (1122-723);[45] (5) Ch'un Ch'iu (Spring and Autum) period (722-481); (6) Chan Kuo (Warring States) period (480-256); (7) Ch'in dynasty (255-206 B.C.).

The following diagram presents in statistical form the data that may be abstracted from Pan Chao's chronological table. The column at the right gives the average "moral rating" which Pan Chao would assign to each of the above seven periods of history, as determined mathematically from Pan Chao's ratings of individual persons. For example, if all the persons within a certain period were to belong to the first group of Sages, their average rating

---

[43] The Chinese names are as follows: (1) *shang shang* 上上: *sheng jen* 聖人; (2) *shang chung* 上中: *jen jen* 仁人; (3) *shang hsia* 上下: *chih jen* 智人; (4) *chung shang* 中上; (5) *chung chung* 中中; (6) *chung hsia* 中下; (7) *hsia shang* 下上; (8) *hsia chung* 下中; (9) *hsia hsia* 下下: *yü jen* 愚人.

[44] The dates here given are in all cases those traditionally assigned, even for periods which we now know to be purely mythical. When making these subdivisions, it was sometimes difficult to decide under which period certain men should be classified, when their lives happened to overlap two epochs.

[45] For purposes of convenience, I have made the Western Chou period end in 723, just before the beginning of the Ch'un Ch'iu period, instead of in 771.

would be 1; it would be 9 if they were all to belong to the ninth group of "stupid men."

| | Number of persons per category | | | | | | | | | | |
|---|---|---|---|---|---|---|---|---|---|---|---|
| Categories | 1 | 2 | 3 | 4 | 5 | 6 | 7 | 8 | 9 | Total persons | Average rating |
| Periods | | | | | | | | | | | |
| Legendary (2852-2206) | 8 | 109 | 10 | | | | | 4 | 9 | 140 | 2.8 |
| Hsia (2205-1766) | 1 | 3 | 13 | 9 | 15 | 3 | 9 | 11 | 4 | 68 | 5.32 |
| Shang (1765-1123) | 1 | 23 | 27 | 26 | 1 | 13 | | 3 | 6 | 100 | 3.93 |
| Western Chou (1122-723) | 3 | 14 | 38 | 37 | 50 | 46 | 39 | 23 | 35 | 285 | 5.23 |
| Ch'un Ch'iu (722-481) | 1 | 17 | 82 | 159 | 183 | 159 | 134 | 146 | 69 | 950 | 5.71 |
| Warring States (480-256) | | 5 | 31 | 76 | 84 | 67 | 53 | 36 | 8 | 360 | 5.42 |
| Ch'in (255-206) | | 1 | 3 | 5 | 11 | 12 | 8 | 6 | 6 | 52 | 6.07 |
| Total | 14 | 174 | 204 | 315 | 340 | 299 | 242 | 232 | 134 | 1955 | 5.35 |

The preparation of the above statistics has been greatly aided by consultation of the *Jen Piao K'ao*, a valuable study on the "Table of Ancient and Modern Men" made by the noted scholar, Liang Yü-sheng (preface dated 1786).[46] This monograph is a treasure house of information, containing detailed notes on each of the 1,955 men (many of them rather obscure figures) listed in the "Table," including references to their first appearance in Chinese literature, discussions of their historicity, etc. In his preface, Liang Yü-sheng also demonstrates that the "Table," as we have it to-day, has suffered certain changes since its original compilation. Thus, by reference to various passages in Chinese literature in which the "Table" is quoted, he proves that at least five names have been lost from it since it was first made,[47] and that ten other names, though

[46] 人表考, by 梁玉繩, in 9 *chüan*. The edition consulted by me is that contained in the *Kuang-ya Ts'ung-shu* 廣雅叢書, printed in 1888.

[47] See his preface, p. 2a. The five persons thus omitted are: Ho Chü 褐拘, Kung Kan 公幹, a Great Officer of Ch'i, Lao Ai 嫪毒, the Marquis of Ch'ung 崇侯, and Ssŭ Kuei 思癸.

they still remain, no longer appear in the same categories under which they were originally grouped.[48] In the compilation of the above statistical summary, these changes have been taken into careful account.

The most striking thing about these data is the very clear way in which they reveal one of the most fundamental Chinese concepts of history: the belief that during the period of remotest antiquity a golden age existed of sage-rulers who governed a happy and contended people, and that history, in later times, has witnessed a constant development of human conflict, disorder, and moral degeneration.[49] Thus the legendary period has the extraordinarily high average of 2.8, which means that, according to the compiler's belief, the important persons of that time, taken as an average, all occupied a position somewhere between that of the "man of wisdom" and the "man of perfect virtue." It possesses eight out of the total fourteen Sages of Chinese history before 206 B. C.; 109 out of the total 174 "men of perfect virtue"; and only nine out of the 134 "stupid men" of the ninth grade.

The following Hsia dynasty falls to the comparatively low average of 5.32. This abrupt drop is difficult to explain, though we may perhaps see in it the realistic impact of the Hsia, the first period which can lay even the slightest claim to historical existence, following in sharp contrast to the preceding, wholly mythical age. Chinese scholars of recent years have established the fact that, once we leave the historically well established Chou dynasty behind us, the farther back we delve into traditional Chinese history, the more

---

[48] See *ibid*. The ten persons, with their ranks as they appear in the present text, and as corrected by Liang Yü-sheng, are as follows:

| Name | Present rank | Corrected rank |
|---|---|---|
| Ch'in Wu-yang 秦舞陽 | 6 | 7 |
| Ching K'o 荊軻 | 5 | 6 |
| Kao Chien-li 高漸離 | 4 | 5 |
| Lin Hsiang-ju 藺相如 | 2 | 5 |
| Lu Chung-lien 魯仲連 | 2 | 5 |
| Marquis of Teng-ch'i 鄧祁侯 | 6 | 7 |
| Meng Tzŭ 孟子 (a eunuch) | 4 | 3 |
| Shih Hui 士會 | 4 | 5 |
| T'ien Tan 田單 | 4 | 5 |
| Yang-ch'u Fu 陽處父 | 3 | 4 |

[49] See Bodde, *China's First Unifier*, pp. 211 f.

detailed and circumstantial become its historical records, yet at the same time the more unreal and idealized become the events which they describe. This phenomenon eloquently testifies to the fact that the records of these early periods are actually of late origin; a fact confirmed in the " Table," not only by the high " moral average " ascribed to the legendary period, but by the large number of 140 persons included in its 646 years, which is a number proportionately greater than that for either the following Hsia or Shang dynasties.

With the Shang dynasty, the average rises from the Hsia average of 5.32 to an average of 3.93, but for all later periods it drops once more well below 5. During the Ch'un Ch'iu period it falls as low as 5.71, and this period also contains a proportionately greater number of men (950 during 241 years) than do any of the others. The reason for both these facts is probably the existence of the great *Tso Chuan* chronological history, which gives us a more detailed and realistic picture of the Ch'un Ch'iu age than we have for any other.

When we come to the final period of all, that of the Ch'in dynasty, we find that it is also the one with the lowest average, 6.07. This is what might be expected, both because of the hatred that the Han scholars felt toward the Ch'in dynasty on account of its burning of the books and other oppressive measures, and because it was actually a period of exceptional unscrupulousness.

The general average for the 1,955 men listed for entire Chinese history down to 206 B. C. is placed at 5.35, that is, somewhat below the figure 5, which would be the absolute average between the first and ninth categories. From this pessimistic fact, we might conclude that Pan Chao (or whoever made this compilation) leaned in her views more toward the Confucian philosopher, Hsün Tzǔ, who maintained that man is by nature evil, than to Hsün Tzǔ's predecessor, Mencius, who believed in the fundamental goodness of human nature. This, however, would be an unwarranted assumption to make on these grounds, as it is highly improbable that when Pan Chao made her historical classifications, she ever imagined that they would some day be subjected to mathematical analysis.

Who, for Pan Chao, were the truly great men of Chinese history? This is a question of interest, not only because she, as the continuator of the *Ch'ien Han Shu*, is one of China's outstanding literary women, but because her views may be taken as representative, to some degree, of the learned world of about A. D. 100 in which she lived.  The fourteen Sages whom she lists are the following:

(1) *Legendary period:*

Fu Hsi (2852-2738)
Shen Nung (the " Divine Farmer ") (2737-2698)
Huang Ti (the " Yellow Emperor ") (2697-2598)

the " Three Sovereigns " (*san huang* 三皇)

Shao Hao (2597-2514)
Chuan Hsü (2513-2436)
Ti Ku (2435-2366)
Yao (2357-2256)
Shun (2255-2206)

the " Five Emperors " (*wu ti* 五帝)

(2) *Hsia dynasty:*

Yü (2205-2198) (founder of the dynasty)

(3) *Shang dynasty:*

T'ang (1783-1754) (founder of the dynasty)

(4) *Western Chou:*

King Wen (1184-1157)
King Wu (1156-1116)
Duke of Chou (1122-1116)

founders of the dynasty

(5) *Ch'un Ch'iu period:*

Confucius (551-479)

Of these Sages, only the last four possess much historical reality. In this connection, a word of explanation must be made about the omission of Lao Tzŭ, who in the text of the " Table of Ancient and Modern Men," as it exists to-day, is with Confucius given a place among the Sages.  The reason for this omission is that, as explained by Liang Yü-sheng, it was only in the year A. D. 742 that Lao Tzŭ was raised in this table, by imperial edict, to the exalted position of Sage which he now holds; before this date, as proved by literary sources, he occupied a place only in the fourth rank.[50]  This eleva-

---

[50] See Liang Yü-sheng, *op. cit.*, *chüan* 1, p. 14b (his discussion on the commentary by Chang Yen 張晏 to the preface of the " Table "), and *chüan* 4, p. 32a (discussion on Lao Tzŭ).  For the edict raising Lao Tzŭ to the first rank, see Teng Chih-ch'eng 鄧之誠, *Chung-hua Erh-ch'ien Nien Shih* 中華二千年史 (Two Thousand Years of Chinese History), Shanghai, 2nd edition, 1935, vol. III , p. 288.

tion came as the result of the cult of Taoism that was practised by many of the rulers of the T'ang dynasty, especially the Emperor, Hsüan-tsung, who believed that Lao Tzŭ was the ancestor of their family.

This tampering with the text largely destroys the significance that would otherwise attach to the fact that in the present text Lao Tzŭ is listed in a place no less than eighty-seven *after* that of Confucius. Were it not for such tampering, this fact would prove that Pan Chao, like most modern scholars, believed that Lao Tzŭ lived later than Confucius, and was not his elder contemporary, as is the traditional view.

The mention of Lao Tzŭ and Confucius leads naturally to the question of what was Pan Chao's attitude toward the various philosophic schools which flourished during the last centuries of the Chou dynasty. Their chief representatives, so far as they are to be found in her table, are the following:

| School | Rank |
|---|---|
| (1) *Confucian:* | |
| Confucius | 1 |
| Hsün Tzŭ | 2 |
| Mencius | 2 |
| Tseng Tzŭ (favorite disciple of Confucius) | 3 |
| Tzŭ Ssŭ (grandson of Confucius) | 2 |
| (2) *Taoist:* | |
| Lao Tzŭ | 4 |
| Lieh Tzŭ | 5 |
| (3) *Mohist:* | |
| Mo Ti | 4 |
| Ch'in Ku-li 禽滑釐 (disciple of Mo Ti) | 4 |
| Hsü Jo 徐弱 } (Later Mohists) | 4 |
| Meng Sheng 孟勝 } | 4 |
| (4) *Legalist:* | |
| Han Fei Tzŭ | 4 |
| Kuan Chung | 2 |
| Li Ssŭ | 6 |
| Shang Yang | 4 |
| Shen Pu-hai 申不害 | 6 |
| Shen Tao 愼到 | 6 |
| (5) *Dialecticians:* | |
| Hui Shih | 6 |
| Kung-sun Lung | 6 |

(6) *School of Five Elements:*

Tsou Yen                                           5

(7) *Miscellaneous:*

Kao Tzŭ 告子 (opposed Mencius on human nature)  4
T'ien P'ien 田駢 (nihilist)                             5
Wei Mou 魏牟 (hedonist)                         6
Yin Wen Tzŭ 尹文子 (pacifist)           4

It is not surprising that the Confucian school, with an average of 2, holds the place of honor. Worthy of note is the fact that both Mencius and Hsün Tzŭ are given the same rating of 2. Hsün Tzŭ, in fact, during the early part of the Han dynasty, seems, if anything, to have been even more popular than Mencius, and it was only many centuries after Pan Chao's time, and especially following the Confucianist revival of the T'ang and Sung dynasties, that Hsün Tzŭ's influence waned, largely because of his pessimistic attitude toward the question of human nature, while Mencius became supreme.

The Mohists, for so many centuries the chief rivals of the Confucians, emerge a rather poor second. Very surprising, however, is the low rating of 4.5 given to the Taoist school, which during the early reigns of the Han dynasty had been the dominant school of thought. Another surprise is the rank of 6 given to the Dialecticians, whose abstract discussions on the "hard and the white," etc., were derided even in their own day, and who by about A. D. 100 had apparently sunk into complete insignificance. The Legalists, with an average of 4.66, fare better than might be expected. But their average would have been further reduced to 5.2, were it not for the inclusion among their number of Kuan Chung, a statesman who lived centuries before the formation of the Legalist school, and whom I have included only because, by the time of the Han dynasty, he was erroneously considered as a Legalist, owing to the false attribution of a Legalistic book to him.

Perhaps the most notable omission among the above mentioned philosophic schools is the name of the great Taoist, Chuang Tzŭ. This omission may simply have resulted from a faulty transmission of the text, as in the cases of the proved omissions which have been pointed out by Liang Yü-sheng. On the other hand, it may confirm the assertion sometimes made as to the relatively low esteem in which Chuang Tzŭ was held during the greater part of the Han dynasty. Taoism, during that time, was associated almost entirely with Lao Tzŭ and with the Yellow Emperor, Huang Ti (who was believed to be the originator of the school), after whose names it was known as the Huang-Lao school. It was only at the very end of the Han dynasty that Chuang Tzŭ replaced Huang Ti in importance, and that the Huang-Lao school of Taoism became known instead as the school of Lao-Chuang.[51]

Of the other omissions, the most notable are those of the egoist, Yang Chu (bitterly opposed by Mencius, and whose school seems to have almost wholly disappeared following the attacks by Mencius) ; Hsü Hsing 許行 (another opponent of Mencius, and believer in a back-to-nature movement) ; and such minor figures as P'eng Meng 彭蒙 and Sung K'eng 宋牼.

Pan Chao's opinion on the *Tso Chuan* controversy is also illuminating. The brief chronological record known as the *Ch'un Ch'iu* (Spring and Autumn Annals) would be of little interest were it not for the three works that have been associated with it: the Kung-yang and Ku-liang commentaries, and the *Tso Chuan*. During the first half of the Han dynasty, the Kung-yang and Ku-liang commentaries were for some reason esteemed high above the infinitely more interesting and detailed *Tso Chuan*, and it was only when Liu Hsin (c. 53 B. C.-A. D. 23) came forward to champion the latter, that it rose to a position of permanent supremacy over the other two works. Hence it is interesting to note that the "Table of Ancient and Modern Men," compiled less than a century after the death of Liu Hsin, fully agrees with the latter's opinion by listing Tso Ch'iu-ming, the supposed author of the *Tso Chuan*, in no less than the second rank, whereas it places Kung-yang Kao and Ku-liang Shu, the authors of the two commentaries, only in the fourth rank.

Before concluding, we may briefly examine Pan Chao's attitude toward the leading statesmen and rulers of the hated Ch'in dynasty. The chief of these are the following:

| *Name* | *Rank* |
| --- | --- |
| Chao Kao | 9 |
| First Sovereign Emperor of Ch'in (Ch'in Shih-huang-ti) | 6 |
| Lao Ai [52] | 7 |

[51] See Fung Yu-lan, *A History of Chinese Philosophy*, I, 174.

[52] This name does not occur in the present text, but has been added

| Name | Rank |
|------|------|
| Li Ssŭ | 6 |
| Lü Pu-wei | 5 |
| Meng T'ien | 4 |
| Sovereign Emperor of the Second Generation (Erh-shih-huang-ti) | 8 |
| Tzŭ-ying 子嬰 (grandson of the First Emperor) | 6 |
| Wang Chien 王翦 (Ch'in general) | 3 |
| Yen Yo 閻樂 (son-in-law of Chao Kao) | 9 |

In view of the general hatred that the Han dynasty scholars bore against the Ch'in, Pan Chao may be considered to have shown remarkable magnanimity, especially when she groups Li Ssŭ, the burner of the books, and his master, the First Emperor, as high as the sixth rank. The fact that she assigns a place in the third rank to Wang Chien, a general who had much to do with the Ch'in conquest of the rest of China, is quite extraordinary. Notable omissions in this part of the table are those of Meng I (brother of Meng T'ien), and Fu-su (eldest son of the First Emperor).

More might be quoted from this strange " Table of Ancient and Modern Men," but enough has been mentioned to indicate its main points of interest. It is a curious and unique example in Chinese literature of Chinese categorical thinking, moralistic in type, as applied to history. It is interesting, besides, because its compilation, if not its inception, is probably in large part the work of a woman; because of the light it throws on the tastes of its author and of her age; and as an illustration of the Chinese belief in an early golden age.

Probably Pan Chao did well to end her work with the year 206 B. C., more than two centuries before her time. Otherwise she might have offended some of the still living descendants of certain men whom she would have been forced to include in her table. Even so, it is inevitable that a work so dependent as this one on subjective criteria, should have met with disfavor in some quarters, and Pan Chao has not escaped strong criticism from certain of the commentators for a few of her judgments. Which, perhaps, is the main reason why, ever since Pan Chao's time, no one else in China has dared to attempt a similar work!

---

because Chang Yen, in his commentary to the preface of the " Table," mentions Lao Ai as appearing in the " Table " in the seventh rank. For other such omissions and changes, see above, notes 47 and 48.

# AUTHORITY AND LAW IN ANCIENT CHINA

LACK OF SPACE COMPELS US to focus our attention almost exclusively on the China of the Chou dynasty, that is, on the span of eight centuries beginning late in the eleventh century B. C. and ending abruptly in 221 B. C. with the creation of a new centralized form of empire.[1] Even within these chronological limits, moreover, we must concentrate, at the risk of possible distortion, on the evolution of but a few key concepts. Concerning the many philosophical theories which, during the second half of the dynasty (sixth century B. C. onward), arose out of the breakup of the old way of life that then took place, we can say extremely little.

Feudalism is the word commonly, and with considerable justice, applied to the political system that operated during the early centuries of the Chou. Only a small part of the country was directly ruled by the Chou kings themselves. The remainder was divided into a host of petty states or principalities, held by titled nobles who were linked to the house of Chou by ties of vassalship. Within each state, most of the land was in turn subdivided among relatives, officials and courtiers of the presiding noble. Beneath this ruling class lived the great mass of commoners, most of whom were peasant serfs hereditarily bound to the lands they cultivated for their overlord proprietors.[2]

The entire population was thus, in theory, integrated into an ascending pyramid capped by the Chou monarch, whose claim to universal sovereignty is graphically expressed in the following passage from the *Book of Odes* (Ode 205):

---

[1] The Chou is traditionally said to have been founded in 1122 B. C., but the actual date was probably almost a century later. Though the dynasty officially ended in 256 B. C., the really decisive break between it and later epochs came only in 221, when its successor dynasty, the Ch'in, achieved the unification of all China.

[2] For a detailed account of this system, see the writer's "Feudalism in China," in Rushton Coulborn, ed.. *The Place of Feudalism in History*, to be published, probably in 1955, by Princeton University Press.

Everywhere under vast Heaven
There is no land that is not the king's.
To the borders of those lands
There are none who are not the king's servants.

A characteristic feature of this political system was its reliance
on custom and personal relationships rather than on any clearly
defined body of law. Its resulting arbitrariness, however, was to
some extent tempered by certain moral and religious considerations.
The aristocracy, for example, were expected to live according to
an elaborate but (in early Chou times) unwritten code of politeness and honor known as *li*—a word that may be variously rendered
as rites, ceremonies, traditional mores, customary morality, etc.
These *li*, however, were excessively refined and laborious to learn,
so that it is questionable whether they affected the commoners,
save indirectly, to any great extent at this time.

Among the psychological factors giving the aristocracy its power
and prestige, probably none was more important than the cult of
the ancestors. Unlike the commoners (who at this period bore no
surnames), each aristocratic clan maintained genealogies through
which it traced descent from famous ancient heroes. To the spirits
of these heroes the clan members offered periodic solemn sacrifice,
in return for which they received powerful aid and protection.

The dominance of this cult probably goes far to explain one of
the most striking differences between early China and many other
ancient civilizations: the absence in the former of a universal
church or a significant priesthood. For this there is a two-fold
explanation. In the first place, the ancestral sacrifices of each clan
were necessarily offered only to its own clan ancestors, not to those
of any other clan. Secondly, these sacrifices, in order to be effective, had to be performed by the clan members in person, not by
priestly proxies. As a result, the ancestral cult was inevitably
divisive rather than unifying in its effects. It could not readily
develop into a national religion with a powerful organized priesthood.

Peculiar to the Chou ruling house was a further important religious sanction for its sovereignty, embodied in the theory of T'ien
Ming, "the Mandate of Heaven." Ming, rendered as Mandate,
literally means "command." T'ien or "Heaven," the supreme Chou
divinity, was undoubtedly originally conceived of in anthropomorphic terms. Already early in the dynasty, however, there are numer-

ous instances in which we find the word depersonalized into the name for a non-anthropomorphic divine power identified as the blue vault of the sky, or even secularized entirely into the everyday designation for the physical sky.[3] According to one plausible explanation, T'ien was perhaps originally a word simply meaning " great man." Then in historic Chou times it came to be used by the Chou more specifically as a collective designation for their own " great men " of the past, i. e., the Chou departed ancestors. Finally it became the name for the realm occupied by these ancestors, i. e., the heavens or sky.[4]

In essence, the T'ien Ming theory asserts that a ruler's political legitimacy depends upon whether Heaven approves of his rule by conferring on him its Ming or Mandate. Thus when the Chou overthrew the preceding dynasty of Shang (also known as Yin), they justified their act by asserting that the final Shang king had been a dissolute tyrant; that he had therefore forfeited Heaven's Mandate; and hence that they themselves, in destroying him, were simply executing the will of Heaven. This idea appears clearly, for example, in the following exhortation addressed by the Chou to the adherents of the fallen dynasty very shortly after the conquest:[5]

Oh ye numerous officials who remain from the Yin! Heaven, unpitying and implacable, has majestically sent down its disaster on Yin, and we of the Chou have [merely] acted to support its Mandate (Ming). Assisting its

---

[3] Numerous examples of all three usages can be found in the *Book of Odes*: (a) As an anthropomorphic divinity (Ode 236): " Heaven (T'ien) gazed below. . . . Heaven made for him a match, . . . fair as a sister of Heaven. . . . There came a command from Heaven, ordering this King Wen," etc. (b) As a non-anthropomorphic supreme power identified with the blue vault of heaven (Ode 121): " O blue Heaven so far away, when will this all be settled? " (c) As the everyday name for the physical sky (Ode 178): " Swoop flew that hawk straight up into the sky (T'ien)." Cf. trans. of Arthur Waley, *The Book of Songs* (Boston and New York, 1937), pp. 262, 156 and 128 respectively.

[4] See H. G. Creel, *The Birth of China* (New York, 1937), pp. 342-344. The ancient graph for T'ien clearly represents a human figure with outstretched arms and legs, i. e., " the great man." A transition such as this is quite conceivable in a language like Chinese, which has no inflection and hence no ready means for distinguishing gender, number, etc.

[5] *Book of History*, V, 14. Cf. translations (here modified) of J. Legge in *Sacred Books of the East*, Vol. III (Oxford, 2nd ed., 1899), pp. 196-197, and of B. Karlgren in *Bull. of Museum of Far Eastern Antiquities*, No. 22 (Stockholm, 1950), p. 55.

brilliant awesomeness, we have effectuated the royal punishment and have correctly dealt with Yin's [Heavenly] Mandate. . . . Oh, ye numerous officials, it is not our small state that has dared aspire to the Mandate held by Yin, but rather it is Heaven that has denied you its trust . . . and has given us its support. . . . How could we ourselves have presumed to seek the throne? . . . It is simply that what we, the people here below, have done, represents the brilliant awesomeness of Heaven.

The vital feature distinguishing this T'ien Ming theory from superficially similar theories elsewhere, such as that of the Divine Right of Kings, is the Chinese insistence on the fact that Heaven may conceivably transfer the Mandate from one ruling house to another. That is to say, even after Heaven has once conferred its Mandate on a certain ruling house, it may thereafter withdraw it at any time, should that house prove to be unworthy. This distinction is important, because it means that in ancient China, unlike some other early civilizations, the king was definitely not regarded as a divine being. On the contrary, he was a man like other men, though one who, because of his superior qualities, had been chosen by Heaven to carry out its divine purpose.[6] This explains why in later times the theory was repeatedly invoked to justify the numerous changes of dynasty that have taken place in China, and why even today the Chinese term for revolution is *ko ming*, which literally means " transferring the Mandate."

The heavy burden of moral responsibility such a doctrine could impose upon a ruler is vividly illustrated by the following statement, issued in the name of the youthful second Chou king (trad. 1115-1079 B. C.) by his regent uncle, the revered Duke of Chou, at a time when the new dynasty was threatened by rebellion:[7]

Unpitying Heaven sends down injury on our house. . . . I am not perfected or wise, leading the people to tranquillity; how much less then should I be able to comprehend the Mandate of Heaven? Yes, I am but a little child; I am like one who must cross deep water. . . . Alas indeed for the widowers and widows! In performing Heaven's service I have been remiss,

---

[6] The fact that, beginning in Chou times, the Chinese sovereign was traditionally known as T'ien Tzu, lit. " Son of Heaven," might at first sight seem to point to a different conclusion. The term becomes readily understandable, however, if we accept Creel's theory, mentioned above, that T'ien had first been the collective designation for the Chou royal ancestors, and only later became transformed into a more generalized divinity.

[7] *Book of History*, V, 7 (Legge, *op. cit.*, pp. 157-159; Karlgren, *op. cit.*, pp. 36-37).

and have greatly thrown trouble on my person. Yet I, the young one, have no self-pity. . . .

This is the prototype of a long series of penitential edicts in which kings and emperors of China, sometimes as recently as the past hundred years, have held themselves accountable not only for human disorders, but also for floods, droughts and other disorders in the world of nature.[8]

The ethical ideas introduced by the T'ien Ming theory were, with the coming of Confucianism (sixth century B. C. onward), enormously strengthened and elaborated. Mencius (379?-281? B. C.), for example, declared flatly that "the people are the most important element" in a state, and that a tyrannical ruler no longer deserves to be called ruler, but should be removed, by force if need be. Heaven, he said, does not actually speak itself, but reveals its choice of a ruler by the manner in which that ruler, through his own exemplary conduct, succeeds in gaining the support of his people. As evidence, Mencius cited the great sage-kings of antiquity who, through sheer force of virtue alone, induced all

---

[8] Cf. the edict of August 22, 1862, issued in the name of the youthful T'ung-chih Emperor by the two co-regent Empresses Dowager: "During the night of the fifteenth of the seventh month, a flight of many shooting stars was suddenly seen moving toward the southwest; on the nights of the twenty-sixth and twenty-seventh, a comet appeared twice in the northwest. That Supreme Blue One [Heaven], when thus sending down its manifestations, does not produce such portents in vain. Moreover, beginning last month and continuing without abatement until now, an epidemic has been rife in the capital. Truly, though we be of tender years, we are filled with deepest dread and apprehension. By the Empresses Dowager we have been instructed that these warnings, transmitted by Heaven to man, are surely indicative of present deficiencies in our conduct of government. . . ." Cf. also the penitential edict of the Kuang-hsü Emperor, issued February 14, 1901, after the disastrous Boxer Rebellion, in which he says that he and the Empress Dowager had wished to commit suicide at the time of their flight from Peking in order to "offer atonement to the spirits of our imperial ancestors." For texts of these edicts, see the *Ta-Ch'ing Li-ch'ao Shih-lu* (Veritable Records of the Great Ch'ing Dynasty for Successive Reigns) [Tokyo, 1937], Mu-tsung Sect., *chüan* 35, pp. 33b-34b, and Te-tsung Sect., *chüan* 477, pp. 13a-16b; English paraphrases in J. O. P. Bland and E. Backhouse, *China under the Empress Dowager* (London, 1910), pp. 486 and 376-381 respectively (where the dates are inexactly given as 1861 and February 13, 1901). I am much indebted to Mr. Joseph Wang, of the Division of Orientalia, Library of Congress, for kindly locating these edicts in the Library's copy of the *Shih-lu*, and copying them for me.

men to be their subjects. In short, for Mencius (and for all the Confucianists), the ruler's goodness, together with the popular support it elicits, become *the* great criteria for judging whether or not he enjoys the Mandate of Heaven.[9]

The championing of these ideas by the Confucianists had two important practical effects. On the one hand, it contributed to the dream, emerging in late Chou times, of a universal empire, ruled by a single Chinese monarch, whose benevolent sway extends to all under Heaven. On the other hand, it contributed to the belief that this monarch should be guided in his rule by an intellectual élite (the Confucian scholars), who through their moral training and knowledge of history are best qualified to interpret to him the meaning of the Heavenly Mandate. This dream and this ideal were partially realized in post-Chou times with the creation of a unified empire whose administrators, aside from the emperor himself, consisted of non-titled, non-hereditary scholar-bureaucrats, recruited through the famous examination system. The cultural egocentrism engendered in this politico-cultural system, with its far-flung empire fringed by tributary dependencies, was to prove one of the major causes for conflict when China entered on large-scale contacts with the West during the nineteenth century.

Before leaving this topic of the Mandate of Heaven, we should stress that the conception of Heaven as an unpitying punishing power—a conception exemplified in the early Chou texts quoted above—becomes greatly softened and even transformed in the thinking of many of the late Chou philosophers. By these men the universe comes to be regarded as an organism that is self-contained, harmonious, and in essence good. It functions solely because of its own inner necessity, without dependence on any kind of an external volitional power. T'ien, therefore, no longer constitutes such a presiding power in this new kind of cosmos. Rather, it becomes simply the name for the non-human aspects of the universe (somewhat equivalent to our word Nature), while T'ien Ming, the Mandate of Heaven, becomes one of several metaphorical designations for its dynamic pattern. The highest function of the ruler in such a universe is to maintain the state of harmonious equilibrium believed to exist between the interlocking spheres of man and nature. To do this, however, he does not, like the Hebrew

---

[9] *Mencius*, esp. Ib, 6 and 8; Va, 5-6; Vb, 9; VIIa, 31; VIIb, 14.

prophets, rely on personal divine revelation. Instead, he studies the way of the ancient sages, for they above all are the men who, through their superior wisdom, were first able to comprehend the organic oneness of man and nature, and on its basis to create our human civilization.[10] Such is the rationalistic and humanistic interpretation which Chinese philosophy, with increasing clarity, gradually gives to the old religious ideas.[11]

It is curious that this philosophical conception of a harmonious universe should have begun to develop precisely during those later centuries of the Chou when intensified interstate wars, coupled with growing social and economic change, were rapidly liquidating the old order. The Chou kings had by now become mere figureheads; most of the little principalities of early Chou times had been annexed by their neighbors, leaving only a handful of giants to struggle for supremacy; men of aristocratic birth had lost their lands and become impoverished, while some of the peasantry, at least, were gaining a measure of emancipation from their age old serfdom. Such is the background of crisis from which sprang the first Chinese written law codes of which we have definite knowledge, those promulgated in the years 536, 513 and 501 B. C. Unfortunately, these codes have not been preserved. Judging from what is recorded concerning them, however, it is clear that they arose in response to purely secular needs, and were primarily penal in character.[12]

[10] Typical of this point of view is the account in Appendix III, *passim*, of the *Book of Changes*, describing how the ancient sages, basing themselves on their examination of natural phenomena, created the eight trigrams and sixty-four hexagrams as graphic symbols of these phenomena, and then proceeded from these symbols to get the ideas for inventing plows, boats, bows and arrows, houses, and other artifacts of civilization. Cf. transl. of Legge in *Sacred Books of the East*, Vol. XVI (Oxford, 2nd ed., 1899), esp. pp. 353-354, 360-361, 371-374, 377-378, 382-385.

[11] For a detailed survey of this world view, which became the dominant one in later Chinese philosophy, see the writer's "Harmony and Conflict in Chinese Philosophy," in Arthur F. Wright, ed., *Studies in Chinese Thought* (University of Chicago Press, 1953), pp. 19-80. It should be stressed that this was the world view of philosophical sophisticates, not necessarily shared by all non-philosophical writers. Even among later philosophical writers themselves, in fact, throwbacks to the earlier, more personalistic ways of thinking can sometimes be found. A good example is Tung Chung-shu (179?-104? B. C.). Cf. *ibid.*, pp. 43-44, 71.

[12] Cf. the *Tso Chuan* (Legge, *Chinese Classics*, V [Hongkong, 1872], pp.

It was not until the fourth and third centuries B. C., however, that a group of statesmen and political theorists known as the Legalists took the final step of exalting law as the one and only arbiter of human conduct. In place of the flexibly-interpreted *li* of antiquity—the traditional mores— they wished to institute a single body of clearly defined law to which all men high and low should be equally subject. In so doing, they were motivated by no burning desire to protect the rights of the individual. On the contrary, their aim was to create an all-powerful state authority which could forcibly put an end to the prevailing disorder. They rejected the concept of a harmonious universe, ridiculed the Confucian ideal of government through virtue, and persistently urged the need for absolutist controls with which to curb what they regarded as the essential selfishness of human nature. Law, in their hands, was merely one of several such controls; others advocated by them included state rewards for public informers, the use of secret police, institution of group responsibility for crime, and suppression of allegedly seditious literature. Thus the law of the Legalists was used to uphold a scale of values very different from the usual morality. Though its exact provisions have not come down to us, we know that they went so far as even to punish privately performed acts of public welfare, provided these had not been specifically authorized by the state.

The Legalists had their triumph in 221 B. C. when the state of Ch'in, employing these principles, subdued its last military opponent and for the first time in Chinese history created a genuinely unified and centralized empire. The triumph was shortlived, however, for the very harshness of the Ch'in brought its speedy collapse. Under the following dynasty Legalism was gradually displaced by Confucianism; government by law was subordinated to government by moral precept. In the words of the late Professor Duyvendak: " While profiting from its work, China has rejected the doctrines of the Law School [the Legalists]. The gulf between law and ethics, created by the Law School, was bridged by again restricting law to merely penal law. . . . Law became again firmly

609, 732, 772). The codes of 536 and 501, belonging to the state of Cheng, were inscribed on bronze vessels and bamboo tablets respectively; that of 513, belonging to the state of Chin, was inscribed on iron tripods.

embedded in ethics; it never acquired authority as an independently regulating norm of conduct." [13]

The Confucian theory that has since prevailed has been democratic in the sense that it has consistently emphasized the ideal of government *for* the people, has tried to counter absolutism by the weight of a morally-educated non-hereditary bureaucracy, and has sanctioned occasional political change as an escape from tyranny. It has been undemocratic, however, in the sense that it has never recognized the need of government *by* the people as a whole, has always regarded such government as the particular preserve of a small ruling élite, and has sanctioned political change only in terms of shifting personalities, not of basic change in the social and political order.

It is understandable why the Confucianists, with their memories of what had happened in Ch'in times, should ever afterward refuse to magnify law lest in so doing they cause moral principle to become subordinated to legal form. We may sympathize with their contention that no government is better than the men who operate it, and hence that the moral training of such men counts for far more than any amount of purely legal machinery. The mistake of the Confucianists, however, as of all advocates of benevolent paternalism, was their belief that a ruling group, even when free from checks such as would be imposed on it by the presence of influential social groups and forces external to itself, can nevertheless long remain true to its ideals. In Confucian China such checks were weak because, aside from the scholar-official class itself, no such influential social group existed. There was in China nothing comparable to the rise of the urban bourgeoisie of the modern West.

Under these circumstances it is scarcely surprising, therefore, that the noble Confucian ideal of government by merit has, despite many triumphs, too often degenerated into a government by privilege. There is a partial similarity at this point between Con-

---

[13] J. J. L. Duyvendak, *The Book of Lord Shang* (London, 1928), pp. 128-129. This is not to deny, of course, that there have been numerous and bulky law codes in later China. They were, however, primarily penal, and played a much less prominent role in Chinese life than that held by law in the West. Professional lawyers, for example, were virtually non-existent in China prior to recent times. For a comprehensive discussion of Chinese law, see Jean Escarra, *Le droit chinois* (Peiping, 1936).

fucianism and the ideology of the men who today control the destinies of China. For these men too, like the Confucianists, proclaim the people's welfare to be their highest aim, yet at the same time insist, again like the Confucianists, that the achievement of this aim depends on the leadership of an élite controlling group— in their case the Chinese Communist Party.[14] This is but one of several significant parallels to be found between these two seemingly sharply antithetical ideologies.[15]

[14] The word "partial" in the preceding sentence deserves stress, in that the Chinese Communists, unlike the Confucianists, not only explicitly advocate, but even insist on, the active participation of the common man in public affairs. Granted that such participation is usually confined to local matters, and is carefully guided from above along lines which severely limit its scope and freedom, it has nevertheless given to many Chinese a hitherto unknown feeling that they have a necessary and appreciated public role to play. Illustrative of the differing Confucian and Communist attitudes toward the people is the Communist slogan, made with regard to their army, that "the soldiers are fish and the people water," as contrasted with the orthodox statement of the Confucian, Hsün Tzu (ca. 298-ca. 238 B. C.), that "the people are the water and the ruler is the boat; the water can support the boat but it can also sink it." Cf. John K. Fairbank, *The United States and China* (Harvard University Press, 1948), p. 205.

[15] This thesis is developed with great skill, though sometimes to excess and with over ingenuity, by C. P. Fitzgerald in his *Revolution in China* (New York, 1952).

# BASIC CONCEPTS OF CHINESE LAW: THE GENESIS AND EVOLUTION OF LEGAL THOUGHT IN TRADITIONAL CHINA *

## 1. THE SCOPE AND SIGNIFICANCE OF CHINESE LAW

WESTERN scholars on China, with only a few distinguished exceptions, have until recently shown but little interest in the study of Chinese law. Today, especially in the United States, this situation is changing, but the stimulus obviously comes much more forcibly from the China of Mao Tse-tung than from the law of pre-Republican (i.e., pre-1912) China. It is the latter, especially in its formal codified aspects, which is the subject of this article.[1]

Good reasons can of course be found to explain the traditional indifference. They include the lack of legal training or interest among all but a handful of former Western sinologists, the formidable difficulties in style and vocabulary of the Chinese legal literature, and the fact that by Chinese scholars themselves this literature was usually regarded as utilitarian only and hence as little worthy of study on aesthetic or moral grounds.

Behind this last point, however, lie other more basic considerations: the fact that the written law of pre-modern China was overwhelmingly penal in emphasis, that it was limited in scope to being primarily a legal codification of the ethical norms long dominant in Chinese society, and that it was nevertheless rarely invoked to uphold these norms except when other less punitive measures had failed. Chinese traditional society, in short, was by no means a legally oriented society, and this despite the fact that, as we shall see, it produced a large and intellectually impressive body of codified law.

The penal emphasis of such law, for example, meant that matters of a civil nature were either ignored by it entirely (e.g., contracts), or were given only limited treatment within its penal format (e.g., property rights, inheritance, marriage). The law was only secondarily interested in defending the rights—especially the economic rights—of one individual or group against another individual or group, and not at all in defending such rights against the state. What really concerned it—though this is to be surmised rather than explicitly discovered in the Chinese legal literature—were all acts of moral or ritual impropriety or of criminal violence which seemed in Chinese eyes to be violations or disruptions of the total social order. The mere existence of the law was intended to deter the commission of such acts, but once they occurred, the restoration of social harmony required that the law be used to exact retribution from their doer. In the final analysis, a violation of the social order really meant, in Chinese thinking, a violation of the total cosmic order, since, according to the Chinese world-view, the spheres of man and nature were inextricably interwoven to form an unbroken continuum.[2]

---

* This paper is an outgrowth of a collaborative course, "Chinese Legal Thought," given at the University of Pennsylvania Law School by Professor Clarence Morris of the Law School, Professor W. A. Rickett of my department, and myself. I am very grateful to Professor Morris for reading the paper in typescript and offering a number of very helpful suggestions.

[1] In the pre-modern field, nontheless, a notable recent contribution is T'ung-tsu Ch'ü, *Law and Society in Traditional China* (Paris and The Hague, Mouton & Co., 1961), which is a revised English version of the author's 1947 work in Chinese. The most comprehensive study in a Western language of Chinese law generally is Jean Escarra, *Le Droit chinois* (Peiping, Henri Vetch, 1936); English translation by Gertrude R. Browne, *Chinese Law*, Works Progress Administration, W.P. 2799, University of Washington, Seattle (Cambridge, Mass., Xerox reprint by Harvard University Law School and East Asian Research Center, 1961). This, an important pioneer work, now stands in need of revision. Among several bird's-eye sketches may be mentioned Karl Bünger, "Die Rechtsidee in der chinesischen Geschichte," *Saeculum* 3 (1952): 192–217, and Franz Michael, "The Role of Law in Traditional, Nationalist and Communist China," *The China Quarterly*, Jan.–March 1962: 124–148.

[2] See especially M. H. van der Valk, *Interpretations of the Supreme Court at Peking, Years 1915 and 1916* (Batavia [Jakarta], University of Indonesia Sinological Institute, 1949), pp. 20–21, and M. J. Meijer, *The Introduction of Modern Criminal Law in China* (Batavia [Jakarta], Koninklijke Drukkerij de Unie, 1949), pp.

For these reasons, the official law always operated in a vertical direction from the state upon the individual, rather than on a horizontal plane directly between two individuals. If a dispute involved two individuals, individual A did not bring a suit directly against individual B. Rather he lodged his complaint with the authorities, who then decided whether or not to prosecute individual B. No private legal profession existed to help individuals plead their cases, and even in the government itself, because law was only the last of several corrective agencies, officials exclusively concerned with the law operated only on the higher administrative levels. On the lowest level, that of the *hsien* or county, which was the level where governmental law impinged most directly upon the people, its administration was conducted by the *hsien* magistrate as merely one of several administrative functions. This meant that, though usually devoid of any formal legal training, he was obliged to act as detective, prosecutor, judge, and jury rolled into one.

Fortunately for the operation of the system, however, the magistrate was commonly assisted in his judicial work by a legal secretary who *did* possess specialized knowledge of the law, and who, on behalf of the magistrate, could prepare cases for trial, suggest appropriate sentences, or write the legal reports which went to higher governmental levels. Yet it is indicative of the Chinese attitude toward law that this secretary did not himself belong to the formal administrative system. He was merely a personal employee of the magistrate, who paid his salary out of his own private purse. Hence the secretary was not permitted to try cases himself or even to be present at the trials. However, to avoid miscarriages of justice on this lowest administrative level, a very carefully defined system of appeals existed which automatically took all but minor cases to higher levels for final judgment—in the case of capital crimes as far upward as the emperor himself.[8]

How law in imperial China became the embodiment of the ethical norms of Confucianism will be discussed later. Here it should be stressed that in China, perhaps even more than in most other civilizations, the ordinary man's awareness and acceptance of such norms was shaped far more by the pervasive influence of custom than by any formally enacted system of law. The clan into which he was born, the guild of which he might become a member, the group of gentry elders holding informal sway in his rural community—these and other extra-legal bodies helped to smooth the inevitable frictions in Chinese society by inculcating moral precepts upon their members, mediating disputes, or, if need arose, imposing disciplinary sanctions and penalties.

The workings of such unofficial agencies were supplemented by complementary procedures on the part of the government itself which, despite their official inspiration, functioned quite separately from the formal legal system.[4] These extra-legal organs and procedures, then, were what the Chinese everyman normally looked to for guidance and sanction, rather than to the formal judicial system *per se*. Involvement in the latter was popularly regarded as a road to disaster and therefore to be avoided at all cost. "Win your lawsuit and lose your money," runs a Chinese proverb. Or again: "Of ten reasons by which a magistrate may decide a case, nine are unknown to the public."[5]

From all this one might conclude that the real reason for the Western neglect of Chinese formal law is that this law inherently does not deserve much attention. Such a conclusion, however, would be unfortunate on several counts. In the first place, law is an important touchstone for measuring any civilization, and its differing role

3-4. For law and the Chinese concept of cosmic harmony, see sect. 11 below.

[8] Good accounts of judicial procedure in imperial times appear, *inter alia*, in R. H. van Gulik, *T'ang-yin-pi-shih*, "*Parallel Cases from under the Pear-Tree*" (Leiden, E. J. Brill, 1956), chap. 3 of Intro., and Sybille van der Sprenkel, *Legal Institutions in Manchu China*, London School of Economics Monographs on Social Anthropology 24 (London, The Athlone Press, 1962), chap. 6. Particularly valuable for its account of the legal secretary and of the legal machinery which operated at the magistrate's level and from there took cases up to higher levels is T'ung-tsu Ch'ü, *Local Government in China under the Ch'ing* (Cambridge, Mass., Harvard University Press, 1962), chap. 6, "Private Secretaries," and chap. 7, "Administration of Justice."

[4] These procedures, which were of a police nature (the *pao-chia* system of registration and crime-reporting), economic (the *li-chia* system for encouraging tax payment, governmental distribution of grain in times of need, etc.), and ideological (hortatory lectures on moral duties, ceremonies in honor of the aged), are described in great detail in Kung-chuan Hsiao, *Rural China, Imperial Control in the Nineteenth Century* (Seattle, University of Washington Press, 1960); also summarized in Dr. Hsiao's article, "Rural Control in Nineteenth Century China," *Far Eastern Quarterly* 12 (1953): 173–181.

[5] See William Scarborough, *A Collection of Chinese Proverbs*, revised and enlarged by C. Wilfred Allan (Shanghai, Presbyterian Mission Press, 1926), pp. 334 and 335, as quoted in van der Sprenkel, *op. cit.*, p. 135.

in China as compared with the West points to basic societal differences between the two civilizations which deserve detailed analysis. In the second place, the various extra-legal bodies for social control mentioned above, despite their obvious importance and the generalized remarks about them to be found in many writings, are very difficult to study with precision. This is because of their scattered and informal mode of operation, and the fact that what they did and said was often either not written down at all, or, if written, not readily available in published form.[6]

The literature on formal Chinese law, by contrast, is large in quantity, fairly readily available, and covers a longer time span than that of any other present-day political entity. It includes the legal sections in various encyclopaedic compilations of governmental institutions, the chapters on legal development in many of the dynastic histories,[7] several large compendia of actual law cases,[8] and above all the voluminous law codes of successive dynasties. The latter, in particular, have a continuity and authoritativeness which make them unrivaled instruments for precisely measuring, dynasty by dynasty, the shifting configurations of Chinese social and political values as officially defined. So far this challenging task has hardly been attempted.[9]

Most recent of these dynastic codes is that of the Ch'ing or Manchu dynasty, compiled in definitive form in 1740 and consisting of 436 statutes and approximately 1,800 sub-statutes.[10] For previous dynasties there also exists a sequence of earlier codes going back to the T'ang code of 653, in 502 articles.[11] Before this date, no codes survive save for scattered quotations in other works. However, a study still in progress has already yielded a wealth of information on the code and judicial procedure of the first lengthy imperial dynasty, that of Han (206 B.C.–A.D. 220).[12]

Prior to the Han and its short-lived predecessor, the Ch'in dynasty (221–207 B.C.), no centralized empire yet existed in China. At that time there were only a number of independent and mutually warring principalities. This pre-imperial age, often called the age of Chinese feudalism owing to its institutional similarities to medieval Europe, is also the age that saw the formative beginnings of Chinese written law. Excluding unreliable myth and legend, the earliest datable evidence of such written law is the promulgation in 536 B.C. of certain "books of punishment" in one of these principalities. About this we shall have more to say in section 4.

## 2. LAW, RELIGION, AND ECONOMICS

A striking feature of the early written law of several major civilizations of antiquity has been

---

[6] It is possible to study the rules of many large clans, however, as preserved in their genealogies. See Hu Hsien Chin, *The Common Descent Group in China and Its Function* (New York, Viking Fund, 1948); Hui-chen Wang Liu, *The Traditional Chinese Clan Rules*, Monographs of the Association for Asian Studies 7 (Locust Valley, N. Y., J. J. Augustin, 1959); and the same, "An Analysis of Chinese Clan Rules: Confucian Theories in Action," in D. S. Nivison and Arthur F. Wright, eds., *Confucianism in Action* (Stanford, Stanford University Press, 1959), pp. 63–96.

[7] Two of the most important of these have been translated by Hulsewé and Balazs (see note 12).

[8] Notably the nineteenth-century *Hsing-an hui-lan* (Conspectus of Penal Cases) which, with its supplements, contains over 7,600 cases dating mostly from the late eighteenth and early nineteenth century. As part of the research on Chinese law currently being conducted at the University of Pennsylvania with the financial assistance of the Law School's Institute of Legal Research, an English translation of selected cases from this huge collection is now in course of preparation. A much smaller compilation, made in 1211 of 144 cases, has been translated in full by van Gulik, *T'ang-yin-pi-shih* (cited in note 3).

[9] Save in Dr. Ch'ü's *Law and Society in Traditional China* (cited in note 1), which, however, may be criticized on the grounds that it unduly emphasizes the unchanging nature of these attitudes. A different approach might reveal significant, though less immediately evident, changes in attitudes.

[10] This is the *Ta Ch'ing lü-li*, available in two partial translations: George Thomas Staunton, *Ta Tsing Leu Lee, Being the Fundamental Laws . . . of the Penal Code of China* (London, T. Cadell & W. Davies, 1810), and Gui Boulais, *Manuel du code chinois*, Variétés sinologiques series 55 (Shanghai, 1924). The former translates all of the statutes (*lü*), but omits the sub-statutes (*li*); the latter, which is more complete and includes the Chinese text, covers (sometimes in abbreviated form only) 372 of the 436 statutes, and many but far from all of the sub-statutes.

[11] This, the *T'ang lü shu-yi*, is as yet untranslated. Though traditionally said to contain 500 articles, the actual number is 502 according to Karl Bünger, *Quellen zur Rechtsgeschichte der T'ang-Zeit*, Monumenta Serica Monograph 9 (Peiping, 1946), p. 31. The code has been analyzed by Ou Koei-hing, *La Peine d'après le code des T'ang* (Shanghai, Université l'Aurore, 1935). For a study and partial translation of one of the codes between Ch'ing and T'ang, see Paul Ratchnevsky, *Un Code des Yuan* (Paris, E. Leroux, 1937).

[12] A. F. P. Hulsewé, *Remnants of Han Law*, Sinica Leidensia 9 (1 v. so far, Leiden, E. J. Brill, 1955), to be followed by a second volume. For the dynasties between Han and T'ang, see the translation and commentary by Etienne Balazs, *Le Traité juridique du "Souei-chou"* (Leiden, E. J. Brill, 1954).

its close association with religion. Not all of these civilizations, to be sure, actually produced systems of written law. When they did so, however, they commonly signalized this achievement by attributing, at least initially, a divine origin to the law they used—one resting on the belief that such law had been given or revealed to mankind by a god or gods.[13]

This belief so obviously underlies Judaic and Islamic law that for them it requires no further elaboration. It is equally apparent, however, in the world's earliest written law as known to us from Mesopotamia. On the stele bearing the famed laws of Hammurabi (ca. 1728–1686 B.C.), for example, a sculptured relief shows Hammurabi receiving from Shamash, god of justice, a divine commission for his writing of the laws. And in the prologue to the laws themselves Hammurabi tells us: "Anum [the sky-god] and Enlil [the storm-god] named me to promote the welfare of the people, me, Hammurabi, the devout, god-fearing prince, to cause justice to prevail in the land, to destroy the wicked and the evil, that the strong might not oppress the weak." [14]

In Egypt, on the other hand, no written law has as yet been found, apparently because the pharoah, as a living god on earth, needed no law other than his own spoken utterance: "He, as a god, *was* the state. . . . The customary law of the land was conceived to be the word of the pharoah. . . . The authority of codified law would have competed with the personal authority of the pharoah." [15] And in India, too, no real equivalent of our idea of law existed in early times. The nearest approach was the concept of *dharma,* a word translatable as "law," but more properly signifying "religious law," and hence *ipso facto* having a divine connotation. Only later did the idea of a purely secular law appear in Kauṭilya's *Arthaśāstra* (ca. 323 B.C.), but this development was short

lived and failed to survive the political disruption following the death of King Aśoka. Since that time, therefore, we are told that the "religious basis of law predominates through the rest of Indian history until modern times." [16]

Turning from Asia to Europe, we find Plato, in the famous opening passage of the *Laws,* making one of his protagonists unhesitatingly attribute the origin of law "to a god." [17] In Rome, similarly, despite its early secularization of law, we find Cicero purporting to quote "the opinion of the wisest men of his day" to the effect that "Law is not the product of human thought, nor is it any enactment of peoples, but something which rules the whole universe. . . . Law is the primal and ultimate mind of God." [18] Even in eighteenth-century England, indeed, after centuries of experience with a secularly-based common law, we find a similar conception persisting in legal theory. Thus we are told concerning Sir William Blackstone, author of the famous *Commentaries* (1765), that he "regarded divine law as the corner-stone of the whole [legal] edifice," "declared that divine law had been specifically revealed to men through inspired writings," and "sought to make secular law approximate to the dictates of God and of nature." [19]

The contrast of China to all this is indeed striking, for in China, as we shall see in the next section, no one at any time has ever hinted that any kind of written law—even the best written law—could have had a divine origin.

Another point worthy of more attention than can be given it here is the possible relationship of law to economic growth in certain civilizations.

---

[13] This theme figures prominently in the excellent study by William A. Robson, *Civilisation and the Growth of Law* (New York, Macmillan, 1935).

[14] See translation by Theophile J. Meek in James B. Pritchard, ed., *Ancient Near Eastern Texts* (Princeton, N. J., Princeton University Press, 1950), p. 164. The same idea goes back to the earliest collection of laws so far discovered, that of Ur-Nammu (ca. 2050 B.C.), the fragmentary prologue of which names Nanna, tutelary deity of the city of Ur, as the god through whose guidance Ur-Nammu "established justice in the land." See Samuel N. Kramer, "Ur-Nammu Law Code," *Orientalia,* n.s., 23 (1954): 40–51 (quotation on p. 46).

[15] John A. Wilson, *The Burden of Egypt* (Chicago, University of Chicago Press, 1951), pp. 49–50.

[16] Daniel H. H. Ingalls, "Authority and Law in Ancient India," in *Authority and Law in the Ancient Orient,* Supplement 17 (1954) of *Journal of the American Oriental Society,* 34–45 (quotation on p. 43).

[17] The Athenian in the book asks his companions: "Do you attribute the origin of your legal system to a god or a man?" To which the Cretan replies: "To a god; undoubtedly we ascribe our laws to Zeus, while in Sparta, the home of our friend here, I believe Apollo is regarded as the first law-giver." Quoted in J. Walter Jones, *The Law and Legal Theory of the Greeks* (Oxford, Clarendon Press, 1956), p. 95; see also Robson, *op. cit.* (note 13 above), p. 32.

[18] Cicero, *De Legibus,* II, iv; translation by Clinton Walker Keyes in Loeb Classical Library edition (Cambridge, Mass., Harvard University Press, and London, William Heinemann, 1948 reprint), p. 381. Also paraphrased in Robson, *op. cit.,* p. 3.

[19] Robson, *op. cit.,* pp. 47–48, summarizing the ideas of Blackstone as expressed in the Introduction to his *Commentaries.*

Mesopotamia, for example, early experienced a very considerable commercial development, reflections of which appear conspicuously in the Hammurabi code. Mesopotamian civilization, in the words of a specialist, was characterized by "the ubiquitous recognition of private property," and a concern for "the rights of the individual in relation to society and the cosmos." [20] The guess may be hazarded that in part, at least, Mesopotamian law may have arisen in response to this insistence upon private property and individual rights.

Here again the contrast with China is instructive. For in China the initial stimulus for law was no more economic than it was religious. Economic growth, to be sure, no doubt played a role in transforming the society of feudal China to the point where it could no longer get along without a written law. When this law appeared, however, it was used neither to uphold traditional religious values nor to protect private property. Rather, its primary purpose was political: that of imposing tighter political controls upon a society which was then losing its old cultural values and being drawn by inexorable new forces along the long road leading eventually to universal empire.

### 3. ANCIENT CHINESE THEORIES OF THE ORIGIN OF LAW

Before entering upon this topic, a brief discussion of terms is necessary. By far the most important word in the Chinese legal vocabulary is *fa*. *Fa* is the usual generic term for positive or written law as an abstraction ("law" or *"the law"*), but it may also be used in the plural to mean separate "laws." The word was already in common use before its appearance in legal contexts. Its root meaning is that of a model, pattern, or standard; hence of a method or procedure to be followed. From this root meaning comes the notion, basic in Chinese legal thinking, that *fa* is a model or standard imposed from above, to which the people must conform.

Another important word, perhaps even more common than *fa* in early legal references, is *hsing*, signifying "punishment" (or punishments), but more specifically "corporal punishment." That the latter is its primary meaning is indicated, among other things, by the inclusion in the written character for *hsing* of the graph meaning "knife." There is every reason to believe that such punish-

ments as nose-cutting, leg-cutting, castration, and the like were current in China well before the enactment of any systems of written law (*fa*). Once written law came into existence, however, the meaning of *hsing* was extended to include not only the punishments *per se,* but also the written prohibitions whose violation would result in these punishments. In this important secondary usage, therefore, *hsing* may be fairly understood in the sense of "penal law" (or laws). The frequency of its occurrence in the early legal passages—both alone and as an alternative for *fa*—is indicative of the antiquity of the Chinese view which sees written law, *fa*, as primarily signifying penal law, *hsing*. Until as recently as the administrative reforms of 1906, this idea was perpetuated in the name of the highest governmental legal organ, the Hsing Pu or Ministry of Punishments.

A third term, *lü*, though very important in the law codes of imperial times (221 B.C. onward), appears only rarely in a legal sense in earlier texts. As used in these codes, it is the technical designation for the major articles into which the codes are divided, and as such may be translated as "statute." It can also, however, refer to the entire body of such statutes as a collective entity, in which case it may conveniently, though a little loosely, be rendered as "code." Aside from its legal significance, *lü* is also the technical designation for the individual "pitch-pipes" (*lü*), twelve in number and of graduated lengths, which were the basis for the Chinese twelve-tone scale. Since the word will not appear again in our discussion, there is no need here to go into the thorny question of how, from this acoustical milieu, *lü* came to acquire its legal connotation. [21]

With these definitions behind us, let us now see how the ancient Chinese viewed the origins of law. A notable feature of Chinese historical and philosophical thinking, apparent already in early times, is its strongly secular tone. In general, it prefers to explain human events in terms of the rational (or what seems to it to be the rational) than in terms of the supernatural. A good example is the fate suffered by Chinese mythology already in the early literature: in case after case, as we read this literature, the fragmentary evidence suggests that

---

[20] See E. A. Speiser, "Early Law and Civilization," *The Canadian Bar Review* Oct. 1953: 863–877 (quotations on pp. 873 and 875).

[21] Answers to this problem are suggested by Hulsewé, *Remnants of Han Law* (cited in note 12) **1**: pp. 30–31, and by Joseph Needham, *Science and Civilisation in China* (4 v. so far, New York, Cambridge University Press, 1954–1962) **2**: pp. 229 and 550–552; in the latter work (pp. 229, 544 ff., and elsewhere) the various meanings of *fa* are also discussed at considerable length.

what at one time must have been the gods, demi-gods, or monsters of full-fledged myth have since become "euhemerized" or "historicized" into the denatured sage-kings, heroes, or rebels of pseudo-history.[22]

When we turn to the legal sphere, therefore, it should not surprise us that here too the atmosphere is entirely secular. What is really arresting, however, especially when we remember the honored status of law in other civilizations, is the overt hostility with which its appearance is initially greeted in China—seemingly not only as a violation of human morality, but perhaps even of the total cosmic order.[23]

An excellent example of this attitude is a story —apparently the historicized fragment of what was once a longer myth—providing probably the earliest explanation for the origin of *fa,* written law. The story appears in a short text entitled *Lü hsing* (Punishments of Lü), itself a section of the important classic known as the *Shu ching* (Document Classic), where it is placed in the mouth of a king who reigned around 950 B.C. Its actual date of composition must surely be several centuries later, but just how much later is hard to say with exactness. However, the fact that it is quoted and mentioned by name in another text of the fourth century B.C. provides us with at least a *terminus ante quem.*[24]

The remarkable feature of this story is that it attributes the invention of *fa* neither to a Chinese

sage-king nor even to a Chinese at all, but rather to a "barbarian" people, the Miao, alleged to have flourished during the reign of the (legendary) sage Shun (trad. twenty-third century B.C.). Thus the key sentence tells us: "The Miao people made no use of spiritual cultivation, but controlled by means of punishments (*hsing*), creating the five oppressive punishments, which they called law (*fa*)." Then the text goes on to say that many innocent people were executed by the Miao, who were the first to administer such punishments as castration, amputation of the nose or legs, etc. Shang Ti or the "Lord on High" (the supreme god of the ancient Chinese), seeing the resulting disorder among the people, felt pity for the innocent and hence exterminated the Miao, so that they had no descendants.[25]

The abhorrence of law expressed in this story no doubt reflects a period in legal development (sixth or fifth century B.C.) when written law was still a novelty and hence viewed with suspicion. In later centuries, when law became more prevalent and the need for its existence became increasingly recognized, various nonmythological and soberly "sociological" explanations of its origin appeared. Though their attitude toward law is no longer hostile, they all agree with the unknown author of the Miao legend in explaining the origin of law in strictly secular terms. The following are three representative examples, the first of which dates from the pre-imperial age (third century B.C.), and the other two from the Han empire (second century B.C. and first century A.D., respectively):

In the days of antiquity, before the time when there were rulers and subjects, superiors and inferiors, the people were disorderly and badly governed. Hence the sages made a division between the noble and the humble, regulated rank and division, and established names and appellations, in order to distinguish the ideas of ruler and subject, of superior and inferior. . . . As the people were numerous and wickedness and depravity arose among them, they [the sages] therefore established laws (*fa*) and controls

[22] See D. Bodde, "Myths of Ancient China," in Samuel N. Kramer, ed., *Mythologies of the Ancient World* (New York, Doubleday Anchor Books, and Chicago, Quadrangle Books, 1961), pp. 369–408, esp. 372–376.

[23] The relationship of Chinese law to the cosmic order will be discussed further in sect. 11. Here it should be mentioned that in purportedly early literature there appears a well-known tradition about a legendary administrator of justice, Kao Yao, which at first sight seems to run counter to the hostile attitude just mentioned. Closer examination, however, shows that the relationship of this tradition to actual written law is a questionable one. See appendix: "Kao Yao and Early Chinese Law."

[24] For translation of the story that follows, see James Legge, *The Chinese Classics* (5 v., Hong Kong University Press reprint, 1960) 3: pp. 591–593; also Bernhard Karlgren (whose version is followed here with modifications), "The Book of Documents," *Bulletin of the Museum of Far Eastern Antiquities* 22 (Stockholm, 1950): 74. The work in which the *Lü hsing* is later quoted is the *Mo-tzu* (compiled by followers of the philosopher of the same name, who lived sometime between 479 and 381 B.C.); see Y. P. Mei, transl., *The Ethical and Political Works of Motse,* Probsthain's Oriental Series 19 (London, 1929), pp. 45–46, 51, and esp. 64 (quoting the same sentence which appears below).

[25] Further fragments of this myth, as found in this and other texts, state that the Lord on High then separated Heaven from Earth so that people could no longer pass from one to the other; also that the Miao, instead of being exterminated, were banished to the extreme northwestern corner of the world, where they continued to exist as a race of winged beings who, despite their wings, were unable to fly. See Bodde, *op. cit.* (cited in note 22), pp. 389–394.

and created weights and measures, in order thereby to prevent these things.[26]

Law (*fa*) has its origin in social rightness (*yi*). Social rightness has its origin in what is fitting for the many. What is fitting for the many is what accords with the minds of men. Herein is the essence of good government. . . . Law is not something sent down by Heaven, nor is it something engendered by Earth. It springs from the midst of men themselves, and by being brought back [to men] it corrects itself.[27]

The sages, being enlightened and wise by nature, inevitably penetrated the mind of Heaven and Earth. They shaped the rules of proper behavior (*li*), created teachings, established laws (*fa*), and instituted punishments (*hsing*), always acting in accordance with the feelings of the people and patterning and modeling themselves on Heaven and Earth.[28]

## 4. THE EARLIEST CHINESE "CODE"

From myth and social theory it is time to turn to the concrete beginnings of Chinese written law as recorded in authentic history. The Chou dynasty (*ca.* 1027–221 B.C.) functioned during its early ʼcenturies under a political system which has often been compared to European feudalism. At the top were the Chou kings, who exercised nominal sovereignty over the entire Chinese cultural world. Under them were vassal lords who held as fiefs from the Chou house a multitude of small principalities. The latter were subdivided in turn into the estates of subordinate lords and officials, while at the bottom of the pyramid came the peasant serfs, hereditarily attached to these estates. In the course of time, however, the vassal principalities broke away from the Chou overlordship and became completely independent states. By

the sixth century B.C., a combination of social, political, economic, and technological forces was bringing about an accelerating dissolution of the old order.

The new forces included, among others, new agricultural techniques which made increases in population possible; the growth of commerce and rise of a money economy; the buying and selling of land and partial freeing of the peasants from their former serfdom; a growing administrative complexity in the state governments; and the appearance of competing schools of philosophy and politics. The final centuries of the Chou dynasty, appropriately known as the Period of the Warring States (403–221 B.C.), saw increasingly bitter warfare between the few large states still surviving, till one of them, the state of Ch'in, succeeded in swallowing up its rivals one by one, and in 221 B.C. finally created the first centralized empire in Chinese history.[29]

Such is the background of interrelated changes against which should be viewed the creation of the first "codes" of written law in the late sixth century B.C. The earliest reliably known to us is the "books of punishment" (*hsing shu*) which Tzu-ch'an, prime minister of the state of Cheng, ordered to be inscribed in 536 B.C. on a set of bronze tripod vessels. His action was followed by similar steps in this and other states in 513, 501, and later. Though the texts of these "codes" have in every case been lost, we may judge of the opposition they aroused from the famed letter of protest which the high dignitary of a neighboring state, Shu-hsiang, sent to Tzu-ch'an upon the promulgation of the Cheng laws:[30]

Originally, sir, I had hope in you, but now that is all over. Anciently, the early kings conducted their administration by deliberating on matters [as they arose]; they did not put their punishments and penalties [into writing], fearing that this would create a contentiousness among the people which could not be checked. Therefore they used the principle of social rightness (*yi*) to keep the people in bounds, held them together through their administrative procedures, activated for them the accepted ways of behavior (*li*),

[26] *Shang chün shu*, chap. 23. This is a third century B.C. work belonging to the Legalist school (on which see below). See translation (here slightly modified) by J. J. L. Duyvendak, *The Book of Lord Shang*, Probsthain's Oriental Series 17 (London, 1928), pp. 314–315.

[27] *Huai-nan-tzu* (The Master of Huai-nan), 9/20a (edition of Liu Wen-tien, *Huai nan hung-lieh chi-chieh*, Shanghai, Commercial Press, 1933). This is an eclectic philosophical work, composed by scholars attached to the court of Liu An, Prince of Huai-nan (died 122 B.C.). The chapter here quoted represents the Legalist school.

[28] *Han shu* (History of the [Former] Han Dynasty), chap. 23 (Treatise on Punishments and Law), written by Pan Ku around A.D. 80. See translation (here slightly modified) in Hulsewé, *Remnants of Han Law* (cited in note 12) 1: pp. 321–322. Though the sages are here said to have "penetrated the mind of Heaven and Earth," they surely did so through their own intelligence and not with the aid of divine revelation. Chinese thinking regularly attributes the creation of civilization to the intelligence of the ancient sages, but never suggests that they received divine revelation.

[29] For a survey of these developments, see D. Bodde, "Feudalism in China," in Rushton Coulborn, ed., *Feudalism in History* (Princeton, N. J., Princeton University Press, 1956), pp. 49–92.

[30] The letter is preserved in the *Tso chuan* history (probably compiled mostly in the third century B.C. from earlier records). See translation of Legge (here modified), *Chinese Classics* (cited in note 24) 5: p. 609. For a rather similar criticism by Confucius of the promulgation of penal laws in the state of Chin in 513 B.C., see *ibid.*, p. 732.

maintained good faith (*hsin*) toward then, and presented them with [examples of] benevolence (*jen*). . . .

But when the people know what the penalties are, they lose their fear of authority and acquire a contentiousness which causes them to make their appeal to the written words [of the penal laws], on the chance that this will bring them success [in court cases]. . . . Today, sir, as prime minister of the state of Cheng, you have built dikes and canals, set up an administration which evokes criticism, and cast [bronze vessels inscribed with] books of punishment. Is it not going to be difficult to bring tranquility to the people in this way? . . . As soon as the people know the grounds on which to conduct disputation, they will reject the [unwritten] accepted ways of behavior (*li*) and make their appeal to the written word, arguing to the last over the tip of an awl or knife. Disorderly litigations will multiply and bribery will become current. By the end of your era, Cheng will be ruined. I have heard it said that a state which is about to perish is sure to have many governmental regulations.

To this criticism, Tzu-ch'an's brief reply was polite but uncompromising:

As to your statements, sir, I have neither the talents nor ability to act for posterity. My object is to save the present age. Though I cannot accept your instructions, dare I forget your great kindness?

This letter is eloquent testimony to the unchanging spirit of conservatism throughout the ages. Shu-hsiang's criticisms of dike and canal building and of bigness in government are recognizably those of any conservative legislator today whenever he attacks public spending and demands a balanced budget. What is uniquely Chinese and therefore most significant about the letter, however, is its insistence upon the moral and political dangers involved in the public promulgation of legal norms. This view of law seems to have no real parallel in any other civilization.

It should not surprise us that Shu-hsiang's letter is strongly Confucian in tone, notably in its use of such Confucian terms as *yi, li, hsin* and *jen*. For though Confucius was but fifteen when the letter was written, these terms and the ideas they connoted were surely already "in the air" when he was young, and were not complete innovations with himself.

## 5. CONFUCIANS AND LEGALISTS

Though Shu-hsiang himself cannot be formally accounted a Confucian, his letter nevertheless epitomizes what may be termed the "purist" Confucian view of law. As we shall see shortly, the Confucians were staunch upholders of the tradi-

tional "feudal" scale of values. Hence it is natural that they should be bitterly hostile to the new law, especially in its early stages. Later, however, as it became increasingly apparent that law had come to stay, the Confucians softened their attitude to the point where they accepted law—although grudgingly—as a necessary evil. Even then, however, they remained Confucian in their insistence that the public enacting of law is not necessary in the ideal state, and that even in the inferior administrations of their own times, government by law should always be kept secondary to government by moral precept and example.[31]

Opposed to the Confucians were men who, because of their ardent advocacy of law, eventually came to be known as the Legalists or School of Law (Fa Chia). Most of them were less theoretical thinkers than tough-minded men of affairs who, as administrators, diplomats, and political economists, sought employment from whatever state would use their services. Their aim was direct and simple: to create a political and military apparatus powerful enough to suppress feudal privilege at home, expand the state's territories abroad, and eventually weld all the rival kingdoms into a single empire. Toward this goal they were ready to use every political, military, economic and diplomatic technique at their disposal. Their insistence on law, therefore, was motivated by no concern for "human rights," but simply by the realization that law was essential for effectively controlling the growing populations under their jurisdiction. In thinking and techniques they were genuine totalitarians, concerned with men in the mass, in contrast to the Confucians, for whom individual, family, or local community were of paramount importance. Yet it would be unfair to regard them merely as unscrupulous power-hungry politicians, for they sincerely believed that only through total methods could eventual peace and unity be brought to their war-torn world. If asked why they did what they did, they would no doubt have echoed Tzu-ch'an's dictum: "My object is to save the present age."

## 6. CONFUCIAN VIEWS OF *LI* AND LAW

As against the Legalists' *fa* or law, the key Confucian term is *li*. This is a word with an extraordinarily wide range of meanings. In its narrow-

---

[31] This shift in Confucian attitude, which it is easy to overlook, is rightly stressed by T'ung-tsu Ch'ü, *Law and Society in Traditional China* (cited in note 1), chap. 6, sect. 3, "The Confucianization of Law," pp. 267 f.

est (and probably original) sense, it denotes the correct performance of all kinds of religious ritual: sacrificing to the ancestors at the right time and place and with the proper deportment and attitude is *li;* so is the proper performance of divination. In this sense *li* is often translated as ritual or rites. In a broader sense, however, *li* covers the entire gamut of ceremonial or polite behavior, secular as well as religious. There are numerous rules of *li* for all customary situations involving social relationships, such as receiving a guest, acquiring a wife, going into battle, and the many other varied duties and activities of polite society. In this sense, *li* is often translated as ceremonial, politeness, etiquette, or rules of proper conduct. Finally, *li* in its broadest sense is a designation for all the institutions and relationships, both political and social, which make for harmonious living in a Confucian society. The *li,* in short, constitute both the concrete institutions and the accepted modes of behavior in a civilized state.

The Confucians believed that the *li* had been created by the ancient sages, and that the disorder of their own age resulted from men's failure to understand or live according to these *li.* A prime Confucian duty, therefore, was to study and interpret the *li* as handed down from antiquity so as to make them meaningful for the present day. This idea led the Confucians to prepare several written compilations of *li* which, however, did not assume final form until near the end of the feudal age and during the early part of the age of empire. During most of the Chou dynasty, consequently, the *li* were transmitted in unwritten form only. At the same time, their large number, complexity, and refinement meant that they were largely an upper-class monopoly. Indeed, what most readily distinguished the Confucian ideal gentleman (the *chün-tzu* or "Superior Man") from ordinary men was his mastery of the *li.*

On the other hand, the Confucians believed that underlying the minutiae of the specific rules of *li* are to be found certain broad moral principles which are what give the *li* their validity. This is so because these principles are rooted in innate human feeling; in other words, they represent what men in general instinctively feel to be right. It is this interpretation of *li* which has caused some modern scholars to suggest that a parallel may be drawn between Confucian *li* and the Western concept of natural law on the one hand, in apposition to a counter parallel which may likewise be drawn between Legalist *fa* and Western positive law.[32]

Finally, and this is an important point, the early *li* were the product of a society in which hierarchical difference was emphasized. That is to say, the *li* prescribed sharply differing patterns of behavior according to a person's age and rank both within his family and in society at large (one pattern when acting toward a superior, another toward an inferior, still a third toward an equal). This idea of hierarchical difference, with resulting differences in behavior and privilege, has remained alive in Confucianism throughout imperial times, despite the disappearance of the pre-imperial feudal society that first gave it birth.[33]

Keeping these ideas in mind, let us now examine the main Confucian arguments in the controversy between them and the Legalists. For the sake of clarity and brevity, we shall use our own words to summarize these arguments, trying, however, to express them as accurately as possible and keeping to what might be called a "purist" Confucian position:

1. Man is by nature good (Mencius, 371?–289? B.C.), or at least is a rational being capable of learning goodness (Hsün Tzu, ca. 298–ca. 238 B.C.). It is by inculcating the *li* that society shapes the individual into a socially acceptable human being. The *li* are thus preventive in that they turn the individual away from evil before he has the chance of committing it, whereas law (*fa*) is punitive in that it only comes into action to punish the individual for evil already committed.

2. A government based on virtue can truly win the hearts of men; one based on force can only gain their outward submission. The *li* are suasive and hence the instrument of a virtuous government; laws are compulsive and hence the instrument of a tyrannical government.

3. The *li* derive their universal validity from the fact that they were created by the intelligent sages of antiquity in conformity with human nature and with the cosmic order. Law has no moral validity because it is merely the *ad hoc* creation of modern men who wish by means of it to generate political power.

4. The five major relationships of Confucianism

---

[32] See especially Needham, *Science and Civilisation in China* (cited in note 21) 2: pp. 519, 530–532, 544 ff.

[33] This point is stressed by T'ung-tsu Chü, *op. cit.,* in his excellent discussion of *li* on p. 230, note 11. See also his entire chap. 6, "The Confucian School and the Legal School."

—those of father and son, ruler and subject, husband and wife, elder and younger brother, friend and friend—are instinctive to man and essential for a stable social order. The *li* reinforce these and similar relationships by prescribing modes of behavior differing according to status, whereas law obliterates the relationships by imposing a forced uniformity.

5. The *li* (meaning at this point primarily rites and ceremony) give poetry and beauty to life. They provide channels for the expression of human emotion in ways that are socially acceptable. Law, on the contrary, is mechanistic and devoid of emotional content.

6. A government based on *li* functions harmoniously because the *li,* being unwritten, can be flexibly interpreted to meet the exigencies of any particular situation. A government based on law creates contention because its people, knowing in advance what the written law is, can find means to circumvent it, and will rest their sophistical arguments on the letter rather than the spirit of the law (see Shu-hsiang's letter).

7. Laws are no better than the men who create and execute them. The moral training of the ruler and his officials counts for more than the devising of clever legal machinery.

To give the flavor of the Confucian spokesmen themselves, the following are offered as a few representative quotations. Included, however, are two of non-Confucian origin, illustrative of the fact that the Confucian distrust of law was shared by other schools of thought, though sometimes for different reasons: [34]

In hearing cases I am as good as anyone else, but what is really needed is to bring about that there are no cases! [35]
Lead the people by regulations, keep them in order by punishments (*hsing*), and they will flee from you and lose all self-respect. But lead them by virtue and keep them in order by established morality (*li*), and they will keep their self-respect and come to you. [36]
The more laws (*fa*) and ordinances (*ling*) are promulgated, the more thieves and robbers there will be. [37]

[34] For another list of such quotations, see Balazs, *Le Traité juridique du "Souei-chou"* (cited in note 12), appen. 9.
[35] Confucius (551–479 B.C.), as quoted in the *Analects,* XII, 13.
[36] Confucius in *Analects,* II, 3.
[37] Lao Tzu, in his chap. 57. Though he is traditionally said to have been an elder contemporary of Confucius, most scholars today believe that the book bearing his name (known also as the *Tao-te ching*) dates from the late fourth or early third century B.C.

Goodness alone [without law] does not suffice for handling government. Law (*fa*) alone [without goodness] cannot succeed in operating of itself. [38]
To have good laws (*fa*) and yet experience disorder—examples of this have indeed existed. But to have a Superior Man (*chün-tzu*) and yet experience disorder—this is something which from antiquity until today has never been heard of. [39]
Laws (*fa*) cannot stand alone, and analogies cannot act of themselves. When they have the proper man, they survive; when they lack the proper man, they disappear. Law is the basis of good government, but the Superior Man (*chün-tzu*) is the origin of the law. Therefore when there is a Superior Man, the laws, though they may be sparing, succeed in being all-pervading. When there is no Superior Man, the laws, though they may be complete, lose their power of orderly enforcement, are unable to respond to the changes of affairs, and suffice only to bring confusion. [40]
The Legalists (Fa Chia) make no distinction between kindred and strangers, nor do they differentiate the noble from the humble. All such are judged by them as one before the law (*fa*), thereby sundering the kindliness expressed in affection toward kindred and respect toward the honorable. Their program might perhaps be followed a single time, but it is not one to be used for long. Hence I say of them that they are stern and deficient in kindliness. [41]
A good government is one that takes benevolence (*jen*) and social rightness (*yi*) as its basic roots, and laws (*fa*) and regulations (*tu*) as its lesser twigs. . . . He who gives priority to the roots, but only secondary place to the twigs, is termed a Superior Man (*chün-tzu*), whereas he who lets his concern for the twigs result in damage to the roots is termed a petty man (*hsiao jen*). . . . To ignore cultivation of the roots while devoting effort to the twigs is to neglect the trunk while giving water to the branches. Law, moreover, has its birth in the upholding of benevolence and social rightness, so that to lay great weight on law while discarding social rightness is to

[38] Mencius (*ca.* 371–*ca.* 289 B.C.), in the work bearing his name, IVa, 1, where he quotes this as a saying of his time. This and the following passages belong to an age when law was coming into wider use. While grudgingly accepting it as inevitable, they emphasize its secondary role in the government of the Confucian ruler.
[39] Hsün Tzu (*ca.* 298–*ca.* 238 B.C.), chap. 9 of the work bearing his name; see translation of H. H. Dubs (here modified), *The Works of Hsüntze,* Probsthain's Oriental Series 16 (London, 1928), p. 123. Repeated in chap. 14 (not translated by Dubs).
[40] *Hsün-tzu,* beginning of chap. 12 (not translated by Dubs).
[41] Ssu-ma T'an (died 110 B.C.), in his essay on the six schools of philosophy, as quoted in the great history begun by himself and completed by his son, Ssu-ma Ch'ien (*ca.* 145–86 B.C.). This is the *Shih chi* (Records of the Historian), chap. 130. See translation of Burton Watson (here modified), *Ssu-ma Ch'ien, Grand Historian of China* (New York, Columbia University Press, 1958), p. 46. Ssu-ma T'an, though something of an eclectic, was more inclined toward Taoism than Confucianism.

value one's cap and shoes while forgetting one's head and feet.[42]

The rules of polite behavior (*li*) do not reach down to the common people; the punishments (*hsing*) do not reach up to the great dignitaries.[43]

## 7. THE LEGALISTS AND LAW

Having given the Confucians their say, we shall now do the same with the Legalists, beginning as before with a summary of their main arguments in our own words:

1. Though a very few persons may be found who are naturally altruistic, the great majority of men act only out of self-interest. This is why stern punishments are necessary. Law is concerned only with the many who are selfish, not with the insignificant few who are good.

2. A government, if it is to be strong, must destroy factionalism and privilege. Hence it is imperative for it to publicize its laws to all and to apply them impartially to high and low alike, irrespective of relationship or rank.

3. Law is the basis of stable government because, being fixed and known to all, it provides an exact instrument with which to measure individual conduct. A government based on *li* cannot do this, since the *li* are unwritten, particularistic, and subject to arbitrary interpretation.

4. A vital principle for reducing particularism and thereby strengthening the state is that of group responsibility. Let the population be grouped into units of five or ten families each, and within each such unit let every individual be equally responsible for the wrong-doing of every other individual, and equally subject to punishment if he fails to inform the authorities of such wrong-doing.

5. Since history changes, human institutions must change accordingly. In antiquity people were few and life was easy, but today the growth of population has resulted in a sharpening struggle for existence. This is why the *li* of the ancients no longer fit modern conditions and

should be replaced by a system of law. Law should certainly not be changed arbitrarily; yet if it is to retain its vitality it should equally certainly be kept ever responsive to the shifting needs of its time.

6. A state that is strong is one that maintains a single standard of morality and thought for its people. All private standards must be suppressed if they do not agree with the public standard as prescribed by law.

7. Men, being essentially selfish, cannot be induced merely by moral suasion to act altruistically. Only by playing on their own self-interest can the state induce them to do what it desires. Hence the wise ruler establishes a system of rewards and punishments in such a way that citizens—especially officials holding important positions—are rewarded if their performance accords exactly with the specific responsibilities attached to their position, but punished when this performance either falls short or exceeds these specified responsibilities.

8. The importance of individual capabilities in government is lessened when there is a good legal machinery. Thus even a mediocre ruler, provided he keeps to his laws, can have a good administration.

9. Laws that are sufficiently stringent will no longer have to be applied, since their mere existence will be enough to deter wrong-doing. Thus harsh laws, though painful in their immediate effects, lead in the long run to an actual reduction of government and to a society free from conflict and oppression.

That the foregoing summary accurately represents the Legalist position should become apparent from the following quotations, in which the Legalists speak for themselves:

For governing the people there is no permanent principle save that it is the laws (*fa*) and nothing else that determine the government. Let the laws roll with the times and there will be good government. Let the government accord with the age and there will be great achievement. . . . But let the times shift without any alteration in the laws and there will be disorder. Let human capabilities multiply without any modification in the prohibitions and there will be territorial dismemberment. This is why, in the sage's governing of men, the laws shift with the times and the prohibitions vary with the capabilities.[44]

---

[42] *Huai-nan-tzu* (cited in note 27), 20/21b–22a, which is one of its Confucian chapters.

[43] *Li chi* (Record of the *Li*), chap. 1; see translation of James Legge (slightly modified) in *Sacred Books of the East* (Oxford, Clarendon Press, 1885) 27: p. 90. This, the best known of the above mentioned Confucian compilations of *li*, did not assume its final form until the first century B.C., but is based upon earlier materials. The statement here made, that the officialdom (to which the Confucians themselves belonged) is not subject to the penalties of the commoners, was to assume key importance, as we shall see, in imperial Chinese law.

[44] Chap. 54 of the writings of Han Fei Tzu (died 233 B.C.), chief theoretician of the Legalist school. See translation of W. K. Liao (here modified), *The Complete Works of Han Fei Tzu*, Probsthain's Oriental Series 25–26 (London, 1939–1959) 2: p. 328.

If the law (*fa*) is not uniform, it will be inauspicious for the holder of the state. . . . Therefore it is said that the law must be kept uniform. It is out of this that preservation or destruction, order or disorder, develop, and this it is that the sage-ruler uses as the great standard for the world. . . . All beings and affairs, if not within the scope of the law, cannot operate. . . . When ruler and minister, superior and inferior, noble and humble, all obey the law, this is called great good government.[45]

What are mutually incompatible should not coexist. To reward those who kill the enemy, yet at the same time praise acts of mercy and benevolence; to honor those who capture cities, yet at the same time believe in the doctrine of universal love; to improve arms and armies as preparation against emergency, yet at the same time admire the flourishes of the officials at the court; to depend on agriculture to enrich the nation, yet at the same time encourage men of letters: . . . strong government will not thus be gained. The state in times of peace feeds the scholars and cavaliers, but when difficulty arises it makes use of its soldiers. Those whom it benefits are not those whom it uses, and those whom it uses are not those whom it benefits. . . . What is today called wisdom consists of subtle and speculative theories which even the wisest have difficulty in understanding. . . . Now in ordering current affairs, when the most urgent needs are not met, one should not concern oneself with what is of no immediate bearing. . . . Therefore subtle and speculative theories are no business of the people.[46]

In his rule of a state, the sage does not rely on men doing good of themselves, but uses them in such a way that they can do no wrong. Within the frontiers, those who can be relied on to do good of themselves are not enough to be counted in tens, whereas if men be used so as to do no wrong, the entire state may be equably administered. He who rules makes use of the many while disregarding the few, and hence he concerns himself not with virtue but with law (*fa*).[47]

When punishments are heavy, the people dare not transgress, and therefore there will be no punishments.[48]

When a ruler wishes to prevent wickedness, he examines into the correspondence between performance and title, words and work. When a minister makes claims, the ruler gives him work according to what he has claimed, but holds him wholly responsible for accomplishment corresponding to this work. When the accomplishment corresponds to the work, and the work corresponds to what the man has claimed he could do, he is rewarded. If the accomplishment does not correspond to the work, nor the work correspond to what the man has claimed for himself, he is punished. Thus when ministers have made great claims while their actual accomplishment is small, they are punished. This is not punishment because of the smallness of the accomplishment, but because the accomplishment is not equal to the name of it. And when ministers have made small claims while the actual accomplishment is great, they are also punished. This is not because no pleasure is taken in the larger accomplishment, but because it is not in accord with the name given to it.[49]

In governing a state, the regulating of clear laws (*fa*) and establishing of severe punishments (*hsing*) are done in order to save the masses of the living from disorder, to get rid of calamities in the world, to insure that the strong do not override the weak and the many do not oppress the few, that the aged may complete their years and the young and orphaned may attain maturity, that the border regions not be invaded, that ruler and minister have mutual regard for each other and father and son mutually support one another, and that there be none of the calamities of death, destruction, bonds and captivity. Such indeed is the height of achievement.[50]

## 8. LEGALIST TRIUMPH BUT CONFUCIANIZATION OF LAW

A reading of the Confucian and Legalist platforms should be enough to tell us what happened. The dynamic and ruthlessly efficient program of the Legalists, as adopted in Ch'in, helped that state to triumph successively over its rivals and in 221 B.C. to found the first universal Chinese empire. Under the new regime the nobles and officials of the former states were taken away from their territories and stripped of power. Their place was taken by a centrally-appointed, non-hereditary, salaried bureaucracy which was to be the model for all dynastic governments from that time onward until the founding of the Republic in 1912. The Legalist law of Ch'in became the law of the entire empire. Finally, in 213 B.C., the Legalist program reached its logical climax

---

[45] *Kuan-tzu*, chap. 45, as quoted (with slight changes) in Fung Yu-lan, *A History of Chinese Philosophy*, translated by D. Bodde (2 v., Princeton, N. J., Princeton University Press, 1952–1953) 1: p. 322. The *Kuan-tzu*, though traditionally ascribed to the statesman Kuan Chung (died 645 B.C.), is actually an eclectic work by anonymous writers. This, one of its Legalist chapters, dates probably from the third century B.C.

[46] *Han Fei-tzu*, chap. 49 (Liao, *op. cit.* 2: pp. 287–288, modified).

[47] *Han Fei-tzu*, chap. 50 (Liao 2: pp. 306–307, modified).

[48] *Shang chün shu*, chap. 18; see translation of Duyvendak (cited in note 26), p. 288. Though attributed to the Legalist statesman Shang Yang (died 338 B.C.), this is actually a composite work by anonymous Legalists, mostly of the third century B.C.

[49] *Han Fei-tzu*, chap. 7 (Liao, *op. cit.* 1: pp. 48–49, modified). For rendition in the first sentence of the important Legalist technical term *hsing-ming* (lit., "punishment and name") as "performance and title," see H. G. Creel, "The Meaning of *Hsing Ming*," in Soren Egerod and Else Glahn, eds., *Studia Serica Bernhard Karlgren Dedicata* (Copenhagen, Ejnar Munksgaard, 1959), pp. 199–211, esp. 205.

[50] *Han Fei-tzu*, chap. 14 (Liao, *op. cit.* 1: p. 124, modified).

with the notorious "Burning of the Books," expressly ordered by the government to destroy the classical texts of antiquity, the writings of the non-Legalist schools of thought, and the historical records of former states other than Ch'in.

Yet the Legalist triumph was amazingly short lived. In 210 B.C. the founder of the Ch'in empire died, and within two years his empire dissolved into rebellion and disorder. Out of the subsequent civil war arose a new empire, that of Han (206 B.C.–A.D. 220), under which the Ch'in bureaucratic government was reestablished and elaborated. At the same time, however, in one of the amazing reversals of history, Confucianism replaced Legalism as the dominant ideology. Already by 100 B.C. Confucianism was beginning to gain recognition as the orthodoxy of the state, whereas Legalism was disappearing for all time as a separate school.

How all this happened cannot be discussed here other than to say that the Confucianism which triumphed in Han times was a highly eclectic thought system—one that borrowed extensively from its philosophical rivals. Since these included Legalism, the eclipse of Legalism as a recognized school by no means meant the complete disappearance of Legalist ideas and practices. On the contrary, these continued to influence the political and economic thinking of Han and later times, probably a good deal more than has been traditionally supposed. Such economic policies, for example, as the "ever-normal granary," various government efforts to equalize private holdings of land, or governmental monopolies of salt, iron, and other products, all probably owe as much or more to Legalism than they do to early Confucianism. Recent study shows that the same may even be true of what has traditionally been thought to be a peculiarly Confucian institution: the civil service examination system used in imperial times to recruit government personnel on the basis of intellect rather than birth.[51]

It would be strange, therefore, if Legalism did not leave a lasting mark on law. Its influence probably explains, for example, the continuing penal emphasis found in all of the imperial codes, and the resulting fact that their treatment even of administrative and other noncriminal matters

usually follows a standard formula: "Anyone who does $x$ is to receive punishment $y$."[52] Or again, the background of Legalism probably explains certain important features of imperial judicial procedure: the nonexistence of private lawyers; the assumption (nowhere explicitly stated but everywhere implied in the treatment of defendants) that a suspect must be guilty unless and until he is proven innocent;[53] or the legal use of torture (within certain specified limits) for extracting confession from suspects who stubbornly refuse to admit guilt despite seemingly convincing evidence against them. Still another idea which probably owes much to Legalism is that of group responsibility (especially conspicuous in treason cases and the like). Here, however, Confucian emphasis on family and communal solidarity has probably also contributed considerably. The earliest roots of the concept, indeed, may well go back to an early communal stage of Chinese social thinking predating either Confucianism or Legalism.

Despite these and other probable survivals from Legalism, the really spectacular phenomenon of imperial times is what has been aptly termed the Confucianization of law—in other words, the incorporation of the spirit and sometimes of the actual provisions of the Confucian *li* into the legal codes. This process got under way during Han times only gradually, and thereafter continued over several centuries. By the enactment of the T'ang code in 653, however, it had effectively closed the one-time breach between *li* and *fa*. Customary law (*li*) achieved official status in the form of positive law (*fa*), or, to reverse the equation and use another interpretation (see text above note 32), positive law (*fa*) achieved moral status as the embodiment of natural law (*li*). As T'ung-tsu Ch'ü rightly points out: "To study the ancient Chinese law we must compare the codes with the

---

[51] See H. G. Creel, *op. cit.* (in note 49), and Creel, "The Fa-chia: 'Legalists' or 'Administrators'?," *Bulletin of the Institute of History and Philology, Academia Sinica,* Extra Volume 4 (Taipei, Taiwan, 1961): 607–636, esp. 632–634. Professor Creel is continuing his research on this important topic.

[52] See van der Sprenkel, *Legal Institutions in Manchu China* (cited in note 3), p. 64.

[53] This point is made by R. H. van Gulik, *T'ang-yin-pi-shih* (cited in note 3), p. 56, where van Gulik comments: "This principle is not based so much on harshness as on the idea that no really good citizen will ever become involved with the law; even a completely innocent person being falsely accused is guilty in so far that he is a party to a disturbance of the peace in the district—which is an affront to the magistrate's administration." After assessing all the factors, van Gulik concludes (p. 63): "All circumstances considered, the old Chinese judicial system worked tolerably well."

books of *li;* only in this way can we trace its origin and real meaning." [54]

The reader is referred to Dr. Ch'ü's book for innumerable illustrations of the truth of this statement. Here we can only summarize the main directions of influence, illustrating each with a few examples. These examples we shall draw from the Ch'ing code of 1740, both because this is readily available in translation, and because a great deal of what it says goes back in essence to much earlier times.

Of all the differences between Legalist *fa* and Confucian *li,* none is more basic than the universalism of the former (its refusal to make exceptions for particular individuals or groups) as against the particularism of the latter (its insistence upon differing treatment according to individual rank, relationship, and specific circumstance). This particularism we find perpetuated in the imperial codes along four major lines. These will be discussed in the following section under the rubrics, "Let the Punishment Fit the Crime," Differentiation by Social Status, Privileged Groups, and Differentiation Within the Family.

### 9. THE IMPERIAL CODES AS EXEMPLIFICATIONS OF *LI*

#### 1. *"Let the Punishment Fit the Crime"*

The codes always endeavor to foresee all possible variations of any given offense and to provide specific penalties for each. Homicide, for example, is differentiated by the Ch'ing code in its treatment of the subject into well over twenty varieties; additional varieties also appear incidentally in other sections of the code in conjunction with such crimes as brigandage or assault and battery.[55]

If we try to discover the *raison d'être* for these manifold differentiations, we find that most of them seem to be classifiable according to one or another of three major criteria. The first is that

of the *motivation* for the homicide, and it is among the varieties belonging to this group that we find the closest analogies with the differentiations familiar to us in Western legal systems. Examples would include premeditated homicide, intentional (but unpremeditated) homicide, homicide in a brawl, by mistake or accident, in roughhousing, by inducing the victim to commit suicide, etc. Other possible examples might include homicide for purposes of witchcraft (killing an individual in order to use his organs for magical purposes), or the killing (usually by a husband) of an adulterous wife and/or her paramour.

The second principle of differentiation seems to be that of the *status,* social or familial, of the killer *vis-à-vis* his victim. This criterion, while not commonly used in modern Western legal systems, is basic to Confucian social thinking and will be discussed in greater detail below. Examples of homicide thus differentiated in the Ch'ing code include parricide, homicide of an official, of a senior by a junior within a family and *vice versa,* of a child by its father, of a husband by his wife and *vice versa,* of a slave by his master and *vice versa,* of three or more persons belonging to the same family, etc.

The third criterion seems to be the *means* or the *situation* through which or under which the homicide is committed. In this group occur what seem to us the least useful and most arbitrary forms of differentiation. Examples would include homicide caused by poison, by improper administering of medicine, by introducing harmful objects into the nostrils, ears, or other openings of the victim's body (shades of Hamlet's ghost!), by depriving the victim of food or clothing, by vehicles or horses, in the course of hunting, etc.

It should be emphasized that these three criteria are nowhere mentioned in the Chinese codes themselves, and have been suggested here solely for purposes of analysis. Thus the Ch'ing code's listing of homicidal offenses seems to follow no readily evident principle of classification: it begins with premeditated homicide, continues with premeditated homicide of an official, and then goes on to parricide, homicide connected with adultery, of three or more persons within a single family, homicide done for purposes of witchcraft, by poison, in a brawl, etc.

It should further be remarked that these and the other kinds of homicide mentioned above by no means exhaust all the possibilities envisaged by the code. Typical of a "situational" homicide, for

---

[54] T'ung-tsu Ch'ü, *Law and Society in Traditional China* (cited in note 1), p. 278. Dr. Ch'ü is the author of the term, "Confucianization of law."

[55] See translation by Boulais, *Manuel du code chinois* (cited in note 10), sect. on homicide, nos. 1211–1343, as well as, in other sects., nos. 1063, 1065, 1380, 1401, 1410, 1424, etc. (Here and below, all references to Boulais are to the statutes and sub-statutes of the Ch'ing code as numbered by him, and not to his page numbers. It should be noted, however, that his arrangement of these statutes sometimes differs slightly from their sequence in the original Chinese text, where no numbers are used.)

example, is the one covered in the following statute: [56]

Whoever, knowing the ford of a river to be deep or miry, falsely asserts it to be level and shallow, or who, knowing a bridge or a ferry boat to be decayed or leaky, falsely asserts it to be firm and solid, thereby causing someone crossing the river to drown, will be sentenced as under the statute concerning homicide or injuries received in a brawl [the sentence for which, when homicide results, is strangulation subject to possible reduction of penalty at the autumn assizes].

The principle of minute differentiation exemplified in the treatment of homicide is generally characteristic of all the subject matter in the codes. Some might argue that in conception it really goes back to the Legalists rather than the Confucians, since the former, as we have seen (point 3 of section 7), were interested in maintaining an exact measurement of individual performance. In view of the universalistic nature of Legalist law, however, as against the Confucian interest in particular differences, a Confucian derivation seems much more likely. The principle of differentiation was no doubt introduced into the codes with the aim of maximizing justice by enabling the law to fit as closely as possible every foreseeable circumstance. In actual fact, however, the principle must often have made justice more difficult, since it compelled the magistrate, faced by a case involving circumstances not exactly covered by any existing statute, to choose as best he could between the several statutes most nearly applicable. [57]

### 2. Differentiation by Social Status

In accordance with the spirit of the *li*, the codes provide penalties which differ sharply according to the relative class status of the offender and his victim. As one of countless examples, let us see how the Ch'ing code treats the offense of striking or beating another person. The lowest degree of this offense, as defined in the code, is a blow or blows delivered solely by the hand or foot and resulting in no wound (defined as inflamation or discoloration of the skin or other more serious injury). Such an act, when occurring between equals (a commoner striking a commoner or a slave a slave), is punishable by twenty blows of the small bamboo. This constitutes the standard

or normal penalty. [58] For a slave who beats a commoner, however, this normal penalty is increased by one degree to thirty blows, wheras for a commoner who beats a slave, it is decreased by one degree to only ten blows. [59] Decapitation is the penalty for a slave who strikes his master (irrespective of whether or not injury results), whereas no penalty attaches to a master who injures a slave, unless this leads to death. [60] The penalty for beating the presiding official of one's own locality is three years of penal servitude, whereas for beating an official belonging to another district the penalty ranges from two years downward depending on the official's rank. [61]

It should be noted in this connection that the number of social gradations recognized in the Ch'ing code is markedly smaller than that found in the T'ang code of 653, owing to the partial social leveling which occurred between these dynasties. Thus the T'ang code has much to say about various serflike groups, collectively known as "bondsmen" (*chien-jen,* literally "mean persons"), whose status varied from group to group but always fell between commoners and slaves. In the Ch'ing code, on the other hand, these groups are scarcely mentioned at all, so that slaves, commoners, and officials are left as the three major categories differentiated by law.

### 3. Privileged Groups

Besides providing penalties that individually differ according to the relative status of offender and victim, the codes recognize entire categories of persons as deserving of special judicial procedure which distinguishes and elevates them as a whole from the great mass of commoners (*liang jen,* literally "good persons"). These categories are known as the *pa yi,* a term literally signifying

---

[56] Boulais, *op. cit.,* no. 1284.
[57] This has been pointed out in slightly differing terms by van der Sprenkel, *op. cit.* (cited in note 3), pp. 64–65.
[58] Boulais, *op. cit.,* no. 1344. Here and below, all references to beating with the light or heavy bamboo are to the *nominal* number of blows which the Ch'ing code, in accordance with earlier codes, continues to prescribe in its statutes, despite the fact that in Ch'ing times the number of blows which was *actually* administered was sharply reduced according to the following ratio: (1) the five degrees of light bambooing, nominally 10, 20, 30, 40 and 50 blows, were in actual practice reduced to 4, 5, 10, 15 and 20 blows respectively; (2) the five degrees of heavy bambooing, nominally 60, 70, 80, 90 and 100 blows, were in actual practice reduced to 20, 25, 30, 35 and 40 blows respectively.
[59] Boulais, *op. cit.,* no. 1381; *cf.* Ch'ü, *op. cit.,* pp. 186–187.
[60] Boulais, nos. 1387 and 1390; Ch'ü, pp. 191 and 193.
[61] Boulais, nos. 1367–1368; Ch'ü, p. 183.

the "eight considerations," but more meaningfully rendered as the "eight groups qualified for consideration." The term originates in the *Chou li* (Rites or Institutions of Chou), one of the major Confucian compilations of *li*.[62] Together with its connotations, it first entered the law of the Wei dynasty (220–265), and has remained in all subsequent codes. Among the eight groups in question are members of the imperial family, descendants of former imperial houses, "persons of great merit," etc., but by far the most significant category is that of high officials (the mandarins) and their immediate family members.

Though the scope of the *pa yi* system changed somewhat from dynasty to dynasty, its general significance was that members of officialdom (and their immediate relatives) could not be arrested, investigated, or tortured without permission of the emperor; that the sentences of those found guilty of an offense were subject to consideration by the emperor with a view to possible reduction; and that the usual punishments inflicted on commoners (light or heavy bambooing, penal servitude of one to three years, life banishment, death) were for the officials commonly (though by no means invariably) commutable to monetary fines, reduction in official rank, or dismissal from the civil service. Thus the law gave formal recognition to the great gap which in other ways separated the mass of commoners (the majority of them illiterate) from the small, highly educated, and theoretically non-hereditary group of scholar-officials.[63]

On the other hand, Confucian morality expected members of the official class to set a moral example to those beneath them, and hence to live according to a code of *noblesse oblige* which for certain offenses exposed them to heavier punishments than were prescribed for the ordinary man. Officials who violated the sumptuary regulations, for example, were punished under the Ch'ing code by 100 blows of the heavy bamboo, whereas the corresponding punishment for nonofficials was only fifty blows. An official who debauched a woman living within his jurisdiction would receive a punishment two degrees greater than the normal punishment for this offense. Likewise, officials who frequented prostitutes were subject to punish-

ment, whereas the code says nothing about commoners who might do the same.[64]

## 4. *Differentiation within the Family*

With the family or clan, especially the joint or extended family consisting of several generations and collateral lines living together (which, however, was always primarily an upper-class phenomenon), we reach the very heart of the Confucian system. It is not surprising, therefore, that the codes should recognize intra-family distinctions based upon sex, seniority, and degree of kinship, which are even more complex than those they recognize for society at large.

Of key importance for determining these distinctions is the system of mourning relationships known as the "five degrees of mourning" (*wu fu*). This means the five kinds of mourning which, in descending order of duration and severity corresponding to the closeness of kinship, are to be observed by any given members of a family upon the death of any other members. Each of the five degrees (of which the second actually comprises four subdivisions, referred to below as 2*a*, 2*b*, etc.) bears the name of the particular mourning garb prescribed for it. In duration, they range from a mourning period of nominally three years (actually only twenty-seven months) for the first degree, down to three months for the fifth. The major relationships covered by the first degree are those of a son or an unmarried daughter who mourn their parents, a wife who mourns her husband or husband's parents, and a concubine who mourns her master. Thereafter, for the lesser degrees, the circle of relationships widens rapidly until at the fifth degree it includes more than forty, among them such unlikely possibilities as male ego's grandfather's spinster first cousin, or female ego's husband's grand-nephew's wife.

An important aspect of the mourning system is that, being based primarily on the superiority of senior generation over junior generation and of male over female, the degrees are by no means necessarily reciprocal. A father, for example, because his generation is senior to that of his son, stands toward the latter in a degree 1 relationship (i.e., he is mourned by the son for twenty-seven months). The son, however, being of a junior generation, stands toward his father only in a degree 2*b* relationship (i.e., he is mourned by the father only for the single year prescribed by the

---

[62] See Edouard Biot, transl., *Le Tcheou-li ou Rites des Tcheou* (2 v., Paris, Imprimerie Nationale, 1851) 2: pp. 321–322.

[63] For a detailed account of the *pa yi* system, see Ch'ü, pp. 177–182.

[64] Boulais, nos. 836, 1617, 1619.

second sub-level of the second mourning degree). Similarly, a husband stands toward his wife in a degree 1 relationship, whereas the relationship of the wife toward her husband is only that of degree 2a.[65]

This system had its origin in the various Confucian compilations of *li*, notably that known as the *Yi li*.[66] Its application to family law almost surely has no parallel elsewhere.

As a concrete example, let us once more examine the Ch'ing code's treatment of the offense of beating, this time within the family. A son who strikes or beats a parent (degree 1 relationship) suffers decapitation, irrespective of whether or not injury results. However, no penalty applies to a parent who beats his son (degree 2b), unless the son dies, in which case the punishment for the parent is 100 blows of the heavy bamboo if the beating was provoked by the son's disobedience, and one year of penal servitude plus sixty blows of the heavy bamboo if the beating was done wantonly.[67] Likewise a wife who strikes her husband (degree 1) receives 100 blows of the heavy bamboo, whereas a husband who strikes his wife (degree 2a) is punished only if he inflicts a significant injury (the breaking of a tooth, a limb, or the like), and if the wife personally lodges a complaint with the authorities; in that case the husband is subject to a punishment two degrees less than the norm, i.e., he receives eighty blows of the heavy bamboo.[68]

At this point it should be stressed that the legal codes go even further than the five-degree mourning system in their differentiations, since in addition to the distinctions based upon generation and sex which are basic to the mourning system, the codes also differentiate according to the respective *ages* of the parties involved. No distinction between older and younger brother, for example, appears in the mourning system; that is to say, since both belong to the same generation, the mourning relationship of each toward the other is identical (degree 2b). In the Ch'ing code, on the contrary, the ages of the two are decisive. Thus if a younger brother beats an older brother, he re-

ceives two and one-half years' penal servitude plus ninety blows of the heavy bamboo, even if no injury results. If, however, an older brother beats a younger one, he incurs no penalty at all.[69] Or again, the penalty for beating a first cousin once removed (degree 4) is one year of penal servitude plus sixty blows of the heavy bamboo, which is increased to one and one-half years plus seventy blows for beating a first cousin (degree 3). These punishments apply, however, *only* if the beater is younger than the cousin; if he is older, he incurs no penalty unless injury results.[70]

An interesting exception to the general principle that closer relationships involve heavier punishments is the treatment of theft within the family: the penalties for this offense are graduated *inversely* to the closeness of relationship, and at the same time made consistently lower than the punishments for ordinary theft outside the family. Thus the penalty for stealing from a fifth degree relative is two grades less than the ordinary punishment; for stealing from a fourth degree relative it is made three grades less; for stealing from a third degree relative it becomes four grades less, etc. The same principle applies even to servants who steal within a family: the punishment is made one grade less than the norm.[71] The explanation, almost surely, lies in the concept, undoubtedly of ancient origin, that within a family property exists for the joint use of everyone and is not the exclusive possession of any single individual. Such, in effect, is what the official commentary on the Ch'ing code itself states. It is confirmed by the fact that should a family theft involve violence, it no longer falls under the statutes on theft but under those concerning the killing or injuring of a relative, wherein the usual principle of punishment increased in ratio to closeness of relationship is followed.[72]

## 10. FILIAL PIETY, LOYALTY, AND HUMANITARIANISM IN LAW

Central to the family values exemplified in the foregoing pages is the Confucian virtue of *hsiao* or filial piety. How influential this was is illustrated by the provision in the T'ang code requiring all officials, upon the death of a parent, to retire from office during the entire mourning period of twenty-seven months (reduced by Ch'ing times,

[65] See, *inter alia*, Boulais, nos. 29–33, or, for a more extended account, Legge's translation of the *Li chi* in *Sacred Books of the East* (cited in note 43) 27: pp. 202–208 and charts.
[66] Chap. 11; see John Steele, transl., *The I-li or Book of Etiquette and Ceremonial*, Probsthain's Oriental Series 8–9 (London, 1917) 2: pp. 9–44.
[67] Boulais, nos. 1419–1420; Ch'ü, pp. 24 and 43–44.
[68] Boulais, nos. 1401 and 1403; Ch'ü, p. 106.

[69] Boulais, no. 1411; Ch'ü, pp. 55 and 61.
[70] Boulais, nos. 1410–1411; Ch'ü, pp. 55 and 61.
[71] Boulais, nos. 1154 and 1156; Ch'ü, p. 68.
[72] Boulais, no. 1155 and note 2; Ch'ü, pp. 68–69.

however, probably for practical reasons, to one year only).[73] Still more extraordinary is another article, also in the T'ang code, providing one year of penal servitude for any couple who conceived a child during the twenty-seven months mourning period. The fact that elsewhere in the T'ang code the same prohibition is listed together with other prohibitions for officials strongly suggests that it was directed toward them rather than toward the general population.[74] If so, it would be a further example of that code of *noblesse oblige* which, as we have seen in the preceding section, was demanded of officials. One is happy to learn that by the founder of the Ming dynasty (reigned 1368–1398) it was strongly criticized as contrary to human nature, with the result that it disappeared from the Ming and Ch'ing codes.[75]

In the world of social relationships outside the family, the correlate of *hsiao,* filial piety, is *chung,* loyalty to superior (meaning above all, of course, loyalty to ruler). Confucianism lays heavy emphasis on both these virtues, but it also teaches that should a conflict arise between the two, *hsiao* is to hold priority; in other words, father and family are to take precedence over ruler and state. This choice is already exemplified in the well-known story in the Confucian *Analects* in which Confucius was told about a person so upright that he had informed the authorities of the fact that his father had stolen a sheep. "With us," Confucius commented drily, "uprightness is different from this. The father conceals the son and the son conceals the father. Therein lies uprightness." [76]

The Legalists, of course, held a contrary opinion. Thus we find the same story quoted by Han Fei Tzu with the added detail that the son was later executed by the authorities on the grounds that the loyalty he showed his ruler in reporting his father's crime was outweighed by the resulting disloyalty to his father. Han Fei Tzu's view of such a judgment is of course quite unfavorable.[77]

The strength of Confucian morality is demonstrated by the fact that what Han Fei Tzu cited as a theoretical possibility became a recognized principle in the law of imperial China. Thus we find that already in Han times close relatives were permitted to conceal the crime of one of their members without legal penalty, and were not compelled to testify in court against him. This idea conflicted of course with the Legalist principle of group responsibility mentioned earlier. In itself it may not seem too unusual, in view of the seeming American parallel that a wife is not permitted to testify against her husband. Added to the Chinese principle, however, is the more extreme provision, also known from Han times onward, that a son who brings an accusation of parental wrong-doing before the authorities is thereby unfilial and hence subject to heavy punishment. Under the Ch'ing code, for example, such an accusation, if false, was punished by strangulation, but even if true, it brought three years of penal servitude plus 100 blows of the heavy bamboo. The same punishments applied to a wife accusing either her husband or her parents-in-law, and lesser punishments applied to less close relatives.[78] Probably China is the world's only country where the true reporting of a crime could entail legal punishment for the reporter.

A notable exception to the right of concealment, however, was its denial in cases of treason or rebellion. When these occurred, the principle of group responsibility was applied with a vengeance, all close relatives of the offender being either executed or permanently banished. Thus we see that when the Confucian state felt its existence to be *really* threatened, it was willing to forego its Confucian precepts.[79]

---

[73] See Ou Koei-hing, *La Peine d'après le code des T'ang* (cited in note 11), p. 43, and *T'ang lü shu-yi* (T'ang code), book 25, article 22; also Boulais, no. 862. The figure of twenty-seven months, though not explicitly stated in this article of the T'ang code, is specified by it elsewhere (book 3, article 2) as the length of mourning for a parent.

[74] Ou, *loc. cit.* See T'ang code, book 12, article 7, and (for the parallel reference) book 3, article 2.

[75] See John C. H. Wu, "Chinese Legal Philosophy: A Brief Historical Survey," *Chinese Culture* 1, 4 (April, 1958): 34, quoting the Ming founder's preface (dated 1374) to the work known as the *Hsiao tzu lu* (Record of Filial Piety and Parental Kindness). The Ming code assumed definitive form in 1397.

[76] *Analects,* XIII, 18.

[77] *Han Fei-tzu,* chap. 49; see translation of Liao (cited in note 44) 2: pp. 285–286.

[78] Boulais, no. 1495. An exception, however, was made for wives severely beaten by their husbands (see text above note 68). In such a case, the wife was permitted to accuse the husband without incurring penalty. See Boulais, no. 181.

[79] Boulais, nos. 1024–1030. On the whole topic of concealment, see also Ch'ü, pp. 70–74, where it is stated (p. 74): "It is clear that when there was no conflict between sovereignty and family, between loyalty to the state and filial piety, both principles were recognized and encouraged. But when the two were in conflict, sovereignty took precedence, and loyalty to the state was the crucial issue." This judgment seems extreme, for the concealment of such a serious crime as murder certainly imposed a considerable limitation upon the state's authority and

On the other hand, another remarkable instance of filial piety in law is the provision that a criminal sentenced to death or long-term servitude, should he be the sole support of aged or infirm parents, might have his sentence commuted in various ways (flogging, monetary redemption, etc.), in order that he might remain at home to care for the parents. In 1769 this principle was broadened to include criminals who were the sole male heirs of *deceased* parents; these too were permitted to remain at home so that they could continue the family sacrifices to the ancestors.[80]

In some respects, the law of imperial China was more humane and intelligent than its Western counterpart. Theft, for example, merited the death penalty only when the theft exceeded a value of 120 ounces of silver, or was thrice committed, the third time in an amount of more than fifty ounces.[81] This compares favorably with pre-industrial England, where only in 1818, and then only after four Parliamentary rejections of the bill, the death penalty was abolished for stealing from a shop goods valued at five shillings.[82] In imperial China all death sentences (with a few specified exceptions), as well as many other major sentences, had to be confirmed by the highest judicial body in the capital and even by the emperor himself before they could be carried out. Many death sentences included the standard formula, "after the assizes," which meant that they could not be executed until reviewed at the autumn assizes annually held in the capital, at which time they were commonly, though not invariably, reduced to a lower sentence. Amnesties, either general or for specified groups or individuals, also occurred fairly frequently.

Confucian humanitarianism further showed itself in the special exemptions and penal reductions provided by law for the aged (seventy and above), the young (fifteen and below), and the physically or mentally infirm.[83] Women, too, were permitted the privilege of monetary redemption for many crimes.[84] The making of anonymous accusations was viewed with abhorrence and punished very severely: strangulation after the assizes for the person guilty of this act, even if the accusation were true, and 100 blows of the heavy bamboo for officials accepting and acting on such accusations.[85] And Confucian confidence in the possibility of human reform underlies the remarkable provision—one going back to T'ang and probably to earlier times—that a criminal who sincerely confesses his guilt to the authorities before his crime becomes known to them will (with certain specified exceptions) be eligible for a reduction or remission of punishment.[86]

In short, the harsher aspects of Chinese law were restricted and blunted more than might at first sight appear by the many exceptions and special circumstances which were the particular contribution of the *li*. Furthermore, the total role of formal law in ordinary life was limited, as indicated in the opening pages, by the prominence of the customary (and largely unwritten) law of clan, guild, council of local gentry, and other extra-legal organs.

On the other hand, excluding from consideration the sanctioning of torture and the other unpleasant aspects of judicial procedure mentioned earlier, it is above all the gross inequalities in the Chinese codes—their insistence upon the sanctity of rank, privilege, and seniority—that probably seem most distasteful to the modern Westerner. Indeed, as he observes the law's harsh punishment of even slight infractions of the system of legalized inequality, he cannot but wonder at the savagery with which the originally "suasive" *li* came to be enforced in Confucian China.[87] He wonders, that

---

hence conflicted with the principle of loyalty to the state, even though it did not necessarily, as did treason or rebellion, directly threaten the security of the state.

[80] Boulais, nos. 96–102.

[81] Boulais, nos. 1119 and 1124–1125. Actually, the so-called death penalty consisted of "strangulation after the assizes," which meant, as we shall see a few sentences below, that usually it would be reduced to a lower penalty (probably life banishment).

[82] See G. F. Hudson, *Europe and China* (London, Arnold, 1931), p. 328. Hudson goes on to comment bitingly: ". . . and soon it was possible to talk about the lack of humane feeling among non-Christian peoples." Likewise, as Hudson points out, Parliament in 1814, after one rejection of the bill, "consented to abolish disembowelling alive as part of the statutory penalty for treason, and henceforth the Englishman could express his disgust at the atrocities of the Chinese penal code."

[83] See Karl Bünger, "The Punishment of Lunatics and Negligents According to Classical Chinese Law," *Studia Serica* 9 (1950) : 1–16.

[84] Boulais, nos. 127–130.

[85] Boulais, no. 1463. To us today, living in an age which has recently added the word "McCarthyism" to its vocabulary, this statute seems particularly impressive.

[86] See George Alexander Kennedy, *Die Rolle des Geständnisses im chinesischen Gesetz* (Berlin, 1939).

[87] Many graphic examples occur among the legal cases preserved in the *Hsing-an hui-lan* (on which see note 8), a considerable number of which are briefly summarized in Boulais, in Ch'ü, and in Ernest Alabaster, *Notes and Commentaries on Chinese Criminal Law* (London, Luzac & Co., 1899).

is, until he remembers the equal savagery with which religious and political nonconformity have been and often continue to be punished in the Christian West.

## 11. LAW AND COSMIC HARMONY

In the opening pages it was suggested that law was traditionally viewed in China—though perhaps not consciously—as primarily an instrument for redressing violations of the social order caused by individual acts of moral or ritual impropriety or criminal violence. It was further stated that such violations, in Chinese eyes, really amounted to violations of the total cosmic order, since the spheres of man and nature were thought of as forming a single continuum.

This concept of law could hardly have started with the Confucians, at least the early Confucians, since law to them was itself a violation of the social order. Nor could it have started with the Legalists, since these men used law quite consciously to destroy and remake the old social order. It is, in actual fact, only a particular facet of the broader concept summed up in the phrase, "the harmony of man and nature." This concept of harmony or oneness, expressed with varying degrees of explicitness, underlies a great deal of Chinese thinking. It is very prominent, of course, in Taoist philosophy. As developed into an elaborate political theory, however, it is particularly the work of the "cosmologists" or "naturalists"—men who tried to explain all phenomena, both natural and human, in terms of the eternal interplay of the positive and negative cosmic principles (the *yang* and the *yin*) and of the Chinese five elements (soil, wood, metal, fire, and water).

The basic theory of these thinkers was that the human and natural worlds are so closely interlinked through numerous correlations that any disturbance in the one will induce a corresponding disturbance in the other. If the ruler, for example, shows an overfondness for women, this will lead to an excess of the *yin* principle in the human world (since the *yin* is feminine), which in turn will cause a corresponding excess of *yin* in the world of nature. Inasmuch as one of the many correlates of the *yin* is water, the concrete result may well be disastrous floods. In order to avoid this kind of situation, therefore, it becomes the ruler's prime duty to cultivate himself morally, to see that his institutions accord with the natural order, and to maintain cosmic harmony by the correct performance of ritualistic observances in which sympathetic magic plays an important part.

This theory developed gradually during the last two centuries of the pre-imperial period and reached a high point during the Han dynasty, when it entered the highly eclectic Confucianism which then achieved orthodoxy. By this time too, as we have seen, law had become an accepted feature of Confucian government and Confucianization of law was gradually getting under way. Parallel to this Confucianization, which meant the subordination of law to Confucian *li*, we may therefore perhaps speak of an analogous "naturalization" of law, meaning by this the subordination of law to the movements of nature.

This "naturalization" process is far less immediately apparent than is that of Confucianization. It is easier to detect in certain features of executive action—the granting of amnesties, for example, which often involved cosmological considerations—than in the content of the laws themselves, the analysis of which from this point of view would require considerable discussion. Here, therefore, we can present as illustration only a single conspicuous example. This is the belief that serious legal proceedings, and especially death sentences, should be carried out only during the autumn and winter months, inasmuch as these are seasons of decay and death, and should be totally avoided during spring and summer, these being seasons of rebirth and growth.

That the genesis of this idea predates the imperial age is strongly suggested by scattered statements found in the *Yüeh ling* or *Monthly Ordinances,* a calendrical text representative of "naturalistic" thinking which was probably written shortly before 240 B.C. The text tells us month by month what human activities are in accord with the natural conditions of that month, and what are the natural disasters that will occur if the wrong activities are carried out. Of legal interest are the following statements: under the second month of spring it is said that the fetters of prisoners are to be removed and criminal cases halted; under the first month of summer that only light sentences are to be pronounced; and under the second month of summer that officials are not to apply punishments. Under the first month of autumn, on the other hand, the text states that laws, prisons, and fetters are to be made ready, and punishments to be applied with firmness, because "Heaven and Earth now begin to be severe"; under the second month that the punishments are to be made more severe; and under the third month that judgments and punishments are to be expedited.[88]

There is abundant evidence that by the Han dynasty the restriction of executions and serious legal proceedings to autumn and winter was not only an idea but an accepted practice— apparently, however, one not always consistently followed, since some of the evidence consists of protests against its violation. In 7 B.C., for example, an official complained that "recently great lawsuits have been tried during the three months of spring," which, he thought, would result in poor harvests. Between 125 and 120 B.C., on the other hand, the *Han shu* (History of the [Former] Han Dynasty) tells us that the stern legal measures of a certain official were so effective that "at the end of the twelfth month there was not even a thief to set the dogs barking." Upon the arrival of spring, however, the official "stamped with his feet and said with a sigh: 'Oh, if winter could be extended by one month, that would have finished my business.'"[89]

In addition to this general ban on spring and summer executions, it seems probable that in Han times, as later, the summer solstice and especially the winter solstice were specifically included in a similar ban. Though this is not clearly stated for the Han dynasty itself, we do know that already then, as later, the solstices were regarded as crucially important days, because on them occurred the transition from the culmination of the *yin* principle (cold and darkness) to the rebirth of the *yang* (heat and light), and *vice versa*. In order, therefore, to prevent any possible human interference with these cosmic changes, governmental activities in general were halted during a period from several days before until several days after each solstice. It seems reasonable to conclude that among these activities executions were included.

Jumping forward to the T'ang code of 653 (the earliest surviving code), we find in it a tremendous proliferation of the periods tabooed to executions. Many of the new taboos are inspired by the then extremely powerful influence of Buddhism, with its opposition to the taking of life. With numerous overlappings, the specified taboos include the following: (1) An unbroken period from the Beginning of Spring (*ca.* February 4 in the Western calendar) to the Autumn Equinox (*ca.* September 23). This thus adds the first six weeks of autumn to the previously tabooed seasons of spring and summer. (2) The first, fifth, and ninth lunar months, these being Buddhist months of fasting. (3) The twenty-four "breaths" or "joints" of the year, these being days occurring throughout the year at fifteen-day intervals, the sequence of which is based on solar reckoning. The most important of them, apart from the already mentioned two solstices, are the two equinoxes and the four days which officially begin the four seasons. (4) Other annual sacrifice days and holidays. A modern scholar has calculated that these totaled fifty-three per year in T'ang times.[90] (5) Days 1, 8, 14–15, 18, 23–24, and 28–30 of each lunar month, these being Buddhist fast days. Coinciding with some of them, but separately listed, are the four days in each lunar month of new and full moon and first and last lunar quarters. (6) Rainy days and night-time.[91]

The many overlaps make it difficult to determine just how many days in a year were forbidden for executions. Even a cursory calculation, however, indicates that the remaining days on which executions *were* permitted must have totaled less than two months annually and probably did not greatly exceed a single month. If, therefore, one *had* to undergo capital punishment, T'ang China would certainly seem to have been the world's best time and place in which to suffer such a fate! It should be noted, however, that in line with usual Confucian thinking, the tabooed periods were not permitted to apply to cases of treason or of slaves who killed their masters. Presumably such acts were regarded as of such social and cosmic enormity that delay in punishing them would be even worse than failure to follow the natural pattern.

On coming to the Ch'ing code of 1740, we find

[88] The *Yüeh ling* was originally a portion of the *Lü-shih ch'un-ch'iu* (compiled *ca.* 240 B.C.), and was subsequently also inserted into the *Li chi* as its fourth chapter. See Legge's translation of the latter in *Sacred Books of the East* (cited in note 43) 27: pp. 259, 271, 275, 284–285, 288, 295.

[89] See Hulsewé, *Remnants of Han Law* (cited in note 12) 1: pp. 103–109, esp. (for the cases cited) 105 and 107.

[90] See Yang Lien-sheng, "Schedules of Work and Rest in Imperial China," in his book, *Studies in Chinese Institutional History* (Cambridge, Mass., Harvard University Press, 1961), pp. 18–42, esp. 22.

[91] See Ou, *La Peine d'après le code des T'ang* (cited in note 11), pp. 85–86, which, however, omits two of the days under (5) and does not explain all entries clearly. Cf. *T'ang lü shu-yi* (T'ang code), book 30, article 14. Unfortunately, this paragraph was written without access to the short study by A. F. P. Hulsewé, *Periodieke executie- en slachtverboden in de T'ang tijd en hun oorsprong* (Leiden, 1948).

the situation drastically changed, with the periods of taboo shrinking to mere symbolic vestiges of their former selves. Thus they now consist only of the first month of spring and last month of summer (i.e., only the first and last months of what had once been a solid half year or more of taboo), plus a period from ten days before until seven days after the Winter Solstice, and another period from five days before until three days after the Summer Solstice. The total time forbidden to executions thus amounts to less than three months.[92]

Near the beginning of this article it was suggested that the successive dynastic codes provide exceptional possibilities for measuring progressive changes in social and political values. Here we see that they can be used to measure changes in cosmological beliefs as well. An analysis of all the surviving codes between T'ang and Ch'ing, plus whatever relevant material is available between Han and T'ang, would surely yield a much more precise graph of these changes in thinking. Even the rough presentation here attempted, however, reveals a weakening belief by Ch'ing times in the doctrine of the oneness of man and nature, such as accords well with what we know from other sources.[93] This loss of conviction may indeed underlie a parallel phenomenon well attested for a quite different field: the unmistakable stereotyping and loss of feeling found in the later stages of Chinese landscape painting—itself the crowning summation in graphic form of the Chinese belief in cosmic harmony.

## 12. CONCLUSION

Many topics less purely ideological than those covered in this survey have had to be omitted despite their inherent interest and importance. Examples are the handling of disputes in feudal China prior to the appearance of written law,[94]

property and contractual relations as treated in the written and customary law of imperial times,[95] or such aspects of imperial judicial procedure as the appellate system and the administration of punishments. Nor have any comparisons been attempted with the legal ideas and procedures operative in China today, despite the added perspective and insight such comparisons would surely provide for the current scene. Even within the purely ideological sphere, in fact, it has not been possible to discuss the important but difficult question of whether or not parallels to the Western ideas of "natural law" and "laws of nature" ever existed in China.[96]

Chinese legal development is in many ways sharply different from that experienced in other civilizations. Through the systematic study of Chinese law, we can learn much of basic importance about Chinese attitudes toward state, society, and family, as well as Chinese views of the universe. Heretofore, apart from a few distinguished exceptions, western scholars have shown little interest in such study.

---

society than was later possible when Chinese government became bureaucratized. It should be noted, however, that our picture is necessarily one-sided, since the disputes of which we have knowledge are all between members of the aristocracy, i.e., between men who were more or less social equals, and do not involve any of the common people.

[95] See Pierre Hoang, *Notions techniques sur la propriété en Chine*, Variétés Sinologiques series 11 (2nd ed., Shanghai, 1920); Henry McAleavy, "Certain Aspects of Chinese Customary Law in the Light of Japanese Scholarship," *Bulletin of the School of Oriental and African Studies* 17 (London, 1955): 535–547; H. F. Schurmann, "Traditional Property Concepts in China," *Far Eastern Quarterly* 15 (1956): 507–516; Jacques Gernet, "La Vente en Chine d'après les contrats de Touen-houang (IXe–Xe siècles)," *T'oung Pao* 45 (1957): 295–391; Edward Kroker, "The Concept of Property in Chinese Customary Law," *Transactions of the Asiatic Society of Japan*, 3rd ser., 7 (1959): 123–146.

[96] This topic, obviously of the greatest importance for comparing Chinese societal and scientific development with that of the West, has been discussed with learning and brilliance, but not absolute finality, by Joseph Needham, *Science and Civilisation in China* (cited in note 21), final chapter of vol. 2. His twofold conclusion is that in the human sphere the Confucian *li* formed a reasonably close Chinese counterpart to the Western concept of "natural law," but that the concept of "laws of nature" in the non-human sphere (laws governing the physical universe, such as the law of gravity) failed to develop in China. For possible exceptions to the second part of this conclusion, which, however, do not destroy its general validity, see D. Bodde, "Evidence for 'Laws of Nature' in Chinese Thought," *Harvard Journal of Asiatic Studies* 20 (1957): 709–727.

---

[92] See Boulais, nos. 35 and 1694.

[93] See D. Bodde, "The Chinese Cosmic Magic Known as Watching for the Ethers," in Soren Egerod and Else Glahn, eds., *Studia Serica Bernhard Karlgren Dedicata* (Copenhagen, Ejnar Munksgaard, 1959), pp. 14–35. This article traces the history of a curious cosmological theory from its beginnings in the first century B.C. until it was declared in the eighteenth century to have reached a "blind alley."

[94] See Henri Maspero, "Le Serment dans la procédure judiciaire de la Chine antique," *Mélanges Chinois et Bouddhiques* 3 (1934–1935): 257–317. The give-and-take spirit apparent in these disputes distinguishes them sharply from the vertically oriented court procedures of imperial times, and suggests a society closer in spirit to Western

We have seen that Chinese written law arose in the sixth century B.C. as a political instrument for coping with the sharpening disorders then resulting from the breakdown of the old social and political order. As such, the earliest law was primarily penal in emphasis, and the same has been true of all later enacted law until recent times. Unlike many other major civilizations, where written law was held in honor and often given a divine origin, law in China was from the beginning viewed in purely secular terms. Its initial appearance, indeed, was greeted with positive hostility by many as indicative of a serious moral decline.

Following the earliest known promulgation of penal law in 536 B.C., the next three centuries witnessed a bitter controversy between Confucians and Legalists. The Confucians advocated the retention in government of the flexibly interpreted and hierarchically oriented body of traditional and unwritten rules of behavior known as *li*, whereas the Legalists wished to replace the *li* by a fixed system of written law (*fa*) which would be equally and sternly applied to all, and would suppress private privilege in favor of a powerful centralized government. The ideas of the Legalists, ruthlessly carried out in the state of Ch'in, helped that state to create the first unified Chinese empire in 221 B.C.

The Ch'in empire collapsed within fifteen years, however, and under the following Han dynasty, beginning around 100 B.C., Confucianism supplanted Legalism as the state orthodoxy. The result in subsequent centuries was a gradual Confucianization of law, in other words, an incorporation into the law codes of the social values originally contained in the Confucian *li*. Thus law in imperial China developed as a hybrid of Legalism and Confucianism. It retained the penal format of Legalist *fa* and something of its harshness, but from Confucianism it adopted the view of society as a hierarchy of unequal components, harmoniously functioning at different levels to form an ordered whole. Only in the present century was serious challenge made of the Confucian doctrine of the natural superiority of the high over the low, of the old over the young, of man over woman.

This Confucianization was paralleled by what might be called the "naturalization" of law. That is to say, law was fitted into the wider doctrine of the oneness of man and nature, which maintained that man should shape his institutions in harmony with the forces of nature. The most conspicuous manifestation of this doctrine in the legal sphere was the idea that death sentences should be carried out only during autumn and winter (these being seasons of decay and death), and should be totally avoided during spring and summer (these being seasons of life and growth).

In conclusion, it would be well to remind ourselves that the controversy between Confucians and Legalists still holds relevance for us today. The concern of the Legalists was political control of the mass man, for which reason they have been termed totalitarian. Yet in their insistence that all men high and low should conform to a single law, they were egalitarian. The concern of the Confucians was moral development of the individual man, for which reason they have been termed democratic. Yet in their insistence that for a graded society there has to be a graded law, they were undemocratic. Throughout history the failing of democracy has been its tendency to accept a double standard: equal rights for those who are its full-fledged members, but discrimination or outright exploitation for those who are not. How to create a society which will uphold the rights of the few, yet not permit these rights to harm the welfare of the many, still remains a major problem.

## APPENDIX

### KAO YAO AND EARLY CHINESE LAW

In section 3 we read the legend in which the Miao, a barbarian people living during the reign of the legendary Shun (trad. twenty-third century B.C.), are said to have created five oppressive punishments (*hsing*), which they then called law (*fa*). It was further stated that this legend (found in the *Lü hsing* section of the *Shu ching* or *Document Classic*) is probably the earliest Chinese explanation of the origin of law.

Another well-known tradition also exists, however, according to which the same ruler, Shun, appointed a model minister, Kao Yao, to have charge of criminal matters. One version of the tradition states that in this post Kao Yao administered the punishments (*hsing*) which Shun had "delineated," whereas another version asserts that it was Kao Yao himself who "made" these punishments.[97] Still a third text of the first century A.D.

---

[97] For the first version, see the *Shu ching*, sects. *Shun tien* (Canon of Shun), *Ta Yü mo* (Counsels of the Great Yü), and *Yi Chi* (Yi and Chi), as translated by Legge, *The Chinese Classics* (cited in note 24) 3: pp. 38–39, 44–45, 58–59, 86, 89–90. For the second version, see the *Chu-shu chi-nien* (Annals of the Bamboo Books), as translated by Legge, *op. cit.* 3: p. 115 of Prolegomena.

does not mention the punishments at all, but instead connects Kao Yao's judicial activities with a mythological animal known as the Hsieh-chai.[98] What the Hsieh-chai was and how it was associated with Kao Yao is summarized in the following modern statement:

The Hsieh-chai is an ancient Chinese supernatural animal, goat-like in appearance but with only one horn. It is endowed with the faculty of detecting the guilty, and can distinguish between the crooked and the upright. . . . When the famous minister Kao Yao tried cases in which guilt was uncertain, he would order the Hsieh-chai to butt the guilty. Those who were in fact guilty it would butt, whereas the innocent it would not butt.[99]

If we compare the *Lü hsing*'s legend of the Miao with these Kao Yao traditions, three points emerge:

1. The *Lü hsing* legend, as we have seen in section 3, supposedly dates from around 950 B.C., but was probably in actual fact written some centuries later, though not later than the fourth century B.C. This would at first sight make it later than the references to Kao Yao in the *Shu ching* and *Chu-shu chi-nien* (see note 97), since these purport to be contemporary or nearly contemporary with Kao Yao himself. The texts in which these references appear, however, most certainly cannot be anywhere near as old as their alleged dating, and in all probability were actually written later than the *Lü hsing*.[100]

2. Whereas the *Lü hsing* explicitly mentions *fa*, written law, this word never appears in the Kao Yao references, which speak instead of *hsing*, punishments, or more specifically of *wu hsing*, the five punishments. This fact weakens any effort to associate Kao Yao with the legendary beginnings of written law, since *hsing*, as we have seen in section 3, primarily denotes the punishments as such, and only secondarily the written penal laws which came to embody these punishments.

3. The argument linking Kao Yao with written law is further weakened by the tradition associating him with the mythical Hsieh-chai, in which no written law is mentioned at all. Conceptually, this tradition points to a magical and therefore probably a pre-legal stage in human thinking. Though textually attested only in the first century B.C., it is quite possible that it already existed at a much earlier time in oral form before then being recorded in writing.[101]

It seems reasonable to conclude, therefore, that Kao Yao's role in legend is not at all that of a lawgiver (a maker and user of written law), but rather that of a supernaturally aided dispenser of justice. It represents, in other words, a magical rather than a legal stage in human development. The legend attributing the origin of written law to the Miao barbarians, on the other hand, belongs to the early period of written law itself, so that it, rather than the Kao Yao traditions, truly represents the early Chinese attitude on the subject.

[98] See Wang Ch'ung (A.D. 27–ca. 100), *Lun heng* (Critical Essays), chap. 52, as translated by Alfred Forke, *Lun-Heng* (2 v., New York, Paragon Book Gallery reprint, 1962) 2: p. 321.

[99] A "life-size" bronze figure of the Hsieh-chai, no doubt unique in the world today, was made in 1962 by the Philadelphia sculptor Henry Mitchell and is now exhibited in the University of Pennsylvania Law School. This quotation is excerpted from the inscription prepared for the statue, which concludes with the motto: "Slow and painful has been man's progress from magic to law."

[100] It is impossible here to go into the extremely complex problem of the dating of the several references, other than to say of the *Ta Yü mo* section of the *Shu ching* that it has long been recognized as a forgery of the third or fourth century A.D., and of the *Chu-shu chi-nien* that it is questionable to what extent its present text agrees with the text originally bearing this name which was first recovered from a tomb toward the end of the third century A.D. The other *Shu ching* references are also "late," but very difficult to date exactly.

[101] That lengthy oral tradition does in fact lie behind some of the mythological themes which first appear in writings of the Han dynasty has already been suggested by Wolfram Eberhard of the University of California. See D. Bodde, "Myths of Ancient China" (cited in note 22), p. 57: "As Eberhard points out, the Han writers could and did utilize long-existent popular oral tradition to a greater extent than did the more aristocratically oriented writers of the [preceding] feudal age."

# PRISON LIFE IN EIGHTEENTH CENTURY PEKING*

Fang Pao (1668–1749), a well known Chinese scholar and official, because of involvement in an allegedly subversive piece of writing produced by a fellow scholar, spent a year (1712–13) in the prison of the highest Chinese judicial organ, the Board of Punishments, in Peking. His *Yü-chung tsa-chi* (Notes on Prison Life) is a short but very graphic account of the prison conditions he experienced. It was first published only in 1851 and is an exceedingly rare document of its sort in the history of Chinese literature. The present article provides additional information concerning the prison of the Board of Punishments during the eighteenth and nineteenth centuries, translates Fang's *Notes*, and discusses its reliability and significance.

## I. FANG PAO AND HIS "NOTES ON PRISON LIFE"

A MAJOR IRONY IN THE STUDY OF CHINESE CIVILIZATION is our ignorance, despite a plethora of written documents, of so many details of daily life, both trivial and important. Did the Chinese, for example, have side-of-the-road traffic regulations before the nineteenth century? With their flair for bureaucratic regularity and hierarchic order, one would think that they would, at least in such great cities as the Ch'ang-an of the T'ang dynasty, then probably the world's largest city. Yet the T'ang penal code of A.D. 653, which has articles punishing riders and drivers who run people down in crowded places, apparently says nothing about which side of the road they are to travel on, nor do later documents.

Our ignorance partially reflects the limited topical scope of most traditional scholarship on China. In much greater measure it stems from the nature of Chinese writings themselves. The users of the written word in imperial China were, by and large, bureaucrats, prospective bureaucrats, retired bureaucrats, or the associates or relatives of bureaucrats; what they wrote naturally reflects the interests, conventions, and limitations of their class. The mundane and especially the seamy aspects of ordinary life were either disregarded as

unworthy of formal description, or alluded to only casually, or idealized from an upper class point of view. Of course important exceptions can be found, especially in Chinese fiction and drama. Even here, however, the scope is usually narrower than that of European literature with its broader social base.

A striking example is our knowledge—or lack of knowledge—of how the prison system functioned in pre-modern China. From official sources we have a few sketchy and pallid statements, some of which, covering the period of this article, will be discussed later. From the millions of Chinese, however, who during more than two millennia of imperial history must have lived and often died in prison, we have disappointingly little. Most of them, of course, were illiterate, or, if literate, incapable of writing about their experiences. But even sophisticated scholar-officials were inhibited by the stigma attached to imprisonment, or by fear of political reprisals.[1]

---

[1] There are a very few and very partial exceptions. For example, the censor Tso Kuang-tou, who was tortured and killed in prison in 1625 at the orders of the eunuch Wei Chung-hsien, wrote a terrifying letter of lamentation to his family, excerpts from which have been translated by Charles O. Hucker, *The Censorial System of Ming China* (Stanford, California, 1966), pp. 284–285. In 208 B.C. the prime minister Li Ssu, a major figure in creating the Ch'in empire, sent a powerful memorial from prison to the new puppet ruler by whom he had been imprisoned when over seventy. See D. Bodde, *China's First Unifier* (Hong Kong reprint of 1966), pp.

---

* Presidential address (delivered in shortened form) at the annual meeting of the American Oriental Society, New York, March 25, 1969. See glossary at the end of the paper for all Chinese characters.

A man who DID dare to write about his prison experience is the early Ch'ing scholar and official, Fang Pao (1668–1749). His *Yü-chung tsa-chi* or "Notes on Prison Life" (literally, "Miscellaneous Notes in Prison") is, despite its brevity, a vivid and moving document.[2] Fang was noted as a scholar and still more as the founder of the T'ung-ch'eng literary school, named after the place in Anhui which was his ancestral home. Fortunately, the facts of his life are well known.[3]

Fang was a native of Nanking who at various times lived and worked as a teacher, scholar, and nominal slave. In 1706 he won his *chin-shih* degree in the metropolitan examination, but in 1711, while in his early forties, he became the victim, either wittingly or unwittingly, of a literary inquisition directed against a work written by a fellow-townsman and former disciple, Tai Ming-shih. To this work, which was alleged by the government to have subversive intent (it is said to have used Ming dynasty reign periods), Fang Pao either signed a preface or the preface was falsely attributed to him.

In the eleventh lunar month of the fiftieth year of the K'ang-hsi reign (December 10, 1711-January 7, 1712), Fang, together with Tai, was arrested in Nanking; by the third month of the following year (April 6–May 12, 1712) he had been brought to Peking and incarcerated in the prison of the highest judicial organ, the Hsing pu or Board of Punishments. There he remained for almost a year until the case was decided in the second month of the fifty-second year (February 25–March 25, 1713). Tai, as a result, suffered execution, but Fang and his family were sentenced to become the nominal slaves of Manchu bannermen. On April 20, 1713, by virtue of Fang's scholarly and literary abilities, he was ordered by the K'ang-hsi Emperor to undertake scholarly work in the Imperial Study (Nan shu-fang). For the next ten years, while still nominally a slave, Fang worked in a variety of imperially-sponsored scholarly enterprises in Peking until, upon the accession of the Yung-cheng Emperor in 1723, he and his family were given complete freedom and allowed to return to their ancestral home. It is unnecessary to trace Fang's further career until his death in 1749.

Fang's "Notes on Prison Life" was almost entirely written during his year in prison. However, undoubtedly for political reasons, it was not included in the 18-*chüan* collection of his essays, the *Wang-hsi hsien-sheng wen-chi* (Collected Writings of Mr. Wang-hsi [Fang Pao]), which was published in 1746 while he was still alive. In the early nineteenth century several scholars collected hitherto unpublished writings by Fang, and in 1851 Tai Chün-heng, a follower of the T'ung-ch'eng school, brought them together in a 10-*chüan* supplemental collection published under the title, *Wang-hsi hsien-sheng wen-chi chi-wai wen* (Writings Supplemental to the Collected Writings of Mr. Wang-hsi). At the same time he republished the original collection. The "Notes on Prison Life" appears in the sixth *chüan* of the supplemental collection which, together with the first collection, is today readily available in three well known editions.[4]

---

50–51. From the year A.D. 566 or 567 we have a document recording the deliberations of officials concerning how much judicial torture should be administered to prisoners in order most effectively to extract confessions. See Etienne Balazs, *Le Traité juridique du "Souei-chou"* (Leiden, 1954), pp. 195–206. These and other such documents, however, provide only very fleeting glimpses of what went on inside prison. From none of them do we get any kind of overall picture of prison life generally.

[2] My knowledge of this document is a debt to the late Arthur Waley, who refers to it in his *Yüan Mei* (London, 1956), p. 115.

[3] See the biography by Fang Chao-ying in Arthur W. Hummel, ed., *Eminent Chinese of the Ch'ing Period (1644–1912)* (2 vols.; Washington, D.C., 1943–44), I, 235–237. This is the basis for the brief account below, supplemented, for the exact dates of Fang's imprisonment, by what he himself writes in his "Notes on Prison Life," plus the *Nien-p'u* (Chronological Biography) attached to the end of his collected writings. For the Tai Ming-shih subversion case in which Fang became involved, see also Luther Carrington Goodrich, *The Literary Inquisition of Ch'ien-lung* (Baltimore, 1935), pp. 77–79.

[4] The editions, together with the locations in their supplemental portions of the *Yü-chung tsa-chi*, are Ssu-pu ts'ung-k'an ed., 6/31a–34b; Ssu-pu pei-yao ed., 6/21b–24b; Kuo-hsüeh chi-pen ts'ung-shu ed., 6/153–156. There is only a single textual variant between the three editions, for which see note 43 below.

"Notes on Prison Life," as indicated by its title, consists, like many Chinese writings, of disconnected notes (seven of them) rather than a single unified essay. They are all quite brief, and arranged in descending order of length. In the translation in section IV below, I have given them numbers and titles which do not appear in the original. Apparently it was only after Tai Chün-heng had collected the first five notes that numbers six and seven became available; these in the Chinese original are printed in smaller type. Note 6 is actually not by Fang Pao but is an anecdote about him supplied by a contemporary, Liu Yen (died 1716; referred to in Tai's editorial comment by his *hao* as Liu Ta-shan). The seventh note is again by Fang and consists of two brief remarks, the first written after his release from prison, the second while he was still confined.

## II. THE PRISON OF THE BOARD OF PUNISHMENTS

Before taking up Fang's "Notes," which is the core of this article, I think it will be helpful if, in the present section, we try to get a picture of the physical layout of the prison of the Board of Punishments and then, in the next section, acquaint ourselves with the daily life-pattern of its prisoners. The translation will thereafter be presented in section IV, followed by a final section of comment.

For the discussion here and in section III, Note 1 of Fang's opus is particularly useful and will always be intended whenever Fang's "Notes" is cited, except for counter indication. What it says must be collated with other sources, however, almost all of them sketchy and sometimes mutually contradictory. On the official side they include the penal code of the Ch'ing dynasty,[5]

descriptions and documents having to do with Ch'ing institutions,[6] and the *Hsing-fa chih* or "Treatise on Penal Law" (abbreviated as "Legal Treatise") which comprises chapters 143–145 of the *Ch'ing shih-kao* (Draft History of the Ch'ing Dynasty).[7]

On the non-official side there are, remarkably, the eyewitness accounts of two British diplomats, Sir Harry S. Parkes and Lord Henry Brougham Loch. Both were members of the Anglo-French military force which in 1860 marched on Peking from Tientsin. In the course of the advance, the two men were captured by the Chinese, separately incarcerated in the prison of the Board of Punishments (September 18), then taken elsewhere (September 29) and finally released (October 8) shortly before the occupation of Peking by the allied forces. The account by Parkes is vivid but brief.[8] Therefore, for our purpose, it will usually be more fruitful to refer to the more detailed account by Loch.[9]

The Board of Punishments occupied an enormous walled enclosure containing a large number of lesser walled compounds, each of which in turn contained one or more one-storey buildings. The Board was located in the southern part of Peking, south of the Forbidden City (a walled complex of

---

[5] The edition used is the *Ta Ch'ing lü-li hui-t'ung hsin-tsuan* (Peking, 1873; Taipei reprint of 1964 with continuous pagination). Hereafter referred to as Code. Partial translations exist by George Staunton, *Ta Tsing Leü Lee, Being the Fundamental Laws . . . of the Penal Code of China* (London, 1810; Taipei reprint of 1966); by Gui Boulais, *Manuel du code chinois* (Shanghai, 1924); and by P. L. F. Philastre, *Le Code annamite* (2 vols.; Paris, 1876; Taipei reprint of 1967). These translations will hereafter be referred to as Staunton, Boulais, and Philastre.

[6] The *Ta Ch'ing hui-tien* (Collected Institutes of the Great Ch'ing Dynasty) and the *Ta Ch'ing hui-tien shih-li* (Items Supplemental to the Collected Institutes of the Great Ch'ing Dynasty), both in their 1899 editions as reprinted in Taipei in 1963 with continuous pagination.

[7] The edition used is the separately annotated and printed *Ch'ing shih-kao Hsing-fa chih chu-chieh* ("Legal Treatise" from the *Ch'ing Draft History* with Annotations), edited by the Legal Research Division, Bureau of Legal Affairs, Council of State (Peking, 1957). Hereafter cited as "Legal Treatise."

[8] Harry S. Parkes, article in the *North-China Herald*, no. 557 (Shanghai, March 30, 1961), p. 51. (Hereafter cited as Parkes, without page reference.) Most of it is excerpted in D. Bodde and Clarence Morris, *Law in Imperial China, Exemplified by 190 Ch'ing Dynasty Cases* (Cambridge, Mass., 1967), pp. 105–106. (This book will hereafter be cited as Bodde/Morris.)

[9] Henry Brougham Loch, *Personal Narrative of Occurrences During Lord Elgin's Second Embassy to China in 1860* (London, 3rd ed., 1900 [1st and 2nd eds., 1869 and 1870]), pp 107–122. (Hereafter cited as Loch.)

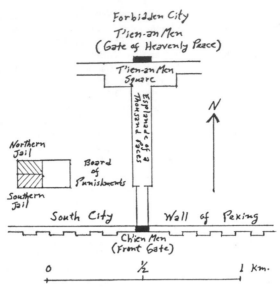

FIG. 1. Location in Peking of the Board of |Punishments and Its Prison |(Comprising Northern and Southern Jails).

imperial palaces in the center of Peking), and somewhat west of a broad north-to-south esplanade known as the Esplanade of a Thousand Paces. The latter, which evenly bisected the southern portion of Peking into east and west sectors, ran southward from the T'ien-an square (just south of T'ien-an Men or Gate of Heavenly Peace, which was the main southern entrance to the Forbidden City) to the major southern city gate of Peking itself. (See Figure 1.)

Many or most of the Board's compounds were used to house the offices and courts where cases coming to the Board from all parts of the empire were adjudicated. Other compounds, however, constituted the Board's prison, wherein were held the offenders who accompanied these cases, and from which such offenders could at any time be readily taken to the Board's courts for interrogation during adjudication of the cases. The Board's prison, *yü*, had two major subdivisions, a northern and a southern. They were known as *chien*, a word which, to distinguish it from *yü*, will be rendered here as "jail." The northern jail was a complex of

compounds occupying the northwestern corner of the Board's enclosure; the southern jail was similarly situated in its southwestern corner.[10]

For graphic evidence concerning the internal arrangements of the jails, we would first of all hope for aid from the great imperially-compiled map of Peking made during the Ch'ien-lung period (somewhere around 1750), on which even individual buildings are indicated. A photographic reproduction of this map, of which the manuscript original is in the Palace Museum in Peking, was made by the Japanese in 1940 during their occupation of the city. Unfortunately, the small scale of the reproduction, as well as the very incomplete labeling of separate buildings, prevent it from helping us even though the enclosure of the Board of Punishments as a whole is clearly indicated.[11] Thus we are compelled to rely entirely on written sources.

---

[10] See Bodde/Morris, pp. 122–123 and 129.

[11] See the *Ch'ien-lung ching-ch'eng ch'üan-t'u* (Complete Map of the Capital During the Ch'ien-lung Period; Peiping, photographic reproduction of 1940), Row 11, sects. 6–7.

A document appended to an edict of 1779, wherein is discussed the question of supplying lamp oil to prisoners (the decision was negative), mentions incidentally that the northern and southern jails had a total of eleven separate compounds or precincts (*ch'u*, lit., "localities"); how many of these precincts there were for each jail it does not say. Each precinct, the document continues, contained five wards (*wu*, lit., "rooms"), which were connected end to end with one another and apparently built in an east-west line along the northern side of the precinct's walled compound. Guards were assigned to each ward and were locked up overnight with the prisoners until morning.[12]

These data are partially confirmed, partially contradicted, and partially expanded by Fang Pao. He says not a word about the northern and southern jails and their eleven precincts, but instead states that the Board's "prison" (*yü*) consisted of five "jails" (*chien*). Four of these, which he calls the "old jails" (*lao chien*), were used, at least in theory, to confine the more serious criminals. The fifth, called by him the "modern jail" (*hsien chien*), was intended for lesser offenders. Additionally, Fang mentions "wooden houses" (*pan wu*) as being used to house either officials under detention or very light offenders. He does not indicate how many such buildings there were or whether they formed part of the "modern prison." It is evident, however, that they were distinct from the old jails, though still within the prison as a whole. Their existence is corroborated by mention in a sub-statute in the Ch'ing Code (see note 32 below).

A reasonable hypothesis is that what Fang calls a "jail" (*chien*) is actually the same as what the document of 1779 terms a "precinct" (*ch'u*). Once this assumption is granted, the conclusion naturally follows that Fang's five "jails" (i.e., precincts) were entirely limited to the particular northern or southern division (northern or southern "jail") in which he himself was staying (and we do not know which one this was). The remaining six precincts (out of the eleven mentioned in the document) would then belong to the other division or jail, whether northern or southern.

This hypothesis is strengthened by the fact that Fang's five "jails" are said by him each to consist of five wards (*shih*); we have seen that the "precincts" of the document likewise each consisted of five wards. (The fact that Fang calls them *shih* and the document calls them *wu* is unimportant. The two words are often used interchangeably and both can signify either a room or a building.) Fang's wards, furthermore—although he does not make this absolutely clear—would seem, like those of the document, to be arranged end to end along a single axis. He does not, however, say whether they were interconnected. Moreover, he describes the centermost of the five as being the living quarters of the guards. This conflicts with the document, which makes no mention of such an arrangement and says instead that the guards stayed at night in the wards of the prisoners themselves. We may perhaps reconcile the discrepancy by assuming that the central ward was a permanent headquarters for the guards, but that some of them, at least, remained at night with the prisoners in the four adjoining wards.

Lord Loch confirms the overnight sojourn of guards with prisoners, adding that at night the door of the ward was "always sealed on the outside with paper bearing the official seal."[13] However, he says nothing about there being FIVE wards in his compound. Rather, he states that on the far side of the courtyard into which he was led there was a long barn-like building (the ward where he was placed), on one side of which, in the foreground, stood some sheds used by the guards as a kitchen, and on the other a small Buddhist shrine.[14] I cannot explain this discrepancy except to suggest, lamely, that perhaps the arrangement of buildings was changed between 1779 and 1860, or perhaps not all precincts were identical in layout.

Fang Pao states further that of the five wards in his precinct, only the central guardhouse had

---

[12] *Ta Ch'ing hui-tien shih-li*, 841/14a (p. 15571 of the 1963 reprint).

[13] Loch, p. 116.

[14] Loch, pp. 108 and 111.

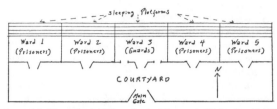

FIG. 2. Prison Precinct with Five Wards (Hypothetical Layout) (Only Guards' Ward Has Windows).

windows. He vividly describes the consequences of the resulting lack of ventilation. From Note 6 of his work we learn how, following his release, he was instrumental in getting new windows installed. A curious detail is that the bars inserted into these windows were not of iron but of wood (*mu ko*).

The official sources state that a standard feature of Chinese prisons generally was a separate section for women (*nü chien*, a women's jail).[15] Obviously, such a section must have existed somewhere in the Board's northern or southern jail or in both, but I have found no explicit reference to it.

We may summarize by saying that the prison (*yü*) of the Board of Punishments consisted of two jails (*chien*), a northern and a southern, situated respectively in the northwest and southwest corners of the Board's enormous enclosure. The two jails, in turn, were divided into a total of eleven separately enclosed precincts (*ch'u*), probably five for the one jail and six for the other, though which had the larger number we cannot say. In the five-precinct jail described by Fang Pao, four, called by him the "old jails" (*lao chien*), were intended for serious criminals; the fifth, which he terms the "modern jail" (*hsien chien*), was for lesser offenders. Each precinct consisted in turn of five ward buildings (*wu* or *shih*), connected with one another and built end to end in an east-west row along the north side of the precinct's walled enclosure. The central ward, according to Fang, was a guardhouse, flanked on either side by two other wards for prisoners. At night, however, some at least of the guards were locked up in each of the flanking wards together with the prisoners. None of the wards in the "old jails," aside from the guardhouses, had windows until, at Fang's initia-

tive following his release, some with wooden bars were installed. External to the "old jails" but somewhere within the prison as a whole existed what Fang calls "wooden houses" (*pan wu*), intended for special categories of favored prisoners. Likewise, although this is not explicitly stated, the prison must have included one or more separate wards or jails for women (*nü chien*).

III. THE PRISONERS OF THE BOARD OF PUNISHMENTS

A complex review system automatically provided that all more serious legal cases originating in districts and departments throughout the empire were, after provisional judgment at that level, sent to the provincial courts for review and then again to the Board of Punishments in Peking for final decision; if the cases called for capital punishment, they were then again sent from the Board to the Emperor for his ratification. Persons involved in these cases were regularly brought with them from the local districts to the provincial courts, and then (though possibly less regularly owing to the longer distances usually involved) from the provincial courts to Peking, where they were housed in the Board's prison. Many other cases came to the Board directly from lower administrative levels in Peking itself, together with numerous prisoners from lower-level Peking jails.[16]

The spectrum of prisoners was wide, ranging from scholar-officials like Fang Pao to illiterates. Besides major offenders, it could and often did include persons only secondarily implicated, as well as witnesses and the protagonists in lawsuits. (Confirmation of these striking facts is supplied by

[15] See, for example, the "Legal Treatise," p. 119.

[16] On these jails, see Fang Pao's Note 1 and footnote 29 below. On the appellate system, see Bodde/Morris, pp. 113–122.

Fang Pao in his Note 1.) This tendency to imprison anyone even remotely involved in a case reflects the official point of view that legal involvement is *ipso facto* a culpable matter, to be avoided whenever possible. It also had the practical convenience, for the government, of making anyone needed at a trial instantly available. Of course, upon the conclusion of a case, all persons arrested on its account but found not guilty were released.

Theoretically, as we have seen, major and lesser offenders were to be varyingly housed in the "old jails," the "modern jail," or the "wooden houses." Very light offenders, witnesses, and so on, were furthermore legally permitted, if they had the necessary funds, to obtain a surety bond (*pao*) allowing them, until the adjudication of their case, to live outside the prison in the custody of a local constable (*ti pao*).[17] Such was the theory, but Fang Pao insists that a tremendous gap existed between reality and theory on these as well as other matters.

A basic principle is that imprisonment *per se* was not recognized as a formal punishment in imperial China. It served merely to keep everyone involved in a case under detention until final adjudication. Nevertheless, the appellate system often meant prolonged incarceration at successive judicial levels before ultimate disposition of a case. Even at the highest level of the Board of Punishments, the waiting period might be considerable. Fang Pao (in his Note 7) tells of one relatively minor case which dragged on for two years in Peking before settlement. In capital cases, moreover, only very serious offenders were sentenced to immediate execution. Many others received sentences calling for execution "after the assizes." Such a judgment meant further judicial review at the autumn assizes held annually in Peking, at which time most such sentences were commuted from death to life exile. A small minority, however, were then placed in a kind of judicial limbo which sometimes kept their recipients in jail for as long as

ten years before a final decision between execution and (more probably) exile was reached.[18]

Our sources make no mention of the existence of single prisoner cells in the Board's prison. Fang Pao states that in what he calls a jail (i.e., a precinct) there were always more than two hundred prisoners. If we accept his further statement that each such jail or precinct consisted of four wards for prisoners and a fifth for the guards, this would mean a figure of fifty or more prisoners in each ward. This figure agrees closely with that given by Loch, who states (p. 113) that in his ward there were forty-eight prisoners. Harry Parkes, however, gives the number for his ward as seventy-three. Accepting Fang's estimate of "more than two hundred" for a single precinct, and multiplying this by the total number of precincts (eleven), we arrive at an overall estimate of 2,200 prisoners as a minimum for the entire prison, with the strong probability that the actual figure was at least 2,500 and may have been considerably higher.

The incarceration of prisoners in large groups rather than in single or dual confinement is a good example of Chinese family- and group-mindedness as against Western individual-mindedness. The Chinese system certainly has the very real psychological advantage that it allows the sharing of misery. An important penological principle in the prisons of the Chinese People's Republic today is the therapeutic value of intensive discussion sessions held among prison cellmates (in groups of half a dozen or so, in contrast to the much larger and completely unstructured groups of the past.)[19]

Occupants of the Board's prison slept crowded together on a low wooden bench which extended about eight feet out from one wall of the ward, sloping slightly toward this wall. Chains suspended from overhead beams were used to confine serious criminals by passing the short chain connecting their handcuffs through a link of the large hanging chain.[20] Of the forty-eight prisoners in

---

[17] See Code, p. 3517. Summarized in Philastre, II, 630, but not included in Staunton or Boulais.

[18] For more details on this complex system, see note 40 below.

[19] A unique eyewitness account of this group-therapy in a modern Chinese prison is by Allyn and Adele Rickett, *Prisoners of Liberation* (New York, 1957).

[20] See Parkes and Loch, p. 108. Fang confirms the

Loch's ward, twenty including himself were chained. About fifteen were nominally in chains but had been imprisoned so long that they were no longer obliged to wear them, and the remaining thirteen were unchained.[21] According to statute, the number of chains to be worn by each chained prisoner differed according to the seriousness of his offense.[22]

The daily regimen of the prisoners is described by Loch (as of September, when he was confined).[23] At sunrise the ward door was opened and the unchained prisoners were allowed to go into the courtyard for exercise; fifteen minutes or half an hour later it was the turn of the chained prisoners to be released from chains and allowed out also. Around seven a.m. the unchained prisoners were brought back to the ward for breakfast, followed around eight a.m. by the chained prisoners. Both groups were later again allowed into the yard and remained there until dinner around three or four o'clock in the afternoon. Following this, they were once more released until the final evening lockup, which took place a little after sunset.

The sources differ somewhat concerning the government's role in feeding its prisoners. A statute in the Ch'ing Code provides punishment for any prison authority neglecting to furnish food to those prisoners not having a family or relatives,

i.e., to prisoners who lack the means to buy food themselves; the implication is clear that prisoners who DO have such means are expected to buy their own food.[24] A sub-statute immediately following, however, states that all prisoners aged seventy or over, fifteen or under, or who are infirm, are to be given one Chinese pint (*sheng*) of grain daily; other ordinary prisoners who do not fall into these categories are to receive only 0.83 of a pint.[25]

When a sub-statute contradicts a statute, the sub-statute, being of later enactment, normally assumes precedence. That this is true of the present sub-statute is indicated by Parkes and by Loch (p. 113), both of whom state that the government was obligated to provide two bowls of millet daily to each prisoner, but that not all prisoners actually ate the millet. Some prisoners, according to the Englishmen (presumably prisoners with private means), received better than ordinary food. Such special food did not come from the government but from one or two well-to-do prison inmates who voluntarily undertook the expense of supplying it in return for a reduction of their sentence. Loch adds that there were two such special kinds of food in addition to the basic government millet ration. Such arrangements must have been made entirely on an *ad hoc* basis because no sanction for them can be found in the Code.

Finally, the Code tells us that prisoners were allowed visits from relatives twice monthly, but that this privilege was denied to robbers. A later sub-statute of 1821 imposes serious limitations by permitting visits only for prisoners whose cases have already been adjudicated and denying them to others whose cases are still undecided.[26]

This background on the physical arrangements and daily life of the Board's prison will, I hope, give more meaning to Fang Pao's "Notes on Prison Life" which follows. In this translation,

---

crowding of the prisoners, but also says of those who were indigent that in winter they "slept on the ground" (*hsi ti erh wo*). *Ti* 'ground' is an ambiguous word which conceivably could refer to the wooden bench as well as to the floor itself. Or should we believe that in Fang's time poor prisoners were actually not allowed to sleep on the raised bench? In itself, this hypothesis is quite plausible. However, it involves the difficulty that all chained prisoners, except during periods when they were unchained, necessarily had to remain below the suspended chains, concerning which we are told only that they were located above the sleeping bench.

[21] Loch, p. 113.
[22] Code, p. 3529; untranslated in Staunton, Boulais or Philastre.
[23] Loch, pp. 110–111 and 113–114. Very probably this regimen was not the same for all seasons. In winter, for example, it is unlikely that prisoners would spend anywhere near as much time in the outside courtyard as is here indicated for September.

[24] See Code, p. 3547; Staunton, no. 301; Boulais, no. 1678; Philastre, II, 648. Boulais, in a comment, notes the same implication.
[25] Code, p. 3550; summarized in Philastre, II, 650–651.
[26] Code, pp. 3551–52 (the first sub-statute) and 3553–54 (sub-statute of 1821); Philastre, II, 649–650 and (in summary only) 650.

footnotes are omitted for matters that have already been covered in this and the preceding section.

## IV. TRANSLATION OF FANG PAO'S "NOTES ON PRISON LIFE"

### 1. Prison Hygiene

In the third month of the fifty-first year of K'ang-hsi [April 6–May 5, 1712], when I was in the prison of the Board of Punishments, I daily saw three or four dead persons taken out through the outlet channel.[27] There was a certain Mr. Tu, prefect from Hung-tung,[28] who engaged me in conversation, saying: "It is contagion that does this. At present, with the equable weather, there are relatively few who die, but in past years there have been as many as ten or more daily."

I asked the reason and Mr. Tu said: "Diseases are so easily transmitted that persons exposed to them, even if they are relatives, don't dare to sleep together. The prison consists of four 'old jails' (lao chien), each having five wards. The middle of these wards, occupied by the guards, has windows on the front side to provide light, and ports under the eaves at the far ends to allow ventilation. But the flanking four wards don't have any, even though there are always more than two hundred prisoners under detention. Every evening, when the locks are closed, all the urine and excrement are left inside to mix their vapors with the food and drink. And with destitute prisoners sleeping on the floor during the height of winter, there are few who don't fall ill when the spring vapors begin to stir. According to the prison's established procedure, locks are opened only at dawn. This means that throughout the night living persons and those who have died sleep next to each other head to head and foot to foot,

without any means of turning away. This is why so many persons suffer contagion.

"Another remarkable thing is that the great robbers who have committed repeated acts of violence or the serious criminals guilty of murder have such strong constitutions that hardly one or two in ten contract disease. Or if they do, they eventually recover. The people who DO die in batches are all light offenders, persons secondarily implicated, or witnesses to whom the law doesn't apply at all."

I said: "The capital has its municipal prison and its five gendarmerie district jails.[29] Why then are so many prisoners held by the Board of Punishments?"

Mr. Tu replied: "With the intensification of litigation in recent years, the authorities wouldn't dare to pass judgment solely at the municipal or the district level. Also, all persons undergoing search, seizure, detention and interrogation by the commandant of gendarmerie are always sent up to the Board of Punishments.[30] And even there, those directors and assistant directors of the Board's fourteen regional departments[31] who are out to get something, as well as its court clerks, prison officials, and guards, all stand to profit from having a lot of prisoners.

"This means that any person the least bit implicated in a case must by various devices be dragged into it, and once he has entered prison, he must, irrespective of guilt or innocence, be fettered hand and foot and put in one of the old jails. After being placed under unendurable sufferings, he is led to

---

[27] Tou is an underground passage, a cavern, an opening, a communication channel, a canal, etc. I presume that it here refers to some kind of exit from the prison precinct through which garbage, trash and sewage were taken away.

[28] Hung-tung is a hsien on the Fen river in southern Shansi. Mr. Tu was, of course, like the author, an offender who had been brought to Peking from the provinces.

[29] For policing purposes, Peking was divided into five districts or "cities" (ch'eng), each under the jurisdiction of a censor who exercised police powers.

[30] These two sentences cover all types of cases submitted to the Board of Punishments from Peking. The first has reference to lawsuits, the second to criminal cases.

[31] Initially, the core of the Board of Punishments consisted of thirteen regional supervisory departments (ssu) named after various provinces (Department of Shantung, etc.), plus a fourteenth ssu dealing with arrests. Shortly after 1723, however, the thirteen regional departments were increased to seventeen, making, with that on arrests, eighteen departments. See the "Legal Treatise" (note 7 above), p. 87, and Bodde/Morris (note 8 above), pp. 124–128.

get a surety bond (*pao*) for himself so that he may leave [the prison] and live outside. Officials and clerks calculate how much they may trim from such a man's family property, and then they take their cut accordingly. In this way prisoners of middle or upper families exhaust their entire fortunes to get a surety bond [allowing them to live outside the prison]. Those next to them in wealth try to be freed from their fetters and to live in the 'wooden houses' outside the jails [but still inside the prison enclosure].[32] For this they still have to spend several tens of taels.[33] It is the very poor who, having no one to call upon, have to remain under fetters without the least clemency so that they can be a warning to others.

"Within the same group of prisoners it sometimes happens that really serious criminals are nevertheless released from prison and stay outside, while lighter offenders and those who are innocent [remain there to] suffer its poisons and accumulate sorrow and resentment. Their ordinary standards of sleeping and eating are disregarded, and should they fall ill, no doctor or medicine is provided. This is why they so often meet their death.

"I have humbly seen that the 'life-loving virtue' of the Sage on High is identical with that of previous sages,[34] so that whenever he deals with a penal sentence, he always seeks for life out of death.[35] And yet the guiltless come to such an extremity! Suppose a man of true humanity (*jen*), a superior man (*chün tzu*), acting in support of the splendid words of the Emperor, were—aside from serious criminals condemned to death or deportation—to set up a separate place of detention for light offenders, persons secondarily implicated, and those whose suits have not yet been concluded. Suppose further that the hands and feet of such persons were to be left unfettered. The lives thus preserved may be imagined!"

Someone else said: "Formerly the prison had five wards called the 'modern jail' (*hsien chien*), which were occupied by persons whose suits had not yet been concluded. If the old documents [concerning the use of these wards] were brought out, it might be possible to make some slight additions to them."[36]

Mr. Tu replied: "Under the Emperor's extended kindness, all officials are to be housed in the wooden houses. Yet today the poor are kept in the old jails, while some at least of the major robbers live in the wooden houses. Here is where minute investigation is called for! The really good thing would be to set up an entirely separate building as a way of 'eradicating the root and stopping up the source.'"[37]

The venerable Mr. Chu my master, who was one of my fellow prisoners, together with a certain Buddhist monk from T'ung-kuan who was also in prison,[38] both contracted disease from which they died; neither of them had deserved heavy punishment. Or again, after a certain person had accused

---

[32] These "wooden houses" (*pan wu*) have been discussed in sect. II above. Their existence is confirmed by a sub-statute in the Code stating that prison guards were forbidden to charge rent to prisoners who occupied the *pan p'eng* or "wooden sheds"—undoubtedly a variant term for the same buildings. See Code, pp. 3552–53 (untranslated in Staunton, Boulais or Philastre). It is possible that Fang's designation, *pan wu*, was influenced by the classical term *pan shih* 'wooden hut' which occurs in the *Book of Odes*, Ode 128, where a lady, lamenting the absence of her husband on a military expedition, states that he has to stay in such a habitation while in the wilds.

[33] The term used here and below is *chin*, lit., "gold," but in this context it signifies a tael (one ounce of silver).

[34] "Sage on High" is a reference to the existing, i.e., the K'ang-hsi, Emperor. "Life-loving virtue" (*hao sheng chih te*) is a phrase from the *Book of History*, Pt. II, bk. 2 (tr. James Legge, *The Chinese Classics*, Hong Kong reprint of 1960–61, III, 59). There, as here, it occurs in a penal context, being used to describe the sage-ruler Shun, who is said to have pardoned inadvertent crimes, dealt lightly with doubtful crimes, and preferred to act irregularly rather than put to death an innocent person.

[35] I.e., the Emperor tries, whenever possible, to lighten the death sentences of condemned criminals. As is well known, all death sentences, save those of bandits and rebels, had to be ratified by the Emperor before they could be carried out.

[36] I.e., to modify their provisions so as to include light offenders, witnesses, etc., among the occupants of the "modern jail."

[37] A phrase from the *Tso chuan*, fourteenth year of Duke Chao, tr. Legge, *Chinese Classics*, V, 656.

[38] T'ung-kuan is a hsien some forty or more miles north of Sian in Shensi. I am unable to identify Mr. Chu, but Fang's description of him sounds as if he were an older associate of Fang, imprisoned at the same time because of involvement in the same affair.

his son of being unfilial, his neighbors were brought [as witnesses] under fetters into one of the old jails, where they wailed and cried until dawn. I was moved by all this and made extensive inquiry about the things Mr. Tu had said. Finding them in agreement with what people in general say, I have written them down.

## 2. Executions and Torture

Whenever there are to be executions, the executioners first wait outside the gate [of the prison precinct] and send their gang in to look around for money—a procedure called "chiselling and netting" (ssu lo). If those [about to be executed] are rich, their relatives are the ones approached [for money], but if they are poor they themselves are talked to face to face. Persons who are to undergo the highest of all penalties [death by slicing] are told: "If you go along with us, we will stab you in the heart first. If you don't, we will completely dismember your four limbs while leaving the heart still alive." Persons who are to undergo strangulation are told: "If you go along with us, we will cut your breath off at the first twisting. If you don't, only by applying a different instrument at the third twisting will you get to die."[39] Even in decapitation cases, in which such demands are impossible [because the head is cut off in one blow], one still has to pay ransom for one's head [in order to assure its recovery for burial with the body]. Thus it is that the rich offer bribes of several tens or hundreds of taels, and the poor, likewise, strip themselves of clothing and personal belongings. People having absolutely nothing at all are dealt with in the manner that has been stated.

Similar behavior characterizes the men who tie up [prisoners for transportation to the execution ground]. If, when they tie somebody up, that person doesn't go along with what they want, the first thing they do is to break his flesh and bones.

At the annual great executions, when fourteen or thirteen persons have been checked off [for death] and [a corresponding] sixteen or seventeen have been held over, they are all of them tied up and sent to the western marketplace to await their fate.[40] Those injured by the bindings, even if lucky enough to be among the persons held over, suffer the effects for several months before recovering. Or sometime in the end they acquire a permanent infirmity.

Once I asked an old employee: "Those whom you execute or tie up are no enemies of yours. Whatever they have you are going to get. So if they really have nothing at all, wouldn't it be humane,[41] at this final moment, to show them a little kindness?"

He replied: "Law (fa) has been established to warn others [by punishing the criminal] and to

---

[39] The Chinese punishment of strangulation was not hanging but the garrotte, that is, it was carried out by twisting a rope ever tighter around the neck of the criminal. On this and the two other standard death penalties here mentioned (death by slicing, given only for a few most heinous crimes, and decapitation, regarded as a more serious punishment than strangulation), see Bodde/Morris, pp. 91–95.

[40] The western marketplace (hsi shih), also known as the vegetable market (ts'ai shih), was the place for public executions in Peking and was located in the western part of the so-called "Chinese City," south of the main city. It is described by L. C. Arlington and William Lewisohn, In Search of Old Peking (Peiping, 1935), pp. 217–218.

Persons whose sentences called for execution "after the assizes" were, at these assizes, which were held annually at Peking in the autumn (see text above note 18), classified under one of several categories, such as "worthy of compassion," "deferred execution," and so on (see note 50 below). All but one such category resulted in immediate or ultimate commutation of the death penalty to exile. The only category leading toward actual execution was that known as "circumstances deserving of capital punishment." Even then, however, a final ceremony existed whereby some of the people so classified succeeded in escaping death. On this occasion the Emperor was presented with a list of names belonging to this category, and at seeming random he touched or checked some of them with his imperial brush but did not touch others. The persons whose names were thus checked off were forthwith executed; the others had to endure the same ceremony several times—most of them for ten consecutive years. If, at the end of this protracted period, their names had still escaped the brush, they then had their death sentence commuted to exile. This checking ceremony is what Fang is here referring to when, taking a hypothetical group of thirty, he says that fourteen or thirteen of them are checked off for death and the remainder (sixteen or seventeen respectively) are held over until the next year. For an account of the whole complex assizes procedure, see Bodde/Morris, pp. 134–143.

[41] Jen shu, lit., "a humane device." The phrase comes from the Mencius, Ia, 7, viii.

caution posterity. If we didn't act like this, people would get the idea that they deserve to have it easy."[42]

The same attitude is found among those who carry out the judicial torture of prisoners. Among three men who, with me, underwent judicial interrogation with the stick, one gave [the interrogator only] thirty taels;[43] his injuries reached as far as his bones and the harmful effects lasted for a month. The second man doubled this amount; his injuries were only to the flesh and by the end of twenty days he had recovered. The third man gave six times as much and by that very evening he was walking normally.

Someone asked about this, saying: "Criminals are unequal in what they have or don't have. Since you are going to get something from ALL of them, why do you still have to grade [your punishments] according to how much you will get?" The reply was: "If we didn't make such gradations, who among them would give much?"

How true the saying of Mencius: "One can't but be careful about the choice of a profession!"[44]

*3. Changes in Sentence*

There was an old employee in the Board of Punishments who hid a false seal in his house, and when documents went down [from the Board] to the provinces, he often secretly altered them, adding or deleting important phraseology which the recipients failed to recognize. However, he did not dare do the same with documents sent up [by the Board] for attention above or transferred by it to other boards.

According to government regulations, major robbers who haven't killed anybody, or other criminals who have jointly plotted to kill somebody—with the exception of the one or two principal plotters [among the latter] who receive immediate execution—are all, by passing through the autumn assizes, to have their sentences reduced one degree [from death] to exile.[45] When, however, there are some sentences calling for immediate execution, the executioners then wait in advance [for the condemned] outside the [prison precinct] gate where, upon the issuance of orders, they instantly bind them up for taking away.

There was a certain pair of brothers who, because of having manipulated the public granary, should, according to law, have undergone immediate execution.[46] Their sentence had in fact been thus drawn up when a certain employee said to them: "Give me a thousand taels and I'll give you life." On being asked how this could be done, he continued: "There's no difficulty. We'll draw up another document and, without changing the sentence itself, will exchange your names in it for those of two companionless and kinless persons

---

[42] *Yu hsing hsin*, lit., "have hearts [expecting] undeserved good fortune."

[43] This is the reading shared by the Ssu-pu ts'ung-k'an and the Kuo-hsüeh chi-pen ts'ung-shu editions, and therefore is probably correct. The Ssu-pu pei-yao edition reads "twenty taels," which is the only variant reading between the three editions in the entire text.

[44] See the *Mencius*, IIa, 7, where Mencius points out that though the arrow maker is fundamentally just as humane as the armor maker, his profession causes him to be concerned lest the arrows he makes fail to inflict injuries, whereas the armor maker's concern is lest the armor he makes fails to protect people against such injuries.

[45] Fang is wrong in saying that the principal plotters in a case of joint premeditated homicide suffer immediate execution. The relevant statute states that the ideological inspirer of premeditated homicide is to suffer decapitation after the assizes, and that other persons who jointly participate in the physical deed are to be sentenced to strangulation after the assizes. Thus both categories of offenders, contrary to Fang's statement, pass through the assizes. See Code, p. 2335; Staunton, no. 282; Boulais, no. 1211; Philastre, II, 164. The punishment for a robber who, without use of violence, steals over 120 taels of silver, is strangulation after the assizes. See Code, pp. 2069–71; Staunton, no. 269; Boulais, no. 1119; Philastre, II, 77.

[46] "Manipulated the public granary" is a rendition of *pa-ch'ih kung-ts'ang*. I have been unable to find a statute precisely covering this offense and punishment. The nearest approach seems to be a provision in the Code, pp. 1131–32 (untranslated in Staunton, Boulais or Philastre), dealing with ex-granary employees who, by virtue of their former positions, deceive and exercise restraints (*pa-ch'ih*) upon persons coming to the granary for grain, thereby extorting money from them. The penalties vary according to the extortion, but the highest, that for extorting over 120 taels, is strangulation after the assizes and not, as stated by Fang, immediate execution.

who are now listed at the end of the case.[47] When the time comes to seal the document and submit it to the throne [for imperial ratification], we'll secretly change it in this way and that will be it."

His fellow employee said: "One may deceive the dead [those who will be brought to death in this way] but one can't deceive the judges [those who have judged the case]. Should the latter [upon discovery of the change] submit a second request to the throne [for nullification of the altered judgment], there would certainly be no way of life left to us."[48]

The first employee laughingly said: "While such a second request would indeed leave us no way of life, it would also mean dismissal for each of the judges.[49] They, however, can't possibly exchange their own official positions for the lives of two men. Thus, after all, the road to death won't be ours."

In the end, the act was carried out. The two men who had been listed at the end of the case suffered immediate execution, while those in charge [i.e., the judges], their mouths gaping and tongues stiff with fear, never dared to investigate.

During my stay in prison, certain prisoners could still be seen to whom everybody pointed, saying: "They are the ones who exchanged their heads with so-and-so." One evening a certain employee suddenly died, and everyone maintained that his punishment had come to him from Hades.

### 4. Freeing of the Guilty

All persons guilty of homicide, if their sentences state that they have acted without premeditation or immediate intent, are, as a result of passing through the autumn assizes, placed in the category of "doubtful on grounds of compassion," and

thereby escape death.[50] Officials use such circumstances to play tricks with the law.

There was a certain Kuo the Fourth[51] who had committed a total of four homicides and yet, by being placed in the category of "doubtful on grounds of compassion," had had his sentence reduced by one degree [from death to exile]. Later he encountered an imperial amnesty, as a result of which he was soon to be released. Together with his [prison] companions, he then nightly drank and sang until dawn. Upon being asked by somebody about his past affairs, he described them each minutely, in the highest of spirits, as if boasting of what he had done.

Depraved indeed are those evil officials whose selling of sentences is endured without reprimand.[52] Thus is the Way (Tao) brought into obscurity.[53] Yet even good officials often regard the pulling of a man from death as a meritorious act, without looking into the facts. How profoundly do they too bring injustice upon the people!

---

[47] These persons were presumably lesser figures sentenced to minor punishment, but the exchanging of their names with those of the two brothers would of course mean an exchange of penalties as well. Furthermore, the fact that they had no relatives would mean that nobody would protest their execution.

[48] I.e., the employees would be executed if the exchange of names were to be reported to the throne in a second memorial.

[49] They would be held negligent for having allowed the transfer to happen.

[50] Fang has here confused two of the categories used to classify offenders at the autumn assizes (see note 40 above). The category of which he speaks (also known as "worthy of compassion") applies to persons guilty of capital crimes who are aged, minors, or disabled. The category which he should properly have cited, because it applies to persons who have committed homicide without premeditation or immediate intent, is called "deferred execution" (see note 55 below).

[51] Kuo Ssu, a name suggesting an ordinary and very possibly an illiterate person.

[52] *Yü yü*, "to sell a sentence," comes from the *Tso chuan*, fourteenth year of Duke Chao, tr. Legge, *Chinese Classics*, V, 656. The term is used here by Fang very appropriately because the text in which it originally occurs describes a lawsuit over land between two nobles, resulting in bribery of the judge by the guilty party, the judge's rendering of an adverse decision against the rightful party, and the latter's killing both of the judge and the guilty party. A famous statesman, brother of the murdered judge, then stepped into the case, stating that his brother had "sold a sentence" (*yü yü*) and that all three parties were equally guilty. He ordered the judge's murderer to be executed, but also punished the dead judge and the other dead noble by having their corpses put on public display in the marketplace.

[53] The phrase used here, *tao chih pu ming*, lit., "non-illumination of the Tao," comes from the *Docrine of the Mean*, sect. 4.

*5. Long–term Prisoners*

There is a great surplus of villains who have long been in prison and get to be hand-in-glove with the jailers. A certain Li of Shan-yin[54] had been imprisoned for homicide. Every year he handed out several hundred taels until, in the forty-eighth year of K'ang-hsi [1709], he was released because of an amnesty. Several months then passed, during which he had nothing to occupy himself with, so that when a fellow villager of his killed somebody, he took the crime upon his own head. The point here is that, according to the Code, unintentional homicide always entails a lengthy detention in prison, without, in the end, leading to the death penalty.[55]

In the fifty-first year [1712], again helped by an amnesty, he had his sentence reduced by one degree to military exile.[56] With a groan he exclaimed: "Now I'll never be able to come back here again!" According to established precedent, persons who are to be sent [from Peking] into military exile are, until this happens, transferred to and detained in [the prison of] the Shun-t'ien prefecture.[57] It being then winter, however, when deportations were suspended, Li drew up a petition begging to remain where he was in the

---

[54] There were two Shan-yin hsien in Ch'ing times, one at the city of Ta-t'ung, Shansi, the other at the city of Shao-hsing, Chekiang.

[55] "Lengthy detention" is somewhat misleading. Cases of unintentional homicide, such as killing by mischance or through roughhousing, were, at the autumn assizes, placed in the category of "deferred execution" (see note 50 above), which means that their nominal death sentence was then usually reduced to less than death. In some difficult cases, however, a final decision was delayed until the assizes three years later, when a reduction of penalty was almost always given. See D. Bodde, "Age, Youth, and Infirmity in the Law of Ch'ing China," sect. 5 (to appear in a symposium volume on premodern Chinese law to be edited by Jerome A. Cohen), correcting the figure of two years erroneously given in Bodde/Morris, p. 138.

[56] *Che jung*. The more precise term is *ch'ung chün*, lit., "to fill the army," on which see Bodde/Morris, pp. 87–91.

[57] The Shun-t'ien prefecture included metropolitan Peking as well as several surrounding districts. It had its own prison separate from the Peking municipal prison and the gendarmerie jails mentioned in Note 1 above.

---

[Board's] prison while awaiting his spring deportation. Only after his request had two or three times been denied did he sadly leave [for the Shun-t'ien prison].[58]

*6. Additional Note by Liu Yen (died 1716) on Fang Pao's Humanitarianism*

When Fang Pao was in prison, it occurred to him that if only the old jails had a window in each wall, this would permit a slight freshening of air. He accordingly had a mason calculate the labor costs. A fellow prisoner said to him: "Those staying in the old jails are mostly 'live people' [they are not guilty of capital crimes], whereas the two of us are 'dead people' [we are thus guilty]. How then can anybody help but laugh when he hears us worrying about the stench from the 'live people'?"

Later, upon [Fang Pao's] release from prison, he was sent in less than twenty days by imperial proclamation to [work in] the Imperial Study (Nan shu-fang), where in a few days he earned seventy taels. [Some of this he sent to] Mr. Kung Meng-hsiung, a second class secretary in the Board of Punishments, who accordingly assumed responsibility [for constructing the windows].[59] A warden of the prison objected, however, and brought a complaint before the Board's Directorate,[60] saying: "If, there being holes in the walls, big robbers and major criminals should escape, who is going to take the blame?"

Mr. Kung replied: "With wooden bars in the windows, how can the prisoners escape?" He then prepared a written statement assuming sole blame for anything that might happen. Thus it was that

---

[58] This result does not support Fang's apparent intent in this Note to show that long-term prisoners enjoyed special privileges. It does indicate (as does Note 4) how important imperial amnesties sometimes were in changing the course of punishment.

[59] I have been unable to obtain further information about Kung Meng-hsiung.

[60] *Liu t'ang*, lit., "six halls," but here referring to the six men who belonged to the "hall" (*t'ang*) or Directorate of the Board of Punishments, which was the highest body of that organ. The Directorate included one Chinese and one Manchu president and two Chinese and two Manchu vice-presidents. See Bodde/Morris, p. 124.

the windows were made. There is nothing surprising in this as far as Fang Pao is concerned, but Mr. Kung's act of rightness should not be forgotten.

### 7. *Two Further Remarks by Fang Pao*
#### *First Remark*[61]

Subsequently, when Mr. Chang of Han-ch'eng again became president of the Board of Punishments and was then succeeded by Mr. Li of Ching-hai, these abuses were all wiped out.[62] Thus when it again happened that an official document was altered and sent under a false seal to Kiangsi province, Mr. Chang drafted the document of annulment with his own hand, and investigation caused a correspondence clerk to admit guilt. Orders were given to prepare a memorial [of impeachment], and the very next day it was ready to be sent up when a departmental director[63] made a request, saying: "According to rule, a government underling while awaiting impeachment should be sent for detention to [one of] the five gendarmerie district jails." Mr. Chang acquiesced, and that very night the underling escaped [from

the new jail to which he had been sent]. The point here is that, should a criminal escape before his punishment has been determined, the penalty incurred by [the heads of] a district jail for allowing this to happen is very light, whereas what they get [in bribes from the prisoner] exceeds all expectations. Therefore they gladly act thus and accept the resulting penalty.

#### *Second Remark*[64]

On another occasion, among prisoners newly arrived [at the Board prison] for adjudication, there was one who had ground down cash coins around their rims so as to collect their metal filings.[65] Though the case might have been decided immediately, it was allowed to drag on for two years, during which time more than seventy secondarily implicated persons and witnesses were pulled into it, and over ten departmental officials successively conducted the prosecution. The same officials would take it in hand and then stop midway, each time bewailing the deceit and depravity of the human mind. Painful it is to see how judicial administrators, despite all their intelligence and display of integrity (*chung*) and love (*ai*), are still incapable of saving the people from oppression.

### V. COMMENTS ON FANG PAO'S "NOTES ON PRISON LIFE"

This unusual text provokes many questions. The central one, that of its reliability, will be discussed presently.

Despite the harrowing conditions under which the work was written, it is composed in a simple and limpid literary Chinese, well studded with

---

[61] This was written after Fang Pao's release from prison early in 1713, and has reference to events following his release.

[62] Han-ch'eng is on the west bank of the Yellow river in Shensi, not far above the point where the river makes its sharp turn toward the sea. Ching-hai is not far southwest of Tientsin. It is possible to identify both men. Mr. Chang of Han-ch'eng is Chang T'ing-shu (died 1729), who had been president of the Board of Punishments in 1709, was removed in 1710 because he commuted sentences on his own authority, again became president in 1713, but in 1723 was degraded five degrees in rank for deliberately giving a criminal too light a sentence. Mr. Li of Ching-hai is Li T'ing-yi (1669–1732), who succeeded Chang as president of the Board of Punishments in 1723, then suggested such reforms as differentiating between the inner and outer quarters of the prison for the respective housing of serious and light offenders, was deprived of his rank because of two judicial errors, but was then allowed to continue in his position and had his rank as president of the Board of Punishments shortly restored. See the biographies of the two men in Hummel, ed., *Eminent Chinese* (see note 3 above), pp. 54 and 490 respectively.

[63] A director of one of the Board's supervisory departments, on which see note 31 above.

[64] This episode presumably belongs to the period when Fang Pao was still in prison.

[65] These were the small copper coins with square holes, of which approximately one thousand, strung together on strings, constituted one tael (ounce) of silver. One wonders how many such cash the offender had to grind down in order to get a tael's worth of money. The crime, in a slightly varied form (grinding off one side of the coin instead of the edges), is a very ancient one, of which complaint was already being made in 120 B.C. See Nancy Lee Swann, tr. and ed., *Food and Money in Ancient China, The Earliest Economic History of China to A.D. 25* (Princeton, New Jersey, 1950), p. 268.

examples of the author's erudition. Classical allusions pop up even in the context of decidedly "unclassical" situations.[66] One wonders, in fact, whether the text's impact might not have been stronger if it had been presented in a less polished medium. The dialogues, in particular, probably lose considerable pungency through transfer from their original colloquial into literary Chinese.

Certain literary conventions are apparent. In Note 1, for example, Fang Pao makes a fellow prisoner, the former prefect Mr. Tu, his spokesman for describing the physical conditions of prison life. In so doing, he has Mr. Tu inform him—the author—of facts which must surely already have been known to him, and which, therefore, are obviously really intended for the reader. For example, it would be needless for Mr. Tu to tell Fang himself that the prison wards had no windows or that their doors were locked from evening until dawn. Granted the literary intent of these and one or two similar remarks, however, there is no reason at all to doubt the essential validity of Mr. Tu's statements as a whole. Other conventions, important for evaluating Fang's general reliability, will be discussed later.

Incidental to Fang's central indictment of prison conditions are interesting bits of prison information. Several have already been discussed in sections II and III. Another concerns a question to which we have no precise answer: how many of the offenders whose sentences called for execution "after the assizes" succeeded, as a result of the judicial review made at the autumn assizes, in gaining commutation to a lower punishment? Among the several categories under which offenders were classified at the assizes, Fang comments meaningfully about the sole one leading toward possible execution: that entitled "circumstances deserving of capital punishment." Out of every thirty persons placed in this category, he says (Note 2), only thirteen or fourteen (forty-three to forty-seven per cent) were actually checked off for execution. Unfortunately, Fang fails to indicate how many in all were thus classified under "circumstances deserving of capital

punishment," as against the other (almost certainly larger) categories leading to commutation of the death sentence. Even so, however, his figures, if we can accept them literally, tend to confirm the opinion of the noted jurist Shen Chia-pen who, in 1907, stated concerning ALL persons who passed through the autumn assizes: "Those who were really marked off for execution every year were no more than ten per cent of the total."[67]

We come now to the vital question of reliability. First of all, it must be admitted that Fang Pao was a very indifferent jurist. He incorrectly lists immediate execution as the statutory punishment for the principal plotters in cases of joint premeditated homicide. He attributes to two brothers a crime—manipulating the public granary—which seems to be non-existent in the Code, at least with the punishment he gives it. He confuses two of the categories used to classify offenders at the autumn assizes. He asserts that unintentional homicide ALWAYS entails lengthy detention in prison—an inexact and misleading statement.[68] In short, he displays about as much—or as little—knowledge of the law as might be expected from an official in a society which had no recognized legal profession. For that matter, many administrators in our own highly legal society would probably not do a great deal better.

Much more serious is what I believe to be a matter of stylistic convention. In his very first sentence, Fang tells us that while in prison he "daily" saw three or four bodies of persons who had died taken away. Assuming an even balance in other respects between inflow and outflow of prisoners, Fang's figures would mean the entire depopulation of his own ward of fifty odd within two to three weeks, and a similar fate for his entire precinct of "more than two hundred" within two to less than two and a half months.

Fang also tells us (Note 7) that as the result of the successive appointments of two new presidents

---

[66] See notes 33, 36, 41, 44, 52 and 53.

[67] Quoted in Bodde/Morris, p. 142, from M. J. Meijer, *The Introduction of Modern Criminal Law in China* (Batavia [Jakarta], 1949), p. 194.

[68] See respectively notes 45, 46, 50 and 55.

of the Board of Punishments, the abuses he had described "were all wiped out." This assertion he then promptly contradicts by telling about the Board employee who again altered an official document and then, through a stupid technicality, was given the opportunity to escape from jail.

This second episode, narrated by Fang with no seeming awareness of its contradictory implications, demonstrates, I think, that in neither instance was he making any deliberate effort to deceive. Rather, he was himself almost surely the victim of a common and deceptive Chinese literary convention. Thus there are two plausible explanations of what he really meant when he chose the word *jih* 'day' or 'daily' to describe the deaths of the prisoners. Either he used it within the mental context of a very specific time span of a few days only—the period when the contagion mentioned by him was at its height—or, if he was in fact thinking in more general terms, he only meant to say that "there WERE days," that is, there were days from time to time, when indeed three or four persons died. If pressed, he would surely have admitted that, in his context, "daily" was used by him for literary emphasis only. It did not and could not mean that day in and day out, month after month, three or four deaths did in fact occur.

Likewise *chieh* 'all' is a word frequently placed for stylistic emphasis after nouns; in some contexts, however, it is evident that it should not be understood literally. What Fang probably really intended to say was that SOME of the abuses he had witnessed were wiped out. In order to state this explicitly, however, he would have had to substitute *huo* 'some' for the more common *chieh*. This would have weakened the positive force of his statement and therefore, probably, would have seemed to him stylistically unsatisfying. More than this, use of the qualifying *huo* instead of the all-encompassing *chieh* would probably have seemed to him to be derogatory toward the two men whom he wanted to praise. Actually there is historical justification for Fang's statement as long as we do not push it to its literal extreme, for it is known that the first president displayed leniency toward at least some of his prisoners, and

that the second advocated certain prison reforms.[69]

All of this leads to a conclusion whose implications transcend the present discussion. There are many common Chinese words—ones like *jih* (daily), *ch'ang* (always or constantly), *chin* (utterly or entirely), *pi* (invariably or inevitably), *chieh* (all), *mei* (each or every), and others— which we may call "total" words because they define an action or situation in total or absolute terms. When we encounter such words we should study their context with great care to determine whether or not we should take them at their full face value. Not infrequently, I believe, it will be found advisable to understand them conventionally rather than literally. (Of course we have many similar usages: "It ALWAYS has to rain when I go to town." Such locutions, however, I believe to be less common in Western formal prose than in that of traditional China.)

Literary convention of a different sort possibly underlies Fang's description (in his Note 2) of how three of his fellow prisoners were subjected to judicial torture. (Typical of Chinese personal reticence is his silence at this point about the details of his own torture despite the fact, attested by himself, that it took place at the same time.) In the neatly graduated correlations made here by Fang between the severity of beatings suffered by the three prisoners and the amounts of their bribes, he may very well have been influenced by the very common Chinese penchant for presenting facts in terms of seemingly precise numerical gradations and categories. If, however, Fang is indeed following convention here, this fact does not invalidate his basic thesis, namely that the severity of judicial torture in his day was more apt to be determined by the size of the sufferer's purse than by the several explicit prohibitions against its arbitrary use specified in the Ch'ing Code.[70]

Aside from such conventions, Fang Pao falls into a contradiction when, in his Note 3, he begins by telling about a Board employee who was ready to alter any kind of document except those going to

[69] See note 62 above.
[70] On these prohibitions, see Bodde/Morris, pp. 97–98.

higher levels, and then continues with the story of the brothers whose names were in fact altered on a document destined for the throne. It is not enough to suggest that the employee guilty of the second act was perhaps different from the first employee. Fang himself does not say so, and without his explicit word, the contradiction remains. It would seem that he, like most people past and present, could be guilty of occasional inconsistencies. It should further be noted that this story, including its dialogue, is entirely hearsay aside from the final sudden death of the guilty employee, which occurred after Fang's arrival in prison.

Are we then to downgrade Fang's accounts as sensational and exaggerated? I for one would strongly object. Despite Fang's strong personal involvement in what he writes, he presents his facts starkly and without sensational embellishment. To me at least they have the ring of truth. (Let us remember that when Fang recorded them he probably did not hope to survive, nor did he think that they would see the light of day.) This is not to deny the possibility that cumulatively speaking, the picture they present may be somewhat overdrawn. On the contrary, I would like to suggest that like the three or four unfortunates whom Fang says died daily, perhaps the deeds he describes of bribery, torture, forgery and the rest were not quite as universal as his unbroken record of them would suggest. Even so, the picture is horrible enough.

The gulf between this picture and the bland statements in the official documents should be enough to make us wary of the latter as records of sociological facts unless supported by corroborating evidence. The "Legal Treatise" in the *Ch'ing Draft History*, for example, asserts that a censor was always sent to investigate any death occurring in the Board's prison.[71] If Fang's statements are even remotely correct, such a provision would have resulted in innumerable visitations. The Ch'ing Code stipulates that sick prisoners were to receive medical attention.[72] Fang (Note 1) denies that such attention was given even to light offenders

and the innocent. The Code states that all prisoners released from prison were to be interviewed by the authorities so as to determine whether, during their imprisonment, they had been subjected to cruel treatment or extortion.[73] Fang, of course, would have laughed if he had heard of this regulation. The Code provides graduated punishments for various kinds of alterations of official dispatches, culminating in decapitation after the assizes for forging an official seal.[74] According to Fang (Note 3), these acts were committed with impunity. The *Collected Institutes of the Great Ch'ing Dynasty* insists that the bringing of liquor into prison was strictly forbidden.[75] Fang (Note 4) tells us of a prisoner who celebrated his imminent release by holding nightly drinking bouts with his prison companions.

How a statement may pass from one official document to another and suffer distortion in the process is illustrated by a legal injunction concerning prisoners which successively appears in three different works. Its first formulation is as a sub-statute in the Code, where we learn, concerning prisoners who are seventy or above, fifteen or below, or infirm, that their fetters are to be regularly washed, their sleeping mats regularly aired, warmed beds are to be prepared for them in winter, and cooling drinks in summer—in short, a regimen more suggestive of a sanatorium than of a prison! Then, turning to prisoners in general, the sub-statute says among other things that they are to receive a padded gown in winter.[76]

The same passage reappears in the *Collected Institutes* (1899 edition), unchanged except that the padded gown is put at the beginning of the list and the entire statement is now made to apply to ALL prisoners and not just to the aged, young, and infirm.[77] From there, the statement as thus revised passes again without further change into

---

[71] "Legal Treatise" (see note 7 above), p. 119.
[72] Code, p. 3550; summarized in Philastre, II, 650–651.

[73] Code, p. 3533; Philastre, II, 636.
[74] See respectively Code, pp. 819 and 3137; Staunton, nos. 71 and 358; Boulais, nos. 300 and 1560; Philastre, I, 346–347 and II, 503.
[75] *Ta Ch'ing hui-tien* (see note 6 above), 56/2a (p. 587 of 1963 reprint).
[76] Code, same reference as in note 72 above.
[77] *Ta Ch'ing hui-tien*, 56/1a (p. 587 of 1963 reprint).

the "Legal Treatise" (twentieth century), except that the order of the warmed beds and cooling drinks is reversed and the stipulations are made particularly to apply to the prisoners in provincial prisons. At this point, however, the author of the "Legal Treatise" appends a realistic note. He laments that abuses proliferated and proved to be incurable despite repeated official criticisms.[78]

It is instructive to compare Fang's "Notes" with Loch's description a century and a half later. Only in Note 1 does the Chinese scholar have much to say about the physical aspects of prison life. Thereafter, as a Confucian, he turns to sociological matters and focuses especially upon what might be called institutionalized bribery and corruption. The Englishman, on the other hand, quite naturally confines himself as a temporary outsider largely to physical facts. Within this limited field, however, there is no basic disagreement between the two men. Both write with restraint and dignity, though the Englishman, true to Western tradition, is more personal in what he says. The following is a masterpiece of British understatement:[79]

The discipline of the prison was in itself not very strict, and had it not been for the starvation, the pain arising from the cramped position in which the chains and ropes retained the arms and legs, with the heavy drag of the iron collar on the bones of the spine, and the creeping vermin that infested every place, together with the occasional beatings and tortures which the prisoners were from time to time taken away for a few hours to endure,—returning with bleeding legs and bodies, and so weak as to be scarce able to crawl,—there was no great hardship to be endured.

Sometimes Loch strongly reinforces what Fang has said, as in the following passage, which should be compared with Fang's remarks (Note 1) about death and crowding in the prison:

The prisoners who were appointed to watch my movements[80] used to take every morning and night a small

rag, and carefully examine and wash my neck and wrists where the ropes and irons had galled my skin. At first I was at a loss to know the reason of their care, but I soon became aware of the fearful consequences which they dreaded might ensue if this precaution had been neglected. There is a small maggot which appears to infest all Chinese prisons; the earth at the depth of a few inches swarms with them. Few enter a Chinese gaol who have not on their bodies or limbs some wounds, either inflicted by blows to which they have been subjected, or caused by the manner in which they have been bound; the instinct of the insect to which I allude appears to lead them direct to these wounds. Bound and helpless, the poor wretch cannot save himself from their approach, although he knows full well that if they once succeed in reaching his lacerated skin, there is the certainty of a fearful, lingering, and agonising death before him. My right-hand neighbour on the bench, where we all slept at night, was dying from the inroads of these insects; his suffering was great, and the relief his fellow-prisoners could afford was of no avail. The crowded state of the gaol brought me in such close contact at night with this poor fellow, that our heads rested on the same block of wood not a foot apart. The thought, as I lay pinioned and ironed, unable to move, during the long, dark nights, that his fate at any moment might be my own, was at times difficult to bear with calmness and with that outward appearance of indifference which it was necessary I should maintain.[81]

A significant difference between the two men is that Fang is outraged by what he sees, Loch (and Parkes as well) is not. The Englishmen are alien intruders who have no emotional involvement in the political system which underlies what they portray. Fang is a Chinese and above all a Confucian scholar. As such he has a feeling of personal betrayal. His attention is far more upon the violations he sees of Confucian morality than upon the men who suffer the effects. Loch, on the other hand, makes some warm remarks about the sufferers themselves as fellow human beings. Here,

---

78 "Legal Treatise," p. 119.
79 Loch, p. 112.
80 I do not believe that the watching was a general practice, or that there is any connection between it and the appointment of cellmates as watchers in Chinese Communist prisons today. It is quite natural that Loch,

as a foreign war prisoner, should be singled out for special attention.
81 Loch, pp. 114–115. See also Loch's account (pp. 108–109) of his condition when he arrived at the prison, and compare with what Fang says (Note 2) about the tying up of prisoners for execution. Prolonged binding, Loch writes, had so destroyed sensation in his left hand that the hand would probably have been lost were it not for the cupidity of one of the jailers who, in order to remove a ring from a swollen finger, carefully rubbed and sucked the finger, thereby restoring circulation.

for example, is what he says of the moment of his release from prison:[82]

> I was not prepared to part from those—villains though they might be——who had, in my hour of trial, shown me kindness and sympathy; therefore . . . I walked up to the prisoners, and beginning on the right of the line passed down and bade farewell to each man. . . . Although the majority of the prisoners were perhaps as great criminals as the world could produce, I knew them only as sharers of my sufferings, and as the authors of many touching acts of most disinterested kindness.

Noteworthy in Fang's recital is the mercenary amorality marking all of its recorded deeds of cruelty. As we read them, we understand the disgust and horror with which jailers and other denizens of the yamens were traditionally regarded in imperial China. Only once does a prison employee attempt an ideological justification of his conduct. "Law (fa)," he says, "has been established to warn others [by punishing the criminal] and to caution posterity. If we didn't act like this, people would get the idea that they deserve to have it easy." No nonsense here about Confucian moral rehabilitation! The sentiment stems directly from the ancient Legalists, grossly vulgarized, however, by the added assumption that extralegal cruelty is justified because it deters wrongdoing. This, of course, is a bowdlerization which the Legalists themselves would never have countenanced.[83]

Fang's "Notes" are given added weight by their date and authorship. Had they been written in the nineteenth century by a white man, we could have shrugged them off either as a predictable description of imperial China in decay or as a tendentious product of Western prejudice. What is impressive is that they were written neither by a foreign missionary, nor a diplomat, nor a businessman, but by a respected Chinese scholar; that they belong neither to the nineteenth century nor even the Ch'ien-lung period, but to the golden age of the K'ang-hsi Emperor! As we ponder these

facts, we get the unhappy feeling that what we have here is no mere temporary aberration but something deeply rooted in the traditional Chinese political system.[84]

Fang's sudden arrest transformed him in the twinkling of an eye from a member of the establishment into an outsider. For the first time he could measure in his own person the gap between the Confucian code as professed by himself and his fellows, and its concrete application to unfortunates for whom no protective civil rights existed. It is notable that his strongest denunciations are directed not against the jailers, executioners and other petty instruments of the penal

---

[82] Loch, p. 122.

[83] See Fang, Note 2. See also Mr. Tu's remark (Note 1) that prisoners who are unable to buy their way out "have to remain under fetters without the least clemency so that they can be a warning to others."

[84] It might be argued, with some truth, that prisons everywhere, and especially pre-modern prisons, are usually bad. See, for example, the recorded personal observations of eighteenth-century British and continental European prisons made by John Howard, *The State of the Prisons in England and Wales, with Preliminary Observations, and an Account of Some Foreign Prisons and Hospitals* (London, 1777; 4th rev. ed., 1792). (I am greatly indebted to Professor R. Morton Smith, of the University of Toronto, for drawing my attention to this extraordinarily informative work.) There are some striking similarities between the European conditions reported by Howard and those in China as described by Fang Pao. Thus Howard variously refers to filth, lack of light and air, "gaol-fever," drinking and carousing in prison, heavy irons, judicial torture, "garnishing" of prisoners, extortions by bailiffs, mixed confinement of hardened criminals with the innocent, and the like. Yet there are also important differences. In eighteenth-century Europe reform was already possible; some of the abuses observed by Howard disappeared even as he was recording them. And among the evils which most aroused his censure, many were at least "legitimate" in the sense that they conformed to the written law of their day; they were not the result of private wrong-doing. By contrast, the unbridled greed, corruption and cruelty which flourished in Fang Pao's prison could not have existed were it not for the indifference of the judicial personnel to the most elementary canons of law and morality alike. Most important of all, it was possible for a determined investigator like Howard to visit prisons throughout Europe and freely publish what he had seen. In China, on the contrary, investigation and criticism remained unthinkable until the first decade of the twentieth century; even then they could not have occurred save as part of the general disintegration of the old way of Chinese life which then took place. For the Chinese penal reform movement, see the book by Meijer cited in note 67 above.

system—the "rapacious underlings" of legal parlance—but against their superiors. It must have cost him much anguish to write his final burning words: "Painful it is to see how judicial administrators, despite all their intelligence and display of integrity (*chung*) and love (*ai*), are still incapable of saving the people from oppression."[85]

Yet despite Fang's disillusionment, it is notable that he retains undiminished confidence in the Confucian doctrine of human perfectibility as manifested in the belief that it is men who reform institutions rather than institutions that debase men. In his final Note 7 he unhesitatingly asserts that merely through the appointments of two new men, the abuses he had experienced "were all wiped out"—this despite the contrary evidence he himself adduces in his next remarks. Apparently, he never gives a thought to the question of what had caused the abuses before the men were appointed, and what might be expected to recur after they were gone.

Revolutions do not happen solely because of human misery. They happen only when enough persons come to believe that the key to removing this misery lies in changing the system rather than in changing leaders. No revolution was possible in China until the penetration of the West brought to the Chinese a knowledge of other ways of life as viable as their own. It would be unfair and unhistorical to criticize Fang Pao the scholar, living in his self-contained Confucian world, for failing to see that the system was at fault. Even in our revolutionary world of today, exposed as we are to a variety of competing ideas, most people still think of social improvement in terms of a superficial change of leaders, not a change of system.

---

[85] See also his bitter remarks at the end of Note 4.

CHINESE GLOSSARY

## I. Titles of Writings

Ch'ien-lung ching-ch'eng ch'üan-t'u 乾隆京城全圖

Ch'ing shih-kao Hsing-fa chih chu-chieh 清史稿刑法志註解

Ta Ch'ing hui-tien 大清會典

Ta Ch'ing hui-tien shih-li 大清會典事例

Ta Ch'ing lü-li hui-t'ung hsin-tsuan 大清律例會通新纂

Wang-hsi hsien-sheng wen-chi 望溪先生文集

Wang-hsi hsien-sheng wen-chi chi-wai wen 望溪先生文集集外文

Yü-chung tsa-chi 獄中雜記

## II. Persons and Places

| | | | |
|---|---|---|---|
| Chang T'ing-shu | 張廷樞 | Nan shu-fang | 南書房 |
| Ching-hai | 靜海 | Shan-yin | 山陰 |
| Chu | 朱 | Shun-t'ien | 順天 |
| Fang Pao | 方苞 | Tai Chün-heng | 戴鈞衡 |
| Han-ch'eng | 韓城 | Tai Ming-shih | 戴名世 |
| Hung-tung | 洪洞 | Tso Kuang-tou | 左光斗 |
| Kung Meng-hsiung | 龔夢熊 | Tu | 杜 |
| Kuo Ssu | 郭四 | T'ung-ch'eng | 桐城 |
| Li Ssu | 李斯 | T'ung-kuan | 同官 |
| Li T'ing-yi | 勵廷儀 | Wei Chung-hsien | 魏忠賢 |
| Liu Yen | 劉巖 (Ta-shan 大山 ) | | |

## III. Terms

| | | | |
|---|---|---|---|
| ai | 愛 | ch'eng | 城 |
| ch'eng | 常 | chieh | 皆 |
| che jung | 讁戍 | chien | 監 |

chin (tael) 金

chin (utterly) 盡

ch'u 處

chung 忠

ch'ung chün 充軍

fa 法

hao sheng chih te 好生之德

hsi shih 西市

hsi ti erh wo 席地而臥

hsien chien 現監

Hsing pu 刑部

huo 或

jen shu 仁術

jih 日

lao chien 老監

liu t'ang 六堂

mei 每

mu ko 木格

nü chien 女監

pa-ch'ih kung-ts'ang 把持公倉

pan p'eng 板棚

pan shih 板室

pan wu 板屋

pao 保

pi 必

sheng 升

shih 室

ssu 司

ssu lo 斯羅

t'ang 堂

tao chih pu ming 道之不明

ti pao 地保

tou 竇

ts'ai shih 菜市

yu hsing hsin 有倖心

yü 獄

yü yü 囹獄

wu 屋

# HENRY A. WALLACE AND THE
# EVER-NORMAL GRANARY*

## CHINESE ORIGIN OF WALLACE'S EVER-NORMAL GRANARY

THE interest that the Far East holds for Henry A. Wallace has been concretely manifested in recent years by the trip which he took to eastern Siberia and China in the early summer of 1944, and by a pamphlet which he wrote at about the same time.[1] Less well known is the fact that this interest, at least along certain lines, is of long standing, and has played an important part in shaping one aspect of his social thinking.

During the past several years I had heard vaguely that among the agricultural measures carried out by Mr. Wallace while Secretary of Agriculture (1933–40), those grouped under the title of "The Ever-Normal Granary" had been inspired by ancient Chinese practice. Because of the importance of Wang An-shih (1021–86) in Chinese economic thought, and because of the existence of a considerable literature on Wang in English, I had supposed that it was he who might have stimulated these measures. On writing to Mr. Wallace for confirmation, however, he very kindly replied to me as follows (letter of August 24, 1945):

* I am deeply indebted to Mr. Wallace for his letter to me that is quoted shortly below, and for permission to quote from his writings and speeches contained in *Wallaces' farmer*, *Democracy reborn* and the *Atlantic monthly;* also to Reynal & Hitchcock, publishers of *Democracy reborn*, and to the publishers of the other above-mentioned two periodicals, for use of these quotations; to Mr. Wallace's private secretary, Miss Mildred M. Eaton, for providing the references to the Ever-Normal Granary contained in *Wallaces' farmer,* as well as otherwise helping me; to Dr. O. C. Stine and his associates, Miss Gladys L. Baker and Mr. Everett E. Edwards, of the Division of Statistical and Historical Research, Bureau of Agricultural Economics, U. S. Department of Agriculture, for supplying me with the publication mentioned in note 16, as well as other pertinent publications, and for giving me the references to the speeches listed in note 18; to Miss Margaret Kelley, of the Office of Information, Field Service Branch, Production and Marketing Administration, Department of Agriculture, who kindly checked the accuracy of the present article's account of the Agricultural Adjustment Act; to the Library of the Bureau of Agricultural Economics, Department of Agriculture, which supplied me with the texts of Mr. Wallace's speeches and of editorials appearing in *Wallaces' farmer;* to Professor Simon S. Kuznets, of the Wharton School, University of Pennsylvania, who brought me in contact with Dr. Stine; and to Dr. K. A. Wittfogel, Director of the Chinese History Project, Columbia University, who wrote to me about references to the Ever-Normal Granary in Wallace's *Democracy reborn*.

[1] Henry A. Wallace, *Our job in the Pacific* (New York: Institute of Pacific Relations, 1944).

I first learned about the Ever-Normal Granary by reading a doctor's degree thesis written by Chen Huan-chang, a Chinese scholar at Columbia University. The title of his thesis was "The Economic Principles of Confucius and His School."[2] As a result I wrote several editorials for *Wallaces' Farmer* during the decade of the twenties entitled "The Ever-Normal Granary."

I didn't become familiar with Wang An-shih until late 1933 or early 1934 as the result of a two-volume work given me by Mrs. Eugene Meyer[3] which was written by an Englishman named Williams and published by the British publishing house of Probsthain and Company.[4] While I am a great admirer of Wang An-shih's work, I don't think I carried out any measures as the result of reading about him. The term "Ever-Normal Granary" traces not to Wang An-shih but to the thesis to which I have earlier referred.

This effectively disposes of the Wang An-shih hypothesis; a discovery that is not surprising in view of the fact that Wang does not seem to have used the term "Ever-Normal Granary" in his own writings, though some of his economic measures embraced the general principles embodied in this ancient Chinese institution.

### CH'EN'S DESCRIPTION OF THE CHINESE EVER-NORMAL GRANARY

Chen [Ch'en] Huan-chang's *Economic principles of Confucius and his school* is a curious work, written with a definitely propagandistic purpose. Ch'en, who was born in 1881, became in his early years a pupil of the famous reformer, K'ang Yu-wei (1858–1927). Following the latter's ideas, he wished to strengthen China against the impact of Christianity and of western thought generally, by transforming Confucianism from a loose system of ethics into a closely knit religious organization supported by the state. Hence, after receiving his Ph.D. from Columbia, he returned to Peking in 1912, where he founded the National Confucian Association.[5]

The propagandistic motivation in Ch'en's book is evident in the exaggerated claims he makes for Chinese culture in his conclusion:[6]

(1) The Chinese have the best religion—Confucianism. ... (2) The Chinese have the highest standard of morality. ... (3) The Chinese have the most widely-

[2] Chen Huan-chang, *The economic principles of Confucius and his school*, Columbia University studies in history, economics and public law, vols. 44–45 (whole number 113) (New York, 1911).

[3] Wife of the former publisher of the *Washington post*.

[4] The actual name of the author is H. R. Williamson. His work is entitled *Wang An Shih, a Chinese statesman and educationalist of the Sung dynasty* (2 vols. London: Probsthain, 1935–37).

[5] Arthur W. Hummel, translator and annotator, *Autobiography of a Chinese historian* (Leyden: E. J. Brill, 1931), p. xiv and note; *Who's who in China* (5th ed. Shanghai: China weekly review, 1936), pp. 27–8. The latter, which contains further details not mentioned above, is the latest reference to Ch'en I have seen.

[6] Chen, *op. cit.*, vol. 2, p. 726.

spoken language. . . . (4) The Chinese have produced the best literature of all kinds. This is beyond dispute. [He concludes his book by saying (p. 730)]:

Under one centralized government, one uniform language, one highly-developed religion, one national idea, China will, without doubt, become a strong nation. . . . But China will not injure anyone not Chinese as the western nations take advantage of other people. After China shall be strong, the Great Similarity of Confucius will come, and the world-state will appear. Then the brotherhood of nations will be established, and there will be no war, but perpetual peace.

Nevertheless, the account Ch'en gives of the Ever-Normal Granary is accurate, on the whole, as well as, apparently, the most detailed that has appeared in English.[7] He begins by describing (pp. 568–70) some precursors of the first actual Ever-Normal Granary of 54 B.C.: (1) When Li K'o[8] became minister of the state of Wei (under Marquis Wen, 424–387 B.C.), he instituted a system whereby the government would buy from the farmers a certain percentage of their grain in years of good harvest, and in times of famine would sell this grain at the normal price. As a result of this program, "even if famine, flood and drought should occur, the price of grain would not be high, and the people would not be obliged to emigrate. . . . When his scheme was carried out in Wei, he not only made the people rich, but also made the state strong." (2) Ch'en quotes Mencius's pointed criticism of King Hui of Liang (370–319 B.C.): "When the grain is so abundant that the dogs and swine eat the food of man, you do not make any collection for storage. When there are people dying from famine on the roads, you do not issue the stores of your granaries for them" (*Mencius*, Ia, 3).

Ch'en then (p. 572) describes how Keng Shou-ch'ang 耿壽昌, in 54 B.C., instituted the first measure actually to be given the name of "Ever-Normal Granary" (*Ch'ang-p'ing-ts'ang* 常平倉):

Keng Shou-ch'ang proposed that all provinces along the boundaries of the empire should establish granaries. When the price of grain was low, they should buy it at the normal price, higher than the market price, in order to profit the farmers. When the price was high, they should sell it at the normal price, lower than the market price, in order to profit the consumers. Such a granary was called "constantly normal granary." As the result was good for the people, the emperor gave Keng Shou-ch'ang the title of marquis.

This is a close paraphrase of the pertinent passage in the *History of the former Han dynasty*, cited by Ch'en as the basis for his account.[9] Ch'en comments further as follows:

[7] Chen, *op. cit.*, vol. 2, ch. 30, "Government control of grain," sect. 1, "Equalizing the price of grain," pp. 568–77.

[8] More properly pronounced Li K'uei. See Giles, *Chinese biographical dictionary*, no. 1164.

[9] *Han shu* (Shanghai: Chung Hua Book Co., edition of 1923), ch. 24a, p. 5a.

This system has continued from the time the constantly normal granary was established . . . to the present day. Although it was sometimes in practice, and sometimes out of practice, according to the political modifications of different ages, its name has nominally existed in nearly all ages. Despite the modifications of this system in later times, the fundamental law of Keng Shou-ch'ang remains the same.

Ch'en cites further instances of its operation, the latest for the year A.D. 1757, and then (pp. 573–77) sums up its chief benefits and weaknesses. It is beneficial, in his opinion, because: (1) Farmers themselves are usually short sighted people, incapable of watching out for their true interests. (2) Unless protected by the government, farmers are helpless and easily exploited by merchants. (3) Grain is a basic necessity of life, so that its price directly affects the welfare of all society. (4) Natural calamities often prevent the price of grain from following the normal law of supply and demand.

As criticism, Ch'en cites the remarks of Ssu-Ma Kuang (1019–86) and Chu Hsi (1130–1200). Ssu-Ma Kuang stated that government magistrates are often corrupt and permit local merchants to use the government-determined prices of grain for speculation purposes. Even if the magistrates are honest, he said, it takes them so long to receive from the capital the government-set price for grain, that by the time it arrives, it no longer fits local conditions. Chu Hsi stated that farmers in distant regions are not benefited by the law, since the government-controlled grain fails to reach them. He further remarked that because of the complexity of the law, it is often not properly administered and the government granaries are left unused.

Before concluding this section, it is worth noting that among the forerunners listed by Ch'en for Keng Shou-ch'ang's Ever-Normal Granary of 54 B.C., he curiously fails to mention two that were probably the most important. These were the closely interrelated systems of "Equable Transport" (*chün-shu*) and "Equalization and Standardization" (*p'ing-chun*), as instituted by the famous economist and statesman, San Hung-yang (143–80 B.C.), in 115 and 110 B.C. respectively. Under the operation of these measures, the key economic products of various regions were bought up by the government, and then transported to and sold in other regions where a need for them existed. Thus the government attempted to maintain fixed prices and an even distribution for the products in question.[9a] Unfortunately, the primary

---

[9a] *Cf.* Esson M. Gale, *Discourses on salt and iron* (Leyden: E. J. Brill, 1931), pp. xxv–xxvi; Chang Chun-ming, "The genesis and meaning of Huan K'uan's 'Discourses on salt and iron'," *Chinese social and political science review*, 18 (April 1934), 21–22; S. C. Chen, "Sang Hung-yang (143–80 B.C.), economist of the early Han," *Journal north China branch royal Asiatic society*, 67 (1936), 161. Chang, by mistake, dates the instituting of the Equable Transport system in 116 instead of 115 B.C.

sources do not tell us, what, precisely, were the commodities thus handled by the government; the wording of the texts, however, makes almost certain the supposition that grain was included. Sang Hung-yang's measures, furthermore, though broader in scope than that of Keng Shou-ch'ang seem to have been based on much the same principles. The term itself, however, Ch'ang-p'ing-ts'ang or Ever-Normal Granary, admittedly was originated by Keng.

Finally, it should be pointed out that this term, translated by Ch'en as "constantly normal granary," is variously rendered by other writers. Thus Lee, in her *Economic history of China*, refers to it at one point as the "constantly normal granary," but elsewhere as the "normally constant granary."[10] Williamson[11] paraphrases it as "Emergency Granary," while it is translated by Dubs[12] as "Constantly Equalizing Granaries." The term Ever-Normal Granary, therefore, which is simpler and better than any of the preceding, seems to have been coined by Mr. Wallace himself.

### THE EVER-NORMAL GRANARY IN WALLACES' FARMER, 1918–27

The lasting impression which Ch'en's book left on Mr. Wallace's thinking is indicated by the three editorials which he wrote on the Ever-Normal Granary while editor of the weekly *Wallaces' farmer* (Des Moines, Iowa). The first, written in 1918, does not actually mention it by name, but obviously refers to the system; in the others, written in 1926 and 1927, the term itself appears.

1. "Storage of Food." (*Wallaces' farmer* 43.49 [December 6, 1918], p. 1772)

The dealers in eggs, butter and other surplus food products are rendering a distinct service both to the producers and the consumers, when they buy these products when they are plentiful and store them up to be used during the time when they are scarce. No doubt it is quite true that some of these men make more of a profit than they ought to make, but certainly their operations tend to equalize the price of food and to make it cheaper than it would otherwise be during that season of the year when the supply is smallest.

If any government shall ever do anything really worth while with our food problem it will be by perfecting the plan tried by the Chinese three thousand years ago;[13]

---

[10] Mabel Ping-hua Lee, *The economic history of China, with special reference to agriculture*, Columbia University studies in history, economics and public law, vol. 99, no. 1 (whole number 225) (New York, 1921), pp. 59, 168. Considering the importance of the Ever-Normal Granary for agriculture, she brushes it aside with amazing celerity in a total of three sentences.

[11] Williamson, *Wang An Shih*, vol. 1, p. 145.

[12] Homer H. Dubs, "Wang Mang and his economic reforms," *T'oung pao*, 35 (1939), 258; *History of the former Han dynasty* (Baltimore: Waverly Press for the American Council of Learned Societies, Washington, D. C. 1944), vol. 2, p. 253.

[13] Two thousand years would be more nearly accurate.

that is, by building warehouses and storing food in years of abundance, and holding it until the years of scarcity.

2. "The Ever Normal Granary" (*Wallaces' farmer* 51.41 [October 8, 1926], p. 1314)

Over a thousand years ago the Chinese had a system which they called the "Ever Normal Granary." A law was passed which provided that when the crops went beyond a certain size and prices below a certain point, the government was empowered to buy grain and put it into the government owned warehouses. Here it stayed until a year came when the crop went below a certain point. The stored grain was then sold to the public. The Chinese, in spite of their rather inadequate crop reporting system and their lack of statistics, seem to have got fairly good results out of this plan for a number of years. Its principle had in it more of statesmanship than can be found in the vast majority of plans suggested for relief of American agriculture.

Of course, an "Ever Normal Granary" is not particularly needed as long as we have a large surplus which must be disposed of to Europe. If, however, we had a really intelligent comprehension of agricultural statesmanship, we would work out in this country a combination of the Chinese idea of an ever normal granary with a common sense handling of our surplus. Doubtless this would involve a certain amount of government meddling for which our people may not yet be ready. Just the same, it must be remembered that the government is continually meddling with agriculture and that it is in large measure responsible for the present surplus of agricultural products because of the experiments which it has conducted and the information which it has put out through the extension service. In times like the present, the government should either stop boosting agricultural production or should go ahead and work out an agricultural program designed to safeguard the future welfare of the nation. There is food for real thought in the Chinese idea of the ever normal granary, even though they themselves made only a partial success of it.

3. "The Ever Normal Granary." (*Wallaces' farmer* 52.3 [January 21, 1927], p. 85)

More than a thousand years ago, one of the Chinese governments worked out a scheme known as the "Ever Normal Granary." It gave very good results for a time, but the statistics of those days were not such as to make the plan altogether satisfactory. A Californian[14] has suggested a variation of this scheme to be applied to cotton as follows:

"Let the federal government each year decide what has been the average price of cotton during the preceding five years, as determined by the open markets of the world. For each 10 per cent of said average price that the current price is below said average price, let the government purchase and store one million bales of cotton, not exceeding five million bales in any one year. For each 10 per cent of said average price that the current price is above said average price for the preceding five years, let the government sell one million bales of its stored supply, until the supply is exhausted. The mathematical rules for buying and selling should be fixed by statute and

[14] I do not know who this is.

work automatically, not being left to the discretion of public officials. The government should carry the interest and warehouse charges as a legitimate contribution to the public welfare. Buying when cotton is down and selling when it is up might alone cover the major part if not all the cost of administration."

There is merit in this idea. It would stabilize prices, and the chief criticism we can see is that it accepts the 1922–26 scale of prices as normal and desirable for farm products. Some day the "ever normal granary" idea will be made to fit modern conditions.

The final words certainly become prophetic in the light of later events. Mr. Wallace's growing concern with the problem of how to regulate the flow of commodities from farmer to consumer is shown by the large number of editorials he wrote in *Wallaces' farmer* during these years, in which he urged individual farmers to control surpluses by storing them themselves until time of need.[15] The increasing dislocation of American agriculture during the 1920's, however, made it more and more evident that such measures of individual self-help were in themselves inadequate, and needed to be supplemented by some sort of government program following the general lines of the Ever-Normal Granary idea in China.

WALLACE'S ADVOCACY OF THE EVER-NORMAL GRANARY, 1934–38

The first Agricultural Adjustment Act, passed by Congress on May 12, 1933, lasted until January 6, 1936, when certain parts of it were invalidated by the Supreme Court. The grounds for invalidation were that it was unconstitutional to finance the administration of the Act by means of taxes levied on the processing of agricultural products. The Act was replaced to a large extent, therefore, on February 29, 1936, by the Soil Conservation and Domestic Allotment Act, which endeavored to encourage farmers to shift production from soil-depleting to soil-conserving crops. This act proved to be inadequate, and so was in its turn amended and expanded, February 16, 1938, by the existing Agricultural Adjustment Act of 1938. The present AAA is far more sweeping in its provisions than either of its predecessors. Because of the Supreme Court decision of 1936, it is financed by special appropriations from the Treasury rather than by processing taxes.[16]

The term, Ever-Normal Granary, seems never to have been used in connection with the first AAA of 1933–36. The reason for this is simple. The

[15] No less than 78 such editorials are collected in the 25-page typescript, "References on farm storing of grain and other food products, taken from *Wallaces' Farmer*, 1912–1932," compiled September 27, 1934, in the Library of the Bureau of Agricultural Economics, Department of Agriculture.

[16] A convenient summary is found in *Achieving a balanced agriculture; how the national farm program meets the changing problem*, prepared by the Division of Special Reports, Office of Information, Department of Agriculture (revised ed. of April 1940), pp. 12–18.

original Act grew out of a situation under which American farmers, for a number of years preceding, had been piling up ever greater surpluses of wheat and other products. These they were unable to dispose of, either domestically or abroad, save at greatly reduced prices. The Act therefore attempted to diminish such surpluses by paying subsidies to farmers who would voluntarily reduce acreage of these products according to certain set quotas. It was not specifically designed for a reversed situation in which drought or other calamity might wipe out the surpluses or cause actual shortage. Thus it differed from the Chinese concept of the Ever-Normal Granary, the intention of which was actually two-fold: (1) through the government's purchasing and storage of the surplus production of good years to prevent gluts and resulting low prices; and (2) through the sale of such stored-up surpluses at fixed prices in years of bad harvest, to prevent scarcity and resulting high prices. Owing to the type of agrarian economy practiced in China (see below, p. 229), the second purpose was probably stronger in the minds of the administrators than was the first.

The terrible drought of the summer of 1934 revealed the need for supplementing an Act thus geared primarily for surpluses rather than shortages. Already on June 6, 1934, Mr. Wallace, foreseeing the effects of the drought, delivered a radio address in which he argued for the establishment of "an ever-normal granary, such as had been used in ancient China and again in Bible times, to carry over the fat yield of good years and provision the people more evenly in times such as these."[17] This address was followed by many others on the same theme, of which only a few of the more pertinent need be cited here.[18] On November 20, 1934, Mr. Wallace summed up the situation succinctly as follows:[19]

For a number of years I have been interested in the concept of the ever-normal granary, a concept not greatly different from that of Joseph, in Bible days, or of the Confucians in ancient China. It is obvious that when we produce very little for export, we have very little to fall back on in years of drought. When we were producing two or three hundred million bushels of wheat annually above domestic needs, an occasional short crop did not endanger our domestic supply; we simply exported

[17] Henry A. Wallace, *Democracy reborn*, selected from public papers and edited with introduction and notes by Russell Lord (New York: Reynal & Hitchcock, 1944), note by Mr. Lord on p. 81. The reference to "Bible times" relates to the measures of Joseph in Egypt, on which see below.

[18] Mr. Wallace argued for the Ever-Normal Granary in speeches delivered on the following dates, in addition to those quoted immediately below: April 17, 1934; May 16, 1935; January 26, February 2 and 9, May 27, October 5, and November 8, 1937. In the Sunday magazine of the *New York times*, November 14, 1937, he wrote an article entitled "Wallace urges 'balanced abundance'; In the 'Ever-Normal Granary' the Secretary sees the salvation of the farm and the city."

[19] "A foundation of stability," speech delivered before the National Grange, Hartford, Conn., and quoted in Wallace, *Democracy reborn*, p. 87.

less. In years when carryover is high, a short crop is likewise no embarrassment. Without either a large exportable surplus or a large carryover, however, a control program must admit the possibility of real shortage. To prevent this would be the purpose of the ever-normal granary.

On August 19, 1936, Mr. Wallace cited not only China and Egypt, but also the Mormons, as support for the Ever-Normal Granary idea:[20]

Joseph was one of the earliest economic statesmen of history. During seven years of good weather, according to the 47th Chapter of Genesis,[21] he stored up the surplus crops to be used when the drought years came. Then, in exchange for stored grain, he accepted from the drought-stricken farmers first, their money; second, their livestock; and third, their land. Apparently he put the farmers on the relief rolls until the drought was over and then gave them back the use of their land in exchange for a very low rent.[22] It was a plan which worked well in ancient Egypt because behind Joseph stood Pharaoh.

In ancient China the followers of Confucius worked out a modification of the same idea which they called the ever-normal granary, and which provided that in the good years the government should buy up a certain percentage of the crops to be stored away until prices had advanced beyond a certain point and the crop had declined below a certain point. The plan was used with moderate success and occasional intermissions for more than 1400 years.

The Mormons, and especially the Mormon women, in the early days of Utah worked out a system of storing the surplus of their wheat against a time when the crops might be unusually short. The system was still operating in Utah in a modified form at the time the World War broke out.

The Federal Farm Board operations brought about considerable storage of wheat and cotton, but the storage was started in response to political pressure and there apparently was little thought as to when or how the surplus would be sold. The experience of the Farm Board was disillusioning both to the farmers and the Farm Board itself. The more the Farm Board dipped into the market to sustain the price of wheat and cotton, the lower the price seemed to sink; and the lower prices went, the less the farmers bought from the people in the cities. So we had the strange paradox of bread lines lengthening almost in proportion to the increasing surplus in storage. The more farmers produced, the less the city people produced.

Today, there is in the United States an unusual opportunity to take advantage of the experience of Joseph, the ancient Chinese, and the Farm Board.

The urgent need for such legislation was heightened by the drought of 1936, which, with that of 1934, largely wiped out previous surpluses and caused serious shortages in some products. The return of good weather in 1937, however, brought renewed surpluses, and this alternation of drought-caused shortage and the production of super-abundance focussed attention

[20] Speech at the Great Lakes Exposition, Cleveland, Ohio; quoted in *Democracy reborn*, p. 117.
[21] But described in more detail in ch. 41.
[22] Twenty per cent of the annual crop, with priests' land tax free, according to ch. 47.

on the need for an all-weather farm program that would give protection against both kinds of hazard. On February 8, 1937, a group of farm leaders from all over the country met in Washington to discuss the situation. They listened to Mr. Wallace's appeal for an Ever-Normal Granary, and then, the following day, unanimously passed a resolution demanding the adoption of such legislation.[23] In the fall of the same year Congress met in special session to enact legislation. The resulting new AAA was signed by President Roosevelt on February 16, 1938. Mr. Wallace was quoted in the *New York times* of February 17 as saying of it: "The Act aims at a more substantial abundance than we have ever had. Various provisions will help, directly or indirectly, in setting up the Ever-Normal Granary plan." And the Act was described by the *Times* itself in the same article as "embodying the most ambitious farm relief experiment the nation has ever attempted."

THE EVER-NORMAL GRANARY IN AMERICAN GOVERNMENT, 1938 TO DATE

Since 1938 the term Ever-Normal Granary has appeared frequently in publications of the U. S. Department of Agriculture. It is commonly used in a general rather than a specific sense, to cover a whole group of broadly related activities, rather than a particular piece of legislation. Some of these activities antedate the AAA of 1938, but they were coordinated by that Act into a comprehensive and unified program. To quote the Department of Agriculture itself:

The Ever-Normal Granary program, in a broad sense, includes the various activities concerned with the supply of agricultural products. It is designed to provide abundance from year to year and in the future with reserves in the store-houses and reserves in the soil. It is concerned with efficiency of production, adjustment of production, conservation, balancing the flow of market supplies, and insuring crop yields.[24]

These five functions may be summarized as follows:

1. *Promoting efficient production:* The Department of Agriculture conducts and sponsors research on crop and livestock selection, tillage methods, commercial fertilizer, etc., designed to improve methods of farm production.

2. *Adjustment of production:* Producers of such staple crops as cotton, wheat, corn, tobacco and rice are asked voluntarily to stay within acreage allotments determined by the Department of Agriculture according to the production of the preceding season, the probable carry-over, and other fac-

[23] *New York times,* February 10, 1937.
[24] *Achieving a balanced agriculture,* p. 23. The following data are abstracted from the same pamphlet, Sect. VI, "The Ever-Normal Granary," pp. 23–31.

tors. Farmers who cooperate in this program earn payments from the government by staying within their acreage allotments, and may also receive parity-payments, if their return on any commodity falls below parity income. "Parity" is determined according to the prices prevailing during the five year period of August 1909–July 1914.

3. *Conservation as a stabilizer of supply:* The foregoing program for adjustment of production operates in coordination with a conservation program, under which the production of unneeded amounts of soil-depleting crops, such as corn, wheat, etc., may be decreased in favor of increased production of soil-conserving crops, such as grasses and legumes.

4. *Balancing the flow of market supplies:* Producers of cotton, tobacco, corn and wheat, if they grow more than can be advantageously marketed at the moment, may receive commodity storage loans from the government, provided that they undertake to hold their surpluses in storage until such time as the crops may be marketed without causing gluts. These loans thus prevent the market from being flooded in years of surplus and insure a sufficiency of supply even in years of poor crops. When total supplies, including reserves, become excessive, farmers must market their production according to fixed quotas, in order to receive such storage loans. These marketing quotas, however, may not be used unless approved by at least two thirds of the farmers voting in referendum on the question. The marketing of surpluses may be facilitated by such devices as the food stamp plan.

5. *Insuring crops:* The government, through the Federal Crop Insurance Act of 1938, as amended, protects wheat, cotton and flax growers from losses caused by bad weather, insects, plant diseases, etc. Insurance premiums are paid by farmers to the government in the form of wheat or cash equivalent. In case of crop failure, the farmers are paid an indemnity by the government.

The above summary shows that the Ever-Normal Granary program, as practised in the United States today, is, in the words of the Department of Agriculture, "much broader than the mere storage of reserves."[25] It thus far transcends the scope of the Ever-Normal Granary in China. Indeed, the basic principle of the latter, that of commodity storage, appears conspicuously only in points four (Balancing the flow of market supplies) and five (Insuring crops, which, to some extent, is simply a particular adaptation of point four).

The primary reason for this is undoubtedly the difference between the Chinese and American types of agriculture. Chinese agriculture is character-

[25] *Achieving a balanced agriculture*, p. 31.

ized by the cultivation of comparatively small plots of land through intensive hand-labor. Its yields per cultivator (though not necessarily per acre) are therefore limited, and its chief danger is that it will not produce enough rather than that it will over-produce. Hence the basic problem of government in such an economy is to protect its people from the harmful effects of scarcity rather than those of over-abundance. American agriculture, on the contrary, is highly mechanized and conducted on large amounts of land, so that it gives a high yield per cultivator. Legislation, to be effective, must therefore not only protect against the old danger of periodic scarcity, but must at the same time, and perhaps even more frequently, deal with the new problem of surplus that arises from an industrial type of economy.

Still another difference between the Ever-Normal Granary in China and in America springs from the paternalistic concept of government that existed in the one country, as compared with the democratic institutions prevailing in the other. In China the Ever-Normal Granary program was carried out *for* the farmers as well as other social groups, but not *by* them. All farmers were compelled to give support to whatever program the government might decide upon. Furthermore, the government itself became a major operator in the agricultural market, for it acquired large quantities of grain which it stored in its own granaries. In America, on the contrary, no farmer need join the Ever-Normal Granary program unless he so wishes, though the government makes it attractive for him to do so by offering financial inducements. Furthermore, it is the farmers themselves who, in return for government loans, store a large part of their produce within their own or other privately owned storehouses, where they may pay off the loans and use or sell the produce. Much less of it, compared with old China, is actually handed over to the government.

Despite these differences, a basic similarity in purpose exists between the two systems. The American Ever-Normal Granary program is "a broad and comprehensive attack on the entire problem of protecting agricultural production and prices against violent fluctuations of the type which have been so harmful in the past."[26] This is a statement which any of the administrators of the Chinese Ever-Normal Granary would have wholeheartedly approved. Thus the American Ever-Normal Granary may fairly be said to have taken not only its name and part of its practice from its ancient Chinese prototype, but to share with the latter much of its underlying philosophy.[27]

---

[26] *Achieving a balanced agriculture*, p. 31.

[27] This does not mean, of course, that other factors did not play an important part in shaping the American concept of the Ever-Normal Granary. It came into existence as a response to the whole situation in which American agriculture found itself in the 1920's and 1930's, by which time, like

By way of conclusion, it is fitting to quote the words written by Mr. Wallace in an article finished just at the time of the Japanese attack on Pearl Harbor:[28]

During the '20's and '30's, when the raw-material producers were in such frequent trouble, various methods were developed to help them adjust themselves to the painful realities of diminishing demand. . . . More than any of the other plans, the Ever Normal Granary in this country recognized consumer needs by setting up huge stockpiles of wheat, cotton, and corn. The stated objective was to carry over the surplus from the fat years to the lean years, thus benefiting the producer in the years of overproduction and very low prices and helping the consumer in years when the supplies otherwise would be short and the prices high. As things turned out, our Ever Normal Granary stocks of corn made possible our quick and heavy shipments of pork and dairy products to Great Britain during this last year. Those of us who formulated the Ever Normal Granary program had in mind that supplies might eventually be very helpful in case of war. But none of us at that time visualized also how important these supplies might be to the war-stricken territories during the years immediately following the declaration of peace.

As part of the effort to win the peace, I am hoping that what might be called the "ever normal granary principle" can be established for a number of commodities on a world-wide scale. It will be remembered that the fourth point of the eight points agreed upon by Roosevelt and Churchill in the Atlantic Charter mentioned the enjoying by all the states, great or small, victor or vanquished, of access on equal terms to the raw materials of the world. To give this lofty ideal a more definite substance should be one of our chief objectives in the months that lie immediately ahead.

This invocation of an ancient Chinese concept as an instrument for international peace would rejoice the heart of Ch'en Huan-chang, the man from whom Mr. Wallace first learned about the Ever-Normal Granary. For it will be remembered that Ch'en, in the conclusion to his book, argued that a re-vivified Confucianism would not only bring renewed greatness to China, but would actualize the ancient Confucian dream of a universal peace. "The Great Similarity of Confucius will come," he predicted in 1911, "and the world state will appear. Then the brotherhood of nations will be established, and there will be no war, but perpetual peace."[29]

other institutions in American economic life, agriculture had reached a point of maturity at which governmental planning was necessary to supplement the old principle of *laissez-faire*. The Chinese Ever-Normal Granary is important, however, because it suggested to Mr. Wallace a promising path along which such planning might proceed. In comparison with it, the examples of Joseph and the Mormons, also cited by Mr. Wallace, are of secondary importance. This is shown by the time lag of more than fifteen years between his first reference to China in 1918 and those he makes to Joseph and the Mormons in 1934, as well as by the very use of the name, "Ever-Normal Granary."

[28] Henry A. Wallace, "Foundations of peace," *Atlantic monthly* (January 1942), 37; quoted in *Democracy reborn*, pp. 183–4.

[29] See above, early part of sect. 2.

As originally written, this article came to an end at this point, but later events have brought very much to the fore the possibility that a world-wide application of the Ever-Normal Granary, as envisaged by Mr. Wallace, may take place in the not too distant future. Thus a United Press dispatch from Washington of August 7, 1946, appearing in the *New York times* of August 8, read in part as follows:

The United Nations Food and Agriculture Organization said tonight that it was proposing an international ever-normal granary so as to keep poorer nations from going hungry while others pile up tremendous unmarketable food surpluses. Such a plan, FAO said, would go a long way toward stamping out conditions existing before the war when half the world's 2,000,000,000 people were chronically underfed and large groups even in the wealthier countries did not get enough to eat.

A companion dispatch from Washington to the *Times* of the same date explained that the plan of the Food and Agriculture Organization calls for establishment of a World Food Board, which would function to:

Stabilize prices of agricultural commodities on the world markets.

Establish a world food reserve adequate for any emergency arising through failure of crops in any part of the world.

Provide funds for financing the disposal of surplus agricultural products on special terms to countries where the need for them was the greatest.

Cooperate with organizations concerned with international credits and agricultural development.

The very next day, however, on August 9, 1946, the *New York times* reported from Washington that this proposal had been unanimously rejected by President Truman's Cabinet, and added that Britain "may support the United States' position at the international conference at Copenhagen on Sept. 2 which will consider the proposed board." It stated further, however, that because of the alluring possibilities of the plan for many countries, "the United States is not expected to have an easy time sidetracking the . . . proposals. The possible help of Great Britain would not avert difficulty, it was said."

The same article described the proposed World Food Board as "an internationalization of the 'ever-normal granary' plan instituted in the United States by Henry A. Wallace, as Secretary of Agriculture, in the 1930's." It attributed its inception to Sir John Boyd Orr, Director General of the United Nations Food and Agriculture Organization, and stated that it "would fix a minimum and maximum permissible price range for each of the controlled commodities, buying them when they fell below the minimum, and selling them when they rose above the maximum. . . . The board would dispose of 'surplus agricultural products on special terms to countries where the need for them is most urgent'." The article attributed the opposition of the United States and Britain to the fact that the plan describes only sketchily how the World Food Board's operations would be financed, and the resulting fear of these countries that much of the burden of this financing would fall on their own shoulders.

As these lines are written, however, a statement by Mr. Wallace has just been issued, strongly denying the truth of the facts asserted in the foregoing article. An Associated Press dispatch of August 13, 1946, from Washington, appearing in the *New York times* of August 14, reads in part as follows:

> Henry Wallace, Secretary of Commerce, said today the President's Cabinet had endorsed the general principle of an international "ever-normal granary" as embodied in the world-food plan recently presented by Sir John Orr. . . .
>
> "Some such plan as this will sooner or later have to be adopted or the plight of the farmers of the world will eventually be worse for a time than it was in either 1921 or 1932," Mr. Wallace said in a statement.
>
> The statement denied published reports that the Cabinet had rejected the food organization director's proposal. It said that the Cabinet accepted the principle "without a dissenting voice and . . . asked that further study be made of this and alternative proposals."
>
> Mr. Wallace's statement presented his personal endorsement of the idea in these words:
>
> "I have long been in favor of the ever-normal granary plan of buffer stocks. In justice both to the farmer and the consumer, I have felt that the internationalization of the ever-normal granary idea is absolutely essential.
>
> "I believe that our own ever-normal granary program made a great contribution to human welfare during the recent war, and I believe that an extension of this program internationally is necessary for continued world peace and prosperity."

Unfortunately, the need of meeting a publication deadline makes impossible the following here of further developments in this effort to gain international acceptance for the ancient Chinese Ever-Normal Granary principle. The discussions of the Orr plan that will take place at the meeting of the Food and Agriculture Organization opening in Copenhagen on September 2, 1946, however, should prove interesting.

### ADDITIONAL NOTE

Since the above was written, Dr. E. A. Kracke, Jr., has kindly drawn my attention to an interesting passage in Leonard D. White, Charles H. Bland, Walter R. Sharp and Fritz Morstein Marx, *Civil service abroad, Great Britain, Canada, France, Germany* (New York & London: McGraw-Hill, 1935). On page 172 of this work, the following statement is made concerning Frederick William I of Prussia (1713–40): "His grain surplus administration bought up at a fixed price whatever the peasants could not sell in fat years, in order to dispose of it in lean years below the market price for the benefit of the lower urban middle class."

It would be an interesting task, but one beyond the scope of this paper, to determine whether any Chinese influence is apparent in what superficially seems to be a striking parallel to the Chinese Ever-Normal Granary. On the face of it, such influence would seem to be not at all impossible, inasmuch as the enthusiasm for China shared by such German thinkers as Leibniz (1646–1716) and Christian Wolff (1679–1754) is well known.[30] Furthermore, Frederick William I seems to have instituted a civil service system in Prussia which in certain basic principles shows interesting resemblances to the Chinese examination system.[31]

On the other hand, there is no doubt that a number of peoples and countries (in addition to Joseph and the Mormons, already cited in this paper) have at various times attempted measures similar to the Chinese Ever-Normal Granary, quite independently of Chinese example.[32] Nowhere else in the past but in China, however, has the institution been applied on anything like such a large scale, nor been maintained (under varying names) over such a long period of time.

[30] For an excellent recent study of this aspect of Leibniz, see Donald F. Lach, "Leibniz and China," *Journal of the history of ideas*, 6 (October, 1945), 436–55.

[31] *Civil service abroad*, pp. 173–5. This work seems to have been overlooked by Teng Ssu-yü in his otherwise excellent study, "Chinese influence on the western examination system," *HJAS*, 7 (September 1943), 267–312.

[32] *Cf.*, for instance, the interesting article by Chester L. Guthrie, "A seventeenth century 'Ever Normal Granary,' the Alhóndiga of colonial Mexico city," *Agricultural history*, 15 (January 1941), 37–43; also bibliography cited in *ibid.*, p. 37, note 2.

# MAN IN THE COSMOS

# HARMONY AND CONFLICT IN
## CHINESE PHILOSOPHY

THE TWENTY-FIVE centuries separating Confucius (551–479 B.C.) from the present day have seen the appearance of many Chinese philosophical schools, of which only a few (Confucianism, Taoism, Buddhism) have survived as organized movements until modern times, though ideas from others have been perpetuated by being absorbed into these three main schools. Despite this long time span, with its numerous and often conflicting bodies of thought, I believe that it is possible to detect certain concepts or patterns which, because of their frequent appearance in widely separated times and contexts, may fairly be regarded as basic in Chinese philosophical thinking.

The purpose of this article is to analyze a few of these patterns, with the hope of demonstrating that, though far from all of them appear with equal prominence in all schools of thought, owing to the inevitable differences of interest among these schools, they nevertheless display sufficient universality and interrelatedness to constitute a homogeneous and therefore significant world view. The title of the article only imperfectly suggests the center of focus of this world view. More fully descriptive, but also more cumbrous and hence ultimately discarded, was the title I had originally planned: "Permanence and Change, Harmony and Conflict, in Chinese Philosophy."

At the outset it should be clearly understood that what we are here primarily concerned with is Chinese thinking on a sophisticated philosophical level rather than its manifestations in such fields as non-philosophical literature, art, or popular religion. It is probably correct to say that ideas in these fields tend, in many cases, to correspond to prevailing philosophical thinking; yet there are also sometimes important deviations—for example, the idea of a personal creator of the universe, which is wholly absent from Chinese philosophy and yet occurs in Chinese popular religion. Even within Chinese philosophical speculation itself, furthermore, the dominance of the thought patterns to be described below has not prevented the appearance of occasional exceptions and countertendencies, some of the more striking of which will be noted as we proceed.

Finally, the reader may wonder why the name of Confucius is mentioned so infrequently in the following pages. The explanation is simple: The ideas of early Confucianism, as preserved in Confucius' own very fragmentary recorded sayings, are usually found expressed with much greater detail and clarity in the works of his two major followers, Mencius and Hsün Tzŭ.*

## 1. The Cosmic Pattern

In a recent article Needham has demonstrated a phenomenon of signal importance which differentiates Chinese from Western patterns of thinking.[1] We in the West, he points out, have been dominated by a world view in which the cosmos, far from being a self-contained, self-operating organism, is conceived of as having been initially created, and since then externally controlled, by a Divine Power who "legislates" the phenomena of the nonhuman natural world. This conception, from which has arisen our idea of the "Laws of Nature," is, of course, not of European origin, being traceable all the way back to ancient Mesopotamia.

In China, on the contrary, quite a different situation prevailed. The most important divinity of the ancient Chinese, to be sure, was a purposeful ruling power known as T'ien, or "Heaven," capable of exercising control over natural and human events alike. Such seems to have been the kind of T'ien believed in by Confucius, and traces of the old conception survive in Mencius (371?–279? B.C.). Even in pre-Confucian literature, however, the anthropomorphic qualities of T'ien were not strongly emphasized, nor was this divinity described as being the creator of the natural universe. Moreover, passages can easily be found in which the word does not have a religious significance at all but is simply used as a name for the physical sky. With the rise of philosophical speculation, therefore, it became possible for the old theistic conception to give way (save for certain exceptions to be discussed later) to a much more naturalistic and depersonalized point of view.

The result, for China, was momentous, for it meant that there, unlike the West, the theory of the "Laws of Nature" failed to gain a foothold. "The Chinese world-view," Needham observes, "depended upon a totally different line of thought. The harmonious cooperation of all beings arose, not from the orders of a superior authority external to themselves, but from the fact that they were all parts in a hierarchy of wholes forming a cosmic pattern, and what they obeyed were the internal dictates of their own natures" (op. cit., p. 230).

In the present section we propose to analyze the nature of this cosmic pattern in terms of its concept of change. For this purpose we shall first turn our attention to the two major cosmological schools of early Chinese philosophy, those of Taoism and of the *Yin* and *Yang* and Five Elements, and then, for later times, to the Confucian New Text school of the Han dynasty (206 B.C.–A.D. 220), to Neo-Taoism (3d–4th centuries A.D.), to Buddhism (4th century onward), and to Neo-Confucianism (11th century onward). Prominent in all these schools is the belief that the universe is in a constant state of flux but that this flux follows a fixed and therefore predictable pattern consisting either of eternal oscillation between two poles or of cyclical movement within a closed circuit; in either case the change involved is relative rather than absolute, since all movement serves in the end only to bring the process back to its starting point.

Perhaps the earliest expression of the oscillation theory is the famous statement by Lao Tzŭ (prob. 4th–3d centuries B.C.): "The movement of the *Tao* (the universal course or Way) is that of reversal" (chap. 40). This general principle explains many of Lao Tzŭ's seeming paradoxes, such as: "Passing on means going far away, and going far away means reverting again" (chap. 25), or "If diminished, it will increase; if increased, it will diminish" (chap. 42).[2]

In the appendixes (prob. 3d–2d centuries B.C.) of the *Book of Changes* —writings representative of the *Yin-yang* school in its early stages—we find a similar concept, expressed, however, in terms of the eternal interplay of two cosmic forces, the *yang* and the *yin*.[3] Thus in Appendix III of this work we read: "The alternation of the *yin* and *yang* is what is called *Tao*" (Legge, p. 355). Or again: "Shutting a door is called *k'un*. Opening a door is called *ch'ien*.[4] One opening following one shutting is called change. The endless passing from one of these states to the other may be called the constant course (of things)" (Legge, p. 372).[5]

For early expressions of the cyclical concept of change, we should turn to the *Chuang-tzŭ* (attributed to the Taoist of the same name, *ca.* 369–*ca.* 286 B.C.), passages from which have been used by Hu Shih to illustrate what he calls ancient Chinese "theories of natural evolution."[6] Such a term is misleading, however, if by it is implied anything similar to modern Western theories of natural evolution, since Chuang Tzŭ himself indicates quite clearly that what he has in mind is a process of endless return within a closed circle rather than of forward movement along a straight line. Thus we read in his twenty-seventh chapter (Giles, p. 365): "All things are species which, through variant forms, pass one into another. Their beginnings and endings are like those in a ring— incapable of being definitely located. This is called the Equilibrium of

Heaven." Or, again, Hu Shih has quoted another passage from the eighteenth chapter (Giles, p. 228), which, though difficult and possibly corrupt, seems to describe a process of biological evolution starting from water-borne germs, passing through a series of plant and animal forms, and culminating when the *ch'eng* (unidentifiable) "produces the horse, which produces man." Here too the significance lies in the closing sentences: "Then again man reverts to the germs. All things come from the germs, and all return to the germs."

In the Five Elements school (originally distinct from the *Yin-yang* school, with which, however, it became amalgamated by the 2d century B.C.), we find other cyclical theories based on the successive flourishing of the Five Elements (earth, wood, metal, fire, and water). One such theory, in which these elements are correlated with historical epochs, will be discussed in the next section. Another theory correlates these same elements with the annual cycle of the four seasons in such a way that each season flourishes owing to the activities of its associated element. In its earliest form this theory is found in the *Yüeh Ling*, or *Monthly Commands*,[7] but it soon reappears, considerably elaborated, in the fifth chapter of the *Huai-nan-tzŭ* (compiled shortly before 122 B.C.). There we find the Five Elements, four seasons, five directions, five colors, ten "stems" or cyclical signs (used for dating purposes), and five notes of the Chinese scale, all correlated in an endlessly recurring cycle to form the following spatiotemporal cosmological framework:

| Element | Season | Direction | Color | Stems | Note |
|---------|--------|-----------|-------|-------|------|
| 1. Wood | Spring | East | Green | *chia* and *yi* | *chiao* |
| 2. Fire | Summer | South | Red | *ping* and *ting* | *chih* |
| 3. Earth | Summer (3d month) | Center | Yellow | *wu* and *chi* | *kung* |
| 4. Metal | Autumn | West | White | *keng* and *hsin* | *shang* |
| 5. Water | Winter | North | Black | *jen* and *kuei* | *yü* |

Numerous variations of this theory occur in the writings of this and later periods down to recent times. Perhaps the most complex is that of Tung Chung-shu (179?–104? B.C.), major representative of the New Text school (the Han dynasty form of Confucianism, which, however, was heavily influenced by the Five Elements and *yin-yang* theories). He accepts the foregoing correlations, save that for him the element earth, being the central of the Five Elements, no longer has its activities confined to the third month of summer but acts throughout the year to assist the other elements in their seasonal duties. Furthermore, he introduces the *yin* and *yang* into his system by conceiving of them as two forces whose annual revolution successively takes them through the four compass points and their associated four seasons. In this way they function, together with the elements stationed at these compass points, to bring about the seasonal changes marking the passage of each year.

A special feature of Tung's system is that the *yang* and *yin*, in doing this, move not in the same but in opposite directions: the *yang* clockwise, the *yin* counterclockwise. Thus the *yang*, starting from the north just after the winter solstice, at which time it is at its lowest ebb, moves clockwise toward the south, passing through spring in the east en route, and steadily growing in strength as it does so, until it reaches its culmination in the south at the time of the summer solstice; thereafter it returns to the north, this time, however, passing through autumn in the west, and steadily diminishing in strength until it arrives once more at the north at the time of the winter solstice. Meanwhile the *yin* follows a contrary course: from the north, where, at the time of the winter solstice, it has reached its topmost power, it moves counterclockwise through the west (from which, however, it does not operate upon autumn but upon spring on the opposite side of the circle); then it continues to the south, there reaching its lowest ebb, after which it again returns to the north, gaining strength as it does so and passing en route through the east (from which, again, however, it does not operate upon spring but upon autumn in the west).

In this way the *yin* and *yang* annually meet each other in the north at the winter solstice, when the *yin* is dominant and the *yang* subordinate, and again in the south at the summer solstice, when the reverse is true. They are annually opposite each other at the spring equinox, when the *yang* is in the east and the *yin* in the west, and again at the autumn equinox, when their positions are reversed; on both occasions they are exactly equal in strength. All this, says Tung Chung-shu, constitutes "the course of Heaven," which, "when it has been completed, begins again."[8]

So far we have not discussed the question of what first set these pulsating or cyclical movements into operation. In other words, how did the universe as a whole come to be what it is now? First of all, it should be stressed that no Chinese thinker who discusses the subject admits the possibility of any initial *conscious* act of creation. By all of them the process bringing the universe from initial simplicity and disorder to its present state of complexity and order is conceived of in purely naturalistic terms. Lao Tzŭ's explanation, for example, is that "*Tao* produced Oneness. Oneness produced Duality. Duality evolved into trinity, and trinity evolved into the myriad things" (chap. 42). In this connection we should keep in mind that for Lao Tzŭ, as for all the Taoists, *Tao* is a wholly spontaneous principle, without any trace of personality. He says of it, for example, that "*Tao*'s standard is the spontaneous" (chap. 25).

When Lao Tzŭ here speaks of *Tao*, he apparently has in mind what he elsewhere calls "non-being," while by "oneness" he means the state of undifferentiated being, and by "duality" the further state in which this same being became differentiated into Heaven and Earth. This, at least, is the deduction we may draw from another passage (chap. 40), in which he says: "Heaven and Earth and the myriad things are produced from being; being is the product of non-being." The *Chuang-tzŭ* (chap. 12; Giles, pp. 143–44) tells us very similarly that "at the Great Beginning there was non-being," that from this non-being there then came oneness, and that this finally resulted in the existing world of separate objects. Many other Chinese thinkers have likewise accepted the theory that the universe as we now have it is the result of a naturalistic process of development starting from an impersonal first cause.[9]

At this point, however, we are faced with a dilemma. If the universe originated from a first cause, this means that in its early stages, at least, it underwent a process of progressive evolution. But if this be true, and if, nevertheless, the cosmic pattern today consists of oscillation or cyclical movement, then we must suppose that at some unknown period in the past the evolutionary process came to a halt and was replaced by the existing one of repetitive movement. How, when, and why did this shift take place?

Most Chinese thinkers do not even seem to have been aware of this problem, which, if faced squarely, would seem to lead logically to the alternative assertion that the whole idea of evolutionary development from a first cause is nothing more than a myth. If the basic pattern of the universe is today that of cyclical movement, then it would be reasonable to suppose that it always has been so in the past.

Hints of such a bold hypothesis are found already in the *Chuang-tzŭ*.[10] However, it is more particularly in a famous commentary on that work, attributed to the Neo-Taoist Kuo Hsiang (d. A.D. 312),[11] that we find such a theory presented with clarity and vigor. Thus in Kuo Hsiang's philosophy the term "non-being" means literally what it says, "nothingness." Hence, for him, there is no such thing as non-being, while being is the only reality. It follows, therefore, that this being could never have been evolved from non-being, as the earlier Taoists maintained, nor can it ever conceivably revert to non-being: "Not only is it that non-being cannot become being, but being also cannot become non-being. Though being may change in thousands of ways, it can never change into non-being. As this is so, there is no time when there is no being; being eternally exists" (Fung 2, p. 209).

Since the universe consists of being, this means that it likewise eternally exists and therefore can have no first cause. On the contrary, as pointed out by Kuo in several passages, one of the basic principles of the universe is that all things in it are self-produced; none of them whatsoever depends for its being on some external Creator:

I venture to ask whether the Creator is or is not? If He is not, how can He create things? If He is, then, (being one of these things), He is incapable of creating the mass of bodily forms. Hence only after we realize that the mass of bodily forms are things of themselves, can we begin to talk about the creation of things. . . . The creating of things has no Lord; everything creates itself. Everything produces itself and does not depend on anything else. This is the normal way of the universe [Fung 2, p. 210].

Thus Kuo's cosmology is one of permanence in change: the individual things of the universe are in a perpetual state of flux—this is its change—but the universe as a whole is eternal and self-creating—this is its permanence.

With the spread of Buddhism in China, this concept was powerfully reinforced, for one of Buddhism's fundamental tenets is that

there has been no single act of divine creation which has produced the stream of existence. It simply is, and always has been, what it is. Even the gods in the Buddhist heavens are attached to the wheel of life and death and are not its creators. Thus the wheel is permanent and unchanging in the sense that it goes on eternally. It is impermanent and changing, however, in the sense that everything in it is in a state of flux.[12]

As a single example of this thesis, let us turn to the Mere Ideation school, as represented in China by Hsüan-tsang (596–664). According to the subjective idealism of this school, all things in our universe, including both the seemingly objective phenomena of the external world and the seemingly subjective ego of the individual, are "mere ideation." That is to say, they are the products of a stream of consciousness which, for each individual, continuously takes its rise from a basic nexus of consciousness known as the *ālaya*, and continuously flows back to that *ālaya* in a closed circuit. The question arises, therefore, whether this stream of consciousness is itself to be regarded as permanent or impermanent? Hsüan-tsang replies, in typically Buddhist manner, that it is neither the one nor the other, by which he really means that it has aspects both of permanence and of impermanence:

It is neither permanent nor impermanent, for it is in perpetual revolution. By "perpetual" is meant that this consciousness, from time without beginning, has constituted a homogeneous successive sequence. . . . By "revolution" is meant that this consciousness, from time without beginning, is born and perishes again from moment to moment, ever successively changing. As cause it perishes and as fruit it is then born. . . . Because these effects are born, it is not impermanent; because these causes perish, it is not permanent. . . . That is why it is said that this consciousness is in perpetual revolution like a torrent [Fung 2, pp. 311–12].

On a more prosaic level, Buddhism shares with other Indian schools of thought a belief in *kalpas*, or "world periods." That is to say, the universe as such is eternal and uncreated, but it passes through recurring cycles of formative growth, organized existence, disintegration, and annihilation, in the course of which successive worlds, including that in which we now live, are born and die. Each phase in this fourfold cycle constitutes one *kalpa* and has a duration of 1,334,000,000 years.[13]

With the rise of Neo-Confucianism, we find this Buddhist theory being taken over by Shao Yung (1011–77), who, however, made it more acceptable to the Chinese mind by replacing the Indian *kalpa* with what he called a *yüan*, or "cycle," and reducing its astronomical length to a more manageable duration of 129,600 years. He furthermore gave the theory a Chinese coloration by expounding it in terms of the alternating growth and decay of the *yin* and *yang*, as symbolized by the hexagrams of the *Book of Changes*. This theory was thereafter widely accepted in Neo-Confucianism, notably by the famous Chu Hsi (1130–1200).[14]

Another famous Neo-Confucian theory of cycles, in which, likewise, no starting point is postulated for the universe, is that of Chang Tsai (1020–77). The entire universe, says Chang, consists only of *ch'i*, or "Ether" (lit., "gas"), which, however, undergoes alternating phases of dispersion and condensation. In its state of dispersion it is invisible and intangible and is then known as the Great Void. At that time, therefore, there is only the Ether as such, but no organized world of discrete objects. But, with the condensation of the Ether, such a world comes into being, only to suffer dissolution, however, at which time the Ether again disperses and reverts to its former state. To quote Chang himself: "The Great Void cannot but consist of Ether; this Ether cannot but condense to form all things; and these things cannot but become dispersed so as to form (once more) the Great Void. The perpetuation of these movements in a cycle is inevitably thus" (Fung 2, p. 497).

This theory is echoed in later times by several thinkers, such as Liu Tsung-chou (1578–1645)[15] and Huang Tsung-hsi (1610–95).[16] Even as late as the nineteenth century, in fact, we find T'an Ssŭ-t'ung (1865–98) enunciating a similar theory, to which, however, under the influence of Western physics, he gives a modern touch by abandoning the word *ch'i* and coining a new term, *yi-t'ai*, which is simply a transliteration of the Western word "ether." This ether, he says, passes through alternating phases of seeming production and destruction, as the result of which individual objects exist and cease to exist. Yet the ether as a whole is never destroyed thereby, and thus the process continues eternally: "If we look at the past, the process of production and destruction has never had a beginning. If we look at the future, the process will never come to an end. And if we look at the present, it is constantly going on. . . . The cycle of production is followed by that of destruction; as soon as there is this destruction, it gives way to production" (Fung 2, pp. 696–97).

## 2. The Pattern of History

In the Christian world, historical events are dated from the birth of Christ; in the Islamic world, from the Hejira; among the Jews, from the Creation. In China, on the contrary, history has no such fixed starting point. Events are dated either according to their occurrence within a recurring sixty-year cycle (each year having its own appellation) or according to their position within the reigns of successive rulers. These chronological techniques are perhaps symptomatic of a Chinese world view which sees the human world as a part of the universal macrocosm and hence as conforming, like the latter, to an inherent pattern of cyclical rather than linear movement.

Besides this cyclical interpretation of history, however, there is another one, equally widespread, which sees the days of the ancient sage-kings as a truly golden age, and all human history since that time as a process of steady degeneration. Between this and the cyclical view there would seem to be a contradiction, inasmuch as the latter denies all forward movement save in relative terms, whereas the former affirms such movement of a sort, though in devolutionary rather than evolutionary terms.

Of the two, that which exalts antiquity seems to be earlier and less philosophical and was no doubt reinforced among its proponents during the late Chou dynasty (6th–3d centuries B.C.) by their sad awareness of the actual political disorder in which they lived. With the rise of the later cyclical theory, we find both views sometimes expressed by the same thinkers without apparent awareness of the possible contradiction between them. Certain men, however, as we shall see, reconcile the two views very simply by maintaining that history does indeed move in cycles but that we moderns are unfortunately living in the downswing of one such cycle. No doubt many other thinkers, if they had been specifically asked, would have given a similar answer to the problem.

Praise of antiquity and disparagement of modernity is so widespread among early Chinese thinkers as to require no extended comment here. For the Taoists, however, its motivation differed from that of the other schools. For them antiquity was golden, not because it was a time of universal government, but because it was one in which government was lacking. All men then lived at peace with one another precisely because they lived in a state of nature which required no government; their subsequent degeneration has been solely due to the increasingly complex and artificial civilization with which they have surrounded themselves.

The Confucians, on the other hand, inevitably reasoned quite differently. For them antiquity was admirable because it was the age of universal rule of the all-wise sage-kings. Hsün Tzŭ (*ca.* 298–*ca.* 238 B.C.), the third major figure in early Confucianism, is no exception to this general Confucian attitude. He, however, perhaps more than any other Chinese thinker, justifies his veneration for the past by a peculiarly static view of history, in which the many are like the one, and past and present are the same. In his own words:

> Abandoned and incorrigible people say: Ancient and present times are different in nature; the reasons for their order and disorder differ. . . . But why cannot the Sage be so deceived? I say it is because the Sage measures things by himself. Hence by himself he measures other men; by his own feelings he measures their feelings; by one kind he measures other kinds. . . . Past and present are the same. Things that are the same in kind, though extended over a long period, continue to have the self-same principles [chap. 5; Dubs, pp. 73–74].

In later times, as one among innumerable examples of continuing reverence for the ancient sages, we need cite only Han Yü (768–824). He maintains that anciently there was an esoteric truth, the *Tao*, which was transmitted through a series of early sage-kings to Confucius, and by him to Mencius (371?–289? B.C.), but that thereafter this *Tao* has ceased to be transmitted (Fung 2, p. 410).

The roots of this theory actually go back to Mencius himself, in whom we find the earliest attempt to reconcile such an exaltation of antiquity with a more sophisticated view of history as a continuing sequence of ebb and flow. "Since the appearance of the world of men," says Mencius (III*b*, 9), "a long time has indeed elapsed, consisting of alternating order and disorder." In this and other passages (II*b*, 13; VII*b*, 38) he further describes history as having already passed through three such periods of order and disorder, each with a duration of roughly five hundred years, and consisting of initial sage-rule, followed by disorder, and then concluded by the rise of new sages. These cycles, as outlined by Mencius, were as follows: (1) from the sage-kings Yao, Shun, and Yü (trad. 24th–23d centuries B.C.) to the founder of the Shang dynasty (trad. 18th century); (2) from the founder of the Shang to the founders of the Chou (trad. 12th century); (3) from the founders of the Chou to Confucius (551–479 B.C.).

Implicit in this theory of Mencius, as in any other theory of cyclical change, are two basic concepts: (1) History is dynamic, not static; it is a continuing process, not a timeless uniformity. (2) Its changes, however, do not occur sporadically but follow a fixed and therefore knowable pattern. There is no doubt that Mencius, inasmuch as he tacitly accepts these two concepts, holds a position much closer to the central stream of Chinese thinking than does Hsün Tzŭ, who rejects them. That his underlying attitude toward history may, in fact, already have been held by Confucius himself is perhaps inferable from the passage in the *Analects* (II, 23) in which, responding to a disciple's question as to whether the future can be foreseen, Confucius replied: "The Yin (i.e., Shang dynasty) perpetuated the civilization of the Hsia; its modifications and accretions can be known. The Chou perpetuated the civilization of the Yin, and its modifications and accretions can be known. Whatever others may succeed the Chou, their character, even a hundred generations hence, can be known."

However, for a theory which for the first time provides a naturalistic interpretation for the existence of historical cycles, we must turn from Confucianism to the Five Elements school. Prominent in this school is the doctrine that human affairs and natural phenomena are closely interlinked, each period of history being under the domination of some one of the Five Elements in an endlessly recurring cycle. For example, the *Shih Chi*, or *Historical Records* (chap. 74), tells us concerning Tsou Yen (3d century B.C.), the founder of this school: "Starting from the time of the separation of Heaven and Earth and coming down, he made citations of the revolutions and transmutations of the Five Powers (Five Elements), arranging them until each found its proper place and was confirmed (by history)" (Fung 1, p. 160). As formulated by his successors, the correlations established between the elements, their accompanying colors, and the early periods of Chinese history were as follows:

| Element | Color | Period |
|---|---|---|
| 1. Earth | Yellow | Yellow Emperor (trad. 3d mill. B.C.) |
| 2. Wood | Green | Hsia dyn. (trad. 2205–1766 B.C.) |
| 3. Metal | White | Shang dyn. (trad. 1766–1123 B.C.) |
| 4. Fire | Red | Chou dyn. (trad. 1122–256 B.C.) |
| 5. Water | Black | Ch'in (255–207 B.C.) or Han dyn. (206 B.C.–A.D. 220)[17] |

In the second century B.C. we find Tung Chung-shu advancing several cycles of his own invention, among which that of the Three Sequences (black, white, and red) is the most important. Equated with actual history, these sequences go as follows:

| Sequence | Dynasty |
|---|---|
| 1. Black | Hsia |
| 2. White | Shang |
| 3. Red | Chou |

Tung also propounds a four-phase cycle consisting of *Shang*, *Hsia*, Simplicity, and Refinement, each of which has either Heaven or Earth as its "guiding principle." (The terms *Shang* and *Hsia*, though identical with the dynasties so named, are abstract conceptions, and hence not to be taken as literally denoting these dynasties.) Equated with history, this cycle operates as follows:

| Sequence | Guiding Principle | Dynasty |
|---|---|---|
| 1. *Shang* | Heaven | Shun (3d mill. B.C. legendary ruler) |
| 2. *Hsia* | Earth | Hsia |
| 3. Simplicity | Heaven | Shang |
| 4. Refinement | Earth | Chou |

Another of Tung's cycles is based upon the alternation of Simplicity and Refinement alone, and he also has cycles consisting of five or nine phases. In all these he explains that the shift from one period to another is to be manifested by various ritualistic changes, such as proclaiming a new color for the official robes and other paraphernalia used at court, instituting a new calendar, building a new capital, and creating new titles of nobility. Such changes, however, all merely serve to demarcate one historical period from another but do not affect their basic principles of government, for "the great source of right principles derives from Heaven; Heaven does not change, nor do these principles."[18]

Wang Ch'ung (A.D. 27–*ca.* 100), iconoclastic member of the Old Text school which followed Tung's New Text form of Confucianism, seems at first sight to stand apart from the general ideological pattern we have been describing. Attacking the prevailing view that the present is inferior to the past, he argues vigorously that "the people of early ages were the same as those of later ages." Indeed, he points out that, judged in terms of size and political stability, his own Han dynasty is even superior to the earlier Chou period.[19] Yet, despite this seeming indorsement of the idea of progress, closer examination shows that he, like most of his countrymen, looks at history in terms of cycles. Thus he writes further in his *Lun Heng*:

> Each age has its prosperity and its decay; the latter, when prolonged, leads to ruin. The case is like that of a man's clothing or food: when first made, (the clothing) is fresh and intact, but after being used for a while it wears out; when first cooked, (the food) is fragrant and clean, but after the lapse of several days it acquires a bad smell. . . . This principle applies to antiquity, and not solely to the present day [chap. 56; Forke, I, 474].

Taking a long jump forward to Neo-Confucianism, we there find expressions of the compromise theory mentioned earlier, namely, that history moves in cycles but that we moderns are living in the downswing of one such cycle. Ch'eng Yi (1033–1108) writes, for example:

> As for successive epochs, those of the Two Emperors (the legendary Yao and Shun) and the Three Kings (founders of the Hsia, Shang, and Chou dynasties) were ones of growth, and later ages have been ones of decay.... There may be some cases in which decay is checked by (momentary) renewed growth, as well as ones in which such revival does not take place.... Generally speaking, however, if we consider the great revolutions of the universe, their principle is one of steady decay and decline (following a peak) [Fung 2, pp. 519–20].

This theory may have been influenced by that of Ch'eng's contemporary, Shao Yung, who, as we have seen in the previous section, took from Buddhism its theory of *kalpas* or world periods and translated it into Confucian terms. According to Shao, the cycle of 129,600 years in which we are today living began at a date corresponding to 67,017 B.C.; living creatures first came into existence *ca.* 40,000 B.C.; and the cycle reached its peak *ca.* 2330 B.C., a period corresponding to the reign of the legendary sage-emperor Yao. Since then there has been a steady decline which has taken mankind through four descending forms of government: those of the sovereign, the emperor, the king, the tyrant (in the Greek sense), and still lesser imitations of these. Living creatures will cease to exist *ca.* A.D. 46,000, and our present world will come to an end in A.D. 62,583. A new cycle will then begin. "From Emperor Yao until today," Shao concludes sadly, there has "sometimes been unity and sometimes division," but "never has there been anyone who could give a (real) unity to the manners and customs for a period of more than one generation" (Fung 2, pp. 474–76).

So far we have been dealing with thinkers all of whom deny the idea of progress by asserting either that the present is inferior to the past or that it is a mere repetition of the past. There are, however, a few conspicuous exceptions to this point of view. Most notable in early times were the Legalists, who, as practical statesmen keenly aware of the forces destroying the feudal system of their day (4th–3d centuries B.C.), were anxious to build a new power structure in its place. They never tired, therefore, of attacking the other schools for their reverence toward the past, and themselves insisted that changing political forms are needed for changing conditions. "Former generations did not follow the same doctrines," they exclaimed, "so what antiquity should one imitate? ... There is more than one way to govern the world, and there is no necessity to imitate antiquity in order to take appropriate measures for the state."[20]

The most famous of the Legalists, Han Fei Tzŭ (d. 233 B.C.), explains the reason for these changes in a passage of his works (chap. 49) which has a curiously Malthusian ring. In ancient times, he says, "there were few people and plenty of supplies, and therefore the people did not quarrel." Hence it was easy to maintain good government without resorting to large rewards or heavy punishments. Today, however, the growth of population is so rapid that "before the death of the grandfather there may be twenty-five grandchildren. The result is that there are many people and few supplies. . . . So the people fall to quarrelling, and though rewards may be doubled and punishments heaped up, one does not escape from disorder" (Fung 1, p. 328). From this it would appear that even the Legalists, despite their insistence on the need for political change, agreed with other schools (though for their own sociological reasons) that conditions of the past were better than those of today. If this interpretation be correct (and perhaps it is unwise to try to read too much into a single passage), it would seem doubtful that the Legalist insistence on the need for change was based on any genuine belief in historical progress.

For such a theory we must turn to the Han dynasty expositors of the *Ch'un Ch'iu*, or *Spring and Autumn Annals*—a small chronicle history of Confucius' native state of Lu covering the years 722–481 B.C., and traditionally, though probably erroneously, attributed to Confucius himself. Tung Chung-shu classifies the 242 years of this history into three groups: events of which Confucius learned through transmitted records (722–627 B.C.); events of which he learned through the oral testimony of older contemporaries (626–542); and events which he personally witnessed (541–481).

Ho Hsiu (A.D. 129–82), a commentator on the *Ch'un Ch'iu*, further elaborates this theory by describing these divisions as constituting the Three Ages of Disorder, Approaching Peace, and Universal Peace. Confucius, he says, when narrating events of the earliest Age of Disorder, of which he learned only through transmitted records, concentrated his attention on his native state of Lu, while dealing only sketchily with the rest of China; in recording the next Age of Approaching Peace, he dealt in detail with China but disregarded the surrounding barbarian tribes; but concerning the third age, which he personally witnessed, "he made evident (in his recording) that there was an order arising of Universal Peace," in which "the barbarian tribes became part of the feudal hierarchy, and the whole world, far and near, large and small, was like one."[21] Devoid though this theory is of historical reality, it seems to be the first in Chinese thought which explicitly recognizes the possibility of positive human progress according to a fixed pattern of historical evolution.

Turning to the Neo-Taoist, Kuo Hsiang, we find him insisting that the principle of change, to which the whole nonhuman world is subject, operates equally strongly in the world of man, and that therefore it is folly for man to try to resist this change:

The events of antiquity have already perished with that antiquity. Though attempts may be made to transmit them, who can cause them to happen again in the present? The past is not the present, and what happened today is already changing. Therefore we should give up the study (of the past), act according to our nature, and change with the times. This is the way to perfection [Fung 2, p. 219].

As a Taoist, Kuo Hsiang refrains from expressing any opinion as to whether this change is for the better or not. Rather than attempt such value judgments, the really important consideration, in his eyes, is that such change is inevitable and natural, and hence that human "perfection" consists in conforming to it. By thus acknowledging, however, that modern social institutions, despite all their complexity, are just as "natural" for their own age as were the simpler forms of life for former days, Kuo diverges significantly from early Taoism, and, in so doing, he undoubtedly reflects centuries of Confucian influence. Yet, by refusing to interpret this growing complexity as necessarily synonymous with human progress, he seems to remain within the prevailing Chinese point of view.

We find a very different situation centuries later when we consider the Confucian, Wang Fu-chih (1619–92), better known as Wang Ch'uan-shan. Not only in his approach to history but also in his nationalism (see Sec. 5 below) he is one of the most "un-Chinese" of all Chinese thinkers. There is nothing accidental, he says, in the shift from one historical epoch to another. Every event is the result of historical forces, which operate according to a definite pattern, irrespective of the intentions of the historical individuals concerned. The actions of these individuals, indeed, no matter how seemingly haphazard and accidental, all contribute in the end to the unfolding of this pattern. Furthermore, the resulting changes are not piecemeal but affect the social institutions of each epoch in their totality. Hence it is futile to argue whether the Chinese bureaucratic empire created in the third and second centuries B.C. was better or not than the feudal hegemony preceding it. Each system was equally inevitable for its own age, and it was likewise inevitable that the one should give way to the other at the precise moment it did. Even a sage, therefore, had he been living in the earlier period, would have been unable to hasten the shift to bureaucratic empire, just as the several attempts at feudal restoration, made soon after the founding of the empire, were all equally doomed to failure.

Not only are such changes inevitable, however, but they belong to a definite pattern of social improvement which has moved China forward from tribalism to feudalism and from feudalism to centralized empire. Though Wang Fu-chih does not deny the greatness of the early sage-kings, he breaks sharply with tradition by asserting that the times in which they lived, despite their efforts, were crude and dark and that there has been a steady subsequent growth in civilization.

When he comes to discuss civilization on a world-wide scale, however, Wang seems to retain a hint of the old cyclical concept. Thus in a remarkable passage he points out that civilization is not the exclusive possession of the Chinese alone, nor does it evolve at the same rate in all places. Hence just as in China itself there has been a gradual cultural shift over the centuries from north to south, so it is possible that in very early times there may have lived non-Chinese peoples as civilized as are the Chinese today, and likewise it is possible that a day will come when the Chinese themselves will revert to barbarism. This view, however, holds only a small place in Wang's total philosophy of history, and elsewhere he vigorously criticizes the cyclical theories of Tung Chung-shu and Shao Yung alike.[22]

For the next exceptions to the prevailing Chinese historical view, we must turn to the nineteenth-century revival of the New Text school of Confucianism, headed by the famous reformer, K'ang Yu-wei (1858–1927). As part of this revival, K'ang refurbished the two-thousand-year-old theory of the Three Ages of Disorder, Approaching Peace, and Universal Peace (originally applied to the *Ch'un Ch'iu*, or *Spring and Autumn Annals*) and, in so doing, brought it up to date and gave it a world-wide context by ascribing the Age of Disorder to the time of Confucius, the Age of Approaching Peace to his own (K'ang Yu-wei's) day, and the Age of Universal Peace to a period yet to come. Not only China, K'ang asserted, but the entire human race, has been steadily moving from Disorder, through Approaching Peace, and thus toward the common goal of Universal Peace, which will inevitably be reached two or three centuries hence. In his *Ta-t'ung Shu*, or *Book of the Great Unity*, K'ang describes the coming millennium with apocalyptic fervor as one in which there will be no political or racial divisions, no social classes, and no exploitation of man by man.[23]

In K'ang's associates, T'an Ssŭ-t'ung (1865–98) and Liao P'ing (1852–1932), we find curious attempts to reconcile this ardent belief in evolutionary meliorism with the prevailing Chinese belief in devolutionary cyclicism. To do this, T'an Ssŭ-t'ung interprets the six lines of the first (*ch'ien*) hexagram of the *Book of Changes* as graphically symbolizing a twofold historical cycle, the first phase of which consists of devolution (prehistoric times to Confucius), and the second phase of evolution (Confucius to an age still in the future). The lower half of the *ch'ien* hexagram, called by T'an its "inner trigram," pertains to its devolutionary phase, and the upper half, called by him its "outer trigram," to its evolutionary phase. This theory (see Fung 2, pp. 699–702) can best be shown through the following table (to be read from bottom to top):

| Lines of *Ch'ien* Hexagram | | Sequence of Three Ages | Absolute Time Sequence |
|---|---|---|---|
| Outer trigram | 6 | Age of Universal Peace | Distant future |
| | 5 | Age of Approaching Peace | Near future |
| | 4 | Age of Disorder | Confucius until today |
| Inner trigram | 3 | Age of Disorder | Hsia dynasty until Confucius |
| | 2 | Age of Approaching Peace | Three Sovereigns and Five Emperors |
| | 1 | Age of Universal Peace | Prehistoric |

Liao P'ing's solution is somewhat different. "The evolution of the world," he writes, "is, culturally, from barbarism to civilization, and, geographically, from the lesser to the greater." Politically, this means that mankind has passed through five ascending forms of government: those of the lord, the tyrant, the king, the emperor, and the sovereign. The process will culminate with "the unification of the entire globe," which "must take place 10,000 years hence."

Confucius, though living long ago, had prophetic insight that this was going to happen and therefore, according to Liao, when editing the classics, used them to convey this information. In so doing, however, he deliberately reversed the true picture, attributing to remote antiquity the Age of Universal Peace, which actually still lies in the future, and portraying the above-mentioned five stages of government in descending rather than ascending order. Confucius' idea in so doing was, says Liao, "to set up an inverted image which, while showing retrogression, would, by telling men about the past, thereby inform them of the future."

As a graphic portrayal of this theory, Liao has a table consisting of two diverging columns of statements, one of which, arranged in usual sequence from top to bottom, is inscribed: "The classics are all abstract words and not real history," while the other, arranged in reverse sequence so that it can be read only by turning the page upside down, is inscribed: "Progress is something actual and historical."[24]

All three of these nineteenth-century Confucianists, as we know, were acquainted to varying degrees with Western literature. Hence there is every reason to suppose that their insistence on progressive

evolution—so at variance with traditional Chinese belief—very probably reflects Western influence, in the form either of scientific writings
on the theory of evolution or of theological literature about a coming
millennium.[25]

It seems fair to conclude, therefore, that, of the men discussed above
as possible exceptions to prevailing Chinese historical theory, some are
only seemingly so, some have expressed their views in rather rudimen-
tary form, some have been under outside influence, and only one—
Wang Fu-chih—has created a really well-rounded theory stressing historical progress.

Most thinkers, on the other hand, when they have expressed themselves on the subject, have either asserted the superiority of antiquity
to later ages or have maintained that historical movement, though an
actual fact, operates only in the form of recurrent cycles. A few have
tried to combine these two prevailing points of view by asserting that
we moderns happen to belong to the downswing of one such cycle. All
such theories, irrespective of other differences, obviously agree in their
implicit denial of the possibility of long-term historical progress. On
the other hand, however, it should be noted that only one major Chinese
thinker—Hsün Tzŭ—has seemingly gone to the opposite extreme by
denying that in history there occurs any appreciable movement at all.

### 3. Good and Evil

In the preceding sections we have seen that the universe, in Chinese
eyes, is a harmonious organism; that its pattern of movement is inherent
and not imposed from without; and that the world of man, being a part
of the universe, follows a similar pattern. What, then, may be asked, is
the origin of evil in such a universe? Before trying to answer this question, it will be helpful if we first survey the prevailing Chinese views on
the subject of human nature.

#### A. THE GOODNESS OF HUMAN NATURE

One of the major problems in Chinese philosophy has been that of the
goodness or badness of human nature. Most of all, it has been a Confucian problem, because the Confucianists, more than others, have been
primarily concerned with the relation of the individual to society. For
the Taoists this problem did not pose itself in the same way, since, in
their eyes, what is good means what is natural, and therefore the extent
of the individual's goodness depends upon the extent to which he is permitted by society to follow his natural instincts. "Do not let what is of
man obliterate what is of Nature," was the Taoist slogan (*Chuang-tzŭ*,

chap. 17; Giles, p. 211). As for the Buddhists, they, if anything, were even less interested in social relationships per se, believing as they did that these are among the ties binding us to the painful wheel of life and death. We shall have something more to say about Buddhist attitudes later.

The Confucianists, on the other hand, were par excellence men whose minds centered on political and social relationships, and therefore it was inevitable that sooner or later they should find themselves confronted with a major problem: to what extent is man's behavior conditioned by the social institutions under which he lives and to what extent does it spring directly from his own innate qualities? Hints of an awareness of this problem may be found already in Confucius, but Mencius (371?–279? B.C.) was the first to venture a clear-cut answer. Man, he maintained—and in so doing it is conceivable, though not provable, that he may have been influenced by Taoist ideas—is a being born for goodness; in him at birth, therefore, there exists a natural tendency for goodness, as inevitable as the natural tendency of water to flow downward (*Mencius*, VIa, 3). This means that social institutions do not produce, but merely give refined expression to, the shoots of goodness already innate in every man.

This optimistic view was far from universally shared in ancient China. Kao Tzŭ, who debated with Mencius on the subject, advanced a theory seemingly closer to the findings of modern psychology. Man's nature, he said, is at birth simply a bundle of instincts, of which those concerned with food and sex are primary; left to itself, therefore, it is as indifferent to either good or evil as water, left to itself, is to the direction it will eventually take when a passage is opened for it either to the east or to the west (*ibid.*).

The Legalists, for their part, were quite uninterested in abstract problems of metaphysics or psychology as such. They were, however, shrewd observers of human behavior as manifested in the disordered China of their time, and, on the basis of what they saw, they concluded cynically that within a state not more than ten people can be found who naturally do good of themselves; almost all men act only through motives of self-interest. This is why, the Legalists argued, no government can be effective unless it be based on a stern system of rewards and punishments, by means of which it can manipulate men's desires and fears for its own purposes (Fung 1, pp. 327–30).

The most formidable opponent of Mencius was, however, his fellow-Confucian of a later generation, Hsün Tzŭ. More than any other Chinese thinker, perhaps, Hsün Tzŭ preached what may be called a philosophy of culture. All morality, he maintained, is a product of culture and education and therefore would not exist were it not for the civilizing institutions created long ago by the sage-kings through their enlightened self-interest. "The nature of man is evil. His goodness is only acquired training." Man at birth possesses desires which, if unchecked, inevitably lead to strife; only under the constant influence of the mores of his group does he gradually learn to do what is right (chap. 23; Dubs, p. 301). In the next section we shall see how Hsün Tzǔ stressed the need for a structured society in order to curb and harmonize the otherwise anarchic desires of the individual.

Hsün Tzǔ's theory influenced many later Confucianists in varying degrees. Tung Chung-shu, for example, tried to harmonize Mencius with Hsün Tzǔ by saying that man's nature initially contains both self-ishness and altruism and therefore can never become wholly good unless subjected to further human training: "Goodness is like a kernel of grain; the nature is like the growing stalk of that grain. Though the stalk produces the kernel, it cannot itself be called a kernel, and though the nature produces goodness, it cannot itself be called good. The kernel and goodness are both brought to completion through man's continuation of Heaven's (work)" (Fung 2, p. 34).

Yang Hsiung (53 B.C.–A.D. 18) asserted somewhat similarly that, "in man's nature, good and evil are intermixed. If he cultivates the good elements, he becomes a good man, but if he cultivates the evil elements, he becomes an evil one" (Fung 2, p. 150). A more deterministic view was expressed by Wang Ch'ung, who said: "There are in truth some (natures) that are good and some that are bad. The good ones are definitely so of themselves, whereas the bad ones may be caused to become good by undergoing inculcation which leads them to exert themselves" (Lun Heng, chap. 4; Forke, I, 374). During the next several centuries of Neo-Taoist and then Buddhist intellectual domination, little more was said on the subject until Han Yü, in the eighth century, proclaimed even more deterministically than Wang Ch'ung that men's natures fall into three categories: the superior, which is wholly good; the medium, which may be made to be either good or bad; and the inferior, which is wholly evil (Fung 2, p. 413).

With the rise of Neo-Confucianism in the eleventh century, however, Hsün Tzǔ's pessimistic view, together with the theories influenced by it, was definitely rejected, and that of Mencius became supreme. From then until recent days all major thinkers, regardless of other differences, have agreed that man is by nature good. The only partial exception is Tai Chen (1723–77), a thinker of materialistic tendencies who reacted strongly against the earlier Neo-Confucianists. Thus he denied their contention that man's nature is a metaphysical principle implanted in man at birth, describing it instead in physical terms as consisting simply of "blood, breath, and the mental faculty." There is a difference, he maintained, between what is natural to man and what is morally necessary, and, though man's nature at birth is potentially good, his ability to rise from the natural to the morally necessary sphere depends upon the extent to which he succeeds in developing his mental faculty. Thus Tai, like Hsün Tzǔ, attaches great importance to education and knowledge as molders of human morality.[26]

### B. ORIGIN OF EVIL

What is the reason for this insistence—well-nigh universal during the last nine centuries—on man's innate goodness? Any consideration of this question must begin with a recognition of the Chinese conviction, already repeatedly referred to, that the universe is a harmony, the basic principle of which is therefore one of goodness; that the human world is an integral part of this harmony; and that man's nature is the vital link between the two.

On this point it is illuminating to contrast the attitudes of Mencius and Hsün Tzǔ. Thus for Mencius, in whom there is a mystical awareness of the oneness of man and the nonhuman universe, the metaphysical justification for the doctrine of human goodness is the fact that man's nature is "what Heaven has given us" (VI*a*, 15). For Hsün Tzǔ, on the contrary, human goodness has no such metaphysical basis but is solely the result of man's own efforts. It is thus unrelated to *T'ien*, or "Heaven," which, by Hsün Tzǔ, is interpreted as simply the name for a wholly naturalistic process.[27]

For this reason Hsün Tzǔ urges men not to exalt and conform to Heaven but rather to depend on themselves and to utilize the manifestations of Heaven for their own advantage (chap. 17; Dubs, p. 183). This denial by Hsün Tzǔ of the cosmic unity of man and nature, together with his theory of human nature and static view of history (see preceding section), represents a world view which in later times was decisively rejected by most Chinese thinkers.

If, however, the universe is actually a natural harmony, and therefore imbued with a principle of goodness which, contrary to Hsün Tzǔ, provides the basis for human goodness, we are then again faced by the question which was raised at the beginning of this section: What is the origin of evil? Is it, as has so often been asserted in the West, a matter of original sin or of a devil—figurative or otherwise—who struggles to gain men's souls? The former thesis is, on the face of it, impossible for anyone who, like Mencius, believes that man is *born* good. But the latter is equally unacceptable to him and his followers, since the very idea of forces of good and evil being engaged in a *struggle* with one another violates the basic concept of a self-contained harmonious universe.

Mencius himself does not analyze the problem from a metaphysical point of view. He merely says that men do wrong because of carelessness—they forget to preserve and nourish the goodness that lies within them and thereby allow it to be stripped from their natures, just as a once-beautiful mountain may be stripped of its trees until it becomes bare and barren. "But is this," Mencius asks, "the (original) nature of the mountain?" (VI*a*, 8). Thus, he says, "if men do what is not good, it is not the fault of their natural powers" (VI*a*, 6).

Though this answer may be unsatisfying in its failure to explain *what it is* that thus causes men to forget their original natures, it at least seems clearly to avoid the idea of good and evil as two contending forces and to point instead toward another conception much more congenial to Chinese thought. This is, that what we call "evil," far from being a positive force trying to destroy the cosmic harmony, is, on the contrary, just as much a part of that harmony, and just as necessary for its functioning, as what we call "goodness." Or, looked at from a slightly different point of view, it is an occasional falling-away from the harmonious centrality of all things—arising, in the case of man, because of his inadequate understanding of the cosmic pattern.

Formulations of this idea occur both in Taoism and in Buddhism. The Taoists, for example, never tire of pointing out that what men call right and wrong, good and evil, are purely relative concepts, without validity from the standpoint of the universal *Tao*. In Chuang Tzǔ's words: "Because of the right there is the wrong, and because of the wrong there is the right. . . . The right is an endless change. The wrong is also an endless change. . . . Therefore the Sage harmonizes the systems of right and wrong, and rests in the Evolution of Nature" (chap. 2; Giles, pp. 18 and 21).

Chinese Buddhism, too, though from its own point of view, denies the existence of evil as a positive force. Men endure the sufferings of life and death simply because of ignorance; they gain release from suffering through an understanding of its true nature. In either case the world itself remains unchanged; the only change lies in the individual's own understanding. Hence sin has no objective existence but is only a state of mind. Indeed, it is even possible for enlightened beings to perform acts without incurring retribution for them, which, if performed by other beings, would certainly be sinful.[28]

The clearest statements on good and evil, however, are those of the Neo-Confucianists. Li Ao (d. *ca.* 844), for example, one of the precursors of Neo-Confucianism, maintains that man's nature per se is wholly good but that, when the nature comes to be externally manifested in the form of the feelings or emotions (*ch'ing*), this goodness becomes obscured. This, however, "is not the fault of the nature," any more than it is the fault of an originally pure stream of water that it later becomes muddied by sediment. To prevent the feelings from operating, therefore, is the way to enable "the nature to gain its fulfilment," whereas "when the movements of the feelings continue unceasingly, it becomes impossible to return to one's nature and to radiate the infinite light of Heaven and Earth" (Fung 2, p. 414). Though Li thus distinguishes sharply between the original nature and its external emotional manifestations, he then goes on to say that "the nature and the feelings cannot exist one without the other"; in other words, that they are not diametric opposites, since both are equally aspects of the same universal whole. This doctrine, as Fung Yu-lan points out (*ibid.*), not only stems back to Mencius, but also owes much to Buddhism.

Chou Tun-yi (1017–73) agrees with Li that, though man's nature is originally good, its manifestations in actual conduct do not always conform to the mean; defective conduct of this sort we then call "evil" (Fung 2, p. 446). At about the same time we find the Ch'eng brothers insisting on the fact that goodness and evil are both inherent in the cosmic pattern and therefore cannot be disassociated from one another. Thus Ch'eng Hao (1032–85) says: "That some things are good and some evil is all equally a result of Heavenly Principle. For in Heavenly Principle it is inevitable that some things be beautiful and some ugly" (Fung 2, p. 518). And Ch'eng Yi (1033–1108) says similarly: "Within the universe, all things have their opposite: when there is the *yin*, there is the *yang*; when there is goodness, there is evil" (*ibid.*). These remarks possibly reflect the views of their uncle, Chang Tsai, who said that "the feelings of love and hatred are both equally products of the Great Void" (Fung 2, p. 483).

In the philosophy of Chu Hsi (1130–1200), the great synthesizer of Neo-Confucianism, there is a dualism between *li*, or "Principle," which is metaphysical, and *ch'i*, or "Ether," which is physical. The *ch'i* is the physical substance of which the universe consists. However, what gives meaning and order to the *ch'i*, and makes an organized universe possible, is the immanence in each physical object, whether animate or inanimate, of the metaphysical *li*, or "Principle." In the case of man, this *li* is known as his nature, which, therefore, in itself is invariably good. As externally manifested, however, this goodness can be actualized only imperfectly, owing to the impediments laid upon the nature by the surrounding physical *ch'i*. This *ch'i* differs in its purity (i.e., in the extent to which it allows *li*, or "Principle," to manifest itself) not only as between different species of creatures but also as between individual human beings. This is the reason for the moral differences externally found among different men. As to why the *ch'i* should thus have such differences, Chu Hsi can say nothing more than that they are natural and inevitable. Thus a disciple once asked: "Since *li* is everywhere good, how is it that the *ch'i* is differentiated into the pure and the turbid?" To which Chu replied: "Because, if one speaks only of the *ch'i*, there is some that of itself is cold and some that is hot, some fragrant and some bad smelling" (Fung 2, p. 553).

Here, as far as the *ch'i* alone is concerned, we find the view expressed that so-called "evil," like so-called "goodness," are both inherent elements in a larger whole. In Chu's greater dichotomy between the *li* and the *ch'i*, however, there seems at first sight to be a dualism of the sort so familiar to us in the West. Yet even here, as we shall see in Section 6, this seeming similarity breaks down on closer examination.

Wang Shou-jen, better known as Wang Yang-ming (1472–1529), was the greatest figure in Neo-Confucianism after Chu Hsi, with whom he differed in many important respects. In his concept of evil, however, he conforms to the general line of thinking we have been describing. Thus he says:

> The highest good is the mind's original substance. Whatever goes beyond this original substance is evil. It is not a case of there being something good, and then of there being something evil standing in opposition to it. Thus good and evil are only a single thing. . . .What we call evil is not original evil, but results either from transgressing or falling short of our original nature [Henke, pp. 156–57].

Somewhat later Yen Yüan (1635–1704) strongly attacks Chu Hsi's dichotomy between the metaphysical *li* as being wholly good and the physical *ch'i* as being the source of evil. Actually, Yen maintains, *li* and *ch'i* are inextricably bound together into "a single continuum," of which, therefore, it is impossible to say that one part is good and another evil. "How then," he asks, "can it be said that Principle (*li*) is uniform and single in its goodness, whereas the physical endowment deviates toward evil?" This would be like saying that the eye's (nonphysical) power of vision is good, whereas the physical eye itself, possessing this power, is evil. In actual fact, however, "it is only when its (the eye's) vision is led astray by improper things, or blocked or beclouded by them, that its view of things becomes wrong, so that evil can first be spoken of." Thus, for Yen, evil is not to be associated solely with the *ch'i*, nor is it a positive quality in itself. Rather, it is simply a deflection from "Heaven's correct pattern," caused by "enticement, delusion, habit, and contagion."[29]

From this survey of Neo-Confucian opinion, let us turn back for a moment to the Han Confucianist, Tung Chung-shu. He, it will be remembered, partially agreed with Hsün Tzŭ by saying that man's nature, at birth, contains selfishness as well as altruism and, therefore, that it cannot be made wholly good save through human institutions and education. His explanation for this initial mixture of good and evil is that man's goodness corresponds to the *yang* principle of Heaven, and his evil to Heaven's *yin* principle. Heaven imposes restraints upon the movements of the *yin*, and man should likewise confine the operation of the evil aspect of his nature, using for this purpose his intelligence, by means of which he creates his civilizing institutions (Fung 2, pp. 32–35).

Here we should keep in mind the thesis first suggested at the beginning of this paper—that in the West the universe has commonly been regarded as under the control of an external Divine Power, whereas in China it has been regarded as a self-contained organism functioning according to its own inherent pattern. At this point, however, it is necessary to make a further qualification by pointing out that this latter conception, while *generally* true of Chinese thinking, is not necessarily invariably true.

The *Yin-yang* and the Five Elements schools, for example, commonly explain the interrelationship alleged by them to exist between natural phenomena and human behavior in terms of an impersonal and automatic sequence of cause and effect. At other times, however, and without any explanation for the resulting contradiction, they interpret abnormal natural phenomena as the deliberate manifestations of a Divine Power, used by it to warn men of their improper behavior (Fung 1, p. 165).

In Tung Chung-shu, who was heavily influenced by the *yin-yang* ideology, a similar contradiction appears (Fung 2, pp. 55–58). Sometimes, as a result, Tung seems to use the word *T'ien*, or "Heaven," in a naturalistic sense, signifying a natural universe whose movements take place through their own inner necessity, without external guidance; at other times, however, he seems to regard *T'ien* as a conscious power, acting deliberately to control the movements of the *yin* and *yang*, the Five Elements, etc.

The latter concept, as we have seen, provides the metaphysical basis for Tung's belief that man's nature initially contains evil as well as goodness, so that the former must be repressed in order to allow the latter to realize its full potentialities. For as soon as one believes that Heaven acts from without to insure the proper functioning of the universe, it would seem to follow that this universe, if left to itself, would no longer function properly. However, Tung Chung-shu is neither clear nor consistent on this point, so that in his philosophy there remains an unresolved contradiction between a teleological and a naturalistic trend of thinking, of which he himself appears to be unconscious.

This leads us to a final consideration of some importance: Hsün Tzŭ, who denies the innate goodness of human nature, also stresses man's separateness from the nonhuman universe, which he conceives of in naturalistic—seemingly almost mechanistic—terms. Tung Chung-shu, on the other hand, while sharing Hsün Tzŭ's views about human nature to a limited extent, nevertheless affirms the unity of man with nature, to which, however, he apparently sometimes attributes volition and even personality. The prevailing Chinese belief in human goodness, for its part, seems to stem from yet a third, peculiarly Chinese, world view, different from that of either of these two men. Unlike that of Hsün Tzŭ, this view asserts that man is an integral part of a larger cosmic pattern, the goodness of which it accepts as axiomatic, simply because it *is* the cosmic pattern; but, unlike Tung Chung-shu's view, it asserts that this goodness is something inherent and spontaneous and not dependent on the volition of any external controlling Power.

### C. UNIVERSAL SALVATION

The natural corollary of the foregoing ideas is a firm belief in the universal perfectibility of all men. This, for the Confucianists, means that every man can become a sage and, for the Buddhists, that every man can achieve Buddhahood. Such, at least, is the theory, though, as clearly realized by Confucianists and Buddhists alike, it is one rarely achieved in actual life.

For the Taoists the situation is somewhat different, since, with their relativistic outlook on human affairs, they not only accept the existence of differences between individual human beings as inevitable but insist that true goodness lies in the preservation rather than the obliteration of these differences. In other words, the Taoists maintain that men are necessarily unequal in their external achievements but that they are nevertheless all equally good in so far as they all equally conform to their true natures. Hence they believe it is folly for anyone to strive to become a sage, unless it is truly in his nature to be such. This point of view explains why the Taoists, unlike the Confucianists and Buddhists, are uninterested in the possibilities of universal sagehood or salvation.

Among Confucianists, on the contrary, the belief in this possibility is shared with few exceptions. It is natural that Mencius should give his hearty approval to a saying possibly already current before his time: "All men may become a Yao or a Shun (legendary sage-rulers)" (VI*b*, 2). More unexpected, however, is Hsün Tzǔ's utterance (chap. 23; Dubs, p. 312) of an almost identical saying: "The man in the street can become a Yü (another sage-ruler)." If Hsün Tzǔ, despite his pessimistic view of man's original moral state, could nevertheless have such confidence in the possibility of human improvement through education, it is not surprising to find almost all later Confucianists voicing similar confidence. Thus Wang Shou-jen, to cite but one example, assures us that "the unifying quality of love is as surely possessed by the little man" as by the great one (Henke, p. 204).

It is the Buddhists, however, especially those representing the more peculiarly Chinese developments in Buddhism, who lay greatest stress on universal salvation. For example, Tao-sheng (*ca.* 360–434), who was very instrumental in shaping Chinese Buddhism, boldly asserted that even the *icchantikas* (nonbelievers in Buddhism), since they are sentient beings, are therefore like other men endowed with the Buddha nature and hence capable of achieving Buddhahood (Fung 2, p. 271).

This trend of thought is most spectacularly developed by the T'ien-t'ai school (6th century onward), in which the startling doctrine is advanced that all beings, even the Buddhas, possess two kinds of nature, the one pure, the other impure, and that these natures, for the Buddhas and other beings alike, remain forever immutable: "The mind-substance of each and every sentient being, and of each and every Buddha, originally contains the two natures, without the slightest distinction for all. Throughout they are exactly of the same sort, and have remained indestructible from antiquity until the present" (Fung 2, p. 379).

The only difference between the Buddhas and ordinary sentient beings, therefore, is that the former check the outward manifestations of the impure nature, whereas the latter do not. Even the Buddhas, however, can merely keep latent, but cannot actually eliminate or change, the impure nature, and, conversely, even depraved beings cannot eliminate or change the pure nature. The necessary corollary is that Buddhahood is open to all beings, provided only that they practice spiritual cultivation. This universalistic theory reached its logical culmination with Chan-jan (711–82), ninth patriarch of the T'ien-t'ai school, who proclaimed that "even inanimate things possess the Buddha-nature." "Therefore," he wrote, "we may know that the single mind of a single particle of dust comprises the mind-nature of all sentient beings and Buddhas. . . . All things, being immutable, are the *Bhūtatathatā* (the Absolute), and the *Bhūtatathatā*, responding to causation, is all things" (Fung 2, pp. 384–85).

This powerful affirmation contrasts significantly with the doctrine of the Mere Ideation school, as propounded in China by Hsüan-tsang. According to this school, the evolutions of all beings throughout successive existences are determined by "seeds"—some of them tainted, others untainted—which are imbedded in the consciousnesses of the beings concerned. These differing kinds of seeds, however, are not distributed among all beings equally: some beings are wholly devoid of the untainted seeds, some possess seeds qualifying them merely for the lower stages of Buddhism, and only a few possess the untainted seeds of Buddhahood itself. This, says the Mere Ideation school, is the reason for the differences in nature found among different beings and explains why not all men, but only a few, are capable of achieving Buddhahood (Fung 2, pp. 307 and 339). It is no mere accident that not only in this respect, but in others as well, the Mere Ideation school is the least Chinese and most purely Indian of all Buddhist schools in China. Indeed, it might better be termed "Buddhism in China" than "Chinese Buddhism."

### 4. Social Harmony

According to Chinese thinking, the world of man is, or should be, a reflection of the nonhuman universe, and man's nature is the essential link between the two. It is time now to examine in detail what has been the major Chinese conception regarding the social order.

Society, in Chinese eyes, consists of a large number of small social units (the family, the village, the guild, etc.), each of which consists in turn of individuals varying greatly in their intellectual and physical capabilities. Because of these inequalities, it is inevitable that class differences should exist. The social order, in other words, is a rationalization of existing human inequalities.

It does not follow, however, that there should be conflict between social classes. On the contrary, the welfare of the social organism as a whole depends upon harmonious co-operation among all of its units and of the individuals who comprise these units. This means that every individual, however high or low, has the obligation to perform to the best of his ability those particular functions in which he is expert and which are expected of him by society. Thus the ruler should rule benevolently, his ministers should be loyal yet at the same time ready to offer if need be their frank criticism, the farmers should produce the maximum of food, the artisans should take pride in their manufactures, the merchants should be honest in their dealings, and no one should interfere needlessly in the tasks of others for which he himself is not qualified. In other words, society should be like a magnified family, the members of which, though differing in their status and functions, all work in harmony for the common good.

It is in Confucianism that we find greatest insistence on this conception of society as a graded but harmonious organism. For example, the typically Confucian idea that government is the function of a specialized ruling group, and that in it, therefore, there can be no popular participation, goes back to Confucius in his assertion: "The people can be made to follow it (probably meaning a policy decreed from above); they cannot be made to understand it" (*Analects*, VIII, 9). Or, again, the view of society as a corporate body of responsible individuals appears in the answer given by him when asked the way of good government: "Let the ruler be ruler, the minister minister; let the father be father, and the son son" (*Analects*, XII, 11). In other words, let each individual fulfil in practice the obligations ideally expected of him according to his social position.

Mencius has given one of the most candid enunciations of Confucian class theory in two passages of his works:

Some labor with their brains and some labor with their brawn. Those who labor with their brains govern others; those who labor with their brawn are governed by others. Those governed by others, feed them. Those who govern others, are fed by them. This is a universal principle in the world [IIIa, 4].

If there were no men of a superior grade, there would be no one to rule the countrymen. If there were no countrymen, there would be no one to support the men of superior grade [IIIa, 3].

But it is Hsün Tzǔ, perhaps more than any other Confucian, who has supplied a theoretical justification for social inequality. Strife arises, he says, because all men are born with desires, whereas things are insufficient to satisfy all these desires equally: "People desire and hate the same things. Their desires are many, but things are few. Since they are few there will inevitably be strife." The primary reason for instituting social distinctions, therefore, is that such distinctions are needed in order to insure an orderly distribution of the good things of life without undue exploitation of one group by another:

If the strong coerce the weak, the intelligent terrorize the stupid, and the people who are subjects rebel against their superiors; if the young insult the aged, and the government is not guided by virtue—if this be the case, then the aged and weak will suffer the misfortune of losing their subsistence, and the strong will suffer the calamity of division and strife. . . . Hence for this reason intelligent men have introduced social distinctions [chap. 10; Dubs, pp. 152–53].[30]

This view of society as an ordered inequality has been taken for granted by all later Confucianists, so that it is sufficient if we quote only the following single typical statement by Tung Chung-shu:

The Sage observes what it is in the nature of the generality of men that leads to disorder. Therefore in his governing of men he differentiates between upper and lower (classes), permitting the rich to have enough to display their noble position, but not to the point of arrogance, and the poor to have enough to support life, but not to reach the point of anxiety. If a harmonious balance be maintained according to this rule, there will then be no lack of material resources, and upper and lower (classes) will be mutually at peace. Therefore good government will be conducted with ease [Fung 2, p. 53].

If we turn from Confucianism to other early schools, we find in Mo Tzŭ (*ca.* 479–*ca.* 381 B.C.) one of the most striking antitheses to the Confucian way of life. In a manner almost Marxian, he emphasizes the fact of conflicting group interests and waxes bitter over "the large state which attacks small states, the large house which molests small houses, the strong who plunder the weak, the clever who deceive the stupid, the honored who disdain the humble" (chap. 16; Mei, p. 87). Nor does he hesitate to make many sarcastic attacks on the "gentlemen of the world" who condone this state of affairs (Mei, pp. 49, 135, 151, 246). Yet, unlike Marx, he draws no conclusion that the weak should unite to dispossess the strong. On the contrary, he remains well within the major current of Chinese thought by upholding the sanctity of the existing class structure and insisting that reform must come from above through moral indoctrination—which, for him, primarily means his famous doctrine of Universal Love, supported by certain religious and political sanctions. In the latter field, indeed, he goes further in the direction of authoritarianism than the Confucians themselves, by urging the complete intellectual conformity of inferior to superior in an ascending hierarchy consisting of clan members, clan patriarchs, state rulers, the king of the Chinese hegemony, and finally the Will of Heaven. This is his well-known doctrine of Agreement with the Superior (chap. 13; Mei, pp. 72–75).

The real totalitarians of ancient China are the Legalists, however, and it is they who are farthest removed from the Confucians in their insistence that men are inherently selfish and that therefore their unquestioning obedience to the state cannot be gained except through fear. Thus the Legalists, while fully as anxious as the Confucianists to maintain a clearly gradated class structure, see it in terms of a rigid conformity based on force rather than of a voluntary co-operation based on suasion. This fact undoubtedly goes far to explain their subsequent disappearance from Chinese thought as an identifiable group, even though certain of their political devices were perpetuated in modified form under the Confucian state.

Among the early Taoists there is a mixed point of view. Whereas the anarchistically minded Chuang Tzŭ would like to do away with government entirely, Lao Tzŭ accepts it, though grudgingly, and with the proviso that it be made as simple as possible. Much of his little book, as a consequence, is intended as advice for the Taoist sage-ruler. Hence when he says that "the Sage rules the people by emptying their minds" (chap. 3) or that he "treats them all as children" (chap. 49), he shows himself as much a believer in class distinctions as any Confucian, though from a different point of view.

A marked mellowing toward social institutions—undoubtedly the outcome of centuries of Confucian influence—appears in the Neo-Taoist Kuo Hsiang. Not merely does he, like Lao Tzŭ, accept organized government and society as unavoidable evils; as we have seen in Section 2, he even goes so far as to find no necessary incompatibility between the order of nature and the growing complexities of human civilization. Thus the following passage, though undoubtedly not intended by Kuo merely to justify the social status quo, nevertheless is as suitable for that purpose as any to be found in Confucian literature:

Error arises when one has the qualities of a servant but is not satisfied to perform a servant's duties. Hence we may know that (the relative positions of) ruler and subject, superior and inferior, . . . conform to a natural principle of Heaven and are not really caused by man. . . . Let the servants simply accept their own lot and assist each other without dissatisfaction, . . . each having his own particular duty and at the same time acting on behalf of the others. . . . Let those whom the age accounts worthy be the rulers, and those whose talents do not meet the requirements of the world be the subjects, just as Heaven is naturally high and Earth naturally low. . . . Although there is no (conscious) arrangement of them according to what is proper, the result is inevitably proper [Fung 2, p. 227].

In another statement Kuo eloquently describes the harmony that emerges from seeming disharmony when the above principle is followed:

Just as the spider and scarab, despite their humble surroundings, can spread their net or roll their ball without seeking the aid of any artisan, so for all creatures, each has that in which it is skilled. Although their skills differ, they themselves are alike in that they all practice these skills. This, then, is the kind of "skill that looks like clumsiness." Therefore the talented employer of men uses those who are skilled in squares to make squares, and those who are skilled in circles to make circles, allowing each to perform his particular skill, and thus to act in accordance with his nature. . . . That is why, being different from one another, their multitude of separate skills seem like clumsiness. Yet because everyone in the world has his own particular skill, the result seems like great skill [Fung 2, pp. 220–21].

Basic in the many attacks made on Buddhism by non-Buddhists during the next several centuries was the conviction that this alien ideology is dangerous to the Chinese way of life. On the one hand, it was felt, the Buddhist teaching that life is suffering is a denial of the Chinese conception of cosmic harmony; on the other, the Buddhist monastic order—an *imperium in imperio*—draws men away from their normal duties and thus destroys the fabric of Chinese society. This attitude appears clearly, for example, in the attacks made by one of the most famous of the critics, Fan Chen (*ca.* 450–*ca.* 515), a man who himself shows both Confucian and Taoist influence. "Buddhism," he begins by pointing out, "is injurious to government and its monks do harm to custom." Then, after going on to criticize the Buddhists for refusing to accept the ordinary round of human existence as natural and therefore desirable, he concludes by saying:

Lesser people should find sweetness in their cultivated acres, and superior men should preserve their quiet simplicity. Let food be grown and it will not be exhausted. Let clothing be spun and it will not come to an end. Let inferiors present their surplus to their superiors, and superiors practice non-interference toward their inferiors. By the use of this principle there will be sufficiency for life and support for the parents; it will be possible to act for oneself and also for others; the country will remain in order and the ruler will be in his place [Fung 2, pp. 291–92].

There is little doubt that Fan's point of view, reiterated by many later critics, was a primary factor in the ultimate decline of Buddhism in China.[31]

It is not until the nineteenth century, therefore, that we find any Chinese so "un-Chinese" as to advocate the transformation of a class society into a classless society. This, however, is precisely the bold proposal made by K'ang Yu-wei and T'an Ssŭ-t'ung, both of whom, as we have seen in the first two sections, were directly influenced by Western thought. Thus K'ang exhorts: "Let us eliminate the class sphere and bring equality to all men. . . . Let us eliminate the sphere of the family and become 'citizens of Heaven.' . . . Let us eliminate the occupational sphere and foster means of livelihood common to all" (Fung 2, p. 689).

With similar fervor T'an Ssŭ-t'ung describes the coming Age of Universal Peace as one in which distinctions between ruler and subject and rich and poor are all to be obliterated: "Poverty and wealth are equalized. Within a thousand or a myriad miles it is as if there were but a single family or a single individual. . . . It is like the Millennium spoken of in Western books, or the Great Unity found in the *Evolutions of Rites*" (Fung 2, pp. 698–99).

Before concluding this section, we should not overlook a seeming contradiction between the Chinese belief in a strongly hierarchical society and the other Chinese belief, discussed in the preceding section, in the universal perfectibility of all men. In other words, there here seems to be a clash between the practical need of the Chinese for social stability and their theoretical advocacy of social mobility, as implied by their belief in the moral worth of the individual. Undoubtedly, the latter concept explains why certain writers have tried to read a "democratic" meaning into Confucianism, even though the former shows clearly why such "democracy" cannot possibly be equated with Western political definitions of the word.

On the theoretical level the Chinese solved this contradiction by recognizing that, whereas classes are necessary to society and must remain forever immutable as such, the possibility always exists for particular individuals to move upward or downward between these classes. Here, therefore, is another manifestation of the Chinese fondness for solutions which permit lesser change to occur within a greater permanency.

On the practical level the exemplification of this concept was the Chinese examination system—a device whereby all members of society, with trifling exceptions, were given the opportunity of entering the ranks of the ruling scholar-bureaucracy. In practice, unfortunately, this institution fell short of its avowed aim, owing to the failure of the Chinese state to provide equally broad opportunities for acquiring the education without which success in the examinations was impossible. This meant that most examination candidates came from a relatively restricted group of gentry families, whose political power, as a result, tended to become hereditary as a class, even though the individual members of this class had to prove their intellectual worth anew from generation to generation. Even this situation, however, is remarkable when compared with prevailing Western conditions before modern times, and to the Chinese mind, with its strong preference for working compromises in place of unworkable absolutes, it must have seemed sufficient. The net result, therefore, is that, though the Chinese social system theoretically left a place open for individual mobility, such mobility was infrequent in practice, save in times of war or political disintegration.

## 5. Peace and War

Since war is the most violent disrupter of social harmony, it is natural enough that it should be overwhelmingly condemned in Chinese philosophy. This is particularly true of the early period, when no unified empire existed, and war between the feudal states was endemic. Thus not only did the Confucians and Taoists denounce war, but also the hitherto unmentioned Dialecticians, whose leaders, Hui Shih and Kung-sun Lung (4th–3d centuries B.C.), were both known as pacifists (Fung 1, pp. 195 and 203). So too were such minor contemporaries as Yin Wen and Sung K'eng, who "proposed disarmament in order to save their generation from war" and preached that "it is no disgrace to be insulted" (Fung 1, pp. 148 ff.). The most famous indictment of war, however, is undoubtedly that of Mo Tzŭ, who in unsparing terms attacked it on both moral and economic grounds. Even for the victors, he said, the cost is so great that "when we consider the victory as such, there is nothing useful about it. When we consider the possessions obtained through it, they do not even make up for the loss" (chap. 18; Mei, p. 102).

Yet it would be incorrect to conclude that all these ancient thinkers were unalterably opposed to war under any circumstances. This, indeed, was made difficult by an embarrassing circumstance, namely, that, among the universally revered sage-kings of early times, several were known to history as having engaged in military campaigns. This fact forced Mencius, Mo Tzŭ, and Hsün Tzŭ alike into the familiar but dangerous doctrine that wars are sometimes "just," provided they be waged by the right person. The ancient sages, these thinkers said, occasionally found it necessary, despite their abhorrence of conflict, to take punitive measures against notorious tyrants or rebels. Such measures, however, would better be described as "chastisement" than as "attack," since their aim, in Hsün Tzŭ's words, was to "stop tyranny and get rid of injury." To this reasoning based on history, Mo Tzŭ added the further argument that the arming of the weak is justifiable as a deterrent to the aggression by the strong. This is why his book, which contains perhaps the most vehement denunciation of warfare in Chinese literature, also contains a group of chapters devoted to the defensive tactics to be used against aggression.[32]

There was only one group of men in ancient China, however, that deliberately exalted war as a political instrument, and this was the Legalists. As followers of *Realpolitik*, engaged in a ruthless struggle for power, they were interested in one thing only: how to create a strong and centralized apparatus of government. To achieve this end, all else must be subordinated, they said, to the two basic occupations of agriculture and war. Yet both, especially the latter, are arduous and poorly rewarded. Therefore, in order to induce people to serve readily in the army, "ordinary conditions should be made so hard for them, that they look upon war as a welcome release from their toil and as a good opportunity for earning rewards. Then they will fight with all their energy."[33] The cold-blooded realism of the Legalists is well expressed in the following passage from the *Han-fei-tzŭ* (chap. 49, middle):

What are mutually incompatible should not co-exist. To reward those who kill the enemy, and at the same time praise acts of mercy and benevolence; to honor those who capture cities, and at the same time believe in the doctrine of universal love; . . . to depend on agriculture to enrich the nation, and on the soldiers to resist the enemy, and at the same time encourage men of letters; . . . strong government will not thus be gained.

Significantly, however, even the Legalists made no attempt to glorify war. For them it was simply a necessary means to a desired end. In the entire range of Chinese philosophy there has been nothing comparable to Nietzsche's exaltation of the superman and praise of war as morally desirable.

Only one later Chinese thinker, so far as I know, in any way compares with the Legalists in his acceptance of warfare. This is Wang Fu-chih, whose militant attitude stems from his nationalism, which, in turn, combines with his view of history (see Sec. 2 above) to set him sharply apart from the general current of Chinese thought. There are good historical reasons for this phenomenon, inasmuch as Wang lived at a time (the seventeenth century) when China was overrun by the Manchus, and this event embittered him so greatly that he spent much of his life in retirement rather than hold office under the alien rulers.

The ideological result, for him, is an ardent nationalism which causes him to extol the glories of the Chinese race and to laud China's periods of military expansion as expressions of manifest destiny. To bring the barbarians under Chinese rule is, he says, "to expand the virtue of Heaven and Earth and establish the apogee of man." Any means toward this end seems to be justifiable to him, the more so as the barbarians, in his eyes, may scarcely be accounted members of the human race at all: "As for the barbarians, destroying them means no lack of benevolence, attacking them means no lack of righteousness, and tricking them means no lack of good faith. Why so? Good faith and righteousness are principles to be practiced between one man and another, but they are not to be extended to an alien species."[34]

Before leaving this topic, there is one matter that should give us pause, and that is the seeming discrepancy between the attitudes we have been describing and those on a more popular and less philosophical level. On the one hand, to be sure, it is quite true that the soldier did not even hold a recognized place among the traditional classes of Chinese society—a fact implied by the well-known saying (rhyming in the original):

> Good iron isn't beaten into nails;
> A good man doesn't become a soldier.

Yet, on the other hand, it is also true that many of the most popular Chinese novels and dramas—from which, until recently, the ordinary man derived much of his knowledge of Chinese history—deal in most colorful fashion with famous wars and military figures of the past. This, no doubt, can largely be explained by fondness—widespread in China as elsewhere—for gallant deeds of derring-do, especially when sufficiently remote from the present as to become enshrouded in a haze of romantic glamour. Another factor of some sociological importance is that many of China's historical military heroes began their careers as bandits and have become identified in the popular mind as Robin Hood–like protagonists of the people against a corrupt social order. Even in these exciting novels and dramas, however, it is noteworthy that chief applause is often reserved for the man who prefers guile to force for gaining the submission of his opponent.[35]

## 6. The Harmonizing of Opposites

By now it should be evident that basic among Chinese thought patterns is the desire to merge seemingly conflicting elements into a unified harmony. Chinese philosophy is filled with dualisms in which, however, their two component elements are usually regarded as complementary and mutually necessary rather than as hostile and incompatible. A common feature of Chinese dualisms, furthermore, is that one of their two elements should be held in higher regard than the other. Here again, therefore, we have an expression of the concept of harmony based upon hierarchical difference, such as we have already seen in the Chinese view of society.

In the following pages we shall discuss only a few of these dualisms: man and nature, being and non-being, quiescence and movement, the *yin* and the *yang*, and *li* and *ch'i*.

### A. MAN AND NATURE

The theme of the oneness of man with nature underlies so much of Chinese art and literature, and is so well known, that it scarcely needs reiteration. Here, therefore, we shall merely cite a few typical examples to illustrate the various ways in which it has been expressed by different schools.

In Taoism, of course, the approach is mystical, as typified by Chuang Tzŭ's statement (chap. 2; Giles, p. 23): "Heaven and Earth came into being with me together, and with me, all things are one." Chuang Tzŭ's contemporary, the Dialectician Hui Shih, expresses a similar sentiment when he says (chap. 33; Giles, p. 451): "Love all things equally; the universe is one." The same theme, expressed in terms of Confucian ethics, is repeated by Mencius (VIIa, 4) in the words: "All things are complete within us. There is no greater delight than to find sincerity (ch'eng) when one examines oneself." The rationalistic Hsün Tzŭ, as we have seen, rejects this mystical approach, but the *Doctrine of the Mean*—a Confucian work probably partially reflecting Mencius' ideas—reaffirms it by saying (chaps. 20 and 22): "Sincerity (ch'eng) is the way of Heaven. To attain to that sincerity is the way of man. . . . (Able to do this), he can assist the transforming and nourishing operations of Heaven and Earth. Capable of assisting in these transforming and nourishing operations, he can form a trinity with Heaven and Earth."

In the *Yin-yang* and Five Elements schools, mysticism gives way to a wholly concrete and matter-of-fact attitude, in which, however, emphasis is given to the delicate balance believed to exist between natural phenomena and human behavior. Thus the *Yüeh Ling*, or *Monthly Commands* (Legge, *Book of Rites*, I, 257), tells us that "if in the first month of spring (the sovereign) follows the regulations pertaining to summer, the rain will be unseasonable, plants and trees will drop (their leaves) early, and the state will constantly have something of which to be afraid. If he follows the autumn regulations, his people will suffer great pestilences." In similar fashion the text goes on to describe the results of other unseasonable behavior for this and other months.

This sort of thinking culminates in Tung Chung-shu, who, with fervor combined with almost painful literalness, proclaims the following correlations, *inter alia*, between man and the nonhuman world:[36]

| Man | Nature |
|---|---|
| head | Heaven's countenance |
| hair | stars and constellations |
| eyes and ears | sun and moon |
| breathing | wind |
| body | Earth's thickness |
| four limbs | four seasons |
| five viscera | Five Elements |
| orifices and veins | rivers and valleys |
| 12 larger joints | 12 months of year |
| 360 lesser joints | 360 days of year |
| ruler's likes and beneficence | warmth of spring |
| ruler's joy and rewarding | heat of summer |
| ruler's dislikes and punishing | coolness of autumn |
| ruler's anger and executing | coldness of winter |
| four official ranks (each with three officials, or a total of 12 officials) | four seasons (each with three months, or a total of 12 months) |

We have already seen how some Chinese criticized Buddhism for its renunciation of life and thereby, in their eyes, its denial of the unity of man with the cosmic process. In part, at least, the reformist Buddhist movement known as *Ch'an* (Japanese *Zen*) was an attempt to answer this criticism. In many ways this school represents the most distinctively Chinese movement in Buddhism. It revolted against the complex cosmological and psychological theories of other Buddhist schools, calling them "arguments which are the ordure of nonsense." Likewise it rejected the deliberate striving for enlightenment through meditation and similar techniques, maintaining instead that "spiritual cultivation cannot be cultivated." By this it meant that enlightenment cannot be forced; it either comes naturally, in the course of one's ordinary humdrum round of life, or it does not come at all. "In carrying water and chopping wood: therein lies the wonderful *Tao*," was the Ch'anist slogan. In the words of Yi-hsüan (d. 867): "You followers of the Way (*Tao*), there is no need for you to devote effort to the Buddhist teaching. Only do the ordinary things with no special effort: relieve your bowels, pass water, wear your clothes, eat your food, and, when tired, lie down. The simple fellow will laugh at you, but the wise will understand."[37]

In this stress on enlightenment as something to be found within the natural round of life (a subject to which we shall recur in Sec. 7), there is much of the spirit of Taoism. In several respects, indeed, the Ch'an school may well be termed a kind of Taoism in Buddhist dress.

Finally, both in Neo-Confucianism and in nineteenth-century Confucianism there are innumerable expressions of a mystic awareness of oneness between man and the nonhuman universe:

Chou Tun-yi is said to have refrained from clearing away the grass from the front of his window, "because," said he, "its impulse is just like my own."[38]

"Heaven and man are to each other as the inner and outer sides (of a garment)," says Shao Yung [Fung 2, p. 468].

"A state of functioning in which differentiation is made between Heaven and man cannot adequately be said to be 'sincerity.' A state of knowledge in which differentiation is made between Heaven and man cannot be considered as the utmost 'enlightenment,' " says Chang Tsai [Fung 2, p. 493].

"The man of love (*jen*) takes Heaven, Earth, and all things as one with himself," says Ch'eng Hao [Fung 2, p. 521].

"The mind of a single person is the mind of Heaven and Earth," says Ch'eng Yi [Fung 2, p. 531].

"It is not the case that man, as the being possessed of the highest intellect, stands alone in the universe. His mind is also the mind of birds and beasts, of grass and trees," says Chu Hsi [Bruce, *op. cit.*, p. 61].

"The universe is my mind, and my mind is the universe," so that "if I can develop completely my mind, I thereby become identified with Heaven," says Lu Chiu-yüan (1139–93) [Fung 2, pp. 573–74].

"The great man is an all-pervading unity with Heaven, Earth, and all things," says Wang Shou-jen [Henke, p. 204].

"The bringing of all things into equable conformity, tranquilizing Earth, giving completion to Heaven, and bringing great harmony to the entire universe: these are my nature's final results," says Yen Yüan [Fung 2, p. 646].

"Heaven is a single spiritual substance, and man too is a single spiritual substance. Though different in size, they both share the vast energy derived from the Great Origin," says K'ang Yu-wei [Fung 2, p. 685].

"The ether functions in its most spiritual and subtle aspects when it constitutes the brain in the human body. . . . It is the electricity in the atmosphere, . . . that unites Heaven, Earth, the myriad creatures, the self, and other men, into a single organism," says T'an Ssŭ-t'ung [Fung 2, pp. 693–94].

### B. BEING AND NON-BEING

The terms "being" (*yu*) and "non-being" (*wu*) occur only sporadically in Confucian literature and then most commonly in the course of diatribes against Taoism or Buddhism. In the latter two schools, on the other hand, both terms are in frequent use, though with a strong and characteristic preference shown for "non-being" as against "being." This preference, as Fung Yu-lan observes, runs quite counter to the Western point of view:

When a student of Chinese philosophy begins to study Western philosophy, he is glad to see that the Greek philosophers also made a distinction between Being and Non-being, the limited and the unlimited. But he feels rather surprised to find that the Greek philosophers held that Non-being and the unlimited are inferior to Being and the limited. In Chinese philosophy the case is just the reverse.[39]

We have already read in Section 1, for example, Lao Tzŭ's statement that "being is the product of non-being" (chap. 40), with which may be compared the passage in the *Chuang-tzŭ* (chap. 23; Giles, p. 304): "All things issue forth from non-being, for since being itself cannot, by means of its own being, cause being, it must necessarily issue forth from non-being." The same idea appears in the Neo-Taoist Wang Pi (226–49), when he says: "Though Heaven and Earth, in their greatness, are richly endowed with the myriad things; though their thunder moves and their winds circulate; though through their evolving operations the myriad transformations come to be—yet it is the silent and supreme non-being that is their origin" (Fung 2, p. 181).

In these and similar Taoist passages, non-being definitely does not mean actual "nothingness." It is simply a convenient name for what is really indescribable and, therefore, strictly speaking, unnamable: the state which is different from, or ontologically prior to, the state of being of our own organized, finite universe. In the same way the Buddhists commonly refer to the world of fluctuating phenomenal existence as that of being, but to the permanent reality underlying this phenomenal flux as non-being.

In the passages quoted so far, being and non-being are apparently regarded as mutually exclusive concepts, whereas, as we have indicated earlier, the long-range Chinese tendency is to merge all such seeming opposites into a higher unity. On the Taoist side, Kuo Hsiang achieves this unity by simply eliminating the concept of non-being from his philosophy entirely. This he does by interpreting the term as actually meaning what it literally says: nothingness. Thus, for him, it becomes equivalent to what we would call a mathematical zero, and so, since there really is no such a thing as non-being, it follows that the only actual existence is that of being. We have already seen in Section 1 how, with this argument, Kuo Hsiang conceives of the universe as an eternal flux of being, self-caused and self-existent, which functions independently of any prior or external agent.

On the Buddhist side, the usual line of reasoning is to say that "non-being," if it really signifies the Buddhist Absolute, cannot be subject to any kind of limitation, such as that implied when it is described as the mere opposite of being. Therefore genuine non-being represents a higher kind of synthesis—one transcending, yet at the same time embracing, both being and non-being as ordinarily conceived.

Perhaps the most striking exemplification of this trend of thought is the Theory of Double Truth as propounded by Chi-tsang (549–623). According to him, there are, for the seeker of Buddhist enlightenment, three ascending levels of truth, each to be found under the two categories of mundane truth and absolute truth. The noviciate begins his spiritual cultivation by rising from mundane truth to absolute truth, as postulated on the lowest level. As his understanding deepens, however, he comes to realize that what, on the lowest level, is absolute truth is no more than mundane truth on the second level. On this higher level, therefore, he again passes from mundane truth to absolute truth, only to be confronted by yet another antithesis of the two on the third or highest level. Thus step by step he progresses in his cultivation until at last he reaches the third and final absolute truth and thereby achieves enlightenment. This process may be schematized as follows (Fung 2, p. 295):

### THREE LEVELS OF DOUBLE TRUTH

| Mundane | Absolute |
|---|---|
| 1. Affirmation of being | 1. Affirmation of non-being |
| 2. Affirmation of either being or non-being | 2. Denial of both being and non-being |
| 3. Either affirmation or denial of both being and non-being | 3. Neither affirmation nor denial of both being and non-being |

Thus, in a manner reminiscent of Hegelian dialectics, being and non-being are gradually merged through a succession of negations of negation, until finally nothing remains to be either affirmed or denied.

#### C. MOVEMENT AND QUIESCENCE

*Tung* ("movement") and *ching* ("quiescence"), or their various rough equivalents, such as *wei* ("activity") and *wu wei* ("non-activity"), are antithetical terms which, like being and non-being, occur frequently in Taoism and Buddhism, especially with reference to human behavior and states of mind. And just as, in the ontological sphere, the Chinese show a strong preference for non-being as against being, so in the human sphere they emphasize the importance of quiescence as against movement. "Quiescence is the lord of movement," says Lao Tzŭ (chap. 26).[40] Therefore, he urges, "Hold fast enough to quiescence, and of the ten thousand things none but can be worked on by you" (chap. 16). Similarly, we are told by Chuang Tzŭ (chap. 13; Giles, p. 158): "Emptiness, quiescence, stillness and non-activity: these are the levels of the universe and the perfection of *Tao* and *Te* (the Power). Therefore true rulers and sages rest therein."

The same emphasis on quiescence as against movement is general in Buddhism, in which, for example, there is the following statement by Liang Su (753–93), an exponent of the T'ien-t'ai school: "What is this Reality? It is the original state of the nature. The failure of things to return to it is caused by darkness and movement. The illuminating of this darkness is called enlightenment, and the halting of this movement is called quiescence" (Fung 2, p. 423).

Both in Taoism and in Buddhism, however, there is a further tendency to merge movement and quiescence into a higher synthesis, for designating which they sometimes use a term other than "quiescence." The Neo-Taoist Wang Pi writes, for example: "The cessation of activity always means quiescence, but this quiescence is not something opposed to activity" (Fung 2, p. 181). Similarly, the Buddhist monk Seng-chao (384–414) has a famous essay, "On the Immutability of Things," in which he discusses the relationship of things past and present. Most people, he says, regard things as in a state of movement, because the events of the past do not reach into the present (they have moved away from the present). He himself, however, regards them as in a state of quiescence, precisely because events of the past do not depart from their positions in the past (they do not move into the present). But then, having thus seemingly spoken in favor of quiescence, he goes on to say that in the final analysis there is no real antithesis between it and movement, inasmuch as they may both be synthesized to form a higher state which he calls "immutability":

In our search for immutability, we surely do not find quiescence by putting movement aside. We must seek for movement in the quiescent, just as we must seek for quiescence in movement. Therefore though (things) move, they are ever quiescent. Because we do not find quiescence by putting movement aside, therefore though (things) remain quiescent, they are ever in movement [*Book of Chao*, chap. 1; Liebenthal, p. 46].

In Neo-Confucianism we find this idea of quiescence continued among certain, though not all, thinkers—primarily they are those in whom Taoist or Buddhist influence is most apparent. Li Ao, for example, uses the Confucian term *ch'eng*, or "sincerity," to describe the state of genuine mental composure of the person who can synthesize the ordinary fluctuations of quiescence and movement. "When there is quiescence," he says, "it must be followed by movement, and when there is movement, it must be followed by quiescence. This uninterrupted (sequence of) quiescence and movement constitutes the feelings." However, "to realize that its (the mind's) original condition is that of the absence of thought; to be separated both from movement and quiescence; and to remain silently immovable: that is the state of sincerity in its utter perfection" (Fung 2, pp. 419–20).

Chou Tun-yi similarly describes the mind, in its highest state of perfection, as having two aspects: that of a quiescent "absence of thought," in which it is "silently immovable," and that of an awakened "penetrating activity of thought," in which, "becoming activated, it thereupon penetrates everywhere." The synthesis of the two is expressed by him in the words: "One's thoughts are absent, yet penetrate everywhere" (Fung 2, p. 450). Ch'eng Hao likewise emphasizes such a mental synthesis, for which, however, he uses the word *ting*, "composure": "What is termed composure is something that persists irrespective of whether there be movement or quiescence. It does not associate itself with anything, nor is there for it anything either internal or external. . . . The normality of the Sage is that his emotions accord with (the nature of) all things, yet (of himself) he has no emotion" (Fung 2, pp. 523–24).

This line of reasoning culminates in Wang Shou-jen's doctrine of the "Unity of Activity (or Movement) and Quiescence," of which he writes:

The mind may neither be said to be active nor quiescent. Its "quiescence" has reference to its (internal) substance (t'i), whereas its "activity" has reference to its (external) functioning (yung). . . . The mind is single and nothing more. Since quiescence refers to its inherent substance, to seek beyond this for yet a further basis of quiescence is to pervert this original substance. And since activity is its functioning, to be fearful of its becoming too readily active is to nullify its functioning. . . . In its state of activity it is active, but in its state of quiescence it is also active. (These two modes) rise and fall as they anticipate things; they follow one another without end [Henke, pp. 387–88].

### D. THE "YIN" AND THE "YANG"

Just as in the foregoing dualisms there is a subordination of one element to another (man to nature, being to non-being, movement to quiescence), so in the interplay of the yin and yang, the former is definitely inferior to the latter. Speaking of them as cosmic forces, for example, Tung Chung-shu says that Heaven "has trust in the yang but not in the yin; it likes beneficence but not chastisement," or again that "the yang is Heaven's beneficent power, while the yin is Heaven's chastising power" (Fung 2, p. 29). Likewise, speaking of them as prototypes of the human social order, he says: "The ruler is yang, the subject yin; the father is yang, the son yin; the husband is yang, the wife yin" (Fung 2, pp. 42–43).

This inferiority of the yin to the yang is accepted—explicitly or implicitly—by all thinkers who adopt the yin-yang ideology. Never, however, is the suggestion made by them that the one can or should wholly displace the other. Hence there is no real analogy with the dualisms based on conflict (light vs. darkness, etc.) so familiar to us in the West. On the contrary, the yin and yang form a cosmic hierarchy of balanced inequality in which, however, each complements the other and has its own necessary function. As we have just seen, comparison is sometimes made with the existing human relationships, by which, indeed, the concept of the yin-yang relationship may to some extent have been inspired. Once formulated, however, this metaphysical relationship was in turn used by the Chinese to justify their existing class society. Such justification appears already, for example, in the appendixes of the *Book of Changes*, where we read in Appendix IV (Legge, p. 420): "Although the yin has its beauties, it keeps them under restraint in its service of the king, and does not claim success for itself. This is the way of Earth, of a wife, of a subject. The way of Earth is not to claim the merit of achievement, but on another's behalf to bring things to their proper issue."

More important than such analogies with human society, however, is the stress on the *yin* and *yang* as cosmic partners without whose joint activities the universal process would be impossible. For example, we are told in Appendix III of the *Book of Changes* (Legge, p. 395): "The *yin* and *yang* unite their forces, and the hard and the soft gain embodiment, thus giving manifestation to the phenomena of Heaven and Earth." Or, again, the same appendix (pp. 355–56) contains a famous statement which was to become basic for all Neo-Confucian cosmological speculation: "One *yin* and one *yang* (i.e., the alternation of the *yin* and *yang*) constitute what is called *Tao*. That which is perpetuated by it is good."

A noteworthy characteristic of the *yin-yang* dualism, and one distinguishing it sharply from those of the being and non-being or movement and quiescence type, is the fact that definite preference is given to the positive element, the *yang*, and not to the negative element, the *yin*. The reason for this becomes apparent as soon as we examine the ancient graphs of the two words, which, respectively, represent light rays streaming from the sun and rain clouds. Thus it is evident that they originally had to do with climatic phenomena—light and darkness, heat and cold, dryness and wetness, etc.—and that only later did they acquire such secondary connotations as activity and passivity, masculinity and femininity, hardness and softness, etc. These climatic associations are dominant in the *yin-yang* cycles of the sort we have described in Section 1, and it would be surprising indeed if the early Chinese, living in North China, with its rigorous winter climate, would have preferred the cold-bringing *yin* to the life-giving *yang*. Yet, confronted by the inexorable diurnal and annual alternation of the two, they were wise enough to see in them a pattern of movement necessary to the cosmic harmony rather than two irreconcilable warring forces.

### E. "LI" AND "CH'I"

In Section 3, when discussing Chu Hsi's interpretation of the problem of evil, we touched briefly on his antithesis between the metaphysical *li*, or "Principle," which is wholly good, and the physical *ch'i* ("Ether," or matter), which is sometimes pure, sometimes turbid. Here again there is a dualism which at first sight looks like those of the West, yet on closer examination it is seen to be typically Chinese. For though Chu Hsi and his followers recognize the ontological priority of *li* over *ch'i*, as well as its precedence in dignity, they also recognize that both are equally necessary, since without either one of them there could exist no organized universe such as that in which we live. Bruce, in his study of

Chu Hsi, has admirably summed up the Sung Neo-Confucian attitude on the subject as follows:

The Dualism, even if we call it Dualism, must be sharply differentiated from certain dualistic theories of the West. For example, in the dualism of the Sung School there is nothing antagonistic in the component elements. On the contrary, they are interdependent and complementary to each other. Law [i.e., *li*] pervades Matter [i.e., *ch'i*] as its directing principle, and Matter furnishes Law with its means of manifestation. It is true that in the dualism of Matter we have the two opposites of the *Yin* and the *Yang*. . . . But even these opposites are complementary not antagonistic. . . . However, a careful study of Chu Hsi's teaching as a whole shows that in his thought the two elements *li* and *ch'i*, coexistent and mutually dependent though they be, are not coequal; that the one is subordinate to the other, and is even derived from it. . . .

To sum up, *li* and *ch'i* are coexistent and inseparable, but *ch'i* is subordinate to *li*, as the source or root from which it is derived. Here, then, we have the answer to the question with which we began. Chu Hsi asserts the essential subordination of Matter to Law as its ultimate source, Chinese Dualism resolves itself into Monism.[41]

In later times there were reactions against even this kind of dualism. The school of Wang Shou-jen, for example, attacked Chu Hsi's dichotomy from an idealistic point of view by acknowledging, with Chu, that man's nature is *li*, but then criticizing Chu's contention that man's mind is merely the physical container of the nature and therefore pertains to *ch'i* and not to *li*. On the contrary, said the Wang school, the mind itself *is* the nature. At the same time, furthermore, it actually holds within itself all the concrete physical things of the external universe. Under A of this section we have already quoted the characteristic statement of Wang's predecessor, Lu Chiu-yüan: "The universe is my mind, and my mind is the universe."

Still later, but this time from a materialistic point of view, men like Yen Yüan and Tai Chen likewise attacked Chu Hsi's dualism. Thus Yen Yüan, as we have seen, maintained that *li* is amalgamated with the *ch'i* "into a single continuum" (Fung 2, p. 637). Tai Chen went still further by saying that man's nature is a product of the physical *ch'i* and that *li*, far from being a metaphysical Principle which is ontologically prior to the *ch'i*, is in reality nothing more than the inherent orderly pattern of the physical things of *ch'i* (Fung 2, pp. 655–58).

## 7. The Sage

The *Sheng*, or "Sage," as the highest ideal for all humanity, figures prominently (sometimes under other names) in Confucianism, Taoism, and Buddhism alike. Here we shall make no attempt to give any detailed description of his many qualities, as conceived by these three schools. Very generally, however, we may say that the Sage is a being who, to a supreme degree, synthesizes in himself antitheses of the sort described in the preceding section. More specifically, he is one in whom there is a merging of "the sublime and the common, the internal and the external, the root and the branch, the refined and the coarse."[42] Unlike the ideal being venerated by some other civilizations, therefore, he does not stand aloof from the world of everyday affairs. In his state of inmost being (sometimes spoken of as quiescence) he rests in the sphere of the sublime; yet in his state of outward functioning (sometimes spoken of as movement or activity) he participates with other men in the practical affairs of daily life.

This synthesis, however, is only the final phase in a process of spiritual development by which the Sage first succeeds in rising from the sphere of the ordinary to the sphere of the sublime and then, instead of remaining in the sublime, returns once more to the world of ordinary humanity. In this process of "withdrawal and return," to use Toynbee's phrase, there thus seems to be another manifestation of that cyclical pattern of thought of which we have already seen numerous examples.

As in many of these previous examples, however, the concept is much less clearly expressed in early Chinese thought than it became later on. Thus in early Confucianism and Taoism alike the Sage is at first conceived of in comparatively narrow terms, expressive of the relative centers of interest of these two schools: man and nature, respectively.

In Confucianism, for example, we find not only the rationally minded Hsün Tzŭ but also the more mystically inclined Mencius, emphasizing the Sage as the supreme exemplar of human relationships. Indeed, for these two thinkers, the very fact that a Sage is a Sage denotes, above all, his supreme ability to formulate and participate in the institutions and relationships of human society. Mencius, for example, tells us that the Sage "is the apogee of the human relationships" (IV*a*, 2). Or again he says: "That whereby man differs from birds and beasts is but small. The mass of the people cast it away, while superior men preserve it" (IV*b*, 19). As illustration, he then cites the legendary Shun as one who "paid discriminating attention to the human relationships."[43] Similarly, Hsün Tzŭ says (chap. 21; Dubs, p. 276) that "the Sage fulfils the duties of the (human) relationships." Or again he remarks: "A ruler is one who is good at organizing society. If this doctrine of forming a social organization is carried out as it should be, . . . the people will be united, and the worthy and good will serve the ruler; it will be the rule of a Sage-king" (chap. 9; Dubs, pp. 137–38).

Among the early Taoists, on the other hand, the true Sage is not someone ever busily organizing human society but rather one who himself conforms as much as possible to the natural, and who, if he be ruler, allows his people to do likewise. Chuang Tzǔ has many sarcastic re-marks (Giles, pp. 108, 113, 117, 125, etc.) about the harm done by such busybodies as Yao, Shun, and other "sages" of the Confucian type. In his first chapter (Giles, pp. 7–8) he speaks of a "spirit man" living on a distant mountain, whose flesh and skin were like ice and snow, who did not eat the five grains but inhaled wind and drank dew, and who wandered beyond the four seas, riding on the clouds and propelled by flying dragons. "Even his dust and siftings," Chuang Tzǔ concludes, "could still be fashioned and molded to form a Yao or a Shun." Lao Tzǔ, too, though less fanciful and more down to earth, stresses the mental detachment of the Sage from the seemingly vital concerns of other men. The Sage, he says, is one who "relies on actionless activity (*wu wei*), and carries on wordless teaching" (chap. 2). He "rules the people by emptying their minds" (chap. 3) and, "in his dealings with the world, cautiously dulls the wits of the world" (chap. 49). His reason for thus acting is that "man's standard is Earth, Earth's standard is Heaven, Heaven's standard is *Tao*, *Tao's* standard is the spontaneous" (chap. 25).

In Neo-Taoism, however, the mellowing attitude toward human in-stitutions, noted earlier, is accompanied by a corresponding change in attitude toward the Sage. "He who reaches the highest point," says Kuo Hsiang, "reverts to what is below," whereas "he who ardently reaches for a position of solitary eminence, and does not put himself on an equality with the ordinary run of men, is a hermit of the mountains and vales, but not one who is unconditioned." Thus, for Kuo, the Sage is not someone who "folds his hands in silence amidst the mountains and forests." On the contrary, he gladly "participates in the affairs of the people" and, "even when occupying the highest place at court, is men-tally no different from the way he is when amidst the mountains and forests." He is one in whom "the without and the within become mutually merged. . . . Therefore the Sage constantly wanders in the without in order to enlarge what is within. . . . Though he works his body the livelong day, his essential spirit is not affected." This, says Kuo, is "the main idea in the writings" of Chuang Tzǔ, whose central purpose it is to "teach us how to ferry over to the ordinary and encom-pass the existing world" (Fung 2, pp. 234–36).

The return of the Sage to the ordinary mortal world is also a con-spicuous theme in Chinese Buddhism. "Though Wisdom lies outside affairs, it never lacks them," says Seng-chao. "Though Spirit lies be-yond the world, it stays ever within it" (*Book of Chao*, chap. 3; Lieben-thal, p. 72). For this reason, "the Sage . . . dwells in the world of change and utility, yet holds himself to the realm of non-activity (*wu wei*). He rests within the walls of the namable, yet lives in the open country of what transcends speech" (*ibid.*, p. 109).

In later Buddhist schools the same idea is expressed in less Taoistic language. For example, we are told by Fa-tsang (643–712), a major figure of the Hua-yen school:

> The experiencing of the Buddha-realm means the emptiness of matter, absence of a personal ego, and absence of phenomenal qualities. . . . However, having experienced entry into this realm, one may not dwell forever after in calm extinction, for this would be contrary to the teaching of the Buddhas. One should teach what is beneficial and joyous, and . . . it is in this realm that one should think about all these things [Fung 2, p. 358].

In an almost contemporary text of the T'ien-t'ai school we read similarly:

> Because of the achievement of cessation, one dwells within the great *Nirvāna*. Yet because of the achievement of contemplation, one stays within (the cycle of) life and death. Or yet again, because of the achievement of cessation, one is not polluted by the world. Yet because of the achievement of contemplation, one is not restricted to silent inactivity [Fung 2, p. 378].

Here again, as in the discussion of good and evil (see Sec. 5, end), there is a contrast between this Chinese point of view and that found in the more purely Indian Mere Ideation school. Thus the latter, while it does not explicitly deny the continued existence of the individual in the phenomenal world after he attains Buddhahood, nevertheless remains conspicuously silent on this point (Fung 2, p. 339).

However, it is in the most purely Chinese expression of Buddhism, that of *Ch'an* or *Zen*, that we find the "humanization" or secularization of the Sage carried to its greatest extent. We have already read the slogan: "In carrying water and chopping wood: therein lies the wonderful *Tao*." The ordinary man wears his clothes, eats his food, and performs other natural physical functions; but, as the Ch'anists are never tired of saying, so does the Sage. The only difference is that his state of mind is no longer the same. In the words of Huai-hai (720–814): "What the man does is no different from what he did before; it is only that the man himself is not the same as he was." The first step of leaving humanity behind and entering sagehood, says Yi-hsüan (d. 867), is that in which "both the man and his surroundings are eliminated," in other words, in which subject and object no longer exist for him. But, having made this step, he then returns from his sagehood to the mortal world, thereby achieving a final synthesis in which, for him, "neither the man nor his surroundings are eliminated." The situation is summed up by P'u-yüan (*ca.* 748–*ca.* 836) when he says: "After coming to understand the other side, you come back and live on this side."[44]

Yet if the wonderful *Tao* is to be found in carrying water and chopping wood, why should it not also be found in the mutual obligations of father and son and ruler and subject, and why should the seeker for enlightenment be obliged to abandon his family and become a monk? These are the questions that underlie many of the Neo-Confucian criticisms of Buddhism. Chang Tsai, for example, remarks of the Buddhists that "as to those who speak about *Nirvāna*, they mean by this a departure which leads to no return," whereas he describes the Confucian Sage as one who "embodies" and "completely understands" the cycle of phenomenal existence (Fung 2, p. 497).

It is not surprising, therefore, that the Neo-Confucianists, unlike the Buddhists, feel under no compulsion to stress the return of the Sage to the ordinary mortal world, since, for them, it is axiomatic that he should always remain within it. In the words of Shao Yung, the Sage is able, on the one hand, "with his mind to represent the meaning of Heaven," but at the same time he is able "to comprehend clearly the affairs of men" (Fung 2, p. 465). The following quotations further illustrate how, for the Neo-Confucianists, the Sage is thus to synthesize "the sublime and the common": [45]

"To be faithful to one's daily round, to be reverent to one's duties, and to be loyal to one's fellow-men: these words reach to the bottom of things both above and below. The Sage from the beginning has had no second way of speaking on these matters," says Ch'eng Hao.

"Men of later times have spoken about the nature and destiny (conferred on man by Heaven) as if they were very special separate matters. Yet the nature and destiny, together with filial piety and the duties of a younger brother, all actually fall into a single category. And as to sprinkling and sweeping floors, responding to demands and answering questions, these too fall into the same category as developing one's nature to the highest and making the very best of one's destiny. There is no 'more important' and 'less important,' no fine and coarse," says Ch'eng Yi.

"He keeps to the place where he is and rejoices in the daily round. . . . Yet his mind wanders freely away to be in direct contact with Heaven and Earth and all things, and in complete accord with what is above and below," says Chu Hsi.

## 8. Conclusion

At this point it is well to reiterate the warning already made at the beginning of this article, namely, that the thought patterns we have been describing, while definitely typical of Chinese thinking on a sophisticated and philosophical level, are not necessarily always equally typical of thinking on other less sophisticated levels; sometimes, indeed, cases of obvious contradiction occur.[46] With this warning in mind, let us now try to recapitulate our findings.

The universe, according to prevailing Chinese philosophical thinking, is a harmoniously functioning organism consisting of an orderly hierarchy of interrelated parts and forces, which, though unequal in their status, are all equally essential for the total process. Change is a marked feature of this process, yet in it there is nothing haphazard or casual, for it follows a fixed pattern of polar oscillation or cyclical return; in either case these is a denial of forward movement, save in proximate terms only.

This cosmic pattern is self-contained and self-operating. It unfolds itself because of its own inner necessity and not because it is ordained by any external volitional power. Not surprisingly, therefore, Chinese thinkers who have expressed themselves on the subject are unanimous in rejecting the possibility that the universe may have originated through any single act of conscious creation. Some, indeed, go still further and deny even the possibility of a more naturalistic process whereby the universe has gradually evolved from a unitary origin into the complexity it has today. For these men the universe is self-created and hence has always existed and always will exist as it does now. Such a belief that the cosmic process in its totality is eternal does not conflict with the possibility that the universe passes through alternating phases of integration and disintegration and, therefore, that our existing world may be only one in a series of such worlds, each representing one of the integrative periods.

Human history belongs to the total cosmic process and, therefore, in the eyes of many Chinese, moves according to a similar cyclical pattern. Another and probably earlier Chinese view, however, sees antiquity as a golden age and all history since that time as a steady process of human degeneration. Some thinkers combine the two theories by saying that history does indeed move in cycles but that we moderns happen to be living during the downswing of one such cycle. Regardless of which of these interpretations is accepted, it is evident that all of them reject the idea of historical progress, meaning by this a process of progressive improvement.

Though the universe is self-acting and not guided by any volitional power, it is far from being merely a mechanistic universe. Indeed, the very fact that its movements result in life is enough to show that in them must be a principle of goodness. More than this, however, even what we humans regard as evil—for example, death—is, from a higher point of view, an integral part of the total cosmic process and therefore inseparable from what we choose to call goodness. In short, whatever *is* in the universe must be good, simply because it *is*.

The vital link between the nonhuman and human worlds is man's nature, and it necessarily follows from the foregoing that this nature must be equally good for all. If, nevertheless, some men fail to actualize the potentialities of their nature, this is because of their inadequate understanding of how the universe operates. This deficiency, however, can be removed through education and self-cultivation, so that the possibility always exists in theory—though admittedly the chances of its ever being actualized in practice are remote—for all men without exception to achieve sagehood. It thus becomes clear that evil, in Chinese eyes, is not a positive force in itself. It is, from one point of view, simply an inherent factor in the universe or, from another, the result of man's temporary distortion of the universal harmony.

Human society is, or at least should be, a reflection of this harmony. Hence it too is an ordered hierarchy of unequal components, all of which, however, have their essential function to perform, so that the result is a co-operative human harmony. This means that the ideal society is one in which each individual accepts his own social position without complaint and performs to the best of his ability the obligations attached to that position. Here there seems to be a conflict between this emphasis on social stability and a belief—implied in the doctrine of the potential perfectibility of all men—in social mobility. The two are reconciled, however, by upholding the sanctity of the class structure, yet at the same time recognizing the possibility of social movement for particular individuals. The Chinese examination system was a unique, though imperfect, attempt to give substance to this compromise on the practical level.

War, as the most violent disrupter of social harmony, is, of course, opposed by all save a very few Chinese thinkers. Even those who have condoned it as a sometimes necessary instrument have never attempted to glorify it—at least on the philosophical level—as has sometimes been done in the West.

Cutting across both the human and the natural worlds there are, in Chinese thinking, many antithetical concepts, among which we have discussed those of man and nature (Heaven, or *T'ien*), being and non-being, quiescence and movement, the *yin* and the *yang*, and *li* ("Principle") and *ch'i* ("Ether"). In each of these dualisms the Chinese mind commonly shows a preference for one of the two component elements as against the other. At the same time, however, it regards both of them as complementary and necessary partners, interacting to form a higher synthesis, rather than as irreconcilable and eternally warring opposites. Thus here again there is a manifestation of the Chinese tendency to merge unequal components so as to create an organic harmony.

The Sage is the man who to the highest degree succeeds in merging these seeming opposites in himself. As portrayed by the Neo-Taoists and Buddhists, he in so doing follows a cycle-like course of withdrawal and return, leading him first from the world of the ordinary to the world of the sublime, but then back once more to the world of ordinary affairs. Among the Neo-Confucianists, owing to their intense concern for human relationships, this idea of withdrawal is not stressed. Nevertheless, they agree with the other two schools that the Sage is both this-worldly and other-worldly, both active and quiescent, so that in him the highest synthesis is achieved.

Though relatively few of these thought patterns occur equally in all the schools we have been discussing, they nevertheless seem sufficiently to complement each other as to form in their totality a homogeneous world view. This homogeneity, naturally, did not spring into being overnight. It is the product of a long evolution, in the course of which certain ideas, and with them entire schools, have been sloughed off, leaving others to interact upon one another during many centuries. Most important in this process have been Confucianism, Taoism, the *Yin-yang* and Five Elements schools, and Buddhism, all contributing to Neo-Confucianism, which thus in a very real sense may be regarded as a summation and synthesis of what had gone before.

It is significant how frequently those thinkers who diverge from one of the strands of thought we have been discussing diverge from others as well. The Legalists, for example, were exceptional in their pessimistic view of human nature, approval of warfare, indifference to any meaningful pattern of history (though as practical men they stressed the need for political change), and reliance on force rather than suasion to achieve an ordered class society. It is not surprising that as a school they totally disappeared, even though certain of their ideas were institutionally perpetuated in later times.

Hsün Tzǔ, likewise, believed that man is born evil, stressed the separateness of man from nature, and held a peculiarly static view of history. Despite his enormous immediate influence, his ideas on all three points, especially the first and second, were ultimately rejected in favor of those of Mencius.

Later on, in Buddhism, we see that the Mere Ideation school, which denied the equal possibility to all men of achieving Buddhahood, also said virtually nothing about the role of the enlightened being in the world of suffering humanity. In other aspects as well (notably its extreme subjective idealism), this was the most Indian and least Chinese of all Buddhist schools in China. Buddhism itself, for that matter, despite its enormous influence, ultimately declined in China owing to the incompatibility of some of its ideas with the prevailing Chinese intellectual pattern.

Centuries later we see that Wang Fu-chih, who believed in historical progress, also preached nationalism and the conquest of the barbarians in the name of manifest destiny. And, finally, in the second half of the nineteenth century, we find a group of men—K'ang Yu-wei, T'an Ssŭ-t'ung, and, to a lesser extent, Liao P'ing—who, under obvious Western influence, break sharply with tradition by affirming historical progress and predicting a future classless society.

As for Tung Chung-shu two thousand years earlier, he presents some curious contradictions. On the one hand, he is a firm believer in the interrelationship of man and nature and the operation in both spheres of recurring cycles. On the other, his attitude toward Heaven seems at times to be a throwback to a much earlier, personalistic conception which, though once general in China, had already by the time of Mo Tzŭ become somewhat old-fashioned.

To attempt any detailed comparison between the prevailing world view of Chinese thinkers and Western thought patterns would require far more space than is here available. Nor would it be easy in view of the enormous diversity of Western thought in different times and places, and the consequent difficulty of determining what, if any, have been its prevailing patterns. Because of this diversity, it is quite possible that Western parallels can be found for many, if not most, of the Chinese concepts we have been discussing. Chinese cyclical theories of the cosmos, for example, are reminiscent of those of Anaximander and other Greek thinkers; the Chinese approach to good and evil suggests the attitude found in Stoic pantheism; and the Confucian theory of society is curiously similar to that found in medieval European thinking.[47]

To attempt isolated comparisons of this sort, however, is a rather fruitless task, for what really counts is the impact of the two bodies of ideas—Chinese and Western—in their totality rather than in their parts. And, if we examine this total impact, two conclusions emerge. One is the much greater homogeneity and total internal consistency of the Chinese world view, as compared with the many thought systems of the West, while the other is the enormous qualitative difference between the two—a difference most pronounced, of course, in the case of modern Western thought, but which goes as far back as ancient Greece. Among the points of difference which, on the Western side, seem to be particularly significant, may be cited the belief in a divine act of creation and a divine Power who decrees laws for a universe subordinate and external to himself; antagonistic dualisms of the good-and-evil or light-and-darkness type; original sin, predestination, and personal salvation; individual and class struggle, glorification of war, and belief in historical progress.

It is worth noting, however, that Western thinking, particularly in such fields as physics, has in recent years tended to move away from some of these traditional concepts toward attitudes and techniques which superficially, at least, bear marked similarity to some of those we have seen for China. This phenomenon is noted, for example, by Lily Abegg in the recent psychological study she has made on Chinese and Japanese thinking.[48] In this work she particularly calls attention to what she calls "the 'new thought form' which is now being talked about in scientific circles," and which is described by her as "based on the complementarity principle, that is to say, on the fact that two diametrically opposed statements can be made about the same thing, both of which can be proved and are correct."

This new approach, she points out, has led some modern scientists into making such paradoxical statements as: "The world is not really finite, neither is it, on the other hand, really infinite"—a statement irresistably reminding us of Chi-tsang's postulations about being and non-being in his Theory of Double Truth (see Sec. 6, B, above). However, as also stressed by Dr. Abegg, the road followed by the West in order to reach such formulations is radically different from that taken by the ancient Chinese thinkers:

> Whereas in the first case [modern physics] it is a matter of drawing the final conclusion from formally logical premises, in the latter case [Chinese thinking] it is a question of the results of a total view of things and total thinking. Modern physics arrives at these conclusions from the outside, the East Asian from the inside. Proceeding from plurality, modern physics thus finds itself faced with an incomprehensible unity and is compelled to make paradoxical statements about it, while the East Asian, proceeding from unity, has known for a very long time that it is not possible to make other than paradoxical statements about unity.

On the social side, though Confucian political and social thought is miles removed from that of a modern democratic society, it is nevertheless interesting to note that modern Western psychology and sociology are moving away from the extreme emphasis on individualism and competition and reaching a position more akin to the Chinese ideal of an integrated social organism based on co-operation. Confucianism, despite its many glaring defects to our modern eyes, proved itself remarkably well adapted to its own agrarian society and in certain respects provided more consistent and equitable answers to the problems of human relations than, let us say, did ancient Greek thinking on the subject. Thus it is a rather curious fact that in ancient Greece, where there was democracy for the few, there was also slavery for the many, whereas in ancient China, where there was no democracy as we think of it, there was also very little slavery.

Of course, in all comparisons of this sort, we should never forget the enormous gap between ideas and practice in China—for example, it certainly did not help the Chinese peasant in his dealings with a rapacious landlord to be told that human nature is good. Similar gaps, however, have likewise always existed in our Western world. Chinese thinking provided a *modus vivendi* for its people during one of the longest spans of human history, but in the process it failed to provide for "progress," and today it is inevitable that it should be cast aside. Western thinking has given the world such progress, but it has also brought it catastrophe, from which it is too early as yet to say whether we shall finally escape.

Rather than attempting value judgments of this sort, however, it is more appropriate in a study such as this to suggest possible reasons *why* Chinese thinking developed along the lines it did. At this point the temptation is strong to make a link between such thinking and the natural, social, and institutional environment of Chinese civilization. There are, for example, the facts that Chinese civilization, though not so autochthonous as once supposed, was founded and thereafter developed in relative isolation from any other civilizations of comparable level; that this was done by a rather homogeneous people, both racially and linguistically; that their terrain was a large continental land mass, much of it plain and most of it remote from the sea, very unlike the mountainous and indented peninsulas and islands of the Mediterranean peoples; that this terrain led them very early toward a strongly monocultural way of life, based almost exclusively on the intensive growing of grain; that, according to one well-known hypothesis, in order to develop this mode of life very far in the dry North China climate, the Chinese were obliged to construct extensive irrigation works, which in turn required the establishment of organized political control over large masses of manpower, thus encouraging the formation of a strongly bureaucratic state; that, as a consequence, commerce and other nonagrarian private enterprise failed to make significant growth, so that the Chinese cities became centers of political power rather than of an independent industrial-mercantile bourgeoisie; and, finally, that the Chinese, because of their concentration on this way of life, became extraordinarily aware of the seasonal rhythm of nature, which, in North China, is marked by a remarkable clocklike regularity.

All these features distinguish China sharply from ancient Greece, as well as from later European culture as a whole. Yet here we come face to face with a consideration which should give us pause: the fact that some of the Western conceptions seemingly most antithetical to those of China—notably those of a universe created and controlled by a divine being, or of various antagonistic dualisms—are not of European origin at all but go back to the cultural complex of the ancient Near East. And yet, socially and politically speaking, this Near Eastern cultural complex, at least from the superficial view of a nonspecialist, seems to resemble more closely what is sometimes called the "oriental bureaucratic state," of which China is a prime example, than it does the patterns of Greece and Europe. How, then, on the grounds we have here postulated, are the sharp ideological differences just mentioned to be explained?

Most writers have simply ignored such problems by speaking vaguely and sometimes mystically about the "oneness of the Orient." A very few, however, notably F. S. C. Northrop, have perceived that vast ideological differences separate Eastern from Western Asia and so have chosen to group Indian with Chinese thinking, on the one hand, as against Near Eastern–European thinking, on the other. As yet almost nobody has pointed out that India and China, despite certain undoubtedly strong ideological similarities, also display differences which, in the final analysis, may be equally significant. To cite only a few examples:

Whereas India is famed for its religions and has always exalted its priestly class, China has produced no world religion, was already in early times dominated by a strongly secular trend, and possessed no important priesthood prior to the advent of Buddhism. Whereas the Indians have a rich epic literature and mythology, the Chinese have very little of either. The Chinese, on the other hand, have been meticulous recorders of historical events and undoubtedly possess the largest historical literature of any long-lived people, whereas the Indians have been notoriously unhistorical. The Chinese have shown a genius for political organization, so that they have repeatedly created durable empires often extending far beyond the borders of China proper, whereas the Indians only rarely and briefly have succeeded in uniting the Indian subcontinent. The Indian caste system has no parallel in Chinese social thinking, even though, as we have seen, Confucianism emphasizes the hierarchical structure of society. Finally, as for Indian philosophy, some of its conspicuous concepts have been reincarnation, life as suffering, *Nirvāna*, subjective idealism, and the universe as atomistic, anarchic, and unorganized; it has also produced a well-developed system of logic. All these ideas were unknown in China prior to Buddhism, and the nearest Chinese approach to a system of logic was that of the Mohists, who, however, were speedily forgotten. Can we then safely accept these many widely divergent ideological manifestations as products of essentially similar ways of thinking or of a common world outlook?

This is not the place to go into a detailed analysis of differences such as these, nor is this writer qualified to do so. What he would like to suggest, however, is that Chinese thought needs not only to be studied internally but also comparatively and that such comparative study, in order to be most fruitful, should not be limited to China and the West alone. Ideally, it should also include the thought systems of other major civilizations, as well as, possibly, some of the preliterate peoples. Furthermore, if it is to achieve its real purpose, it must study these thought systems in the full context of their institutional background (social, political, and economic) rather than merely *in vacuo*.

This, of course, is a gigantic undertaking, for which, no doubt, data on the individual systems concerned are as yet inadequate. However, as a possible first step in its direction, thought might be given to the feasibility of preparing a small list of key concepts or themes, formulated with sufficient flexibility so that they could be applied to all the thought systems concerned. By using them as a guide, it might then be possible to extract from these systems a body of data which, being grouped around a common set of themes, would be sufficiently homogeneous to lend itself readily to comparative analysis.

## NOTES

\* Bibliographical Note.—A few Chinese works, because of the brevity of their chapter or paragraph divisions, are cited simply according to these divisions, as follows:

|  |  |
|---|---|
| *Analects* of Confucius | *Doctrine of the Mean* |
| *Lao-tzŭ* | *Mencius* |

The following works, available in Western translations, have been cited according to these translations, whose wording, however, has often been modified by me in the interests of consistency or greater accuracy:

*Book of Changes:* James Legge's translation in *Sacred Books of the East*, Vol. XVI (2d ed.; Oxford, 1899)
*Book of Lord Shang:* J. J. L. Duyvendak, *The Book of Lord Shang* (London, 1928)
*Chuang-tzŭ:* H. A. Giles, *Chuang Tzŭ* (2d ed.; Shanghai, 1926)
*Hsün-tzŭ:* H. H. Dubs, *The Works of Hsüntze* (London, 1928)
*Huai-nan-tzŭ:* Evan Morgan, *Tao the Great Luminant* (Shanghai, 1934)
*Lü-shih Ch'un-ch'iu:* Richard Wilhelm, *Frühling und Herbst des Lü Bu We* (Jena, 1928)
*Mo-tzŭ:* Y. P. Mei, *The Ethical and Political Works of Motse* (London, 1929)
Seng-chao's *Chao Lun*, or *Book of Chao:* Walter Liebenthal, *The Book of Chao* (Peiping, 1948)
Wang Ch'ung's *Lun Heng*, or *Critical Essays:* Alfred Forke, *Lun Heng* (2 vols.; Berlin and London, 1907 and 1911)

Wang Shou-jen's writings and conversations: Frederick Goodrich Henke, *The Philosophy of Wang Yang-ming* (Chicago and London, 1916)
*Yüeh Ling*, or *Monthly Commands:* James Legge's translation in *Sacred Books of the East*, Vol. XXVII (Oxford, 1885), pp. 249–310.

Many other works, unavailable in Western translation, are, for the sake of easy reference, cited according to the quotations made from them in Fung Yu-lan, *A History of Chinese Philosophy*, translated from the Chinese by Derk Bodde (Princeton: Princeton University Press, 1952–53). The two volumes of this work are referred to as "Fung 1" and "Fung 2."

1. Joseph Needham, "Human Laws and Laws of Nature in China and the West," *Journal of the History of Ideas*, XII (1951), 3–30, 194–230.
In making this contrast between the Chinese world view and the Western concept of the "Laws of Nature," what Needham is concerned with on the Western side is, of course, the traditional body of theological belief associated with the words "Laws of Nature" and not the changed meaning assumed by this term in rather recent times. As to the theological concept, he points out (*op. cit.*, p. 3): "Without doubt one of the oldest notions of Western civilization was that just as earthly imperial lawgivers enacted codes of positive law, to be obeyed by men; so also the celestial and supreme rational creator deity had laid down a series of laws which must be obeyed by minerals, crystals, plants, animals and the stars in their courses." Elsewhere (p. 229) he stresses the fact that "in the outlook of modern science there is, of course, no residue of the notions of command and duty in the 'laws' of Nature. They are now thought of as statistical regularities."

2. Cf. the many similar quotations in Fung 1, pp. 182–85.

3. Embodiments, respectively, of light, heat, masculinity, movement, dryness, etc., and of darkness, cold, femininity, quiescence, wetness, etc.

4. *Ch'ien* and *k'un* are the names of the two primary of the sixty-four hexagrams in the *Book of Changes* and are graphic representations of the *yang* and *yin*, respectively.

5. Cf. the many similar quotations in Fung 1, pp. 384–90.

6. Hu Shih, *Development of the Logical Method in Ancient China* (Shanghai, 1928), pp. 134–36.

7. A little almanac contained both in the *Lü-shih Ch'un-ch'iu* (compiled just prior to 235 B.C.) and in the slightly later *Book of Rites*.

8. Cf. the exposition in Fung 2, chap. 2, secs. 4–5, and especially the diagram on p. 28. For the quotation see p. 24.

9. Cf. the *Lü-shih Ch'un-ch'iu* (V, 2; Wilhelm, p. 58): "Great Oneness produced the Two Forms. The Two Forms produce the *yin* and *yang*"; the *Book of Changes* (Appendix III; Legge, p. 373): "In the *Changes* there is the Supreme Ultimate, which produced the Two Forms"; the *Huai-nan-tzŭ*'s seven stages of cosmogonic evolution (chap. 2; Morgan, pp. 31–33); Tung Chun-shu's *Yüan*, or "Origin," which "existed before Heaven and Earth" (Fung 2, p. 20); Yang Hsiung's (53 B.C.–A.D. 18) *Hsüan*, or "Mystery," which underwent successive tripartite divisions whereby it evolved into the three *fang*, nine *chou*, twenty-seven *pu*, and eighty-one *chia* (Fung 2, pp. 140–42); Chou Tun-yi's (1017–73) famous *T'ai-chi T'u* ("Diagram of the Supreme Ultimate"), which graphically portrays the stages of cosmic evolution, beginning with the Supreme Ultimate, and passing through the *yin* and *yang*, the Five Elements, and thus to all

things (Fung 2, pp. 435–38); and, finally, Yen Yüan's (1635–1704) Way of Heaven, which acts through the *yin* and *yang* to produce the four powers, which, in turn, by means of their sixteen forms of transformation, produce thirty-two basic conditions or factors, as the result of which all things arise (Fung 2, pp. 636–38).

10. Cf. the conversation between the shadow and the penumbra (chap. 2; Giles, p. 32) and the difficult passage (chap. 22; Giles, p. 291) beginning: "Was what existed prior to Heaven and Earth a thing?"

11. Actually this commentary seems to have been the joint work of Kuo Hsiang and Hsiang Hsiu (*ca.* 221–*ca.* 300), but for the sake of convenience we will refer to it here simply under the former's name.

12. Note by Bodde in Fung 2, p. 237.

13. For an expression of this theory in Chinese Buddhism see Tsung-mi (780–841) as quoted in the Chinese edition (Shanghai, 1934) of Fung 2, 793–94 (revised at this point for the English edition, in which, therefore, this passage does not appear).

14. For Shao's theory see Fung 2, pp. 469–74, and for Chu Hsi's acceptance of it see Fung 2, pp. 546–47, 549–50.

15. "Pushing backward, (we see that) there has never been a time when there has not been the Ether, and turning forward, that there will never be a time when it is not here. Being contracted, it then passes from 'non-being' to 'being,' but this 'being' does not result in (permanent) being; being expanded, it then passes from 'being' to 'non-being,' but this 'non-being' does not result in (permanent) non-being" (Fung 2, p. 640).

16. "In the great process of evolutionary change there is only the single Ether, which circulates everywhere without interruption, . . . and so continues in an endless cycle. . . . The Sage, because this process of rise and fall never loses its sequence and order, refers to it as Principle (*li*)" (Fung 2, pp. 640–41).

17. There was a dispute during the Han dynasty as to whether or not the Ch'in had been a legitimate dynasty, and therefore whether or not it had really enjoyed the support of the element water. It will be noticed that the sequence of the elements here given differs from that as correlated with the seasons (see Sec. 1), in which wood (symbolizing new plant growth) goes with spring, fire (symbolizing heat) with summer, etc.

18. Fung 2, pp. 62–63. For an exposition of Tung's whole theory of cycles see Fung 2, chap. 2, sec. 1.

19. Cf. his *Lun Heng*, or *Critical Essays*, chaps. 56 and 57 (Forke, I, 471–76; II, 200).

20. *Book of Lord Shang*, chap. 1 (Duyvendak, pp. 192–73).

21. Cf. the exposition in Fung 2, pp. 82–84.

22. Cf. Hsi Wen-fu, *Ch'uan-shan Che-hsüeh* ("The Philosophy of Wang Ch'uan-shan") (Shanghai, 1936), Part II. It should be noted that though Wang's theory of historical progress makes him quite exceptional in the total range of Chinese philosophy, certain similar tendencies are discernible in a few other scholars of his and the next century, such as Ku Yen-wu (1613–82), Huang Tsung-hsi (1610–95), and Chang Hsüeh-ch'eng (1738–1801).

23. Cf. Fung 2, pp. 679–91.

24. Cf. Fung 2, pp. 710–14, esp. the table on p. 714.

25. Cf. preceding section for T'an's theory of the *yi-t'ai* or ether, and Sec. 4, near end, for his reference to "the Millennium spoken of in Western books."

26. Cf. Fung 2, pp. 657–63, and, for the comparison of Tai with Hsün Tzŭ, pp. 669–72. In his theory of the nature, Tai was anticipated in part by Ch'en Ch'üeh (1604–77). Cf. Fung 2, pp. 659–60.

27. Fung Yu-lan goes so far as to assert that "Hzün Tzŭ's Heaven . . . differs entirely from that of Mencius, inasmuch as it contains no ethical principle" (Fung 1, p. 286). This statement, however, is nowhere explicitly confirmed by Hzün Tzŭ himself, being merely inferential from his total philosophy. In fact, it seems to be contradicted by a passage in Hsün Tzŭ's nineteenth chapter (Dubs, p. 223), in which, in the course of describing the *li* (rites, rituals, rules of correct behavior, traditional mores, etc.), he gives to them a cosmic significance: "They are that whereby Heaven and Earth unite, whereby the sun and moon are bright, whereby the four seasons follow their sequence, whereby the stars move in their courses, whereby all things prosper, whereby love and hatred are tempered, whereby joy and anger keep their proper place."

The mystical tone of this passage, however, accords poorly with Hsün Taŭ's usual humanistic outlook. Indeed, at the very beginning of the same chapter in which it appears (Dubs, p. 213), Hsün Tzŭ gives an entirely rationalistic explanation for the origin of the *li*, saying that they were originally instituted by the early kings in order to put an end to human disorder. On the other hand, the passage is reminiscent of certain metaphysical interpretations of the *li* found in such Confucian compilations as the *Li Chi*, or *Book of Rites* (see Fung 1, pp. 343–44). As a matter of fact, it happens to be one of several passages in the *Hsün-tzŭ* which also appear almost verbatim either in the *Li Chi* or the closely analogous *Ta Tai Li Chi*. The thesis has already been advanced, on grounds other than those given here, that all or most of such passages do not actually come from Hsün Tzŭ's hand at all but have been incorporated at a later time into the work now bearing his name from these ritualistic texts, rather than the other way round, as traditionally assumed. See Yang Yün-ju in Lo Ken-tse (ed.), *Ku Shih Pien* ("A Symposium on Ancient Chinese History," Vol. VI [Shanghai, 1938]), pp. 138–42.

28. Cf. "On the Explanation of Retribution," by Hui-yüan (334–416), in which, after citing such acts, he concludes: "Thus the retributions of punishment or blessing depend upon what are stimulated by one's own (mental) activities. They are what they are according to these stimuli, for which reason I say that they are automatic. By automatic I mean that they result from our own influence. How then can they be the work of some other Mysterious Ruler?" (Fung 2, p. 274). Cf. also the ninth-century Ch'an (Zen) monk, Hsi-yün, who, on being asked whether certain acts were sinful or not, replied: "It cannot definitely be said that they are sinful or not sinful. Whether there is sin or not depends on the man. . . . The mind should be like a void emptiness. . . . Then to what can sin have attachment?" (Fung 2, p. 404). Cf. also Sec. C below.

29. Fung 2, pp. 644–46. In the following century a somewhat similar view was expressed by Tai Chen (cf. Fung 2, pp. 666–68). As pointed out by Fung Yu-lan, however, neither man wholly succeeded in avoiding certain logical inconsistencies in their attempts to break away from Chu Hsi's system.

30. Cf. also H. H. Dubs, *Hsüntze, the Moulder of Ancient Confucianism* (London, 1927), chap. xiv on "Inequality," which is an excellent exposition of the whole Confucian approach to the subject.

31. Cf. also Kenneth Ch'en, "Anti-Buddhist Propaganda during the Nan-ch'ao," *Harvard Journal of Asiatic Studies*, XV (1952), 166–92; Arthur F. Wright, "Fu I

and the Rejection of Buddhism," *Journal of the History of Ideas*, XII (1951), 33–47, esp. pp. 43–44.

32. Cf. Y. P. Mei, *Motse, the Neglected Rival of Confucius* (London, 1934), pp. 96–99, and Dubs, *Hsüntze*, pp. 269–70.

33. J. J. L. Duyvendak, *The Book of Lord Shang* (London, 1928), Introduction, p. 83.

34. Hsi Wen-fu, *op. cit.*, pp. 97 and 99.

35. Cf. the famous "stratagem of the empty city," recounted in C. H. Brewitt-Taylor (trans.), *San Kuo, or Romance of the Three Kingdoms* (Shanghai, 1925), II, 371–73. In this episode the sagacious leader Chu-ko Liang (181–234) finds himself, with only a handful of his troops, trapped in a city by an opponent commanding a huge army. He meets the situation by throwing open the gates of the city and calmly sitting on top of the city wall, where he plays his lute in full sight of the enemy. His opponent, convinced that this is a trick and that within the city must be concealed a large force of soldiers, thereupon marches his soldiers away without even venturing an attack.

36. Abstracted from quotations in Fung 2, pp. 30–32, 47–51. For innumerable similar correlations see the *Po Hu T'ung*, attributed to Pan Ku (A.D. 32–92), and translated by Tjan Tjoe Som as *Po Hu T'ung: The Comprehensive Discussions in the White Tiger Hall* (2 vols.; Leyden, 1949, 1952).

37. For these quotations see Fung 2, pp. 393, 396, 402.

38. Quoted in J. Percy Bruce (trans.), *The Philosophy of Human Nature, by Chu Hsi* (London, 1922), p. 68.

39. Fung Yu-lan, *A Short History of Chinese Philosophy*, ed. D. Bodde (New York, 1948), p. 24.

40. The word here used for "movement" is not *tung* but *tsao*, "hasty or impetuous movement" (Mathews' *Chinese-English Dictionary*, No. 6729). It appears again in chap. 45 in apposition to *ching* but did not succeed in establishing itself as a technical term in later Taoist literature.

41. J. Percy Bruce, *Chu Hsi and His Masters* (London, 1923), pp. 121–24.

42. Fung Yu-lan, *The Spirit of Chinese Philosophy*, trans. E. R. Hughes (London, 1947), p. 200.

43. Cf. also VI*b*, 2, where Mencius says of Shun and of another Sage, Yao, that "their course was simply one of filial piety and fraternal duty."

44. Cf. the quotations in Fung 2, pp. 396, 403, 405; also Sec. 6, A, above.

45. Quoted in Fung, *Spirit of Chinese Philosophy*, p. 200 (translation slightly modified by me). Cf. also *ibid.*, p. 201, for a Taoist-like poem by Ch'eng Hao, as well as Fung, *Short History of Chinese Philosophy*, pp. 291–93, for the same poem and a similar one by Shao Yung.

46. These emerge clearly, for example, when we compare Taoism as a philosophy (the kind of Taoism we have been discussing here) with Taoism as a popular organized religion. Thus in philosophical Taoism the emphasis is on the subordination of man to nature, whereas in religious Taoism the goal is the acquisition of human immortality through magical means, in other words, the gaining by man of control over natural forces; likewise in philosophical Taoism any idea of divine causation is rigidly excluded, whereas in religious Taoism the universe is peopled by a vast host of anthropomorphic deities.

47. On this last point, cf. Tawney's description of European medieval social theory, which reads almost as if it might have been written by a Confucian scholar: "The facts of class status and inequality were rationalized in the Middle Ages by a functional theory of society. . . . Society, like the human body, is an organism composed of different members. Each member has its own function. . . . Each must receive the means suited to its station, and must claim no more. Within classes there must be equality. . . . Between classes there must be inequality. . . . Peasants must not encroach on those above them. Lords must not despoil peasants. Craftsmen and merchants must receive what will maintain them in their calling, and no more" (R. H. Tawney, *Religion and the Rise of Capitalism* [London, 1926], pp. 22–23).

48. Lily Abegg, *The Mind of East Asia*, trans. from the German by A. J. Crick and E. E. Thomas (London and New York, 1952). The quotations that follow are taken from pp. 36, 39, and 40.

# Chinese "Laws of Nature": A Reconsideration

A S suggested by the title, this article is a sequel to one by the present writer called "Evidence for 'Laws of Nature' in Chinese Thought," which was published in *HJAS*, 20 (1957), 709–27. The earlier article was in turn inspired by Joseph Needham's illuminating and detailed analysis of the same subject in his *Science and Civilisation in China*.[1] Indeed, the final pages of that article consisted of interchanged comments between Dr. Needham and myself, based upon the views expressed in the main body of the article, which had been sent to Dr. Needham in advance of publication.

Similarly, the present article is an outgrowth of three years of work by the present writer in Cambridge, England (1974–77), largely spent preparing a draft of most of the next-to-last section for publication in the future seventh volume of *Science and Civilisation in China*. This section, dealing with the many intellectual and social factors which may have favored or hindered the development of science in premodern China, contains a subsection entitled "Man and Nature,"

---

[1] Hereafter referred to as *SCC*. See Section 18, "Human Law and the Laws of Nature in China and the West," in *SCC*, II (Cambridge: Cambridge Univ. Press, 1956), 518–83. A still earlier version of the same study was published by Dr. Needham under the same title and with only slight textual changes in *Journal of the History of Ideas*, 12 (1951), 3–30 and 194–230.

and it is in this subsection that the thorny question of Chinese "laws of nature" arises once more.

In his 1956 study of the subject, Dr. Needham distinguishes sharply between "natural law" and "laws of nature." The former, he points out, is wholly juridical and hence applicable only to the human world; this is so even though some of its past proponents may have viewed it as having had a divine origin, and subsequently as having early gained embodiment in the immemorially accepted customs of their particular society. "Laws of nature," on the other hand, solely pertain to the nonhuman sphere, for they consist of those fixed physical regularities (such as the law of gravity) which men have discovered to be constantly operative in the world of natural phenomena. It is Dr. Needham's belief that in Western society the concepts of these two kinds of law go back in large part to a common root, namely, the Judeo-Christian belief in the existence of a Supreme Being who initially created the universe and laid down laws for it, some of them peculiarly applicable to mankind, others regulating the functions of nonhuman creatures and natural phenomena generally. In his own words:[2]

One of the oldest notions of western civilisation was that just as earthly imperial lawgivers enacted codes of positive law, to be obeyed by men, so also the celestial and supreme rational creator deity had laid down a series of laws which must be obeyed by minerals, crystals, plants, animals and the stars in their courses.

Dr. Needham believes that in China, however, a radically different course of development occurred. After analyzing, with negative results, a number of early Chinese texts in which parallels to the Western concept of "laws of nature" might at first sight be expected to be present, he concludes that little or no development of the idea of "laws of nature" took place in China. By contrast, the ancient Chinese had an important word, *li* 禮 (propriety, politeness, traditional mode of behavior, etc.), which in several respects presents a fairly good parallel to the Western concept of "natural law." The major reason, he believes, for the nonappearance of "laws of nature" in Chinese traditional thinking was the relative absence therein of the idea of a creative divinity:[3]

[2] *SCC*, ii, 518.
[3] *SCC*, ii, 582.

The development of the concept of precisely formulated abstract laws capable, because of the rationality of an Author of Nature, of being deciphered and re-stated, did not . . . occur. The Chinese world-view depended upon a totally different line of thought. The harmonious cooperation of all beings arose, not from the orders of a superior authority external to themselves, but from the fact that they were all parts in a hierarchy of wholes forming a cosmic pattern, and what they obeyed were the internal dictates of their own natures.

The consequences of these differing viewpoints in East and West were profound for both civilizations, Dr. Needham maintains. In the West, the secularization of the concept of "laws of nature" by the seventeenth century, and its clear differentiation from that of "natural law," helped enormously to promote the rapid growth of the new science which took place from that time onward. But in China, where the concept of "laws of nature" hardly existed, there was also very little growth of the physical sciences during those same centuries.

The conclusions reached in my own 1957 *HJAS* article are some-what less assured. Most of the article is devoted to six passages from Chinese texts (all of them different from those earlier discussed by Needham) whose terms or ideas seem at first sight to be consonant with the concept of "laws of nature." Though four of the six are shown to be either negative or ambiguous in this respect, the remaining two (Passages 5 and 6) provide evidence which, to quote the article itself,[4] is

quite sufficient, in my opinion, to demonstrate that at least a few early Chinese thinkers viewed the universe in terms strikingly similar to those underlying the Western concept of "laws of Nature." On the other hand, I do not feel that it [this evidence] suffices to overthrow Needham's main contention: namely that the prevailing trend of Chinese speculation moved along a very different path—that of a self-contained, self-operating, "organismic" universe.

In recent years other passages in early Chinese texts have come to light which (contrary to Dr. Needham's opinion stated in the final pages of my 1957 article) seem likewise to express ideas not too far removed from those which in Europe led to the concept of "laws of nature." Of the nine passages given below, seven belong to this new body of material; the other two (Passages 4 and 6) are repetitions

---

[4] *HJAS*, 20 (1957), 722.

of the two more important passages in the 1957 article and are presented here in simpler form.

THE NINE PASSAGES

**Passage 1.** The first passage comes from Chapter 19 of the *Mo-tzu* 墨子 (late fourth or early third century B.C.):[5]

When it came to [the time of] King Chieh of the Hsia, Heaven had its harsh commands (*ming* 命): that sun and moon should be untimely (*pu shih* 不時), that cold and heat should arrive irregularly (*tsa chih* 雜至), that the five grains should die of drought, that demons (*kuei* 鬼) should shout within the capital, and that cranes should cry out for ten days. Heaven then commanded (*ming*) T'ang in the Piao Palace to assume and exercise the Great Mandate (*ta ming* 大命) of Hsia.

Here is Mo Tzu's version of how the Mandate of Heaven was transferred, traditionally in 1766 B.C., from Chieh, the allegedly tyrannical last ruler of the Hsia dynasty, to T'ang, founder of the Shang. That Heaven commands (*ming*) mankind, and especially mankind's appointed rulers, to conduct themselves in various ways, and that it also punishes wrongdoers who violate its commands are commonplaces of early texts such as the *Shu ching* (*Documents Classic*) and *Shih ching* (*Poetry Classic*). But it is quite exceptional for Heaven also, as here, to command the objects and forces of nature to change their usual patterns of operation. In European thinking it was only in the sixteenth and seventeenth centuries, coincident with the rise of modern science, that the idea of God's reign over the world was gradually transferred from consideration of the exceptions in nature (the comets and monsters which had disturbed medieval equanimity) and came to be identified with its unvarying rules.[6] In this *Mo-tzu* passage, though no laws of nature are actually mentioned, there seems to be a Chinese parallel to the pre-sixteenth century European approach.

---

[5] Cf. Yi-pao Mei, tr., *The Ethical and Political Works of Motse* (London: Arthur Probsthain, 1929), p. 112, considerably modified. Here and below, although references are given to existing Western translations of Chinese texts whenever available, it should be noted that the translations actually presented are in each case my own, and often differ markedly from the cited translations.

[6] See *SCC*, II, 542.

**Passage 2.** The second passage, too, comes from the *Mo-tzu*:[7]

Moreover there is a basis for my knowing how generously Heaven loves the people. It is the fact that it [Heaven] has orbited[8] the sun, moon, and stars in order to illumine and lead them [the people]. It has instituted (*chih* 制) the four seasons of spring, autumn, winter, and summer in order to guide and untangle them.[9] It sends down snow, frost, rain and dew, to grow the five grains, hemp and silk, thereby enabling the people to gain and be benefited by them. It has laid out the mountains, streams, gullies, and valleys, and allocated various activities [to be carried out by people in these different localities], so that it may oversee the people's goodness or lack of goodness [in the way they carry out these activities].[10] It has created kings, dukes, marquises, and earls, causing them to reward the worthy and punish the violent. It depletes its metals, woods, birds, and animals, and allows the five grains, hemp and silk to be worked upon, so as to provide materials for the people's clothing and food.

This is the same passage in which Mo Tzu, a few lines earlier, describes Heaven (*t'ien* 天) as a beneficent deity ruling over a man-centered universe. "Heaven," he states, "loves the whole world universally. Everything is prepared for the good of man. Even the tip of a hair is the work of Heaven."[11] In Passage 2 we see this loving Heaven of Mo Tzu acting consciously to place the heavenly bodies in their orbits and to "institute" the four seasons, while at the same time creating human institutions, all for the good of man. It is not surprising that Mo Tzu's strong theism should thus lead to statements very reminiscent of those which in European thinking led to the formulation of "laws of nature," even though he never uses the term.

**Passage 3.** The third passage comes from the *Lü-shih ch'un-ch'iu* 呂氏春秋 (*Mr. Lü's Springs and Autumns*; compiled 240 B.C.).[12] Here the text begins by identifying "Supreme Oneness" (*t'ai yi* 太一) as

---

[7] Chap. 27; cf. Mei, p. 145, again considerably modified.

[8] Emending *mo* 磨 to *li* 歷.

[9] "Guide and untangle" is an inadequate rendition of *chi kang* 紀綱, a term which, used as a noun, means "net" or "nexus." It is one of several technical terms covered by Needham in his discussion of possible Chinese equivalents of "laws of nature." See *SCC*, II, 554–56.

[10] This rather obscure sentence seems to mean that Heaven has allocated various occupations, such as farming, hunting, fishing, foresting, etc., to the people to perform according to the varying kinds of terrain which Heaven has provided for them.

[11] Cf. Mei, p. 145.

[12] Chap. 22; cf. Richard Wilhelm, tr., *Frühling und Herbst des Lü Bu We* (Jena: Eugen Diederichs, 1928), pp. 56–57.

another name for the *Tao* or Way. Then it says of it: "Supreme Oneness produced the Dual Forms, and the Dual Forms produced the *Yin* and *Yang*." Here the "Dual Forms" (*liang yi* 两儀) are probably Heaven and Earth.[13] The text goes on to describe how from the permutations of the *Yin* and *Yang* the many aspects of nature came into existence. Then, after apostrophizing the *Tao* in rhymed clauses very similar to descriptions of it in the *Lao-tzu*, the text says again of Supreme Oneness: "Therefore Oneness instituted ordinances which the Dualities follow and obey."[14] In other words, the *Tao*, under the name of Supreme Oneness, here replaces Mo Tzu's personal Heaven as the originator of the universe, and then institutes ordinances or orders (*ling* 令) for Heaven and Earth (here thought of as physical entities) to obey.

**Passage 4.** The *Kuan-tzu* 管子 contains an interesting definition of *tse* 則, "rule"—one of the several technical terms discussed by Needham in his search for Chinese "laws of nature."[15] The passage reads:[16]

What are basic to the [*Yin* and *Yang*] vital forces (*ch'i* 氣) of Heaven and Earth, to the harmonious balance between cold and heat, to the properties of water and soil, to the existence of human beings, birds, animals, plants, and trees; and which things, despite their extreme abundance, all possess as standards (*chün* 均), yet which never undergo change [themselves]—such are called "rules" (*tse*).

Here we are told that *tse* are basic to human, animal, and plant life, to climatic phenomena and inorganic matter. All things, despite their multiplicity, possess these *tse* as standards, and yet the *tse* themselves never undergo change. Unfortunately, the text fails to indicate how these *tse* themselves originate. Are they imposed on natural things and phenomena by a transcendent being or power acting as a legislator for created beings? If so, we seem to be in the presence of a concept close to what in the West would be called "laws

---

[13] See Fung Yu-lan, *A History of Chinese Philosophy*, tr. Derk Bodde, 2 vols. (Princeton: Princeton Univ. Press, 1952–53), I, 384. A few lines later, however, Fung also cites a closely parallel passage from the Great Appendix of the *Yi ching* (tr. James Legge in *Sacred Books of the East*, III [Oxford: Oxford Univ. Press, 1899], 373), wherein the Dual Forms are perhaps to be identified as themselves constituting the *Yin* and *Yang*.

[14] *Ku yi yeh che chih ling, liang yeh che ts'ung t'ing* 故一也者制令两也者從聽.

[15] *SCC*, II, 559–62 and 565–70.

[16] *Kuan-tzu*, opening section of Chap. 6; tr. and discussed in Bodde, pp. 720–21.

of nature." Or, are the *tse* perhaps thought of instead as *internal* rules which the things and phenomena enumerated in the text obey simply because the *tse* are proper to the natures of these things and phenomena?

There is no way of conclusively deciding between these alternatives. However, it should be pointed out that in the purely human sphere, the word *tse*, as used in other passages, commonly refers to a man-made rule or law, and in the few instances in which it occurs in the term *t'ien tse* ("rule of Heaven"), it seems to signify the rules or laws which Heaven has promulgated for man to follow. In either case it is a norm or standard imposed from above upon those who are subjected to it. This seems to suggest that in the present *Kuan-tzu* passage, in which the *tse* are referred to in broader terms as being basic to the nonhuman as well as the human world, the word has a universality and objectivity such as in the human world would be attributed to codes of law. On the other hand, if the passage simply has to do with internal rules proper to the natures of the beings and things specified, one wonders why some other term less legal than *tse* was not used. More appropriate, one would think, would be words like *hsing* 性, "nature" (especially, but not exclusively, human nature), or *ch'ing* 情, "quality."

**Passage 5.** This is another *Kuan-tzu* passage, this time from Chapter 64. Remarkable is the way in which it correlates the words *li* 理 (pattern, principle of organization) and *fa* 法 (law) with one another, in the course of establishing a macrocosmic-microcosmic parallelism between the natural and human worlds. Ordinarily, of course, *li*, as a term of central importance in the dominant Chinese organismic view of the cosmos, would never be equated with *fa* in this way. The passage reads:[17]

Heaven covers over the myriad creatures.[18] It regulates (*chih* 制) heat and cold. It moves (*hsing* 行) the sun and moon. It sequentially arranges[19] the stars. Such are

---

[17] *Kuan-tzu*, Chap. 64; cf. W. Allyn Rickett, tr., *Kuan-tzu, a Repository of Early Chinese Thought* (Hong Kong: Hong Kong Univ. Press, 1965), I, 122–23, where the significance of this passage with regard to "laws of nature" has already been pointed out. The final sentence is a repetition of a sentence in the *Kuan-tzu*, Chap. 2, on which this whole passage in Chap. 64 is a commentary.

[18] As a bird covers and shelters with its wings. See *Shih ching* No. 245.

[19] *Tz'u* 次, used as a verb, literally, "it sequences . . ."

Heaven's regularities (ch'ang 常). It governs (chih 治) these matters by means of its principles (li 理), starting them anew when they have reached their end.[20]

The ruler shepherds his myriad people. He governs (chih 治) all-under-Heaven. He supervises his hundred officials. Such are the ruler's regularities (ch'ang). He governs (chih) these matters by means of his laws (fa 法), starting them anew when they have reached their end.

The text goes on to list a series of paired "regularities" (ch'ang), such as those of father and mother, ministers and their inferiors, son and his wife. It then concludes:

Therefore so long as Heaven does not disregard (shih 失) its regularities (ch'ang), cold and heat will have their proper season, and the sun, moon, and stars will have their proper order. . . . Therefore when these regularities are made to function, there is good order; when they are disregarded, there is disorder. Heaven has never yet changed that whereby it governs (chih). That is why it is said that Heaven does not change its regularities (ch'ang).

In later cosmological thinking, especially that of Neo-Confucianism, li, "principles," are usually thought of as inherent patterns of organization for the objects, beings, and forces to which they pertain. In the present anonymous passage, however, probably belonging to the first century B.C.,[21] they function as instruments used by Heaven to maintain its regularities (ch'ang) in such matters as the alternation of cold and heat, movements of sun and moon, and orderly sequence of the stars. By analogy, the ruler is pictured as similarly using his fa, "laws," to maintain the regularities in his governing of the human world. Probably the reason why fa is used here only to refer to human government and not to Heaven's administrative activities, is the traditional prejudice (especially powerful among Confucians) against the whole idea of fa or positive law. This prejudice was of course intensified by the harsh way in which the Legalists had used fa to establish a powerful centralized state (the Ch'in empire) in 221 B.C.[22] Yet despite this reluctance to apply the word for human law to the world of nature, it would seem that the

---

[20] I.e., the movements of sun and moon, etc., operate cyclically, and are started anew by Heaven at the end of each cycle.

[21] See Rickett, p. 121.

[22] At this point it is well to distinguish clearly between li 理, "principle," which is the word used by the Kuan-tzu writer, and li 禮, "traditional mores, good custom," which the Confucians had wanted to retain in place of fa.

author of this *Kuan-tzu* passage comes rather close to what in European thought would be referred to as "laws of nature."

**Passage 6.** Because this passage, a rather lengthy excerpt from the *Huai-nan-tzu* 淮南子 (compiled around 139 B.C.),[23] was translated and discussed at length in my 1957 article on "laws of nature,"[24] and subsequently retranslated with considerable change by Dr. Needham,[25] it will be presented here in summary form only. Most of the fifth chapter, of which this passage forms the conclusion, is verbally identical, or nearly identical, with the noted calendrical text, the *Yüeh ling* 月令 (*Monthly Ordinances*), originally contained in the *Lü-shih ch'un-ch'iu* and reproduced from there in the *Li chi* (*Record of Rites*). As in the manner of the *Yüeh ling* (a product of the five-elements cosmologists), the *Huai-nan-tzu*'s fifth chapter describes, month by month, the natural phenomena and human behavior proper to each month and the dire consequences (snow in summer and the like) of practicing in one month the behavior prescribed for another.

The chapter bears the suggestive title, "Shih tse hsün 時則訓" ("Teachings on the Rules for the Seasons"), on which Kao Yu 高誘 (fl. 205–12) comments: "*Tse* (rules) are *fa* (laws). They are fixed laws (*ch'ang fa* 常法) for the four seasons, for cold and heat, and for the twelve months. Hence they are spoken of as rules for the seasons, [which phrase] is accordingly used as the title for the chapter."[26]

The conclusion of the passage, which is what concerns us and which is not paralleled by the *Yüeh ling*, deals with the regulating (*chih* 制) and measuring (*tu* 度) of the *Yin* and *Yang*, i.e., of meteorological phenomena, as carried out by Heaven, Earth, and the four seasons; these six powers are respectively symbolized by the carpenter's marking-line[27] (Heaven), the water level (Earth), the drawing compass (spring), the steelyard (summer), the carpenter's square (autumn), and the balance (winter). Acting in the manner of these

---

[23] See edition of Liu Wen-tien 劉文典, *Huai-nan hung-lieh chi-chieh* 淮南鴻烈集解 (Shanghai: Commercial Press, 1933), 5.19b–20a.

[24] Bodde, pp. 714–20.

[25] *SCC*, IV, pt. 1 (1962), 15–16.

[26] Liu Wen-tien, 5.1a. It should be noted that the word *ling* 令, "ordinance," which occurs in the corresponding title of the *Yüeh ling*, carries, like *tse*, a legal connotation.

[27] "Marking-line" is a better rendition for *sheng* 繩 than is "plumb-line," the interpretation found both in Bodde, p. 715 and *SCC*, IV, pt. 1, 15.

six kinds of measuring instruments, Heaven, Earth, and the four seasons are each said, with much poetic imagery, to "regulate" and "measure" the *Yin* and *Yang*, and to align, even, and otherwise fit all things of the world into their proper relationships. In this way, says the text, the seasonal movements of natural phenomena will be made to occur smoothly and without hitch.

Two sentences in particular are of crucial importance but are unfortunately ambiguous. At the end of the several sentences describing the work of the heavenly marking-line, the text reads: "This is why *shang ti* 上帝 uses [or used] it [the marking-line] as the progenitor [prime standard] of things."[28] Again at the end of the sentences describing the operations of Earth's water level, there is a parallel sentence: "This is why *shang ti* uses [or used] it [the water-level] as the equalizer of things."

The question here is whether *shang ti* is to be translated as the name of a unitary deity, "Lord on High," which is the meaning the term regularly has in early Chou texts, or should rather be pluralized and secularized to mean "the rulers of old" (taking *shang*, "above," in the secondary sense of "ancient"), which is a meaning very occasionally attested for it in Han texts. The former interpretation suggests that the whole passage describes the activities of a personal divine engineer, the "Lord on High" of ancient Chinese belief, who uses Heaven and Earth (and by analogy the four seasons, though this is not explicitly stated) as his instruments for operating the universe. This interpretation brings us close to the idea of "laws of nature."

The second interpretation destroys this conclusion, because it means that these functions were performed by the "rulers of old," i.e., by human beings, even though beings of more than ordinary human qualities. Semantically, both interpretations are possible, in that *ti*, originally the name of a divinity, had by late Chou times

---

[28] "Progenitor" is the rendition in my 1957 article as against "prime standard" in Dr. Needham's translation (see preceding note). "Progenitor" seems closer to the original word, *tsung* 宗, the more so as Kao Yu glosses it: "*Tsung* means *pen* 本 (origin)" (Liu Wen-tien, 5.20b). There seems to be an echo here of the *Lao-tzu*, Chap. 4, which says of the *Tao* that "it is as it were the progenitor (*tsung*) of the myriad creatures (*wan wu* 萬物)." Cf. Arthur Waley, *The Way and Its Power* (London: Allen & Unwin, 1934), who translates: ". . . the very progenitor of all things in the world" (p. 146).

also come to be a title applied to human rulers of exceptional powers ("emperors").

*Shang ti*, in the sense of "rulers of old," occurs thrice in the Han medical text, *Huang-ti nei-ching su-wen* 黃帝內經素問 (*The Yellow Emperor's Manual of Internal Medicine: Candid Questions*),[29] where the *shang ti* or "rulers of old" are said to have been interested in taking the pulse and performing other medical activities. In early Chou texts, on the other hand, *shang ti* was indubitably the name of a unitary deity. The question is whether this original meaning was still current as late as the second century B.C., when the *Huai-nan-tzu* was compiled. To reach an answer, it will be helpful to study the history of a longer title in which the words *shang ti* appear.

Sometimes in early Chou texts *shang ti* was coupled with *t'ien*, Heaven, to form the compound name of what was still regarded as a single deity, the well-known *huang t'ien shang ti* 皇天上帝 or "August Heaven Lord on High." By the end of the Chou this lengthy title had no doubt become somewhat archaic. Yet it continued to be used occasionally both then and in Han texts, and when this happens there can be no doubt that *shang ti* meant only "Lord on High," never "rulers of old."

*Huang t'ien shang ti* occurs twice in this way in the *Yüeh ling*,[30] and therefore also in the corresponding places in the *Huai-nan-tzu*'s fifth chapter, preceding the passage in which we are interested. The same title also appears in a proclamation issued by Wang Mang in A.D. 7 in response to the rebellion of Chai Yi; the *Ch'ien Han shu* (*History of the Former Han Dynasty*) explicitly says of this proclamation that it was archaistically modelled on one of the chapters in the *Shu ching* (*Documents Classic*). Later in the same proclamation the term *shang ti ming*, "mandate of *shang ti*," likewise occurs and is there glossed by the T'ang commentator Yen Shih-ku 顏師古 (581–645) as equivalent to *t'ien ming*, "mandate of Heaven." There can be no doubt, therefore, that when Wang Mang refers in his proclamation either to *shang ti*

---

[29] Once in Chap. 9 and twice in Chap. 13 (*chüan* 3.5a, 4.32, and 4.3b of the *SPTK* ed); cf. Ilza Veith, tr., *Huang Ti Nei Ching Su Wen* (Baltimore: Williams & Wilkins, 1949), pp. 136 and 149; cited also in *SCC*, IV, pt. 1, 15.

[30] Under the last months of summer and winter; see James Legge, tr., *The Li Ki*, in *Sacred Books of the East*, XXVII (Oxford: Oxford Univ. Press, 1885), 278 and 309.

or *huang t'ien shang ti*, he has in mind only the "Lord on High" of antiquity, not the secular "rulers of old."[31]

Although an absolute judgment is impossible, the weight of the foregoing evidence seems to favor the interpretation of *shang ti* in our passage as "Lord on High" rather than the much less frequently mentioned "rulers of old." And this in turn confirms the interpretation of the passage as having to do with a supreme deity who guides and regulates natural phenomena by means of measuring instruments. Admittedly this is not quite the same as a deity who actually legislates such phenomena. Nevertheless, a similarity undoubtedly exists, just as the words "law" and "measure" are semantically linked by the fact that every law has a certain quantitative aspect.[32] Such a view is further strengthened by the title of the *Huai-nan-tzu's* fifth chapter, "Teachings on the Rules (*tse*) for the Seasons," and Kao Yu's gloss of *tse* as equivalent to *ch'ang fa*, "fixed laws." Both he and the author of the chapter (or at least the editor who devised its title) obviously recognized a close connection between the idea of using measuring instruments to control natural phenomena and of using rules or laws to do the same.

**Passage 7.** This passage is gratifyingly brief. Tung Chung-shu (179?–104? B.C.), in his *Ch'un-ch'iu fan-lu* 春秋繁露 (*Luxuriant Gems of the Spring and Autumn*), in the course of speaking about the *Yin* and *Yang*, uses an administrative term, *chih* 制, which has already been encountered several times in the sense of "regulating" or "instituting."[33] The sentence in question reads: "That the *Yang* is noble and the *Yin* mean: this is Heaven's institution (*chih*)."[34] Here again it is quite conceivable that Tung, as a prominent Confucian, prefers to use the word *chih* rather than *fa*, "law," because of the Confucian prejudice against the latter word. Actually, however, the two words are close in meaning in this particular context. Like many other Chinese thinkers—though more strongly than most—Tung views the universe as consisting of a macrocosmic natural world and,

---

[31] For the proclamation, see *Ch'ien Han shu*, 84.14b and 84.17b (Po-na ed.).

[32] This point is discussed in *SCC*, II, 553.

[33] In Passages 2, 3, 5 and 6 above.

[34] *Ch'un-ch'iu fan-lu*, Chap. 46, end. For *chih* 制 some editions read *hsing* 刑, "punishment," which yields no sense.

closely parallel to it, a microcosmic human world.[35] It is not surprising, therefore, that he cites the alleged cosmic inferiority of the *Yin* to the *Yang* as justification for the social inferiority of woman to man which in his own time and later actually characterized Chinese society.[36] Because of his prevailing tendency to view Heaven as a personal deity,[37] it is easy for him to imagine the hierarchy of the cosmic *Yin* and *Yang* principles as having been institutionalized by Heaven as an example for mankind to follow.

**Passage 8.** In A.D. 6, after Wang Mang established himself as Acting Emperor, a memorial was submitted to him which included the words: "You have established the Pi Yung 辟雍 and set up the Ming T'ang 明堂 to propagate the laws of Heaven (*t'ien fa* 天法) and to spread the influence of the sages."[38] The Pi Yung or Hall of the Circular Moat was in Han times closely associated with the Imperial Academy, and consisted of an open-air structure where, on occasion, the emperor himself might lecture on scholarly matters. The Ming T'ang or Cosmic Hall was a building consisting of rooms corresponding to the months of the year and oriented around a central axis so as to face the compass points corresponding to the months. At monthly intervals, within the appropriate room, the emperor, following the prescriptions laid down in the *Yüeh ling* (*Monthly Ordinances*) and clad in colors appropriate to the particular season, allegedly performed the ceremonies designed to accord with the cosmic conditions of that month.[39]

It is impossible to know for certain whether the "laws of Heaven" for whose propagation the Hall of the Circular Moat and the Cosmic Hall are said to have been established were thought of only

[35] See especially *Ch'un-ch'iu fan-lu*, Chap. 56, as quoted in Fung, II, 30–31; also *SCC*, II, 299.

[36] See Fung, II, 42–43, citing especially *Ch'un-ch'iu fan-lu*, Chap. 53.

[37] See Fung, II, 19 and 29–30.

[28] *Ch'ien Han shu, ch.* 99A; cf. H. H. Dubs, tr., *The History of the Former Han Dynasty*, III (Baltimore: Waverly Press, 1955), 227.

[39] The first Pi Yung and Ming T'ang of Han times were erected by Wang Mang in A.D. 4 at Ch'ang-an, the Former Han capital, but were destroyed by fire when Wang was overthrown and killed there in A.D. 23. See Dubs, III, 80, 191 and 462. In A.D. 56, new buildings of the same name were built at the Later Han capital of Lo-yang. See Hans Bielenstein, "Lo-yang in Later Han Times," *BMFEA*, 48 (1976), 65–69. On the functioning of the Ming T'ang, see also *SCC*, II, 287.

as Heaven-given norms for *men* to follow, or also included celestial regulations governing *natural phenomena*. Mention of the Cosmic Hall, however, suggests that possibly the latter as well as the former were intended. The only other textual reference to *t'ien fa*, "laws of Heaven," known to us is less ambiguous. It occurs in the *Tso chuan* history under the year 515 B.C., where there is little doubt that it relates to human affairs only, and therefore is comparable to "natural law" rather than to "laws of nature" in the scientific sense.[40]

**Passage 9.** The final example occurs in Ko Hung's *Pao-p'u-tzu* 抱朴子 (*The Master Who Embraces Simplicity*; compiled around A.D. 320), where we read:[41]

The *Tao* serves internally to control the body and externally to conduct the state. It is able to order (*ling* 令) the Seven Agents (*ch'i cheng* 七政, i.e., the sun, moon, and five planets) to hold to their degrees of measurement,[42] the two vital forces (*ch'i* 氣, i.e., the *Yin* and *Yang*) to be in harmonious accord, the four seasons not to lose [their proper times], cold and warmth to keep their limitations,[43] and wind and rain not to act with violence.

Ko Hung's approach to nature was diverse and unusual. He believed strongly in animism,[44] and was confident that the vitalistic forces of nature could be controlled or changed by the intervention of human techniques. But he also began his book with a rhapsodic invocation of the *Tao* as "the Mystery,[45] the first ancestor of Spon-

[40] Needham discusses this passage in *SCC*, II, 547.

[41] *Nei p'ien* 內篇, Chap. 10; cf. James R. Ware, tr., *Alchemy, Medicine, Religion in the China of A.D. 320: The Nei P'ien of Ko Hung (Pao-p'u-tzu)* (Cambridge, Mass.: M.I.T. Press, 1966), p. 168.

[42] *Tu* 度, the technical term for the measured movements of the heavenly bodies. See *SCC*, II, 553–54.

[43] Curiously, there is no verb in this clause, which literally reads: "the limitations of cold and warmth." However, the meaning is surely that cold and warmth should not transgress the levels of intensity expected of them during the normal course of the year.

[44] To cite only a very few of many examples, Ko Hung believed that spirits are present in mountains, rivers, plants, trees, wells, water holes, and pools, as well as the human body. See *Pao-p'u-tzu, Nei p'ien*, Chap. 6; tr. Ware, p. 116. Ko Hung described the spirit of one such mountain as having the shape of a small boy and hopping backward on one foot, that of another mountain as resembling a red drum, and still a third as an anthropoid nine feet high, wearing fur-lined clothing and a straw hat. He also believed that some of the huge trees on mountains were capable of speech. See ibid., Chap. 17; tr. Ware, pp. 282 and 287.

[45] *Hsüan che* 玄者. In the *Lao-tzu*, Chap. 1, the *Tao* is referred to in an indirect way as "the mystery of mysteries."

taneity (*tzu jan* 自然), the great progenitor[46] of the myriad different things.''[47] In view of his wide range of thinking, it should not surprise us to find him likewise affirming the power of the *Tao* to order the *Yin* and *Yang*, as well as various meteorological agents, to keep to their courses and otherwise function harmoniously. This seems a rather close approach to the idea of "laws of nature" even though the term itself is lacking.

## CONCLUSION

The foregoing nine passages come from seven different sources,[48] having a total time span of perhaps seven centuries (probably fourth century B.C. to ca. A.D. 320). In only one of them (the eighth) does *t'ien fa*, the literal equivalent of "laws of nature," occur, and its exact significance there is uncertain. In other passages, however, several supreme agencies—Heaven (*t'ien*), the Lord on High (*shang ti*),[49] or the *Tao* (also referred to as Supreme Oneness)—are said by means of their commands or orders, institutions or regulations, or simply through their own direct action, to cause various celestial bodies (the sun, moon, and stars) to follow their proper orbits, the *Yin* and *Yang* to operate harmoniously, the four seasons to come in due succession, heat and cold and other meteorological phenomena to be equable, and the five grains to be available for human needs. In one of the passages (the sixth, from the *Huai-nan-tzu*) the Lord on High is said to use Heaven, Earth, and the four seasons (respectively symbolized by the carpenter's marking-line, the water level, drawing compass, and other measuring tools) as the agencies for carrying out various cosmic functions. In another passage (the fifth, from the *Kuan-tzu*) no supreme operator is mentioned, but *tse*, "rules," are described as basic standards for the functioning of the *Yin* and *Yang*, cold and heat, and animal and plant life, as well as that of humans.

---

[46] *Tsung*, the same word which appeared in the sixth passage above (that from the *Huai-nan-tzu*) at note 28.

[47] *Nei p'ien*, Chap. 1; cf. Ware, p. 28.

[48] The *Mo-tzu* and *Kuan-tzu*—two from each—as well as the *Lü-shih ch'un-ch'iu*, *Huai-nan-tzu*, Tung Chung-shu, a memorial to Wang Mang, and Ko Hung.

[49] Accepting the interpretation of *shang ti* in Passage 6 as "Lord on High" rather than "rulers of old."

Here a significant difference between Chinese and Western think-ing should once more be noted. In Europe, prior to the secularization of the concept of "laws of nature" in the seventeenth century, the idea of a supreme deity who *legislates* cosmic phenomena seems to be never far away from that of a supreme deity who *creates* the universe. In the nine cited Chinese passages, on the contrary, the idea of creat-ing is conspicuously lacking. The sole exception is the third (from the *Lü-shih ch'un-ch'iu*), in which the *Tao*, partially personified as Supreme Oneness, is said to have "produced" (*ch'u* 出, literally, "put forth") the Dual Forms, namely Heaven and Earth. The relative weakness of the idea of creation in Chinese thinking, and thus the relative weakness of the idea of a truly all-powerful deity, is a probable major reason (as said earlier) why the concept of "laws of nature" developed no further in China than it did.

Does the new evidence invalidate Dr. Needham's strongly argued thesis that the concept of "laws of nature" was alien to Chinese philosophical thinking? Probably not, as far as the overwhelming bulk of Chinese philosophical writing is concerned. What it does oblige us now to recognize, however, is that in addition to the domi-nant viewpoint argued for by Dr. Needham, a minority viewpoint also existed, expressed by a very few early Chinese thinkers, which was a good deal more congenial to the ideas underlying the "laws of nature" than would at first thought be suspected. On second thought it would, indeed, be strange if within an intellectual tradition as rich and varied as that of China, no trace whatever should have appeared of a concept which in the European environment was to prove so persistent and significant.

Not surprisingly, the embryonic beginnings of "laws of nature" are particularly apparent among those relatively early thinkers— Mo Tzu, who in Chou times advocated "universal love," the Han Confucian Tung Chung-shu, and the Chin alchemist Ko Hung— who thought in strongly theistic or animistic terms. On the popular level it is very probable that such ideas long remained widespread. Quite remarkably, however, they failed to gain more than a tem-porary and minority position in the main stream of Chinese philo-sophical speculation. Although traces of "laws of nature" may possibly occur in philosophical writings after the time of Ko Hung, they have so far not been discovered by me. In any event, one may doubt that they could long have survived the rise of Neo-Confucianism from the eleventh century onward.

Just as in Chinese philosophy, despite its overwhelmingly organismic view of the universe, a very few thinkers are to be found who interpret cosmic phenomena as being controlled or legislated by an all-powerful but beneficent deity, so in Western philosophy, despite its overwhelming acceptance of the idea of monotheistic creation and consequently of "laws of nature," there are a very few thinkers whose minds move in the direction of a noncreated, self-contained, and self-regulating "organismic" universe. The earliest such in Europe were perhaps the Stoics, followed very much later by men like the Cambridge Platonists (seventeenth century) and, more especially, by Leibniz around the same time. The latter's organic philosophy, Dr. Needham believes, may well have been influenced by Chinese organicist thinking, especially that of Neo-Confucianism, about which Leibniz had considerable knowledge. And following Leibniz there appeared increasing numbers of other "organic" philosophers and scientists, including, in the present century, men like Whitehead and Einstein.[50]

Had the above-mentioned two minor intellectual currents proved stronger and more enduring at an early time in China and Europe alike, the results for science and for general social development on the two sides of Eurasia would probably have been incalculable. But this is a very complex story which cannot be further pursued here.

[50] See the account in *SCC*, II, 496–505. It should be noted that Needham's thesis of the influence of Chinese philosophy on Leibniz's organicism is by no means universally accepted. See, for example, Olivier Roy, *Leibniz et la Chine* (Paris: J. Vrin, 1972), pp. 116–17, and David E. Mungello, *Leibniz and Confucianism, the Search for Accord* (Honolulu: University Press of Hawaii, 1977), pp. 14 and 99.

# THE CHINESE VIEW OF IMMORTALITY: ITS EXPRESSION BY CHU HSI AND ITS RELATIONSHIP TO BUDDHIST THOUGHT*

IN THE LONG HISTORY of Chinese thought, one of its greatest figures has been the Neo-Confucianist, Chu Hsi (A.D. 1130-1200). For several centuries before his time most of the best minds of China had devoted themselves to Buddhism, while Confucianism, though accepted as a basis for political institutions, had shown little ideological development. Beginning about A.D. 1000, however, a strong revival of Confucianism took place, fostered by a brilliant group of men who showed themselves usually antagonistic to Buddhism, even though, at the same time, they were indebted to it for many of their own concepts. Chu Hsi was easily the most important of this group, and it is chiefly owing to his genius that the scattered ideas of his predecessors were welded into a coherent, all-inclusive system of thought, which speedily became accepted as the basis of Chinese orthodoxy. The Neo-Confucianism of Chu Hsi, therefore, has for somewhat more than seven hundred years, until the last four or five decades, exerted an incalculable influence upon the minds of the vast majority of well educated Chinese.

There has recently appeared elsewhere a fairly lengthy account of Chu Hsi's philosophy, translated by myself from a history of Chinese philosophy written by Fung Yu-lan, a well known contemporary Chinese historian of philosophy.[1] In the seventh section of that account, Professor Fung presents an exposition of Chu Hsi's criticisms on Buddhism. The present article is an attempt on my part to expand certain of the ideas there presented in passing, and to relate them to the general stream of Chinese thought.

Before doing this, however, it is necessary, for the sake of intelligibility, to sketch very briefly one or two of Chu Hsi's main concepts. According to Chi Hsi, the universe is a dual one. On the

---

* I am indebted to Dr. W. Norman Brown, Professor of Sanskrit at the University of Pennsylvania, for having read this article and checked upon its use of Sanskrit terms.

1. Fung Yu-lan, "The Philosophy of Chu Hsi," translated with introduction and notes by Derk Bodde, *Harvard Journal of Asiatic Studies*, VII (1942), 1-51.

one hand, there exists a physical world of concrete matter; on the other, a metaphysical world made up of abstract *li* (translated by me as Law). This *li* or Law is multiple, so that for every single class of objects that belong to the physical world of matter, there exists a corresponding Law or principle in the metaphysical world, which is described by Chu Hsi as being "above form." These innumerable Laws, however, are not only transcendent; at the same time they directly manifest themselves within the individual things (both man-made and natural) of our phenomenal world. It is they, indeed, that give order and form to the world of matter. Without them there could exist no separate physical objects having specific characteristics and functions; there would, in fact, be only a mass of undifferentiated and inchoate ether. To give an example: it is the metaphysical Law that pertains to boats that causes such boats (as found in our physical world) to move only on water and not on land, just as it is the Law pertaining to carts that causes carts to move only on land.

When found immanent in this way in material things, these Laws or *li* are known as *hsing*. This word has a long history in Chinese philosophy, in which it usually means human nature. In Chu Hsi's system, however, it is evident that not only men, but also animals and even inanimate things, have their own *hsing* or individualized Law, since all things possess Law. The term, therefore, is translated by me simply as the Nature (that pertains to any specified object). In human beings this Nature manifests itself via the Mind (*hsin*), which is conceived by Chu Hsi as belonging wholly to the physical world of matter, but as, at the same time, acting as a temporal container or lodging-place for the metaphysical and universal Law.

With the above by way of introduction, we may now turn to consider some of the reasons for Chu Hsi's criticism of Buddhism. One of his leading points of attack, as outlined by Professor Fung in section 7 of his article, is the accusation that the Buddhists fail to understand the true character of the Nature (*hsing*), and confuse it with Mind. Chu Hsi quotes with approval (cf. Fung, *op. cit.*, p. 49) the saying: "What the Buddhists call the Nature is exactly what the (Confucian) Sage calls Mind, and what the Buddhists call Mind is exactly what the Sage calls Thought." On the surface, this may seem like a mere quibbling over terms; actually it represents a basic difference between Neo-Confucianism and Buddhism, or, at least, between

Neo-Confucianism and what Chu Hsi seemed to regard as Buddhism.

For Law, according to Chu Hsi, pertains to the permanent and unchanging metaphysical world that is "above form," and hence is itself necessarily universal and impartial. Its manifestation (under the name of *hsing* or Nature) within any given object of our physical universe, therefore, is a purely temporary phenomenon, which is ever taking place within an infinite number of separate objects simultaneously. Thus the Law that pertains to human beings, for example, manifests itself simultaneously within all existent human beings alike, and endures permanently quite regardless of the life or death of any particular one of these human beings. In other words, the fact that any physical thing (such as a human being, in the example just given) is a temporary sharer of the Law pertaining to that class of things, in no way gives to the particular thing in question a personal entity of its own that will endure after the physical disintegration of that thing.

In the case of Mind, however, quite a different situation prevails. Mind is something concrete and physical, which belongs to the transitory world of matter that is "below form." It is individual and unique, therefore, for every separate being that possesses it. For the very same reason, however, it, like the beings that possess it, is equally subject to change and dissolution, so that its existence within any given individual being cannot give to that individual a permanent entity of its own.

With these points clearly understood, it is easy to see why Chu Hsi objected to what he considered the confusion made by the Buddhists between the Nature and the Mind. For to designate as the Nature something that really has the characteristics of the Mind, is to attribute to what is permanent and universal (Law, which comprises the Nature) the quality of individuality that properly pertains only to Mind. In other words, it is to ascribe to individual objects an entity which is falsely called the Nature, and which is erroneously regarded both as permanent, and yet at the same time (unlike the true Nature) as being separate for each object.

The same point of view underlies Chu Hsi's statement (cf. Fung, p. 48) that "the Confucianists maintain that Law (*li*) undergoes neither creation nor destruction. The Buddhists maintain that there is a Spiritual Intelligence (*shên shih*) that undergoes neither creation nor destruction." In the note on this latter term in my translation of

Fung's article, I have explained that it is a Buddhist name for the soul. It is used, for example, in one Buddhist text as follows: "At the time of the end of the world, fierce flames will appear filling the entire universe. The souls (*shên shih*) of the dead will then crash down from their flight and be carried on the smoke to enter a boundless hell." It is evident, therefore, that Chu Hsi is here accusing the Buddhists of believing in the existence of a personalized soul, while at the same time denying the existence of an impersonal and universal principle which he calls *li* or Law.

This raises the question as to what were Chu Hsi's own views on immortality. Such views do not assume a prominent place in his philosophy. Nevertheless, they are to be found expressed in a letter (in which he also deals with what he considers to be the Buddhist position on the subject), replying to a disciple, Lien Sung-ch'ing, who had addressed him on the matter. Chu's letters reads as follows:[2]

You have stated: "The Nature (*hsing*) of the universe[3] is my own Nature. How, then, can death be accompanied by sudden annihilation?"

As regards this doctrine, it is not, to be sure, quite incorrect. Nevertheless, I do not know whether in propounding it, you regard (the Nature of) the Universe as primary, or do you regard that of the ego (*wo*) as primary?[4] If you regard that of the Universe as primary, it follows that this Nature is then a Principle (*tao li*) common to the entire Universe, in which there are therefore no divisions as to what pertains to men and what to creatures, what to the "that" and what to the "this"; nor are there any distinctions as to death or life, antiquity or modern times. Although one is then to say that there is no annihilation at death, this does not mean that there is a survival of a personal ego.

But if you regard (the Nature of) the ego as being primary, this simply means that you recognize as existing in your own body a spiritual (*ching shên*), soul-like (*hun p'o*) something, having cognition and consciousness, which you look upon as being your Nature, and to which you cling in all its operations unto death, unwilling to let it go. To call such a thing "death

2. Cf. the *Chu-tzŭ wên-chi* (Collected Writings of Chu Hsi), *Ssŭ-pu ts'ung-k'an* edition, bk. (*chüan*) 41, p. 686, of the continuously paginated version bound in western fashion. The passage here quoted was originally pointed out to me by Professor Fung when I was attending his lectures on Chinese philosophy at Ts'ing Hua University, Peiping, in 1934-35.

3. Lit., "of Heaven and Earth," the usual Chinese term meaning universe. The reference here is to some sort of cosmic soul or spirit.

4. I.e., is the Nature (i.e., spirit or soul) of the individual to be regarded as subordinate to and forming part of the universal world Nature or soul, or is it free and self-sufficient?

without annihilation," is the height of egotistical thinking. How, then, may it merit, nevertheless, being included among the discussions on the theories of life or death, or the principles of the Nature (*hsing*) and of Destiny (*ming*)?

The doctrines of Buddhism are also fundamentally of this sort. Those of its devotees who are clever are themselves ever cognizant of the meanness of this (doctrine), which they therefore disparage and avoid discussing. On the contrary, they poke their heads into other doctrines pertaining to all sorts of mysterious and abstruse principles, so vast, like a boundless sea, that they cannot be approached for investigation. And yet the starting point of them actually does not lie outside this (doctrine of a personal ego, described above).

But if such (a doctrine) were really true, it would mean that within the single Nature (*hsing*) belonging to the Universe there were to exist innumerable other separate Natures of men and creatures. Each of these Natures would have its own particular domain, without impinging one upon the other. (The creatures possessing these Natures would), with a change of their name and surname, each be born of itself and die of itself.[5] (Such creatures), furthermore, would not be formed out of the creative activities of the *yin* and the *yang* in the Universe; nor would these *yin* and *yang* of the Universe have anything into which to infuse their creative activities.[6]

As you have taken the trouble to ask me on this question, I have accordingly answered following the receipt of your letter.

The question of whether Chu Hsi has here fairly represented the Buddhist position will be discussed later. At this place I should like to stress the point that Chu Hsi's general approach to the problem of immortality is in striking accord with that of well-nigh all other non-Buddhist Chinese thinkers who have ventured to discuss it. It is a really remarkable fact that, for millenia, China has been a stronghold of the so-called worship of ancestors, a cult presumably based upon a belief in the immortality of the soul; that it has been a country in which superstitious beliefs in spirits and ghosts of all kinds are rife among the common people; and yet that, when we study what China's sophisticated thinkers have had to say on the subject, we find either that they have hesitated to admit the possibility of immortality at all,

---

5. This is a difficult sentence, and I am not certain that I have caught the exact meaning. If I have, it would seem to refer to the Buddhist doctrine of successive rebirth, the rebirth of any given creature being regarded as occurring entirely separately and independently from that of any other creature.

6. The *yin* and the *yang* are respectively the principles of negation, quiescence, darkness, moisture, cold, etc., on the one hand, and of positiveness, activity, light, dryness, heat, etc., on the other, the interaction of which create all physical phenomena.

or have conceived of it only in general semi-pantheistic terms, rather than in terms of a personal survival. This should become clear after reading the brief survey that follows.

Confucius (B.C. 551-479), as is well known, was very reluctant to discuss matters of the other world. Once, on being asked by a disciple about man's duty to the spirits, he replied: "When still unable to do your duty to men, how can you do your duty to the spirits?" Likewise, when the same disciple ventured to ask about death, Confucius replied: "Not yet understanding life, how can you understand death?"[7]

Some three centuries or so later, we find the Confucian scholars adopting a very sophisticated attitude toward the subject, when they compiled the classic known to us today as the *Book of Rites*, a bulky work devoted to detailed descriptions of the ancient rituals and ceremonies. These very elaborate ceremonials were connected, to a large degree, with the burial and mourning rites, and sacrifices to the dead. Yet such rites are not, say the Confucians, performed for the benefit of the dead themselves, for the dead are dead, and therefore cannot possibly enjoy such things. The real reason for the existence of these ceremonies is that they provide an outlet for the emotions of the living. Through their observance, the bereaved relatives are permitted to express, in a sincere yet civilized manner, the grief which they experience on the loss of a beloved one. The performance of these ceremonies, in other words, acts as a catharsis for the emotions; yet at the same time, by serving as a fixed ritualistic framework within which such emotions may express themselves, the ceremonies prevent the emotions from running to excess and thus doing injury to those who experience them.[8]

Turning to the Taoist school, we find there quite a different point of view. Its greatest representative, Chuang Tzŭ (ca. B.C. 369-ca. 286), does, to be sure, express himself in one passage in a manner which seems to preclude any possibility of immortality. "Man," he writes in the second chapter of his book, "may say: there is immortality. But what is the use of this saying? When the body is decomposed, so with it is the spirit. Can it not be called very deplorable?"[9] In the

7. *Analects* XI, 11.
8. Cf. Fung Yu-lan, *A History of Chinese Philosophy*, I: *The Period of the Philosophers (from the Beginnings to circa 100 B.C.)*, translated from the Chinese by Derk Bodde (Peiping, 1937), ch. 14, esp. 344-46.
9. Cf. translation of Fung Yu-lan, *Chuang Tzŭ* (Shanghai, 1933), p. 47.

following chapter, nevertheless, he writes apropos of the death of the Taoist sage, Lao Tzŭ, as follows: "The fingers may be unable to supply further fuel.[10] But the flame is carried onward, and we know not when it may come to an end."[11]

These words seem to hint at some form of continued life after death. Actually, however, they are only an expression of Chuang Tzŭ's pantheistic and mystical view of the universe. This is a point made fully evident by other passages in his book, and hence Fung Yu-lan, in his comment on the present passage, is entirely correct when he interprets it as follows:[12] "This is Chuang Tzŭ's conception of immortality. His conception does not presuppose a spiritualistic universe. . . . The body of the individual must die; so does his soul, which is the function of the body. But the universe as a whole must eternally exist; so do those who identify themselves with the whole."

In fact, the general attitude of the Taoists toward immortality may be summed up as follows: In the universe there is only one all embracing stream of existence (called the Way or *Tao*); life and death are merely differing phases of this single existence; after death, therefore, we continue to exist as integral parts of this single stream of existence which never dies, but this in no way may be interpreted as signifying a personal form of immortality.[13] Such a concept is basic in the following passage from the *Huai-nan-tzŭ* (ch. 7).[14]

Heaven and Earth, in their revolutions, permeate each other, and the "ten thousand things" combine to form the One. If we understand this One, there is no single thing that we cannot understand, but if we do not understand this One, there is no single thing that we can understand. For example, living in the world, I too am a thing. Can I not then realize that with me the things in the world are made complete, and that without me these things are incomplete? . . . In life I am added to the kind that have form, just as in death I am submerged among the kind that are formless. Yet the number of things (having form) is not increased by my life, nor is the thickness of the earth increased by my death. . . . The Creator's

10. I.e., the matter which forms our physical frames may come to an end.
11. Cf. Fung, *op. cit.*, p. 71.
12. *Ibid.*, pp. 71-72.
13. Cf. also Fung Yu-lan, *A History of Chinese Philosophy*, pp. 236-39.
14. A work largely of Taoist inspiration, compiled under the patronage of Liu An, Prince of Huai-nan (died B.C. 122). Cf. translation of Evan Morgan, *Tao the Great Luminant* (Shanghai, 1934), pp. 62-63. This translation is often unreliable, and my own differs from it in a number of respects.

moulding and guidance of things is like a potter's kneading of the clay.[15] The earth which he has taken and formed into basins and bowls is in no wise different from that which he has left in the ground. And when the vessels which he has created become broken, they are dispersed and return to their source, where they are in no wise different from the basins and bowls as they were made.

Without the above passage as a guide, the following words from the *Huai-nan-tzŭ,* which occur only a few pages later on, might easily be open to misinterpretation:[16]

The body may die, but the spirit never undergoes change. With this absence of change it replies to the never ending thousand shifts and ten thousand turnings of the flux (of the universe). What undergoes change reverts to the formless, but what does not undergo change remains co-existent with Heaven and Earth.

If we turn now from Confucianism and Taoism to the minor schools of thought, we find expressed in various ways the same basic denial of a future personal existence. The famous egoist and hedonist, Yang Chu, for example, has many bitter remarks on the inevitable ending of all things by death, and the consequent futility of all striving during life. Here is one example:[17]

In life the myriad creatures all differ from each other, but in death they are reduced to a single uniformity. In life they may be virtuous or degenerate, honorable or despicable: that is how they differ from each other. But in death they will stink and rot and decompose: that is how they are all equal to each other. . . . Perhaps it may be ten years or perhaps a hundred years . . . they will all nevertheless die. They may be virtuous and sage, or they may be evil and degenerate; quite regardless they will die. In life they may be Yao or Shun;[18] in death they will only be rotting bones. In life they may be Chieh or Chou;[19] in death they too will be

15. References to the Creator (*tsao wu chê*) occur a number of times in Taoist writings. They are not to be taken literally as indicating a belief in a personal Creator, however, but merely as poetic metaphors.

16. Morgan, *op. cit.,* p. 68.

17. Cf. translation of Anton Forke, *Yang Chu's Garden of Pleasure* (London, 1912), pp. 40-41 (rather loosely translated). Yang Chu lived during the fifth century B.C. The little treatise here quoted bears his name and comprises the seventh chapter of the *Lieh-tzŭ,* a Taoist work. By many modern Chinese scholars, however, it is regarded as a forgery written by some unknown person of the third or fourth centuries A.D. But for our present study the question of its precise date or authorship is unessential.

18. Legendary sage emperors of antiquity noted for their virtue.

19. Tyrant rulers of antiquity noted for their cruelty.

rotting bones. In being rotten bones they are all alike. Who, then, will be able to distinguish their (former) differences?

As a final example, let us examine the views of the iconoclast, Wang Ch'ung (A.D. 27-ca. 97), who wrote a large work, the *Lun-hêng* (Critical Essays), to dissipate what he considered the irrationalties of his age. In his chapter, "On Death," he writes as follows:

Human death is like the extinction of fire. When a fire is extinguished, its light does not shine any more, and when man dies, his intellect does not perceive any more. The nature of both is the same. If people nevertheless pretend that the dead have knowledge, they are mistaken.[20]

A few lines below he expresses a view which is not far removed from that of the Taoists, though his is based upon a purely material-istic approach, whereas theirs is derived from a mystical awareness of the oneness of the universe:

During the months of the depth of winter, the cold air prevails and water freezes into ice. At the approach of spring, the air becomes warm, and the ice melts to water. Man's life in the universe is like the ice. The *yang* and the *yin* fluids[21] crystallize to produce man. When his years are concluded and his span is exhausted, he dies and thus reverts to these fluids. As spring water cannot freeze again, so the soul of a dead man cannot become a body again.

The above survey may suffice to indicate that Chinese philosophers either: (1) simply deny the survival of a soul after death; or (2), if they do speak of immortality, conceive of it never in personal terms, but only in the sense that the universe as a whole is never destroyed, and that therefore we, being parts of the universe, continue, after the bodily dissolution that accompanies death, to participate (in newly constituted forms) in the existence of that universe. Mo Tzŭ (ca. B.C. 479-ca. 381), indeed, remains the only non-Buddhist of really outstanding importance who has championed the idea of a personal immortality.[22] And Mo Tzŭ's school, as we know, completely dis-

20. Translation of Alfred Forke, *Lun-hêng*, in *Mitteilungen des Seminars für Orientalische Sprachen*, IX (1906), 376.

21. The negative and positive forces that create all physical phenomena. Cf. above, note 6.

22. Cf. his chapter, "On Ghosts," translated by Mei Yi-pao, *The Ethical and Political Works of Motse* (London, 1929), pp. 160-74. In this, Mo Tzŭ recounts many of the ghost stories current in his day as one of his "proofs" for the existence of spirits.

appeared a few centuries after his death, leaving almost no trace on later Chinese thought.

Chu Hsi's attitude toward immortality may thus be seen to be in harmony with that of the great bulk of non-Buddhist (especially Taoist) Chinese thinkers before his time. His attribution to the Buddhists, however, of a belief in personal survival, will come as something of a shock to those who remember that one of the most important tenets of early Buddhism was the denial of the existence of a personal ego or ātman. It may be questioned, however, how literally we should understand such a doctrine. Sir Charles Eliot, for example, warns us that

the universality of the proposition really diminishes its apparent violence and nihilism. To say that some beings have a soul and others have not is a formidable proposition, but to say that absolutely no existing person or thing contains anything which can be called a self or a soul is less revolutionary than it sounds. It clearly does not deny that men exist for decades and mountains for milleniums; neither does it deny that before birth or after death there may be other existences similar to human life. It merely states that in all the world, organic and inorganic, there is nothing which is simple, self-existent, self-determined, and permanent; everything is compound, relative and transitory.[23]

Certainly it is true that, during the early centuries of Buddhism in China, the practical and realistic Chinese found it difficult to accept a philosophy which stresses the theory of karma and reincarnation, not only in the human but also in the animal and spirit worlds, yet at the same time denies the existence of a self or ātman that may pass through these stages of successive rebirth. Most of them, as a consequence, reversed the early Buddhist theory of anātman (non-ātman) by attributing to the Buddhists a belief that a definite self or soul does, indeed, survive through countless existences. This fact, which has not, so far as I know, been properly emphasized in western writings on Chinese Buddhism, is clearly brought out by the Chinese scholar, T'ang Yung-t'ung, who states quite categorically:

From the very beginning the Chinese failed to comprehend the deep meaning of Buddhism [as to the non-existence of the ātman] . . . Buddhism

23. Sir Charles Eliot, *Hinduism and Buddhism, an Historical Sketch* (London, 1921), I, 191.

spoke about the endless cycle of transmigration. Because of this, the doctrine that the soul does not perish, but is carried on as a result of karma, became a current belief [among the Chinese].[24]

Among the several quotations cited by Professor T'ang in support of this statement, one of the earliest and most interesting is found in the *Li-huo lun* (The Raising of Doubts), a little work, also known after its supposed author as the *Mou-tzŭ*, which was written toward the end of the second century A.D. as a refutation of the anti-Buddhists.[25] In the twelfth chapter of this book, the supposed critic of Buddhism is represented as objecting to the author: "Buddhism says that after a man dies he must live again. I do not believe in the truth of such a judgment." To which the author counters: "The soul certainly does not die. It is only the body which decomposes. The body is like the stalk or leaf of the five kinds of grain, while the soul is like the germ or seed of those grains. The stalk and leaves, having been born, must inevitably die, but how can the germ or seed ever perish?"[26]

In later times this topic remained a subject of fierce debate between Buddhists and agnostic non-Buddhists, especially the Confucian scholars. Soon after the year A.D. 500, one of the latter, a man named Fan Chên, wrote a famous tract entitled the *Shên-mieh lun* (Essay on the Extinction of the Soul). In this he hotly attacked the Buddhist belief in an enduring soul, and raised many arguments against its survival after death, of which the following is a fair example:

The body supplies the material stuff for the soul; the soul gives function to the body. . . . The relationship of the soul to the material stuff (of its body) is like that of sharpness to a knife. The relationship of the body to its functions is like that of a knife to its sharpness. The sharpness is not the same as the knife, nor is the knife the same as the sharpness. Nevertheless, without sharpness there will be no (true) knife, and without the knife there will be no sharpness. I have never heard of sharpness having been

24. T'ang Yung-t'ung, *Han Wei Liang-Chin Nan-pei-ch'ao fo-chiao shih* (History of Buddhism during the Han, Wei, Two Chin, and Northern and Southern Dynasties) (Shanghai, 1938), pp. 89, 91. (This is a history of Chinese Buddhism from its introduction into China in the first century A.D. to about A.D. 600. It is easily the best Chinese work on the subject that has yet appeared.)
25. On this work cf. Paul Pelliot, "Meou-tseu ou les doutes levés," *T'oung pao*, 2nd series, XIX (1918-19), 255-433, esp. 255-86.
26. Pelliot, *op. cit.*, p. 301. The seed, which is produced from one plant and in its turn gives birth to another, represents the Buddhist idea of successive rebirth through karma.

preserved after the knife has been destroyed. How, then, can we suppose that the body becomes extinct, but that the soul continues to exist?[27]

Despite this and other attacks, belief in the existence of a permanent soul continued in later times to be widely held by Chinese Buddhists. Wei Shou (A.D. 506-572), for example, in the chapter on Buddhism contained in his *Wei shu* (History of the Wei Dynasty), expressly states that, according to Buddhist belief, "the soul is never destroyed."[28]

It is evident, therefore, that such a belief was for centuries common among the Chinese, at least among those who accepted Buddhism as a popular religion without delving into its higher abstrusities. Against this, Chu Hsi counters with his concept of a wholly impersonal type of immortality, according to which Law or *li*, though itself universal, becomes temporarily manifested as the Nature in an infinitude of ever changing physical objects, departing again upon the extinction of

27. For this and other such passages, cf. T'ang Yung-t'ung, *op. cit.*, pp. 470-73; also Alfred Forke, *Geschichte der mittelalterlichen chinesischen Philosophie* (Hamburg, 1934), pp. 266-74.

It may be remarked here parenthetically that, both in the case of this analogy and that of the seed of grain just quoted from the *Mou-tzŭ*, certain realistic and practical objections may be raised, i.e., that the seed under certain conditions may be destroyed (for example, it may be eaten), or that there may sometimes exist a knife that has lost its sharpness. The argument by analogy, however, which plays a very important part in Chinese philosophy, should not be judged too strictly from the point of view of realistic exactitude. It is not intended to serve as an absolutely water-tight proof, covering all possible alternatives in the case being argued. Rather it is a clarifying marker or beacon, erected by the writer to throw light upon the train of thought which he is trying to expound. If, under the normal conditions postulated for it by the writer, the analogy is an apt one, it helps to bring conviction to the mind of the reader. The latter will, in any case, not try to twist it to fit abnormal or unnatural situations, for he knows that the analogy was never designed to cover such situations, but only to represent a particular train of ideas. Thus, in the case of the analogy of the knife, a Chinese reader would not bother to argue that some knives are dull, for he knows that this is an accidental condition that lies outside the basic point being made, namely: that the purpose of all knives is to cut, and that therefore every knife, speaking from an ideal point of view, must possess sharpness if it is to be a true knife. The success of the analogy depends upon the extent to which it convinces the reader that, just as sharpness is a quality indivisible from the knife, so is the soul indivisible from the body, and hence must perish together with that body.

For further discussion of this and other favorite types of Chinese argument, cf. my *China's First Unifier* (Leiden, 1938), pp. 223-32, and "Types of Chinese Categorical Thinking," *Journal of the American Oriental Society*, LIX, 2 (1939), 200-19.

28. Cf. translation of James R. Ware, "Wei Shou on Buddhism," *T'oung pao*, 2nd series, XXX (1933), 113. It is interesting to note that, in this passage, the term for soul is *shih shên* (lit., "Intelligent Spirit"), which is a mere transposition of the words *shên shih* ("Spiritual Intelligence") used by Chu Hsi, in his criticism of Buddhism quoted above, to designate the Buddhist concept of soul.

these objects, but continuing to exist ever unchanged within the metaphysical world of Law which transcends our sensory universe. In formulating such a theory, it seems clear that Chu Hsi was simply following the attitude generally held by Chinese philosophy, especially Taoism, while adapting it to his own particular metaphysical framework.

It is still questionable, nevertheless, whether Chu Hsi, in his criticism, has correctly apprehended the Buddhist point of view regarding the ego. It will be remembered that, in his letter, he asserts that if the doctrine of an enduring personal self "were really true, it would mean that within the single Nature (*hsing*) belonging to the Universe there were to exist innumerable other separate Natures of men and creatures. Each of these Natures would have its own particular domain, without impinging one upon the other," etc.

Such a picture of an anarchistic world of individual and unrelated Natures or personalities is surely a gross misrepresentation of the Buddhist point of view. Chu Hsi does not, to be sure, actually attribute it to the Buddhists themselves. He merely implies that such a picture represents the logical culmination of the Buddhist view if it is accepted. Such may have been his own honest opinion, but it is doubtful whether he could have found any prominent Buddhist who would have agreed with him. Buddhism, in fact, has, on the contrary, ever tended to stress the absolute interrelationship of all things in the universe, regardless of whether such relationship is to be conceived as taking place on the noumenal or the phenomenal plane. Even in early times, indeed, one of the chief arguments against the belief in a self or ātman was the assertion that every supposedly separate entity is really only a composite combination of other things; for example, what we call a chariot is not, in itself, a single entity, but is simply a convenient appellation for an aggregate of separate parts, such as wheels, shafts, body, etc.

Likewise Mahāyāna Buddhism, as developed in China, though it may have permitted, for popular purposes, the belief in the existence of a separate self, nevertheless always maintained that this self exists in close interrelationship with other selves and with the universe as a whole. Sometimes this belief took the form expressed by the *Nirvāṇa sūtra* (first translated into Chinese in A.D. 423), which maintained that the Dharmakāya or "Law-body" (i.e., the true essence of being or the absolute) is the sole unchanging reality that underlies all changing phenomena, and is actually contained within all physical creatures. To quote a modern Chinese scholar on the subject:

Not only is it the case that the Law-body of the Buddha eternally remains; the Law-body of each and every one of us sentient beings is moreover in no wise different from the Law-body of the Buddha. Because of this, "All sentient beings possess the Buddha-nature." . . . [The proponents of such a theory] maintained that the Buddha actually possesses a "Greater Ego" (*ta wo*). This doctrine, when it was heard of, horrified and startled those who maintained that there exists no ego (ātman).[29]

Another conception is that of "Mind-only," as found, for example, in the *Laṅkāvatāra sūtra* (first translated into Chinese ca. A.D. 420). According to this work, there is an ālayavijñāna or "all-conserving mind," psychologically somewhat akin to our concept of the subconscious, the activities of which cause all sensory phenomena to appear, so that the entire universe, as we see it, is a product of our own minds. This ālayavijñāna, though superficially it seems to be a sort of a personal ego, is actually "the store or totality of consciousness, both absolute and relative, impersonal in the whole, temporarily personal or individual in its separated parts."[30] It is, therefore, something quite distinct from the usual concept of a personal ātman.[31]

There are, of course, an infinite number of variations of these doctrines as developed in the various schools of Mahāyāna Buddhism. Some, no doubt, could even be found approaching fairly closely the position taken by Chu Hsi himself, though a usual difference between the Buddhists and the Neo-Confucianists (including Chu Hsi) is that the former regarded the physical world as we see it to be illusory and therefore "void" or "empty"; the latter, on the contrary, regarded both the physical world of matter and the metaphysical world of Law as equally "real" and existent, even though the one undergoes constant change, whereas the other exists eternally unchanging.

29. Translated from Chiang Wei-ch'iao, *Chung-kuo fo-chiao shih* (A History of Chinese Buddhism), 2nd ed. (Shanghai, 1933), I, 20a.
30. William Edward Soothill and Lewis Hodous, *A Dictionary of Chinese Buddhist Terms* (London, 1937), p. 292a.
31. Cf. D. T. Suzuki, *Studies in the Lankavatara Sutra* (London, 1930), esp. pp. 241-98. For literature on the Yogācārya school, which developed this doctrine, cf. the Introduction by Clarence H. Hamilton to his translation of the *Wei shih er shih lun, or the Treatise in Twenty Stanzas on Representation-only*. American Oriental Series, vol. XIII (New Haven, 1938).

It would seem, therefore, that Chu Hsi, although he is said to have studied Buddhism in his youth, has been led by his antipathy toward it into a misinterpretation of the Buddhist doctrine at this point. This is not said with any aim of belittling his true greatness. The fact is that such misinterpretation was probably an almost inevitable consequence of the age and intellectual environment in which he lived. For in the China of the twelfth century, Buddhism, as a dynamic philosophical force, had already passed its peak, and had crystallized (with the possible exception of the Ch'an or Zen sect) into comparatively static dogma. It still, of course, held a powerful appeal for many millions of Chinese. Its higher philosophical speculations, nevertheless, were no longer attracting the attention of the best minds of China, many of whom were turning toward Neo-Confucianism, which in several ways represented a sort of philosophical nationalism. And with the rise and flowering of Neo-Confucianism, there came a reassertion of the ever latent tendency of Confucian scholars to look with distrust, or even active disapproval, upon whatever lies outside the realm of Confucian orthodoxy.

It is little wonder, therefore, that though the Neo-Confucian philosophers were undoubtedly deeply influenced by the general conceptions of Buddhism, probably few of them troubled to acquire a really broad and penetrating knowledge of Buddhism's more abstruse refinements. Especially would this be true of Chu Hsi, coming as he did at a time when Neo-Confucianism had already been raised by his predecessors to a position of dominance, and when Buddhism consequently was losing prestige. Chu Hsi's contemptuous reference to the Buddhists, therefore, as men who "poke their heads into other doctrines pertaining to all sorts of mysterious and abstruse principles," and his description of these principles as "so vast, like a boundless sea, that they cannot be approached for investigation," are not only a typically Confucian outburst of impatience with what cannot be conveniently fitted into the Confucian view of things; they are also to some extent an unconscious admission of misunderstanding and ignorance.

# SOME CHINESE TALES OF THE SUPERNATURAL

## KAN PAO AND HIS *Sou-shên chi*

### INTRODUCTION

The curious combination of realism and fancy, practicality and credulity, often characteristic of Chinese thought, is nowhere better exemplified than in the innumerable tales of the supernatural that occupy so many pages of Chinese literature. Even in those stories which make the greatest demands upon the imagination, their author usually takes pains to preserve an appearance of historical verisimilitude by carefully noting not only the surnames and personal names of his heroes and their locale, but also in many cases their exact dates and other realistic details.

Such stories go back early into Chinese literature, and a number appear incidentally in the pages of such historical works as the *Tso chuan* and *Kuo yü*. In the first century A. D. the famous iconoclast, WANG Ch'ung, recorded many of the legends current in his own day, with the express purpose of heaping ridicule on them.[1] It was only in later centuries, however, that the "ghost" story attained to the dignity of a separate genre in Chinese literature. Men with a taste for the fantastic, often scholars who lacked official employment, amused themselves and their friends by writing collections of such short stories, all being magical or supernatural in character. Some had long been handed down among the people; others were pure inventions of the authors themselves. The culminating collection of such stories is undoubtedly the *Liao-chai chih-i*,* by P'U Sung-ling (1630-1715),[2] translated in part by H. A. GILES under the title, *Strange Stories from a Chinese Studio*.

---

[1] Cf. for example the many stories contained in his two chapters, "Spook Stories" and "All About Ghosts" (trans. FORKE, *Lun-Heng*, in *MSOS* 10[1907]1-30).

* [For V. M. ALEKSEEV's translations from this collection cf. *JA* 230.323-325.]

[2] These are the dates given in T'AN Chêng-pi 譚正璧, *Chung-kuo wên-hsüeh-chia ta-tz'ŭ-tien* 中國文學家大辭典, no. 5401. GILES, *Chinese Biographical Dictionary* 1668, gives a birth date of 1622 and no death date.

The man who initiated this type of literature in its crude beginnings seems to have been the Chin dynasty writer, KAN Pao 干寶, who during the first half of the fourth century A. D. compiled a work in twenty *chüan* called the *Sou-shên chi* 搜神記. It may be roughly translated as " Researches into the Supernatural." [3] This little book, to be sure, was prepared by its author for a purpose far more serious than that of mere entertainment, as was the case with later examples of its class, and it cannot, like them, be considered as pure fiction. Nevertheless, it remains their prototype, inasmuch as it seems to be the first conscious attempt in Chinese literature to make a systematic collection of stories dealing exclusively with events in the realm of the supernatural, the magical, and the fantastic. As we shall see, its terminal date of composition may be placed roughly at A. D. 350.

The little that we know of KAN Pao's life is derived from his biography in the *Chin shu* (History of the Chin Dynasty).[4] This informs us that he was a native of Hsin-ts'ai 新蔡 (corresponding to the present place of the same name in south-eastern Honan), that his *tzǔ* was Ling-shêng 令昇, and that he came of good family, his grandfather having been a marquis. He himself was summoned by the Chin government to a post in the Bureau of History, and later was enfeoffed as a Kuan-nei Marquis 關內侯. Under Emperor Yüan (A. D. 317-322) he was made head of the Bureau of History and commissioned to write a history covering the reigns of the earlier Chin rulers from the founding of the dynasty in 265 to the year 316. This work, called the *Chin chi* 晉記, in twenty *chüan*, brought him wide acclamation, but is today known only in quotation. The biography's mention here of Emperor Yüan gives us the only fixed dates in KAN Pao's life, and it says little concerning the rest of his official career, though it mentions him as holding several different offices. It does state, however, that he wrote other books, including a work on the *Tso chuan*, the

---

[3] KAN Pao is sometimes incorrectly referred to as Yü Pao, owing to the graphic similarity between the characters *kan* 干 and *yü* 于. Thus WYLIE, *Notes on Chinese Literature*, p. 192, erroneously speaks of him as Yü Pao, and the *Combined Indices to Twenty Historical Bibliographies* (Harvard-Yenching Institute Sinological Index Series no. 10) 2, p. 82, gives a cross reference from Yü Pao to KAN Pao.

The text of his *Sou-shên chi* used for this article is that edited and punctuated by HU Huai-ch'ên 胡懷琛, published by the Commercial Press, 3rd ed., 1935 (1st ed., 1931). In this edition the pagination is continuous for the entire book, instead of following the usual practice of beginning anew for each *chüan*. [For a brief account of the *Sou-shên chi* cf. also H. MASPERO, *BEFEO* 9. 597-8.]

[4] *Ssǔ-pu pei-yao* ed. 82. 7b-8b. [*Chin-shu chiao-chu* was not available to the author.]

*Tso-shih i wai-chuan* 左氏義外傳; commentaries on the *Book of Changes* and the *Rites of Chou*; and his *Collected Writings* (*Wên chi* 文集). All of these have since been lost, and it is the *Sou-shên chi* to which KAN Pao owes his reputation today.

If we are to believe the biography, the circumstances under which KAN Pao compiled this work were, to say the least, peculiar. According to the biography, KAN Pao's father had had a certain maidservant who had been his special favorite, and who, as in so many similar cases, had incurred the jealousy of the legitimate wife, i. e., of KAN Pao's mother. This mother, when the father died, cruelly caused the maid-servant to be thrust alive into a tomb (presumably that of the father), an event which happened at a time when KAN Pao and his brothers were still too young to interfere. Ten odd years later, however, when the mother herself died, the tomb was opened and, to the amazement of all, the body of the maidservant was found to be perfectly preserved as if in life. After several days the maidservant actually recovered consciousness and explained that throughout her ten years of sojourn in the tomb, she had been carefully supplied with food and drink by the father. She was thereupon married to someone and ultimately gave birth to several children.

As if this startling experience were not enough, the biography also states that on another occasion KAN Pao's elder brother once fell ill, during which time his breathing was interrupted for several days, yet his body did not become cold. Later he too recovered consciousness, and stated that during this period of suspended animation he had seen, as if in a dream, wondrous things in heaven and earth, and had had no realization that he had died.

The biography tells us that KAN Pao, deeply moved by these events, " thereupon collected from ancient and modern times (instances of) supernatural and awe inspiring anomalies, and changes and transformations in men and creatures. (The resulting work), in twenty *chüan*, he named the *Sou-shên chi* 搜神記 (Researches into the Supernatural)." So excellent was the result that later, when he showed the completed work to a friend, LIU T'an 劉惔 (of whom more hereafter), the latter admiringly exclaimed: " You may be said to be the TUNG Hu 董狐 of demons!" This TUNG Hu is renowned as an historian of the seventh century B.C. once reputedly praised by Confucius for his fearless honesty.[5]

[5] Apropos of TUNG Hu's recording of the murder of a certain duke in 607 B.C., Confucius, according to the *Tso chuan* (LEGGE, *Chinese Classics* 5.291), said of him:

While today we may remain skeptical of the circumstances that caused KAN Pao to compile his book, his surviving preface for it certainly testifies to the fact that the book was not written for any mere purpose of entertainment, but had the very serious mission of proving to a skeptical world the actual existence of spirits. In this preface KAN Pao first attempts to absolve himself for any errors of fact the book may contain. "Although," he writes, "I have made careful examination of what is recorded in ancient writings and have taken from traditions that are current at the present day, these are probably not matters such as a single ear or eye (in every case) hears or sees for itself. How, then, may I dare say that there are no instances which deviate from the truth?" For, he goes on to defend himself, cases also exist in which mistakes have been committed by historians of the past, who nevertheless have retained respect because their mistakes have been few, whereas the truth that they have preserved has been great. "And if, then," he continues, "among the affairs of the present age which I have culled out and investigated, there be some that are empty or untrue, I beg that the blame for this may be shared in part by those talented men and scholars of antiquity. As for what I have recorded, it will still suffice to show that the 'way of the spirits'[6] is not a delusion."

With this background in mind, it can be seen that the *Sou-shên chi* is not fiction in the sense that the *Liao-chai chih-i* and other examples of its type are fiction; hence it also largely lacks the literary qualities that grace these later works. Instead, it consists simply of a series of several hundred bald and matter-of-fact recitals of supernatural occurrences, usually derived from earlier sources, many of which, including the *Tso chuan, Kuo yü,* and other historical works, can be identified. The entire sixth *chüan* of the *Sou-shên chi,* for example, is borrowed with little change from records of various anomalous manifestations found in the two "Treatises on the Five Elements" contained in the *Han shu* (ch. 27) and *Hou Han shu* (chs. 23-28).[7] Some of the stories,

"Of old, TUNG Hu was an excellent historian. In his writings he had the rule of not concealing (the truth)."

[6] *Shên tao* 神道, the same term used for the Japanese Shintō.

[7] The editors of the *Ssŭ-k'u ch'üan-shu tsung-mu* (Ta-tung 大東 Book Co. lithographic ed. of 1930, 142. 3b-4a) erroneously state that the seventh *chüan* is also derived from the same two sources. This seventh *chüan,* however, while similar in subject matter to the sixth, deals entirely with events after A. D. 220, i. e., subsequent to the close of the Later Han dynasty.

again, closely resemble each other, and are evidently merely differing versions of the same tradition. These facts, plus what KAN Pao himself expressly states in his preface, make it improbable that any of the stories is the pure invention of KAN Pao himself.

None of the stories are long, some being less than forty characters in length, and even the longest extending to less than five hundred characters. In subject matter they are very diverse. Some deal with a multitude of different kinds of spirits and demons, both malevolent and otherwise; others with divine rewards bestowed upon exemplars of filial piety; still others with supernatural dragons, tigers, birds and other animals; others again with miraculous births, resuscitations from death, etc., etc. A certain amount of classification is apparent in the way these different types of story have been arranged in the book. Elements of folklore appear in some of the stories, and despite KAN Pao's reliance upon other sources for his material, his book remains of considerable interest today as a broad picture of many of the popular beliefs of his time. It is also valuable in another way, because many of its sources have since become lost, leaving the *Sou-shên chi* as the only, or at least earliest, version of certain stories and legends, a few of which are still current at the present time.

Before translating some of these stories, a word must still be said as to the present-day condition of the *Sou-shên chi* and the nearest possible date when it may have been compiled. On the first point, the editors of the great eighteenth century bibliography, *Ssŭ-k'u ch'üan-shu tsung-mu*,[8] adduce a number of quotations which are to be found in later works, and which agree substantially with our present-day text. On the other hand, they also adduce other such quotations which are not to be found in the existing text. These facts indicate that the *Sou-shên chi* as we have it today, while authentic as far as it goes, is incomplete.

In their attempt to date the compilation of KAN Pao's work, however, the usually reliable *Ssŭ-k'u*° editors have fallen into a curious error. They point to the fact that one of the stories in the *Sou-shên chi* (2. 16-17) concerns itself with a contemporary of KAN Pao, a certain HSIEH Shang 謝尚 (308-357), who is mentioned there as being Commander (*chiang chün* 將軍) of Chên-hsi 鎭西 (a place in eastern Sinkiang). This title, as the *Ssŭ-k'u*° editors observe, was acquired by HSIEH Shang under Emperor Mu of the Chin dynasty, i. e., between the years 345 and 356.

[8] See above, note 7.

It will be remembered in this connection that the only fixed dates in KAN Pao's biography are those of the period 317-322, during which time Emperor Yüan commissioned him to write his history of the earlier Chin rulers. It will also be remembered, however, that when the *Sou-shên chi* was completed, KAN Pao showed it to his friend, LIU T'an. Now this LIU T'an, according to the *Ssŭ-k'u*° editors, died during the T'ai-ning period (323-326), i. e., some twenty years before HSIEH Shang acquired his title of Commander of Chên-hsi. Therefore, they conclude, the story of HSIEH Shang, at least, must be an interpolation that has been added to the *Sou-shên chi* after KAN Pao's time.

This reasoning, while correct in itself, is based on an inexplicable error concerning the date of LIU T'an's death. Thus when we turn to LIU T'an's biography in the *Chin shu* (75. 6a-6b), we find no mention of his death as having occurred during the T'ai-ning period. We do find, however, the statement that he was made a minister at the beginning of the rule of Emperor Chien-wên. Chien-wên reigned officially from 371 to 372, but much earlier, in the year 345, a momentary and unsuccessful attempt was made to seat him on the throne. There is no doubt that when the text speaks here of the beginning of his reign, it refers to this brief period in 345, and not to his official rule of 371-372. This can be readily proved by the following facts: (1) LIU T'an's biography states that LIU died at the age of thirty-six *sui*, i. e., thirty-five years in our western reckoning. (2) It also states that he was poor when young, so that only WANG Tao 王導 then recognized his merits. This WANG Tao died in the year 330, a date that corresponds well with LIU T'an's presumed promotion to minister in 345, but which antedates by more than thirty-five years the other hypothetical date of 371-372. (3) After mentioning how LIU T'an became a minister at the beginning of the reign of Emperor Chien-wên, his biography states that he protested against the machinations of HUAN Wên 桓温, when the latter captured Szechuan in the year 347. This date once more harmonizes well with that of 345, and immediately following it, the biography announces the death of LIU T'an in such a manner as to show that this probably occurred soon after 347.

We may conclude, therefore, that LIU T'an died shortly after 347, and probably not later than 350, as any subsequent date would make him less than fifteen years old when he was befriended by WANG Tao. From this, furthermore, we may conclude that KAN Pao completed his *Sou-shên chi* some time between the year 345 (the beginning of the period when HSIEH Shang, mentioned in his book, became Commander of Chên-hsi) and the year 350 (by which time LIU T'an had presumably died). In summary, therefore, we may say that the *Sou-shên chi*, as it exists today, is probably for the most part the same as KAN Pao's original work, save that certain parts have been lost from it; also, that the terminal date for its composition is probably not later than the year 350.

## TRANSLATIONS FROM THE *Sou-shên chi*

The following are a few stories from the *Sou-shên chi*, selected for their interest or humor, or because they are characteristic of the work. The titles given to them here do not occur in the original text, in which they simply follow each other as a succession of paragraphs.

### 1. The Hindu Magician

#### (*Chüan* 2, pp. 13-14)

This is one of the least representative stories in the entire collection, because there is really nothing " supernatural " in it. It is translated here, however, as an interesting account of how one Hindu, at least, no doubt actually earned his living in fourth century China. While there is no evidence that this man was himself a Buddhist monk, he was probably one of the many hangers-on of Buddhism who came to China with that religion from India and Central Asia during these centuries, and whose arts closely remind one of those miracle-working Buddhist monks who, as described in the *Kao-sêng chuan* (Biographies of Eminent Buddhist Monks), performed all kinds of magical tricks in order to impress their Chinese converts.[9]

The Yung-chia period (307-312), mentioned at the beginning of the text, is that tragic epoch during which hundreds of thousands of Chinese fled from their homes in North China and crossed the Yangtze river to escape the invasions of the northern Tatars.

During the Yung-chia period (307-312) of the Chin dynasty, there was a foreigner from India who came travelling south of the Yangtze river. He had magical arts by means of which he was able to cut off his tongue, join it together again, and to spit out fire. Wherever he went, people gathered to watch him.

When he was about to cut off (his tongue), he would first stick out the tongue and show it to the assembly. After that he would cut it off with a knife so that blood poured forth and covered the ground. He would then place it in a vessel, which he would hand around to the audience for inspection, showing them that half of his tongue was

[9] Cf. T. K. CHUAN, " Some Notes on *Kao Seng Chuan*," *T'ien Hsia Monthly*, 7, 5 (Dec., 1938), 452-468, especially pp. 459-464.

apparently there. After that he would take it back, put it in his mouth, and join it together once more. After a brief space of time, the people seated there could see that his tongue was as it had been before, so that they could not tell whether it had actually been cut off or not.

In (the trick of) joining together some object which had been cut in two, he would take a thin silk cloth. This he would give to another man so that each held one end, and then with scissors he would cut it in two at the center. This having been done, he would take the two severed parts and display both of them. But then the silk cloth would again be joined together into one piece, so that it was nowise different from its original condition. Many people of the time suspected that this was an illusion, yet when they secretly tried to do it themselves, they found the cloth actually to be cut in two.

When he spat fire, he would first have a powder placed in a vessel. He would ignite a bit of this, and swallow it [10] together with some millet sugar. Then after puffing and blowing two or three times, he would open his mouth, the whole inside of which would be filled with fire. He would use the heat thus generated to cook something, in this way having a (cooking) fire.

He would also take such things as book-paper or string and throw them into the fire, with all the crowd looking on. When they had seen that these things were completely burned up, he would stir the ashes and bring the things forth, whereupon they would be in their original condition.

### 2. The Spirit of the Rice Pestle, Hsi-yao

#### (Chüan 18, p. 135)

This is one of a group of stories in the Sou-shên chi dealing with spirits who inhabit houses, walls, and other human constructions. A closely parallel story is that of the Taoist priest, Hsieh Fei 謝非, to be found in chüan 19, pp. 147-148. According to Hu Huai-ch'ên, editor of the Commercial Press edition of the Sou-shên chi used here, the same Hsi-yao story is still current at the present time. The name, Hsi-yao 細腰, meaning " narrow waisted," is no doubt an allusion to the shape of the rice pestle.

CHANG Fên 張奮 was a native of the Commandery of Wei.[11] His family had originally been great and rich, but it suddenly suffered reverses, its wealth became dissipated, and so he sold his house to

---

[10] The ho 合 (to unite) of the text is probably a misprint for han 含 (to swallow).

[11] 魏郡. There were several commanderies of this name. This may be the one established under the Chin dynasty at the present Chiang-ning 江寧 hsien in Kiangsu.

Ch'êng Ying 程應. When Ying occupied it, his entire family fell ill, and so he in his turn sold it to a neighbor, Ah Wên 阿文.

Wên first went alone carrying a large sword, and at sunset he entered the northern hall [12] and climbed up onto the central roof beam. During the third watch [13] a person suddenly appeared, more than ten feet tall, wearing a high cap and yellow clothes. He ascended the hall and cried out: " Hsi-yao! " Hsi-yao replied, and the person continued: " How is it that in the house there is the aura of a living man? " " There is none," came the answer, whereupon the person disappeared.

After a while another person wearing a high cap and green clothes appeared, followed by a second one wearing a high cap and white clothes. The questions and responses between these two were like those that had preceded.

When day was about to break, Wên climbed down into the hall, and in the manner that had been followed previously, he called out, asking: " Who is the one wearing the yellow clothes? " " Gold," was the reply, " below the western wall of the house."

"And who is the one wearing green clothes? " " Cash coins," was the reply, " five paces to the side of the well in front of the hall."

"And who is the the one wearing white clothes? " " Silver," was the reply, " below the pillar in the north-east corner of the wall."

"And who may you be? " " Oh, as for me," was the reply, " I am the rice pestle. At present I am underneath the stove."

When it became light, Wên accordingly dug for these things. He found five hundred pounds of gold and silver and ten million strings of cash. He furthermore took the pestle and burned it up. From this time onward he enjoyed great wealth, while the house was henceforth peaceful and undisturbed.

### 3. The Goddess of Silkworms

#### (Chüan 14, p. 104)

This, so far as I know, is the earliest version of a curious bit of folklore invented to explain the origin of the silkworm. Like many folk stories, it is not entirely consistent, inasmuch as it seems to imply that before the appearance of the first silkworm, some other kind of silkworm had already existed. E. T. C. Werner, in his *Dictionary of Chinese Mythology* (Shanghai, 1932, pp. 517-518), gives the same story in slightly different form, and writes concerning its strange heroine, the Goddess of Silkworms: " In the temples her image is to be seen covered with a horse's skin. She is called

---

[12] The main hall of the house.

[13] I. e., around midnight. The third watch lasts from 11 p. m. to 1 a. m.

Ma-t'ou Niang 馬頭娘, ' the Lady with the Horse's Head,' and is prayed to for the prosperity of mulberry trees and silkworms. The worship continues even in modern times. The sacrifice is performed on the third day of the third moon."

There is an old story that in ancient times a certain master went away on a distant journey, leaving no one at home save a single daughter, together with a stallion of whom she herself took care. Living a long time in this lonely spot, she was filled with thoughts about her father, and so said to the horse in fun: " If you can get my father to return to me, I will marry you." When the horse heard these words, it broke away from its halter and went straight off to where her father was. On seeing the horse, her father was surprised and delighted, and took it and rode on it. But the horse kept constantly looking in the direction from which it had come and made neighs of lamentation. The father said: " This horse has never acted like this before. Must there not be some reason for it at home? " And so he hurriedly rode home on it.

There, because the creature had such remarkable qualities, he gave it increased rations of fodder. Yet the horse refused to eat, and each time it saw the girl appear or disappear, it immediately pulled impetuously (on its halter), showing either pleasure or displeasure. This happened more than once, until the father, in wonder, privately inquired about it of his daughter. The latter told him everything that had happened, saying that that must be the cause. Her father replied: " Don't say anything about this, for I fear it may bring shame on our house. Moreover, you are not to move about (where the horse is)." So saying, he lay in ambush with a crossbow, with which he shot and killed (the horse). Its skin he set out to dry in the courtyard.

When the father (again) went away, his daughter, in company with the girls of the neighborhood, played about with the skin and trampled on it with her feet, saying: " You, a brute animal, wished to take a human being for a wife! Thus you yourself brought on this butchering and flaying, and have caused for yourself such suffering! " But before she had finished speaking, the horse's skin arose with a bound, wrapped itself around the girl, and made off with her. The other girls of the neighborhood, filled with fear, did not dare to save her, but ran away to tell her father. Yet by the time her father returned and looked for her, she had already disappeared.

Later when several days had elapsed, both the girl and the horse's skin were found among the branches of a great tree, where she had been completely transformed into a silkworm which was spinning in the tree. The threads of its cocoon were thick and large and quite different from those of ordinary silkworms. The women of the neighborhood took it and reared it, and (the amount of silk) which they received from it was several times more (than the ordinary). Therefore they named its tree the " mulberry." The word " mulberry " (*sang* 桑) is here equivalent to the word " mourning " (*sang* 喪).[14]

From this time onward all the people have vied with each other to produce this (kind of silkworm). It is the same as that raised at the present time, and the so-called " mulberry silkworm " (of today) is descended to us from that ancient silkworm.

## 4. The Slaying of the Fox Fairy

### (*Chüan* 18, p. 141)

This is one of several tales in the *Sou-shên chi* dealing with that famous character in Chinese ghost stories, the fox fairy. A story with similar theme appears on the following page of the text.

The essential characteristic of the fox fairy is, of course, its power to transform itself, either into a horrible demon, as in the present story, or into a human being (preferably a beautiful woman) who does mischief to mankind. Such a belief, however, appears not to have become developed before the late third or early fourth century A. D., and before that time the fox seems to have been regarded merely as a creature of ill omen, without clearly defined magical powers. Such, at least, is the conclusion to be reached through a perusal of the large amount of material that J. J. M. DE GROOT has collected on the subject.[15] The *Sou-shên chi* is the earliest work, I believe, in which stories of fox fairies assume a prominent place, while the first definite statement that I have found of the ability of the fox to change its form is that made by the famous Taoist alchemist, Ko Hung (ca. 250-ca. 330), in his *Pao-p'u tzŭ*:[16] " The fox and the wolf

---

[14] This is one of the typical popular etymologies often established in Chinese writings for words accidentally the same in sound. It is, of course, completely devoid of any scientific foundation.

[15] Cf. his *The Religious System of China* (Leyden, 1901), 4. 188-196; 5. 576-600. Of the many citations made by him, only a very few (cf. pp. 576-577 and 592) go back before the late third century. He makes numerous references to the *Sou-shên chi*, incidentally falling into the common error of calling its author Yü Pao instead of KAN Pao.

[16] *Ssŭ-pu pei-yao* ed. 3. 2a (a passage overlooked by DE GROOT, *op. cit.*). The dates of Ko Hung's life are uncertain. I follow those given by T'AN Chêng-pi *op. cit.* (see ftn. 2) no. 356. These dates are confirmed by CHIANG Liang-fu 姜亮夫, *Li-tai ming-jên nien-li pei-chuan tsung-piao* 歷代名人年里碑傳總表, p. 37, who states that Ko Hung died at the age of eighty-one *sui* some time during the Hsien-ho period (327-334). The dates of ca. 281-361, however, are suggested by WU Lu-ch'iang and Tenney L. DAVIS, " An Ancient Chinese Alchemical Classic, Ko Hung on the Gold Medicine and on the Yellow and White," *Proceedings Amer. Acad. Arts and Sciences*, 70. 6, Dec. 1935, p. 221.

both live to an age of eight hundred years, and when they reach five hundred years they are clever at changing themselves into human form." It is curious in this connection that the wolf, while mentioned in later Chinese folklore, has not shared there the important position of the fox.[17]

The word translated as "demon" in this and the two following stories is the Chinese *kuei* 鬼.

In the western suburbs outside Nan-yang[18] there was a lodge for travellers where no one could stay, because anyone who did so would be sure to suffer some calamity. But once a native of that city, SUNG Ta-hsien 宋大賢, stopped overnight at that lodge, inasmuch as it happened to be just on the road from his own place. There he sat, without having prepared any weapons, playing his lute in the night. Toward midnight a demon suddenly appeared, who climbed up the stairs and began talking to Ta-hsien. He had staring eyes, grinding teeth, and a horrible face.

Ta-hsien continued playing his lute as before. The demon thereupon went off to the city, where he found the head of a dead man which he brought back with him. Then he again spoke to Ta-hsien, saying: "Would it not be better to sleep a little?" And with this he threw the dead man's head in front of Ta-hsien. "Splendid indeed!" exclaimed Ta-hsien. "I had no pillow to sleep on, and was just wishing for something like this."

Again the demon went away, and after a long time once more returned, saying: "Could we not have some boxing together?"[19] "Excellent!" exclaimed Ta-hsien, and before he had finished speaking, while the demon was yet standing in front of him, he laid hold of the latter's waist. The demon could only cry out impetuously that he would die, but Ta-hsien thereupon slew him. The next day, when he looked at him, he saw that he was a fox. From that time onward there were no more supernatural doings in the travellers' lodge.

## 5. The Righteous Mei Demon

### (*Chüan* 17, pp. 131-132)

The Mei 魅 demon, like the fox fairy, figures prominently in several of the stories in the *Shou-shên chi*. It appears already in early works such as the *Tso chuan*, where it is always coupled with the word *ch'ih* 魑 as the Ch'ih-mei demon. GRANET, in his

---

[17] DE GROOT (*op. cit.*, 5. 563-570) discusses lycanthropy in China, but admits that it has been in no way comparable there with the belief in supernatural foxes.

[18] 南陽, at the present hsien of the same name in Honan.

[19] *Shou po* 手搏, lit., "striking with the hands."

*Danses et légendes de la Chine ancienne* (Paris, 1926, p. 316 and note 2 on p. 490), discusses the meaning of Mei and explains that it is a term for the ensemble of aged things that have become malevolent; also that it is a general term for prodigies of various kinds. A more detailed analysis, citing the various early texts in which the Mei or Ch'ih-mei is mentioned, together with the remarks of the commentators on these texts, is to be found in KIANG Chao-yuan, *Le voyage dans la Chine ancienne* (translated from the Chinese by FAN Jên, Shanghai, 1937, pp. 168-172). Among the often conflicting and vague statements of the commentators quoted there, the clearest describes the Mei as being a malevolent creature, either having bestial form, or with human face and animal body, and born from the supernatural emanations of mountains and forests.

In the *Sou-shên chi* the Mei is usually conceived of as at least in part animal, and is often identified with the fox fairy. Likewise it is generally malevolent, so that the manner in which the Mei in the present instance rectifies a case of human injustice, gives a surprising twist to this story. The story is also of interest for its account of the exorcizing activities of the Taoist priest.

During the Wu period (222-280) there was a certain NI Yen-ssǔ 倪彥思 who lived in the village of Yen 埏 in the western part of Chia-hsing hsien,[20] where he once suddenly noticed a Mei demon enter his house, talk with the people there, and eat and drink like a man. Its body, however, remained invisible. Among Yen-ssǔ's maidservants were some who had the habit of secretly slandering everybody, and who now said that they were going to speak about this. But Yen-ssǔ kept them in check so that none of them dared to speak ill of (the demon).

Yen-ssǔ had a concubine whom the Mei followed about and sought after, so Yen-ssǔ invited in a Taoist priest [21] to exorcize him. No sooner had the wine and food been prepared (for the ceremony), than the Mei smeared them over with filth which he took out of the privy. The Taoist then fiercely beat upon a drum to summon spirits (to drive away the Mei). Thereupon the Mei grasped the " crouching tiger " that stood on the spirit-seat, and blew into it in the note of *chiao*.[22]

[20] 嘉興縣, south of the present Kashing hsien in Chekiang.

[21] *Tao shih* 道士.

[22] 角, the third of the ancient five note scale, corresponding to the western note of E. The " crouching tiger " (*fu hu* 伏虎) is explained in the *Tz'ŭ-yüan* and *Tz'ŭ-hai* under the term *chiang lung fu hu* 降龍伏虎, " descended dragon and crouching tiger." According to these dictionaries, both Buddhist and Taoist priests have the power to induce dragons to descend from the sky into their alms bowls; also, with their priestly staffs, to separate tigers locked in deadly combat, and cause them to crouch in respectful submission. The " crouching tiger " here referred to was no doubt a figure of such an animal used by the Taoist priest as part of his paraphernalia for exorcism ceremonies, and set up on the seat or altar which the assisting spirits were supposed to occupy.

A moment later the Taoist suddenly felt a chill on his back, and leaping up in alarm, pulled off his clothes. There was the " crouching tiger "! At this the Taoist desisted from his efforts and departed.

During the night Yen-ssŭ secretly discussed the matter with his wife beneath the bed clothes. They were both terrified by this Mei. The Mei thereupon from the roof beam of the house said to Yen-ssŭ: " You have been talking about me to your wife! I am going to break off the roof beam of your house." And with this there was a tremendous rumbling sound. Yen-ssŭ was frightened lest the roof beam be broken in two. He seized a light to look around, whereupon the Mei at once extinguished the light. The sound of the breaking of the beam continued even more ominously than before. Yen-ssŭ was afraid that the house would collapse, and everyone, both big and small, ran outside. Again they took a light to look around, only to see that the beam was still as before. Then the Mei let out a loud laugh and asked Yen-ssŭ: " Now are you going to talk about me again? "

The Intendant of Agriculture of the Commandery heard of this and said: " This spirit must surely be a fox creature." The Mei at once went to the Intendant of Agriculture and said: " You as an official take for yourself many hundred bushels of grain, which you store away in a certain place. As a functionary you have been corrupt and wicked, and yet you dare to talk about me! Now you must vacate your office and let the people take back the grain which you have stolen from them."

The Intendant of Agriculture, greatly terrified, thanked him, and from that time onward there was no one who dared talk about him. Three years later he departed, and no one knows where he has located himself.

### 6. A Ghostly Encounter

#### (*Chüan* 16, p. 122)

This, one of the most amusing stories in the collection, well illustrates the humanized form in which the Chinese often conceive their spirits. Indeed, so cooperative and good natured is the demon whom we encounter here, that we cannot but feel sorry for him when he meets his sorry fate. Perhaps, however, we should not be too surprised by his human characteristics, since he is, after all, a true ghost who had once been a man, and not, like the Mei, a monstrous creature " born from the supernatural emanations of mountains and forests."

This story is one of a number in which human beings succeed in outwitting their ghostly opponents. It contains the interesting folk belief that the only thing feared by ghosts is to be spat upon by a man.

SUNG Ting-po 宋定伯, a native of Nan-yang,[23] once in his youth was travelling by night, when he encountered a demon. On questioning the demon, the latter replied: " I am a demon," and then asked: " And who are you? " " I too am a demon," said Ting-po falsely. " Where are you going? " the demon asked again. " To the city of Yüan," he replied.[24] The demon said: " I too am going to the city of Yüan." And with this they continued walking.

After several miles the demon said: " To walk on foot is too tedious. How would it be if we each alternately carry the other? " " Very good," replied Ting-po.

Thereupon the demon first carried Ting-po for several miles, but finally said: " You, sir, are too heavy. It must be that you are not a demon." " I have only recently become a demon," Ting-po replied, " and that is why my body is so heavy."

Ting-po then in his turn carried the demon, who weighed almost nothing at all. And this was done a second and a third time. Then Ting-po again said: "As I am only a new demon, I don't yet know what I should be afraid of." " The only thing that will give you discomfiture," replied the demon, " will be to have a man spit on you." And with this they continued together.

Along the road they came to a stream, where Ting-po told the demon to cross first. Yet as he listened, (the demon) seemed to make no sound at all. When Ting-po himself crossed, however, he made a great splashing noise. The demon again asked him: " How is it you make such a noise? " " Because," Ting-po replied, " having only recently died, I am not yet accustomed to fording streams. So don't be surprised at me."

When they had almost reached the city of Yüan, Ting-po, who was then carrying the demon on his shoulders, suddenly seized him. The demon raised a tremendous yell, but (Ting-po) tied him up with a rope and paid no more attention to him. Then (Ting-po) went with him straight to the center of the city of Yüan, where on setting him down upon the ground, he became transformed into a sheep. (Ting-po) thereupon sold him (as a sheep), but being afraid that he might (again) transform himself, he spat upon him. He obtained fifteen hundred cash for him, and then departed.

[23] See above, note 18.
[24] 宛, in the present Nan-yang hsien, Honan.

At that time SHIH Ch'ung [25] had a saying about this: " Ting-po once sold a demon, for whom he obtained fifteen hundred cash! "

### 7. The People with Disembodied Heads.

#### (*Chüan* 12, p. 92)

This is one of the tall " travellers' tales " to be found the world over, and in Chinese literature suggestive of the accounts contained in such works of pseudo-geography as the *Shan-hai ching* (Classic of Mountains and Seas). No doubt it is inspired by one of the many aboriginal tribes in south and south-west China with whom the Chinese came into extensive contact in the course of their southward expansion during the early centuries of the Christian era.

During the Ch'in period (255-207 B. C.), there existed in the south a " People with Disembodied Heads," [26] whose heads had the ability of flying around. This race of people derived its name from the fact that they practised a sacrifice known as that of the " fallen insects." [27]

During the Wu period (A. D. 222-280), General CHU Huan [28] obtained a maidservant whose head, every night after she had gone to sleep, would immediately fly away. It would come and go, sometimes through the small door for the dog, sometimes through the skylight, and its ears would act as wings. When day was about to break, it would return to her again. This happened time after time.

The neighbors, mystified by this, once came with a lamp during the night to look at her, and found that only her body was there, but no head. The body was feeble and cold and its breathing had almost stopped. Thereupon they covered it over with blankets.

At daybreak the head returned, but, being hindered by the blankets, was unable to gain its resting place. Twice and thrice it moved around, and then sank to the floor. Heartrending groans came forth, and the body breathed in quick gasps and looked as if it were about

---

[25] 石崇, a wealthy official and marquis of the Chin dynasty who was fond of ostentation, and who was executed in A. D. 300 when he refused to surrender a beautiful concubine to a certain favorite of a powerful prince. Cf. GILES, *Chinese Biographical Dictionary*, 1709.

[26] *Lo t'ou min* 落頭民, lit., " people whose heads fall off."

[27] *Ch'ung lo* 蟲落. The only apparent resemblance in the two terms is the common occurrence in both of them of the word *lo*, " to fall " or " fall off." It is quite possible that the characters represent the sounds of some term in the language of one of the non-Chinese aboriginal tribes of South China.

[28] 朱桓, hot tempered but brave and honest officer of the state of Wu who died in 238. Cf. GILES, 448.

to die. They then removed the blankets, at which the head again leaped up and joined itself to the neck. After a short time everything was peaceful as before.

Huan was tremendously astonished by this, and feared that it would be impossible for him to put up with such a thing, so he dismissed her. But when she had explained the matter clearly to him, he realized that it was simply something innate in her nature.

At the present time, the great generals who make expeditions to the south also frequently find such people. Cases, moreover, have occurred when (the neck of these people) has been covered over with a bronze basin, so that the head could no longer approach (the body), where-upon they have died.

## 8. The Great Gibbons of Szechuan

### (*Chüan* 12, p. 93)

This again is a story of the travellers' type, closely following in the text that given above. Shu 蜀, the locality referred to, is roughly equivalent to the modern Szechuan. Positive identification of the curious creature here described as the great gibbon is provided by the third of the three names attached to it, that of *ch'üeh-yüan* 玃猨 Bernard E. READ, *Chinese Materia Medica: Animal Drugs* (Peiping, 1931), says of the *ch'üeh* under no. 400a: " It probably denotes the great gibbon, *Hylobates,* W." In the same work, no. 401a, he defines the *yüan* as " the gibbon, *Hylobates agilis.*" Under no. 400a he furthermore throws light on the folklore touched on in the present story by his statement (derived from Chinese writers) that this gibbon " steals people's property and is a great observer. There are no females so it goes after women for a mate who bear its young."

The other two terms applied in the text to the great gibbon, those of *chia-kuo* 猳國 and *ma-hua* 馬化, are more difficult to explain. Literally they respectively mean " pig country " and " horse transformation," which are unintelligible, so that it is obvious that they must be incorrect phonetic equivalents for the true characters. In the case of *chia-kuo*, I would suggest that *chia* 猳, " pig," is a mistake for *chia* 犲, which the K'ang-hsi Dictionary, quoting the *P'ien-hai* 篇海 (compiled under the Chin dynasty, 1115-1234; revised in the sixteenth century), defines as another name for the *ch'üeh.* The latter, as we have seen, is the great gibbon. Likewise I would suggest that the second part of the name, *kuo* 國, " country," is a mistake for *kuo* (果 or 猓), as used in the name *kuo-jan* (果然 or 猓然). READ, *op. cit.,* no. 402, defines the *kuo-jan* as " the Proboscis monkey, *Semnopithecus larvatus,*" and quotes various Chinese authors as saying that " it is larger than a gibbon " and is " like a gibbon, white face with black jaws, a long beard."

The name *ma-hua,* however, is more puzzling. The only hypothesis I can offer is that *ma* 馬, " horse," may conceivably be equivalent to *ma* 犸, which the K'ang-hsi Dictionary, quoting the *Chi-yün* 集韻 (seventh century), merely defines as being some sort of quadruped. I can give no suggestion as to the word *hua* 化, " to transform."

Nor, finally, can I explain why the unfortunate Szechuan bearers of the surname YANG should be singled out in this story as the descendants of the great gibbon.

On the tops of the lofty mountains in south-western Shu, there lives a creature similar in kind to the monkey. It is seven feet tall, can act like a human being, and is good at running and pursuing people. It is named the *chia-kuo*, and is also known as the *ma-hua* or the great gibbon.[29] It lies in ambush for beautiful women walking along the road, and immediately seizes and makes off with them in such a manner that no one knows about the matter. With a long rope it pulls in all travellers who pass by, so that they are firmly bound [30] and unable to escape.

This creature is able to distinguish between the odor of men and women. Therefore it seizes women, but men it does not take. If it captures a married woman, it sets up house with her. Those (women) who then remain childless, are to the end of their lives not permitted to return (to their original homes), and after ten years they become similar to it in form and their minds also become confused, so that they no longer think of returning.

But if (a captured woman) should get a child, she is at once sent back to her home. The children who are thus produced are like human beings in form, and any mother who does not rear them will suffer sudden death. Being afraid of this, there are no (mothers) who do not so rear them.

(Such children), when they grow up, are no different from ordinary human beings, and all of them assume the surname of YANG 楊. Therefore the many Yangs who today live in the south-west of Shu are for the most part descendants of the *chia-kuo* or *ma-hua*.

### 9. Other Stories

Other *Sou-shên chi* stories of interest to the folklorist or students of mythology might also be cited, such as that of the goddess of the manure pile, Ju-yüan 如願 ("As you like it"), who is sacrificed to on the fifteenth day of the first month (*chüan* 4, p. 32); or that of the sacrifice made to the God of the Hearth by the filial son, YIN Tzŭ-fang 陰子方 (*chüan* 4, p. 33). These, however, are not translated here because I intend to treat them in connection with another work in which the same stories are mentioned.[31]

---

[29] For these names, see the discussion above.

[30] *Ku* 故 is probably to be taken here in the sense of *ku* 固, " firm."

[31] The sixth century book on annual customs, *Ching-ch'u sui-shih-chi* 荆楚歲時記, a translation of which I am now preparing. It was in the course of making this trans-

Other stories of interest are those describing the supernatural origin of certain races. Notable among these is the myth of P'an-hu 盤瓠 (*chüan* 14, pp. 101-102), the dog who was a pet of the legendary Chinese emperor Ti K'u 帝嚳 (ca. 2400 B. C.). This dog succeeded in bringing to his imperial master the head of a certain troublesome barbarian general, and was thereupon, in accordance with the reward previously promised by the emperor, given the emperor's own daughter as wife. The dog then carried off the daughter to the fastnesses of the southern mountains, where she gave birth through him to six children, who became the progenitors of the present day Miao and Yao tribes of Kweichow.

Another story is that of Tung-ming 東明 (*chüan* 14, p. 102), the hero who was born somewhere in northern Manchuria or southern Siberia, when the maidservant of the king of that country became pregnant because a strange emanation, resembling a chicken's egg, entered her womb from Heaven. The king, considering the boy thus born to be inauspicious, cast him into a pig sty and then into a horse corral, but in each case the pigs and horses sheltered him and kept him alive by breathing upon him. Therefore the boy was allowed to grow up and became a skilful archer, until the king, becoming alarmed for his own safety, again wished to kill him. Thereupon Tung-ming fled southward until he reached a river, where, on striking the water with his bow, the fish and turtles rose to the surface and conveniently formed a bridge on which he crossed, thus eluding his pursuers. There, in the part of Manchuria lying roughly between Harbin and Mukden, Tung-ming established the country of Fu-yü 夫餘, from which the Koreans trace their origin.

Both these stories appear with only minor verbal variations in the *Hou Han shu*,[32] from which they have already been translated into English; hence only summaries of them are presented here.[33] It might be pointed out, however, that the scholars who have discussed the *Hou Han shu* versions of these myths appear to have overlooked the *Sou-shên chi* entirely, although that work was compiled almost one century prior to the *Hou Han shu*, the author of the latter history, FAN Yeh, having lived from 398

---

lation that I had occasion to read through the *Sou-shên chi*, and so came to write the present article.

[32] *Ssǔ-pu pei-yao* ed., beginning of ch. 116, and sect. on Fu-yü country in 115. 3a-3b, respectively.

[33] The P'an-hu myth has been translated by Berthold LAUFER, "Totemic Traces among the Indo-Chinese," *Journal of American Folk-lore* 30 (1917), 419-420; by LI Chi, *The Formation of the Chinese People* (Cambridge, Mass., 1928), 243-244; by LIU Chungshee Hsien, "The Dog-Ancestor Story of the Aboriginal Tribes of Southern China," *Journal of Anthropological Institute* 62 (1932), 361-368; and by LIN Yüeh-hwa, "The Miao-Man Peoples of Kweichow," *HJAS* 5 (1941), 333-334. LIU's article has not been available to me for consultation, but of the others, LAUFER's is by far the most detailed, translating as it does not only the text proper of the *Hou Han shu*, but also the accompanying statements of the commentators, including a passage quoted from KAN Pao's now lost history of the Chin dynasty, the *Chin chi*.

The Tung-ming myth has been translated by Alexander WYLIE in his translation of *Hou Han shu* 115, "History of the Eastern Barbarians," *Revue de l'extrême orient*, no. 1, 1882. Another account of the myth, with added details from Japanese sources, appears in William Elliot GRIFFIS, *Corea, the Hermit Nation* (New York, 1882), 19-21.

to 445. The P'an-hu myth, as a matter of fact, can be carried back at least still another century, since the commentary to its *Hou Han shu* version quotes a reference to it taken from the now lost *Wei lüeh* 魏略, a work which was compiled between the years 239 and 265.[34]

[Ed.'s note: There would seem to have been other *Sou shên chi* differing from KAN Pao's. There is one at the end of Lo Chên-yü's *Tun-huang ling shih* 敦煌零拾, and *The Chinese Repository* contains translated excerpts from one attributed to a Ming dynasty author: 10. 84-87, 185-191, 305-309 (second signature so paginated; not the first and immediately preceding one), 18. 102-109, and 19. 312-317. The latter would seem to be abridged in *Tao tsang* 1105-6 as well as in an illustrated Ming text entitled 出像增補搜神記 now in the Harvard-Yenching Institute Library. Cf. also WYLIE, *Notes* 193.

---

[34] For this dating cf. CHAVANNES, Les pays d'occident d'après le Wei Lio, *TP* 6 (1905), 519-520.

# THE CHINESE COSMIC MAGIC KNOWN
## AS WATCHING FOR THE ETHERS

## I. Introduction

Despite its familiarity, it may be helpful to begin with a brief reminder of the salient features of the prevailing Chinese world-view, especially as it was formulated during the Han dynasty (206 B.C.–A.D. 220). The universe, according to this view, is a harmoniously functioning organism consisting of multitudinous objects, qualities and forces which, despite their seeming heterogeneity, are integrated into coherent patterns by being subsumed under one or another of many numerical categories. (The best known such category, of course, is that in sets of fives, such as the five elements, five directions, five colors, etc.) Among items belonging to a common category, a particular affinity exists between those having the same relative position within their respective sequences. For example, the property common to such diverse items as fire, summer, south, bitter taste, burning smell, heat, the planet Mars, feathered creatures, beans, the hearth sacrifice, the lungs, the tongue, joy, and

### Bibliographical Note

References to the dynastic histories are all to the Chung-hua Book Co.'s 1923 photolithographic reprint of the 1739 Palace edition.
The following abbreviations are used:

SPPY      Ssu-pu pei-yao edition (Shanghai: Chung-hua Book Co., 1927–35)
SPTK      Ssu-pu ts'ung-k'an edition (Shanghai: Commercial Press, 1920–35)
TPYL      *T'ai-p'ing yü-lan* encyclopaedia (comp. 983), SPTK edition
TSCC      Ts'ung-shu chi-ch'eng edition (Shanghai: Commercial Press, 1936–39)
YHSFCYS   *Yü-han shan-fang chi-yi-shu* 玉函山房輯佚書, compiled by Ma Kuo-han 馬國翰 (1794–1857), Changsha edition of 1883.

For the sake of the printer, the Chinese characters of well known works (the dynastic histories, the classics, compilations like TPYL), well known persons (Tu Fu or Chu Hsi), and major place names or names of dynasties and rulers, have been omitted.
I am deeply indebted to Dr. A. Kaiming Chiu, Librarian of the Chinese-Japanese Library, Harvard University, for the bibliographical information acknowledged on p. 28, note 2; p. 30. note 1; p. 33, notes 2 and 3.

many more, is that each of them is number two within its particular sequence of five. Affinities of this kind should be thought of as functioning more along lines of spontaneous response (the response of one stringed instrument to another the same in pitch) or of mutual attraction (the attraction between iron and the lode stone), than of mechanical impulsion (the impact of one billiard ball upon another).

It is evident that such correlations not only cut across the usual categories of time and space, the abstract and the concrete, but also bridge the apparent gap between the human and the natural worlds. These two worlds, in fact, actually merge to form a single continuum, the halves of which are so closely interwoven that the slightest pull or strain on the one spontaneously induces corresponding pull or strain on the other. A primary function of the ruler is to prevent or relieve such pulls and strains by the correct performance of periodic rituals designed to reinforce the normal affinities between the two halves.

One of the most curious manifestations of this world-view is the practice known officially as "watching for the ethers" (hou ch'i 候氣), or, less officially, as the "blowing of the ashes" (ch'ui hui 吹灰). The "ethers" or "vital forces" in question are, of course, those of the yin (negative) and yang (positive) principles, as they ceaselessly interact to generate the eternal round of cosmic phenomena. Within the year, this round follows a two-phase cycle: that from the winter solstice in the eleventh lunar month (which therefore begins the Chinese astronomical year) to the summer solstice in the fifth month, during which period the yang ether grows from nadir to zenith, while the yin ether correspondingly declines; and that from the summer solstice back to the winter solstice again, during which the process is reversed.

The theory of "watching for the ethers" rests on the belief that though the yin and yang ethers are themselves impalpable and invisible, their "arrivals" (chih 至) during the successive months of the year can be visually detected by means of the musical tubes known as lü 律 or "pitch-pipes". These tubes, as is well known, are twelve in number and graduated in length according to a mathematical progression which begins with the longest and lowest-pitched tube, huang-chung 黃鍾 (9 Chinese inches long), and ends with the shortest and highest-pitched, ying-chung 應鍾 ($4^{20}/_{27}$ inches). The tubes may be made either of bamboo, jade or bronze, and are blown vertically. While not themselves used as musical instruments, they cover a range of exactly one octave and thus provide the twelve half notes of the untempered chromatic scale. As pointed out by Chavannes more than half a century ago, this scale is identical with that of Pythagoras and is mentioned in Chinese literature only in the second half of the third century B.C. These facts, plus other data, caused him to argue that it might have been carried to Asia and eventually[1] to China through the conquests of Alexander the Great[1].

The fact that the pitch-pipes are twelve in number naturally induced the Chinese to correlate them with the twelve months and with the compass points with which these months are themselves correlated. These correlations begin with the longest pipe, *huang-chung* (equated with the eleventh month and with the north), and end with the shortest, *ying-chung* (equated with the tenth month and with north northwest)[2]. During the Han dynasty, when the pitch-pipe lore was greatly elaborated, the dimensions of the primary *huang-chung* tube were also made the basis for deriving the standard Chinese measures of length, capacity and weight[3]. In view of this central importance of the pitch-pipes for music, the calendar, and the system of weights and measures alike, it is not surprising that they should also come to be regarded as instruments whereby to observe the cosmic movements of the *yin* and *yang* ethers.

The basic procedure for so doing is to construct a roofed chamber carefully protected from all extraneous disturbances (especially wind currents) by three surrounding walls. Within this chamber, on the bare earth, the pitch-pipes are arranged in a circle according to their months and corresponding compass directions. They are buried vertically (or almost vertically) in the soil with their open upper ends either even with, or projecting slightly above, the surface; these open ends are then filled with very fine ashes made by burning the pith of reeds. The theory is that at each month the *yin* or *yang* ether of that month will rise from below the ground toward the surface. As it does so, it enters the lower end of the particular pitch-pipe of that month (but of none other), thereby causing its ashes to fly forth from the upper end. Though the pipes are never said to emit any sound when this happens, the idea of the ethers "blowing" into them and thereby expelling their ashes is no doubt based on the analogy of the human breath (also known as *ch'i*) that passes through them when they are musically sounded.

Before turning for specific details to the texts themselves, two further points should be made clear. The first is that the *yin* and *yang* ethers, though loosely equated with the months of the lunar calendar, should more properly be thought of in conjunction with the well known cycle of days, based on solar reckoning, which occur at approximately

[1] E. Chavannes, "Des rapports de la musique grecque avec la musique chinoise", Appen. II in *Mémoires historiques de Se-ma Ts'ien* (Paris, 1895–1905), III, 630–645.

[2] For a diagram showing the correlations, see Fung Yu-lan, *A History of Chinese Philosophy*, tr. D. Bodde (Princeton University Press, 1952–53), II, 15.

[3] See H. H. Dubs, "Standard Weights and Measures of Han Times", Appen. 1 of Chap. IV in *History of the Former Han Dynasty* (Baltimore, 1938–55), I, 276–280.

fifteen-day intervals throughout the year. These are known, significantly, as the twenty-four *ch'i* ("ethers" or "breaths" of the year), among which the two solstices and two equinoxes are primary. With these *ch'i* the lunar calendar is correlated in such a way that two of the *ch'i* always occur in each lunar month, the second in each pair being known as that month's *chung* 中 or "middle" *ch'i*. It is upon the twelve specific dates of these "middle breaths", rather than during their entire corresponding months, that the arrival of the *yin* or *yang* ether was expected and watched for[1]. The following are the names of the "middle breaths", their corresponding lunar months, and the approximate dates for them in our Western calendar:

| Lunar Month | Middle Breath | Western Calendar | Lunar Month | Middle Breath | Western Calendar |
|---|---|---|---|---|---|
| 11 | Winter Solstice | Dec. 22 | 5 | Summer Solstice | June 21 |
| 12 | Great Cold | Jan. 22 | 6 | Great Heat | July 23 |
| 1 | Rain Water | Feb. 20 | 7 | Stopping of Heat | Aug. 23 |
| 2 | Spring Equinox | March 20 | 8 | Autumn Equinox | Sept. 23 |
| 3 | Grain Rain | April 20 | 9 | Frost's Descent | Oct. 23 |
| 4 | Grain Full | May 21 | 10 | Slight Snow | Nov. 22 |

The other general point is that, during the Han dynasty, certain exponents elaborated the basic twelve-note pitch-pipe scale into sixty different sequences or scales, known, for the sake of convenience, as the sixty pitch-pipes[2]. With these it thus became theoretically possible to watch for the ethers not merely once a month, but at intervals of approximately *six* days each (since 6 × 60 approximates the number of

---

[1] Though this fact is made explicit only by later expositors, it is strongly implied in the earlier texts. Examples are the reference to the two solstices at the end of Ts'ai Yung's account (see p. 19, note 2 below); the equating of the first of the pitch-pipes, *huang-chung*, with the first of the "middle breaths", the winter solstice, in the passage attributed to Yang Hsiung (see p. 20, note 3); and the equating of Hsin Tu-fang's twenty-four revolving fans with the twenty-four *ch'i* or "breaths" (see p. 24, note 1), from which it would follow that the pitch-pipes, being half this number, would go with the twelve "middle" *ch'i* in the same series. The only possible exception appears to be the writer of the document of 589 (see p. 22, note 1), who, unlike the others, speaks of the ethers as arriving irregularly, or continuing to operate over periods of several days.

[2] How this was done is too complex to be explained in detail here. Suffice it to say that each of the twelve notes of the basic pitch-pipe scale was correlated with each of the five notes of the parallel Chinese pentatonic scale, thereby resulting in sixty varying sequences (5 × 12), all using the same basic notes, but starting on different levels. See Wang Kuang-ch'i 王光祈, *Chung-kuo yin-yüeh shih* (A History of Chinese Music) [Shanghai: Chung-hua Book Co., 1934], I, 66–67.

2

days in a year). Such is the system alluded to at the end of our first text below. So complex is it, however, that one seriously wonders whether it does not represent a theoretical abstraction rather than something ever actually put into practice.

## II. History of "Watching for the Ethers" Until the Seventh Century

Though we do not know with absolute certainty just how and when the theory of "watching for the ethers" originated, it seems probable that Ching Fang 京房 (79–37 B.C.), the well known Han specialist on the pitch-pipes and the *Book of Changes*, was at least in part responsible. Thus the *History of the Later Han Dynasty*, in its "Treatise on the Pitch-pipes and Calendar", quotes in summary a treatise by Ching Fang in which, after enumerating the above-mentioned sixty scales (which were Ching's special creation), it continues with what are probably Ching's own words: "Tubes are cut (from bamboos) to make the pitch-pipes. One blows these in order to examine their tones, and sets them forth (on the ground) in order to make manifest the ethers"[1].

Besides this apparently earliest reference, there is also a possibility— attended, however, by serious difficulties—that a slightly later con-temporary of Ching Fang, the famous writer Yang Hsiung 揚雄 (53 B.C.– A.D. 18), may have written upon the theory[2]. Be that as it may, the *Later Han History*, after quoting Ching Fang's treatise, goes on to say that in A.D. 177, when scholars were asked to put the pitch-pipes into

---

[1] *Hou Han shu*, 11/4b; repeated in *Chin shu*, 16/2b. As cited in *Hou Han shu*, the quotation is so far removed from the beginning of Ching Fang's treatise by the intervening enumeration of the sixty scales that one wonders whether it still belongs to this treatise. The corresponding text in *Chin shu*, however, is telescoped in such a way (with the sixty scales omitted) as to leave no doubt that by the *Chin shu's* author, at least, the two sentences were regarded as part of the treatise. For the *Hou Han shu's wu* 物, "thing", which yields no sense, I adopt the parallel reading of *hsiao* 效, "to make manifest", found in *Chin shu*.

[2] *Chin shu*, 16/5b, and *Sung shu*, 11/2a, both introduce a passage with the words, "Yang Tzu-yün 子雲 (i.e., Yang Hsiung) says", and then, after fifty-three intervening characters, go on to say: "When the *yin* and *yang* are in harmony, the shadow (of the gnomen) reaches (the length proper to it when, at the winter solstice, it is annually measured). When the ethers of the pitch-pipes give response, the ashes (of these pitch-pipes) disappear". Here again, however, it is questionable whether these two sentences still form part of the passage introduced earlier by the words, "Yang Tzu-yün says", the more so as in *Hou Han shu*, 11/5a, where the same two sentences are quoted, no such attribution is made and the preceding passage of fifty-three characters is omitted entirely. Another text, though likewise attributed (in a much later work) to Yang Hsiung, is, as we shall see, quite probably the work of a different Yang who lived two and a half centuries later. See p. 20, note 3.

good order, they had difficulty in doing so because the only techniques still transmitted were "the general derivation (of the pitch-pipes from one another) according to fixed numbers (i.e., according to a fixed mathematical progression), and the 'watching for the ethers' "[1]. From this we may conclude that the latter technique had by then already been known for a considerable time.

A few lines after this episode, the *Later Han History* gives us the first detailed technical description of how to "watch for the ethers". From parallel versions in several other texts, we know with reasonable certainty that this *locus classicus* comes from the hand of the noted ritual specialist Ts'ai Yung 蔡邕 (133–192). More specifically, it is from his commentary on the famous calendrical text, *Yüeh ling* (Monthly Ordinances). Here is the way it reads in its *Later Han History* version[2]:

As to the procedure for watching for the ethers: A triple-walled chamber (*shih san ch'ung* 室三重) is prepared, the doors of which bar it off (from the outside world) and (the walls of which) must everywhere be closely covered over with plaster[3]. Within the chamber a covering of reddish silk (*t'i man* 緹縵) is spread[4]. Stands are made out of wood, one for each pitch-pipe, which extend deep down within (the ground) and high up outside (the ground)[5]. The pitch-pipes, in accordance with their compass points, are mounted upon these[6]. Ashes from the pith of reeds (*chia fu hui* 葭莩灰) are stuffed

---

[1] *Hou Han shu*, 11/5a.

[2] *Hou Han shu*, 11/5a, which I take as standard because it is the most detailed and seemingly most accurate. With minor variants and some shortening, the same text appears in *Chin shu*, 16/5b, and *Sung shu*, 11/2b, but in none of these three histories is it explicitly attributed to Ts'ai Yung. It does have such attribution, however, when also quoted in the T'ang sub-commentary on the *Yüeh ling* chapter in the *Book of Rites* (first month, under the statement naming the pitch-pipe of that month). See *Li-chi chu-su* 禮記注疏, 14/7a (SPPY ed.). Likewise it is quoted in part in the *T'ai-p'ing yü-lan* (TPYL) encyclopaedia (comp. 983), 16/6a, where it is attributed directly to Ts'ai Yung's *Yüeh ling* commentary, the *Yüeh-ling chang-chü* 月令章句. It is furthermore included among the fragments of this work collected by Ma Kuo-han (1794–1857) in his YHSFCYS, 24/3b.

[3] The idea is to insulate the chamber against all outside drafts.

[4] As interpreted by Ch'en Yang a thousand years later (see p. 28, notes 2 and 3), this covering was probably spread like a tent within the chamber, and the pitch-pipes placed beneath it, in order to be further protected from air disturbances.

[5] My translation follows the interpretation of K'ung Ying-ta 孔穎達 (574–648) in *Li-chi chu-su*, 14/7a: "They are buried in the ground so that their lower part within the ground extends deep down and the part emerging from the ground extends high up".

[6] K'ung Ying-ta explains further: "The *huang chung* tube is buried at the position *tzu* 子 (the north), with its upper end tilted toward the south. By extension,

into the inside (of each pitch-pipe), and in accordance with the calendar, a watch is kept upon them. Whenever one (of the pitch-pipes) is reached by the ether (of its corresponding month), its ashes move[1]. Those ashes that are thus caused to move by the ethers are scattered, whereas those (accidentally) moved by persons or wind remain together.

Within the palace, when thus watching (for the arrival of the ethers), twelve pitch-pipes of jade are used and only at the two solstices does the watching take place. At the Spirit Terrace, however, sixty pitch-pipes of bamboo are used, and the days for watching are those corresponding to these pitch-pipes.[2]

The chief interest of the next passage lies in the possibility that it *may* have been written by the afore-mentioned Yang Hsiung (53 B.C.– A.D. 18), in which case it would be the earliest technical account of our subject. There are serious objections to this attribution, however, and it seems quite likely that it actually comes from the pen of another lesser known Yang, Yang Ch'üan 楊 泉 (whose surname is written with a slightly different character, and who flourished around the year 265):[3]

(the positions of) all the remaining tubes may be known". In other words, the wooden stands, together with the pitch-pipes mounted on them, are set in the ground in a circle in which each pitch-pipe is located according to its compass direction, with its upper end tilted in the opposite direction, i.e., toward the center of the circle.

[1] The *Li-chi chu-su* version is a little more detailed here: "When the ether of a given month arrives, the ashes (of the pitch-pipe of that month) fly around so that their tube is emptied". With these words, the *Li-chi chu-su* ends its account.

[2] On the sixty pitch-pipes, see p. 18 above, where it was suggested that this paragraph may represent only a theoretical ideal rather than actual practice. The "Spirit Terrace" (Ling T'ai 靈 臺) was the imperial observatory south of the palace, where the watching would naturally be done more intensively than in the palace itself. I have emended the reading of *li* 曆, "calendar" (found in the Palace ed. of *Hou Han shu*), to *lü*, "pitch-pipes", as given in other editions, which yields better sense.

[3] In TPYL, 16/7b, where this passage is quoted, it is attributed to "Yang Tzu-yün (i.e., Yang Hsiung), *T'ai-hsüan ching*"; again in 28/6b, where it also appears, it is cited simply as "*T'ai-hsüan ching*". The difficulty is that there is no such passage in the existing version of Yang Hsiung's well known *T'ai-hsüan ching* 太 玄 經, and that a book of the same name was also written by Yang Ch'üan, of which, however, only scattered fragments survive. Moreover, as demonstrated by the text following this one, Yang Ch'üan himself was definitely interested in our subject. These facts, plus the close similarity between the names of Yang Ch'üan and Yang Hsiung, suggest the possibility that the TPYL editors may have quoted from Yang Ch'üan's work while mistakenly believing that they were quoting from the better known work of the same name by Yang Hsiung. It should be added, however, that Ma Kuo-han does not include this passage among the fragments of Yang Ch'üan's *T'ai-hsüan ching* collected by him in YHSFCYS, 68/21a–22a.

To correlate the pitch-pipes, bamboos are measured so as to be made into tubes, and the pith of rushes is made into ashes. These are laid out within the nine barriers, where, immobile and silent, the faintest wind does not arise and the finest dust does not form. Then, on midnight of the winter solstice, the *huang-chung* (pitch-pipe) gives response[1].

Concerning the provenance of the bamboos and reed pith thus used, the above-mentioned Yang Ch'üan informs us briefly as follows:[2] "One takes bamboos from the Golden Gate Mountain in Yi-yang hsien in Hung-nung to make the tubes, and the pith of reeds from Ho-nei to make the ashes"[3].

For our next important account we must jump three centuries to the commentary on the *Yüeh ling* written by Hsiung An-sheng 熊安生 (ca. 500–ca. 585):[4]

As to the "blowing of the ashes", the meaning is that twelve pitch-pipes are made, and are buried (in the ground) within a chamber at the positions of the four seasons (i.e., of the months of these seasons). The pith of reeds is burned into ashes which are stuffed into the pitch-pipes, and these are covered with silk gauze. When the ether (of a given month) arrives, it blows the ashes (of that month's pitch-pipe) and thus moves the gauze. A small movement means that the ethers are harmonious. A large movement is an indication that the ruler is weak, his ministers strong, and that they are monopolizing the government. Non-movement of the gauze is an indication that the ruler is overbearing and tyrannical.

[1] The term "nine barriers" (*chiu pi* 九閉) is difficult. (The alternate reading in TPYL, 28/6b, is *chiu chien* 間, "nine spaces or sections"). Probably it is a poetical way of saying that the chamber containing the pitch-pipes is closed off in all directions from the outside world, the number nine having reference to the eight main compass points plus the center.

[2] Cited in *Chin shu*, 16/5b, where it is ascribed to the *Yang Ch'üan chi* 記 (Records of Yang Ch'üan). The statement is also quoted in TPYL, 16/7a, 42/5a, 871/8b and 962/7a, where it is ascribed to another (now lost) work by Yang Ch'üan, the *Wu-li lun* 物理論 (On the Principles of Things).

[3] The "Golden Gate Mountain", etc. 弘農宜陽縣金門山 was southwest of the present Lo-ning 洛寧 hsien, itself some 80 kms. southwest of Loyang in Honan. Ho-nei 河內, "Within the River", was roughly equidistant from Loyang in the opposite direction, north of the Yellow river. The fact that these two sites are located in the general region of the Later Han capital of Loyang (and not Ch'ang-an of the Former Han) faintly suggests that only in Later Han times did the cult of the ethers really become current.

[4] Quoted in *Li-chi chu-su*, 14/7a. Essentially the same passage, though somewhat differently worded, appears in *Chin shu*, 16/5b, where it is merely introduced by the words: "Someone says".

Here we are supplied with several new points: (1) Ts'ai Yung's large silk covering (presumably spread like a tent over the pitch-pipes, see p. 19, n. 4) is no longer mentioned, but instead we are told that each individual pitch-pipe is to be covered with silk gauze (obviously so that the movements of its ashes may be more readily detected). (2) More important philosophically is the correlation asserted to exist between the movements of the ethers and human government. This is a natural outgrowth of the strong Chinese conviction that a close interaction exists between the human and the natural worlds. (3) From the parallel version in *Chin shu* (not quoted) we learn further that the pitch-pipes are to be buried *level* with the surface of the ground, i.e., with their upper ends even with the surface. This again differs from Ts'ai Yung's statement that the tubes should project above the surface, but agrees with all later accounts.

Of these accounts, by far the most significant is that of the *History of the Sui Dynasty*, in its "Treatise on the Pitch-pipes and Calendar"[1]. There we are told that in 589, when Emperor Wen, founder of the Sui dynasty, unified the country, he commanded Mao Shuang 毛 爽, together with Ts'ai Tzu-yüan 蔡 子 元, Yü P'u-ming 于 普 明 and others, to "watch for the periodic ethers"[2]. Here is their procedure:

In accordance with antiquity, within a triple-walled secret chamber, twelve stands made of wood are prepared for the musical tubes. The latter are set up on the stands in accordance with the twelve points of the compass, and are buried in earth so that their tops are level with the ground. Ashes of reed pith are stuffed into them and the mouths of the pitch-pipes are covered over with thin reddish silk gauze. Then, upon the arrival of the ether of each month, and the mysterious communion between it and the pitch-pipe (of that month), the ashes (of that pipe) fly forth so that they hit the gauze and scatter outside. However, the responses to the ethers are sometimes early, sometimes late, and the ashes flying about are sometimes abundant, sometimes sparse. Sometimes the response to the ether may occur at the beginning of the month, whereas sometimes it occurs only during (that month's) middle or final decade. Sometimes the ashes become completely expended after flying forth during three or five nights, whereas sometimes the entire month may end with only a small amount having flown forth.

[1] *Sui shu*, 16/3b–4a (sect. entitled *Hou ch'i*, "Watching for the Ethers").

[2] This no doubt was one of Emperor Wen's many attempts to use religious and philosophical ideas as sanctions for his new dynasty. See Arthur F. Wright, "The Formation of Sui Ideology, 581–604", in John K. Fairbank, ed., *Chinese Thought and Institutions* (University of Chicago Press, 1957), pp. 71–104.

Emperor Wen, we are told, was astonished and inquired of the ritual specialist Niu Hung 牛 弘 (545–610), who gave the following explanation:[1]

> When half of the ashes fly forth, it is a harmonious ether that is blowing. When all the ashes come forth, it is a fierce ether that is blowing. And when the ashes are unable to come forth at all, it is a weak ether. Response (of the ashes) to a harmonious ether signifies that the government is tranquil. Response to a fierce ether signifies that the ministers are out of control. Response to a weak ether signifies that the ruler is oppressive.

To this the emperor made a very sensible objection: Changes in the quality of government usually occur only gradually, not abruptly. How then can there be such a correlation between these changes and the abrupt monthly fluctuations in the ethers? Niu Hung, we are told, was unable to reply, and so ordered Mao Shuang and his colleagues to prepare a report on the subject, which they did under the title of *Lü p'u* 律 譜 (Repertory on the Pitch-pipes). This report, as summarized in the *Sui History*, narrates the history of the pitch-pipes since earliest times. More especially, it lists some of the efforts since the Han to use them for watching for the ethers. Here are its pertinent highlights:

(1) Tu K'uei 杜 夔 (who died just after the fall of the Han, between the years 220–226), "constructed pitch-pipes with which to watch for the ethers, but the ashes all failed to fly"[2].

(2) Following this failure, there seems to have been a long quietus until the sixth century, when several attempts were made. Of these, the most interesting is that by Hsin Tu-fang 信 都 芳 (died during 543–550), a mathematician and inventor of strange mechanical devices. What the *Sui History* says of him provides a brief but fascinating picture of proto-scientific activity in medieval China:

> He had clever ideas and was able by means of the (musical) tubes to watch for the ethers.... Once while talking to someone he pointed to the sky and said: "The ether of the first month of spring has arrived". The man went to examine the tubes and (found that) their flying ashes had already given response. Each month, in (Hsin's) statements about watching (for the ethers), there was never any error.
>
> He also made twenty-four revolving fans (*lun shan* 輪 扇), which he buried in the ground in order to measure the twenty-four ethers

---

[1] Niu's biographies in *Sui shu*, ch. 49, and *Pei shih*, ch. 72, refer to his general interest in the pitch-pipes, but do not report this particular episode.

[2] This statement is not confirmed in Tu's biography in *San Kuo chih*, *Wei chih*, 29/2b, though from it we see that he was an expert on music.

(of the year)[1]. Each time one of these ethers became active, one of the fans would move of itself, whereas all the other fans remained still. Their responses corresponded to those of the ashes in the tubes like the two halves of a tally[2].

(3) During the reign of Emperor Wu of the Liang (502–549), there still existed an ancient jade pitch-pipe allegedly recovered from the same tomb which, when opened in the year 280 or 281, had yielded the *Bamboo Books* and other early texts. During the time of King Ts'ang-wu 蒼梧 (473–477) of the Sung period, this jade pitch-pipe had been mutilated by being bored with holes so that it could be played horizontally (an interesting confirmation, incidentally, of the assertion that the ancient pitch-pipes were blown vertically and not horizontally). Because, however, its essential dimensions were still preserved, it was possible, when Emperor Wu ordered a certain Mao Ch'i 毛栖 to construct a new set of pitch-pipes, for the latter to do so, using this tube as a model. The result was that "from this time onward the ashes of the pitch-pipes flew again"[3].

(4) Upon the outbreak of Hou Ching's 侯景 rebellion in 551, a son of Mao Ch'i, Mao Hsi 喜, obtained his father's pitch-pipes from the Liang

---

[1] i.e., the twenty-four *ch'i* or "breaths" (Winter Solstice, Great Cold, etc.), on which see p. 17 above.

[2] Unlike the other historical data, this account does not appear in Mao Shuang's report itself, but is taken from the earlier part of the same section in *Sui shu* in which Mao's report is recorded. The story is given somewhat differently in Hsin's biographies in *Pei Ch'i shu*, 49/1b, and *Pei shih*, 89/4a–b (which is especially detailed). These tell us that Hsin, on being asked whether he could revive a technique that had long been lost, thought it over for ten days and finally exclaimed: "I've gotten it!" He then added, however, that success would be impossible without the use of pith ashes obtained from reeds of Ho-nei. The first attempt, made in violation of this warning, failed, but a second attempt, in which the proper ashes were used, worked perfectly. Because, however, the art was not properly valued by the age (*Pei Ch'i shu* inadvertently drops the negative and so reads: "was valued by the age"), it was subsequently discontinued and thus lost. Hsin's third biography in *Wei shu*, 91/3b, does not mention the story but does state that Hsin was the inventor of several strange contrivances (including, apparently, a seismograph). It likewise gives the period of his death. Hsin was also author of a treatise entitled *Yüeh shu* 樂書 (Book of Music), but its few surviving fragments (collected in YHSFCYS, 31/19a–22a) contain nothing pertinent. On an important surviving text by Hsin, see p. 28, note 3 below.

[3] There is an anachronism in Mao Shuang's report at this point, since it also states that Mao Ch'i had inquired about the pitch-pipes from the calendar specialist, Ho Ch'eng-t'ien 何承天, whose dates are 370–447. That Mao Ch'i held office under the Liang dynasty, and hence could scarcely have been acquainted with Ho, is confirmed by what is said of him in the opening lines of the biographies of his son, Mao Hsi (on whom see below). Perhaps the anachronism is a result of the telescoping of Mao Shuang's report by the *Sui shu*.

Bureau of Music. After the Ch'en dynasty was founded in 557, he privately used them to watch for the ethers, with effective results. Under Emperor Hsüan (569–582) he became an official and wished to memorialize the throne on the subject. Apparently this was not done, however, and when this ruler died, Mao left the capital to become a provincial official. Subsequently he retired and left the tubes to his children, and with the downfall of the Ch'en in 589, the tubes were lost[1].

(5) In the same year of 589, as we have seen, Mao Hsi's younger brother, Mao Shuang (for whom there is no biography), was asked by the Sui founder to restore the art of watching for the ethers, with the results already described. Mao Shuang's report to the emperor, after giving the historical data here summarized, continues with technical details about the pitch-pipes, but fails completely to answer the emperor's fundamental objection.

(6) Perhaps for this reason the *Sui History* says nothing further on the subject save that in 618, during the disorders at Chiang-tu 江 都 (the present Yangchow) attending the assassination of Emperor Yang and collapse of the Sui dynasty, the pitch-pipes were destroyed.

## III. Later History of "Watching for the Ethers"

With the downfall of the Sui dynasty, what may be called the formative period in the history of watching for the ethers comes to an end. During the next several centuries nothing further of importance was written (with one significant exception, on which see p. 28, note 3), nor does the theory ever seem to have been subjected to actual test. By this time a knowledge of it had become part of the intellectual baggage of educated men, showing itself in the form of literary clichés in the poems of some of the greatest T'ang writers. There is no evidence, however, that any of these men personally witnessed what they so casually mention.[2]

With the growth of scholarly and scientific activity during the Sung dynasty, however, there comes renewed interest in the theoretical aspects

---

[1] These facts are not confirmed in Mao Hsi's biographies in *Ch'en shu*, 29/1b, and *Nan shih*, 68/3a.

[2] The following are two representative examples: (1) Tu Fu (712–770), in a poem about the winter solstice, writes that on that day the ashes of "the reed are blown, and the six jade pipes agitate the floating ashes". (Six of the twelve pitch-pipes are supposed to be *yang*, the other six *yin*; it is the former of which Tu here speaks.) See *Concordance to the Poems of Tu Fu* (Peiping: Harvard-Yenching Sinological Index Series, Supplement No. 14, 1940), II, 515 (*chüan* 32, poem 42). (2) Han Yü (768–827) says in a poem supposedly written on the day following the spring equinox: "I remember yesterday, when the *chia-chung* 夾 鍾 pipe first blew its ashes". See *Han Ch'ang-li ch'üan-chi* 韓 昌 黎 全 集, 3/14b (SPPY ed.).

of the subject, and consequent attempts to explain it in "scientific" terms. Of these the most detailed and interesting is that by Shen Kua (1030–94), found in the same remarkable book in which he gives us the first clear accounts of the magnetic compass and of printing by movable type[1]:

> People all wonder how it is that, though the spot where the pitch-pipes are placed extends no more than several feet, an ether's arrival causes only its own particular pitch-pipe to respond. Some say that the ancients had their own art for this, some that it is the lengths (of the pitch-pipes) in their numerical ratios that cause the mysterious communion (between ethers and pitch-pipes) to produce changes, and some that it is their compass-point locations that automatically induce mutual reactions. All these (theories) are wrong....
>
> As to the procedure: A single chamber is first prepared, the ground of which is made perfectly level. Then the pitch-pipes are buried so that all are even at the top, whereas the depth to which they enter the ground differs (according to their respective lengths). At the winter solstice the *yang* ether, (then beginning its upward expansion from underground), stops at a point nine inches from the surface of the ground; and inasmuch as it is only the single *huang-chung* tube that reaches to such (a depth), it is therefore *huang-chung* that responds (at this time). But in the first month the *yang* ether, (continuing its upward course), stops at a point eight inches from the surface of the ground. *T'ai-ts'ou* 太簇 (pipe of the first month), together with its (two) predecessors, all extend (to this depth), but (these predecessors), *huang-chung* and *ta-lü* 大呂, have already been emptied (of their ashes). Hence it is only the single *t'ai-ts'ou* pitch-pipe whose ashes then fly forth. The case is like someone who uses a needle to probe into the channels (of the ethers in the human body): these ethers, in compliance with the needle, will then issue forth[2].
>
> Since there are inevitable differences in the looseness or compactness of the ground (on which the pitch-pipes are set), it should first be partitioned off (from these pitch-pipes) by means of the wooden stands, and then soil should be filled in above the stands in such a way that it is made everywhere the same in hardness and compactness. Its surface is levelled off by a water (level), and then the

---

[1] Shen Kua 沈 括, *Meng-hsi pi-t'an* 夢 溪 筆 談, 7/51 (TSCC ed.).

[2] The reference is probably to acupuncture, the purpose of which is to relieve the body of the pressure caused by excessive localized concentration of the ethers believed to be within.

pitch-pipes are buried in it. In this way, even though (the ground) beneath them may be either loose or compact, yet, it being cut off (from the pipes) by means of the wooden stands, their ethers are therefore automatically equalized (in their movements). (The secret) simply consists in rendering uniform the soil that lies on top of the stands.

This final paragraph possibly implies, though it does not explicitly state, an important innovation: namely, that the twelve individual stands (as mentioned by all earlier writers) are to be replaced by a single stand made large enough to cover the entire permanent ground, and itself covered by a layer of soil of uniform density, into which the pitch-pipes are then set. (The word *an* 案 in the text can of course be translated in the singular or plural either as "stand" or "stands".) For otherwise it is hard to see how the pitch-pipes can really be kept insulated from the permanent ground beneath, as Shen Kua insists they should be. But once insulated in this way by an intervening wooden barrier, does not this very fact upset that spontaneous "mysterious communion" (*ming fu* 冥符) between ethers and pitch-pipes which is the philosophical basis for the whole theory ?

Another serious objection is that the sequence of the pitch-pipes and the movements of the *yin* and *yang* do not really correspond. For whereas the pitch-pipes are arranged in a steadily shortening progression, beginning with *huang-chung* in the eleventh month and ending with *ying-chung* in the tenth, the *yin* and *yang*, during the same period, pass through a two-phase cycle of expanding *yang* and contracting *yin* (from winter solstice to summer solstice), followed by expanding *yin* and contracting *yang* (from summer solstice back to winter solstice)[1]. This discrepancy means, if Shen's theory be accepted, that the *yin's* upward expansion during the second half of the year begins at a level much nearer to the ground's surface than that at which the *yang* began six months earlier, and higher even than that at which the *yang* ceases its expansion.

It is somewhat astonishing that despite these objections, even the great Chu Hsi (1130–1200) seems to accept Shen's theory (though without mentioning him by name). For example, Chu Hsi says: "Now the tubes, though buried close to one another, nevertheless differ in length and in the depth to which they enter the ground. This is why the responses to the ethers come earlier or later. It has nothing to do with the positions (of the tubes themselves)". Or again: "*Huang-chung*, being the longest, is therefore deepest (in the ground) and so the first

[1] This incongruity has already been pointed out by Fung Yu-lan, *A History of Chinese Philosophy*, II, 15 and 121.

to respond. *Ying-chung*, being the shortest, is therefore shallowest and so the last to respond"[1].

Of the many specialized treatises on the pitch-pipes and music produced from Sung times onward, we can give only a sampling. For the most part they quote and re-quote what has already been said, with only occasional excursions into new ground. Hence their chief interest for our subject lies in the light they throw upon the intellectual outlook of their own age. One of the earliest and largest of such treatises is Ch'en Yang's *Yüeh shu* or *Book of Music* (presented to the throne in 1101)[2]. In it he offers the following theory as to how the doors leading into the "triple-walled chamber" should be arranged: "A chamber is made with triple walls, each pierced by a door. The locations of these doors are such that the outermost one is at *tzu* 子 (the north), the middle one at *wu* 牛 (the south), and the innermost one again at *tzu*". Obviously, the purpose of this labyrinthine approach is to eliminate all possibility of air currents reaching as far as the inner chamber.

Ch'en Yang likewise differentiates between the "covering of reddish silk", said by Ts'ai Yung to be spread within the chamber, and the silk gauze said by later writers to be placed over the individual pitch-pipes: "A reddish silk covering is spread within the chamber, round above and square below. The pitch-pipes, in accordance with their compass-points, are buried (beneath this covering) in such a way that their (upper) ends are level with the ground; these are covered over with thin gauze". We may deduce from this that the covering of reddish silk (whose color significance remains obscure) is erected like a tent over the pitch-pipes within the chamber, no doubt in order to protect them still further from air disturbances. Ch'en's statement that it should be round above and square below reflects the traditional Chinese belief that Heaven is shaped like a circle, Earth like a square. The following diagram depicts the triple-walled chamber as conceived by Ch'en Yang, with its alternating doors, tent-like covering, and the pitch-pipes arranged according to their numbered months beneath this covering[3].

---

[1] *Chu-tzu ch'üan-shu* 朱子全書, 41/20b and 26a (Hung-tao T'ang 宏道堂 ed.).

[2] See Ch'en Yang 陳暘, *Yüeh shu* 樂書, 102/4b–5a (Canton ed. of 1876), for the quotations that follow. I am greatly indebted to Dr. A. Kaiming Chiu, Librarian of the Chinese-Japanese Library at Harvard, for checking the references to this work, which was not available to me.

[3] Adapted from the diagram in *ibid.*, p. 4a. It is also reproduced in Liu Chin 劉瑾 (late Yuan dynasty), *Lü-lü ch'eng-shu* 律呂成書, 1/3 (TSCC ed.).

*Additional remark*: To Dr. Joseph Needham, of Cambridge University, I am deeply indebted for drawing my attention, after the completion of this article, to a forerunner of Ch'en Yang's diagram to be found in *Yüeh-shu yao-lu* 樂書要錄,

## TRIPLE-WALLED CHAMBER FOR
## WATCHING FOR THE ETHERS

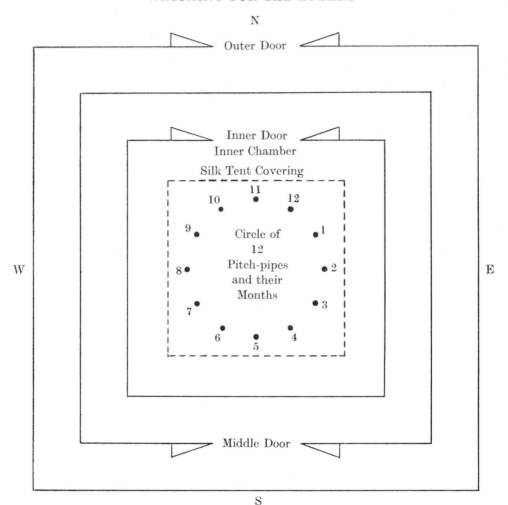

N

Outer Door

Inner Door
Inner Chamber
Silk Tent Covering

11
10    12

9

Circle of
12
Pitch-pipes
and their
Months

8    2

7    3

6    4
5

W    E

Middle Door

S

6/54 (TSCC ed.). It agrees closely with Ch'en's work save in its reversed orientation of the doors (outer and inner doors facing south, middle door facing north). The *Yüeh-shu yao-lu* is attributed, in the bibliographical treatises of the two T'ang histories, to the famous T'ang Empress Wu (684–704), and no doubt it was compiled by scholars during her reign. In China itself, however, it was lost at an early date, so that the incomplete and often corrupt version today extant derives from a single copy brought from China to Japan in 735. (See postface by Hayashi Jussai 林 述 齋 to the first printed edition of this work, contained in his *Yi-ts'un ts'ung-shu* 佚 存 叢 書, First Series of 1799). These facts suggest the possibility that Ch'en Yang, when preparing his own diagram of 1101, may have been ignorant of this predecessor produced four centuries earlier.

The *Yüeh-shu yao-lu* is also noteworthy for its citation, on the pages following the diagram (pp. 55–58), of the *Yüeh-shu chu-t'u fa* 注 圖 法, a text it attributes

To the traditional motivation of watching for the ethers in order to ensure continuing harmony between the natural and human worlds, Sung and later writers add a secondary practical consideration: that of using the known times of arrival of the ethers as a means for checking upon the accuracy of measurements of a newly constructed set of pitch-pipes. We find this motivation expressed with great cogency, for example, by Ts'ai Yüan-ting (1135–98):[1]

> One blows (the pitch-pipes) in order to examine their tones, and sets them forth (on the ground) in order to watch for the ethers. These (techniques) both seek (to determine the correctness of) *huang-chung* on the basis of whether its tone is high or low and whether its ether (arrives) earlier or later; they are ideas used by the ancients for the making (of the pitch-pipes).
>
> When a pitch-pipe is long, its tone is low and its ether arrives early; but if overly long, it makes no tone at all and the ether does not respond. When a pitch-pipe is short, its tone is high and its ether arrives late; but if overly short, it makes no tone at all nor does the ether respond. This is the general principle.
>
> If now one wishes to find the middle tone and ether, but there is nothing available as a standard, the best thing to do is to cut several bamboos for determining the (correct) tube for *huang-chung*, making some of them shorter and some longer. For every tenth of an inch within their range of length, one tube is made, with nine inches being

to that same Hsin Tu-fang, of revolving fans fame, whom we have already encountered. This text consists of Ts'ai Yung's classical description of watching for the ethers, coupled to which is a commentary presumably containing Hsin's own words. In what it says about the orientation of the doors, the commentary agrees with the diagram, thus making it probable that the latter, though prepared by the T'ang editors, was based on Hsin's ideas. Further concrete details are also supplied by the commentary: The color of the tent-like silk covering above the pitch-pipes, described by us as being "reddish", is actually orange 赤 色 黃 也, and made by dyeing plain white silk. The stands on which the pitch-pipes are mounted each have a hole bored in their base, into which their respective pitch-pipes are inserted, and enclose these pipes in an upward bulging flare, thus being apparently shaped somewhat like elongated egg-cups. At the center of the pitch-pipe circle, we are told further, a larger stand or stool is provided for the watchman who, lantern in hand, sits there during the five days preceding and following the expected arrival of the ethers, waiting to detect their precise movements.

[1] Ts'ai-Yüan-ting 蔡 元 定, *Lü-lü hsin-shu* 律 呂 新 書, *chüan* 2, sect. 1. Contained in *Hsing-li ta-ch'üan* 性 理 大 全, comp. by Hu Kuang 胡 廣 (1370–1418), 24/2b–3a (ed. of 1551). Here again I am indebted to Dr. Chiu for checking this reference.

taken as the (approximate) standard of length for all, and their circumference and diameter being measured (from this basis) according to the rules for (making) *huang-chung*.

If, this having been done, one blows them one by one, the middle (i.e. correct) tone will then be obtained, and if one sets them more or less deeply (in the ground), the middle (i.e. correct) ether may then be verified. When its tone is harmonious and its ether responds, the *huang-chung* is really a *huang-chung* indeed! And once it is really a *huang-chung*, then (from it) may be obtained the (other) eleven pitch-pipes, as well as the measures of length, capacity, and weight (likewise based upon it). Later generations, not knowing how to go about this, have sought (to construct accurate pitch-pipes) only by measuring with the footrule.

Ts'ai's preference for mechanical trial-and-error, rather than mathematical formula, is, one suspects, typical of a good deal of Chinese scientific activity. His views are warmly echoed by several later writers, notably Liu Chin of the late Yuan dynasty (see p. 28, note 3).

At first sight it seems rather remarkable that ever since the sixth century no one apparently ever tried to prove or disprove the theory of the ethers through actual experiment, and virtually everyone writing on the subject (including even Chu Hsi) seemingly accepted it without question—this despite the rise of the great rationalistic movement known as Neo-Confucianism. Perhaps, however, we should not really be so surprised when we stop to recall the state of science in Europe during the same period. At any rate, it seems to be only well along in the Ming dynasty—more specifically, in the sixteenth century—that serious doubts arise. Prominent among the early skeptics is Hsing Yün-lu (*chin shih* of 1580), who in his large *Ku-chin lü-li k'ao* includes a scathing attack on the theory[1].

Hsing begins with the typically Chinese argument that the theory is nowhere mentioned in the classics. From this, however, he proceeds to more concrete objections: How can a particular ether affect only one of several pitch-pipes when what happens to be "north" for their group would immediately become "south" were the chamber containing them to be shifted merely a few feet farther north? Or again, how can the *yang* ether, at the winter solstice, possibly be expected to rise to a point only nine inches below the ground's surface, when in northern climes at that time the entire ground freezes to a depth of several feet? After several further such objections, Hsing advances his own vigorous ex-

---

[1] Hsing Yün-lu 邢雲路, *Ku-chin lü-li k'ao* 古今律歷考, 35/525–528 (TSCC ed.). The quotations below are from p. 528.

planation of what really happened in the case of Hsin Tu-fang's revolving fans and the Mao family's flying ashes (both of the sixth century):

> I understand it! The movements of the fans and flying of the ashes were all (based on) mechanisms. With such mechanisms connected to the openings (through which the ethers were claimed to pass), and with men operating these mechanisms, the fans would move and the ashes would fly without fail, at the appointed times. These false things were secretly done in order to deceive the ruler of men.

Such contrivances, Hsing goes on, have long been known and continue to exist. Then he makes a truly astonishing assertion:

> Unto the present day, officials of the Imperial Board of Astronomy go to (the offices of) the Shun-t'ien Prefecture[1], and (there), using mechanisms, manufacture a false watching for the ethers with ashes. At such periods of the year as the Beginning of Spring (ca. Feb. 6) they make announcement, saying: "The ashes have flown!" By submitting such an announcement,... whom are they going to deceive? They deceive only Heaven![2]

Taken at its face value, this allegation seems incredible. If, however, we can stretch Hsing's "present day" (*chin* 今) to mean something like "recent times", and if, furthermore, we can assume that what he had in mind were isolated episodes rather than a continuing practice, then there are two such episodes—one in 1539, the other (if it occurred at all) probably in 1581 or 1582—which could conceivably have given Hsing the pretext for his accusation. For the first of them we must turn to the *Ming History's* "Treatise on Music"[3].

There we are told that in 1530 a certain court official, Chang Ô 張 鶚, urged that Ts'ai Yüan-ting's trial-and-error method be used for making an accurate set of pitch-pipes. Apparently nothing came of this, for nine years later (in 1539) we read that Chang repeated his proposal. This time it was approved by members of the Board of Ceremonies, who suggested that a chamber be constructed for the purpose just outside the inner enclosure of the Altar of Heaven in Peking's south suburb. The suggestion was followed by the emperor, with results which the *Ming History* discreetly glosses over. It merely says that the technique proved to be vague and confused, and could not in the end be successfully

---

[1] The metropolitan prefecture in which Peking, the capital, was located. Its administrative offices were situated in the northeast section of Peking, east of the Drum Tower.

[2] In the sense that their false action is a violation or betrayal of the natural order.

[3] *Ming shih*, 61/4a and 5a.

applied. Another less canonical text, however, tells us what actually happened: after the proposal was adopted, "those in the know privately laughed", with the result that work on the chamber was halted and the actual experiment never took place[1]. This clearly indicates the strong change in attitude that had occurred by 1539.

Another even more bizarre episode is narrated by Li Shih-ta 李世達 (1531–99), in his preface to the book of a younger contemporary, Yüan Huang 袁黃[2]. The protagonists of the story are Yüan himself and a man whom Li calls Chang Chiang-ling 張江陵, but who is actually none other than the famous Ming prime minister, Chang Chü-cheng 居正 (1525–82)[3]. According to Li, the episode took place when Yüan was the tutor of Chang's children. We can date it as probably occurring in 1581 or early 1582, since Li concludes by stating that "shortly afterward" Chang died, and it is known that his death occurred on July 9, 1582.

According to the story, Chang had a triple-walled chamber constructed in order to perform Ts'ai Yüan-ting's technique for testing the pitch-pipes. The results, however, were completely negative, and so he asked Yüan to examine the chamber, which the latter did and declared to be defective in five ways: (1) In order to maintain the purity of the ethers, the chamber should be built in a quiet spacious site, whereas the ground of this one was choked with stones and rubble. (2) In order to keep the ethers concentrated within the chamber, its outer wall should be built 3 feet down into the ground, its middle wall 1 ft. 6 inches down, and its inner wall $7^6/_{10}$ inches, all of which specifications were disregarded in the present structure. (3) The outer door should be at the north, the middle one at the south, and the inner one again at the north, whereas all doors of the present structure faced south (the usual orientation in Chinese buildings). (4) The pitch-pipe tubes lacked the proper mathematical ratios to one another. (5) Because of the principle of magnetic declination,

[1] This is narrated in the *Yüeh lü chih* 樂律志 or "Treatise on Music and the Pitch-pipes" (comp. by Huang Ju-liang 黃汝良 in 1633; see *Ming shih, loc. cit.,* last line). The *Ming shih* says that this treatise failed to achieve wide circulation, and I do not know whether it is still extant. The passage in question is quoted, however, in the *Ch'in-ting Hsü Wen-hsien t'ung-k'ao* (Imperially Complied Continuation to the *Wen-hsien t'ung-k'ao,* of 1747), 107/3750c (Commercial Press photolithographic ed. of 1936); in the same work (pp. 3747a–3750c) the two memorials of Chang Ô are quoted *in extenso.*

[2] This book, *Li-fa hsin-shu* 歷法新書, according to Dr. Chiu, exists only in a Ming edition which is nowhere available in the United States. Fortunately, however, Li's preface has been reproduced by Chiang Yung 江永 (1681–1762) in Chiang's *Lü-lü hsin-lun* 律呂新論, B/87 (TSCC ed.).

[3] For this identification I am indebted to Dr. Chiu. Chiang-ling is not a "style" or a "courtesy name", but the name of Chang Chü-cheng's native city on the Yangtze.

the *huang-chung* tube should not be located precisely according to magnetic north, but rather a few degrees to the west of this position[1].

Li says further that Chang accordingly had a new chamber built a little south of the Altar of Heaven, in which Yüan's specifications were followed. "And when, according to the proper procedure, a watch was made, the flying ashes all responded". Chang, greatly pleased, wished to make Yüan Huang Director of Music, but a falling out between the two over a question of reforming the calendar led to Yüan's retirement on the pretext of illness. Soon after this, according to Li, Chang Chü-cheng himself died.

Can we believe that this story—or at least events sufficient to give it a plausible basis—actually occurred? On the one hand it is not inherently impossible, for Chang Chü-cheng, as prime minister, certainly had the power to carry out such a project if he wished, even within the sacred precincts of the Altar of Heaven itself. On the other hand, it is well known that many unfair stories about Chang were circulated after his death, and the wording of this one is certainly intended to place him in an unfavorable light. Furthermore, it is striking that the story is recorded nowhere save in Li's preface (and what we know elsewhere about Yüan Huang's life is unfortunately very sketchy). This last point is stressed by Chiang Yung (1681–1762) as the reason why he (Chiang), in his own book (see p. 33, n. 2), reproduces Li's preface so that its knowledge will not be lost. A few lines earlier, Chiang himself shows a very healthy skepticism regarding the whole ethers theory. Yet after quoting the preface he is constrained to admit: "I don't know whether this really happened or not". For us today there seems little alternative but to accept this inconclusive verdict.

This seems to be the last attempt of which there is record. By the Ch'ing dynasty, when Chiang Yung was writing, the ethers theory was on its last legs, and by the eighteenth century it would appear to be quite dead. Illustrative of the prevailing disbelief are the editorial comments in the imperial bibliography, *Ssu-k'u ch'üan-shu tsung-mu* (comp. 1782), made on the writings of Ts'ai Yüan-ting and Liu Chin. Thus the editors say about Ts'ai: "In what he says about watching for the ethers, he shows the greatest confusion". And about Liu's ardent advocacy of Ts'ai's ideas: "To discard the verifiable tones (as a method for determining the pitch-pipes) and seek instead to examine into the vague and unknowable ethers is indeed a blind alley"[2].

---

[1] This fifth point, as quoted in Li's preface, is far from being as simple as it is presented here, and it would take considerable space to explain its precise wording. There seems no doubt, however, that it is based on the principle of magnetic declination.

[2] Lit., "is indeed the final extremity" 斯亦末矣. See *Ssu-k'u ch'üan-shu tsung-mu* (Shanghai: Ta-tung Book Co., 1930), 38/2b and 4a.

The theory of watching for the ethers probably originated in the first century B.C., as a natural and logical application of the fundamental Chinese belief in the harmony and interrelatedness of man and nature. During the next six or seven centuries it was elaborated and sporadically put into practice, especially during the sixth century. Thereafter, however, it became a crystallized element in China's intellectual heritage, seemingly believed in by most, refined in some minor details by a few, and subjected to actual test by almost no one. The sixteenth century saw another flare-up of interest, resulting in two alleged attempts at testing. By this time, however, the tide of thought was beginning to run strongly against it, and by the eighteenth century it was possible for official opinion to declare it to have reached a blind alley. With this final unequivocal rejection, we may safely take our leave of this curious chapter in the history of Chinese cosmic speculation and pseudo-scientific endeavor.

SEXUAL
SYMPATHETIC
MAGIC IN
HAN CHINA

In an overwhelmingly agrarian civilization like that of China, it is
scarcely surprising that prayers and rituals for securing rain should be
among the earliest and most enduring of religious practices. They are
mentioned in inscriptions of Shang date (before 1000 B.C.), and numerous references to them occur in the *Spring and Autumn Annals* and
other texts of the Chou dynasty (*ca.* 1027–221 B.C.). Only in the Han
dynasty (206 B.C.–A.D. 220), however, does the first really detailed
and systematic description of them appear. It is the essay, *Ch'iu yü*[1]
or "Seeking Rain," written by the famous Confucian scholar Tung
Chung-shu (179?–104? B.C.) as the seventy-fourth chapter of his
*Ch'un-ch'iu fan-lu* ("Rich Dew of the Spring and Autumn").

The highly schematized form of this essay makes it improbable that
it is really a sociologically exact account of the rain-making ceremonies actually performed by the general populace either before or
during Tung Chung-shu's time. Much more likely is the assumption
that in its main lines, at least, it is Tung's own scholastic formulation
of what such ceremonies ideally *ought* to be, derived from the cosmological theories which he himself did so much to propagate. This is

---

[1] For the Chinese characters corresponding to these transliterations of Chinese
terms, see the list on page 375.

evidenced by the fact that his essay actually describes not one but several rituals, each intended for a particular season and having its own direction, color, and numerical formula, in accordance with the system of correlations based upon the five elements. At the same time, however, other forms of sympathetic magic are also mentioned, some perhaps stemming from genuine folk tradition, others almost surely of his own invention. A town suffering from drought, for example, should close its southern gates and open those on the north, the reason being that south is the direction of the *yang* cosmic principle, which is hot and dry, whereas north is the direction of the complementary *yin* principle, which is cool and moist. Women, because they pertain to the *yin*, should appear in public places, whereas men, being *yang*, should remain in seclusion. Rain should be induced to fall by placing pots and other open-mouthed vessels on the streets to receive it, and the lighting of fires should be prohibited.[2]

Here, however, our concern is only with a single sentence which comes in the brief summarizing remarks at the very end of Tung's essay. This sentence reads: "In all of the four seasons, on the *keng-tzu* days, all husbands and wives among officials and commoners are ordered to cohabit."[3]

Neither Su Yü (died 1914) nor any of the other standard commentators offers any help in explaining this sentence.[4] Its key term, *ou-ch'u* ("to cohabit"; lit., "to dwell in pairs"), is exceedingly rare, and possibly unique, as shown by the fact that the *P'ei-wen yün-fu* thesaurus of 1711, a great compendium of phrases taken from all periods of Chinese literature, cites for it only this single passage.[5] After so doing, however, the same work goes on to quote an explanatory sentence from an unnamed commentary: "To cohabit (*ou-ch'u*) when praying for rain has the idea of securing harmony between the *yin* and the *yang*."[6]

Whoever the author of this unnamed commentary may have been,[7] there is no doubt that he has correctly understood the purport of

---

[2] Tung's essay is summarized in Otto Franke, *Studien zur Geschichte des konfuzianischen Dogmas und der chinesischen Staatsreligion* (Hamburg, 1920), pp. 270–72, which, however, does not deal with the particular sentence discussed below.

[3] *Ssu-shih chieh yi keng-tzu chih jih ling li min fu-fu chieh ou-ch'u.* See Su Yü, ed., *Ch'un-ch'iu fan-lu yi-cheng* (1910), 16/12a.

[4] To Dr. A. Kaiming Chiu, Head of the Chinese-Japanese Library at Harvard University, I am much indebted for confirming this point by examining some ten editions of the *Ch'un-ch'iu fan-lu* available at Harvard.

[5] See *Wan-yu wen-k'u* edition (Shanghai: Commercial Press, 1937), p. 1635.1, s.v.

[6] *Tao yü erh ou-ch'u ch'ü yin-yang ho chih yi.*

[7] See the "Additional Note."

## CHINESE CHARACTERS
### CHARACTERS FOR WELL-KNOWN TERMS AND TITLES OMITTED

#### A. WORDS AND PHRASES

| | | | |
|---|---|---|---|
| keng (again, to change) | 更 | ou-ch'u (to cohabit) | 偶處 |
| keng (cyclical stem) | 庚 | sang (mourning) | 喪 |
| keng-tzu (cyclical day) | 庚子 | sang (mulberry) | 桑 |
| ming (blind, benighted) | 冥 | tzu (cyclical branch) | 子 |
| ming (insect grub) | 螟 | tzu (to engender) | 孳 |

#### B. SENTENCES

Ssu-shih chieh yi keng-tzu chih jih ling li min fu-fu chieh ou-ch'u.

四時皆以庚子之日令吏民夫婦皆偶處.

Tao yü erh ou-ch'u ch'ü yin-yang ho chih yi.

禱雨而偶處取陰陽和之義.

#### C. PERSONS

| | | | |
|---|---|---|---|
| Chang Yen | 張晏 | Su Yü | 蘇輿 |
| Chu Mu-chieh | 朱睦㮮 | Tung Chung-shu | 董仲舒 |
| Huang Yü-chi | 黃虞稷 | Wu P'eng-chü | 吳鵬舉 |
| Ling Shu | 淩曙 | Wu T'ing-chü | 吳廷舉 |
| Lu Wen-ch'ao | 盧文弨 | Yeh Te-hui | 葉德輝 |

#### D. BOOK TITLES AND EDITIONS

Ch'ien-ch'ing-t'ang shu-mu

千頃堂書目

Kuan-ku-t'ang shu-mu ts'ung-k'o

觀古堂書目叢刻

Ch'iu yü  求雨

Li yen  例言

Ch'un-ch'iu fan-lu

春秋繁露

Po hu t'ung

白虎通

CCFL chieh-chieh  節解

Shih-yüan ts'ung-shu

適園叢書

CCFL yi-cheng  義證

Fan-lu chieh-chieh

繁露節解

Wan-chüan-t'ang shu-mu

萬卷堂書目

Tung's statement. The term *ou-ch'u*, as used here, can only be a euphemism for sexual intercourse, and what Tung Chung-shu is advocating, therefore, is that on every *keng-tzu* day, that is, on every thirty-seventh day throughout the year of the recurrent sixty-day cycle, all married couples throughout the country should have sex relations. By so doing they will insure a proper balance between the *yin* and *yang* principles in the human world, which, because of the intimate interrelationship between man and nature, will bring about a corresponding balance between the two forces in the world of nature. Since droughts (and, it might be added, floods as well) are the result of an imbalance between the *yin* and *yang*, it is obvious that these will be prevented in this way.

It remains to determine why Tung Chung-shu should have singled out *keng-tzu* as the particular day of the cycle for the performance of this mass sympathetic magic. The answer, though not provable with absolute finality, rests in all probability upon word plays of a sort popular in Han times.

These word plays held a definite, though somewhat minor, place in the total world picture of the Han cosmologists. According to this picture, the multitudinous components of the universe—those of time and space, living creatures and inanimate objects, natural phenomena and human institutions, natural and human attributes and concepts—though seemingly heterogeneous, are in actual fact classifiable under a series of parallel sequences or categories. Within each such category, the component members are held together by sympathetic attraction or by mutual action and response, as within a common electrical field. Between the various categories, in turn, interactions occur according to a fixed temporal and spatial sequence. Thus the cosmos is interwoven by a network of relationships which, because they bridge the seeming gap between the natural and human spheres, therefore merge the two into a single continuum. It has been plausibly suggested that this concept of an integrated "total" universe may have been inspired, or at least strengthened, by the political reality which the Han inherited from the preceding Ch'in dynasty: a "universal empire" having a highly centralized bureaucracy, and, in Han times, an increasingly pervasive set of common social values.[8]

The starting point of the attempt to classify all natural and human phenomena into categories lay of course in the polarized antithesis between the *yin* and *yang* principles. Equally important was the system

[8] See Joseph Needham, *Science and Civilisation in China*, II (Cambridge: Cambridge University Press, 1956), 338.

of the five elements, with its many correlated sequences in fives. Equated with the second element, fire, for example, were such disparate items as south, summer, the smell of burning, a bitter taste, the number 7, the musical note *chih*, the sun, the planet Mars, heat, the ruler King Wen (of the Chou dynasty), the divinity Chu-jung, the hearth sacrifice, the feathered category (i.e., birds) among living creatures, the chicken among domestic animals, beans among the cereals, the lungs and the tongue among the five viscera and five sense organs respectively, joy among the five affective states, and many more. Other numerical sequences were also important, notably those of eights (based upon the eight trigrams of the *Yi Ching* or *Classic of Changes*) and of nines.

Besides such number systems, the Han Chinese looked for other means to establish correlations. One procedure—much facilitated by the large number of homophones in the Chinese language—consisted in the postulating of semantic relationships between words having the same or nearly the same pronunciation. Such etymologies—some of them well founded, many others quite arbitrary and fanciful—appear in various Han writings, among them scholarly commentaries on the classics, the *Shuo-wen* dictionary of circa A.D. 120, or the exegesis of rites and institutions entitled *Po hu t'ung* ("Comprehensive Discussions in the White Tiger Hall") of circa A.D. 80. Of the following two examples, the first is also of interest as illustrating the Han belief in the interrelationship between human behavior and natural phenomena.

The *Shuo-wen* dictionary, in its definition of *ming*, "insect grub," connects this word with another different *ming* meaning "dark, blind, benighted, obtuse," etc. Thus we read: "*Ming* (insect grub) is an insect which eats the hearts of grain. When government functionaries benightedly (*ming*) violate the law, these grubs (*ming*) are born."[9] Similarly, the word *sang*, "mulberry," is correlated with *sang*, "mourning," by the famous commentator on the classics, Cheng Hsüan (A.D. 127–200), in his explanation of a passage in one of the ritual texts wherein, apropos the mourning ceremonies to be followed by the lower aristocracy, we are told that the hair of the deceased is to be knotted with a hairpin made of mulberry wood. Cheng's commentary on this reads: "The function of the mulberry (*sang*) is to call attention

---

[9] See *Shuo-wen chieh-tzu Tuan chu* ("*Shuo-wen chieh-tzu* with Tuan's Commentary"), 13A/30a (*Ssu-pu pei-yao* ed.). Most editions of the *Shuo-wen* read "leaves of grain" instead of "hearts of grain," but as pointed out by Tuan Yü-ts'ai (1735–1815) in his commentary, the correctness of the "hearts of grain" reading is attested by early citations in other works.

to the mourning (*sang*). Its use for making use hairpins derives from its name."[10]

It should not surprise us, therefore, on turning to the question of the possible significance of the term *keng-tzu*, to find that each of its components could in Han times be correlated with a homophonous equivalent. Thus concerning *keng*, name of the seventh cyclical stem, we are told by various writers that it may stand for a differently written *keng*, a word which, according to context, variously means either "again" or "to change."[11] Likewise, concerning *tzu*, name of the first cyclical branch, we learn that it may be equated with a differently written *tzu* which means "to engender."[12] Adoption of these two borrowed meanings, therefore, allows us to convert *keng-tzu*, normally the designation of a day in the sexagenary cycle, into a punning phrase, "again to engender," which may in turn be interpreted as a wish: "May we again engender." Obviously, sex relations performed every sixty days throughout the country on that particular day of the cycle bearing this felicitous borrowed connotation will inevitably result in increased human births and, through extension, in greater crop fertility and good fortune generally.

There is, besides this, a secondary possible reason for Tung's selection of *keng-tzu:* the fact that the cyclical branch *tzu*, in addition to designating a point of time in the sexagenary cycle, is also used spatially to designate the north, direction of the element water. Hence *keng-tzu*, in this sense, may be interpreted as signifying "again the north," that is, "again the element water," which once more becomes a wish: "May there again be water."

Beliefs in the interrelationship of human and natural fertility are, of course, common throughout the world. Usually, however, they belong to immemorial group tradition rather than to the conscious theorizing of known individuals. What makes the present instance remarkable,

---

[10] See commentary on *Yi li*, sec. xii (text proper translated by John Steele, *The I-li or Book of Étiquette and Ceremonial* [London, 1917], II, 49). Word plays of this sort remained popular in later China and were often represented symbolically in art. See Schuyler Cammann, "Types of Symbols in Chinese Art," in Arthur F. Wright, ed., *Studies in Chinese Thought* (Chicago: University of Chicago Press, 1953), pp. 195–231, esp. 224–25.

[11] See *Po hu t'ung*, chap. ix (translated by Tjan Tjoe Som, *Po Hu T'ung, the Comprehensive Discussions in the White Tiger Hall* [Leiden, 1949–52], p. 434): "*Keng* [cyclical stem] means that the things 'change' *keng.*" A similar statement is made by Chang Yen (probably third century), as quoted in H. H. Dubs, *History of the Former Han Dynasty*, I (Baltimore, 1938), 225, n. 1.

[12] See *Po hu t'ung*, chap. ix (Tjan, *op. cit.*, p. 435): "*Tzu* [cyclical branch] means *tzu* 'to engender.'" Similar statements appear in *ibid.*, chaps. i and xxix (p. 270, n. 33, and p. 561). See also references in the *Huai-nan-tzu* (second century B.C.), chap. iii, and *Shih chi* or *Historical Records* (ca. 85 B.C.), chap. xiii, as cited by J. J. L. Duyvendak in a book review in *T'oung Pao*, XXXVIII (1945), 337.

therefore, is not so much its existence per se as the fact that it should have been deliberately created by an individual scholar, drawing for this purpose upon a complex philosophical world-view. Confucianism, as is well known, has generally been prudish in its attitude toward sex (which perhaps explains why this particular sentence by Tung Chung-shu has been ignored by all the standard commentators). That Tung should have disregarded this prudishness in his efforts to maintain cosmic harmony illustrates the great difference between the syncretic version of Confucianism promulgated by him, with its emphasis upon the use of ritual to integrate man with nature, and either pre-Han early Confucianism or the several forms of Confucianism which developed in post-Han times.

Finally, it should be noted that this particular instance of Tung's advocacy of sexual sympathetic magic almost surely never passed beyond the stage of theory. For if it had ever been actually attempted, solid government support would of course have been necessary, and this, if really supplied, would in all probability have been recorded in some way in the Han dynastic histories.

ADDITIONAL NOTE[13]

Concerning the identity of the unnamed commentator quoted in the *P'ei-wen yün-fu*, I can hazard only some guesses rather than any firm conclusions. Su Yü (died 1914), in the *Li yen* section (p. 5*b*) prefacing his *Ch'un-ch'iu fan-lu yi-cheng*, states that the earliest commentary on the *Ch'un-ch'iu fan-lu*, with one exception, is that by Ling Shu (1775–1829). The exception is a work entitled *Fan-lu chieh-chieh*, in one *ts'e* (volume), by a certain Wu T'ing-chü,[14] which is listed in the sixteenth century bibliography by Chu Mu-chieh, the *Wan-chüan-t'ang shu-mu*.[15] This work, Su Yü goes on to say, he has not seen himself—a fact which, in view of Su's eminence as a specialist on Tung Chung-shu, strongly suggests that it was already no longer extant in his day.

Other bibliographies, however, list a still earlier work whose title, *Ch'un-ch'iu fan-lu chieh-chieh*, is identical with the foregoing save for the addition of the two initial words, *Ch'un-ch'iu*. This second work, in ten *chüan* (books or parts), is ascribed to a certain Wu P'eng-chü

[13] In preparing this note, I am again indebted to Dr. Chiu for certain bibliographical data.

[14] Presumably the Wu T'ing-chü who died about 1524. See biography in *Ming shih* ("Ming Dynastic History"), 201/1b–2a, which, however, says nothing about his authorship of such a work.

[15] 1/6a of the edition contained in Yeh Te-hui, *Kuan-ku-t'ang shu-mu ts'ung-k'o* (Changsha, 1903).

of the Yuan dynasty (1280–1367), about whom I have been unable to find further information. It is listed both in Huang Yü-chi's (1629–91) *Ch'ien-ch'ing-t'ang shu-mu*,[16] and (possibly derived from this) in Lu Wen-ch'ao's (1717–96) *Pu Liao Chin Yüan yi-wen-chih* ("Supplemental Treatise on Liao, Chin and Yuan Literature").[17] This too is probably lost today.

It is truly extraordinary that two men, belonging to successive dynasties and differing in their names by only a single character (Wu P'eng-chü and Wu T'ing-chü), should have produced commentaries on the same work bearing virtually identical titles and otherwise outwardly differentiated only by the inconclusive statements that the one consisted of ten *chüan* (books or parts) and the other of a single *ts'e* (volume). Nevertheless, in the absence of concrete evidence to the contrary, we must assume that they were separate works. We may therefore hazard the guess that the unnamed sentence of commentary quoted by the *P'ei-wen yün-fu* thesaurus comes from one or the other of them, or possibly was contained in both. And inasmuch as the compilers of the *P'ei-wen yün-fu* did not always go to the original sources for their quotations, but sometimes relied on citations contained in secondary works, it is conceivable that both of the Wu treatises had themselves already been lost by 1711, the year when the *P'ei-wen yün-fu* was published.

---

[16] *Shih-yüan ts'ung-shu* edition, 2/51a.

[17] Contained in *Erh-shih-wu shih pu-pien* ("Supplemental Compilations on the Twenty-five Dynastic Histories" [Shanghai: K'ai-ming Book Co., 1936]), p. 8494.3.

# TEXT STUDIES

# A PERPLEXING PASSAGE IN THE CONFUCIAN ANALECTS

ONE OF the most baffling passages in the Confucian *Analects* is *Analects* IX, 1, which Legge translates: "The subjects of which the Master seldom spoke were—profitableness, and also the appointment (of Heaven), and perfect virtue" (*Tzu han yen, li, yü ming, yü jen*).[1] The difficulty here is not primarily a grammatical one, for such a translation may be read from the text without trouble, but rather lies in the fact that the statement made runs counter to everything that the rest of the *Analects* tells us concerning Confucius. It may be granted, to be sure, that *li*[2] (Legge's "profitableness") is not a subject that appears very frequently in the *Analects*. It is almost always disparaged, or attacked outright in the places where it does occur,[3] and in the one instance in which it is really regarded favorably, it assumes a special meaning having reference to public welfare.[4]

The same thing, however, can hardly be said about *ming*[5] (Legge's "appointments (of Heaven)"), which appears frequently in the *Analects* bearing the same metaphysical connotation that it possesses in this passage (as distinct from its other meanings, such as "command," "commission," "life," etc.).[6] But it is with the word *jen*[7] (Legge's "perfect virtue"), which forms the keystone of Confucian ethics, that the greatest obstacle to our understanding arises, an obstacle so great as to force Legge to admit: "With his not speaking of *jen* there is a difficulty which I know not how to solve. The fourth Book is nearly all occupied with it and no doubt it was a prominent topic in Confucius's teachings."

Despite such a manifest contradiction between this single passage and the entire remainder of the *Analects*, western sinologists, such

---

[1] 子罕言, 利, 與 命, 與 仁.
[2] 利.
[3] *Ana.* IV, 12; 16; XIII, 17, etc.
[4] *Ibid.*, XX, 2.
[5] 命.
[6] *Ana.* II, 4; VI, 8; XI, 18; XII, 5; XVI, 8; XX, 3.
[7] 仁.

as Zottoli, Couvreur, Chavannes, Soothill and Wilhelm, all translate in exactly the same manner as does Legge. So, for that matter,
does the Chinese translator, Ku Hung-ming.[8] In this they are but
following what the majority of Chinese scholars have long accepted
as the orthodox interpretation.

Attempts, of course, have not been wanting to find a rational
explanation for this puzzling passage. Thus, concerning the strange
inclusion of the word *jen* (" perfect virtue "), Ho Yen of the Wei
Dynasty (220-265 A. D.) says: " Few are able to attain to it [*jen*].
Therefore [Confucius] rarely spoke of it." [9] And Chu Hsi (1130-
1200) writes in similar strain: " Ch'eng Tzu says ' Planning for
profit is injurious to righteousness; the workings of heavenly
decree are abstruse; the way of *jen* is vast. On all these the Master
rarely spoke.'" [10]

But all this is merely explaining the language away. It is
absurd to suppose that Confucius hesitated to impart even his most
abstruse ideas to such a man as his beloved disciple Yen Hui, at
whose death Confucius exclaimed, " Alas! Heaven is destroying
me! Heaven is destroying me! " [11] And the essential difficulty
persists that *jen*, when all is said and done, remains one of the
commonest topics to be found in the *Analects*.

The passage has been generally accepted by Chinese scholars as
being free from textual corruption, and in Ssu-ma Ch'ien's *Shih chi*
it appears word for word the same as in the *Analects*.[12] The
problem lies, then, in finding a reading for the chapter which,
without disturbing the existing text, will harmonize itself with
what the remainder of the *Analects* tells us.

In the *Hsüeh chai chan pi*, a book of the Sung Dynasty, there
seems to lie an answer to the problem, despite Wylie's condemnation of it as " only . . . a work of second rate standing." [13] This

---

[8] *Loc. cit.*, Couvreur, *Les Quatres Livres*; Ku Hung-ming, *Discourses and
Sayings of Confucius*; Soothill, *Analects of Confucius*; Wilhelm, *Kung-tse*.
Also Zottoli, *Cursus Litteraturae Sinicae*, Vol. II, p. 279, and Chavannes;
*Mémoires Historiques*, Vol. V, p. 405.

[9] 寡 能 及 之, 故 希 言 也.

[10] 程 子 曰, 計 利 則 害 義. 命 之 理 微. 仁 之 道 大. 皆 夫
子 所 罕 言 也.

[11] *Ana.* XI, 8.

[12] Cf. Chavannes, *op. cit.*, in note 8 above.

[13] Wylie, *Notes on Chinese Literature*, p. 161 (1902 edition).

work, which appeared about the middle of the thirteenth century, was written by Shih Sheng-tsu,[14] a follower of Wei Liao-weng (1178-1237),[15] who is noted as being the founder of a school of classical criticism continuing the Confucian teachings of Chu Hsi. Though it deals for the most part with doubtful questions concerning the *I ching,* there is one section that specifically discusses the problem involved in *Analects* IX, 1.[16]

Concerning this passage, Shih Sheng-tsu points out the impossibility of the orthodox interpretation, following much the same reasoning as that given above, and then continues: " In short, what the Master rarely spoke on is profit and nothing more. From this clause [i. e., which begins with the beginning of the passage as a whole, and ends with the word *li,* (profit)] must be made a single [separate] meaning. As regards *ming* [heavenly decree] and *jen,* these are both what he [Confucius] constantly held forth upon. And this clause [i. e., which follows the word *li,* embraces these two terms, *ming* and *jen,* and extends to the end of the passage as a whole] forms a separate single meaning." [17] Shih Sheng-tsu then adds an important grammatical note: " The [two] characters *yü* [are to be taken in the sense of] *hsü* [a word which may be translated as " to allow," " grant," " give up to," etc.]." [18]

Thus what, according to the orthodox interpretation, is a single sentence, now becomes cut up into two entirely separated sentences through the mere insertion of a period instead of a comma after the character *li*; while the two *yü* characters, which served as connectives (Legge's " an also . . . and . . .") become verbs meaning " to give forth " or " share." Thus the passage, newly translated, becomes: " The Master rarely spoke of profit. (But) he gave forth (his ideas concerning) the appointments (of Heaven), (and also) gave forth (his ideas concerning) perfect virtue." This is not only grammatically correct, but gives a translation thoroughly in accordance with the spirit of the *Analects* as a whole.

---

[14] 學 齋 佔 畢. by 史 繩 祖. It appears in the 12th 集 of the 學 津 討 原 (edited by 張 海 鵬), of which I have consulted the 昭 曠 閣 刻 本 edition, published in 1805.

[15] 魏 子 翁.

[16] Cf. section 子 罕 言 利, in chüan 1, pp. 18b-19b.

[17] 蓋 子 罕 言 者, 獨 利 而 已. 當 以 此 句 作 一 義. 曰 命, 曰 仁, 皆 平 日 所 深 與. 此 句 別 作 一 義.

[18] 與 者, 許 也.

To explain how the character *yü* may thus be metamorphosed from a conjunction into a verb, in what may seem to some a rather surprising fashion, Shih Sheng-tsu quotes analogous examples from the *Analects*, which translated by Legge are: "There is nothing which I do that is not *shown to* you." "The Master said, 'I *admit* people's approach to me. . . . If a man purify himself . . . I *receive* him so purified.'" "The Master . . . said, 'I *give my approval to* Tien.'" "If I *associate* not with these people . . . with whom shall I *associate*?"[19] In these examples the character *yü* conveys the idea, not easily translated into exact words, but readily grasped in the original, of sharing, or associating, oneself and one's ideas with others, or perhaps of holding forth on (in the sense that an orator holds forth), which last meaning fits well into Shih Sheng-tsu's interpretation of *Analects* IX, 1, and which I have ventured above to use in translating the character *yü* where it appears in Shih's own explanation.

To this exposition of Shih's views, let us add a final proof of our own. The use of the conjunction "and" is in general avoided in Chinese, both in the written and spoken languages. Yet if we accept the traditional interpretation for *Analects* IX, 1, we find that the character *yü* occurs twice in this short sentence with this meaning—something most unusual. Legge senses this peculiarity when he translates: "The subjects . . . were—profitableness, *and also* the appointments (of Heaven), *and* perfect virtue." The second "and" is passable, but the "and also" is certainly most clumsy and unnecessary.

If we look through the *Analects*, we find a number of sentences of a type very similar in structure to the one under discussion, in which things and ideas are grouped in the same way into categories. Thus we have: "The Master's frequent themes of discourse were—the Odes, the History, and the maintenance of the Rules of Propriety." "The subjects on which the Master did not talk, were—extraordinary beings, feats of strength, disorder, and spiritual beings." "There were four things which the Master taught—letters, ethics, devotion of soul, and truthfulness." "There were four things from which the Master was entirely free. He had no foregone conclusions, no arbitrary predeterminations, no obstinacy, and no egoism."[20]

---

[19] *Ana.* VII, 23; 28; XI, 25; XVIII, 1. The character 與 occurs twice in the second and fourth examples.

[20] *Ibid.*, VII, 17; 20; 24; IX, 4.

Comparing these four sentences, we make a most interesting discovery. In not one of them does the character *yü* occur, either in the meaning of "and," or with any other meaning whatsoever! The "and's" that occur in the translations have been added by Legge solely in order to conform to the demands of English idiom. It seems hardly possible, then, that in *Analects* IX, 1, which coincides almost exactly with these examples in sentence structure, two *yü* characters would appear gratuitously, unless they were intended to play a definite part in determining the meaning of the sentence, a part far more important than a mere superfluous conjunction such as "and," or "and also." Translation of the character *yü* according to the formula laid down by Shih Sheng tsu would seem, then, to be the only possible alternative to falling into a glaring inconsistency.

It is difficult to account for the fact that Chinese scholarship should for the main have disregarded an explanation of a puzzling passage which, when once understood, appears quite logical and natural. Shih Sheng-tsu lived a little too late to have his researches adopted by Chu Hsi and so receive the stamp of orthodox approval. Nevertheless, an extract from his explanation of this passage appears in the *Huang ch'ing ching chieh*, published by Yüan Yüan in 1829, which Legge praises so highly, but which the eminent translator of the Chinese classics evidently must have overlooked when he studied the passage under consideration.[21]

In any case, *Analects* IX, 1, affords an interesting example of some of the difficulties besetting the student of Chinese, while Shih Sheng-tsu's explanation exemplifies the use in China of a true scientific method, as applied to textual criticism, at a time when Europe had not yet emerged from the Middle Ages.

---

[21] 皇 清 經 解 published by 阮 元. Cf. the section 四 書 考 異 beginning of chüan 459.

## TWO NEW TRANSLATIONS OF LAO TZU *

PROFESSOR DUYVENDAK's untimely death on July 9, 1954, coming when he was still at the height of his powers, takes from us yet another of the giants of European sinology. All who are familiar with his writings have long recognized his eminence as a Chinese scholar. But to friends and students (among whom I was privileged to be one) he was more than this as well: a morally big human being. This bigness he displayed in the everyday affairs of ordinary life: his self-effacing simplicity, his friendly warmth, his endless patience to all who approached him; and in time of crisis he displayed it again when, during the Nazi occupation of Holland, he suffered imprisonment for the " crime " of having opened his home to Jewish refugees.[1]

Many members of this Society, of which Duyvendak was an honorary member, probably still remember his after-dinner talk at the Society's annual meeting in New York in 1946, when, speaking with the humor, charm, and modesty so typical of him, he described how he and his fellow countrymen had lived during the war years. In those " times of troubles," when boiled tulip bulbs became the food of many, it is altogether natural that this European scholar of Chinese civilization should turn for solace to that ancient " treasure house of wisdom," the *Tao Te Ching* of Lao Tzu. The result was a Dutch translation, published while the war was still in progress.[2] And now it is again altogether fitting that his subsequent

French and English translations—based upon, but amplified and otherwise considerably modified from that Dutch version—should become his final published works.

### The French and English Versions Compared

Both versions begin with a brief but admirable introduction, giving one of the best discussions of the *Tao Te Ching* and of Taoist key ideas yet seen by this reviewer. Thereafter, in the main body of the French version, each of the *Tao Te Ching*'s eighty-one chapters receives a spread of two facing pages (sometimes a little more) arranged as follows: (1) on the right hand page appears a photographic reproduction of the traditional Chinese text, and next to it, on the same page, a reconstituted Chinese text (photographed from handwritten copy) embodying Duyvendak's numerous emendations of the traditional text; (2) on the facing left hand page appears Duyvendak's French translation (based on the reconstituted text), and underneath it, in smaller type, his detailed commentary. The book then concludes with a numbered list of all Chinese characters mentioned in the commentary, followed by a one-page table of all the textual transfers between chapters of the traditional text made by Duyvendak in the course of establishing his reconstituted text.

The English edition includes all of the above features save that it omits the two all-important parallel Chinese texts. For this reason, of course, the French edition must remain primary for everyone who reads Chinese. Aside from this, the commentary of the English edition also embodies a very few minor additions or other modifications.[3]

Not often, however, does it happen that, as here, the same text is translated by the same scholar into two different languages. This, not surprisingly, has resulted in occasional verbal differences which it is instructive to compare. On the whole,

---

* *Tao Tö King, Le livre de la Voie et de la Vertu.* Texte chinois établi et traduit avec des notes critiques et une introduction par J. J. L. DUYVENDAK. (Librairie d'Amérique & d'Orient.) Pp. xiii + 187. Paris: ADRIEN-MAISONNEUVE, 1953.—

*Tao Te Ching, The book of the Way and its Virtue.* Translated from the Chinese and annotated by J. J. L. DUYVENDAK. (The Wisdom of the East Series.) Pp. vi + 172. London: JOHN MURRAY, 1954.

[1] For an excellent obituary, including a ten-page bibliography of his writings, see Paul Demiéville, " J. J. L. Dukvendak (1889-1954)," *T'oung Pao*, 43 (1954), 1-33.

[2] *Tau-te-tsjing, Het boek van Weg en Deugd* (Arnhem, 1942; 2nd rev. ed., Arnhem, 1950). Though the first edition bears the imprint of May 1942, it did not actually appear until May 1943. Cf. Duyvendak in *T'oung Pao*, 38 (1945), 334, n. 3.

[3] Examples are the new archaeological evidence cited under 11 for the thirty-spoke chariot wheel of Chou times, the reference to the *Han-shih-wai-chuan* under 49, and the quotation from Shakespeare's *Tempest* under 80. (Here and below, numbers refer to the chapters of the *Tao Te Ching*, not to pages.)

my impression is that the French version tends to be a little more literal than does the English; this, however, is by no means always true. Here we can cite only a few examples:

In 13, for *ching* 驚, French " choses effrayantes " becomes English " goads " (probably under the influence of Arthur Waley, who in translating the same passage uses " goad " as a verb). In 21, for *ching* 精, French " germes " becomes English " essence," and *yu* 有, literally translated as " il y a," becomes much more freely rendered as " latent " (probably again under Waley's influence). In 27, for *hsi ming* 襲明, French " illumination ambivalente " seems considerably more " ambivalent " and less meaningful than English " twofold understanding." [4] Likewise, in the context of 41, I prefer English " gentleman " to French " noble " for *shih* 士. In 59, on the other hand, some mistake seems to have happened in allowing " La ' mère ' par laquelle on possède le royaume " to become " The ' mother ' of possessing the kingdom."

### Textual Emendations

The truly revolutionary feature of Duyvendak's work, sharply distinguishing it from almost all its predecessors, is his recognition, not merely that the present *Tao Te Ching* is occasionally corrupt in individual words (as other translators have acknowledged), but that considerable portions of its text have become seriously disarranged from their original sequence. Most of this scrambling, he believes, occurred in Han times (or very shortly thereafter), when the text was edited so as to conform to its present number of eighty-one chapters (which, as he points out, is a magic number in Taoism). In this editing it was easy for the narrow bamboo slips (on which Chinese books were then written) to lose their proper sequence, and, once this had happened, the errors were difficult to correct, owing to the inherent obscurities of the text itself.

In order to restore what he believes to have been the original sequence, therefore, Duyvendak has not hesitated to delete, or to transfer from one chapter to another, passages ranging in length from one to thirty or more characters, and affect-

---

[4] This, incidentally, is one of several instances (others will be discussed later) in which Duyvendak's interpretation differs radically (and, in my opinion, quite justifiably) from those of his predecessors; cf., for this same phrase, Legge's " hiding the light," Waley's " resorting to the light," Lin Yutang's " stealing the light," etc.

ing no less than twenty-seven chapters. In so doing he has followed two general principles: (1) When, as happens fairly frequently, the same, or nearly the same, passage appears in two different chapters, it is deleted from that to which it seems less appropriate, while retained in the other; the reason for this is that, as pointed out by Duyvendak, it seems quite unlikely that such a considerable number of repetitions would appear in a text as brief as that of the *Tao Te Ching*. (2) When, as happens even more frequently, a passage seems ideologically and stylistically out of place in its present chapter, but fits well into another, it is accordingly deleted from the former and shifted to the latter. Fortunately, such transfers are facilitated not only by the general syntactic features (balance, parallelism, contrast, etc.) shared by the *Tao Te Ching* with other classical Chinese texts, but also by the numerous rhymes which are its own particular characteristic (though these, as Duyvendak points out, are by no means always infallible guides).

The resulting rearrangement provides a text indubitably smoother, more natural and more meaningful than the traditional one, and one that in case after case carries conviction as to its correctness. After reading it, indeed, one wonders how other translators could have remained content with the traditional arrangement, or how Waley could have described the text as " at least as satisfactory as that of other early Chinese works." [5]

The rearranging of any long-accepted text, however, carries obvious dangers, for once embarked on, it inevitably raises the question: where to stop? Here we should stress that relatively few of Duyvendak's changes are wholly original with him; for most of them he follows proposals made by modern Chinese scholars, notably Ma Hsü-lun in his *Lao-tzu Ho-ku* (1924). Yet Ma, in Duyvendak's opinion, is too " radical " in his approach to the text. " In numerous cases," writes Duyvendak (English ed., pp. 3-4), " I do not agree with him; I only accept alterations if they seem to be absolutely necessary." Now here, of course, he is expressing a subjective opinion, for obviously what may appear " necessary " to one scholar may appear equally " unnecessary " to another. It is quite conceivable, indeed, that to some readers (I am not one of them) who have

---

[5] Arthur Waley, *The Way and Its Power* (London, 1934), p. 131.

been brought up on the traditional text, Duyvendak will seem just as much of a radical as Ma Hsü-lun seems to him. Such is the situation that inevitably arises when, as here, textual changes are executed primarily on the basis of internal criteria, with only occasional support from external evidence.

Illustrative of these difficulties is the passage, "stop its (his) apertures, close its (his) doors," which, since it is repeated in two chapters (52 and 56), should therefore be theoretically deleted from one of them. In the case of 52, however, this is impossible, since deletion there would leave the next several words grammatically dangling in the air, and would furthermore destroy the antithesis now found between the opening clause of our doubtful passage ("stop its apertures") and the counter clause ("open its apertures") that begins the following paragraph. Yet if we turn to 56, deletion also becomes difficult, since this would destroy the alternating rhymes that now exist between the final words of the two clauses of our passage (t'ui, "apertures," and men, "doors") and the corresponding words in the two clauses that follow (jui, "sharpness," and fen, "tangles"). As a result, Duyvendak is reluctantly obliged to retain the passage unchanged in both chapters, even though in so doing he violates his usual rule.

Of considerably greater philosophical import is Duyvendak's bold deletion, in 42, of the opening three words in the famous chain statement: "Tao produced one; one produced two; two produced three; three produced the ten thousand things." Here, contrary to most cases, he has external justification: the fact that in the Huai-nan-tzu, where the same passage is quoted, the words "Tao produced one" do not appear.[6]

This emendation is very tempting philosophically, because the statement, "Tao produced one," in itself seems to run counter to the general tenor of Taoist thinking. This it does because, especially in the context of the statements that follow, it makes it appear as if the Tao were some sort of an initial creative agent, standing anterior and external to the train of creation which it sets in operation, whereas according to prevailing Taoist speculation, I believe I am right in asserting that the Tao is definitely not thus regarded as an external creative agent. On the contrary, it itself embraces—indeed, is identical with—the entire range of creative evolution in all its multiple phases, beginning with the undifferentiated "oneness" which the Taoists also describe as "Non-being" (wu), and evolving from this into the growing complexity of what they call "Being" (yu).[7] Perhaps it is unwise to insist too much on logical consistency in a probably composite text like the Tao Te Ching. Because it is so well known, however, the statement, "Tao produced one," has given trouble to later commentators, and it would be exceedingly convenient if it could be eliminated.[8]

On the other hand, a radical emendation such as this, based on the mere fact of textual omission in later quotations, seems a risky business, especially in view of the support for the traditional reading seemingly supplied by a passage in Chuang-tzu, chap. 12 (trans. Giles, p. 143): "At the Great Beginning (t'ai ch'u) there was Non-being (wu). It had neither being nor name and was that from which came the One. When the One came into existence, there was the One but still no forms. . . ." This agrees with Tao Te Ching 42 in saying that prior to the One there was something else, even though, for it, this "something else" is wu or "Non-being," whereas for

[6] Actually, though Duyvendak does not say so, this truncated version of the passage appears not once but twice in the Huai-nan-tzu: in 3.21a and 7.1b of Liu Wen-tien's edition of 1923.

[7] Support for this interpretation is provided by the passage in Huai-nan-tzu 3.21a, just prior to citation there of our Tao Te Ching passage, in which we read that "Tao started in the One" 始於一. This, it seems to me, is quite different from saying that the Tao "produced" 生 the One; it simply means that the evolutionary process to which we give the name Tao starts with a Oneness. This interpretation is confirmed when we read further that "with the One, there was (as yet) no production; therefore a division into the yin and yang occurred; through the union between the yin and yang, the ten thousand things were produced." Cf. also the second citation of our Tao Te Ching passage in Huai-nan-tzu 7.1b, where, in explanation of the statement, "One produced two," the commentator Kao Yu (fl. 205-212) explicitly states: "The One means Tao." For an interesting discussion of the relationship of "one" to two and other numbers, see Bernard S. Solomon, "'One is no number' in China and the West," Harvard Journal of Asiatic Studies, 17 (1954), 253-260, esp. (for the metaphysical viewpoint which is our concern here) 257-258.

[8] Cf. Fung Yu-lan, A History of Chinese Philosophy, II (Princeton, 1953), 183, where we see how Wang Pi (226-249), in commenting on this statement, is forced to contradict his own system of thought, according to which the Tao itself is to be equated with the One.

the *Tao Te Ching* it is the *Tao*. Tempted though I am to accept Duyvendak's emendation, I must confess that I can do so only with considerable hesitation—a hesitation typical of that constantly encountered in one's study of this baffling text.

### The Translations as Translations

Judged solely as translations, without regard for problems of textual rearrangement, these two works, it seems to me, not only display exceptional ease and clarity of style, but more specifically excell along three particular lines: (1) their feeling for the concreteness of expression which is such a prominent characteristic of classical Chinese; (2) their similar feeling for those vital syntactic features (parallelism, contrast, etc.), the slurring over of which in translation so often leads to semantic as well as merely stylistic distortion; (3) their ability to seize unusual meanings of Chinese words when the ordinary ones fail to fit the particular context. Here there is space only to illustrate this third point by two examples:

The phrase in 62, *chin tz'u tao* 進此道, has traditionally been translated transitively as "to send in (or present, or bring forward) this *Tao*"; cf. Waley: "Better were it, as can be done without moving from one's seat, to send this Tao." In its context, however, this is not very meaningful, and Duyvendak is almost surely right when he takes *chin* as intransitive ("to move forward") and therefore translates: ". . . it would be better for them to sit still and make progress in the Way."

In 70, likewise, there is a two-clause passage, the second being introduced by *tse* 則, which, in such a position, almost always means "then, thereupon, in that case." This, indeed, is the way the word has previously been handled here; cf. Waley (who, however, renders the entire passage quite loosely): "Few then understand me; but [*tse*] it is upon this very fact that my value depends." Duyvendak, however, takes for *tse* a much rarer verbal meaning ("to model or pattern oneself upon"), and so translates entirely differently: "Those who understand me are rare, those who pattern themselves [*tse*] after me are highly prized." Unquestionably he is right, because by so doing he secures a neat balance between initial verbal *tse* and initial verbal *chih*, "to understand," of the preceding clause. No doubt he was helped here by his keen feeling for Chinese syntax.

Sometimes, however, I feel that his search for unusual meanings leads to translations which, while philologically acceptable, are ideologically improbable. A case in point is the word *po* 博 in 81, which ordinarily means "broad, comprehensive, universal," but also occurs rather rarely as the name of a kind of backgammon, and can then be used as a verb meaning to play this game. Duyvendak elects to use this technical meaning here and therefore translates: "He who knows, does not game [*po*]. He who games [*po*], does not know." This he does on grounds that the traditional interpretation of the statement (" he who knows, is not universal [*po*]," said here with reference to the Taoist adept) is clearly "contradictory to the character of the Way which gives 'universal' knowledge instead of specialized ability."

In the Confucian *Analects*, however, *po* occurs three times in the expression *po hsüeh* 學, "to study widely" or "widely studied." Thus we read in VI, 25 (here and below I follow Waley's renderings): "A gentleman who is widely versed [*po hsüeh*] in letters . . . is not likely . . . to go far wrong"; IX, 2: "Master K'ung is no doubt . . . vastly learned [*po hsüeh*]"; XIX, 6,: "One who studies widely [*po hsüeh*] and with set purpose, . . . will . . . achieve Goodness"; cf. also the analogous use of *po* alone in IX, 10: "He has broadened [*po*] me with culture, restrained me with ritual."

In view of these examples, I think we are well justified in assuming that the *po* of *Tao Te Ching* 81 is an allusion to *po hsüeh*, Confucian "wide learning," in contrast to *chih* 知, "knowledge," which here surely refers to the "genuine" knowledge of the Taoist. Such an interpretation accords very well with the Taoist viewpoint, according to which there is nothing really "broadening" in the "wide learning" of Confucianism, but only an arid pursuit of book learning and a tedious preoccupation with the minutiae of ceremonial behavior. The attempt to equate *po* with "gaming" here, on the other hand, seems trivial and irrelevant, and Carus has neatly captured the true antithesis when he translates: "The wise [*chih*] are not learned [*po*]; the learned are not wise." [9]

Much more important, philosophically, is Duyvendak's unusual translation of the two opening

---

[9] Waley's translation is similar (though, as not infrequently in his *Tao Te Ching* renderings, more prolix and less precise): "True wisdom is different from much learning; Much learning means little wisdom."

lines of 1: " The Way that may truly be regarded as the Way is other than a permanent way [uncapitalized]. The terms that may truly be regarded as terms are other than permanent terms." This runs directly counter to the usual interpretation: " The Way that may be called the Way [10] is not the invariable Way. The names [i. e., terms] that may be called names are not the invariable names."

Duyvendak's unorthodox rendering requires a semantic extension of *k'o* 可, usually " may " or " can," into " may truly," and of *fei* 非, usually " is not," into " is other than." Above all, however, it rests upon what I believe to be a misunderstanding of the word *ch'ang* 常 (" permanent " in his translation; " invariable " in mine). For in contrast to other scholars, who take *ch'ang* as referring here to the true metaphysical Way of Taoism, Dukvendak interprets it as a derogatory epithet descriptive of the " ordinary " (this is another possible rendering of *ch'ang*) and mundane ways (uncapitalized) of everyday life. " The characteristic feature of an ordinary way or road," he writes, " is the fact that it is unchangeable and permanent. However, the Way, which is being discussed here, is characterized by the very opposite: this Way is never-ending change. Being and Non-being, life and death, alternate constantly. Nothing is impermanent and unchangeable. The very concept of ' way ' therefore acquires an opposite meaning."

This argument overlooks the philosophical objection that, granted that the universe is in a state of never-ending change or flux, this does not mean that the Way or *Tao* should be categorized as impermanent and changing, at least in the same sense. On the contrary, the very fact that change is *constant* in the universe implies that the principle (i. e., Way or *Tao*) of change is likewise " constant " or " invariable." In other words, the one unchanging constant in an ever-changing universe is precisely its character of never-ending change.

In the second place, Duyvendak's argument falls on philological grounds: the fact that *ch'ang* is an important technical term in the *Tao Te Ching*, frequently used to designate precisely what is permanent and genuine from a Taoist point of view. Thus, just as in 1 (if my interpretation is correct) the true *Tao* is described as *ch'ang* or " invariable," so in 28 the same adjective is ap-

plied to that other major concept of Taoism, *Te* (" Power," " Virtue "). In several chapters, moreover, *ch'ang* appears as a noun in its own right, " the Invariable," in which cases it is linked with another important word, *ming* 明 , " enlightenment " or " to be enlightened." Thus we read in 16: " Return (i. e., acquiescence) to what is fated is called the Invariable (*ch'ang*); to know the Invariable is to be enlightened (*ming*) "; [11] in 52: " Revert to one's (state of) enlightenment (*ming*). . . . This is called practising the Invariable (*ch'ang*) "; [12] and in 55: " Understanding of the natural harmony is called the Invariable (*ch'ang*); understanding of the Invariable is called enlightenment (*ming*)." [13]

The same misconception of *ch'ang* leads to a further mistake in the fourth paragraph of 1, where " *ch'ang wu* . . . *ch'ang yu* " (which simply means " invariable Non-being . . . and invariable Being ") is translated as " the constant alternation between Non-being and Being." " Alternation " here is gratuitous, since *ch'ang* has reference to Being and Non-being per se, and not to their functions. Nor do I see how the similar passage cited by Duyvendak from the *Chuang-tzu* in support of his interpretation does anything to strengthen his case. [14]

### Misprints

In the French edition, between the third and fourth sentences of the translation of 21, one sentence has been inadvertently omitted (fortunately corrected in the English edition, where the corresponding sentence reads: " Though vague and intangible, latent in it are things "). In 15 of the French edition, first line of commentary,

---

[10] Or " that may be trodden "; the phrase lit. reads: " that may be *tao*-ed."

[11] This (my rendering) seems to me preferable to Duyvendak's " Surrendering one's trust is called the constant (law). He who knows this constant (law) is called enlightened."

[12] Duyvendak: " If . . . one resorts to one's vision, . . . this is called ' practising what is constant.' "

[13] Duyvendak: " To understand the natural harmony means being constant. To understand being constant means being enlightened." For a detailed discussion of these and other occurrences of *ch'ang* in the *Tao Te Ching*, see Fung Yu-lan, *A History of Chinese Philosophy*, I (Peiping, 1937; 2nd ed., Princeton, 1952), 180-182.

[14] Cf. *Chuang-tzu*, chap. 33 (Giles, p. 447), which says of Lao Tzu that he built his doctrine " on the principle of invariable (*ch'ang*) Non-being and invariable (*ch'ang*) Being," but which Duqvendak interprets as meaning that he " built it on the principle of constant (alternation of) Non-being and Being."

lxvi is a mistake for lxv (the same error is repeated in the English edition), and in 63, last line of second paragraph of commentary, lxxxix is a mistake for lxxix (corrected in the English edition).

The one really major blemish of the French edition, however, is its extraordinary number of errors in the reconstituted (handwritten) Chinese text, sixty-six characters of which have been omitted entirely in copying, and three more copied incorrectly, affecting a total of fourteen chapters. This is particularly unfortunate inasmuch as it is precisely this reconstituted Chinese text that gives the French edition its primary importance for scholars. The blame, however, should not be attached to Duyvendak himself; it is simply a case of having been poorly served by his Chinese copyist, whose work he acknowledges in his introduction.

Of the omitted characters, more than half (those in 28, 38, 60, 61, 74) occur in passages consisting of identical (or closely similar) phraseology repeated in successive clauses, of which, therefore, the copyist has obviously overlooked the one while copying the other. The same principle explains two of the three miscopied characters, two of which, however, are also close graphic variants of the characters they are intended to reproduce. That so many gross errors can occur in a text expressly intended for a modern scholarly publication, should warn all of us to be very cautious before accepting the numerous textual variants commonly adducible for almost every ancient text. For while many of these are no doubt entirely justified and useful, many others are probably nothing more than careless scribal errors.

The following is a list of the reconstituted text's miscopied characters; headings indicate the chapter, column, and character number (position in a column) of the characters in question:

| Chap. | Col. | Char. no. | Error | Correction |
|---|---|---|---|---|
| 31 | 5 | 14 | 徧 | 偏 |
| 78 | 1 | 15 | 不 | 能 |
| 78 | 3 | 3 | 主 | 王 |

The following is a table of the omitted passages, headings being the same as before save that "*Char. no.*" this time refers to that character in the existing reconstituted text *immediately following which* the omitted passage in question is to be inserted:

| Chap. | Col. | Char. no. | Omission |
|---|---|---|---|
| 7 | 3 | 6 | 私 |
| 13 | 4 | 8 | 貴 |
| 20 | 5 | 10 | 沌沌兮 |
| 27 | 1 | 8 | 瑕 |
| " | 2 | 3 | 不 |
| " | " | 9 | 約 |
| " | 3 | 16 | 善 |
| 28 | 4 | 1 | 爲下天谷 |
| 34 | 1 | 14 | 而 |
| 38 | 2 | 7 | (24 chars.) 下德爲之 · · · 上義 · · · 有以爲 |
| 51 (between cols. 4 and 5) | | (13 chars.) | 功成 · · · 不去 (to be transferred from chap. 2) |
| 54 | 4 | 12 | 家 |
| 60 | 2 | 8 | 神不傷人 |
| 61 | 2 | 12 | 取則小國 |
| 74 | 3 | 10 | 夫代大匠斲 |

\* \* \*

These rather lengthy remarks very far from exhaust all the jottings originally put down in preparation for this review. Yet from them, I trust, two major points are made abundantly clear: Why, on the one hand, these translations are so excitingly different from all previous Western study on the *Tao Te Ching* and open for it revolutionary new possibilities; yet why, on the other hand, they cannot be regarded as "definitive" translations and fail to make the work of previous translators obsolete. Duyvendak himself, indeed, would be the last to advance such a claim, for in his own words (English ed., p. 5): "I do not flatter myself with the belief that I have successfully surmounted all the difficulties. There are passages which do not satisfy me, and of which the translation remains uncertain." This statement, I believe, would still hold good even were all the problems surrounding the proper arrangement of the text to be successfully resolved.[15]

We must, in short, accept the fact that the *Tao Te Ching*, by its very nature, is not susceptible to any really "definitive" translation. So laconic is it, so deliberately esoteric, so peculiar in some of its syntactic forms, that though its general mean-

---

[15] Cf. 32, which in its traditional form is obviously badly scrambled and fails to yield good sense, yet still remains unsatisfactory, so it seems to me, even after Duyvendak's drastic rearrangement.

ing is clear enough, many of its individual statements must probably remain forever veiled in uncertainty. This is what makes it at once so fascinating and at the same time so exasperating to the
translator. Yet what else can reasonably be expected from a writer who waits until the very last
chapter of his book to warn his readers: " He who
knows does not speak; he who speaks does not
know "? [16]

[16] Traditionally, these words belong to 56, where, however, they are badly out of context. Duyvendak, therefore, is surely right in transferring them to 81, where
there is a series of similar parallel paradoxes, one of
which (" he who is wise is not learned; he who is
learned is not wise ") has already been discussed above.

## ON TRANSLATING CHINESE PHILOSOPHIC TERMS

THE perennially fascinating problem of translating Chinese into Western languages (or vice versa) has evoked considerable discussion in recent years.[1] My excuse for adding to it here is that Professor Boodberg, in his review (see foregoing note) of my translation of Fung Yu-lan's *History of Chinese Philosophy,* has raised questions which, while addressed specifically to my rendering of certain Chinese philosophic terms, at the same time bear importantly on the larger problems of Chinese translation as a whole. In the following pages, therefore, I shall begin by commenting—I trust in a spirit of friendly discussion—on what Professor Boodberg has said about these terms (indicating in parentheses for each of them the English equivalents used by me in my translation, the two volumes of which will hereafter be cited as Fung 1 and 2). Then, using some of these as illustrations, I shall comment on the theories of translation presented by Professor Boodberg in his own article on "semasiology," as well as that by Professor Schafer on "two sinological maladies" (both cited in note 1 above). And having done this, I shall finally try to formulate a few general conclusions of my own.

1. *Yu* 有 (Being) and *Wu* 無 (Non-being)

Against these renderings for *yu* and *wu* (especially when used in non-Buddhist textual environment), as against several of the other renderings to be discussed later, Boodberg's general criticism is that they are "idiosyncratic and peculiarly supercharged terms of the Occidental philosophical vocabulary." With regard to *yu* and *wu*, he continues more specifically that these words "preserved as verbs a transitiveness of meaning which kept them within the

[1] Cf. the articles in Arthur F. Wright, ed., *Studies in Chinese Thought* (Chicago, 1953): Arnold Isenberg, "Some Problems of Interpretation"; I. A. Richards, "Toward a Theory of Translating"; Achilles Fang, "Some Reflections on the Difficulty of Translation"; Arthur F. Wright, "The Chinese Language and Foreign Ideas." Cf. also Edward H. Schafer, "Chinese Reign-names—Words or Nonsense Syllables?", *Wennti* no. 3 (July 1952), 33–40, and Schafer, "Non-translation and Functional Translation—Two Sinological Maladies," *Far Eastern Quarterly* 13 (1954), 251–60. Likewise Peter A. Boodberg, "The Semasiology of Some Primary Confucian Concepts," *Philosophy East and West* 2.4 (January 1954), 317–32, and Boodberg, Review of my translation of Fung Yu-lan, *A History of Chinese Philosophy,* Vol. II (Princeton, 1953), in *Far Eastern Quarterly* 13 (1954), 334–7.

category of 'having' (or a French '*il y a*') and scarcely permitted them to masquerade effectively as equivalents of our 'to be or not to be.' "

This is no doubt true. The difficulty, however, is that *yu* and *wu*, used philosophically, no longer operate as transitive verbs, but as nouns, and that this happens in Chinese texts long before the coming of Buddhism to China. In such cases, terms like "being and non-being" or "existence and non-existence," despite their admittedly supercharged Occidental associations, seem the closest—indeed almost the only—feasible equivalents. What then are the translators to do if they are to be denied their use? Their reply has been well nigh unanimous, as shown, for example, by the way in which they have handled the passage in *Lao-tzu*, chap. 2: *Yu wu hsiang sheng* 有無相生, "*Yu* and *wu* generate one another." Thus in French we find for this:

"L'être et le non-être" (Julien, Wieger, Duyvendak[2]).

In German:

"Sein und Nichtsein" (Strauss, Richard Wilhelm, Forke[3]).

In English:

"Existence and non-existence" (Legge, Lionel Giles, John C. H. Wu,[4] Erkes, Hughes[5]);

"Being and Not-being" (Waley);

"Being and non-being" (Lin Yutang[6]).

This list, though far from exhaustive, contains some rather impressive names.[7] Rather than believe that none of these men was aware of the difficulties involved, I personally find it far easier to suppose that they translated the way they did because they could find no real alternative. Boodberg himself, unfortunately, has failed to suggest any such alternative.

2. *Hsing erh shang* 形而上 (What is above shapes) and
*Hsing erh hsia* 形而下 (What is within shapes)

These phrases occur once in the *Yi Ching* and, more frequently, in Neo-Confucianism. In the *Yi Ching* they are rendered by Legge as "that which is antecedent to the material form" and "that which is subsequent to the material form,"[8] while by Wilhelm they are rendered (in close agreement with my own version) as "what is above form" and "what is within form."[9] As found in

---

[2] *Tao Tŏ King* (Paris, 1953), 7.
[3] *Geschichte der alten chinesischen Philosophie* (Hamburg, 1927), 263.
[4] In *T'ien Hsia Monthly* 9 (1939), 404.
[5] *Chinese Philosophy in Classical Times* (London & New York, 1942), 145.
[6] *The Wisdom of China and India* (New York, 1942), 584.
[7] The only exceptional reading I have found is that of Carus, whose "to be and not to be" would surely be objected to by Boodberg. Yet even Carus elsewhere (e.g., *Lao-tzu*, chap. 40) translates "existence and non-existence."
[8] *Sacred Books of the East*, XVI, 377.
[9] Richard Wilhem, *I Ching* (English translation by Cary Baynes, New York, 1950), I, 347.

Neo-Confucianism (Chu Hsi), Le Gall translates them either as "imperceptible" and "corporel" or as "supérieur à la forme" and "matériel,"[10] while Bruce translates "the corporeal" and "the incorporeal,"[11]

Boodberg, however, comments that "parallel passages immediately following our phrases in the *Yi ching* require considering *erh* as an interverbal conjunction and *hsing* and *shang* (*hsia*) as verbs. Is then the first phrase to be understood as 'what is shaped (or: shapes) and transcends (become supernal?),' and if so, what did that exactly mean?"

I am afraid I cannot satisfactorily answer this question. This does not greatly disturb me, however, because I believe there is excellent grammatical ground for rejecting the interpretation entirely as far as the *Yi Ching* (let along Neo-Confucianism) is concerned. This becomes apparent as soon as we reproduce the *Yi Ching* text in which our two key phrases appear, followed by the allegedly "parallel passages":

形而上者謂之道
形而下者謂之器
化而裁之謂之變

(Then follow two other lines essentially parallel to line 3.)

It is apparent that the seeming parallelism between these several lines is destroyed by one vital difference: the presence in lines 1 and 2 of the particle *che* 者, clearly making noun phrases out of the preceding *hsing erh shang* (*hsia*), in contrast to the accusative pronoun *chih* 之 of line 3 (and the following two unquoted lines), which equally clearly gives verbal force to the corresponding three preceding words. Legge senses this distinction when he translates these latter words as "transformation and shaping" (in contradistinction to his "that which is antecedent... and that which is subsequent" for lines 1 and 2). And though this distinction appears less clearly in Wilhelm's translation ("that which transforms things and brings them together"), he goes even further than Legge by suggesting that line 3 and the two lines following have been wrongly transposed to their present position in the text, and really belong to a passage two paragraphs lower down where the wording is very similar. Thus for him, as for Legge, it is plain that they do not constitute true parallels to the *hsing erh shang* (*hsia*) lines that precede.

3. *T'i* 體 (Substance or Essence)
   and *Yung* 用 (Functioning)

Here again there is considerable unanimity on the part of the translators: "substance and function" (Levenson[12] and Hellmut Wilhelm[13]); "substance, or

---

[10]Stanislas Le Gall, *Le philosoph Tchou Hi* (Shanghai, 2nd ed., 1923), 81 and 90.
[11]J. P. Bruce, *The Philosophy of Human Nature* (London, 1922), 274.
[12]In Wright, *op. cit.* (note 1 above), 155.
[13]In *Journal of the History of Ideas* 12 (1951), 55.

body, and function; the fundamental and phenomenal" (Soothill and Hodous[14]); "substance and operation" (Bruce[15]); "substance and application" (Liebenthal[16]); "essence and function" (Nivison[17]). Boodberg, however, objects that "Chinese *t'i* never developed the subtlety of our 'essence' and 'substance,' having remained close to the level of 'embodiment' or 'form.'"

The important consideration here is that "embodiment" and "form," while usually entirely satisfactory for *t'i* when occurring alone, are entirely too concrete and physical in their connotations to express the added rather metaphysical overtones it acquires as soon as it appears in the famous phrase, *t'i* and *yung*. In this formula, *t'i* signifies the inherent, enduring and fundamental (hence "internal") qualities of a thing or situation, in contrast to *yung*, which has reference to its functional, fluctuating and secondary (hence "external") manifestations.

This distinction of "inner" and "outer" is, as pointed out by Liebenthal (*loc. cit.*), clearly expressed in the *Tz'u-hai* dictionary's definition of *t'i-yung* (*sub t'i*, definition 10): "What is visible externally is *yung*; what is self-complete (*chü* 具) internally is *t'i*." Something of the same extended connotation for *t'i* also occurs in the term *pen-t'i lun* 本體論 (discussion on fundamental or original *t'i*), the modern Chinese coined equivalent for the "ontology" of Western philosophy. "Substance" certainly seems here more apposite for it than either "embodiment" or "form."

That *t'i* should thus acquire metaphysical overtones in certain contexts should not surprise us when we remember that the term *t'i-yung* itself, while popular in Neo-Confucian and later writings, is probably of Chinese Buddhist origin.[18] There it often occurs in conjunction with a third term, *hsiang* 相 (*laksana*), as, for example, in the opening paragraphs of the *Awakening of Faith*, where the three words are respectively rendered by Suzuki as "quintessence," "activity" and "attributes."[19] Elsewhere in Buddhism, however, *t'i* and *yung* are paired together without *hsiang*, as, for example, in the definition given for them by Chih-k'ai (538–597): "*T'i* refers to the (non-phenomenal) Reality (*shih-hsiang* 實相), which lacks all differentiation; *yung* refers to the

---

[14]Cf. their *Dictionary of Chinese Buddhist Terms* (London, 1937), 488b.

[15]*Philosophy of Human Nature*, 4.

[16]Walter Liebenthal, *The Book of Chao* (Peiping, 1948), 19.

[17]In Wright, *op. cit.*, 118.

[18]Cf. the citations in Fung 2, pp. 366 and 375. Though T'ang Yung-t'ung, in his study of the Neo-Taoist Wang Pi, himself uses the term *t'i-yung* to describe Wang's thinking, this term does not seem to be actually present in Wang's own writings (nor have I found it in other early non-Buddhist writings). See T'ang's article (transl. by Walter Liebenthal) in *Harvard Journal of Asiatic Studies* 10 (1947), 143.

[19]D. T. Suzuki, *Açvaghosha's Discourse on the Awakening of Faith in the Mahāyāna* (Chicago, 1900), 53. This is a translation of the version of the *Ch'i-hsin Lun* by Śikṣānanda, 652–710 (*Taishō* ed. no. 1667; vol. 32, p. 584b), but the same terms also appear in the version attributed to Paramārtha, 497–569 (*ibid.* no. 1666; vol. 32, p. 575c).

totality of (phenomenal) *dharmas* (*fa* 法), which are non-identical in their graded distinctions."[20] Nor is it surprising to find the term *pen-t'i* (fundamental or original *t'i*) likewise recorded in the Buddhist dictionaries as a Buddhist expression.

In such Buddhist contexts, therefore (and, by extension, in later non-Buddhist contexts as well), it seems evident that words like "embodiment" or "form" cannot adequately express the full significance of *t'i*.

### 4. *Jen* 仁 (Love)

In his study of the historical evolution of the Confucian virtue *jen*, Dubs has shown that its essential significance is "love for others"; sometimes, however, the word has been narrowly interpreted to signify primarily the *graded* kind of love deemed appropriate for a Confucian hierarchical society, whereas at other times it has been broadened into a much more impartial and universalistic concept.[21] My own rendering of *jen* simply as "love," therefore, was an attempt to find a convenient mean between these interpretations, most readily covering its shifting meanings throughout its long history. This rendition is not unique, for it has also been used or suggested by such scholars as Bruce[22] and Tjan Tjoe Som.[23]

Boodberg, however, prefers the more specific terms "humanity" or "co-humanity."[24] "With Bodde's 'love' made so much of by every Confucian writer," he remarks, "the non-sinological reader will keep wondering as to their motivation in persistently rejecting the Mohist doctrine of 'comprehensive love' (*chien-ai*, here 'love' is an entirely legitimate rendering), when he is not trying to brush off the familiar connotations of Agape, Eros, or Amor Dei that come to hover over *jen*...."

My justifications for "love" are four in number:

(1) By explicitly stating in the Preface to my translation (Fung 2, pp. xvi-xvii) that *jen* does not, like *ai* mi, include the idea of sexual love, and that, in its narrowest sense, it denotes a *graded* love, I had hoped to save the reader from the ambiguities feared by Boodberg.

(2) Boodberg's argument for "humanity" or "co-humanity" rests primarily on the semantic equation between *jen* and its homophone *jen* ("man"), occurring three times in the Confucian classics in the formula: "*Jen* (humanity)

---

[20] *Statements on the Lotus Sūtra* 法華文句, *chüan* 3b (*Taishō* no. 1718; vol. 34, p. 38a).

[21] H. H. Dubs, "The Development of Altruism in Confucianism," *Philosophy East and West* 1.1 (April 1951), 48–55.

[22] In his *Philosophy of Human Nature* and *Chu Hsi and His Masters* (London, 1923).

[23] In his translation of the *Po Hu T'ung* (2 vols.; Leyden, 1949, 1952), esp. I, 292–3, where he offers justification for this rendering.

[24] Both terms are suggested by him in his review. However, in his earlier "Semasiology of Some Primary Confucian Concepts," 330 (cited in note 1 above), he definitely gives preference to "co-humanity" on the ground that this avoids the European and non-Chinese connotations evoked by "humanity."

means *jen* (man or mankind)."[25] Readers familiar with this formula, however, may be surprised to realize that in an even greater number of cases *jen* is defined, or at least referred to in the classics, in terms of that very word *ai*, for which Boodberg himself concedes "love" to be a legitimate rendering. Thus we read: "It (*jen*) means to love (*ai*) others" (*Analects*, XII, 22); "The man of *jen* loves (*ai*) others" (*Mencius*, IVb, 28); "For the man of *jen*, there is nobody (or nothing) that he does not love (*ai*)" (*ibid.*, VIIa, 46); "He is content with his circumstances and genuine in his *jen*, therefore he can practice love (*ai*)" (*Yi Ching*, Appen. III; Wilhelm, I, 317);"*Jen* serves to love (*ai*) them (the people)" (*Book of Rites*, chap. 17; Legge, XXVIII, 98).

Similar statements, moreover, are common in the non-classical literature of Chou and later times, e.g., the Later Mohists,[26] the *Kuo-yü*,[26a] the *Huai-nan-tzu*,[27] Tung Chung-shu (at least four times! ),[28] the *K'ung-tzu Chia-yü*,[29] Han Yü,[30] Ch'eng Yi,[31] Chu Hsi,[32] and, in the nineteenth century, the eclectic T'an Ssu-t'ung.[33] Thus many Chinese thinkers have explicitly described *jen* in terms of *ai*, "love."

(3) As already indicated, there is a definite advantage, when translating a term with extended meanings like *jen*, to use a similarly broad English term like "love," rather than narrower words like "humanity" or "co-humanity" which, admirable though they be in certain contexts, hardly fit at all in others. What are we to do, for example, when told by Tung Chung-shu (Fung 2, p. 52)

---

[25]*Mencius*, VIIb, 16; *Doctrine of the Mean*, chap. 28; *Book of Rites*, chap. 7 (Legge, *Sacred Books of the East*, XXVIII, 333).

[26]Cf. their definition (cited in Fung 1, p. 275): "*Jen* is to love (*ai*)."

[27]Chap. 20: "What is called *jen* is the love (*ai*) of others." Cited in Tjan Tjoe Som, *op. cit.*, I, 293.

[28]Cf. *Ch'un-ch'iu Fan-lu*, chap. 29: "The standard for *jen* lies in showing love (*ai*) to others, not the self" (cited in Fung 2, p. 38, and Tjan, *loc. cit.*); chap. 30: "*Jen* without wisdom means love (*ai*) without discrimination" (cited in Fung 2, p. 39); chap. 58: "If we examine the purpose of Heaven, (we see that) it is boundless and infinitely *jen* .... The purpose of Heaven is ever to love (*ai*) and confer benefit" (cited in Fung 2, pp. 52–53); chap. 59: "*Jen* means to love (*ai*) others" (cited in Tjan, *loc. cit.*). These definitions scarcely support Boodberg in his decision to render *jen* as "co-humanization" when speaking of "Tung Chung-shu's great formula for the 'co-humani-zation' of the universe."

[29]Cf. R. P. Kramers, *K'ung Tzu Chia Yü* (Leyden, 1950), sect. 9, p. 242, where three disciples of Confucius, on being asked by him to define *jen*, reply respectively that it is "to make others love (*ai*) yourself," "to love (*ai*) others," "to love (*ai*) yourself."

[30]"A love (*ai*) for everyone is called *jen*." Cited in Fung 2, p. 409.

[31]Cf. citation in Fung 2, p. 517, where Ch'eng Yi states that from a man's "feeling of distress, which is linked to love (*ai*),...one may deduce that he (innately also) possesses the quality of *jen*."

[32]Cf. Chu's commentary on *Analects*, I, 3: "*Jen* is the Principle (*li*) of love (*ai*), it is the virtue of the heart." Cited in Soothill, *Analects of Confucius* (1910), 104.

[33]Cf. citation in Fung 2, p. 693: "There is something supremely great and supremely subtle .... It has no name, but we call it the 'ether.' As made manifest in action, Confucius...referred to it as *jen* .... Mo Tzu referred to it as universal love (*chien ai*). The Buddha referred to it...as compassion and mercy. Jesus referred to it...as loving (*ai*) others as oneself.... The scientists refer to it as the power of love (*ai*) and attraction."

that "the beautiful expression of *jen* lies in Heaven, for Heaven *is jen*"? Or when Wang Shou-jen (Fung 2, p. 599) says of the great man that "when he sees plants and trees being torn and broken, he will certainly experience a feeling of sympathy and compassion...because in his *jen* he is one with the plants and trees"? In these contexts "love" certainly seems to hit the mark better than do Boodberg's narrower alternatives.

(4) Finally, there is the stylistic convenience that "love" can much more readily be converted into a verb or adjective than can "humanity" or "co-humanity."[34] This is no small advantage when translating a text the size of Fung Yu-lan's, in which *jen*, functioning as verb or adjective, occurs many times.

5. *Yi* 意 (Idea) and *Yi* 義 (Righteousness,
   or, very occasionally, Concept)

Here again Boodberg's objection is that these words belong to the "super-charged" vocabulary of Western philosophy. "*Yi* [the first *yi*]," he says, "never acquired the pregnant richness of the 'idea' of Western tradition, and the other *yi*, mistranslated 'righteousness' and 'concept,' hardly ever trans-cended the meaning of 'congruity.'"

The difficulty here is that, not only in "idea" but also in its Chinese coun-terpart *yi* (the first *yi*), we have to do with words that can operate both on philosophical and non-philosophical levels of meaning. On the non-philosophical level, there seems to be no objection to equating the two, as, for example, in the statement about Yang Hsiung (Fung 2, p. 137): "Nor would he do anything that did not accord with his own ideas (*yi*)."

What are we to do, however, in those admittedly rare cases where *yi* seems to be used as a technical philosophic term—for example, when Wang Pi (Fung 2, p. 184) talks about the relationship of *yi* to *hsiang*, "symbols," and *yen*, "words"? How are we to handle *yi* here, unless we translate it by that same word "idea" which we elsewhere give for it in ordinary non-philosophical contexts? Unfortunately Boodberg offers no suggestions at this point, and I myself have none.

As for the other *yi*, "mistranslated 'righteousness,'" let us grant that it may originally have meant something like "congruity." Creel says of it, for example: "Its sense is not simply that of what is 'right' or 'righteous' in the ordinary meaning of these words. It means rather that which is fitting and suitable."[35]

[34]On p. 330 of his "Semasiology," Boodberg suggests "co-human" and "co-humanize [oneself]" as variant forms for "co-humanity," yet on p. 328 he correctly points out that *jen* as a verb functions transitively. But to "co-humanize [oneself]" is scarcely transitive!

[35]H. G. Creel, *Confucius, the Man and the Myth* (New York, 1949), 134.

As used in Confucianism, however, *yi* means a good deal more than merely the passive conformity of the individual to a social norm, such as might be inferred from a word like "congruity." Rather, *yi* characterizes the conduct of those individuals who are consciously aware of the existence of certain moral standards and obligations, and who strive in their every act to live up to them to the best of their ability. In the words of Creel (*op. cit.*, 135): "It is a regulator of conduct similar to *li* and the Way; and one that constantly places his own responsibility squarely before the individual. For whereas the Way is general, and one may look to others for some guidance concerning it, the question of what is suitable in each given situation is one that the individual must decide for himself."

In the case of *yi*, as of *jen*, probably no single English term (such as "righteousness," "rightness," "justice," "moral duty") can fully convey the moral ramifications of the original. Any one of these, however, at least warns the reader that he is dealing with a positive moral concept, which is certainly not true in the case of such a colorless and amoral term as "congruity."[36]

### 6. *Li* 理 (Principle)

Though approving of this rendering, Boodberg then goes on to say: "One would wish we could devise an English rendering more faithfully registering the semantic range of *li*. Perhaps 'Ingrain' or '(Archetypal) Venation' would not be too awkward." My only comment is that I wish I could share this optimism. As far as "Ingrain" is concerned, I am even uncertain whether it is a noun, though I do know that a noun is certainly called for if we are to translate *li* at all.

### 7. *Liang Yi* 兩儀 (Two Forms)

Here at last I am glad to be able to agree that—at least in Neo-Confucian context—"Two Forms" is not too happy for *liang yi*, for which Boodberg's "paired congruities" may well be better. In its original *Yi Ching* context, however, I am less sure, since there the *liang yi* are generally understood to be the two primary lines (one divided, the other undivided) from which have been evolved the eight trigrams. Legge accordingly translates "two Forms," and it was probably overdependence on him which caused me to adopt the same rendering even in Neo-Confucian contexts.[37]

[36]Perhaps I am not being fair here, and perhaps Boodberg, despite his reference to "congruity," does not mean that he would actually use it as a translation for *yi*. In his "Semasiology," for example, after analyzing *yi* at length, he concludes (pp. 330-1): "Most Chinese contexts would become perfectly clear if *yi* were translated 'self-shipful compropriety' or 'proper selfshipfulness.'" "To this I must reply with regret that as far as I am concerned, even "congruity" seems preferable to neologisms such as these, concerning which I shall have more to say presently.

[37]Cf. Legge, *Sacred Books of the East*, XVI, 373. Wilhelm, *I Ching* (English ed., I, 342), translates a little differently: "two primary forces."

As used in Neo-Confucianism, however (especially in Chou Tun-yi's *Diagram of the Supreme Ultimate Explained*), the *liang yi* are usually interpreted as the *yin* and the *yang* which, since they do not have any definite physical shape, cannot very appropriately be described as the "Two Forms." Better is the term "Two Modes," extensively used by other translators of Chou's *Diagram Explained.*[38]

How tricky such terms can be, however, is exemplified by none other than Chu Hsi himself, who, though obviously well aware that Chou Tun-yi's *liang yi* are the *yin* and *yang*, in one passage of his *Conversations* elects to define them along quite different and more concrete lines such as would there justify the rendering "Two Forms." Thus he tells us, using some of the very phraseology of Chou's *Diagram Explained* (Fung 2, p. 546): "There is a division into the *yin* and the *yang*, and the Two Forms (*liang yi*) are thus established. These Two Forms are Heaven and Earth, and are different in meaning from the Two Forms associated with the pictured trigrams."

## CONCLUSION

I have already several times referred to Boodberg's article, "The Semasiology of Some Primary Confucian Concepts" (cited in note 1 above). This article now calls for closer examination, since its assumptions underlie many of the criticisms we have been discussing. What, precisely, does Boodberg mean when he speaks of "semasiology"? In his own words (*op. cit.*, 320), it is a

methodology...which combines the meticulousness of scientific observation and computation in establishing the range, frequency of occurrence, and environmental reflexes of a given logoid with a naïve but unshakable belief that within the diffuse and viscous cytoplasmic mass of its connotations there lurks an ascertainable and definable etymonic karyosome. To that belief is to be added the conviction that, once the nucleus of a Sinitic word is delineated with reasonable precision, a patient search through the rich catalogue of the contour forms of the etyma of our Mediterranean heritage would finally yield a silhouette of sufficiently congruous perimeter...

If this means, as I think it does, that we should try to establish phonetically, graphically and historically, the precise significance of a Chinese term, and then with equal care search our Indo-European linguistic treasury for that term most nearly coinciding with its contours, there seems to be nothing unreasonable here or even startlingly revolutionary. Indeed, as applied by Boodberg himself, the method results in some translations which, stylistically at

[38] E.g., Bruce, *Chu Hsi and His Masters*, 130, and C. P. Hsu, *Ethical Realism in Neo-Confucian Thought* (Peiping, 1933), 26; also Forke, *Geschichte der neueren chinesischen Philosophie* (Hamburg, 1938), 48: "die beiden Modi"; Le Gall, *op. cit.*, 36, and Chow Yih-ching, *La philosophie morale dans le Néo-Confucianisme* (Paris, 1954), 42: "les deux modes." Gabenlentz's *Thai-Kih-Thu* (Dresden, 1876) was not available to me.

least, are perfectly comprehensible and usable: "lordling" for *chün-tzu* (ordinarily "superior man," "gentleman"), "regimen" for *cheng* ("government"), "Form" for *li* ("rites," "propriety"), "co-humanity" for *jen*.

As against these, however, it also yields "translations" which I regretfully find it hard to describe other than as neologistic monstrosities: "enrectivity, arrectivity" for *te* (ordinarily "virtue," "power"), "compagination" for *hsing* ("punishments"), "selfshipful compropriety, proper selfshipfulness" for *yi*. To me, at least, there is something wrong with a methodology when it results in translations which must themselves be translated before they can be properly understood.

A basic difficulty, it seems to me, is Boodberg's apparent conviction that a translation can be adequate only if it maintains *etymological* (and not merely *conceptual*) congruency with the original term. Unfortunately, in languages as far removed from each other as Chinese and English, the attempt to find such etymological congruencies can only sometimes be successful; in many other cases it inevitably imposes such a strain on the recipient language as to compel the translator to resort to bizarre neologisms of the sort noted. A basic canon of translation, in my opinion, is that it should pay careful heed to the peculiar genius of *both* the languages between which it operates, and not over-arbitrarily try to force the one into the Procrustean bed of the other. On this point it is instructive to see the way in which Chinese has translated many modern Western terms: because of its concreteness, it often tends to translate nominally terms which, in their original languages, have verbal derivation, for example, "(railroad) train," which in Chinese becomes *huo ch'e*, lit. "fire vehicle."

I do not mean to imply, of course, that the attempt to discover Chinese etymologies should be abandoned. Unless readily translatable and understandable, however, I believe that such etymologies should be restricted to footnotes or explanatory comment, and not compressed into topheavy neologisms then erroneously called "translations." At this point, moreover, we need the further warning that the search for meanings should not neglect the possible semantic evolution undergone by a term in the millennia following its earliest occurrence. "Lordling," for example, *may* be an adequate rendering for *chün-tzu* in its pre-Confucian setting, but it certainly fails completely to convey the rich connotations accumulated by that term from Confucius onward (when "superior man" or "gentleman" become *conceptually* far more appropriate).[19] To translate *chün-tzu* as "lordling" in such cases would be like translating

[19]I question, however, whether even in pre-Confucian times *chün-tzu* had the possibly "perjorative value" suggested for it by Boodberg on p. 322 of his article. On the contrary, I believe that many passages could be cited from pre-Confucian literature to show that *chün-tzu* was then a respected designation. As only one example, cf. *Book of Odes* no. 251 (Waley transl., p. 182): "All happiness to our *Chün-tzu*, Father and mother of his people."

"science" as "knowledge" in a modern textbook, simply because "knowledge" is what we know the word originally meant.

Something of Boodberg's approach to translation appears also in Edward H. Schafer's article, "Non-translation and Functional Translation—Two Sinological Maladies" (see note 1 above), where we read (p. 251): "The chief if not the sole responsibility of the scholarly translator...is to convey, as precisely as he may in a different tongue, the sense of the *language* of the original." By this Schafer means that it is the literal wording of a phrase that holds primary importance and should be inserted in the translated text itself, whereas any paraphrastic significance it may have in its particular context—what I would call its "dictionary meaning"—should be subordinated to a footnote.[40]

Schafer's principle operates constructively as long as he applies it to terms whose literal meaning is readily translatable and understandable. In other cases, however, it leads to such weird results as "Penetralian," "Auriporphyrian," and "Protonotary Stimulant," suggested by him (p. 260) as renderings for certain official titles. The difficulty here, it seems to me, lies in Schafer's insistence on the universality of his principle, without making allowance for several pertinent considerations:

(1) What type of term is it that is being translated? Geographical names, official titles, and the like (which are the main concern of Schafer's article) are as a rule easier to translate literally than are philosophical and psychological terms (for which, in many cases, no really "literal" translation is possible).

(2) How important is the term being translated to the translation as a whole? A political scientist, for example, reading a Chinese historical text, may conceivably welcome "Officiant Penetralian" as the more-or-less literal rendering of *shih-chung* 侍中 . I strongly suspect, however, that a student of Chinese thought, reading a philosophical text in which the identical title happens to occur, will be more than happy to settle for such looser but more immediately understandable "dictionary" renditions as "President" or "Secretary," permitting him the sooner to get back to his philosophical reading.

(3) Does a term's literal meaning still exist as a living reality in the minds of the persons who use it (and who hear or read it)? Or has its vividness faded into a mere cliché or convention, used unthinkingly whenever one wishes to evoke the "real," i.e., the "dictionary" meaning of the term? A case in point

---

[40]I have doubts about the way in which Schafer uses "connotation" and "denotation" to describe these two kinds of meaning, but I shall not discuss them here. Instead, for the sake of simplicity, I shall use the terms "literal meaning" and "dictionary meaning" (i.e., the meaning which a dictionary or other authoritative source or evidence would indicate a term as really having in a specific context, irrespective of its usual "literal meaning"). For example, "of Scotland or its inhabitants" is the literal meaning of the word "Scotch," but "whiskey" and "parsimonious" are both recognized "dictionary meanings" for it when it occurs in certain contexts.

is the colloquial *yao-fan-ti*, whose literal meaning, "demander of food," has become entirely swallowed up in its dictionary meaning of "beggar." I doubt whether one in a thousand of the Chinese who use this term ever stops to think of its literal meaning. Why, therefore, unless one wants to be pedantic (or is writing a philological treatise), translate it other than as "beggar"? In such a familiar case, indeed, even a footnote reference to "demander of food" seems superfluous.

(4) What kind of text is it that is being translated? A work in which literary style is of the essence—for example a T'ang poem—would seem to call for a different approach, and a different kind of literalness, than would a text—say the chapter of a dynastic history—in which it is the content, not style, that is important.

(5) For whom is the translation primarily intended? Philological details that may seem desirable to the sinologist may well repel the less specialized reader, especially when he finds them interfering with his ready comprehension of the text as a whole.

Perhaps, having said all this, we can now try to formulate a few general conclusions of our own. A good translation, it seems to me, should ideally try to meet at least three criteria:

(1) *Stylistic intelligibility, simplicity and naturalness.* This means avoidance of clumsy locutions, awkward or hard-to-understand neologisms, exoticisms, and the other faults that often arise from over-labored and over-literal adherence to the original text. Such over-literalness, however, need not always spring from scholarly over-caution, for there is another variety as well, deliberately cultivated by certain translators in the hope thereby of enhancing the quaintness and color of their work. For such translators *yao-fan-ti* will always be "demander of food," never "beggar," and this despite the fact that the image evoked by the original term is far paler than that evoked by it for Westerners in its literal English dress.

The rule here might be: translate colorfully only what is authentically intended to be colorful in the original; for the rest, be content with more sober (but for that reason often more idiomatic and more comprehensible) language. And if, having done this, the translator still feels the literal wording to be important, footnotes are always available for that purpose.

(2) *Consistency.* This means that a technical vocabulary consistently used in the original should as much as possible be reproduced by a similarly consistent vocabulary in the translation. This is why, as I have pointed out, I prefer an unprecise English word like "love" for a similarly unprecise Chinese word like *jen*, rather than other narrower and therefore less widely usable words. And if, as often happens, consistency becomes unfeasible despite all efforts, it is then the translator's duty to warn the reader of this fact. Here I gladly accept Boodberg's reproof for not having always followed this principle

myself, e.g., when, on p. 521 of my translation, I without notice rendered *li*—elsewhere "Principle"—as "truth."

(3) *Accuracy.* By this I do not merely mean accuracy of meaning—vital though such accuracy of course is—but also fidelity to the spirit and form in which the original is written. From this point of view, as I have tried to show, a merely literal translating of the *language* of the original does not always achieve its purpose. Nor does a translation which considers only a word's earliest etymology, without examining the semantic evolution it may have undergone in later times. We have seen, for example, the troubles that "embodiment" or "form" give us when we come to translate *t'i* in the phrase *t'i-yung.*

At the heart of our problem, as far as philosophical translation is concerned, is that we are not there dealing with sticks or stones, official titles or place names, but with ideas, ideals and convictions bearing highly charged emotional and intellectual overtones, the verbal expressions of which therefore equally consist of "idiosyncratic and peculiarly supercharged terms." This, of course, is just as true of Chinese as of Occidental philosophy.

The translator consequently finds himself in the unenviable position of having to grapple, on both sides of his translation, with vocabularies that are not merely supercharged, but *differently* supercharged, owing to the divergent linguistic and cultural backgrounds from which they spring. No matter how much he would like to escape from this predicament, he finds himself compelled in a large percentage of cases, owing to the very nature of his subject—the fact that he is dealing with ideas and not with things—to use precisely those supercharged terms of the one civilization in order to translate the equally (but differently) supercharged terms of the other. Obviously the risk involved is great, yet equally obviously it is one he must assume, since all too often the only alternative to thus translating supercharged Chinese term A by the almost (but not quite) congruent supercharged Western term $A^1$ is either not to translate at all or to invent bewildering neologisms of his own. The same problem, of course, arises in reverse in translating Western or other non-Chinese ideas into Chinese.[41]

Among techniques for circumventing, or seeming to circumvent, some of these difficulties, the easiest but least satisfactory is not to translate at all, but merely transliterate, troublesome terms. Save for a few terms scarcely translatable (such as *yin* and *yang*), or those with obscure or debatable meanings, I fully agree with Schafer's condemnation of this practice as one of our commonest "sinological maladies." Far better is it in cases of doubt to provide the reader with both the literal and "dictionary" meanings of the term, plus whatever further information is deemed desirable.

[41]Cf. Arthur F. Wright, "The Chinese Language and Foreign Ideas," cited in note 1 above.

Had I myself done this more extensively in my translation of Fung Yu-lan's *History*, I suspect that I might have obviated some of Boodberg's criticisms. Here, however, I was confronted by special inhibiting considerations: the fact that the text was already formidably long, that it was the work of a contemporary Chinese scholar whose narrative I did not wish to interrupt more than minimally necessary, and that my translation was intended for the educated layman as well as the specialist. Certainly it seems true that detailed semantic investigations are technically far more feasible in specialized monographs than in broad surveys of the Fung Yu-lan type.

Obviously, no sustained translation from a language and civilization as alien as those of China can ever meet with equal satisfaction *all* the criteria we have been discussing. Translation necessarily represents a compromise between several competing desiderata, in the reaching of which, since it is not a science but an art, the translator must rely more on flexibility of judgment and a sense of balanced values than on any slavish adherence to fixed rules.[42] Under the best of circumstances, frustration remains one of his major occupational hazards, and often he must think bitterly of the truth of Kumārajīva's dictum, that translating is like the pre-chewing of food that is to be fed to others: in either case the product is bound to be poorer in taste and quality than the original.

Yet despite all the frustrations and facile criticisms to which the translator is exposed, certain positive compensations remain for him. One is the insight his work gives him into a civilization other than his own, and the sharpened insight into his own civilization that this experience affords. Another is the intellectual satisfaction coming from successfully pulling a little closer together ideas belonging to divergent cultural traditions, and from his consciousness that in so doing he is doing what only few people can do well. And a third is the moral satisfaction of knowing that he is thereby contributing—if only in small measure—to the world's store of knowledge.

[42] If I myself have seemed onesided in stressing the dangers of over-literalness, it is because scholarly translators often appear less conscious of these than of the opposite dangers of under-literalness. Most of us are quick enough to condemn translators whose laziness or ignorance allows them to be content with loose paraphrase, or those other translators who (sometimes for love of fame or money) are ready to glamorize and "jazz up" their work by filling it with modern idioms and ideas hopelessly alien to the original.

# LIEH-TZU AND THE DOVES:
## A PROBLEM OF DATING

Concerning the dating of the Taoist work *Lieh-tzŭ* 列子 there is, as is well known, a wide divergence of opinion, for whereas most Western scholars accept it as a work of the third century B.C., modern Chinese scholarship tends to regard it as a forgery of the third or fourth century A.D. Among the passages used to support the latter dating is that from chapter eight, describing the release of living doves on New Year's day, in which some scholars believe there is a Buddhist influence. The passage in question, whose setting is the city of Han-tan (capital of the state of Chao) in the fifth century B.C., reads as follows:[1]

The people of Han-tan (had the habit), on New Year's day, of presenting (live) doves to Chien-tzŭ.[2] This greatly pleased Chien-tzŭ, who liberally rewarded those (who made the donations). To a stranger who asked the meaning of this (custom), Chien-tzŭ explained that the release of living creatures (*fang-shêng* 放生) on New Year's day was a manifestation of kindness. "But," said the stranger, "if the people, knowing of Your Lordship's desire to release them, compete with one another in catching them, those that die in the process must indeed be numerous. If you really wish to let them live, the best way would be to prohibit the people from catching them at all. For if they have to be caught in order to be released, the kindness does not compensate for the cruelty." Chien-tzŭ acknowledged that he was right.

Another less developed version of the same story appears in the seventeenth chapter of *K'ung Ts'ung-tzŭ* (a work of Later Han or post-Han date); in it sparrows (*ch'iao* 雀) take the place of doves (*chiu* 鳩), and the setting, while still Han-tan, is shifted from the fifth to the third century B.C.:[3]

---

[1] Translation slightly modified from that of L. Giles, *Taoist Teachings from the Book of Lieh Tzŭ* (London, 2nd printing, 1925), pp. 118, 119.

[2] *I.e.*, Chao Chien-tzŭ 趙簡子, head of the Chao clan in the state of Chin, who died in 458 B.C. See E. Chavannes, *Mémoires historiques de Se-ma Ts'ien* (Paris, 1905), v, 40. Han-tan 邯鄲 was some ten *li* south-west of the present city by that name in southern Hopei.

[3] *K'ung Ts'ung-tzŭ* 孔叢子, 5/8a–b (Ssŭ-pu pei-yao ed.).

The people of Han-tan (had the habit), on New Year's day, of presenting (live) sparrows to the King of Chao, which they tied together with varicoloured cords. This greatly pleased the King, and Shen-shu reported it to Tzŭ-shun,[4] . . . saying: "The releasing of them on New Year's day is a manifestation of the giving of life."

Dr. Waley, who accepts the early dating of *Lieh-tzŭ*, writes as follows about the anecdote from it we have just quoted:[5]

In certain passages of *Lieh Tzŭ* critics have seen references to Buddhism; thus the anecdote (viii, 24) about "release of living things" as part of a New Year ceremony has been interpreted as referring to the Buddhist custom of *fang-shêng* ("release of live things"). It remains to be proved that this Buddhist custom was known in China at anything like so early a date as the third or fourth century A.D., the period to which critics attribute the forging of *Lieh Tzŭ*.

Dr. Waley is unquestionably right in denying the possibility of Buddhist influence, for the Buddhist practice to which he alludes does not seem to have become widespread before the T'ang dynasty, and is apparently first referred to only during the reign of Emperor Wu of the Liang (early sixth century).[6] Does this fact in itself, however, in any way prove the counter thesis that this *Lieh-tzŭ* passage is actually a product of the third century B.C.? Obviously it does not, and therefore, in what follows, we shall look for external datable evidence in an effort to determine whether any specific period can be found which, more than others, possessed a cultural milieu favouring the appearance of a story of this kind. The Han dynasty, as we shall see, constituted such a period, for during it there developed what might almost be called a cult of doves (*chiu*), as evidenced not only in the alleged custom of releasing doves on New Year's day, but in other stories and practices as well.

### 1. *The presentation of dove-staffs to the aged*

During the Later Han dynasty, annually in the eighth month, according to *Hou Han-shu*, 15/2b, a "registration of households" (*an hu* 案 戶) took place throughout the empire, in the course of which the populace of

---

[4] *I.e.*, K'ung Tzŭ-shun 孔 子 順, a seventh-generation descendant of Confucius who was councillor to King An-hsi (276–243) of Wei during the latter part of that ruler's reign. See Chavannes, *op. cit.*, v, 431, note 5.

[5] Arthur Waley, *Three Ways of Thought in Ancient China* (London, 1939), p. 258.

[6] See citations in Ting Fu-pao, comp., *Fo-hsüeh ta-tz'ŭ-tien* (Great Dictionary of Buddhism) [Shanghai, 2nd ed., 1929], *sub fang-shêng*. The earliest of these is the biography of Hsieh Cheng 謝 徵 in *Liang shu*, 50/5a, where it is stated that Hsieh "composed an 'Essay on Releasing Living Things' (*Fang-shêng wên* 文), for which he was conferred favours by the world." This statement is immediately followed by a date corresponding to 529. (References to the dynastic histories are to the Chung-hua Book Co.'s 1923 photolithographic reprint of the 1739 Palace edition.)

each prefecture was ranked according to age. On this occasion the local authorities held a reception for the aged, at which persons over seventy were given millet gruel, while those over eighty were in addition presented with staffs, the handles of which were decorated with the figure of a dove. The explanation for this dove figure, as given by the text, is that "the dove is a bird which has no difficulty in swallowing (its food), and the wish here is that the aged should (likewise) have no difficulty in swallowing."

Without discussing the plausibility of this explanation, we should note that this practice of conferring dove-staffs is apparently unmentioned in texts dealing with the Former Han dynasty, so that it seems to be of Later Han origin. Like many official ceremonies inaugurated under the Later Han, however, it was undoubtedly inspired by statements in the ritualistic texts, specifically, in its case, by what is said in the *Yüeh-ling* (Monthly Commands) under the eighth month: "In this month, support is given to the decrepit and aged. They are presented with stools and staffs, and distribution is made to them of millet gruel, drink and food."[7] Though this says nothing about the staffs being decorated with doves, the idea for so doing may possibly derive from another passage in *Chou-li* (where, however, the reference is to the second and not the eighth month): "In the middle (month) of spring, he (the Netter of Birds) nets the spring birds. He presents doves to nourish the aged of the country."[8]

Apart from what is said in *Hou Han-shu*, the existence of dove-staffs in Later Han times is attested by such writers of the day as Wang Ch'ung 王充 (A.D. 27-ca. 100),[9] Ying Shao 應劭 (ca. 140-ca. 206),[10] and Kao Yu 高誘 (fl. dur. 205-12).[11] Moreover, it is also evidenced by two objects of Han date of which Laufer, in separate publications, has provided illustrations. The first is a pottery hill-jar, on whose cover, moulded in low relief, appears a man leaning on a staff; a side panel of the same jar shows a similar figure, holding, however, not an ordinary staff, but what appears to be a bird-like object. Laufer, in commenting on its possible meaning, draws attention to the *Hou Han-shu* passage about dove-staffs we have just cited.[12]

---

[7] Cf. *Li chi*, ch. 4; tr. J. Legge in *Sacred Books of the East* (Oxford, 1885), xxvii, 287–88. Also contained in *Lü-shih ch'un-ch'iu*, viii, 1; tr. R. Wilhelm, *Frühling und Herbst des Lü Bu We* (Jena, 1928), p. 92.

[8] *Chou-li*, xxx; tr. E. Biot, *Le Tcheou li* (Paris, 1851), ii, 211.

[9] *Lun hêng*, ch. 36 (tr. A. Forke, *Lun-Hêng*, Berlin, 1911, ii, 84), in which Wang wonders why the staffs presented to aged persons should be surmounted by a dove rather than some other kind of bird.

[10] In the passage quoted from him below, on which see note 14.

[11] In his commentary on *Yüeh-ling*, as found in *Lü-shih ch'un-ch'iu* (see note 7), where he writes: "This (practice mentioned in *Yüeh-ling*) is the same as the present ranking of households, with its distribution to the aged of dove-staffs and gruel."

[12] B. Laufer, *Chinese Pottery of the Han Dynasty* (Leiden, 1909), Plate LVI, Fig. 2, and remarks on pp. 205, 206 (where he gives a somewhat garbled version of the *Hou Han-shu* passage). Unfortunately, Laufer's photograph is not clear enough to let us see for ourselves the bird which he says is there.

Likewise, in his other publication, Laufer reproduces, from a Chinese catalogue of bronzes, a drawing of a bronze staff handle, topped by a dove, which by the catalogue is labelled a "Han dove staff-head".[13]

## 2. *How doves saved the life of the Han founder*

There is a Han story according to which Kao-tsu, founder of the dynasty, while campaigning against Hsiang Yü in 205–204 B.C., was once saved by doves from capture by his opponent. This story is unknown in the accounts of his campaigns given by *Shih-chi* and *Han-shu*, and seems to have become current in written literature only toward the end of the Later Han, though many references to it occur in post-Han texts as well. The earliest version I have found is that by Ying Shao (ca. 140-ca. 206), in his *Fêng-su t'ung-yi* 風俗通義 :[14]

> It is popularly said that when Kao-tsu was battling with Hsiang Yü between Ching and So, he hid himself in a thicket of reeds. (Hsiang) Yü pursued him, but just then some doves were cooing above him, so that the pursuers believed surely nobody was there. Thus (Kao-tsu) succeeded in escaping, and so when he mounted the throne, he singled out this bird (for special attention). Hence (during the Han dynasty there arose the custom of) making dove-staffs for presentation to aged men.

The battle here mentioned is presumably that of June, 205 B.C., which took place between Ching 京 and So 索 , south of Jung-yang 滎 陽 (near the modern Chengchow, Honan). In the histories, however, it is recorded as a victory for Kao-tsu, with no mention of his having had to hide from Hsiang Yü.[15] Whereas this version of the story makes it the inspiration for the practice of conferring dove-staffs on the aged, another version, slightly changed in locale and date, links it to the custom (described in *Lieh-tzǔ* and *K'ung Ts'ung-tzǔ*) of releasing doves on New Year's day. The earliest example of this second version found by me is that in *San Ch'i*

---

[13] Laufer, "The Bird-Chariot in China and Europe", in *Boas Anniversary Volume* (New York, 1906), p. 419, reproducing the drawing found in the eighteenth century catalogue of imperial bronzes, *Hsi-ch'ing ku-chien* 西 清 古 鑑, 38/19a–b (Shanghai: 1926 photolithographic reprint of the 1751 ed.). (In Laufer's article the reference is mistakenly given as 38/39.)

[14] Edition of the Centre franco-chinois d'études sinologiques, *Le Fong sou t'ong yi* (Peiping, 1943), p. 87. The story in question does not occur in the text proper of *Fêng-su t'ung-yi* now extant, but has been added to it from quotations found in several other works, of which the earliest is Li Tao-yüan's (d. 527) *Shui-ching chu* (Commentary on the Water Classic), 7/11b (Ssu-pu ts'ung-k'an ed.). Forke, in his translation of *Lun-hêng*, ii, 84, note 4, has already noted the passage.

[15] See H. H. Dubs, *History of the Former Han Dynasty* (Baltimore, 1938), i, 8c, 81.

*lüeh-chi* 三齊略記, a work by an unknown Chin author, today known only in quotation:[16]

> At Jung-yang there is a Well of Escape (Mien-ching 免井), and when the Duke of P'ei, (founder) of the Han, was fleeing from Hsiang Yü, he took refuge in this well. (At that time) there was a pair of doves perching above it. Someone said that the Duke of P'ei had fled into the well, but (Hsiang) Yü replied: "Were someone in the well, the doves would not be perching above it." Thereafter the Duke of P'ei saved himself from his danger. It is probably because of this that later, during the Han era, (there arose the custom of) releasing doves on New Year's day.

The events described here are presumably those of June/July, 204 B.C., when Kao-tsu was besieged by Hsiang Yü at Jung-yang, and succeeded only with great difficulty in escaping from the city.[17] The same story, in a somewhat telescoped form, also appears in the *Ti-li shu* 地理書, by Lu Têng 陸澄 (425–494):[18]

> Jung-yang has a well inside which the King of Han hid from Hsiang Yü. A pair of doves flew and perched on the well, so that (Hsiang) Yü supposed no one was there. Thus the Duke of P'ei succeeded in escaping, and on this account (the well) acquired its name (of Well of Escape). It is because of this that, during the Han era, (there arose the custom of) releasing doves on New Year's day.

Other versions of the story also exist (some in local gazetteers of relatively recent date), in which the well is variously named Well of Distress (Ô-ching 厄井), Well of Yao (Yao-ching 堯井), or Well of Pigeons (Po-ko-ching 鵓鴿井); its location, though usually placed in the general vicinity of Jung-yang, is in one case (that of the Well of Pigeons) shifted all the way to the neighbourhood of Lin-ch'êng 臨城 (in south central Hopei), *i.e.*, far north of the scene of Kao-tsu's actual campaigns against Hsiang Yü.[19]

### 3. *The dove-chariot*

Very occasionally, in Chinese writings on bronzes, references are made to certain small bronze objects termed *chiu-ch'e*, "dove-chariots", which are

---

[16] See *T'ai-p'ing yü-lan*, 29/5b (Ssu-pu ts'ung-k'an ed.), where it is quoted as *San Ch'i lüeh*. On this lost work see *Pu-Chin-shu yi-wên-chih* (Supplemental Treatise on Literature for the Chin History), in the K'ai-ming Book Co.'s *Êrh-shih-wu-shih pu-pien* (Supplemental Compilations on the Twenty-five Histories), iii, 3741, top.

[17] Dubs, *op. cit.*, i, 84, 85.

[18] Now lost, but quoted (as *Ti-li chih* 志) in *T'ai-p'ing yü-lan*, 921/6b.

[19] See the citations in *T'ai-p'ing yü-lan*, 189/9a; the *T'u-shu chi-ch'êng* encyclopaedia, ts'e 517, 29/27b (Chung-hua photolithographic ed. of 1934); and *P'ei-wên yün-fu*, p. 2116.1, *sub* Ô-ching (Commercial Press: Wan-yu wên-k'u ed. of 1938). Most of these recount only the story itself, without explicitly linking it either to the dove-staffs or the freeing of doves.

said in the texts to have been used as toys. They consist of the figure of a dove mounted between two chariot-like movable wheels, with the dove's tail being sometimes supported on a third smaller wheel. Usually a baby dove sits on the back of the adult bird, while others sometimes perch on her tail or breast. In the Chinese catalogues of bronzes picturing these dove-chariots, they are said to have originated in the Han dynasty and to have continued being made until the T'ang. Aside from the drawings found in these works, a very few actual specimens are extant in bronze collections today. In the West they have been illustrated and discussed in some detail by Laufer and Seligman, as well as, recently and more briefly, by Hentze.[20]

Despite the fact that Seligman wrote in ignorance of Laufer's earlier study,[21] the two men come to remarkably similar conclusions. Both point out that the Chinese dove-chariots are not unique, being paralleled in Europe by bird-chariots found at various Bronze Age sites. Though the European examples apparently vary considerably in date (Laufer assigns one to probably the eighth century B.C., whereas Seligman would date his examples around 1300), they are surely considerably older than the earliest Chinese examples, provided these do belong, as traditionally stated, to the Han dynasty.[22] It is the common conclusion of Laufer and Seligman, therefore, that the bird-chariot probably originated in Europe and spread from there to Han China (according to Laufer, probably via Siberia).

*Conclusions*

1. The *Lieh-tzŭ* anecdote about releasing doves on New Year's day has nothing to do with the Buddhist practice of *fang-shêng*, "releasing living things", since the latter is not mentioned before the sixth century A.D., whereas the latest date suggested for *Lieh-tzŭ* is only the third or fourth century A.D.

2. The Han dynasty saw the development of an interest in doves which manifested itself in: (a) the distribution to aged persons of staffs, the handles of which were decorated with the figure of a dove; (b) the alleged

---

[20] Laufer, "The Bird-Chariot in China and Europe" (see note 13); C. G. Seligman, "Bird-Chariots and Socketed Celts in Europe and China", *Journal of the Royal Anthropological Institute of Great Britain and Ireland*, n.s., vol. 23 (1920), 153–58; Carl Hentze, "Le symbolisme des oiseaux dans la Chine ancienne", *Sinologica*, vol. v, no. 2 (1957), 74, 75. All three articles contain good illustrations, but whereas Laufer and Seligman focus their attention on the bird-chariots *per se*, Hentze discusses these only in the context of a much broader theory, whose speculative nature and lack of precise documentation make it difficult for me to accept its conclusions.

[21] In a postscript, Seligman states that he became aware of the latter only after writing his own paper.

[22] The studies of Laufer and Seligman were made many years ago, and further research on this subject would be desirable.

custom of releasing doves on New Year's day; (c) the story of how the Han founder, Kao-tsu, while campaigning against Hsiang Yü, was saved from capture by the presence of doves above his hiding place (a story variously used to explain the practice both of a and b); and finally (d) the making of small bronze dove-chariots, believed by Laufer and Seligman to have originated in Bronze Age Europe and to have passed from there to China of the Han dynasty.

3. None of the datable texts cited in support of the foregoing developments is earlier than the first century A.D.; those connected with the Kao-tsu story, indeed, first appear only toward the end of the Later Han and continue into much later times. The evidence, therefore, points strongly to the first and second centuries A.D. (and not the Former Han) as the period when the cult of doves first really gathered momentum. In view of this fact, it seems extremely unlikely that the *Lieh-tzŭ* anecdote could have been written as early as the third century B.C., and much more probable that it too belongs to the first or second century A.D. Conceivably, indeed, it (as well as the parallel in *K'ung Ts'ung-tzŭ*) could have been written somewhat later, *i.e.*, sometime during the third or fourth century, which is where modern Chinese opinion has tended to date the *Lieh-tzŭ* as a whole. The Later Han, however, seems on the whole a more probable period, since it is then that most of the dove references occur.

4. I have no ready explanation as to why Han-tan is made the locale of the *Lieh-tzŭ* and *K'ung Ts'ung-tzŭ* stories, but appears in no other text. We have already seen, however, that the Kao-tsu story, though usually located in the general region around Jung-yang in Honan, is in one instance shifted to a place in Hopei well north of Han-tan.

5. The fact that the *Lieh-tzŭ* dove anecdote probably dates only from the Later Han, or, conceivably, is even post-Han, does not in itself, of course, necessarily invalidate the thesis that the *Lieh-tzŭ* as a whole belongs to the third century B.C. Such a thesis can be proved or disproved, however, only by painstakingly analysing the other stories in the book, and then synthesizing the resulting data.

## Marshes in *Mencius* and elsewhere

### A lexicographical note

Everyone who reads Professor Creel (hereafter Herrlee in these pages) knows that he can never be dull. To his writings he always brings a disciplined imagination, a limpid style, an unerring ability to focus on vital issues, and a concommitant ability to stimulate the mind of the reader—sometimes quite controversially so. Such is the stuff of great scholarship.

It is not Herrlee the scholar but Herrlee the pedagogue, however, who has quite unwittingly stimulated the writing of the present article. This he did long ago by preparing, with his collaborators Chang Tsung-ch'ien and Richard C. Rudolph, the three volumes of *Literary Chinese by the inductive method* (Chicago, 1938-39, 1952) on which generations of students of classical Chinese have been raised. Despite competition in recent years from other texts, as well as certain recognized weaknesses of its own, I have remained faithful to *Literary Chinese* for one all-compelling reason: the fact that it, more than any other textbook in its field I know, provides a genuinely cultural, as well as linguistic, introduction to Chinese civilization. Indeed, a very fitting subtitle for it might be *Chinese culture by the inductive method.*

In the third volume, that of *The Mencius,* I have nonetheless always regretted the decision to stop with the first three books, thereby depriving the student of some of the most famous chapters, notably the debates between Mencius and Kao Tzu on human nature. However, though there are some arid stretches in these first books which might have been deleted, they are of course balanced by other chapters of outstanding importance. One of the best is IIIa, 4, with its lengthy debate between Mencius and the follower of the agriculturalist Hsü Hsing. This provides one of the most vivid statements of Confucian social and economic theory, but besides this, the chapter is peppered with other cultural tidbits. At the very beginning the mention of the curious agricultural implements *lei* 耒 and *ssu* 耜 (wrongly rendered by Legge and others as "plow handles and shares" or the like) allows the teacher to say something about early Chinese agricultural technology. A little later, the iron implement used by Hsü Hsing gives opportunity to mention the beginning of the iron age in China. The "shrike-tongued barbarian of the south" who appears near the end vividly illustrates how intolerant Confucian culturalism could sometimes be. And somewhat earlier comes the unexpected excursion into Chinese mythology, with its description of the primeval flood, the conquest of which enabled the world to become fit for sedentary (and therefore, for the Chinese, civilized) human habitation.

In this same paragraph (the seventh in James Legge's arrangement) there is a sentence that has always puzzled me. It reads, in Legge's translation:[1]

> Shun committed to Yih the direction of the fire to be employed, and Yih set fire to, and consumed, *the forests and vegetation on* the mountains and *in* the marshes, so that the birds and beasts fled away to hide themselves. [Legge's italics]

How, one wonders, could marshes be set on fire? The commentators give no help—after all, there is nothing ethically or philosophically significant in a marsh—and the translators, for the most part, do no better. Thus, from the latter, we have the following renditions of the key second part of the sentence: "I mit le feu dans les montagnes et les marais et les purifia par l'incendie" (Couvreur).[2] "Yi fired the hills and bogs, and burnt them" (Lyall).[3] "Yih then burned away the undergrowth of mountain and marsh" (Giles).[4] "He then set fire to the mountains and marshes so that they were reduced to ruins" (Ware).[5] "Shun sent Yi with a burning torch to set fires in the hills and fens, and to burn them off" (Dobson).[6] The only translators who seem to be tacitly aware of the problem are Richard Wilhelm and D. C. Lau. The former translates: "I legte Feuer an die Berge und Dschungeln und verbrannte die Urwälder."[7] And Dr. Lau writes: "Yi set the mountains and valleys alight and burnt them."[8] Neither scholar, however, warns the reader that there is anything peculiar about the word paraphrased as "jungles" or "valleys."

---

[1] James Legge, *The Chinese classics*, II (Hong Kong & London, 1861), 126.

[2] Séraphin Couvreur, *Les Quatre livres* (Ho Kien Fou, 1895), 423. I am indebted to Professor Hans Bielenstein of Columbia University for sending me the wording of Couvreur's rendition.

[3] Leonard A. Lyall, *Mencius* (London & New York, 1932), 78.

[4] Lionel Giles, *The book of Mencius* (London, 1942), 60.

[5] James R. Ware, *The sayings of Mencius* (Mentor Books, 1960), 85.

[6] W.A.C.H. Dobson, *Mencius* (Toronto, 1963), 117.

[7] Richard Wilhelm, *Mong dsi (Mong ko)* (Jena, 1916; 2nd printing, 1921), 56. I am indebted to Professor Emeritus Hellmut Wilhelm of the University of Washington for sending me the wording of his father's rendition.

[8] D. C. Lau, *Mencius* (Penguin Books, 1970), 102.

The word in question is *tse* 澤, which during most of its history has normally signified "marsh" but today is undoubtedly best known as the first syllable in the personal name of Mao Tse-tung. In Herrlee's *Mencius,* vocabulary entry no. 712 defines *tse* as: "A marsh, a pool, moisture. Favor, kindness, beneficial influence. To moisten, to enrich, to benefit, to anoint. Smooth, glossy, slippery." These definitions are in general agreement with the standard dictionaries. In what follows, we will confine our discussion to the two primary concrete meanings of "marsh" and "pool" (broadening the latter, however, to include "pond/lake"), together with any further concrete meanings that may develop from these.

In Chou dynasty texts it is evident that *tse* was a general designation for almost any stationary, and probably usually shallow, expanse of water. Sometimes the *tse* was so shallow and covered with reeds and grasses as to be a real marsh, but at other times it was deep enough to permit the movement of boats or erection of fish-weirs; in such instances it seems better to term it (depending on size) a pool, pond, or lake. The former situation is illustrated by a speech in the *Tso chuan* under the year 522 B.C., in which the statesman Yen Tzu tells the duke of Ch'i: "The trees of the mountain forests are maintained [for your use] by the Heng-lu [an official title], the reeds and rushes of the marshes (*tse*) by the Chou-chiao [another title], and the fuel for fire of the thickets by the Yü-hou [still another title]."[9] The situation in which a *tse* corresponds to a lake is illustrated by a sentence in the *Chuang-tzu* describing the age of pristine perfection: "In that age the mountains had no paths or trails, the lakes (*tse*) no boats or fish-weirs."[10]

The distinction between *tse* as "marsh" and as "pool/pond/lake" is sometimes so vague that any precise translation becomes arbitrary.[11] The ambiguity of the word emerges clearly in another statement in the *Tso chuan* where we read: "When a stream is blocked up, it becomes a *tse.*"[12] Generally

[9] Chao 20: Legge, *Chinese classics,* V (London, 1872), 683b; Couvreur, *Tch'ouen Ts'iou et Tso Tchouan* (Ho Kien Fou, 1914), III, 323.

[10] Chap. 9: *Ssu-pu pei-yao* ed. (hereafter *SPPY*), 4/7a; Burton Watson, *The Complete works of Chuang Tzu* (New York & London, 1968), 105. The word liang 梁, translated "fish-weirs," is rendered by Watson as "bridges," but there are many passages in which it occurs in conjunction with *tse* and refers to a dam or other barrier built into the water to trap fish. See the decisive statement in the *Mo-tzu,* chap. 9: *SPPY* 2/3b; Y. P. Mei, *The ethical and political works of Motse* (London, 1929), 37, which tells how the virtuous administrator collects taxes on "the profits (*li* 利) of the mountain forests and of the lake weirs (*tse liang* 澤梁)," "Profits" can only signify fish profits here. See similarly *Mencius,* Ib, 5 (Legge, 38), as well as passages in other works.

[11] See, for example, the *Tso chuan* passage cited at note 16 below, where Legge translates *tse* as "marshes" and Couvreur as "bords des lacs." Actually, as we shall see, both renditions are probably inaccurate.

[12] Hsüan 12 (597 B.C.): Legge, 317b; Couvreur, I, 618.

speaking, however, it would seem, on the basis of many occurrences not cited here, that in early Chou times *tse*, in the meaning of "marsh," was somewhat less common than in later times, but in the meaning of "pool/pond/lake" was considerably more common. A possible reason, suggested here only very tentatively because much more research would be needed, is that *tse* meaning "marsh" was rivaled in early Chou times by another and possibly more popular word, *hsi* 隰, "swamp," which later declined in importance.[13] *Tse* as "pool/pond/lake," on the other hand, started by having the field pretty much to itself; from late Chou times onward, however, it was more and more replaced by *hu* 湖, a word that eventually became the standard designation for "lake" but, because of its southern origin, is not found in the early Chou literature.[14]

The basically aquatic significance of the word *tse* is of course indicated by the occurrence in the written character of the graphic element meaning "water." It is natural enough, therefore, that *tse* should usually be thought of in conjunction with low-lying terrain. The classical expression of this idea— formulated in a deliberately reversed manner for paradoxical effect—occurs in one of the famous riddles enunciated by Hui Shih: "Heaven is as low as the earth; mountains and *tse* are on the same level."[15] Other texts can be found, however, in which *tse* seems to have very little connection with water, and there are even rare instances in which the word's associations seem to be with heights rather than depths. Illustrative of the second point is a *Tso chuan* passage stating (in Legge's translation) that certain officers of the Chin army were sent to "examine all the difficult places in the hills and marshes (*tse*)." As translated by Couvreur, the officers are said to have explored "les passages escarpés dans les montagnes et sur les bords des lacs (*tse*)."[16] The key word here, *hsien* 險, can, in a secondary sense, signify "dangerous" or "difficult" (hence Legge's "difficult places"). Its primary meaning, however, is "steep or rugged terrain" and the like, and this is surely what the word means when, as

[13] According to the Harvard-Yenching *Concordance to Shih Ching, hsi* appears in no less than fifteen poems (nos. 38, 58, 84, 115, 126, 132, 148, 163, 164, 204, 210, 227, 228, 250, 290), whereas *tse*, in its concrete primary meanings, occurs in only three (nos. 145, 181, 261). However, there is some ambiguity about the word *hsi* itself, because although it does mean "swamp" in many contexts, in some others it apparently simply means "lowland."

[14] *Hu* does not occur in the *Shih ching, Shu ching, Lun yü* or *Tso chuan.* However, it occurs once in the *Mo-tzu,* chap. 15: *SPPY* 4/5a, Mei, 85; once in the *Kuan-tzu,* chap. 84: *SPPY* 24/16b; Lewis Maverick (ed.), *Economic dialogues in ancient China, selections from the Kuan-tzu* (Carbondale, Illinois, 1954), 202; and seven times in the *Chuang-tzu* (see the Harvard-Yenching *Concordance to Chuang Tzu*). In the *Kuan-tzu* and *Chuang-tzu, hu* is invariably linked with another well-known word of southern origin, *chiang* 江, "river."

[15] *Chuang-tzu,* chap. 33: *SPPY* 10/20b, Watson, 274.

[16] Hsiang 18 (555 B.C.): Legge, 478b; Couvreur, II, 335-36.

here, it occurs in conjunction with *shan* 山, "mountains." Hence Couvreur's "passages escarpés" is much better than Legge's "difficult places"; by the same token, however, his "bords des lacs" for *tse* is fully as incongruous as Legge's "marshes." The decisive factor is that the word *tse* is conjoined here *both* with *shan* and with *hsien* (the phrase in question, *shan tse chih hsien* 山澤之險, literally means "the *hsien* of mountains and of *tse*"). The only reasonable conclusion, it seems to me, is that these *tse* were located *among* the mountains, rather than below and away from them.

Even more conclusive, though many centuries later, is a passage wherein Fan Yeh (398-446), in his *Hou Han shu* [Later Han history], describes the early habits of the Southern Barbarians (in modern Hunan).[17] Here, having narrated the origin of these "barbarians" from the union between a dog and the daughter of the mythological Chinese sage ruler Ti K'u, Fan Yeh says of them: "They loved to enter mountain gorges but did not enjoy flat expanses. The Sovereign [i.e. Ti K'u], in accordance with their notions, bestowed on them famous mountains and broad *tse*." The stated preference here for "mountain gorges" (*shan ho* 山壑, translated by Streffer as "tiefe Gebirgstäler") as against "flat expanses" (*p'ing k'uang* 平曠, translated by Streffer as "offenem Flachland"), followed by the linking of "famous mountains" (*ming shan* 名山) and "broad *tse*" (*kuang tse* 曠澤) with one another, makes it impossible, in my opinion, for the latter to be thought of as either low-lying "marshes" or "lakes" that are below the mountains. Surely they must be plateau-like expanses among the mountains themselves. Streffer, I think, is on the right track when he translates (though without comment): ". . . weitem fruchtbaren Boden bei berühmten Bergen."

As to the usually aquatic associations of *tse*, passages can nevertheless be found wherein flora and fauna seemingly quite out of place in a damp environment are associated with *tse*. The *Kuan-tzu*, for example, says in a passage in which the very term just cited, *kuang tse*, appears: "The tiger and the leopard are the most ferocious of beasts. So long as they dwell in deep forests and broad *tse* (*kuang tse*), men will be fearful of their awesomeness and respect them."[18] The *Chuang-tzu*, likewise, speaks about "the *tse* pheasant" (*chih* 雉, the ring-necked pheasant), which Burton Watson translates incongruously as "swamp pheasant."[19] It would seem that in both passages,

---

[17] *SPPY* 116/1b. Translated in Johanne Michael Streffer, *Das Kapitel 86 (76) des Hou Han Shu* (Göppingen, West Germany: Verlag Alfred Künmerle, 1971), 80. The reading of this passage with students several years ago first suggested to me that *tse* might have meanings other than those found in the dictionaries.

[18] Chap. 64: *SPPY* 20/3a. See W. Allyn Rickett, *Kuan-tzu, a repertory of early Chinese thought*, I (Hong Kong, 1965), 125, where he conventionally translates *kuang tse* as "broad marshes."

[19] *Chuang-tzu*, chap. 3: *SPPY* 2/3a, Watson, 52.

grasslands would fit the situation better than would swamps or marshes.

Other references seem to indicate, however, that these grasslands—if they were indeed such—could on occasion grow shrubs, bushes, and even trees in addition to grass. Thus the *Chuang-tzu*, in a passage to be quoted later (see note 25), associates the Chinese oak (*shu* 杼) and Chinese chestnut (*li* 栗) with what it calls the "great *tse*" (*ta tse* 大澤)—apparently a *tse* of considerable extent. And the *Kuan-tzu*, in a passage likewise cited below (see note 32), describes what it calls "the northern *tse*" in the state of Ch'i (modern Shantung) as an important source of cooking fuel. The term rendered "fuel" is actually a binom, *hsin jao* 薪蕘, which Yin Chih-chang (d. A.D. 718), commentator on the *Kuan-tzu*, explains by saying: "What is large is *hsin*, what is small is *jao*." It is evident that *hsin* (the standard word for "firewood") here refers to pieces of wood of larger size, while *jao* is the term covering smaller branches, twigs, shrubs, and grasses.

The word *tse* occurs a number of times in the *Tso chuan* as a suffix in place names; Legge usually translates by the formula, "at the marsh of X," while Couvreur, more cautiously, usually leaves *tse* untranslated as part of the place name ("at X-*tse*"). It happens more than once that these *tse* are the locales for military or political events such as would ordinarily never be imagined as occurring either in a "marsh" or a "lake." In 638 B.C., for example, when the viscount of Ch'u had gained an important victory over Sung, the two wives of the earl of Cheng offered him a congratulatory feast at a place in Cheng called "the *tse* of K'o."[20] In 580 the son of a deceased ruler of Cheng signed a treaty with the state of Chin at the *tse* of Hsiu.[21] Other treaties, between other states, were likewise signed in 579 and 570 at the *tse* of So and *tse* of Chi respectively.[22] In 549 the viscount of Ch'u besieged the capital of Cheng at its eastern gate, for which purpose he camped his army at the *tse* of Tz'u.[23] And in 505, somewhat similarly, the Lu army marched through the capital of Wei and then halted at the *tse* of T'un.[24] In each instance, the actions make excellent sense if we visualize them as occurring at a meadow, heath, or other expanse of non-wet open land.

Not only could *tse* be the locales for treaty-signings and military encampments, however. Sometimes recluses or primitives lived in them as well. The *Chuang-tzu*, with characteristic humor, tells how Confucius, after learning Taoist wisdom, "said goodbye to his friends and associates, dismissed his disciples, and retired to the great *tse*, wearing furs and felted clothing and

[20] Hsi 22: Legge, 183b; Couvreur, I, 336.
[21] Ch'eng 11: Legge, 373b; Couvreur, II, 83.
[22] Ch'eng 12 and Hsiang 3: Legge, 378a and 420a; Couvreur, II, 94 and 193.
[23] Hsiang 24: Legge, 508b; Couvreur, II, 414.
[24] Ting 5: Legge, 762b; Couvreur, III, 527.

living on acorns and chestnuts."[25] And the *Huai-nan-tzu*, in a description of primitive man, states that "the people of old lived in *tse* in covered-over pits." Because, however, they suffered from cold and damp in winter and heat and insects in summer, the sages proceeded to build houses of clay and wood for them.[26] These "covered-over pits" (*fu hsüeh* 復穴) are mentioned already in the *Shih ching*, where it is said that Tan-fu, ancient ancestor of the Chou people, formed coverings (*fu*) and pits (*hsüeh*) for his people at a time when houses as such did not yet exist.[27] The terms at once suggest the pit dwellings whose foundations have been uncovered at various Chinese Neolithic sites. Further, their mention in the poem in conjunction with Tan-fu (in Northwest China) suggests that the *tse* where the *Huai-nan-tzu* says the ancients had their "covered-over pits" may also have been located in the northwest loess highlands.

By now so much has been said about various kinds of *tse* that the reader may almost have forgotten the original context. The key words in *Mencius*, IIIa, 4 read (in my rendition): "Yi ignited the mountains and *tse* and burned them off." This theme of a sage who anciently clears the land by fire is by no means unique. The *Kuan-tzu*, in two successive chapters, attributes the same act to Huang Ti, the Yellow Sovereign, and then to Yü, founder of the Hsia dynasty. In both cases the sentences run: "He set fire to the mountain forests, destroyed the dense thickets, and burned off the luxuriant *tse*."[28] Regardless of which sage is involved, it is evident that the theme is that of clearing the land from primeval growth and thus making the world suitable for settled human habitation. In other words, it is a culture myth symbolizing the formation of sedentary agrarian civilization.

The same act of burning off the land, devoid of any mythological associations, is also mentioned quite casually in a number of other passages. Thus the *Kuan-tzu*, in the course of enumerating several matters about which the ruler should be particularly careful, mentions among them that of "the mountains and the *tse* not being saved from fire; plants and trees not being planted."[29] The *Huai-nan-tzu* warns similarly that "when fire is released in a *tse*, the [neighboring] forest becomes anxious [lest it catch fire]."[30] And the *Chuang-tzu* remarks poetically of the Taoist adept: "The Perfect Man is godlike. Though the great *tse* burns, it cannot roast him; though the Ho and

---

[25] Chap. 20: *SPPY* 7/12a, Watson, 214. This is the passage, mentioned earlier, which implies that oaks and chestnuts grew in the *tse*.

[26] *Huai-nan-tzu, SPPY* 13/1a.

[27] *Shih ching*, no. 237.

[28] *Kuan-tzu,* chap. 78: *SPPY* 23/4b, Maverick, 151; chap. 79: *SPPY* 23/4b, Maverick, 160-61. The sentence is repeated no less than three times in the second reference.

[29] Chap. 4: *SPPY* 1/13b, Maverick, 42.

[30] *SPPY* 16/7a.

Han rivers freeze, they cannot chill him."[31]

Of particular interest is yet another passage from the *Kuan-tzu*, one of the many in which the model minister, Kuan Chung, advises his ruler, Duke Huan of Ch'i (r. 685-643 B.C.).[32] It begins with the statement: "The northern *tse* in Ch'i was set on fire." The text then goes on to say that when this happened, Kuan Chung congratulated his ruler, saying: "Our cultivated lands (*t'ien yeh* 田野) will now be extended, and the peasants will be sure to have a hundred-fold profit." His prediction proved accurate, for by the ninth month of that year all the grain taxes had been collected and the quality of the grain was excellent. On being asked the reason, Kuan Chung explained: "Whether it be a state of a myriad or a thousand chariots, no one can cook without fuel. Now with the burning of the northern *tse*, there has been no continuation [of the former supply of fuel from that area], so that the peasants have been able ... to sell their fuel at ten times more per bundle [than formerly]." This, he concludes, has given them the means effectively to carry out their agricultural work (by hiring additional labor?), which is why they have been able to bring in their tax grain so early. Not only, as mentioned earlier, does this passage indicate that some trees, at least, grew in the *tse* besides shrubs and grasses. It also implies that the burning of the *tse* led to its conversion into agricultural land ("Our cultivated lands will now be enlarged"). Unless the burning were in fact followed by drainage operations—and there is no mention of these in the text—it is hard to see how the *tse* from which the new lands were converted could possibly have been either a marsh or a lake.

Two technical terms occur in the texts to describe the act of burning. The primary one is *fen* 焚, the graph of which appropriately consists of the elements signifying "fire" and "forest." *Fen* appears in the *Mencius* passage, the first of the *Kuan-tzu* passages, and the *Chuang-tzu* quotation; in each instance I have rendered it as "burn" or "burn off." The other, more general, term is *shao* 燒, found in the first and third *Kuan-tzu* passages, where I have translated it as "set fire to" or "set on fire." Yin Chih-chang, commenting on the third *Kuan-tzu* passage, explains: "To circulate fire for hunting is called *shao*." That *shao* and *fen*, used technically, are practically synonymous is indicated by the *Shuo-wen* dictionary, which says under *fen*: "*Fen* is to set on fire (*shao*) for hunting."[33] Though there is ample evidence that fire was

---

[31] Chap. 2: *SPPY* 1/21b, Watson, 46, who translates: "Though the great swamps blaze." We have already encountered the term *ta tse*, "great *tse*," in an earlier quotation from *Chuang-tzu* (see at note 25).

[32] Chap. 80: *SPPY* 23/14b, Maverick, 169-70. This is the passage referred to earlier because of its mention of the firewood and other fuel derived from the *tze*.

[33] *Shuo-wen chieh-tzu, Ssu-pu ts'ung-k'an* ed., 10A/8b.

used in early China to drive out the game in mass hunts,[34] our texts clearly suggest that it was also used—probably not only prehistorically but much later as well—to clear the land for agriculture. Perhaps the process was similar to the "slash and burn" agriculture still practiced in parts of Southeast Asia today.

The foregoing evidence, I hope, supports the conclusion that the word *tse* anciently covered a considerable range of meanings. Starting as a designation for a low-lying area of either marsh or outright water, the word—no doubt because of the concept of openness ever present in it—was extended to cover other kinds of open terrain as well. Some of these had probably little or nothing to do with water, and some seem to have been located quite high in the mountains. For the most part, no doubt, these non-aquatic *tse* consisted of open meadow or grassland, but in some instances such land was apparently interspersed to some extent by bush and even trees. While many *tse* were presumably small, certain ones were probably large enough to be measured in miles. English words that come to mind as possible synonyms include grassland, meadow, heath, moor, bush, plateau, alpine meadow.

Before concluding, it is worth pointing out that our own word "marsh" provides an interesting semantic parallel when used as a dialect word in southwestern England. In Somersetshire, for example, the word carries with it "no implication of bog or swamp. 'The marshes' are some of the richest grazing land in Somerset." And in southern Devonshire the word is "applied loosely to meadows by the riverside, whether dry or marshy."[35] From this part of England these dialect usages apparently passed to Australia, and more specifically to Tasmania, where a resident informs us: "A 'marsh' here is what in England would be called a meadow."[36]

What this article has discussed is admittedly of no great consequence. Though the excuse for writing it has been the desire to explain a puzzling passage in a textbook prepared by Herrlee Creel, the result in no way pretends to match the intellectual interests of the man to whom it is affectionately dedicated. If there is any general moral to be drawn, it is simply that no easy shortcuts are possible for the serious study of classical Chinese civilization and language. Resort to the dictionaries and similar aids is not enough. They must

[34] See, *inter alia*, the account of the hunt in *Shih ching* no. 78, which (in Bernhard Karlgren's rendition, *The Book of odes* [Stockholm, 1950], 53) speaks of "rows of fires" that "surge everywhere."

[35] See Joseph Wright (ed.), *The English dialect dictionary* (6 vols.; London, Oxford & New York, 1898-1905), IV, 44, *sub* "marsh (4)."

[36] Mrs. Louisa Anne Meredith, *My home in Tasmania during a residence of nine years* (2 vols.; London, 1852), I, 163. Quoted in Edward E. Morris, *Austral English, a dictionary of Australasian phrases and usages* (London, 1898), 287, s.v.

be supplemented at every turn by eternal readiness to do one's own exploring —usually laboriously, often unproductively, and not infrequently leading into obscure byways as well as along the better-known highways. Herrlee's every writing testifies to his full awareness of this principle and his lifelong commitment to the task of exploring.

# BIBLIOGRAPHY OF DERK BODDE

## Abbreviations

AHR    *American Historical Review*
FEQ    *Far Eastern Quarterly* (later *JAS*)
FES    *Far Eastern Survey*
HJAS    *Harvard Journal of Asiatic Studies*
JAOS    *Journal of the American Oriental Society*
JAS    *Journal of Asian Studies* (earlier *FEQ*)

## A. Books, Pamphlets and Articles

1923    1. "A Boy's Trip to an East Indian Volcano." *St. Nicholas Magazine* (December 1923), 134-137. Reprinted in E. Ehrlich Smith, Orton Lowe, and I. Jewell Simpson, comps., *Adventures in Reading, Fourth Year* (Garden City, N.Y.: Doubleday, Doran & Co., 1928), pp. 190-200.

1925    2. "My House-boat Trip in China." *St. Nicholas Magazine* (January 1925), 276-283.

1926    3. "My Trip to the Great Wall of China and the Ming Tombs." *St. Nicholas Magazine* (April 1926), 570-577.

1927    4. "Thundering Waters!" *St. Nicholas Magazine* (January 1927), 170-176.

       5. "The Dragon Speaks." *St. Nicholas Magazine* (July 1927), 683-685.

1930    6. *Shakspere and the Ireland Forgeries*. Harvard Honors Theses in English No. 2. Cambridge, Mass.: Harvard University Press, 1930. Pp. 68. Reprinted in James Dow McCallum, comp., *The Revised College Omnibus* (New York: Harcourt, Brace & Co., 1939), pp. 268-283 (appendix in original omitted). Further reprints, Folcroft, Pa.: Folcroft Library Editions, 1973; New York: Haskell House, 1975; Norwood, Pa.: Norwood Editions, 1975.

1933    7. "A Perplexing Passage in the Confucian Analects." *JAOS*, 53.4 (1933), 347-351.

1934    8. *"Tso chuan* yü *Kuo yü"* [The *Tso chuan* and the *Kuo yü*]. *Yenching hsüeh-pao* [*Yenching Journal of Chinese Studies*], 16 (December 1934), 161-167.

1936    9. "The Attitude toward Science and Scientific Method in Ancient China." *T'ien Hsia Monthly*, 2 (February 1936), 139-160.

     10. *Annual Customs and Festivals in Peking, As Recorded in the Yenching Sui-shih-chi*. By Tun Li-ch'en. Translated and annotated by Derk Bodde. Peiping: Henri Vetch, 1936.

Pp. xxii, 147. Reprint with new introduction and correction of typographical errors, Hong Kong: Hong Kong University Press, 1965.

*1937*    11. *A History of Chinese Philosophy*, Vol. I: *The Period of the Philosophers (from the beginnings to circa 100 B.C.).* By Fung Yu-lan. Translated by Derk Bodde with introduction, notes, bibliography and index. Peiping: Henri Vetch, 1937. Pp. xx, 454. See also no. 52 for second edition of 1952.

*1938*    12. *China's First Unifier: a Study of the Ch'in Dynasty as Seen in the Life of Li Ssu (280?-208 B.C.).* Sinica Leidensia Series, Vol. III. Leiden: E. J. Brill, 1938. Pp. viii, 270. Reprint with new introduction and correction of typographical errors, Hong Kong: Hong Kong University Press, 1966.

*1939*    13. "The Far East at the Meeting of the American Oriental Society in Baltimore." *Notes on Far Eastern Studies in America*, 5 (1939), 15-17.

14. "Some Fundamental Differences between China and Japan." *T'ien Hsia Monthly*, 9 (September 1939), 156-168.

15. "Types of Chinese Categorical Thinking." *JAOS*, 59.2 (1939), 200-219.

16. "Our New Chinese Collection." *University of Pennsylvania Library Chronicle*, 7.3-4 (1939), 60-65. See also no. 33.

*1940*    17. *Statesman, Patriot, and General in Ancient China: Three Shih-chi Biographies of the Ch'in Dynasty (255-206 B.C.).* American Oriental Series, Vol. 17. New Haven: American Oriental Society, 1940. Pp. xi, 75. Reprint with correction of typographical errors, New York: Kraus Reprint Corporation, 1967.

*1941*    18. "Far Eastern Institute of America: a Proposal for a Permanent Organization." *Notes on Far Eastern Studies in America*, 8 (1941), 8-11.

*1942*    19. "Peking Man and a New Theory of Human Evolution." *Far Eastern Leaflets, Numbers 1-6* (Washington, D.C.: American Council of Learned Societies, 1942), 8-10.

20. "A 'Totalitarian' Form of Government in Ancient China." *Far Eastern Leaflets, Numbers 1-6* (Washington, D.C.: American Council of Learned Societies, 1942), 23-25.

21. "The Chinese Language as a Factor in Chinese Cultural Continuity." *Far Eastern Leaflets, Numbers 1-6* (Washington, D.C.: American Council of Learned Societies, 1942), 28-29.

22. "Some Chinese Tales of the Supernatural: Kan Pao and His *Sou-shen chi*." *HJAS*, 6 (February 1942), 338-357. See also no. 29.

23. "Hsü Ti-shan (1893-1941)." *HJAS*, 6 (February 1942), 403-404.
24. "Early References to Tea Drinking in China." *JAOS*, 62 (March 1942), 74-76.
25. "The New Identification of Lao Tzu Proposed by Professor Dubs." *JAOS*, 62 (March 1942), 8-13. See also no. 32.
26. "The Philosophy of Chu Hsi." By Fung Yu-lan. Translated with introduction and notes by Derk Bodde. *HJAS*, 7 (April 1942), 1-51. See also nos. 28, 39, and 52.
27. "The Chinese View of Immortality: Its Expression by Chu Hsi and Its Relationship to Buddhist Thought." *Review of Religion*, 6 (May 1942), 369-383.
28. "The Rise of Neo Confucianism and Its Borrowings from Buddhism and Taoism." By Fung Yu-lan. Translated with notes by Derk Bodde. *HJAS*, 7 (July 1942), 89-125. See also nos. 26, 39, and 52.
29. "Again Some Chinese Tales of the Supernatural: Further Remarks on Kan Pao and His *Sou-shen chi*." *JAOS*, 62 (December 1942), 305-308. See also no. 22.
30. "Dominant Ideas in the Formation of Chinese Culture." *JAOS*, 62 (December 1942), 293-299. Reprinted in *Harvard Educational Review*, 13 (March 1943), 127-139. Reprinted with slight changes in Harley F. MacNair, ed., *China* (United Nations Series, Berkeley & Los Angeles: University of California Press, 1946), pp. 18-28.
31. *China's Gifts to the West*. Asiatic Studies in American Education, No. 1. Washington, D.C.: American Council on Education, 1942. Pp. vi, 40. See also no. 41.

1944
32. "Further Remarks on the Identification of Lao Tzu, a Last Reply to Professor Dubs." *JAOS*, 64.1 (1944), 24-27. See also no. 25.
33. "Our Chinese Collection." *University of Pennsylvania Library Chronicle*, 12 (April 1944), 38-43. See also no. 16.

1946
34. "Henry A. Wallace and the Ever-normal Granary." *FEQ*, 5.4 (August 1946), 411-426.
35. "China's Muslim Minority." *FES*, 15 (September 11, 1946), 281-284.
36. "Japan and the Muslims of China." *FES*, 15 (October 9, 1946), 311-313.
37. "Chinese Muslims in Occupied Areas." *FES*, 15 (October 23, 1946), 330-333.
38. "Sinological Literature in the United States, 1940-1946." *Quarterly Bulletin of Chinese Bibliography*, n.s. 6 (March-December 1946), 1-27.

1947
39. "A General Discussion of the Period of Classical Learning." By Fung Yu-lan. Translated and annotated by Derk

Bodde. *HJAS*, 9 (February 1947), 195-201. See also nos. 26, 28, and 52.

40. "Chinese Philosophy and the Social Sciences." *Pacific Affairs*, 20 (June 1947), 199-204.

1948   41. *Chinese Ideas in the West*. Asiatic Studies in American Education, No. 3. Washington, D.C.: American Council on Education, 1948. Pp. viii, 42. See also no. 31.

42. *A Short History of Chinese Philosophy*. By Fung Yu-lan. Edited by Derk Bodde. New York: Macmillan, 1948. Pp. xx, 368. Paperback edition, 1960. See also nos. 53 and 61.

1949   43. "Report on Communist China." *FES*, 18 (November 16, 1949), 265-269.

44. "Why the Communists Have Won in China." *Foreign Policy Bulletin*, 29 (December 30, 1949).

1950   45. "Deadline Here for U.S. Decision on China." *Foreign Policy Bulletin*, 29 (January 6, 1950).

46. "The Red Dynasts vs. Chinese Tradition." *The Reporter*, 2 (January 3, 1950), 20-22.

47. "Notes on Cultural Activities in Peiping." *FEQ*, 9 (February 1950), 195-198.

48. "Price Fluctuations in Tientsin, August 1948-August 1949." *FES*, 19 (April 19, 1950), 78-80.

49. *Tolstoy and China*. By Derk Bodde. With the collaboration of Galia Speshneff Bodde. The History of Ideas Series, No. 4. Princeton, New Jersey: Princeton University Press, 1950. Pp. vi, 110. Reprint, New York: Johnson Reprint Corporation, 1967.

50. *Peking Diary, a Year of Revolution*. New York: Henry Schuman, 1950. Pp. xxi, 292. British edition, London: Jonathan Cape, 1951. Paperback reprint with new foreword, Greenwich, Conn.: Fawcett Premier Books, 1967. Further reprint, New York: Octagon Books, 1976. See also no. 51.

1952   51. *Peking-Tagebuch, ein Jahr Revolution in China*. Translated by Max Müller. Wiesbaden: Eberhard Brockhaus, 1952. Pp. 334. See also no. 50.

52. Second edition of Fung Yu-lan, *A History of Chinese Philosophy*, Vol. I (see no. 11), with added section, "Revisions and Additions for the Second Edition," pp. xxi-xxxiv. Princeton: Princeton University Press, 1952. See also no. 55.

53. Fong Yeou-lan, *Précis d'histoire de la philosophie chinoise*. D'après le texte anglais édité par Derk Bodde. Traduction de Guillaume Dunstheimer. Préface de Paul Demiéville. Paris: Payot, 1952. Pp. 373. See also nos. 42 and 61.

*1953*   54. "Present Status of the Study of Chinese Philosophy and Religion in American Universities." *Philosophy East and West*, 2 (January 1953), 358-362.

55. *A History of Chinese Philosophy*, Vol. II: *The Period of Classical Learning (from the second century B.C. to the twentieth century A.D.)*. By Fung Yu-lan. Translated by Derk Bodde with introduction, notes, bibliography and index. Princeton: Princeton University Press, 1953. Pp. xxv, 783. See also nos. 26, 28, 39, and 52.

56. "Harmony and Conflict in Chinese Philosophy." In Arthur F. Wright, ed., *Studies in Chinese Thought* (Chicago: University of Chicago Press, 1953), pp. 19-80. Paperback reprint, University of Chicago Press, Phoenix Books, 1967.

*1954*   57. "Authority and Law in Ancient China." In *Authority and Law in the Ancient Orient*, Supplement No. 17 (July-September 1954), 46-55, of *JAOS*. Reprinted in *Silver Jubilee Volume of the Zinbun-Kagaku-Kenkusyo* (Kyoto, 1954), pp. 34-42.

58. "Two New Translations of Lao Tzu." *JAOS*, 74 (October-December 1954), 211-217.

*1955*   59. "On Translating Chinese Philosophic Terms." *FEQ*, 14 (February 1955), 231-244.

*1956*   60. "Feudalism in China." In Rushton Coulborn, ed., *Feudalism in History* (Princeton: Princeton University Press, 1956), pp. 49-92, 404-407.

61. Fung Yu-lan, *Storia della Filosofia Cinese*. A cura di Derk Bodde. Unica traduzione autorizzata dall'Inglese di Mario Tassoni. Milano: Arnoldo Mondadori Editore, 1956. Pp. 375. See also nos. 42 and 53.

*1957*   62. "Needham on Chinese Philosophy and Science." *JAS*, 16 (February 1957), 261-272.

63. *China's Cultural Tradition: What and Whither?* New York: Holt, Rinehart & Winston, 1957 (and many later printings). Pp. vi, 90.

64. "Evidence for 'Laws of Nature' in Chinese Thought." *HJAS*, 20 (December 1957), 706-727. See also no. 91.

*1958*   65. "Comment on Professor Schafer's Review of *China's Cultural Tradition*." *JAOS*, 78 (January-March 1958), 57-59.

66. "Letter to the Editor." *JAS*, 18 (November 1958), 183-184.

67. "Chinese Classics." *Encyclopaedia Britannica*, edition of 1958, V, 565-566 (and later editions through 1965).

*1959*   68. "China: Old Society and New Forces." In *Asia in Perspective* (Philadelphia: Philomathean Society of the University of Pennsylvania, 1959), pp. 28-40.

69. "The Chinese Cosmic Magic Known as Watching for the

Ethers." In Søren Egerod and Else Glahn, eds., *Studia Serica Bernhard Karlgren Dedicata, Sinological Studies Dedicated to Bernhard Karlgren on His Seventieth Birthday October Fifth, 1959* (Copenhagen: Ejnar Munksgaard, 1959), pp. 14-35.

70. "Lieh-tzu and the Doves: a Problem of Dating." *Asia Major*, n.s. 7.1-2 (Arthur Waley Anniversary Volume, 1959), 25-31.

1960    71. "Hsün-tzu." *Encyclopaedia Britannica*, edition of 1960, XI, 854-855 (and later editions through 1972).

Paperback reprint of *A Short History of Chinese Philosophy*, (see no. 42).

1961    72. "Myths of Ancient China." In Samuel Noah Kramer, ed., *Mythologies of the Ancient World* (Chicago: Quadrangle Books, 1961; paperback edition, Garden City, N.Y.: Doubleday Anchor Books, 1961), pp. 367-408. Reprinted in Chun-shu Chang, ed., *The Making of China: Main Themes in Premodern China* (Englewood Cliffs, N.J.: Prentice-Hall, 1975), pp. 16-37. See also no. 88.

1963    73. "Comments on the Paper of Arthur F. Wright" [entitled "On the Uses of Generalization in the Study of Chinese History"]. In Louis Gottschalk, ed., *Generalization in the Writing of History* (Chicago: University of Chicago Press, 1963), pp. 59-65.

74. "Basic Concepts of Chinese Law: th. Genesis and Evolution of Legal Thought in Traditional China." *Proceedings of the American Philosophical Society*, 107 (October 15, 1963), 375-398. Reprinted with slight changes as chapter 1 in no. 79.

75. "The Term *Ming-ch'i*." *Ars Orientalis*, 5 (1963), 283.

1964    76. "Sexual Sympathetic Magic in Han China." *History of Religions*, 3 (Winter 1964), 292-299.

1965    77. "Shih Huang Ti." *Encyclopaedia Britannica*, edition of 1965, XX, 514-515 (and later editions through 1972).

78. "Li Ssu." *Encyclopaedia Britannica*, editions of 1965 and 1972, XIV, 100.

Reprint of *Annual Customs and Festivals in Peking* (see no. 10).

1966    Reprint of *China's First Unifier* (see no. 12).

1967    Reprint of *Statesman, Patriot, and General in Ancient China* (see no. 17).

Reprint of *Tolstoy and China* (see no. 49).

Paperback reprint of *Peking Diary* (see no. 50).

Paperback reprint of *Studies in Chinese Thought* (see no. 56).

79. *Law in Imperial China, Exemplified by 190 Ch'ing Dynasty Cases . . . with Historical, Social, and Judicial Commentaries.* By

Derk Bodde and Clarence Morris. Cambridge, Mass.: Harvard University Press, 1967. Pp. xiv, 615. Paperback reprint, Philadelphia: University of Pennsylvania Press, 1973.

1968  80. "Chinese Folk Art and the Russian Sinologist V. M. Alexeev." By Derk Bodde and Galia S. Bodde. *JAS*, 27 (February 1968), 339-347.

81. "Comments" [on Ping-ti Ho, "Salient Aspects of China's Heritage"]. In Ping-ti Ho and Tang Tsou, eds., *China's Heritage and the Communist Political System*, Volume One, Book One of *China in Crisis* (Chicago: University of Chicago Press, 1968), pp. 50-58.

1969  82. "Prison Life in Eighteenth Century Peking." *JAOS*, 89 (April-June 1969), 311-333.

1970  83. "Homer Hasenpflug Dubs, 1892-1969." *JAOS*, 90 (October-December 1970), 633-634.

1973  84. "Age, Youth, and Infirmity in the Law of Ch'ing China." *University of Pennsylvania Law Review*, 121 (January 1973), 437-470. Reprinted with slight changes as no. 92.

85. "Introduction to the History of China." In Bradley Smith and Wan-go Weng, *China: a History in Art* (New York: Harper and Row, 1973; Doubleday, 1979), pp. 10-13.

86. "Legal Sources." In Donald D. Leslie, Colin Mackerras and Wang Gungwu, eds., *Essays on the Sources for Chinese History* (Canberra: Australian National University Press, 1973), pp. 99-103.

Paperback reprint of *Law in Imperial China* (see no. 79).

Reprint of *Shakspere and the Ireland Forgeries* (see no. 6).

1975  87. *Festivals in Classical China, New Year and Other Annual Observances during the Han Dynasty, 206 B.C.-A.D. 220.* Princeton: Princeton University Press and Hong Kong: Chinese University of Hong Kong, 1975. Pp. xvi, 439.

1976  Reprint of *Peking Diary* (see no. 50). Two reprints of *Shakspere and the Ireland Forgeries* (see no. 6

1977  88. *Mifologii Drevnego Mira.* Moscow: "Nauka" Publishing House, 1977. Pp. 456. Russian translation of *Mythologies of the Ancient World* (see no. 72), with a new introduction by I. M. Diakonoff.

89. "Han Festivals." *JAS*, 37 (November 1977), 185-186.

1978  90. "Marshes in *Mencius* and Elsewhere: a Lexicographical Note." In David T. Roy and Tsuen-hsuin Tsien, eds., *Ancient China: Studies in Early Civilization* (Hong Kong: Chinese University Press, 1978), pp. 157-166.

1979  91. "Chinese 'Laws of Nature': a Reconsideration." *HJAS*, 39 (June 1979), 139-155. See also no. 64.

1980  92. "Age, Youth, and Infirmity in the Law of Ch'ing China."

In Jerome A. Cohen, Randle Edwards and Fu-mei Chang Ch'en, eds., *Essays on China's Legal Tradition* (Princeton: Princeton University Press, 1980), pp. 137-169. See also no. 84.

FORTHCOMING

93. "Obituary: Boris Ivanovich Pankratov, 1892-1979." *Newsletter of the American Oriental Society.*

94. "Forensic Medicine in Pre-imperial China." *JAOS*, 102 (1982).

95. "Intellectual and Social Factors" [which may have fostered or inhibited the development of science in China before approximately 1600]. In Joseph Needham et al., *Science and Civilisation in China*, Vol. VII: *The Social Background* (Cambridge: Cambridge University Press), sect. 49.

96. "The Ch'in State and Empire." In *The Cambridge History of China*, Vol. I: *Ch'in and Han*, edited by Denis Twitchett and Michael Loewe (Cambridge: Cambridge University Press), chap. 1.

## B. Book Reviews

For review articles, see A-58, 62, and 80.

*1939* 1. H. H. Dubs, trans., *History of the Former Han Dynasty*, Vol. I. In *AHR*, 44 (April 1939), 641-642.

*1940* 2. Rudolf Löwenthal, *The Religious Periodical Press in China*. In *JAOS*, 60 (December 1940), 584-585.

*1941* 3. Woodbridge Bingham, *The Founding of the T'ang Dynasty*. In *JAOS*, 61 (December 1941), 293-295.

*1942* 4. William C. White, *Chinese Temple Frescoes*. In *JAOS*, 62 (March 1942), 83-84.

5. Edward H. Hume, *The Chinese Way in Medicine*. In *FEQ*, 1 (May 1942), 288-289.

*1943* 6. Lin Mousheng, *Men and Ideas: an Informal History of Chinese Political Thought*. In *FEQ*, 2 (May 1943), 308-310.

7. E. R. Hughes, *The Great Learning and the Mean-in-Action*. In *Review of Religion*, 8 (March 1943), 277-281.

*1946* 8. Lin Yueh-hwa, *The Golden Wing, a Family Chronicle*. In *American Anthropologist*, n.s. 48 (January-March 1946), 112-114.

9. "Recent Swedish Studies on Chinese Archaeology and Kindred Topics: a Review of the *Bulletin of the Museum of Far Eastern Antiquities*, Stockholm, Nos. 14-17 (1942-1945)." In *American Anthropologist*, n.s. 48 (July-September 1946), 441-450. Reprinted in *Quarterly Bulletin of Chinese Bibliography*, n.s. 7 (March-December 1947), 10-20.

10. Gung-hsing Wang, *The Chinese Mind*. In *Pacific Affairs*, 19 (September 1946), 313-314.

1947   11. *Bulletin of the Museum of Far Eastern Antiquities*, 18 (1946). In *American Anthropologist*, n.s. 49 (July-September 1947), 477-480.

1948   12. *Spoken Chinese, a Course with Phonograph Records and Text Book*. In *FES*, 17 (January 28, 1948), 26.

13. Leonard Olschki, *Guillaume Boucher: a French Artist at the Court of the Khans*. In *FEQ*, 7 (February 1948), 213-214.

14. *Bulletin of the Museum of Far Eastern Antiquities*, 19 (1947). In *American Anthropologist*, n.s. 50 (October-December 1948), 682-683.

1950   15. II. G. Creel, *Confucius, the Man and the Myth*. In *JAOS*, 70 (July-September 1950), 199-203.

16. *The I Ching or Book of Changes*. The Richard Wilhelm Translation, rendered into English by Cary F. Baynes. In *JAOS*, 70 (November-December 1950), 326-329.

1951   17. James Hightower, *Topics in Chinese Literature*, and Yang Lien-sheng, *Topics in Chinese History*. In *JAOS*, 71 (February-March 1951), 92.

18. Michael Lindsay, *Notes on Educational Problems in Communist China*. In *FEQ*, 10 (May 1951), 343-344.

19. Freda Utley, *The China Story*. In *Saturday Review of Literature* (June 2, 1951), pp. 17, 32.

20. Robert Elegant, *China's Red Masters*. In *General Magazine and Historical Chronicle*, 54 (Philadelphia, Autumn 1951), 61-62.

21. John DeFrancis, *Nationalism and Language Reform in China*. In *JAOS*, 71 (October-December 1951), 279-281.

22. Osvald Sirén, *Gardens of China*. In *JAOS*, 71 (October-December 1951), 281-282.

1952   23. Karl A. Wittfogel and Feng Chia-sheng, *History of Chinese Society: Liao (907-1125)*. In *Journal of Economic History*, 12 (Winter 1952), 63-65.

24. Lily Abegg, *The Mind of East Asia*. In *The Nation*, 175 (November 1, 1952), 410-411.

25. Achilles Fang, trans., *The Chronicle of the Three Kingdoms*. In *AHR*, 57 (July 1952), 1044-1045.

26. James Robert Hightower, trans., *Han Shih Wai Chuan*. In *United States Quarterly Book Review*, 8 (December 1952), 365-366.

1954   27. Joseph R. Levenson, *Liang Ch'i-ch'ao and the Mind of Modern China*. In *AHR*, 60 (1954), 191.

28. Witold Jablonski, Janusz Chmielewski, and Olgierd Wotasiewicz, trans., *Cxuang-tsy, Nan-hua-czen-king*. In *FEQ*, 14 (November 1954), 100.

29. Teng Ssu-yü and John K. Fairbank, *China's Response to the West*. In *United States Quarterly Book Review*, 10 (December 1954), 478-479.

1955  30. Joseph Needham, *Science and Civilisation in China*, Vol. I. In *Annals of the American Academy of Political and Social Science*, 297 (January 1955), 178-179.

31. E. Stuart Kirby, *Introduction to the Economic History of China*. In *Journal of Economic History*, 15.1 (1955), 57-58.

32. John K. Fairbank and Masataka Banno, *Japanese Studies of Modern China*. In *FES*, 24 (October 1955), 159.

33. Edwin O. Reischauer, *Ennin's Travels in T'ang China* and *Ennin's Diary*. In *Annals of the American Academy of Political and Social Science*, 302 (November 1955), 199-200.

1956  34. Peter Townsend, *China Phoenix, the Revolution in China*. In *FES*, 25 (March 1956), 48.

35. O. Brière, *Fifty Years of Chinese Philosophy, 1898-1950*. In *FES*, 25 (October 1956), 159.

1958  36. John K. Fairbank, ed., *Chinese Thought and Institutions*. In *AHR*, 63 (April 1958), 684-686.

37. *Revue bibliographique de sinologie, première année, 1955*. In *Pacific Affairs*, 31 (March 1958), 91-92.

38. V. I. Avdiev and N. P. Shastin, eds., *Ocherki po Istorii Russkogo Vostokvedeniya* [Sketches from the History of Russian Orientology]. In *JAOS*, 78 (October-December 1958), 304-305.

39. Holmes Welch, *The parting of the Way: Lao Tzu and the Taoist Movement*. In *HJAS*, 21 (December 1958), 180-184.

1959  40. *Sovetskoye Kitayevedeniye* [Soviet Sinology]. In *JAS*, 18 (May 1959), 428-431.

41. Arthur F. Wright, *Buddhism in Chinese History*. In *Annals of the American Academy of Political and Social Science*, 325 (September 1959), 171.

1960  42. David S. Nivison and Arthur F. Wright, eds., *Confucianism in Action*. In *JAS*, 19 (August 1960), 447-448.

43. W. K. Liao, trans., *The Complete Works of Han Fei Tzu*, Vol. II. In *JAS*, 20 (November 1960), 100-101.

44. Bruno Belpaire, trans., *Petits traités chinois inédits, No. 1, Le catéchisme philosophique de Yang-Hiong-Tsé*. In *Artibus Asiae*, 23.1 (1960), 73.

45. William Theodore de Bary et al., comps., *Sources of Chinese Tradition*. In *Artibus Asiae*, 23.3-4 (1960), 254-255.

1961  46. Hellmut Wilhelm, *Change: Eight Lectures on the I Ching*. In *JAOS*, 81 (1961), 53-54.

47. Kung-chuan Hsiao, *Rural China: Imperial Control in the Nineteenth Century*. In *Annals of the American Academy of Political and Social Science*, 338 (November 1961), 175-176.

48. Arthur F. Wright, ed., *The Confucian Persuasion*. In *Artibus Asiae*, 24.2 (1961), 134-136.

49. A. C. Graham, trans., *The Book of Lieh-tzu*. In *Bulletin of the School of Oriental and African Studies*, 24.3 (1961), 598-599.

1962   50. A. Shifman, *Lev Tolstoi i Vostok* [Leo Tolstoy and the Orient]. In *JAS*, 21 (May 1962), 363-364.

1963   51. Joseph Needham, *Science and Civilisation in China*, Vol. IV, Pt. 1. In *Pacific Affairs*, 36 (Fall 1963), 298-299.

1964   52. W. F. Wertheim and E. Zürcher, eds., *China Tussen Eergisteren en Overmorgen* [China between the Day before Yesterday and the Day after Tomorrow]. In *Pacific Affairs*, 37 (Spring 1964), 83-84.

1965   53. Joseph Needham, *Science and Civilisation in China*, Vol. IV, Pts. 1 and 2. In *Science*, 149 (August 20, 1965), 848.

54. Raymond Dawson, ed., *The Legacy of China*. In *Pacific Affairs*, 38 (Summer 1965), 183-184.

1967   55. E-tu Zen Sun and Shiou-chuan Sun, trans., *T'ien-kung K'ai-wu: Chinese Technology in the Seventeenth Century*. In *Annals of the American Academy of Political and Social Science*, 369 (January 1967), 187-188.

56. David S. Nivison, *The Life and Thought of Chang Hsüeh-ch'eng*. In *AHR*, 72 (January 1967), 667-668.

57. Nicole Vandier-Nicolas, *Le Taoïsme*. In *JAOS*, 87.1 (1967), 82-83.

1969   58. L. S. Perelomov, *Kniga Pravitelya Oblasti Shan (Shan Tszyun Shu)* [The Book of the Lord of the Shang Region (Shang Chün Shu)]. In *JAS*, 28 (August 1969), 847-848.

59. Donald J. Munro, *The Concept of Man in Early China*. In *JAS*, 29 (November 1969), 160-162.

1970   60. Yen Chih-t'ui, *Family Instructions for the Yen Clan, Yen-shih Chia-hsün*, translated by Teng Ssu-yü. In *JAS*, 3.2 (1970), 169-170.

61. Nathan Sivin, *Chinese Alchemy: Preliminary Studies*. In *Bulletin of the History of Medicine*, 44 (March-April 1970), 178-179.

1971   62. Joseph Needham, *Clerks and Craftsmen in China and the West*. In *Bulletin of the History of Medicine*, 45 (July-August 1971), 390-391.

1972   63. *Tu-li ts'un-i ch'ung-k'an pen* [New Typeset Edition of the *Tu-li ts'un-i*]. Compiled by Hsüeh Yün-sheng. Edited and punctuated by Huang Ching-chia. In *JAS*, 31 (May 1972), 650-651.

64. *Istoriko-Filologicheskie Issledovaniya, Sbornik statey k semidesyatiletiyu akademika N.I. Konrada* [Historical-Philologi-

cal Studies, a collection of articles for the seventieth anniversary of the Academician N.I. Konrad]. In *JAOS*, 92.4 (1972), 560-561.

1973   65. Yu. L. Krol et al., eds., *Strany i Narody Vostoka* [Countries and Peoples of the East], Vol. XI. In *JAOS*, 93 (1973), 404-405.

1974   66. *Tretya Nauchnaya Konferentsiya "Obshestvo i Gosudarstvo v Kitae," Tezisy i Doklady* [Third Scholarly Conference on "Society and State in China," Theses and Reports]. In *JAS*, 33 (May 1974), 459-461.

67. Shigeru Nakayama and Nathan Sivin, eds., *Chinese Science: Explorations of an Ancient Tradition*. In *AHR*, 79 (December 1974), 1609-1610.

1975   68. *Syma Tsyan, Istoricheskie Zapiski* [Ssu-ma Ch'ien, Historical Records], Vol. I. Translated and commented on by R. V. Viatkin and V. S. Taskin. Edited by R. V. Viatkin. Introductory article by M. V. Kriukov. In *JAOS*, 95.1 (1975), 118.

1976   69. Joseph Needham, *Science and Civilisation in China*, Vol. V, Pt. 2. In *JAS*, 35 (May 1976), 488-491.

70. Herrlee G. Creel, *Shen Pu-hai: a Chinese Political Philosopher of the Fourth Century B.C.* In *HJAS*, 36 (1976), 258-269.

1980   71. Holmes Welch and Anna Seidel, eds., *Facets of Taoism: Essays in Chinese Religion*. In *AHR*, 85 (1980), 444.

72. Charles Wei-hsun Fu and Wing-tsit Chan, *Guide to Chinese Philosophy*. *JAOS*, 100 (1980), 88-89.

73. P. M. Thompson, *The Shen Tzu Fragments*. *T'oung Pao*, 66 (1980), 309-314.

FORTHCOMING

74. A. C. Graham, *Later Mohist Logic, Ethics and Science*. *JAOS*, 101 (1981).

75. Michael Loewe, *Ways to Paradise: the Chinese Quest for Immortality*. *HJAS*, 42 (1982).

# INDEX

All Chinese words and names in this book are transcribed according to the standard Wade-Giles romanization system except for: a. Wade-Giles syllable *i*, which is often but not invariably here transcribed as *yi*, so that both spellings should be looked for; b. the spellings preferred by some modern Chinese scholars when writing their names in Western languages, which are therefore those always given in this book even when sometimes diverging from the Wade-Giles forms (e.g. Fung Yu-lan, preferred by Fung himself to Wade-Giles Feng Yu-lan); c. well-known place names, which follow the spellings established long ago by the Chinese Post Office (e.g. Peking, not Pei-ching).

In the arrangement of Chinese words, no distinction is made between *u* and *ü* or between aspirated and nonaspirated syllables (e.g. *pan* and *p'an*). Terms and names consisting of more than one syllable are arranged in the alphabetical sequence of the several syllables, irrespective of whether these are hyphenated.

The index covers both text and footnotes of the entire book save for its Bibliography (pp. 427-438). It includes virtually all personal names mentioned in the book, as well as all titles of Chinese writings published before 1912, but not those of post-Republican (post-1912) Chinese writings or of any writings in non-Chinese languages.

Certain ancient Chinese texts that bear the same names as their putative authors are listed together with these authors under single author-title entries (Chuang Tzu/*Chuang Tzu*). Similar joint entries, supplemented by cross references, are used to list those texts which in some parts of this book happen to be cited by Chinese title but in others by English equivalent (e.g. *Lun yü*/*Analects*). Slight typographical variations, sometimes found in different parts of the book when citing the same texts, are ignored in this index (e.g. *Shih Ching*/*Shih ching*).

Certain terms and names occurring ubiquitously throughout the book (notably Confucianism, Taoism, Buddhism) are listed in the index only selectively.

**Library of Congress Cataloging in Publication Data**

Bodde, Derk, 1909-
  Essays on Chinese civilization.

  Bibliography:  p.
  Includes index.
    1.  China—Civilization—Addresses, essays, lec-
tures.    I.  Le Blanc, Charles.    II.  Borei, Dorothy.
III.  Title.
DS721.B613        951.05        80-20812
ISBN 0-691-03129-0
ISBN 0-691-00024-7 (pbk.)

*Derk Bodde is Professor of Chinese Studies Emeritus at the University
of Pennsylvania. Charles Le Blanc is Director of the Centre d'Etudes de
l'Asie de l'Est at the University of Montreal. Dorothy Borei is Assistant
Professor of Far Eastern History at Guilford College.*